Studies in Tectonic Culture:
The Poetics of Construction in Nineteenth and Twentieth Century Architecture

Graham Foundation for Advanced Studies in the Fine Arts

Chicago, Illinois

The MIT Press

Cambridge, Massachusetts

London, England

Publication of this book has been supported by a grant from the
Graham Foundation for Advanced Studies in the fine Arts.

This book was set in Helvetica Neue by Graphic Composition, Inc.,
and was printed and bound in the United States of America.

Library of Congress Cataloging-in-Publication Data

Frampton, Kenneth.
    Studies in tectonic culture : the poetics of construction in
nineteenth and twentieth century architecture / Kenneth Frampton ;
edited by John Cava.
        p.   cm.
    "Graham Foundation for Advanced Studies in the Fine Arts, Chi-
cago, Illinois."
    Includes bibliographical references and index.
    ISBN-13: 978-0-262-06173-5 (hc : alk. paper)   978-0-262-56149-5 (pb : alk. paper)
    1. Signs and symbols in architecture.   2. Architecture,
Modern—19th century.   3. Architecture, Modern—20th century.
I. Cava, John.   II. Title.
NA642.F72   1995
724′.5—dc20   95-9812
                                                    CIP

10   9   8   7

Contents

Foreword

In a recent novel by Phillip Lopate the somewhat intrepid attempt of the leading character to write a doctoral dissertation on Gottfried Semper ends with a nervous breakdown. The erstwhile graduate student never quite recovers. He first withdraws into a dreary shop in which he sells Persian carpets, then into an emotional aporia in which he is no longer able to connect with friends and family or to divert his failing business from bankruptcy. Like some whorl in an Oriental arabesque, his life circles feverishly in an eddy of nondirectional space; ultimately he loses the capacity to make the simplest decision and retreats into the calm of a psychological stupor.[1]

Architectural theory can be a heady experience, as a few adventurous souls have taken the occasion to discover. It is perhaps for this reason that so many of our architectural educators have gone to such lengths to exclude it from the architectural curriculum, to shunt the student out of harm's way, as it were. When schools of architecture do offer the pretense of engaging in weighty matters of philosophical import, it is generally limited to carefully diluted readings of Heidegger or Foucault or Derrida (certainly no one from the discipline of architecture), and these measured doses are taken sparingly in the privacy of the design studio where they can be shielded from contact with that other nemesis to "creative" design—architectural history. Hence in a rather perverse and arcane way, theory in these instances becomes a pretext to ignore, or at least to downplay, architecture's legitimate intellectual development. One of the merits of this book by Kenneth Frampton is that it seeks to redress this bias or imbalance.

It may seem axiomatic to define architecture simply as the "poetics of construction," but Frampton does precisely this. In a time when the profession increasingly gravitates toward pedantic gamesmanship and neo–avant-gardism, it is salutary to recall that architecture was once rendered as a more substantial art. It is also refreshing to be reminded that architecture can be evaluated by an entirely different set of criteria, involving the appreciation of craft and an expressive emphasis on what Frampton terms its tectonic and tactile dimension. But this focus on architecture's tangible materiality, which must be distinguished from cruder efforts at artistic materialism, is at the same time fraught with certain dangers. How do we follow Frampton and Giorgio Grassi in stressing this art's tectonic basis (and consequently de-emphasizing the supposed nihilism of its technology) without at the same time undermining architecture's capacity for representational values? How do we articulate a building's corporeal presence without diminishing the allusive poetics of its form?

The partial answer to this dilemma can be found, I think, at the point where the author's historical panorama begins: in the late eighteenth and first half of the nineteenth century. The better architects of this period—from Jacques-Germain Soufflot to John Soane to Henri Labrouste—would hardly have viewed this issue as a dilemma in the first place. Karl Friedrich Schinkel, for example, accepted it as apodictic that an edifice conveys cultural meaning on various levels: not only in the capacity of tectonic form to portray its constructional logic but also in the efficacy of the building to function inconographically and didacti-

cally. Thus while the exposed brick piers and castellated cornice of his Bauakademie (structurally necessary to anchor the interior system of fireproof vaults)
pay homage to the innovative tectonic system, the building comes to be defined
on another level by the terra-cotta tapestry that Schinkel wove into the surrounds of the doors and principal windows, in which he depicted, through a series of narrative panels, the mythological and constructional history of this art.

It is also easy to overlook the fact that the giant Ionic colonnade of the Altes Museum was rationalized by Schinkel simply as a hierarchic plastic response to its
location on the Lustgarten, opposite the honorific mass of the royal palace. The
principal facade of the building, however, was the recessed wall of this urban
stoa, on which were painted four colossal murals, two of which were one story
high and six in length, portraying his intensively artistic vision of the cosmological and cultural history of mankind. Even seemingly ancillary details, such as the
ornamental railings of the upper vestibule of the fountain placed in front, were
scrupulously crafted to expound his grander vision of allegory. It was only
through the rationalist filter of an Augustus Welby Pugin or Eugène Emmanuel
Viollet-le-Duc that the modern concern with enhancing or articulating the logic
of construction began to overshadow these others forms of tectonic expression.

But this graphic impulse did not entirely expire. Carl Bötticher elevated this tendency to another level of theoretical refinement with his distinction between the
Kernform (core form) and *Kunstform* (symbolic art form), that is, by interpreting
the degree of curvature of a Greek entablature molding more abstractly as an
artistic response to the intensity of the load placed upon it. Friedrich Theodor
Vischer and Robert Vischer circumscribed this animistic thesis of Bötticher (and
Schopenhauer) with the psychological notion of "empathy," which they defined
as the mostly unconscious projection of human emotion, of our "mental-sensory
self," into sensuous form. Only later in the century, in fact around 1900, did architects (forever condemned, it seems, to search beyond their own discourse
for ideological inspiration) again take an interest in exploring the potent empathetic expressiveness of what Frampton now calls ontological form. This notion
of empathy for Robert Vischer (and later, in 1886, for Heinrich Wölfflin) was in no
way a merely figurative reading of form. It presumed both our physiological and
emotional engagement with the world and therefore was corporeal and emotive
rather than conceptual or intellectual.

It is this empathetic sensitivity to form and its material expression—the
nineteenth-century Germanic notion of *Formgefühl*—that elevates Frampton's
tectonic thesis well above the plane of vulgar materialism and leads it back to
its complementary touchstone of representation. The author does not wish to
deprive architecture of other levels of iconic expression but rather to reinvest a
design with a now largely understated layer of meaning, one perhaps more primitive or primordial in its sensory apprehension. When he brings this theoretical
perspective to his analyses of such twentieth-century architects as Auguste Perret, Frank Lloyd Wright, Mies van der Rohe, Louis Kahn, Jørn Utzon, and Carlo
Scarpa, Frampton at the same time posits elements of a new paradigm by
which we might once again draw history and theory closer to one another—or
rather, view one more properly as the critical engagement of the other. He seeks
in this way to reaffirm that very ancient connection between the artificer and the
artifice, between the designer's initial conception and design's hard-won ingenuity. In such a view ornament indeed becomes, as he interprets Scarpa's work, a

"kind of writing," but it is now an embellishment more germane and indeed intrinsic to the tectonic process. It is manifest in the creative act rather than in its figurative appropriation.

In one of the more astute architectural analyses of the nineteenth century, written in 1898, the Munich architect Richard Streiter, after surveying the major directions of nineteenth-century Germanic theory from Bötticher to Otto Wagner, decided that architecture could only renew itself by becoming emphatically "realist," which he defined as the most scrupulous fulfillment of the demands of function, convenience, health, and *Sachlichkeit,* in addition to taking into account the local materials, landscape, and historically conditioned ambiance of a building's milieu. This prescription of Streiter is not so different from Frampton's almost quixotic task to unite vitality with calm, in order "to create a still yet vital point within the whirlwind." It seems that about every 100 years or so we have to be reminded of the cogency of our sensuous discourse with the world. This book, with its rich and palmate array of ideas, may not put an end to the affected disenchantment that so often insinuates itself into our "post-postmodern" architectural discourse (as some, sadly, are already referring to it), but it will certainly give a tangible start to this art's deepening and further elaboration.

Harry Francis Mallgrave

Acknowledgments

These studies have their origin in the inaugural Francis Craig Cullivan lecture
that I had the honor to give in 1986 at Rice University in Houston, Texas. In this
regard I have to thank the faculty of architecture at Rice University, without
whom this book would never have been started. I wish also to extend my particular gratitude to Professor Anderson Todd of Rice for his patience and tireless
support and to Alan Balfour who, while chairman of the same faculty, was able
to arrange for further financial assistance. In terms of the actual production I
would also like to acknowledge my profound debt to John Cava of the University of Oregon at Eugene, for his constant and invaluable help during the seemingly endless period of research and preparation that preceded the publication
of this text. I have also to thank Claudia Schinkievicz, who not only translated
this text into German but also effected its initial publication in German in 1993.
While the present text is virtually the same, subsequent minor corrections and refinements have been made and new insights have inevitably emerged. Particular
acknowledgments have to be given to Harry Mallgrave and Duncan Berry for
their invaluable help in the development of the material embodied in chapter 3.
I must also thank Karla Britton and Karen Melk for their untiring assistance in
the countless reworkings to which this text has been subjected, not to mention
the various students of the Graduate School of Architecture, Planning and Preservation at Columbia University who have on occasion assisted with the preparation of certain study models. There are a number of other scholars and
architects who indirectly, through their work, have played a key role in the conceptual development of this book. Among these particular credit should be accorded to Stanford Anderson, Robert Bartholomew, Barry Bergdoll, Rosemarie
Bletter, Massimo Cacciari, Peter Carter, Peter Collins, Francesco Dal Co, Hubert
Damisch, Guy Debord, Kurt Forster, Marco Frascari, Scott Gartner, Roula Geraniotis, Vittorio Gregotti, Wolfgang Herrmann, Eleftherios Ikonomou, Richard
Francis Jones, Aris Konstantinidis, Sergio Los, Robin Middleton, Ignasí de Sola-
Morales, Fritz Neumeyer, Bruno Reichlin, Colin Rowe, Eduard Sekler, Manfredo
Tafuri, and Giuseppe Zambonini. It should go without saying that there are
countless others to whom I am also equally indebted and whose specific contributions are acknowledged, as it were, in the footnotes. Last, but not least, I
would like to salute the production staff and editorial direction of the MIT Press
and above all the Graham Foundation in Chicago, whose timely grant enabled
us to proceed with the publication of this present book.

We don't ask to be eternal beings. We only ask that things do not lose all their meaning.

Antoine de Saint-Exupéry

Studies in Tectonic Culture

1   Introduction:
Reflections on the Scope of the Tectonic

The history of contemporary architecture is inevitably multiple, multifarious even; a history of the structures that form the human environment independently of architecture itself; a history of the attempts to control and direct those structures; a history of the intellectuals who have sought to devise policies and methods for those attempts; a history of new languages which, having abandoned all hope of arriving at absolute and definitive words, have striven to delimit the area of their particular contribution.

Obviously the intersection of all those manifold histories will never end up in unity. The realm of history is, by nature, dialectical. It is that dialectic that we have tried to pin down, and we have done what we could not to smooth over conflicts which are cropping up again today in the form of worrisome questions as to what role architecture itself should or can have. It is useless to try to reply to such questions. What needs to be done, instead, is to trace the entire course of modern architecture with an eye to whatever cracks and gaps break up its compactness, and then to make a fresh start, without, however, elevating to the status of myth either the continuity of history or those separate discontinuities.
Manfredo Tafuri and Francesco Dal Co, L'architettura contemporanea, 1976

The great French architectural theorist Eugène-Emmanuel Viollet-le-Duc would compile his magnum opus of 1872, his *Entretiens sur l'architecture,* without once using the term space in a modern sense.[1] Twenty years later nothing could be further from the structuralism of Viollet-le-Duc's thought than the primacy given to space as an end in itself in August Schmarsow's *Das Wesen der architektonischen Schöpfung (The Essence of Architectural Creation),* first published in 1894.[2] Like many other theorists before him, Schmarsow would advance the primitive hut as the primordial shelter, only this time he would see it as a spatial matrix, or what he would call the *Raumgestalterin,* the creatress of space.[3]

To a greater extent perhaps than any other late nineteenth-century theorist, including the sculptor Adolf von Hildebrand, who gave primacy to kinetic vision, and Gottfried Semper, from whom Schmarsow derived his thesis, Schmarsow came to see the evolution of architecture as the progressive unfolding of man's feeling for space, what he called *Raumgefühl.* Between 1893 and 1914 Schmarsow's identification of space as the driving principle behind all architectural form coincides with the evolving space-time models of the universe as these were successively adduced by Nikolai Ivanovich Lobachevsky, Georg Riemann, and Albert Einstein. As we know, such paradigms would come to be deployed early in this century to rationalize in various ways the appearance of dynamic spatial form in the field of avant-gardist art.[4] This conjunction was reinforced through the experience of speed and the actual transformation of space-time in an everyday sense, due to the mechanical inventions of the last half of the century: the familiar Futurist technology of the train, the transatlantic liner, the car, and the plane.

Space has since become such an integral part of our thinking about architecture that we are practically incapable of thinking about it at all without putting our main emphasis on the spatial displacement of the subject in time. This quintessentially modern viewpoint has clearly underlain innumerable texts treating the intrinsic nature of modern architecture, ranging from Sigfried Giedion's *Space, Time and Architecture* of 1941 to Cornelis van de Ven's *Space in Architecture* of 1978. As van de Ven shows, the idea of space established a new concept that not only overcame eclecticism through a relativizing of style, but also gave priority to the spatio-plastic unity of interior and exterior space and to the nonhierarchical assimilation of all instrumental forms, irrespective of their scale or mode of address, into one continuous space-time experience.

Without wishing to deny the volumetric character of architectural form, this study seeks to mediate and enrich the priority given to space by a reconsideration of the constructional and structural modes by which, of necessity, it has to be achieved. Needless to say, I am not alluding to the mere revelation of constructional technique but rather to its expressive potential. Inasmuch as the tectonic amounts to a poetics of construction it is art, but in this respect the artistic dimension is neither figurative nor abstract. It is my contention that the unavoidably earthbound nature of building is as tectonic and tactile in character as it is scenographic and visual, although none of these attributes deny its spatiality. Nevertheless we may assert that the built is first and foremost a construction and only later an abstract discourse based on surface, volume, and plan, to cite the "Three Reminders to Architects" in Le Corbusier's *Vers une architecture* of 1923.[5] One may also add that building, unlike fine art, is as much an everyday experience as it is a representation and that the built is a thing rather than a sign, even if, as Umberto Eco once remarked, as soon as one has an object of "use" one necessarily has a sign that is indicative of this use.

From this point of view, we may claim that type form—the received "what" deposited by the lifeworld—is as much a precondition for building as craft technique, however much it may remain open to inflection at different levels. Thus we may claim that the built invariably comes into existence out of the constantly evolving interplay of three converging vectors, the *topos,* the *typos,* and the *tectonic.* And while the tectonic does not necessarily favor any particular style, it does, in conjunction with site and type, serve to counter the present tendency for architecture to derive its legitimacy from some other discourse.

This reassertion of the tectonic derives in part from Giorgio Grassi's critical polemic as this was advanced in his essay "Avant Garde and Continuity" of 1980, in which he wrote:

As far as the architectural vanguards of the Modern Movement are concerned, they invariably follow in the wake of the figurative arts. . . . Cubism, Suprematism, Neo-plasticism, etc., are all forms of investigation born and developed in the realm of the figurative arts, and only as a second thought carried over into architecture as well. It is actually pathetic to see the architects of that "heroic" period, and the best among them, trying with difficulty to accommodate themselves to these "isms"; experimenting in a perplexed manner because of their fascination with the new doctrines, measuring them, only later to realize their ineffectuality.[6]

Despite the retardataire implications of this Lukacsian critique, Grassi's observation nonetheless challenges the prestige that still seems to attach itself to the figurative in architecture. This challenge comes at a time when architecture appears to oscillate uneasily between a deconstructive aestheticization of its traditional modus operandi and a reassertion of its liberative capacity as a critical form. It is perhaps a measure of Grassi's professional alienation that his work remains somewhat hermetic and indeed paradoxically removed, when built, from the poetics of craft construction. This is all the more inexplicable given the care that he takes in developing the constructional details of his work (fig. 1.1). No one perhaps has made a more judicious assessment of the contradictory aspects of Grassi's architecture than the Catalan critic Ignasí de Sola Morales:

Architecture is posited as a craft, that is to say, as the practical application of established knowledge through rules of the different levels of intervention. Thus, no notion of architecture as problem-solving, as innovation, or as invention ex novo, *is present in showing the permanent, the evident, and the given character of knowledge in the making of architecture.*

. . . The work of Grassi is born of a reflection upon the essential resources of discipline, and it focuses upon specific media which determine not only aesthetic choices but also the ethical content of its cultural contribution. Through these channels of ethical and political will, the concern of the Enlightenment . . . becomes enriched in its most critical tone. It is not solely the superiority of reason and the analysis of form which are indicated, but rather, the critical role (in the Kantian sense of the term), that is, the judgement of values, the very lack of which is felt in society today. . . . In the sense that his architecture is a metalanguage, a reflection on the contradictions of his own practice, his work acquires the appeal of something that is both frustrating and noble.[7]

Etymology

Greek in origin, the term tectonic derives from the word *tekton,* signifying carpenter or builder. The corresponding verb is *tektainomai.* This in turn is related to the Sanskrit *taksan,* referring to the craft of carpentry and to the use of the axe. Remnants of a similar term can be found in Vedic poetry, where it again refers to carpentry. In Greek it appears in Homer, where it alludes to the art of construction in general. The poetic connotation of the term first appears in Sappho, where the *tekton,* the carpenter, assumes the role of the poet. In general, the

1.1
Giorgio Grassi, restoration and reconstruction of the Roman theater of Sagunto, Valencia, 1985. Cross section.

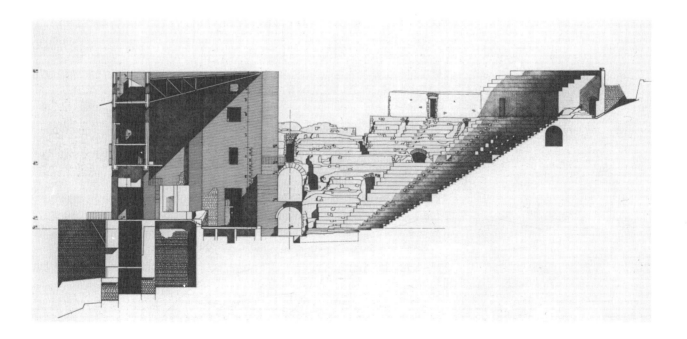

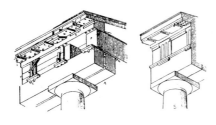

1.2
Auguste Choisy, the derivation of the Doric order from timber construction, from *Histoire de l'architecture,* 1899.

term refers to an artisan working in all hard materials except metal. In the fifth century B.C. this meaning undergoes further evolution, from something specific and physical, such as carpentry, to a more generic notion of making, involving the idea of *poesis.* In Aristophanes it would seem that the notion is even associated with machination and the creation of false things, a transformation that would appear to correspond to the passage from pre-Socratic philosophy to Hellenism. Needless to say, the role of the *tekton* leads eventually to the emergence of the master builder or *architekton.*[8] That the term would eventually aspire to an aesthetic rather than a technological category has been remarked on by Adolf Heinrich Borbein in his 1982 philological study:

Tectonic becomes the art of joinings. "Art" here is to be understood as encompassing tekne, *and therefore indicates tectonic as assemblage not only of building parts but also of objects, indeed of artworks in a narrower sense. With regard to the ancient understanding of the word, tectonic tends toward the construction or making of an artisanal or artistic product. . . . It depends much more upon the correct or incorrect applications of the artisanal rules, or the degree to which its usefulness has been achieved. Only to this extent does tectonic also involve judgment over art production. Here, however, lies the point of departure for the expanded clarification and application of the idea in more recent art history: as soon as an aesthetic perspective—and not a goal of utility—is defined that specifies the work and production of the* tekton, *then the analysis consigns the term "tectonic" to an aesthetic judgement.*[9]

The first architectural use of the term in German dates from its appearance in Karl Otfried Müller's *Handbuch der Archäologie der Kunst* (Handbook of the Archaeology of Art), published in 1830, wherein he defines *tektonische* as applying to a series of art forms "such as utensils, vases, dwellings and meeting places of men, which surely form and develop on the one hand due to their application and on the other due to their conformity to sentiments and notions of art. We call this string of mixed activities tectonic; their peak is architecture, which mostly through necessity rises high and can be a powerful representation of the deepest feelings." In the third edition of his study Müller remarks on the specifically junctional or "dry" jointing implications of the term. "I did not fail to notice that the ancient term *tektones,* in specialized usage, refers to people in construction or cabinet makers, not however, to clay and metal workers; therefore, at the same time, it takes into account the general meaning, which lies in the etymology of the word."[10]

In his highly influential *Die Tektonik der Hellenen* (The Tectonic of the Hellenes), published in three volumes between 1843 and 1852, Karl Bötticher would make the seminal contribution of distinguishing between the *Kernform* and the *Kunstform;* between the core form of the timber rafters in a Greek temple and the artistic representation of the same elements as petrified beam ends in the triglyphs and metopes of the classical entablature (fig. 1.2). Bötticher interpreted the term tectonic as signifying a complete system binding all the parts of the Greek temple into a single whole, including the framed presence of relief sculpture in all its multifarious forms.

Influenced by Müller, Gottfried Semper would endow the term with equally ethnographic connotations in his epoch-making theoretical departure from the Vitruvian triad of *utilitas, fermitas,* and *venustas.* Semper's *Die vier Elemente der*

Baukunst (Four Elements of Architecture), published in 1851, indirectly challenged the neoclassic primitive hut as posited by the Abbé Laugier in his *Essai sur l'architecture* of 1753.[11] Based in part on an actual Caribbean hut that he saw in the Great Exhibition of 1851, Semper's primordial dwelling was divided into four basic elements: (1) the earthwork, (2) the hearth, (3) the framework/ roof, and (4) the lightweight enclosing membrane. On the basis of this taxonomy Semper would classify the building crafts into two fundamental procedures: the *tectonics* of the frame, in which lightweight, linear components are assembled so as to encompass a spatial matrix, and the *stereotomics* of the earthwork, wherein mass and volume are conjointly formed through the repetitious piling up of heavyweight elements. That this last depends upon load-bearing masonry, whether stone or mud brick, is suggested by the Greek etymology of stereotomy, from *stereos,* solid, and *tomia,* to cut. This tectonic/stereotomic distinction was reinforced in German by that language's differentiation between two classes of wall; between *die Wand,* indicating a screenlike partition such as we find in wattle and daub infill construction, and *die Mauer,* signifying massive fortification.[12] This distinction will find a certain correspondence in Karl Gruber's 1937 reconstruction of a typical German medieval city, which illustrates the difference between heavyweight battlements built of masonry and lightweight residential fabric framed in wood and filled with wattle and daub (*Fachwerkbau*) (fig. 1.3).[13]

This distinction between light and heavy reflects a more general differentiation in terms of material production, wood construction displaying an affinity for its tensile equivalent in terms of basketwork and textiles, and stonework tending toward its substitution as a compressive material by brickwork or *pisé* (rammed earth) and later by reinforced concrete. As Semper was to point out in his *Stoffwechseltheorie,* the history of culture manifests occasional transpositions in which the architectonic attributes of one mode are expressed in another for the

1.3
Karl Gruber, reconstruction of a typical medieval city, 1937.

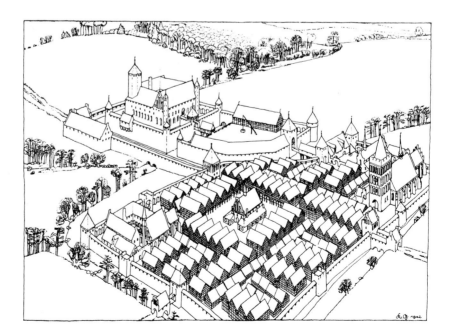

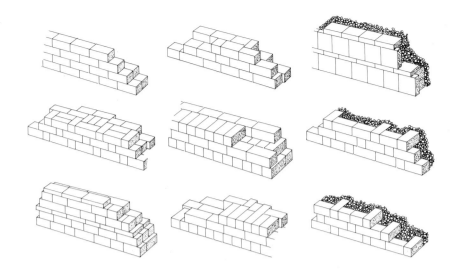

sake of retaining traditional symbolic value, as in the case of the Greek temple, where stone is cut and laid in such a way as to reinterpret the form of the archetypal timber frame. In this regard we need to note that masonry, when it does not assume the form of a conglomerate as in *pisé* construction, that is to say when it is bonded into coursework, is also a form of weaving, to which all the various traditional masonry bonds bear testimony (fig. 1.4).[14] The woven overlapping thin tiles or *bóveda* of traditional Catalan vaulting point to the same end (fig. 1.5).

The general validity of Semper's *Four Elements* is borne out by vernacular building throughout the world, even if there are cultures where the woven vertical screen wall does not exist or where the woven wall is absorbed, as it were, into the roof and frame, as in, say, the North American Mandan house (fig. 1.6). In African tribal cultures the enclosing vertical screen covers a wide range of expression, from primitive infill walls, plastered on the inside only, as in the Gogo houses of Tanzania (fig. 1.7), to precisely woven wall mats that line the exterior of the chief's hut, as we find in Kuba culture. Moreover according to climate, custom, and available material the respective roles played by tectonic and stereotomic form vary considerably, so that the primal dwelling passes from a condition in which the earthwork is reduced to point foundations, as in the boulder footings of the traditional Japanese house (fig. 1.8), to a situation in which ste-

1.4
Methods of Roman brick bonding.

1.5
Antoni Gaudí, brick and Catalan vaulting in the Casa Vicens, Barcelona, 1878–1880.

1.6
Mandan house, American Indian, section.

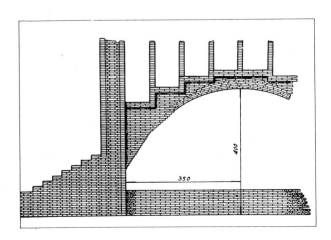

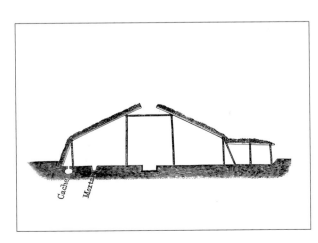

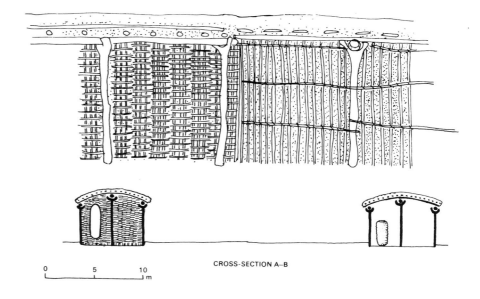

CROSS-SECTION A–B

0   5   10
|____|____| m

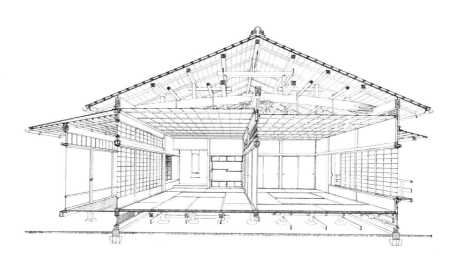

1.7
Gogo houses of Tanzania, detail of infill walls.

1.8
Traditional Japanese one-story house.

reotomic walls are extended horizontally to become floors and roofs, made up of the same material although reinforced with brushwood or basketwork (fig. 1.9). Alternatively the basic cell is covered by a vault of the same material, both techniques being equally prevalent in North African, Cycladic, and Middle Eastern cultures.

It is characteristic of our secular age that we should overlook the cosmic associations evoked by these dialogically opposed modes of construction; that is to say the affinity of the frame for the immateriality of sky and the propensity of mass form not only to gravitate toward the earth but also to dissolve in its substance. As the Egyptian architect Hassan Fathy was to point out, this is never more evident than in mud brick construction, where the walls tend to fuse with the earth once they fall into ruin and disuse. However, untreated wood is equally ephemeral when exposed to the elements, as opposed to a well-bedded stone foundation that tends to endure across time and thus to mark the ground in perpetuity.[15]

Topography

No one has argued more persuasively as to the cosmogonic implications of the earthwork than the Italian architect Vittorio Gregotti, who in 1983 wrote:

The worst enemy of modern architecture is the idea of space considered solely in terms of its economic and technical exigencies indifferent to the ideas of the site.

. . . Through the concept of the site and the principle of settlement, the environment becomes [on the contrary] the essence of architectural production. From this vantage point, new principles and methods can be seen for design. Principles and methods that give precedence to the siting in a specific area. This is an act of knowledge of the context that comes out of its architectural modification. The origin of architecture is not in the primitive hut, or the cave or the mythical "Adam's House in Paradise."

Before transforming a support into a column, a roof into a tympanum, before placing stone on stone, man placed the stone on the ground to recognize a site in the midst of an unknown universe: in order to take account of it and modify it. As with every act of assessment this one required radical moves and apparent simplicity. From this point of view, there are only two important attitudes to the context. The tools of the first are mimesis, organic imitation and the display of complexity. The tools of the second are the assessment of physical relations, formal definition and interiorization of complexity.[16]

It is difficult to find a more didactic modern example of this last than the acknowledged masterwork of the Greek architect Dimitris Pikionis. I have in mind his Philopapou hillside park, laid in place during the second half of the 1950s on a site adjacent to the Acropolis in Athens (fig. 1.10). In this work, as Alexander Tzonis and Liane Lefaivre have remarked, Pikionis created a topographic continuum that was removed from any kind of technological exhibitionism. This serpentine causeway, passing across an undulating rock-strewn site, constituted, in essence, a stone tapestry, bonded into the ground through irregularly coursed pavers, furnished with occasional seats, and studded here and there with iconic signs.[17] Collaged rather than designed, it reinterprets the *genius loci* as a mythic

1.9
Traditional construction from the towns of Mzab in Algeria:

1. masonry foundation walls
2. mud brick
3. *timchent* rendering
4. smooth rendering
5. palmwood lintel
6. clay gargoyle
7. *timchent* roof finish
8. small stone vaults
9. *timchent* rendering
10. palm branch beams
11. stone arch
12. palm nervures centering

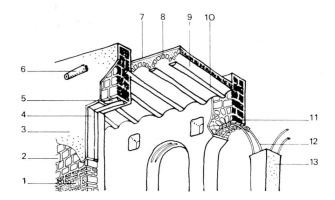

1.10
Dimitris Pikionis, detail of park paving, Philopapou Hill, Athens, 1951–1957.

narrative, part Byzantine, part pre-Socratic, a promenade to be experienced as much by the body as by the eyes. That this was always central to Pikionis's sensibility is evident from a 1933 essay entitled "A Sentimental Topography":

We rejoice in the progress of our body across the uneven surface of the earth and our spirit is gladdened by the endless interplay of the three dimensions that we encounter with every step. . . . Here the ground is hard, stony, precipitous, and the soil is brittle and dry. There the ground is level; water surges out of mossy patches. Further on, the breeze, the altitude and the configuration of the ground announce the vicinity of the sea. [18]

Pikionis's work testifies to the fact that the earthwork tends to transcend our received perceptions about both aesthetics and function, for here the surface of the ground is kinetically experienced through the gait, that is to say through the locomotion of the body and the sensuous impact of this movement on the nervous system as a whole. There is moreover, as Pikionis reminds us, the "acoustical" resonance of the site as the body negotiates its surface. One recalls at this juncture Steen Eiler Rasmussen's *Experiencing Architecture* and the remarkable chapter entitled "Hearing Architecture," where he notes the all but imperceptible acoustical character of built form. [19] Rasmussen reminds us that the spatial reflection or absorption of sound immediately affects our psychological response to a given volume, so that we may find it warm or cold according to its particular resonance rather than its appearance. Similar psycho-acoustical effects have been remarked on by Ulrich Conrads and Bernhard Leitner in a 1985 essay in which they comment on the spiritual aura evoked by the reverberation time of the Taj Mahal and, rather coincidentally, on the way in which Mediterranean vernacular forms appear to be suited to the articulation of certain diphthongs and vowels and not others, with the result that such dwellings prove unsuitable as vacation homes for people speaking northern languages. [20] That even formal integrity may depend in part on acoustical effect is confirmed by Luis Barragán's San Cristóbal horse farm realized in the suburbs of Mexico City in 1967, wherein the central reflecting pool and the sound of its water fountain jointly assure the unity of the whole.

Corporeal Metaphor

The capacity of the being to experience the environment bodily recalls the notion of the corporeal imagination as advanced by the Neapolitan philosopher Giambattista Vico in his *Scienza nuova* of 1730. Against the rationalism of Descartes, Vico argued that language, myth, and custom are the metaphorical legacy of the species brought into being through the self-realization of its history, from the first intuitions deriving from man's primordial experience of nature to the long haul of cultural development running across generations. In his 1985 study Michael Mooney had this to say about Vico's conception of this metaphorical process:

In a moment of stirring oratory, Vico held, when the beauty of a conceit overwhelms the spirit as its truth impresses the mind, both speaker and listener are caught up in a rush of ingenuity, each making connections that were not made before, their spirits fused by the freshness of the language, their minds and finally their wills made one. So here, too, analogously to be sure, the first dim seeing of Jove is an event in which body through language becomes conscious, the poetry of a thundering sky evoking in response the poetry of giants made men, struck dumb with awe.

What occurs is an exchange in metaphor, the image of providence in a thundering heaven passing into the bodies of awestruck men. The physical universe of deus artifex, *itself a poem, everywhere written in conceits, becomes in the bodies of clustered men a poet, henceforth a maker of self; the passive ingenuity of the universe comes to life in the mind (however unrefined it yet is) and the spirit (however passionate and violent it may be) of man, and man, now standing erect, becomes the* artifex *of his own existence.*[21]

Vico's concept of the enactment and reenactment of man through history is not only metaphorical and mythical but also corporeal, in that the body reconstitutes the world through its tactile appropriation of reality. This much is suggested by the psycho-physical impact of form upon our being and by our tendency to engage form through touch as we feel our way through architectonic space. This propensity has been remarked on by Adrian Stokes, in discussing the impact of time and touch on the weathering of stone.

Hand-finish is the most vivid testimony of sculpture. People touch things according to their shape. A single shape is made magnificent by perennial touching. For the hand explores, all unconsciously to reveal, to magnify an existent form. Perfect sculpture needs your hand to communicate some pulse and warmth, to reveal subtleties unnoticed by the eye, needs your hand to enhance them. Used, carved stone, exposed to the weather, records on its concrete shape in spatial, immediate, simultaneous form, not only the winding passages of days and nights, the opening and shutting skies of warmth and wet, but also the sensitiveness, the vitality even, that each successive touching has communicated.[22]

That such a purview stands in total opposition to all our more recent attempts to impose upon cultural experience a consciously distanced and exclusively semiotic character has been remarked on by Scott Gartner.

The philosophical alienation of the body from the mind has resulted in the absence of embodied experience from almost all contemporary theories of meaning in architecture. The overemphasis on signification and reference in architectural theory has led to a construal of meaning as an entirely conceptual phenomenon. Experience, as it relates to understanding, seems reduced to a matter of the visual registration of coded messages—a function of the eye which might well rely on the printed page and dispense with the physical presence of architecture altogether. The body, if it figures into architectural theory at all, is often reduced to an aggregate of needs and constraints which are to be accommodated by methods of design grounded in behavioral and ergonomic analysis. Within this framework of thought, the body and its experience do not participate in the constitution and realization of architectural meaning.[23]

Metaphor, rather than being solely a linguistic or rhetorical trope, constitutes a human process by which we understand and structure one domain of experience in terms of another of a different kind.[24] This concept surely lies behind Tadao Ando's characterization of the *Shintai* as a sentient being that realizes itself through lived-in space.

Man articulates the world through his body. Man is not a dualistic being in whom spirit and the flesh are essentially distinct, but a living corporeal being active in the world. The "here and now" in which this distinct body is placed is what is first taken as granted, and subsequently a "there" appears. Through a perception of that distance, or rather the living of that distance, the surrounding space becomes manifest as a thing endowed with various meanings and values. Since man has an asymmetrical physical structure with a top and a bottom, a left and a right, and a front and a back, the articulated world, in turn, naturally becomes a heterogeneous space. The world that appears to man's senses and the state of man's body become in this way interdependent. The world articulated by the body is a vivid, lived-in space.

The body articulates the world. At the same time, the body is articulated by the world. When "I" perceive the concrete to be something cold and hard, "I" recognize the body as something warm and soft. In this way the body in its dynamic relationship with the world becomes the shintai. *It is only the* shintai *in this sense that builds or understands architecture. The* shintai *is a sentient being that responds to the world.*[25]

This concept parallels similar arguments advanced by Schmarsow and later by Merleau-Ponty,[26] particularly Schmarsow's thesis that our concept of space is determined by the frontalized progression of the body through space in depth. Similar spatio-corporeal connotations are evident in Adolphe Appia's disquisition on the interplay between body and form on the stage, in his *L'Oeuvre d'art vivant* of 1921.[27] A similar phenomenological awareness is also evident in Alvar

1.11
Alvar Aalto, Säynätsalo Town Hall, 1949–1952. Plan, section through council chamber, and longitudinal section.

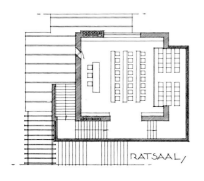

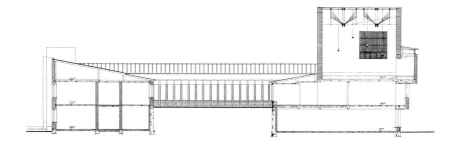

1.12
Alvar Aalto, Säynätsalo Town Hall, stair to the council chamber.

1.13
Ogre's Night at the turn of the year, Kyushu. Ritual raising and burning of the *hashira*.

Aalto's Säynätsalo Town Hall (1952) where, from entry to council chamber, the subject encounters a sequence of contrasting tactile experiences (fig. 1.11). Thus, from the stereotomic mass and relative darkness of the entry stair (fig. 1.12), where the feeling of enclosure is augmented by the tactility of the brick treads, one enters into the bright light of the council chamber, the timber-lined roof of which is carried on fanlike, wooden trusses that splay upward to support concealed rafters above a boarded ceiling. The sense of arrival occasioned by this tectonic display is reinforced by various nonretinal sensations, from the smell of polished wood to the floor flexing under one's weight together with the general destabilization of the body as one enters onto a highly polished surface.

Ethnography

Semper's theory of tectonics was profoundly rooted in the emerging science of ethnography. Like Sigfried Giedion after him, Semper tried to reground the practice of architecture in what Giedion would call "the eternal present," in his 1964 study of this title. This search for a timeless origin is directly evoked in the Prolegomenon to *Der Stil* where, in a manner uncannily reminiscent of Vico, Semper writes of the cosmogonic drive as an archaic impulse continually changing across time (fig. 1.13).

Surrounded by a world full of wonder and forces, whose law man may divine, may want to understand but never decipher, which reaches him only in a few fragmentary harmonies and which suspends his soul in a continuous state of unresolved tension, he himself conjures up the missing perfection in play. He makes himself a tiny world in which the cosmic law is evident within strict limits, yet complete in itself and perfect in this respect; in such play man satisfies his cosmogonic instinct.

His fantasy creates these images, by displaying, expanding, and adapting to his mood the individual scenes of nature before him, so orderly arranged that he believes he can discern in the single event the harmony of the whole and for short moments has the illusion of having escaped reality. Truly this enjoyment of nature is not very different from the enjoyment of art, just as the beauty of nature . . . is assigned to the general beauty of art as a lower category.

However, this artistic enjoyment of nature's beauty is by no means the most naive or earliest manifestation of the artistic instinct. On the contrary, the former is undeveloped in simple, primitive man, whereas he does already take delight in nature's creative law as it gleams through reality in the rhythmical sequence of space and time movements, is found once more in the wreath, the bead necklace, the scroll, the circular dance and the rhythmic tone that attends it, the beat of an oar, and so on. These are the beginnings out of which music and architecture *grew; both are the highest purely cosmic nonimitative arts, whose legislative support no other art can forgo.*[28]

Although we cannot dwell here on all the ethnographic evidence that may be summoned in support of Semper's thesis, I will cite nonetheless two examples that testify to the way in which the two basic modes of building, the compressive mass and the tensile frame, have been deployed throughout time in such a way as to create a lifeworld that is cosmogonically encoded.

The first instance is taken from Pierre Bourdieu's 1969 study of the Berber house, in which he demonstrates how the entire domain is organized in terms of sectional displacement and material finish in such a way as to distinguish the *upper/dry/human* from the *lower/wet/animal* parts of the dwelling (fig. 1.14). On the opposing transverse axis the same space is ordered about a main entrance, invariably oriented toward the east, and a weaving loom that, in being set opposite the open door and the rising sun, is analogously seen as the sun of the interior. On the basis of this cosmic cross axis the house and its surroundings are divided into a homological hierarchy in which every value is counterbalanced by its opposite. Thus, the attributes of the external world are reversed on the interior; the southern exterior wall becomes the "northern" interior wall, and so on.

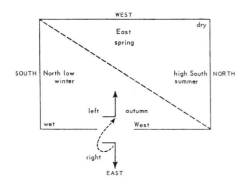

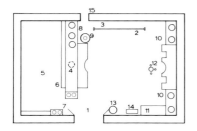

1.14
Berber house, seasonal orientation and internal/external inversion according to the cardinal points:
1. threshold
2. loom
3. rifle
4. *thigejdity*
5. stable
6. trough for oxen
7. water pitchers
8. jars of dried vegetables, etc.
9. hand mill
10. jars of grain
11. bench
12. *kanun*
13. large water jar
14. chest
15. back door

Associated with dawn, spring, fertility, and birth, the loom, before the "eastern" interior wall, is regarded as the female place of honor and is seen as the spiritual nexus of the dwelling. It is balanced by the male object of honor, namely the rifle, that is stacked close to the loom. That this symbolic system is reinforced by the construction itself is confirmed by Bourdieu's testimony.

In front of the wall opposite the door stands the weaving loom. This wall is usually called by the same name as the outside front wall giving onto the courtyard (tasga), or else the wall of the weaving-loom or opposite wall, since one is opposite it when one enters. The wall opposite this is called the wall of darkness, or of sleep, or of the maiden, or of the tomb. . . . One might be tempted to give a strictly technical explanation to these oppositions since the wall of the weaving-loom . . . receives the most light and the stone-flagged stable is, in fact, situated at a lower level than the rest. The reason given for the last is that the house is most often built perpendicularly with the contour lines in order to facilitate the flow of liquid-manure and dirty water. A number of signs suggest, however, that these oppositions are the center of a whole cluster of parallel oppositions, the necessity of which is never completely due to technical imperatives or functional requirements. In addition to all this, at the center of the dividing wall, between "the house of human beings" stands the main pillar, supporting the governing beam and all the framework of the house. Now this governing beam which connects the gables and spreads the protection of the male part of the house to the female part . . . is identified explicitly with the master of the house, whilst the main pillar on which it rests, which is the trunk of a forked tree . . . is identified with the wife . . . and their interlocking represents the act of physical union.[29]

Bourdieu proceeds to show how this same symbolic system differentiates in a categorical way between the lower and upper parts of the house; that is, between the sunken, stone-flagged stable regarded as a space of darkness, fertility, and sexual intercourse and the upper dry, light space of human appearance, finished in polished cow dung.

Our second example is drawn from Japanese culture, in which weaving and binding emerge from archaic time as the primary element in a number of agrarian renewal and ground-breaking rites that still survive today throughout the country (fig. 1.15). In an essay on these rituals, Gunter Nitschke shows how Japanese archaic land-taking/agricultural rites are invariably initiated by knotted or bound signs, known generically as *musubi,* from *musubu,* to bind (fig. 1.16).[30] Nitschke argues that building/binding as a cyclical activity takes priority over religion in the archaic creation of order out of chaos, citing by way of evidence the etymological origin of the word religion in the Latin verb *ligare,* to bind. In contrast to the Western monumental tradition with its dependence on the relative permanence of stereotomic mass, the archaic Japanese world was symbolically structured through ephemeral tectonic material, knotted grasses or rice straw ropes known as *shime-nawa,* literally "bound ropes" (fig. 1.17), or more elaborately through bound pillars of bamboo and reed called *hashira* (fig. 1.18). As Nitschke and others have shown, these Shinto prototectonic devices exercised a decisive influence on the evolution of Japanese sacred and domestic architecture through its various incarnations, from the earliest Shimmei shrines dating from the first century through to the seventeenth-century *shoin* and *chaseki* versions of Heian wooden construction. Due to the relative perishability of untreated wood, Japanese honorific structures were everywhere subject to cyclical rebuilding, the most famous instance being the monumental Naiku and Geku precincts at Ise that, with their attendant buildings, are rebuilt in their entirety every twenty years. On these occasions a new shrine is built on the adjacent site of a previous shrine, this sacred domain having lain dormant over the intervening twenty-year period (fig. 1.19).

Aside from the evident differences separating stereotomic and tectonic construction in archaic building culture, two common factors may be seen as obtaining in both of these examples. The first is the primacy accorded to the woven as a place-making agent in so-called primitive cultures; the second is the universal presence of a nonlinear attitude toward time that guarantees, as it were, the cyclical renewal of an eternal present. This premodern seasonal perception of the temporal finds reflection in the fact that as late as a century and a half ago the

1.15
Ritual tools on display in the course of a Shinto ground-breaking ceremony.

1.16

Musubi. Japanese knotted-grass land marking and land taking compared to the configuration of Western script.

1.17

Shime-nawa. The bound rice straw, apotropaic signs and talismans of Shinto culture.

Japanese day was not divided into twenty-four hours.[31] Instead, it was broken down into six equal periods whose lengths varied according to the seasons of the year. Even after they were imported, in the sixteenth century, Western clocks had to be mechanically adjusted to suit the old system of time.

Confirming the preeminence that Semper would give to textiles as the first cosmogonic craft, Japanese building and place-making practices seem to have been interconnected throughout history. Thus, to a greater degree perhaps than in other cultures, metalinguistic forms and spatio-temporal rhythms are bound up with the act of building in Japan. That this culture is quite literally woven throughout is further substantiated by the dovetailing interrelationship of every conceivable element in the traditional Japanese house, from the standard tatami mat of woven rice straw construction (fig. 1.20) to the *kyo-ma* and *inka-ma* method of modular building.[32]

Representational versus Ontological

The concept of layered transitional space as it appears in traditional Japanese architecture (fig. 1.21) may be related indirectly to the distinction that Semper draws between the *symbolic* and *technical* aspects of construction, a distinction that I have attempted to relate to the *representational* and *ontological* aspects of tectonic form: the difference, that is, between the skin that re-presents the composite character of the construction and the core of a building that is simultaneously both its fundamental structure and its substance. This difference finds a more articulated reflection in the distinction that Semper draws between the *ontological* nature of the earthwork, frame, and roof and the more *representational,* symbolic nature of the hearth and the infill wall. In my view, this dichotomy must be constantly rearticulated in the creation of architectural form, since each building type, technique, topography, and temporal circumstance brings about a different cultural condition. As Harry Mallgrave has suggested, Semper remained somewhat undecided as to the relative expressivity of structure and cladding, hesitating between the symbolic expressivity of construction as a thing itself—rationally modulated from both a technical and an aesthetic standpoint—and a symbolic elaboration of the cladding irrespective of its underlying structure. According to this last rubric, cladding is conceived as an overriding decorative or metalinguistic means for enhancing form so as to represent its status or latent value. Mallgrave posits a reconciliation of this split in which first the symbolic (the representational) and secondly the constructional (the ontological) are alternatively revealed *and* concealed. He writes:

Konrad Fiedler, in an 1878 essay that took its starting point in Semper's theory, suggested a peeling away of the dressing of antique architecture to exploit in modern works the wall's purely spatial possibility. This suggestion was taken

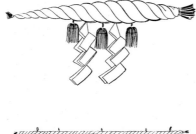

1.18
Typical *hashira* or bound column prepared for a Japanese agrarian renewal rite.

1.19
Naiku shrine, Ise. The two *temini* side by side; the one occupied and the other dormant.

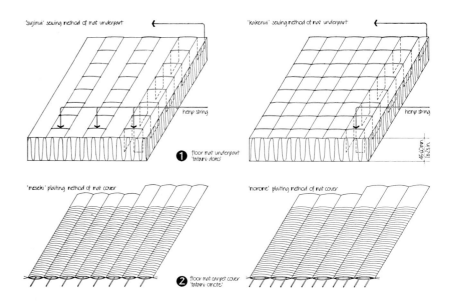

*up and greatly developed by August Schmarsow in a 1893 lecture, in which he
specifically rejected the decorative attributes of the "art of dressing" (Beklei-
dungskunst) in favor of architecture's abstract capacity to "create space"
(Raumgestalterin). The history of architecture is now to be analyzed as a "feeling
for space" (Raumgefühl). Schmarsow's proposal was effectively canonized by
the Dutch architect Hendrik Berlage in his important lecture of 1904, in which he
defined architecture as the "art of spatial enclosure." In the addendum he
attached to the publication of his lecture Berlage argued that the nature of the
wall was surface flatness, and such constructive parts as the pillar and capitals
should be assimilated into it without articulation. Semper's figurative masking of
reality is transposed in Berlage's conception into a literal mask, in which surface
ornamentation, materials, and structural components represent, as it were, their
own constructive and nonconstructive roles as surface decoration.*[33]

This dialogue between the constructive and the nonconstructive would be denied by Adolf Loos in his somewhat biased interpretation of Semper's *Bekleidungstheorie,* which may explain why structure and construction play such a
negligible role in his architecture. In his 1898 essay entitled "Das Prinzip der Bekleidung" (The Principle of Cladding) Loos stresses the primacy of cladding over
all other considerations.[34] Even so, he will still insist on the authenticity of material, so that contrary to Renaissance practice he will argue against the use of
stucco to imitate stone or, even more ironically, against the "graining" of wood
so as to resemble wood of a higher quality. Loos's habitual application of thin
marble revetment on the grounds that it was the cheapest wallpaper in the
world, since it would never need to be replaced, tended to remove him, as his
work would suggest, from Semper's initial preoccupation with the articulation of
the frame and its infill. Like the dissimulating rhetoric of the *Gesamtkunstwerk* to
which he was so opposed, Loos embraced an atectonic strategy in that his spatially dynamic *Raumplan* could never be clearly expressed in tectonic terms.
Indeed, this masking of the actual fabric so that its substance cannot be dis-
cerned is perhaps the sole attribute linking Loos to his rival, the Secessionist architect Josef Hoffmann. The fact that Loos revered tradition makes this affinity
all the more paradoxical, particularly since the aura of tradition emanating from

his marble cladding served to conceal as much as to reveal the harsh reality lying beyond the confines of the bourgeois house. At the same time, as Mallgrave remarks, Peter Behrens's 1910 dismissal of Semper as a positivist will prove quite decisive for modern building culture in that, strongly influenced by the counterthesis of Alois Riegl, the central preoccupations of German architects will shift away from the tectonic to the abstractly atectonic, bordering on the graphic, thereby assisting in that transformation which Robert Schmutzler will call the crystallization of the Jugendstil.[35]

Tectonic/Atectonic

In a 1973 essay entitled "Structure, Construction, and Tectonics," Eduard Sekler defined the tectonic as a certain expressivity arising from the statical resistance of constructional form in such a way that the resultant expression could not be accounted for in terms of structure and construction alone.[36] Sekler proceeded

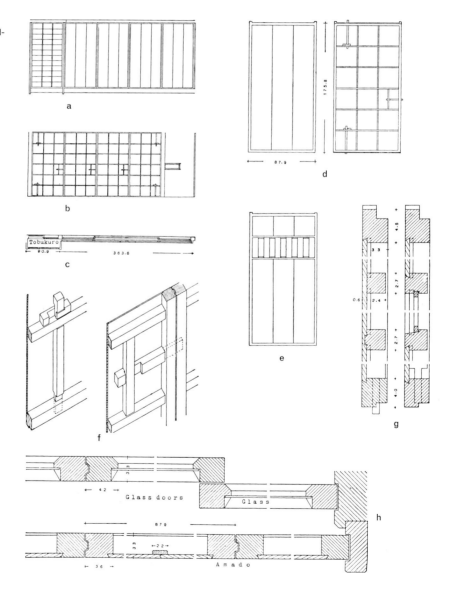

1.21
Details of traditional and modern *amado* sliding wooden shutters.

to show how similar combinations of structure and construction could become the occasion for a subtle variation in expression, as in the various corner details that appear in the American work of Mies van der Rohe. He went on to note that a given expression may be at variance with either the order of the structure or the method of construction, citing as an example the concealed flying buttresses of the Baroque. However, when structure and construction appear to be mutually interdependent, as in, say, Paxton's Crystal Palace of 1851, the tectonic potential of the whole would seem to derive from the eurythmy of its parts and the articulation of its joints. Even here, however, statical capacity and representational form can be said to diverge, albeit imperceptibly, since Paxton's modular cast-iron columns of standard diameter are brought to sustain different loads by varying their wall thickness.

In a subsequent essay dealing with Josef Hoffmann's masterwork, the Stoclet House, built in Brussels in 1911 (fig. 1.22), Sekler would introduce the counter-concept of the *atectonic,* as made manifest in this instance by the cable moldings deployed throughout.

At the corners or any other places of juncture where two or more of these parallel mouldings come together, the effect tends towards a negation of the solidity of the built volumes. A feeling persists as if the walls had not been built up in a heavy construction but consisted of large sheets of thin material, joined at the corners with metal bands to protect the edges. . . . The visual result is very striking and atectonic in the extreme. "Atectonic" is used here to describe a manner in which the expressive interaction of load and support in architecture is visually neglected or obscured. . . . There are many other atectonic details at the Stoclet House. Heavy piers have nothing of adequate visual weight to support but carry a thin, flat roof as at the entrance and over the loggia on the roof terrace. . . . In this connection it is equally significant that windows are set flush into the fa-

1.22
Josef Hoffmann, Stoclet House, Brussels,
1911. Main hall.

1.23
Peter Behrens, AEG turbine factory, Berlin,
1909.

*cades, even slightly protruding, not in recesses which would betray the thickness
of the wall.*[37]

Similar weightless effects can be found in a great deal of German architectural
production at the beginning of this century, most notably perhaps in Peter Behrens's AEG turbine factory built in Berlin in 1909. Here, the massive Egyptoid
corner bastions stop short of supporting the roof that otherwise appears to rest
on them. In this unique work, tectonic and atectonic patently coexist; in the first
instance, the ontologically tectonic, pin-jointed steel frames that run down Berlichingenstrasse, in the second the representationally atectonic corner bastions,
of in situ concrete that, while supporting their own weight, pointedly fail to carry
the oversailing cantilever of the roof (fig. 1.23).

It is ironic that this architectonic ambivalence should emerge in Behrens's symbolization of technological power, particularly since he envisaged architecture as
serving power throughout history—the thesis advanced in his essay "What Is
Monumental Art?" of 1908. Perhaps this psycho-cultural ambivalence arises directly out of his rather willful (*Kunstwollen*) attempt to render the factory shed as
a kind of crypto-classical barn in order to signify what Ernst Jünger would later
call the *Gestalt* of the worker—the "will to power" of the workers who had already been transformed from an agrarian labor force into a highly skilled proletariat, indentured in the service of the industrial *Kartel*.[38]

Technology

There is perhaps no twentieth-century philosopher who has responded more
profoundly to the cultural impact of technology than Martin Heidegger, and
while there can be little doubt that there are reactionary aspects of his thought,

21

his work amounts to a fundamental break with positivism; above all, perhaps, through his notion of "thrownness," the idea that each generation has to confront its own destiny within the long trajectory of history.[39] At the same time he has articulated a number of specific insights that are of relevance to the arguments advanced here. The first of these concerns the topographic concept of the bounded domain or place, as opposed to the space endlessness of the megalopolis. This was first broached by him in an essay entitled "Building, Dwelling, Thinking" of 1954:

What the word for space Raum, Rum, *designates is said by its ancient meaning.* Raum *means a place cleared or freed for settlement and lodging. A space is something that has been made room for, something that is cleared and free, namely within a boundary, Greek* peras. *A boundary is not that at which something stops, but, as the Greeks recognized, the boundary is that from which something begins its presencing. . . . Space is in essence that for which room has been made, that which is let into its bounds. That for which room is made is always granted and hence is joined, that is, gathered, by virtue of a location. . . . Accordingly spaces receive their being from locations and not from "space." . . . The space that is thus made by positions is space of a peculiar sort. As distance or "stadion" [in Greek] it is what the same word* stadion *means in Latin, a* spatium, *an intervening space or interval. Thus nearness and remoteness between men and things can become mere distance, mere intervals of intervening space. . . . What is more the mere dimensions of height, breadth, and depth can be abstracted from space as intervals. What is so abstracted we represent as the pure manifold of the three dimensions. Yet the room made by this manifold is also no longer determined by distances; it is no longer a* spatium, *but now no more than* extensio—extension. *But from space as* extensio *a further abstraction can be made, to analytic-algebraic relations. What these relations make room for is the possibility of the purely mathematical construction of manifolds with an arbitrary number of dimensions. The space provided for in this mathematical manner may be called "space," the "one" space as such. But in this sense "the" space, "space," contains no spaces and no places.*[40]

The implications of this for tectonic form are perhaps self-evident, namely the need for human institutions to be integrated with the topography in such a way as to offset the rapacity of development as an end in itself. For Heidegger the problem with technology does not reside in the benefits that it affords but in its emergence as a quasi-autonomous force that has "stamped" the epoch with its *Gestalt.* It is not primarily the environmentally degrading aspects of industrial technique that concern him, but rather the fact that technology has the tendency to transform everything, even a river, into a "standing reserve," that is to say, at one and the same time, into a source of hydroelectric power and an object of tourism.

For Heidegger the rootlessness of the modern world begins with the translation of the Greek experience into the edicts of the Roman imperium, as though the literal translation of Greek into Latin could be effected without their having had the same experience. Against this misunderstanding that culminates for him in the productionist philosophy of the machine age, Heidegger returns us, like his master Eduard Husserl, to the phenomenological presence of things in themselves.

That which gives things their constancy and pith but is also at the same time the source of their particular mode of sensuous pressure—colored, resonant, hard, massive—is the matter in things. In this analysis of the thing as matter, form is already co-posited. What is constant in a thing, its consistency, lies in the fact that matter stands together with a form. The thing is formed matter.[41]

To the extent that architecture remains suspended between human self-realization and the maximizing thrust of technology, it must of necessity become engaged in discriminating among different states and conditions; above all perhaps among the durability of a thing, the instrumentality of equipment, and the worldliness of human institutions. The tectonic presents itself as a mode by which to express these different states and thereby as a means for accommodating, through inflection, the various conditions under which different things appear and sustain themselves. Under this precept different parts of a given building may be rendered differently according to their ontological status. In a 1956 essay entitled "On the Origin of the Work of Art," Heidegger conceives of architecture as having the capacity not only of expressing the different materials from which it is made but also of revealing the different instances and modes by which the world comes into being.

In fabricating equipment—e.g. an axe—stone is used and used up. It disappears into usefulness. The material is all the better and more suitable the less it resists perishing in the equipmental being of equipment. By contrast the temple-work, in setting up a world, does not cause the material to disappear, but rather causes it to come forth for the very first time and to come into the Open of the work's world. The rock comes to bear and rest and so first becomes rock; metals come to glitter and shimmer, colors to glow, tones to sing, the word to speak. All this comes forth as the work sets itself back into the massiveness and heaviness of stone, into the firmness and pliancy of wood, into the hardness and luster of metal, into the lighting and darkening of color, into the clang of tone and into the naming power of the word.[42]

This essay contains further insights that are of pertinence to the tectonic. The first turns on the related but etymologically distinct notion of *techne,* derived from the Greek verb *tikto,* meaning to produce. This term means the simultaneous existence of both art and craft, the Greeks failing to distinguish between the two. It also implies knowledge, in the sense of revealing what is latent within a work; that is to say it implies *aletheia,* or knowing in the sense of an ontological revealing. This revelatory concept returns us to Vico's *verum, ipsum, factum,* to that state of affairs in which knowing and making are inextricably linked; to a condition in which *techne* reveals the ontological status of a thing through the disclosure of its epistemic value. In this sense one may claim that knowledge and hence beauty are dependent upon the emergence of "thingness." All of this is categorically opposed to connoisseurship, where works of art are offered solely for aesthetic enjoyment or where alternatively by virtue of their curatorial preservation they are withdrawn from the world. Of this last Heidegger writes, "World-withdrawal and world-decay can never be undone. The works are no longer the same as they once were. It is they themselves, to be sure, that we encounter there, but they themselves are gone by."[43]

Heidegger asserts a fertile and necessary opposition between the *artifice* of the world and the *natural* condition of the earth, realizing that the one is symbiotically conditioned by the other and vice versa. *Measure* and *boundary* are two terms by which he tries to articulate this relationship. His thinking in this regard, combined with his later emphasis on dwelling, caring, and letting-be, have led a number of commentators to see him as a pioneer of "eco-philosophy."[44] Technology was disturbing to Heidegger inasmuch as he saw it as being devoid of any respect for the intrinsic nature of things. He considered that neither nature nor history nor man himself would be able to withstand the unworldliness of technology if it were released on a planetary scale.

Tradition and Innovation

The notion of mediating instrumental reason through an appeal to tradition, as an evolving matrix from within which the lifeworld is realized both materially and conceptually, is echoed by the Italian school of thought known as *pensiero debole*.[45] One of the key precepts in "weak thought" is the a priori value attached to the fragmentary. This seems to be particularly relevant to the practice of architecture in that the *métier* has no hope of being universally applied in the sense that technoscience achieves such an application. One has only to look at the spontaneous megalopolitan proliferation of our times to recognize the incapacity of the building industry, let alone architecture, to respond in any effective way. Where technology, as the maximization of industrial production and consumption, merely serves to exacerbate the magnitude of this proliferation, architecture as craft and as an act of place creation is excluded from the process.[46]

Seen from this standpoint, the radically new, as an end in itself, loses its claim to perpetual validity, particularly when it is set against the "thrownness" of history. This *Geschick* as Heidegger calls it embodies not only a material condition, specific to a given time and place, but also the legacy of a particular historical tradition that, however much it may be assimilated, is always in the process of transforming itself through what Hans Georg Gadamer has characterized as the "fusion of horizons."[47] For Gadamer, critical reason and tradition are inextricably linked to each other in a hermeneutical circle in which the prejudices of a given cultural legacy have to be continually assessed against the implicit critique of "other" traditions. As Georgia Warnke has written: "it is not that Gadamer no longer identifies the dialectical or dialogical process with the possibility of an advance on the part of reason; it is rather that Gadamer refuses to foreclose this advance by projecting a point of absolute knowledge at which no further dialogic encounters can develop that rationality."[48]

Such a transformational concept is necessarily opposed to the triumph of one universal method. It is, by definition, unstable and specific in a fragmentary sense. Unlike technoscience that regards the past as a series of obsolete moments along the ever-upward trajectory of hypothetical progress, the so-called human sciences cherish the lived past as an *Erlebnis* that is open to being critically reintegrated into the present. As Warnke puts it:

The way in which we anticipate the future defines the meaning that the past can have for us, just as the way in which our ancestors projected the future determines our own range of possibilities. Thus for Gadamer, Vico's formula entails that we understand history not simply because we make it but also because it has made us; we belong to it in the sense that we inherit its experience, project a future on the basis of the situation the past has created for us and act in light of our understanding of this past whether such understanding is explicit or not.[49]

This formulation seems to be echoed in the famous apodictic statement of the Portuguese architect Alvaro Siza that "architects don't invent anything, they transform reality."[50] Unlike fine art, all such transformations have to be rooted in the opacity of the lifeworld and come to their maturity over an unspecified period of time. The way in which such transformations are at once, however imperceptibly, transformed in their turn means that neither a hypostasized past nor an idealized future carries the conviction that they once had in the heyday of the Enlightenment. The decline of utopia denies the validity of the *novum* as an end in itself. As the Italian philosopher Gianni Vattimo puts it in his book *The End of Modernity,* once progress in either science or art becomes routine it is no longer new in the sense that it once was. He remarks, after Arnold Gehlen, that "progress seems to show a tendency to dissolve itself, and with it the value of the new as well, not only in the effective process of secularization, but even in the most extremely futuristic utopias."[51] While the crisis of the neo-avant-garde derives directly from this spontaneous dissolution of the new, critical culture attempts to sustain itself through a dialectical play across a historically determined reality in every sense of the term. One may even claim that, critique aside, critical culture attempts to compensate, in a fragmentary manner, for the manifest disenchantment of the world. The transformed, transforming real is thus constituted not only by the material circumstances obtaining at the moment of intervention but also by a critical intersubjective deliberation upon or about these conditions, both before and after the design and its realization. Material constraints aside, innovation is, in this sense, contingent upon a self-conscious rereading, remaking, and re-collection of tradition (*Andenken*), including the tradition of the new, just as tradition can only be revitalized through innovation. It is in this sense that we may come to conceive of Gehlen's *post-histoire* as the domain of the "bad infinite," to borrow Gadamer's phrase.[52]

Such a hermeneutical model presupposes a continual intersubjective self-realization on the part of the species and a kind of "cantonal" decentralization of power and representation in the field of politics, not to mention the imperative of raising the general level of education throughout society. Under such circumstances we might begin to entertain a possible convergence between Jürgen Habermas's ideal speech situation, his concept of undistorted communication, and Gianni Vattimo's formulation of hermeneutical legitimation as this ought to be applied to the realization of an architectural project. Of this last we find Vattimo writing in terms that seem uncommonly close to those of Habermas:

If therefore, in architecture, as also in philosophy, in existence in general, we renounce any metaphysical, superior, transcendent legitimation (of the kind reaching ultimate truths, redemption of humanity, etc.), all that is left is to understand legitimation as a form of the creation of horizons of validity through dialogue, a dialogue both with the traditions to which we belong and with others.[53]

Irrespective of the inroads of the media, that is to say, of the distortions of mass communication that condition such a large sector of everyday life in the late twentieth century, Habermas's "ideal speech situation" seems to be a prerequisite for an intelligent cultivation of the environment, for as every architect knows, without good clients it is impossible to achieve an architecture of quality.[54] Apart from this, architectural practice has little choice but to embrace what one may call a double hermeneutic, one that, first, seeks to ground its practice in its own tectonic procedures, and second, turns to address itself to the social and to the inflection of what Hannah Arendt termed "the space of public appearance."[55] Vittorio Gregotti reflects on these two aspects in the following terms:

In the course of [the last] thirty years, during which the obsession with history emerged and developed, the belief has taken root that architecture cannot be a means for changing social relationships; but I maintain that it is architecture itself that needs, for its very production, the material represented by social relations. Architecture cannot live by simply mirroring its own problems, exploiting its own tradition, even though the professional tools required for architecture as a discipline can be found only within that tradition.[56]

Elsewhere Gregotti returns to the problem of land settlement, to his earlier preoccupation with the territory of architecture,[57] effectively touching on what may be the ultimate consequence of global mobilization: the simple fact that we have yet to arrive at any pattern of "motopian" land settlement that could be possibly regarded as *rational.*[58]

I believe that if there is a clear enemy to fight today, it is represented by the idea of an economic/technical space indifferent in all directions. This is now such a widespread idea that it seems almost objective. . . . It is a question of a shrewd, modernistic enemy capable of accepting the latest, most fashionable proposal, especially any proposal capable of selling every vain formalistic disguise, favorable only to myth, redundancy or uproar, as a genuine difference.[59]

With remarkable perspicacity Gregotti implies the manner in which tectonic detail may be combined with traditional type forms, modified in light of today's needs but free from gratuitous novelty, in such a way as to articulate the qualitative *difference* separating irresponsible speculation from critical practice. The difficulty of realizing this *répétition différente* is at no point underestimated by Gregotti.[60]

After Auguste Perret's famous slogan "Il n'y a pas de détail dans la construction," Gregotti maintains that detailing should never be regarded as an insignificant technical means by which the work happens to be realized. The full tectonic potential of any building stems from its capacity to articulate both the poetic and the cognitive aspects of its substance. This double articulation presupposes that one has to mediate between technology as a productive procedure and craft technique as an anachronistic but renewable capacity to reconcile different productive modes and levels of intentionality. Thus the tectonic stands in opposition to the current tendency to deprecate detailing in favor of the overall image. As a value it finds itself in opposition to the gratuitously figurative, since to the degree that our works are conceived as having a long duration "we must produce things that look as if they were always there."[61]

In the last analysis, everything turns as much on exactly *how* something is realized as on an overt manifestation of its form. This is not to deny spatial ingenuity but rather to heighten its character through its precise realization. Thus the presencing of a work is inseparable from the manner of its foundation in the ground and the ascendancy of its structure through the interplay of support, span, seam, and joint—the rhythm of its revetment and the modulation of its fenestration. Situated at the interface of culture and nature, building is as much about the ground as it is about built form. Close to agriculture, its task is to modify the earth's surface in such a way as to take care of it, as in Heidegger's concept of *Gelassenheit* or letting be. Hence the notion of "building the site," in Mario Botta's memorable phrase, is of greater import than the creation of freestanding objects, and in this regard building is as much about the topos as it is about technique. Furthermore, despite the privatization of modern society, architecture, as opposed to building, tends to favor the space of public appearance rather than the privacy of the *domus*.[62] At the same time, it is as much about place-making and the passage of time as it is about space and form. Light, water, wind, and weathering, these are the agents by which it is consummated. Inasmuch as its continuity transcends mortality, building provides the basis for life and culture. In this sense, it is neither high art nor high technology. To the extent that it defies time, it is anachronistic by definition. Duration and durability are its ultimate values. In the last analysis it has nothing to do with immediacy[63] and everything to do with the unsayable. What was it Luis Barragán said? "All architecture which does not express serenity fails in its spiritual mission."[64] The task of our time is to combine vitality with calm.

2 Greco-Gothic and Neo-Gothic:
The Anglo-French Origins of Tectonic Form

Ornament is the secret that **Baukunst** *keeps to allow the* **Tekton** *to display the values of which he is guardian. And to conclude this point, it may be useful to remember one of Mies's more felicitous aphorisms. When the architect states that architecture begins where two bricks are carefully joined together, our attention should not fall on the curious, reductive image of the "two bricks," but on what is required for their joining to create something architecturally significant: "carefully" is the key word here. Planning, building, and* **Baukunst** *imply continual care. And such attention demands dedication, "idleness," and time—irrevocable decisions, as Nietzsche instructs. To build is thus to provide protection for the possibility of the event; it is a rejection of the "new" and a love of tradition.* **Baukunst,** *finally, is the* art of time.
Francesco Dal Co, Figures of Architecture and Thought, *1990*

The roots of the Greco-Gothic ideal go back to the seventeenth century inasmuch as they are ultimately traceable to Claude Perrault's retranslation of Vitruvius published in French in 1673, and to his *Ordonnance des cinq espèces de colonnes selon la méthode des anciens* of a decade later. Perrault's Cartesian doubt was to have a lasting impact on French architecture since he repudiated the mythic proportions of the Renaissance, along with the almost divine status accorded to the five orders, asserting instead a theory of positive and arbitrary beauty that was to have a subversive impact on the French classical tradition. The tectonic implications of Perrault's position are evident from his contention that style belongs to the realm of arbitrary beauty, whereas symmetry, richness of materials, and precision of execution are the only indisputable constituents of a positive and universal form of beauty. Where we may elect to regard style as atectonic by virtue of its representational emphasis, positive beauty may be seen to be tectonic inasmuch as it is based on material substance and geometrical order.

Perrault's cultural universalism was further developed by Michel de Frémin in his *Mémoires critiques d'architecture* of 1702. Frémin was the first author to challenge the truism that familiarity with the five orders was necessarily an indication of architectural competence. He was also one of the earliest theorists to regard the Gothic as being fundamental to the development of a structural architecture. In advocating a synthesis of Gothic intercolumnar and Greek trabeated form, the Abbé de Cordemoy would follow Frémin's lead in his *Nouveau traité de tout l'architecture* of 1706, which was significantly subtitled *l'art de bâtir utile aux entrepreneurs et aux ouvriers* (the art of building useful for contractors and craftsmen). In his seminal essay of 1962, "The Abbé de Cordemoy and the Graeco-Gothic Ideal," Robin Middleton stresses the critical importance of Cordemoy in the evolution of French classical tradition:

Interpreting the old Roman theorist [Vitruvius] with unusual rigor, impelled by the conviction that antique architecture was more pure in form than the architecture of the Renaissance cared to admit, Cordemoy proposed an architecture of simplified geometric forms, set one in relation to another, to result in a unified whole. But while he insisted on the unity of the whole, he demanded that each element should retain an air of independence—"le dégagement," he called this quality. He vigorously condemned the bas relief effect of contemporary architecture and rejected scornfully the numerous motifs that were scattered over the surfaces of buildings, blurring their outlines with continuous and uneasy modelling. He attacked especially the court facade of the Louvre. Three superimposed orders were, he considered, excessive, even if sanctioned by antique example. He liked plain masonry surfaces. And, in accord with Frémin, he discouraged the use of ornament. He went even further; he declared that pedestals, applied orders of columns and pilasters should be dispensed with, although he conceded that pilasters could be used *in antis* or to express the external junction of walls. When pilasters were to be used, however, he insisted (and here once again he showed his allegiance to Perrault) there was to be no diminution in their width from top to bottom. He desired, above all, a simplified rectangular architecture. He disliked acute angles and all curves. He approved only of rectangular door and window openings. He liked roof lines to be horizontal. Demanding the use of flat roofs or, as a more practical alternative, Mansart roofs, he sought to do away with the pediment altogether.[1]

It is necessary to mention that Cordemoy insisted on the hierarchical principles of propriety in architecture, arguing that all utilitarian structures should be left entirely devoid of ornament, thereby serving to express the difference in cultural stature between everyday building and works of institutional and symbolic import. It is difficult to adequately represent the cultural complexity of the synthesis that Frémin, Cordemoy, and Laugier successively sought to achieve in their drive to promote a hypothetical Greco-Gothic architecture embodying the character of *dégagement,* that is, columnar articulation within the ordinance of Neoplatonic form. All three theorists wanted to eliminate the elliptical vault and the flying buttress from the syntax of architecture along with the organic excesses of Gothic tracery and detailing—what Frémin called *un amas confus de figures monstrueuses et déréglées.* The touchstone for all of them was the freestanding column that was common to both the Gothic cathedral and the Greek temple.

Dégagement plays an absolutely fundamental role in Abbé Laugier's characterization of the ideal Greco-Gothic church as this appears in his *Essai sur l'architecture* of 1753.

Let us choose the most common form, that of the Latin Cross. I place all around the nave, transept and choir the first Order of isolated columns standing on low socles; they are coupled like those of the portico of the Louvre in order to give more width to the intercolumniations. On these columns I place a straight architrave terminated by an ogee of moderate projection and erect over this a second Order, consisting, like the first one, of free-standing and coupled columns. This second Order has its complete straight entablature and, directly over it without any sort of attic, I erect a plain barrel vault without transverse ribs. Then, around the nave, crossing, and choir, I arrange columned aisles which form a true peristyle and are covered by flat ceilings placed on the architraves of the first Order. . . . This is then my idea and here are the advantages: (1) A building like this is entirely natural and true; everything is reduced to simple rules and executed according to great principles: no arcades, no pilasters, no pedestals, nothing awkward or constrained. (2) The whole plain wall is nowhere to be seen, therefore nothing is superfluous, nothing is bulky, nothing is offensive. (3) The windows are placed in the most suitable and most advantageous position. All intercolumniations are glazed, above and below. There are no more plain lunettes cutting into the vault as in ordinary churches, but ordinary large windows. (4) The two Orders placed one above the other bring nave, crossing and choir to *a height which is in no way irregular and does not require columns of an exorbitant scale. (5) The vault, although barrel vault, loses all heaviness through this height, especially since it has no transverse ribs which would appear to weigh down heavily. (6) Splendor and magnificence could easily be added to the* dégagement, *simplicity, elegance and dignity of such a building.*[2]

In the frontispiece of his *Essai sur l'architecture,* Laugier was to state this paradigm in more aboriginal terms, inasmuch as the hut was of skeletal timber construction and its roof was pitched rather than vaulted. It was ideologically significant of course that this last was more compatible with the form of the

2.1
The primitive hut. Frontispiece from the second edition of Abbé Laugier's *Essai sur l'architecture,* engraved by Ch. Eisen, 1755.

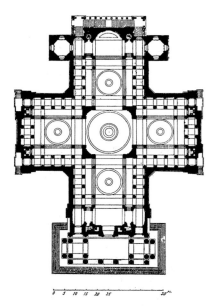

2.2
Jacques-German Soufflot, Ste.-Geneviève,
Paris, 1755–1789 and 1791–1812. Plan.

2.3
Jacques-Germain Soufflot, Ste.-Geneviève,
axonometric (from Choisy).

Greek temple than the Gothic church (fig. 2.1). It is commonly accepted that this paradigm, both as a description and as a drawing, saw its conceptual realization in Jacques-Germain Soufflot's (1713–1780) Ste.-Geneviève church, under construction in Paris from 1755 to 1812 (figs. 2.2, 2.3).[3] Soufflot's achievement of the main body of this structure by 1770 was a triumph for the neoclassical adherents of the Greco-Gothic ideal, although it was also an occasion on which they were compelled to recognize the contradictory nature of this cultural project from a statical point of view; the literal stability of its form being in question throughout the period of construction. Soufflot's Ste.-Geneviève was radical at two different levels. On the one hand, it fulfilled the rationalistic mission of the Greco-Gothic ideal by combining vaulted and trabeated structural forms in a new spatial unity; on the other, it stretched the art of reinforced masonry construction to its technological limits. As Werner Oechslin points out, Ste.-Geneviève was a revolutionary innovation and its ultimate realization was to be of as much interest to mathematicians and engineers as to architects.[4] Indeed, Ste.-Geneviève would have been incapable of completion had it not been for certain engineers from the Ponts et Chaussées; men such as Charles-Augustin de Coulomb, who invented much of modern statical theory, and his colleague Emiland-Marie Gauthey, who was to defend Soufflot's unorthodox, freestanding, columnar dome supports against the criticism coming from the circle of Pierre Patte. Gauthey tested the compressive stress of every stone that went into the masonry supports of the dome. To facilitate this he would devise an on-site testing machine, a device later refined by Jean Rondelet. Rondelet was to serve his apprenticeship as a stonemason under Soufflot at Ste.-Geneviève, and after his master's death in 1780 he stayed on to finish the church, seeing its final completion in 1813. It seems that the spalling and cracking of the columns under the

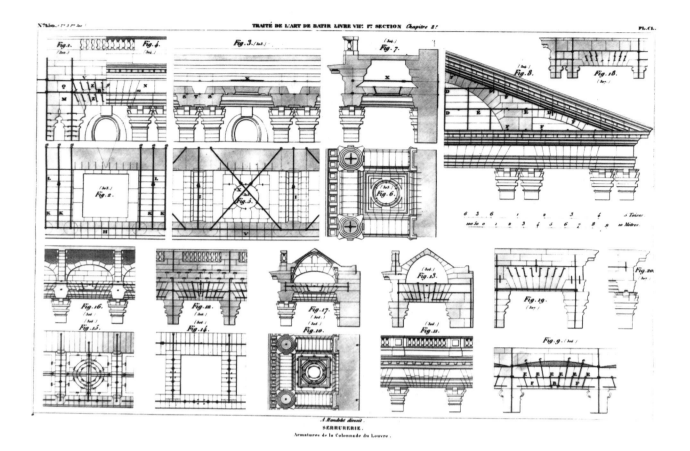

A. Rondelet direxit.
SERRURERIE.
Armatures de la Colonnade du Louvre.

2.4
Claude Perrault, colonnade, east facade of the Louvre, Paris, 1665. Medieval wrought-iron cramping techniques applied to wide-span trabeated construction.

pendentives of the dome was due to the uneven settlement of hard and soft stone, a defect that he rectified by adding stonework to the sides of the triangular piers at the base of the columns and thereafter binding the whole assembly together with wrought-iron bars.

Elaborate iron cramping had already been used by Claude Perrault when building the disengaged trabeated colonnade along the east facade of the Louvre (1665) (fig. 2.4), and Soufflot would employ a similar system in constructing the reinforced stone portico to Ste.-Geneviève in 1770. Rondelet's analytical drawing of this pronaos, as published in his *Traité théorique et pratique de l'art de bâtir* of 1802–1817, reveals the inherent contradiction of pursuing tectonic order with stereotomic means (fig. 2.5). Aside from the concealed relieving stone arches, which resemble the hidden flying buttresses used elsewhere, the density and complexity of the wrought-iron reinforcement seems to anticipate François Hennebique's final perfection of the reinforced concrete frame (fig. 5.1).

Ste.-Geneviève was a hybrid work from both a typological and a structural point of view; first for its synthesis of Greek and Latin cross plans and second for the contradiction between the concealed buttresses and the orthogonal order of the internal peristyle. The technical difficulties encountered in the erection of this church testify to the willfulness of neoclassical doctrine, most evident perhaps in Ste.-Geneviève where there is a discrepancy between the structural vaults

Greco-Gothic and Neo-Gothic

33

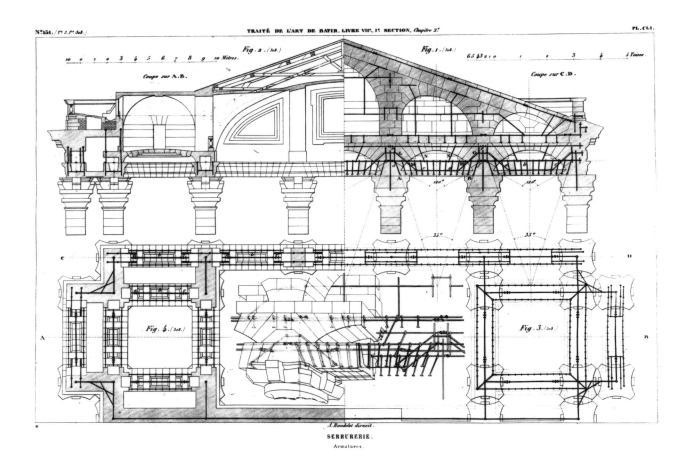

SERRURERIE.
Armatures.

carrying the main loads at the crossing of the church and the representative semicircular arches employed throughout the internal volume (fig. 2.6).

Where the Greco-Gothic movement was almost exclusively French, the Gothic revival of the nineteenth century was Anglo-French in that it arose out of the careers of two figures who were mutually influential: the Comte Charles de Montalembert, who published his Catholic tract *De l'état actuel de l'art religieux en France* in 1839, and the Anglo-French Augustus Welby Northmore Pugin (son of the French émigré Augustus Charles Pugin), who published his pro-Catholic cultural polemic in 1836 under the title *Contrasts: Or a Parallel between the Noble Edifices of the Fourteenth and Fifteenth Centuries and Similar Buildings of the Present Day; Showing the Present Decay of Taste.* There were other contemporary Anglo-French intellectuals who pursued similar goals, notably the Cambridge polymath Robert Willis, who, influenced like Pugin by A. F. Frézier's study of medieval stereotomy, advanced his own thesis in 1842 "On the Construction of Vaults in the Middle Ages," and the French scholar Arcisse de Caumont, who in 1824 published his pioneering archaeological study *Sur l'architecture du Moyen Âge.*[5]

With the exception of a didactic comparison between Gothic and Romanesque, one that will favor the former for its aspirational height, Pugin's *Contrasts* gives little indication as to how ecclesiastical architecture might be renewed. It is a pro-Catholic diatribe against a degenerate present rather than an architectural thesis, and it is only after Pugin has achieved a number of works himself—some twenty churches in the space of five years—that he is able to give more cogent advice as to the manner in which a truly Catholic architecture might be revived. This comes with his *True Principles of a Christian or Pointed Architecture* published in 1841, in which he characterizes the reductive form of the typical nineteenth-century church or chapel as little more than a room full of seats facing the street (fig. 2.7).

The critical but regressive nature of Pugin's *Contrasts* is evident from his desire to turn the clock back. Catholic convert at the age of 23 and henceforth desirous of being affiliated with Cardinal Newman's Oxford Movement, Pugin was never able to exorcise his nostalgia for the golden age of Christendom. Like Henri Saint-Simon in his influential book *The New Christianity* of 1825, Pugin was to regard himself as an untimely witness to the decay of European Christian culture, not only the decay induced by the Reformation in all its forms but also the inner decay of the Catholic Church as a sociocultural institution. While Pugin was critical of Catholicism in its decline, he was against those emerging forms

2.5
Jacques-Germain Soufflot, Ste.-Geneviève, pronaos. Rondelet's cutaway elevation and isometric reveals only too clearly the extent to which the masonry is reinforced by a wrought-iron armature as well as by stone anchors that are hidden behind the sculptured pediment.

2.6
Jacques-Germain Soufflot, Ste.-Geneviève, partial section through base of dome.

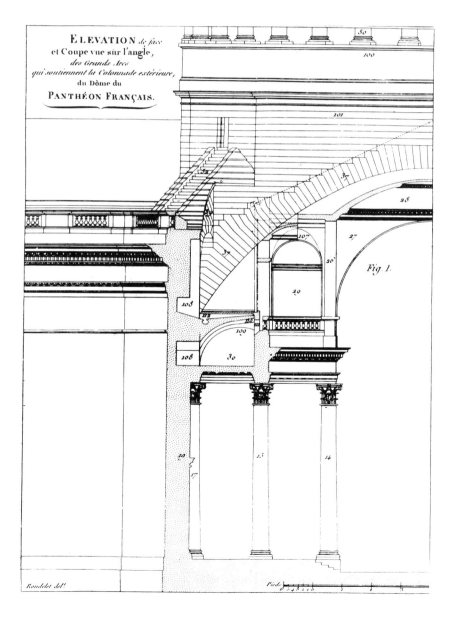

of modern social welfare advanced by such utilitarian reformers as Sir Robert Peel, founder of the police force, and Jeremy Bentham, the inventor of the Panopticon. Pugin's opposition to any kind of authoritarian secular reform also served to distance him from Saint-Simon, since the latter, as the founder of the Napoleonic Ecole Polytechnique, favored a technocratically administered welfare state as opposed to Pugin's ideal of a benevolent theocracy.

While convinced of the possibility of recovering a lost harmony through architecture, Pugin is initially unable to articulate this project in any detail. In 1835, while designing the neo-Gothic details for Charles Barry's Palace of Westminster, Pugin can do little more than rant against Catholic decadence in the first edition of *Contrasts*. His polemic is sharpened considerably in the second edition of 1841, when he criticizes a whole range of utilitarian practices, from Benjamin's Panopticon to the habit of dissecting the bodies of the poor in the name of medical research (fig. 2.8). Pugin's ultimate contrast, drawn between the generic cities of 1440 and 1840, enables him to reject as barbarous the brick-faced, vaulted, iron-framed, fireproof mill construction of the late eighteenth century.[6]

Opposed to the rhetorical architecture of the Counter-Reformation and hence as anti-Baroque as the Jesuit, Greco-Gothic movement, Pugin was incapable of countenancing the slightest trace of what he called classical paganism in architectural form. For Pugin architecture was a religious and ethical affair, and his passionate commitment to the moral rigor of early Christendom was to lead him into constant conflict with the more worldly members of the British Catholic hierarchy. However, despite the contentious nature of his polemic, his evident talent assured him a wide patronage and enabled him to realize nearly a hundred buildings, many of them churches, before his untimely death in 1852 (fig. 2.9).

While Pugin's ability as an antiquarian draftsman recommended him to Barry as a Gothic delineator for the Palace of Westminster, he was not trained as an architect in the usual sense. This lack of schooling makes it all the more remarkable that, after leaving Barry in 1837, he was able to build with such conviction and assurance. Part of this was no doubt due to the training he had received at an early age from his father, and part was also probably due, as Phoebe Stanton has suggested, to his familiarity with A. F. Frézier's *La Théorie et la pratique de la coupe des pierres et des bois pour la construction des voûtes* (1737–1739). Pugin's *True Principles* of 1841 was based on two fundamental axioms that, aside from serving as the guiding precepts for his own practice, were to be followed throughout the rest of the century as the protofunctionalist principles of the Gothic Revival. These precepts, which also served as the basic underpinning of the Arts and Crafts movement, read as follows: "First, that there should be no features about a building which are not necessary for convenience, construction or propriety; second, that all ornament should consist of the enrichment of the essential construction of the building."[7] Pugin distinguished applied ornament from the decorative elaboration of tectonic features and argued for the precise significance of the smallest detail in this last regard. He was convinced that tectonic form should be largely determined by the nature of the material and that all these conditions had been best met in the English Gothic manner of the fifteenth century, irrespective of whether the work in hand was a cathedral or an almshouse. In the course of this thesis Pugin will pass from a warm appraisal of the Gothic to a deprecation of the Greek temple, above all for its misapplication of stone to forms deriving from timber construction.

Grecian architecture is essentially wooden in its construction; it originated in wooden buildings and never did its professors possess either sufficient imagination or skill to conceive any departure from the original type. . . . This is at once the most ancient and most barbarous mode of building that can be imagined; it is heavy and, as I before said, essentially wooden; but is it not extraordinary that when the Greeks commenced building in stone, the properties of this material did not suggest to them some different and improved mode of construction?

Pugin proceeds to contrast this lack of development with the architects of the Middle Ages who "with stone scarcely larger than ordinary bricks, threw their lofty vaults from slender pillars across a vast intermediate space, and that at an

2.7
A. W. N. Pugin, plate from *True Principles,* 1841. The utilitarian chapel as a decorated shed.

2.8
A. W. N. Pugin, plate from *Contrasts,* 1841.

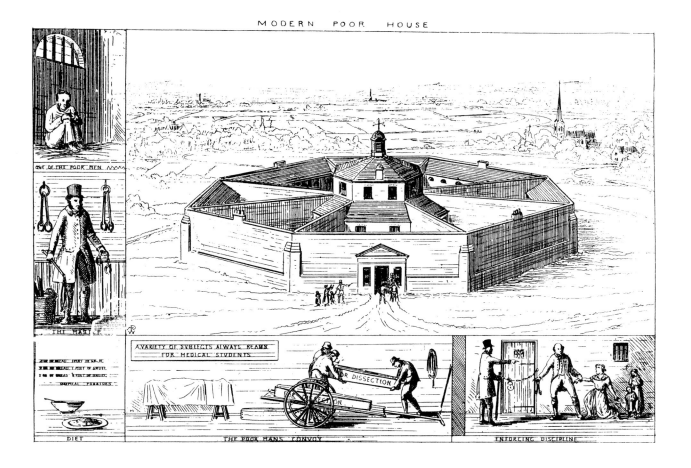

amazing height, where they had every difficulty of lateral pressure to contend with. This leads me to speak of buttresses, a distinguishing feature of Pointed Architecture."[8]

From this contrast between trabeated and vaulted stereotomic form, we may assume that Pugin was at least familiar with some of the Greco-Gothic arguments advanced by Cordemoy and Laugier. Like the Greco-Gothicists, Pugin is convinced that a column should be a freestanding, load-bearing support, but unlike them he proceeds to praise the tectonic virtues of the pointed arch and the flying buttress and to point out that in St. Paul's cathedral, London, Christopher Wren, far from dispensing with flying buttresses, merely built a screen wall to conceal them (compare Soufflot's Ste.-Geneviève) (fig. 2.10).

Pugin's subsequent appraisal of the Gothic groin vault follows a similar line of reasoning, in which he argues in favor of its lightness, its techno-aesthetic unity (its ribs wedged into position by a central boss), and its aspirational height. This last is contrasted to the decadence of the English Decorated style as this appears in Henry VII's chapel in Westminster, with its structurally redundant fan vaulting and its vulgarly rhetorical stone pendants. He applies a similar logic to

2.9
A. W. N. Pugin, Church of St. Augustine, Ramsgate, 1842.

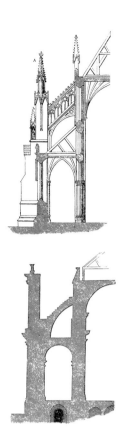

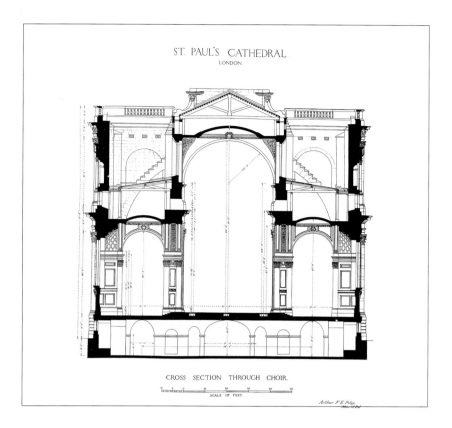

ST. PAUL'S CATHEDRAL
LONDON.

CROSS SECTION THROUGH CHOIR.

SCALE OF FEET.

Arthur F. E. Poley.

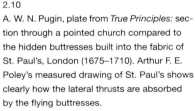

2.10

A. W. N. Pugin, plate from *True Principles:* section through a pointed church compared to the hidden buttresses built into the fabric of St. Paul's, London (1675–1710). Arthur F. E. Poley's measured drawing of St. Paul's shows clearly how the lateral thrusts are absorbed by the flying buttresses.

the design of spires, arguing that their form should be derived directly from their construction, as opposed to the false Baroque dome of Wren's St. Paul's or the equally empty bulbous timber steeples of the continental Baroque (fig. 2.11).

Pugin would rationalize what the Greco-Gothicists had criticized as the excrescences of the Gothic. Thus, he justified the pinnacle as an essential counterweight to the thrust of the buttress and in much the same vein, but to different ends, deprecated the flat-topped church tower, first because it was a secular form and second because it was yet another symptom of post-Gothic decadence, since a flat-topped tower was insufficiently aspirational in a religious sense. Pugin saw the pitched roof as the sine qua non of a pointed architecture, particularly where this pitch conformed to the 60-degree angle of the equilateral triangle; that is to say, where it was sufficiently steep to throw off snow without imposing too much strain on the tile fixings. The forms of Gothic moldings are adduced according to similar logic. Thus, splayed jambs and arches to doors and windows are advocated for the provision of easy access and for the admission of light, while sloping profiles are rationalized on the grounds of their draining water away from apertures, etc. Elsewhere Pugin insists that moldings must recede from the face of the jamb rather than project, in order to preserve the tectonic severity of the form, while hooded moldings are to be employed exclusively for the purpose of weathering.

Pugin observed that in Gothic the different details are multiplied with the increased scale of the building, whereas in the classic they are merely magnified. And just as Pugin despised the tendency of post-Renaissance architecture to conceal and disguise the essential structural body of the work, so he also loathed the pompous scalelessness of classical magnification.

Greco-Gothic and Neo-Gothic

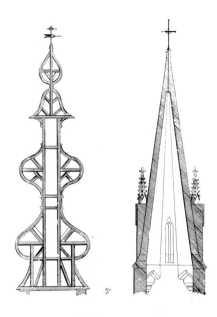

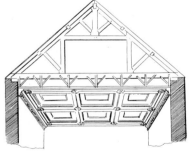

2.11
A. W. N. Pugin, plate from *True Principles*: section through an early stone steeple compared to the typical Flemish steeple in timber.

2.12
A. W. N. Pugin, plate from *True Principles*: ornamented medieval wooden truss roof compared to the concealment of trusswork by a suspended ceiling. This is an implicit critique of Wren's Sheldonian Theatre of 1663–1669.

As we have already seen, the buttressless exterior of St. Paul's is to be paralleled in Soufflot's Ste.-Geneviève. But the preponderance of scenographic effect is not the only cause for Pugin's dissatisfaction with the classic and the baroque, for symmetry itself is regarded as an anathema to the extent that it is not an organic or natural principle, as a passage written in 1841 makes clear: "The mediaeval builders made their plans in such a way as they were essentially convenient and suitable to the required purpose, and decorated them afterwards." Their beauty is "so striking because it is natural."[9]

Unlike Karl Friedrich Schinkel and Gottfried Semper, and even unlike Eugène Viollet-le-Duc, who in many respects will succeed him as the leading nineteenth-century theorist of structural rationalism, Pugin is not interested in the development of an appropriate nineteenth-century style. Anti-Vitruvian and anti-utilitarian to an equal degree, Pugin displays minimal concern for the integration of new methods and materials, although he does indeed introduce iron into his details. In short Pugin, unlike the Gothic Revivalists who came after him, was against the project of an evolving style. Thus he will come to regard the flat, four-centered arch of the English Decorated manner as a symptom of the cultural decadence that would lead inevitably to the concealed buttress of St. Paul's. For Pugin, load-bearing masonry was an ethical precondition, although timber trusswork could be admitted for the support of spires and roofs. Once again, the timberwork had to be revealed, in contradistinction to the concealment of the roof truss as evident, say, in Wren's Sheldonian Theatre completed at Oxford in 1669 (fig. 2.12). Pugin is quite specific about which dimensions and materials are or are not conducive to a constructed architecture. Thus, large stones as commonly employed in Greek and neoclassical masonry are undesirable because they weaken the strength of the structure and misrepresent its scale. Cast iron is rejected (at least in theory) because it is intrinsically disproportionate, devoid of modeling, and detrimental to the vitality of craft production due to its modular repetition. As we have already noted, the use of wrought and even occasionally cast iron introduced a contradictory element into Pugin's cultural program, above all because it led to the wholesale production of Gothic Revival accoutrements in cast iron and other materials (fig. 2.13). This departure from the original medieval materials and methods led to a highly organized form of craft production that Pugin set up with several manufacturers, such as John Hardman (metal), George Meyers (stone and wood carving), Herbert Minton (tiles), and John Grace (furniture). It was exactly these fabricators that enabled him to design and furnish his prodigious output. He appears not to have felt that there was any discrepancy between the repetitive mass production of these "ecclesiastical warehouses" and the essential craft base of his much-admired medieval culture. Accepting steam locomotion and industrial technology as among the necessary improvements of his age, Pugin elected to ignore the ideological contradictions implicit in his double standard. Thus, while nothing was more antithetical to him than Joseph Paxton's modular Crystal Palace of 1851, the mass production of modular parts is nonetheless a common denominator that serves to bring under a single rubric both Paxton's Palace and Pugin's Palace of Westminster, arguably the two most canonical British buildings of the mid-nineteenth century (figs. 2.14, 2.15). The full irony of this paradox was to be played out in the Great Exhibition itself, wherein Pugin, with the aid of Hardman, set up his medieval court as a display of their mutual generative capacity. This exhibition of "modern" Gothic detail was much admired by Semper (fig. 2.16). Its neo-

Gothic enclosure opened onto an implicit but dematerialized ceiling provided by the floating ferro-vitreous construction of Paxton's palace, as detailed, significantly enough, by the railway engineers Fox, Henderson & Partners (fig. 2.17). We may take it that such cultural confrontations brought Pugin to write to Hardman at the end of his life in 1851: "As we gain knowledge conviction of failure is inevitable. It quite gets on my mind. I believe we know too much. Knowledge is power but it is misery. Dear me, a few years ago I felt quite satisfied with things we now look upon as abominable. Still, I almost sigh for the old simplicity when I thought all the old cathedral men fine fellows. It is all delusion. Everything is deception and unreal vanity and vexation of spirit."[10]

At this juncture, our account of the neo-Gothic tectonic shifts back to France, for the next major figure within the Greco-Gothic line is Henri Labrouste who, thirteen years older than Viollet-le-Duc, was thoroughly trained in the French academic system, first in the Ecole des Beaux-Arts and then in the French Academy in Rome.

As is evident from his Cours de Cassation, a Grand Prix student project of 1829, Labrouste had been trained in the Ecole des Beaux-Arts according to planning precepts similar to those advanced by Jean-Nicolas-Louis Durand in his typological manual *Précis des leçons d'architecture données a l'Ecole Polytechnique,* published between 1802 and 1805 (fig. 2.18). Opposed to sublime monumentality, despite his apprenticeship with Etienne Boullée, Durand took an anti-Laugier position, insisting that buildings should be assembled about or upon a series of orthogonal type forms or matrices, to be varied in scale, deportment, and representational expression according to the status of the work. While Labrouste followed similar precepts, he augmented such typological rigor with tectonic invention and symbolization that went well beyond the abstractions of Durand. Thus, while displaying little affinity for the Gothic *in se,* his designs for the Bibliothèque Ste.-Geneviève (1838–1850) (fig. 2.19) and the Bibliothèque Nationale (1854–1875) (figs. 2.20, 2.21) amounted to a rationalized and articulated neoclassical architecture that was to serve as a link between the intercolumniated space theorized by the Greco-Gothic intellectuals and the structurally rationalist, Gothic-inspired architecture to be elaborated later by Viollet-le-Duc. At the same time, as David Van Zanten reminds us, Labrouste's Bibliothèque Ste.-Geneviève demonstrated the virtues of a simplified stone architecture as it might have been imagined by Cordemoy.

Labrouste's ornamental articulation of this simple, spatial and structural scheme brings out its particular qualities rather than filtering them through the conventional columnar dress of neoclassicism. There are no breaks in the wall plane or pediments or pavilions on the silhouette. There are no pilasters or projecting window surrounds . . . the only capitals are collars of Labrouste's invention around the piers of the reading room window arcade. Otherwise, ornament has sunk back into the structural surfaces. Instead of the richly varied shadows of a deeply sculpted neoclassical building surface, Labrouste used the flat, even shadows cast by bevels, right-angle projections, and simple cyma rectas to make palpable the solidity of the actual stone surfaces.[11]

With the completion of this library, Labrouste demonstrated a model and a method that Viollet-le-Duc would turn to a few years later, namely the insertion of a prefabricated, fireproof iron armature into a masonry shell tectonically prepared for its reception. In this instance, the iron framework comprised a double

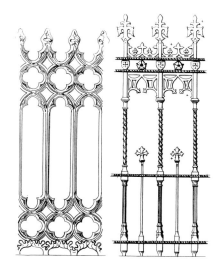

2.13
A. W. N. Pugin, plate from *True Principles:* a comparison between cast- and wrought-iron railings intended to show the mechanical coarseness of the former.

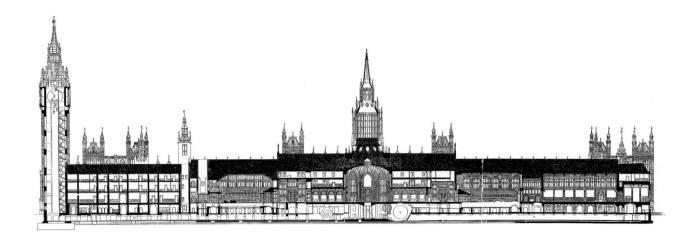

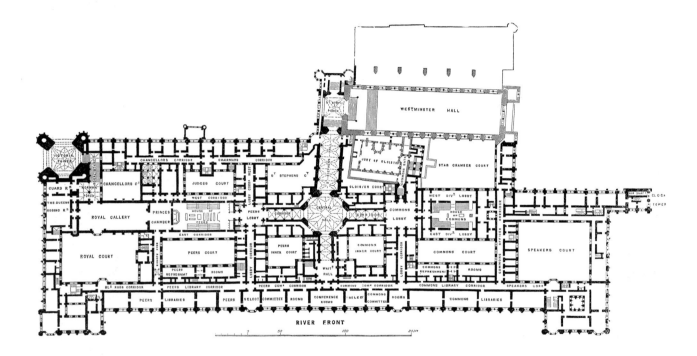

2.14
A. W. N. Pugin and Sir Charles Barry, Westminster New Palace, London, 1836–c.1865. Longitudinal section and plan.

2.15
Joseph Paxton (with Fox and Henderson, consulting engineers), Crystal Palace, Hyde Park, 1851.

2.16
Joseph Paxton (with Fox and Henderson), Crystal Palace, the medieval court.

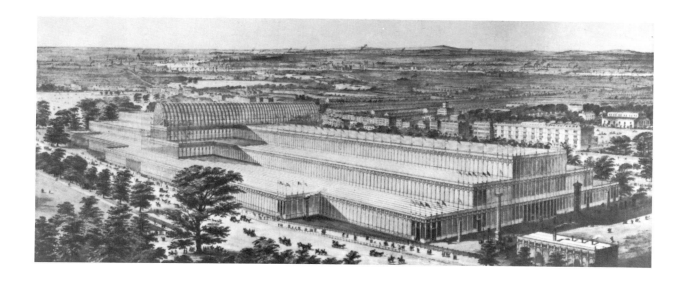

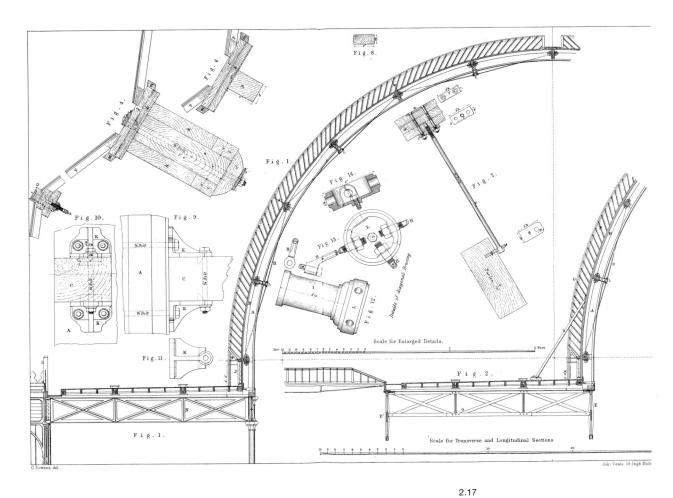

2.17
Joseph Paxton (with Fox and Henderson),
Crystal Palace, construction details.

2.18
J. N. L. Durand, horizontal combinations.
Plate from *Précis des leçons d'architecture,*
1823.

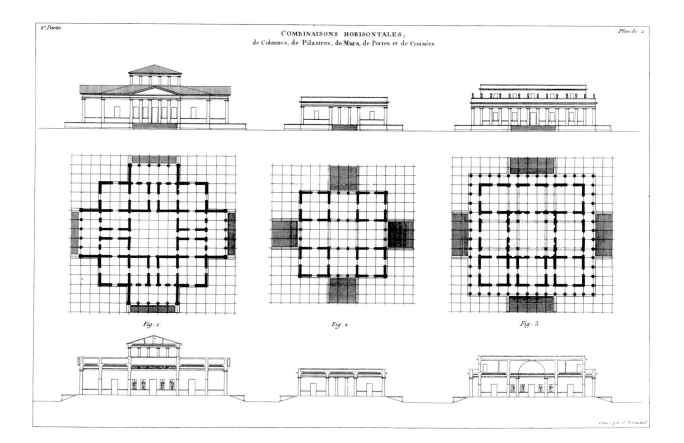

COMBINAISONS HORISONTALES,
de Colonnes, de Pilastres, de Murs, de Portes et de Croisées

Fig. 1.   Fig. 2.   Fig. 3.

barrel-vaulted roof, made up of lightweight iron sheets, with its roof loads carried on a skeleton of fretted, openwork iron ribs. This assembly rested in part on a central line of cast-iron columns and in part on brackets corbeling out from the masonry perimeter. It is of the utmost importance, as Herman Hertzberger has remarked, that the arcuated iron ribs go around the corner at the end of the long volume, thereby unifying the space and forestalling a reading of the library structure as two parallel lines of vaults (fig. 2.22).[12] Not least among the expressive subtleties of this encased armature is the way its structural module is reflected on the exterior. Iron tie rods, connected to the foot of each iron rib, extend through the thick masonry walls to terminate in circular cast-iron anchor plates, visible on the facade (fig. 2.23). A similar permeation of the thick masonry case by a metallic tectonic can be found elsewhere in the fabric, above all in the cast-iron beams that support the floor above the entry colonnade and the sundry rails, radiators, and light fittings that furnish the reading room.

Labrouste would amplify this approach in his Bibliothèque Nationale begun in 1854. In this instance "encasement" was unavoidable, since the respective wrought-iron armatures of the stacks and the reading room itself had to be installed within the existing masonry shell of the Palais Mazarin. The exact manner in which this operation was carried out is significant, from the grillwork and catwalks of the cast-iron book stacks to the sixteen cast-iron columns carrying the armature of the wrought-iron reading room roof. In the first instance, we have a dematerialized top-lit "engine room" space of astonishing lightness and precision; in the second we are presented with shell vaults covering a nine-square plan. These last comprise cupolas, built up out of terra-cotta panels and pierced by oculi. While providing light for the reading room, their assembly rests on a grid of riveted latticework iron arches that in turn take their support from the slender cast-iron columns. It is of the utmost import that *each* of these columns is a freestanding element, including those lining the perimeter, for this fur-

2.19
Henri Labrouste, Bibliothèque Ste.-Geneviève, Paris, 1838–1850. Transverse section.

2.20
Henri Labrouste, Bibliothèque Nationale, Paris, 1854–1875. Plan, section, and details.

2.21
Henri Labrouste, Bibliothèque Nationale, perspective.

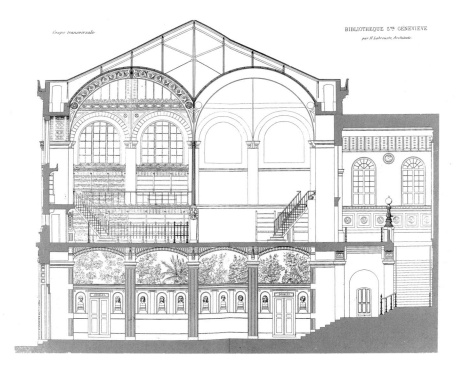

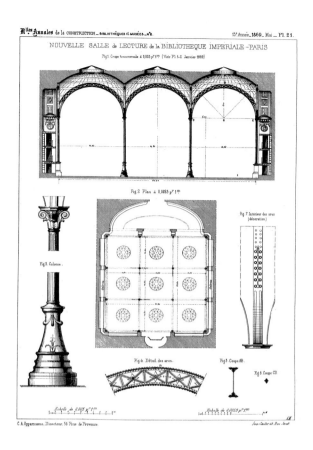

NOUVELLE SALLE de LECTURE de la BIBLIOTHÈQUE IMPÉRIALE _ PARIS

Fig 1. Coupe transversale à 0,005 p.º 1ᵐ (Voir Pl. 1-2 Janvier 1869)

Fig 2. Plan à 0,0025 p.º 1ᵐ

Fig 3. Colonne.

Fig 7. Intérieur des arcs (décoration)

Fig 4. Détail des arcs.

Fig 5. Coupe AB.

Fig 6. Coupe CD.

Echelle de 0,005 p.º 1ᵐ

Echelle de 0,0025 p.º 1ᵐ

C. A. Oppermann, Directeur, 56 Rue de Provence.   Imp. Caillot 43, Rue Jacob.

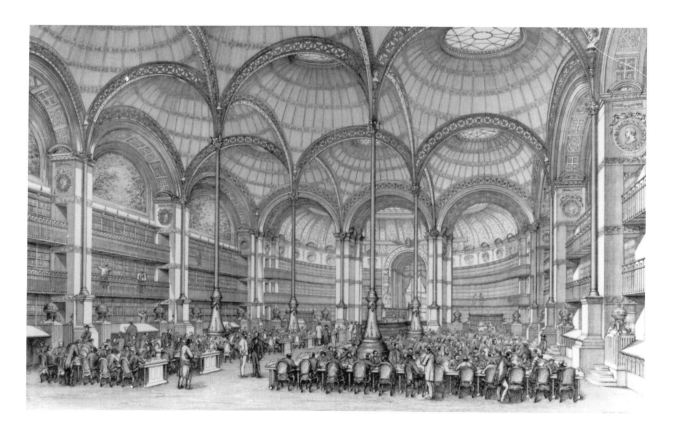

ther exemplifies the Greco-Gothic tradition. This complete articulation of the tectonic skeleton is a more complete demonstration of the proposition that Labrouste had first advanced in his Bibliothèque Ste.-Geneviève. Such a self-contained, lightweight columnar armature will come to be repeated later, in the work of both Viollet-le-Duc and Auguste Perret.

It is typical of Labrouste's sophisticated sensibility that this space would be conceived as a Roman *velarium,* that is to say, as a top-lit space that, amongst its other metaphorical readings, was intended to recall a tented membrane, suspended in high summer over an antique courtyard. This metaphor could hardly be more ambiguous, for where, on the one hand, the space is evidently vaulted, on the other, these vaults may be fancifully interpreted as the folds in a billowing canvas, held down by cast-iron guy ropes. Thus Labrouste's reading room seems to oscillate between a transcendental triumph over gravity through its freestanding columns and the evocation of an *al fresco* space that has been temporarily covered. This last, as in the entry of the Bibliothèque Ste.-Geneviève, is reinforced by Poussinesque murals that decorate the perimeter of the room.

One may note, after Peter McCleary, how these two successive masterworks of Labrouste's career amount to a technological transition, as one passes from the craft empiricism of the cast-iron, pin-jointed, foliated arches of the Bibliothèque Ste.-Geneviève to the wrought-iron, riveted, trussed arches of the Bibliothèque Nationale. In both instances, Labrouste strove for a consistent tectonic expression, one in which the ornamentation would be derived directly from the process of construction.[13]

Viollet-le-Duc began his independent career as an architect in 1840, receiving no less than twelve commissions for the restoration of medieval monuments between 1842 and 1845, among them the prestigious task of restoring Notre-Dame de Paris. He was not, however, a Gothic Revivalist in the same nostalgic and moralistic sense as Pugin. Indeed, far from being "anti-pagan" (to use Pugin's terminology), Viollet-le-Duc accorded equal respect to both the Gothic and the Greek, arguing after Saint-Simonian cultural theorists that both of these tectonic forms were the direct issue of healthy, organic societies. He sought "with some desperation an architecture Gothic in inspiration, but recognizably of the nineteenth century."[14] This quest was ultimately to be satisfied in theoretical rather than practical terms, for while he realized over forty buildings in almost as many years of practice, he never succeeded in evolving a convincing mode of

2.22
Henri Labrouste, Bibliothèque Ste.-Geneviève, axonometric of iron ribs within masonry shell.

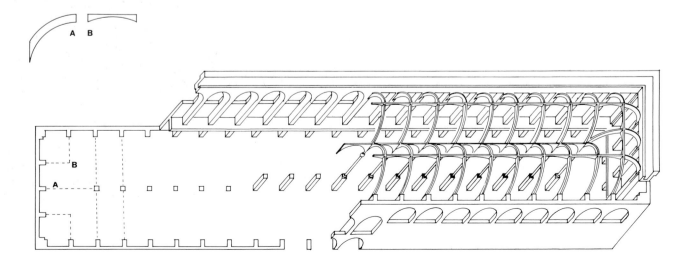

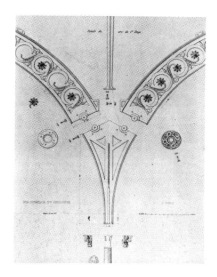

2.23
Henri Labrouste, Bibliothèque Ste.-
Geneviève: the wrought-iron arches are an-
chored back into the masonry encasement
through wrought-iron tie rods passing
through the thickness of the wall. A metal
boss indicates the presence of the iron armature on the exterior.

contemporary architecture for himself. His wide influence as a theoretician dates from the publication of his *Dictionnaire raisonné de l'architecture française du XI au XVI siècle,* which began to be published in 1854, and his *Entretiens sur l'architecture,* the first volume of which came out four years later, both works being completely published by 1872.

Viollet-le-Duc's *Entretiens* may be characterized as an encyclopedic polemic, since the overriding aim of this two-volume magnum opus was to discredit scenographic eclecticism, and to establish in its stead architecture as an *art* of construction, predicated on logic, climate, economy, and the pragmatic precepts of intelligent craft production. The *Entretiens* is a polemically discursive work in the modern sense, for, as its author was to point out with regard to the grecophile culture of the Roman Empire, "the Romans were necessarily *classic,* in the modern acceptance of the word; for nothing assimilates better with administrative direction than classicism, as we now conceive it, and nothing is more contrary to the administrative spirit than discussion."[15]

Viollet-le-Duc opened the first volume of the *Entretiens* with a frontal attack on the then popular archaeological theory (later to be replicated by Auguste Choisy) that the Greek Doric manner was a petrification of an earlier mode of wooden temple construction. In so doing, he also attempted to discredit one of the Platonic tenets of the Greco-Gothic ideal, namely, Laugier's model of the primitive hut as advanced in his *Essai sur l'architecture.* Viollet-le-Duc argued, on the basis of anthropological evidence, that most primitive huts were conical or pyramidal in shape rather than four-square, rectangular, and pedimented.

Throughout the *Entretiens* Viollet-le-Duc is at pains to distance himself from Gothic Revivalism, which may well explain his equally surprising omission of any reference to the Comte de Montalembert, whom he had known and who, as we have already seen, was an influence on Pugin. Thus, while Viollet-le-Duc was to adduce from French twelfth-century Gothic a set of principles that were not that different from those set forth in Pugin's *True Principles of Pointed or Christian Architecture* (1841), he nonetheless insisted, unlike Pugin, on using these principles to evolve a relatively untried approach toward the generation of structural form. Viollet-le-Duc was not afflicted with Pugin's ecclesiastical angst. Indeed, he was at pains to distance himself from the *partie cléricale,* and while he was every bit as literary as Pugin, his procedure was syntactic, open, and additive, rather than semantic and closed. Again unlike Pugin, pagan culture was of seminal importance for him, above all Rome, largely because he saw Roman walling as an economic and technically sound principle of assembly in which fair-faced revetment was effectively keyed into a rubble stone backing. Closer to Gottfried Semper's ethnographic *Bekleidung* theory that pointed to the lightweight brick or tile cladding of heterogeneous structures, Viollet-le-Duc distanced himself from the ontological tectonic of Pugin's masonry principles.[16]

Throughout the two volumes of his *Entretiens* Viollet-le-Duc encourages the dynamic assembly of different materials, techniques, and resources, in order to evolve an effective and engaged mode of building for the given moment. By such an assembly, however, he did not intend a simpleminded transposition of different technologies, as in, say, the inarticulate substitution of cast-iron columns for stone supports, without reconsidering the interactive and contingent character of the entire assembly. This aversion to mere juxtaposition led him to be critical of the nineteenth-century railway terminus with its characteristic split between the classic, heavy palatial front and the light, ferro-vitreous shed to the rear. By a similar token, but at a different scale, he did not accept the concealed cramping of trabeated, fair-faced stonework that was the indispensable technique of the Greco-Gothic mode of building, as we have already seen in the case of Soufflot's Ste.-Geneviève.

To the extent that he took Michel de Frémin's *Mémoires critiques d'architecture* of 1702 as his own point of departure, Viollet-le-Duc was influenced by the Greco-Gothic line of reasoning. It is this that leads him to recognize the diseconomy of the flying buttress and later to invent an isometric architecture of equilibrated, mixed-media construction. This dynamic, synthetic approach is as evident in his analysis of the Roman basilica at Fano as it is the inspiration for his iron-reinforced 65-foot-span vaulted hall to be erected without buttresses. In this audacious proposal for a slender masonry wall reinforced by cast-iron tubes, he provides for absorption of the lateral thrust through a combination of cast-iron compression members and wrought-iron tie bars. In this instance the resultant force acts as a counterthrust delivered to the masonry footing at the base of the wall. Of this he wrote:

It is plain, however, that had the mediaeval builders possessed cast or rolled iron of considerable dimensions, they would not have employed such a material as they employed, stone. . . . It is likewise evident, however, that they would not have failed to take advantage of the principles of elasticity which they were already applying to buildings of stone. . . . This organism *is undoubtedly less simple than was that which consisted of a series of massive stone buttresses, however it is less expensive, as this combination of iron stays cannot cost so much as the buttresses with their foundations; besides, less space is taken up.*[17]

More precisely concerned with the economy of structure than the theorists of the Ecole des Beaux-Arts, Viollet-le-Duc pursues lightweight hollow or reticulated metal construction as an agent for transforming every conceivable tectonic element, from window shutters to metal roofs. This ferro-vitreous syntax leads him away from the reiteration of historical forms, and henceforth he proposes a series of ever more elaborate equilibrated structures, combining load-

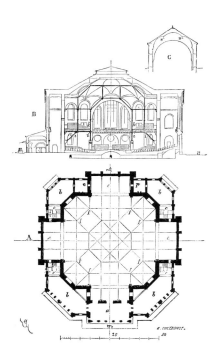

2.24
Eugène-Emmanuel Viollet-le-Duc, project for a 3,000-seat hall, from the *Entretiens,* 1872. Plan and section.

bearing masonry encasement, Roussillon vault construction, cast-iron tubes, rolled-iron ribs, wrought-iron tie rods, and eventually lightweight soffits made out of pleated metal or plaster of Paris and hung from vaulted metal skeletons, reminiscent of the ribs used in Gothic construction. This idea of "iron network vaulting," as he called it, was to be further developed by his pupil, Anatole de Baudot, and elaborated into a series of projects for large exhibition spaces. Of this proto-space-frame principle, Viollet-le-Duc was to write:

Solid bodies such as polyhedrons, consisting of plane surfaces, appear to suggest the elementary forms applicable to the structure of mingled iron and masonry where vaulting is in question. The nature of the metal and the forms in which it can be manufactured do not favor the construction of iron arches. . . . But if we regard plate-iron as a material specially adapted for resisting tension, if the masonry in conjunction with it be so combined as to prevent distortion of the iron-work, if we consider iron as easy to employ and connect in straight pieces; and if of these separate pieces we form a kind of independent network, and on this network of girders we rest the vaulting in separate parts, we shall thus have contrived a system of iron framework consistent with the nature of the material, and a method for covering wide spaces by means of a series of distinct vaults. [18]

This is the prescription for his famous 3,000-seat hall, roofed by an iron armature, having a 140-foot clear span, and set within a load-bearing neo-Romanesque masonry case (fig. 2.24). As we have seen, this heavyweight encasement of lightweight iron construction had already been achieved by Henri Labrouste in his two Parisian libraries. However, the famous perspectival view of Viollet-le-Duc's octagonal hall, together with its polygonal roof structure and statically determinate iron members, demonstrates for the first time the principles of structural rationalism (fig. 2.25).

With these exhibits before us we may recapitulate the basic tenets of Viollet-le-Duc's argument; first, that the essential materials of paleotechnology, namely cast and wrought iron, are the unprecedented and unique resources from which the constituent elements of a nineteenth-century architecture must be developed; second, that this new architecture must arise out of a complementary synthesis of traditional and innovative elements, for, as he was to put it, "buildings of masonry offer advantages which those constructed solely of iron and glass do not afford"; [19] third, that this new architecture, like all great architecture and, above all, like twelfth-century Gothic, must express its fundamental interaction with nature, that is to say, it must reveal the way in which it resists gravity. For Viollet-le-Duc this dialogue between culture and nature is to be articulated in terms of vault, strut, tie rod, and joint. This crystalline, ossiferous project follows Labrouste and anticipates that subtle synthesis of the theories of Viollet-le-Duc with those of Semper as this appears later in the work of Hendrik Petrus Berlage (fig. 2.26).

For Viollet-le-Duc, statical logic and the rationality of the constructional procedure were inseparable. It was as though the one were the necessary proof of the other and vice versa. Thus, of a rational procedure for the construction of a medium-span dome, he would write:

Suppose a dome 65 feet in diameter at the base, whose circumference at the base will consequently be 195 feet; we divide this circumference into sixty parts, and making a templet of a slice of the dome thus divided, we cut this slice into a

51

E. GUILLAUMOT.

certain number of panels. . . . Nothing can be easier, especially if we have several
of these domes to cover in, than to have made in a workshop, moulded in plaster of Paris or pressed concrete, the requisite quantity of these panels . . . there
would be only seven different patterns of panels; and if sixty be required for the
lower zone, a similar number will also be necessary for each of the zones. These
panels, prepared in advance, even in winter, and sufficiently dried, may be raised
into place like voussoirs and set with plaster of Paris or cement. Each zone as it
is set, forms a concentric ring which cannot give way, and the next may be immediately superposed. It need not be added that the panels may be moulded into
sunk compartments, so as to form an interior decoration.[20]

This conjunction of received know-how and critical intellect, so typical of his writing, fails nonetheless to do justice to the full consequences of his thought, of which he was perhaps only partially aware himself. Of this, no one has written more perceptively than Hubert Damisch in his critique of Viollet-le-Duc's *Dictionnaire*:

The movement through which Viollet-le-Duc eliminated the theory of architecture from the illusions, so dear to academics of former times, is one which, turning away from the outward appearance in order to probe the real essence of a work of art, claims the architectural phenomenon as an object of science. The "beauty" of a building cannot be measured by the quality of the outer covering: if the word "beauty" has any meaning—and it must have one if we are to speak of architecture and not merely of construction—it implies the idea of truth, of the equal value of form and reality. . . . From Viollet-le-Duc's point of view, the phenomenological approach could in no circumstances prevail over structural analysis, and could only indirectly lead us to the "essential being" of a building, that area where the architectural form flows out of the constructed reality. . . . But, by distinguishing between the essential being and its appearance, between phenomena and numena, surely Viollet-le-Duc reintroduced into architectural theory a new aspect of that same transcending illusion which he denounced in official teaching? . . . Which is another way of saying that the "truth" of a building is not to be found in bricks and mortar any more than in the outer form.

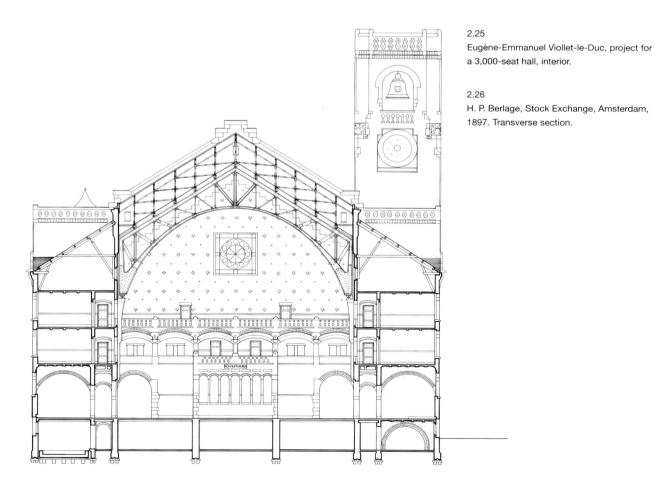

2.25
Eugène-Emmanuel Viollet-le-Duc, project for a 3,000-seat hall, interior.

2.26
H. P. Berlage, Stock Exchange, Amsterdam, 1897. Transverse section.

No, it lies in the space between them, that which makes them complementary, in that space where style is born, in that gap between things which is intimated in the absence of a logical link between the two propositions that open the article on Construction: Construction is the means; architecture the result. . . . *And perhaps it is there, between those two small propositions, separated by an ambiguous semi-colon, that we should seek the secret of the still relevant impact of the* Dictionnaire *and its educational value.*[21]

Be this as it may, the *Entretiens* would become a more prospective study, above all for the way in which it exploited the cultural history of construction as a means for adducing an appropriate mode for the emerging present. The range of Viollet-le-Duc's knowledge, combined with the intensity of his cultural concern and his capacity for practical application, makes the *Entretiens* a unique treatise in which the author is able to pass from reflections on the philosophy of history to the pragmatics of construction without there being any noticeable interruption in the fluidity of his thought.

While Viollet-le-Duc was to have a wide and lasting influence as a theoretician, there are, aside from a whole range of general practitioners,[22] only two figures that can be identified as direct followers; the one dedicated to practice and the other to theory. I have in mind Joseph Eugène Anatole de Baudot (1834–1915), whose St.-Jean de Montmartre church was completed in Paris in 1904, and Auguste Choisy, whose influential *Histoire de l'architecture* was published in 1899. We are reminded here of the close affinity obtaining between Labrouste and Viollet-le-Duc, above all because when the former closed his atelier in 1856, he recommended that his prime student de Baudot should go and study with the master of structural rationalism.

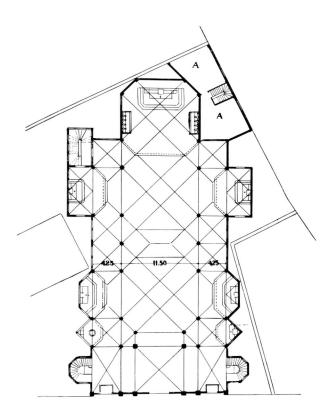

De Baudot's first independent work, the church of St.-Lubin, Rambouillet, completed in 1869, deployed cast-iron columns in the manner of Viollet-le-Duc. Thereafter, however, disaffected with exposed metal armatures, de Baudot began his search for a more homogeneous but nonetheless equally tectonic expression. He continued to use iron, however, for the two large exhibition halls that he projected for the world exhibitions held in Paris in 1878 and 1889, presumably because he felt that ferro-vitreous construction was an appropriate material for the fabrication of large-scale temporary exhibition structures. These two projects, the one circular, the other rectangular, were attempts to realize Viollet-le-Duc's "iron network vaulting" on a grand scale. They could hardly compare, however, in either span or expressive grandeur with the great ferro-vitreous halls of the epoch, de Dion's 116-foot-span Galerie des Machines of 1878 and Dutert's 180-foot-span Galerie des Machines of 1889.

In 1890, some seventeen years before François Hennebique's decisive reinforced concrete patents of 1907, the engineer Paul Cottancin perfected his own reinforced masonry system known as *ciment armé*.[23] This title would later serve to distinguish Cottancin's invention from Hennebique's coinage of *béton armé* by which the latter established the monopoly of his reinforced concrete method.[24] While Hennebique's patent process came to be universally adopted within a decade, Cottancin's labor-intensive system was virtually obsolete after 1914. In contrast to Hennebique's in situ concrete construction necessitating the erection of timber formwork, Cottancin's *ciment armé* employed wire-reinforced, perforated brickwork as the permanent formwork of a cement armature, together with thin, lightweight cement shells. In Cottancin's system, the wire reinforcement and cement infill were considered as acting independently, the former in tension, the latter in compression, and by this separation Cottancin was able to avoid the fundamental weakness of all other contemporary reinforced concrete patents, namely the incalculability of the adherence between the metal reinforcement and the concrete. This, together with the economy of the permanent formwork in brick, gave Cottancin's stressed masonry method an initial advantage that lasted until the turn of the century, when the evident economy and less skilled craftwork demanded by the Hennebique system won the day.

2.27
Anatole de Baudot, St.-Jean de Montmartre, Paris, 1894–1904. Plan.

2.28
Anatole de Baudot, St.-Jean de Montmartre, longitudinal section.

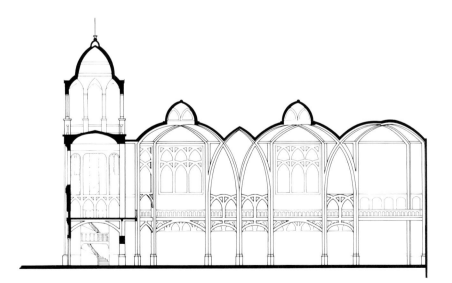

The commission of St.-Jean de Montmartre and Cottancin's patent happened to coincide, and de Baudot was prompt in utilizing a method that would allow him to combine light isostatic construction with bonded brickwork. The result was a somewhat oriental, diagonally ordered system of vaults rising from thin brick walls and piers enclosing narrow channels of interior space (figs. 2.27, 2.28). Twenty-six square piers (50 centimeters by 50 centimeters) in reinforced brickwork rose some 25–30 meters from the crypt, to support nave vaults with spans of up to 11.5 metres and double-vaulted shell roofs each 7 centimeters thick with a 4-centimeter insulation space in between. Even more surprising from a structural point of view was the 5-centimeter floor separating the upper from the lower church.[25] De Baudot wrote: "As can be seen, there is no question here of applying known forms of vaulting, but of demonstrating structural and visual relationships resulting from a system absolutely unfamiliar before now."[26] Obstructed by a bureaucracy that was alarmed by its unorthodox construction, St.-Jean de Montmartre was not finished until 1904, some two years after de Baudot had proposed one of the most radical structures of his career, a polygonal exhibition hall for the Exposition Universelle of 1900. This proposal consisted of a large vaulted space to be constructed exclusively in *ciment armé*. Paradoxical as it may seem for a pupil of Viollet-le-Duc, *ciment armé* would dominate de Baudot's thought for the remainder of his career, culminating in a prophetic *salle des fêtes* projected in 1910 (fig. 2.29). This square structure was to be carried on sixteen cylindrical supports, resembling Gothic cluster columns. These columns are shown supporting a horizontal space frame of extraordinary complexity. This flat, shallow-domed, lightweight roof truss can be seen as anticipating by some 45 years Pier Luigi Nervi's comparable, isostatic reinforced concrete structure built outside Rome in 1953 to house the Gatti wool factory (fig. 2.30).

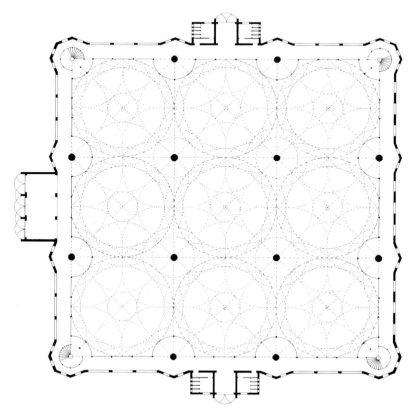

Other than a common Saint-Simonian passion for the application of objective analysis to the history of architecture, François Auguste Choisy and Viollet-le-Duc had little in common. However, this intellectual background plus a brief shared experience in the Franco-Prussian War seem to have prompted Viollet-le-Duc to acknowledge Choisy in the last volume of the *Entretiens,* above all for Choisy's work on the optical corrections employed in the Parthenon. Choisy, for his part, emulated Viollet-le-Duc to the letter, particularly in his first book, *L'Art de bâtir chez les Romains,* published in 1873. Apart from being written by an engineer, this was the first architectural history to explain the origin of tectonic form in terms of the materials available, the structural systems employed, and the state of craft production. Choisy's subsequent fieldwork in Turkey led, a decade later, to his second historical opus, *L'Art de bâtir chez les Byzantines* published in 1883. By then he was already established as a technocratic academic, first in the Ecole des Ponts and Chaussées and after 1881 in the Ecole Polytechnique. The next sixteen years of research and writing resulted in his magnum opus, his two-volume *Histoire de l'architecture* published in 1899.

The overriding thesis of Choisy's *Histoire* was simple enough. He tried to show how each great civilization arrived at its apogee when, subject to geographical and material conditions, its essence was expressed collectively in tectonic form. Once the prime point of synthesis had been achieved, however, there was a tendency for the culture to decay through excessive formal variation until it became little more than a parody of the original. In two successive maps Choisy attempts to show how Romanesque and Gothic building cultures were diffused along different trade routes in France between the tenth and thirteenth centuries.

2.29
Anatole de Baudot, *salle des fêtes,* c. 1910.
Plan and interior.

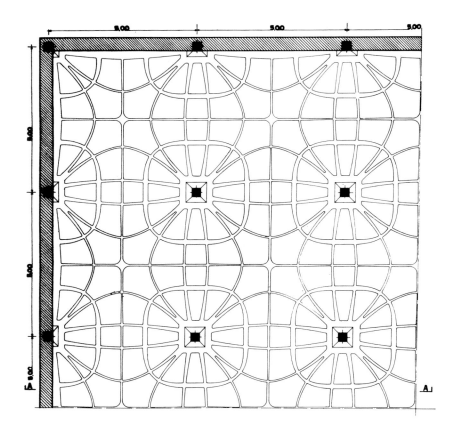

Choisy's isometric representational method had an inherent disadvantage, in that it tended to inhibit a sufficiently precise analysis of the structural articulation of the given tectonic form. This was particularly true of skeletonal structures that did not submit as well to his method as those of load-bearing masonry construction.[27] It was as though all the examples that he analyzed were forged out of the same homogeneous substance, as we find this, say, in brick, mud, rammed earth, or reinforced concrete construction. Choisy's accompanying text, however, was more analytical and sophisticated, and this more than made up for the slightly schematic nature of his illustrations. It is clear for example from his discussion of the origins of the Doric that he was aware of the German debate on the aboriginal structural authority of the Greek orders as this had been challenged by Heinrich Hübsch in his book *In welchem Style sollen wir bauen?* (1828). All in all Choisy sees little pragmatic justification for the Vitruvian thesis that the Doric order was derived from trabeated wooden construction. His skepticism in this regard seems to have been bolstered by the technologically inconsistent detailing that had been found in a number of Greek temples. From this Choisy concludes that it took many years before the pragmatics of masonry construction could be successfully reconciled with the aboriginal image of a trabeated construction in wood. In the end, he opted for a subtle reconciliation of the two theories, namely, that while the order may well have derived from timber construction it also derived from the technical demands of building in masonry.[28]

The enduring influence of Choisy's *Histoire* was due as much to the revelatory aspect of his didactic isometric projections as to the precision of his analytical text (fig. 2.31). Realizing that conventional orthographic and perspectival methods were inadequate and misleading, Choisy opted for a comparative method and a mode of projection by which the essence of the construct could be both represented and classified. Resorting to a projective graphic technique previously reserved for the representation of iron castings and machine tools, he aspired to an objective characterization of his subject matter, and it was exactly these typified abstractions that led to his extensive influence on the architects of the machine age, from Le Corbusier to Louis Kahn. Restricted by his method from entering fully into the pragmatics of any specific technology, Choisy presented tectonic tropes as complete entities wherein the space form was inseparable from the mode of construction and where subcomponents were presented as set pieces derived from the influences of climate, material, and cross-cultural interaction. In this way, as Cornelis van de Ven has argued, Choisy attempted to bridge between the typological plan forms of Durand and the structural rationalism of Viollet-le-Duc.[29] Apart from Auguste Perret, who was his follower in many ways, Choisy seems to have been the last theorist of the Greco-Gothic ideal, as we may judge from his two-volume encyclopedic history that devoted a third of the first volume and a third of the second to Greek and Gothic architecture respectively. In one upward-looking isometric after another, in which the corporeal volume was depicted as being homogeneous with its columnar supports, Choisy seems to have anticipated reinforced concrete as the sole technique that would prove capable of overcoming the age-old schism and fusing into a single entity the two great lines of Western building culture.

2.30
Pier Luigi Nervi, Gatti wool factory, Rome, 1953. Partial plan.

2.31
Auguste Choisy, Beauvais cathedral, from *Histoire de l'architecture,* 1899.

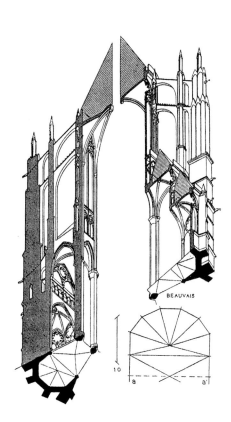

3 The Rise of the Tectonic:
Core Form and Art Form in the German
Enlightenment, 1750–1870

Two examples illustrate the cultural conjunction of nature and architecture within the panoramic scope of Schinkel's view. Just when he was preparing the final plan for the museum, he also started to work on a painting, View of Greece in Its Flowering, *which betrays a deep conceptual affinity with the museum vestibule. Comparably elevated onto the porch of a Greek temple under construction, the viewer looks out onto a large ancient town that descends from the slopes toward a gulf. A wide awning shields from the sun the workmen and sculptors on the right, while the crowns of tall trees shade a landscaped terrace to the left. These natural and artificial umbrellas, enhanced by subtle color correspondences, complement one another and bracket the field of vision. The main activity in the painting, the construction of a great monument, centers on a sturdy scaffolding in the middle of the picture: the scaffolding is, of course, a temporary device, required merely for construction, but its prominence and pivotal role surely signify the activity of building as much as its material result. Construction is indeed the very building of social and cultural fact. This image of ancient building also lends its framework to Schinkel's example of modern architecture. The general conditions have changed, but the similarity of Schinkel's images—the temple in ancient culture, the museum in modern—also reveals a telling distinction. A comparable double row of Ionic columns, a narrative frieze appropriately transferred from sculpture to wall painting, and* spectators *rather than* workmen *at once liken the Berlin museum to ancient architecture and contrast the* modern *consumption of that culture to the image of its ancient production. Subsuming and transcending all of these distinctions is, of course, the fact that nature no longer provides the foil of culture but has yielded that role to the cityscape.*
Kurt Forster, "Schinkel's Panoramic Planning of Central Berlin," 1983

From 1750 onward the antique Greek world exercised a fundamental hold over the German imagination, from the time of J. J. Winckelmann's appraisal of the serenity of the Apollo Belvedere to J. C. F. Hölderlin's poetic preoccupation with Greece; a country that he, like Winckelmann, never visited. Hölderlin's hypersensitive career epitomizes many of the dilemmas that confronted the intellectuals of the *Sturm und Drang* period, above all their intense nostalgia for the spirit and life of a lost golden age, for an age that was as divorced from the historical experience of Germany as it was distant from the political and moral aims of the *Aufklärung.* Thus, while Friedrich Schiller admitted the unsurpassable greatness of Greek art, he nonetheless believed that the liberative aims of the Enlightenment would be better served by a dramatic art form that would be ethically superior to Greek tragedy. In 1792, he wrote: "In this branch alone our civilization will perhaps be able to make good the theft which it has committed on art as a whole."[1]

In his seminal *Geschichte der Kunst des Altertums* (History of Ancient Art) of 1764, Winckelmann was the first to introduce the notion of cyclical growth and decay into the history of civilization, a paradigm that would be transformed into a dialectical system by Hegel in his aesthetic lectures given between 1818 and 1829.[2] Winckelmann divided Greek art into four periods, the archaic period, the sublime moment of Phidias, the idealism of Praxiteles, and, finally, the deliquescence of Hellenism. He believed that the naturalistic beauty of Greek art arose out of two basic causes: the temperate nature of the Greek climate and the liberative political order of the Greek state.[3] Winckelmann's appraisal of this dichotomous legacy seems to have indirectly affected the character of the Prussian Enlightenment, dividing it as it did into two related but antithetical impulses: the expressivist and the rationalist.

The former can be traced as a recurrent theme that runs through the writing of Herder and Goethe. Both men felt that a Germanic culture comparable to that of ancient Greece could only arise out of the intrinsic character of the people, the climate, and the nordic landscape. As Charles Taylor has written: "We are here at the point of modern Nationalism. Herder thought that each people had its own peculiar guiding theme or manner of expression, unique and irreplaceable, which should never be suppressed and which could never simply be replaced by any attempt to ape the manners of others, as many educated Germans tried to ape French *philosophes.*"[4] Herder's concern for autochthonous culture partially accounts for Goethe's initial preference for the Germanic character of Gothic architecture over the alien rationality of Greek classicism, before he moved to Weimar in 1775 and embraced Palladianism as the touchstone of progressive culture.[5] Thus for all his youthful enthusiasm for Strassbourg's cathedral, as this appears in his essay "Von deutscher Baukunst, D. M. Erwin von Steinbach" of 1772, published in Herder's *Von deutscher Art und Kunst,* Goethe's cultivated preference for the classical at the end of the eighteenth century would parallel the teachings of the art historian Aloys Hirt, who was so convinced of the spiritual superiority of Greek culture as to strive for its full embodiment in the emerging Prussian state.

Notwithstanding its classicizing proclivities, German idealistic philosophy saw the Enlightenment as a radical break for which one had to evolve a new set of ethical and cultural values appropriate to a rational and scientific age. The most prominent figure after Kant to advance this position was Hegel, who attempted to formulate a dialectical view of world culture. In Hegel's protean scheme, architecture emerges as a primordial manifestation within the changing spectrum of cultural form. For Hegel, beauty in art, as opposed to natural beauty, derives from the extent to which the evolving spirit and its corresponding form are interrelated; his three stages of cultural development arose out of the different degrees to which this synthesis of form and content was achieved. In this system, architecture first makes itself manifest as an apotheosis of *symbolic* form, a stage that was epitomized by the Egyptian pyramids, whose construction is expressed through the mute character of massive monumental form. Hegel saw such an art as essentially oriental, as opposed to the subsequent occidental apotheosis of Greek art, with its sensuous, sculptural representation of anthropomorphic form. This moment of *classical* balance between art and life and presumably between form and spirit begins to disintegrate with the eventual demise of the Greek city-state. For Hegel this collapse will have the ultimate consequence of engendering *romantic* art, wherein form and content veer apart, due in large measure to the dematerializing aspirations of Christianity.

In the Hegelian system, art comprises a dichotomy consisting of the idea and its material embodiment. Subject to the changing nature of the dominant form, the history of art passes through the same three successive stages of symbolic, classical, and romantic. Within this overview, sculpture is seen as the liberative, anthropomorphic embodiment of human individuality, as opposed to the universality of symbolic art as this appeared when architecture was the primary artistic manifestation. The romantic period is initiated by the advent of Gothic architecture; only later does it develop into the dominant expressive modes of painting, music, and poetry.

Painting, music and poetry are three preeminently romantic arts (although Gothic architecture is essentially romantic). This is so for two reasons. Firstly, romantic art is concerned with action and conflict, not repose. Architecture cannot represent action at all, sculpture very little. . . . Secondly, the material media of painting, music and poetry are more ideal, more removed from the purely material plane of architecture and sculpture. Painting uses only two dimensions and presents merely the appearance of matter without its reality. Music abstracts from space altogether and subsists in time only. . . . Poetry, lastly, has for its medium the wholly subjective and inward forms of the sensuous image. Romantic art has the germ of its dissolution within itself. Art is according to its very notion the union of spiritual content and outward form. Romantic art has to some extent already ceased to be art, by virtue of the fact that it breaks up the harmonious accord of the two sides that are present in classical art.[6]

In viewing his own time as quintessentially romantic, Hegel predicts the ultimate disappearance of art. Architecture seems to be specially privileged within his tripartite system, however, as each of the three phases has its equivalent expression in architectonic form. Thus, while the quintessence of the symbolic epoch in architecture would remain the achievement of Egyptian civilization, Hegel opposes to this the classical apotheosis of the Greek temple as the sanctuary of an anthropomorphic godhead together with the politically liberative form of the *polis.* This last is seen as totally antithetical to the Gothic, which Hegel regards as epitomizing the introspective dematerializing obsessions of romanticism.

The cruciform shape, the spires, the general trend of the building upwards into vast and aspiring heights,—all is symbolical. Yet the spirit of this symbolism is throughout romantic. These forests of spires and points rising one above the other, the upward-pointed arches and windows, the vast height of the buildings, represent the upward aspirations of the soul which has withdrawn from the outward world into its own self-seclusion. The essential feature of romantic art is, as we have seen, precisely this withdrawal of the soul from the external and sensuous world into the subjectivity of its own inner soul-life. And this in general is what the Christian Church represents. The Greek temple with its walks and colonnades is open to the world. It invites ingress and egress. It is gay and pleasant. It is flat, low, and wide, not, like the Christian Church, narrow and high. This flatness and horizontal extension represent extension outward into the external world. All these features are reversed in the Gothic Church. The pillars are not outside but inside. The whole is entirely enclosed, forming an abode of the soul shut off in self-seclusion from the outside world. The sun enters in a glimmer through the stained-glass windows. Everyone comes and goes, prays upon his knees and moves away. . . . The absorption of all this life as in these infinite silent spaces, represents, in sensuous fashion, the infinity of the spirit and its aspirations. What is emphasized here, then, is the inner soul-life, cut off from the world, the subjectivity which is the essential principle of romantic art.[7]

The term "classical romanticism" thus comes to imply a good deal more than a stylistic characterization, for it expresses precisely that synthesis of Greek and Christian cultures with which intellectuals such as Hegel and the architect Karl Friedrich Schinkel would attempt to sublimate their nostalgia for a lost golden age, through their separate formulation and representation of Prussia as a rational, Christian nation. Schinkel's architecture comes to fruition in that post-Napoleonic moment of reconciliation between the rational and the ideal, wherein

3.1
Aloys Hirt, plate from *Die Baukunst nach den Grundsätzen der Alten,* 1809.

public works are projected and realized in order to embody the enlightened institutions of the modern, liberal state.

Given the prevailing Greek influence, the emergence of the tectonic idea in Prussia was bound up with an attempt to reinterpret the antique world in modern form, as we may judge from the title of Aloys Hirt's influential book *Die Baukunst nach den Grundsätzen der Alten* (Architecture According to the Basic Principles of the Ancients) that appeared in 1809 (fig. 3.1). In 1793, sixteen years prior to the publication of Hirt's book, David Gilly founded the Bauschule in Berlin. Gilly's son, Friedrich, and the art historian Hirt were among the first members of the faculty of this school, later known as the Bauakademie, the former passing from the status of student to teacher by the time he was twenty.

Before coming to Berlin in 1788, the elder Gilly had practiced in Pomerania, both as an architect and a pedagogue, founding his private architectural school in Stettin in 1783. French building technology exercised a strong influence first on Gilly and later on his son, with the latter studying French construction methods during his stay in Paris in 1798, shortly before his premature death two years later (fig. 3.2). Father and son seem to have been equally preoccupied with French framing techniques dating back to the time of Philibert Delorme, and David Gilly would exploit a French timber roofing method, known in German as *Bohlendach,* in a military gymnasium that he built in Berlin in 1800. Gilly the elder possessed what others of his generation lacked, namely, a feeling for simplicity and practical economy in building. These values were evident in his numerous publications and in the character of his teaching in the Bauschule. In this he was later influenced by the typological, modular economy of J. N. L. Durand, whose *Précis des leçons d'architecture données à l'Ecole Polytechnique* was published from 1802 to 1805. Durand's influence on the Bauschule curriculum brought it closer to the practical engineering standpoint of the Ecole Polytechnique than to the emerging postrevolutionary rhetoric of the Ecole des Beaux-Arts.

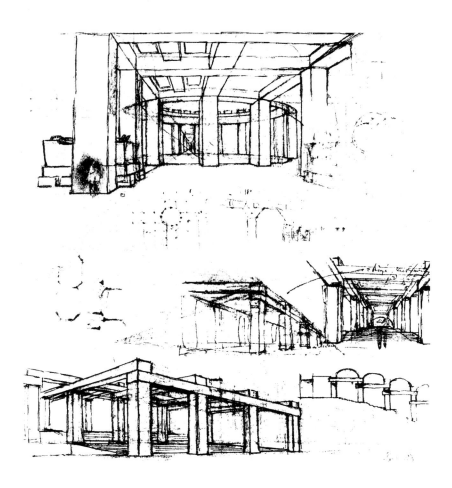

The younger Gilly was fired by the idea of an emergent Germanic identity, as is evident from his design for the monument to Frederick the Great in Leipziger Platz, Berlin. Despite his hypersensitivity and the rich legacy that he left to the Bauschule (fig. 3.3), Friedrich Gilly was as much a constructor as his father, as is evident from the last design of his life, his project for the Hundebrücke in Berlin, to be executed later in a different and more rhetorical form by Schinkel (figs. 3.4, 3.5).[8] As Hermann Pundt has remarked:

Where Gilly's Hundebrücke design comprised three spans of cast iron mounted on simple abutments and on hydraulically profiled stone bases, Schinkel's Schlossbrücke projected for the same site in 1822 was entirely rendered in masonry. We are already witness here to the way in which Schinkel would transform the legacy of Friedrich Gilly and turn even the commission for a bridge into an occasion for a representative urban monument.[9]

Schinkel, for his part, would remain suspended throughout his career between the conflicting demands of ontological and representational tectonic form. The representational aspect predominates in his Singakademie project of 1821, where an interior peristyle is created through the encasement of freestanding timber stanchions in such a way as to simulate a Doric colonnade (fig. 3.6). A similar but more ontologically valid tectonic will appear in the castellated brick cornice of his building for the Bauakademie, completed in Berlin in 1836 (figs. 3.7, 3.8). The lower line of projecting corbels in this cornice alludes to the size

3.2
Friedrich Gilly, studies (rue des Bons Enfants), Paris, 1798. Gilly notes the details of roof lights, stairwells, and the *Bohlendach* roof construction.

3.3
Friedrich Gilly, design for a mausoleum, c. 1798.

3.4
Friedrich Gilly, Hundebrücke, Lustgarten, Berlin, 1800.

3.5
Karl Friedrich Schinkel, Schlossbrücke, Berlin, 1824.

3.6
Karl Friedrich Schinkel, Singakademie, Berlin, 1821.

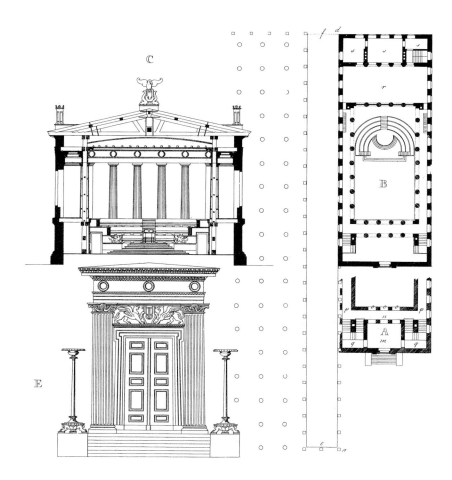

and spacing of the rafter system supporting the roof, and may thus be read as the metaphoric representation of the real structure hidden within. It is significant that the Bauakademie was the most astylistic of Schinkel's works in that its "utilitarian" form was all but totally free of historical allusion. It was indebted in this regard to British industrial mill construction of the last quarter of the eighteenth century.

Goethe's uncertainty as to the necessary destiny of German architecture—his lifelong vacillation between the Classic and the Gothic culminating in his mature appreciation of the neo-Gothic (see his later reworking of *Von deutsche Baukunst* of 1823)[10]—had the effect of initiating a more general quest for a reconciliatory "third style" appropriate to the modern age and the embodiment of the emerging German state. This hypothetical third style was first formulated in Hübsch's essay *In welchem Style sollen wir bauen*? (In What Style Should We Build?) of 1828, in which he advanced the so called "round-arch style" as an antithesis to both the Grecophilia of Hirt's academic classicism and the *Spitzbogenstil* of the Gothic that Hübsch distanced himself from much like the Greco-Gothicists, in part because of its grotesque complexity and in part for its inapplicability to secular tasks. In the spirited debate that ensued, Hübsch's thesis was first taken up by Rudolf Wiegmann, who initially criticized Hübsch for his historicizing materialism and then defended him as he recognized the emerging *Rundbogenstil* as the interrupted, underevolved Romanesque or Byzantine manner of the thirteenth century as this had been eclipsed before its prime by

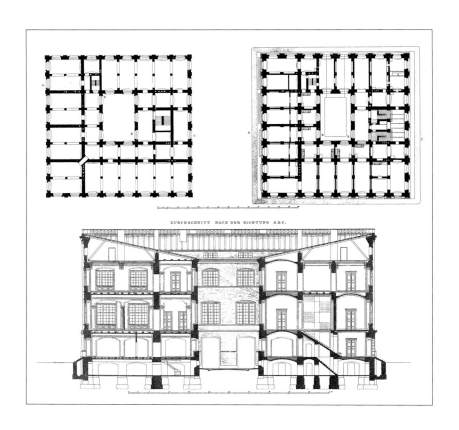

3.7
Karl Friedrich Schinkel, Bauakademie, Berlin,
1836. Note that the centers of the rafters correspond to the centers of the indented corbels on the cornice of the building.

3.8
Karl Friedrich Schinkel, Bauakademie.

3.9
Page from Schinkel's diary of July 16–18,
1826: factories and mills at Manchester,
England.

3.10
Page from Schinkel's diary, 1826.

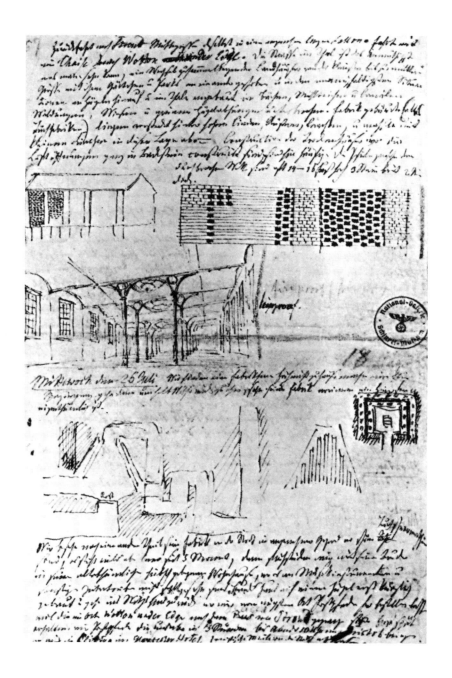

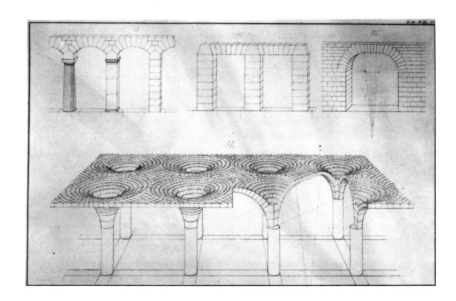

Karl Friedrich Schinkel, plate from the *Architektonisches Lehrbuch,* 1826. This seems to be an adaptation of a system of Catalan or Roussillon vaulting in flat tile.

3.12
Karl Friedrich Schinkel, plate from the *Architektonisches Lehrbuch.*

3.13
Karl Friedrich Schinkel, plate from the *Architektonisches Lehrbuch.*

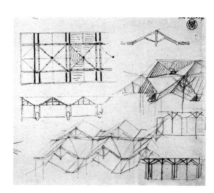

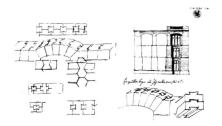

the Gothic. This was virtually the same argument that Gottfried Semper would advance in his defense of his neo-Romanesque Nikolaikirche projected for Hamburg in 1845.[11]

Despite his passing affinity in the 1830s for the technostatics of Hübsch's *Rundbogenstil,* Schinkel was drawn to the stylistic potential of the new technology, particularly as he encountered this on his visit to Britain in 1826, when, as his travel diaries indicate, he was more interested in advanced iron technology and mill construction than in the civic aspects of contemporary English architecture (figs. 3.9, 3.10). Having become professor of building at the Berlin Bauakademie, formerly the Bauschule, Schinkel went to England as an official Prussian emissary in the company of his friend and colleague Peter Christian Beuth.[12] Their joint brief was to study not only museums but also British industrial production. Beuth's interest lay in the field of "industrial design," long before such a profession existed, as we may judge from his founding of the Technischer Gewerbeschule in 1821 and from his joint editorship with Schinkel of a pattern book for applied artists and craftsmen, published in the same year under the title *Vorbilden für Fabrikanten und Handwerker.*[13] They later became jointly involved in writing the program of the Bauakademie that was designed to accommodate both an architectural school and Beuth's Gewerbeinstitut. It is interesting to note that at midcentury the building's ground-floor show windows were filled with what were presumably ideal production items from the point of view of high-quality design, as we may judge from Eduard Gärtner's painting of the Bauakademie, dating from 1868.

Despite his reservations about the tectonic status of iron, designs for exposed ferro-vitreous construction appear with increasing frequency in the pages of Schinkel's *Architektonisches Lehrbuch* from the 1820s on.[14] This unfinished textbook, his sole pedagogical legacy, becomes an ever more fertile catalogue of the various ways in which one might impart tectonic significance to engineering technique (fig. 3.11). Thus the *Lehrbuch* contains many examples of differently articulated structural assemblies, rendered in different materials. In the main, these sketches are ontological rather than representational in character, that is to say the tectonic system itself is emphasized rather than the cladding of its form, or, to put it in terms of Kàrl Bötticher's later formulation, the *Kernform* (core form) rather than the *Kunstform* (art form) predominates. Nevertheless, in certain drawings the two aspects are interrelated, as in Schinkel's 1830 studies for the application of stone relieving arches to a multistory warehouse. This same page shows a progressive increase in the width of supporting piers as a wall descends toward its foundation (fig. 3.12). A comparable sense of corporeal articulation appears in his studies for the internal drainage of glass roofs (1831) (fig. 3.13). Where the appointment of the work is civic and monumental, representational elements come to be emphasized, as in Schinkel's sketches for a *Volksfestsaal* dating from 1820.

Schinkel's interest in nineteenth-century engineering technology is reflected in the stepped and battered walls of the Neuer Packhof warehouse, built in Berlin between 1829 and 1832 (fig. 3.14). A comparable involvement with advanced engineering technique occurs in the double-layered, glass facades of his bazaar project for the Unter den Linden, Berlin, of 1827 (fig. 3.15). This drive toward expressive construction, irrespective of the status of the building, even appears in Schinkel's more monumental works, as in the articulated elemental stairway of the Prince Karl Palace (fig. 3.16) or in the exposed timber rafters that take their support off masonry piers in the open gable ends of the Charlottenhof built in Potsdam in 1832 (fig. 3.17).

In his Friedrich Werder Church, completed in Berlin in 1830, Schinkel fully articulates the difference between the outer casing of the building and its inner lining (fig. 3.18). The former is a load-bearing brick barn structure with a trussed timber roof, a typical *Hallenkirche,* while the latter is a lightweight, self-supporting Gothic shell, the pillars of which conform to the spacing of the outer structural brick piers (figs. 3.19, 3.20). If one studies the drawings carefully one can see that there is a subtle interrelation between the brick outer casing (pierced by pointed windows) and its inner Gothic shell.[15] The fact that the Gothic lining is nothing more than a scenographic layer is indicated by the oculus set into the crown of each vault, a feature emphasizing the absent boss, which, in traditional Gothic construction, would assure the integrity of the vault. By maintaining a parallel articulation between the fenestration of the encasement and the rhetorical openings of the nave, Schinkel inverts the opposition between the core form and the art form; that is to say, the core form is on the outside and the art form

3.14
Karl Friedrich Schinkel, Neuer Packhof, warehouse, Berlin, 1829–1832. Note the battering of the building and the gradual diminishment of the walls in section.

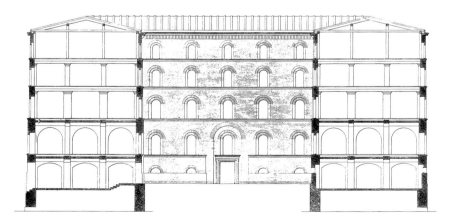

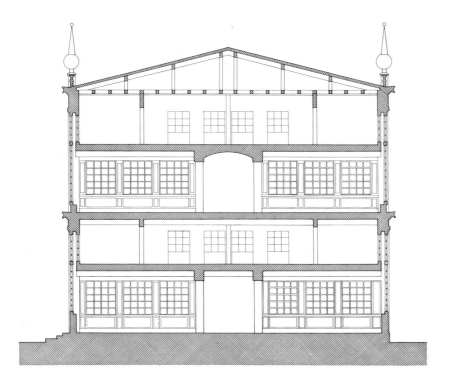

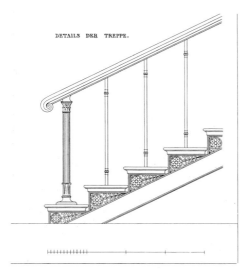

DETAILS DER TREPPE.

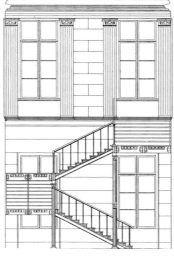

3.15
Karl Friedrich Schinkel, design for a *Kauf-haus,* Unter den Linden, Berlin, 1827. Section. A shopping bazaar with two floors of shops and two mezzanines for dwellings.

3.16
Karl Friedrich Schinkel, palace for Prince Karl, vestibule and stair detail. It is typical of Schinkel that light metal construction appears everywhere in his classical work, even in palatial structures. One might compare these staircases to the typical stair details applied by Mies van der Rohe at IIT.

3.17
Karl Friedrich Schinkel, Court Gardener's House, Charlottenhof, Potsdam, 1833. Note the isolated pier supports for the long beams at the gable ends of the building.

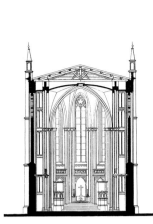

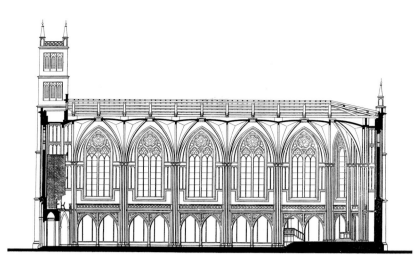

3.18
Karl Friedrich Schinkel, Friedrich Werder
Church, Berlin, 1825–1830.

3.19
Karl Friedrich Schinkel, Friedrich Werder
Church, the nave as a representative shell.
Note the absence of bosses in the centers of
the vaults, indicating the nonconstructional
nature of the Gothic structure.

3.20
Karl Friedrich Schinkel, Friedrich Werder
Church, plan.

3.21
Karl Friedrich Schinkel, Friedrich Werder
Church, alternate proposal: a Roman shell
inserted inside the same basic masonry
encasement.

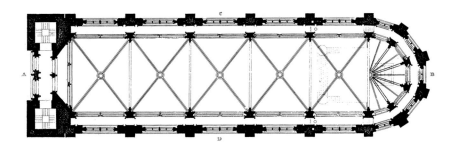

is on the inside. More than any other undertaking of his career, this work reveals the self-conscious scope of Schinkel's eclecticism. As in the later theoretical elaborations of Bötticher, the articulation of essence in relation to the appearance was of more consequence for Schinkel than the choice of any particular style. This is suggested by the alternative arcuated Roman interior projected for the same church (figs. 3.21, 3.22). This play with alternative representational schemes laid over the same basic parti points to the influence of Durand. Durand is equally present in Schinkel's Schauspielhaus completed in 1821, despite the manifest displacement that occurs between the modular grid of the exterior and the load-bearing walls that subdivide the internal volume (fig. 3.23).[16] This shift has its origin in the fact that Schinkel was compelled to build on preexisting foundations. As a reflection of this modular accommodation, a didactic interplay is set up on the side facades between the regularity of the repetitive module and four giant pilasters that refer symbolically to the freestanding peristyle that crowns the entry (fig. 3.24). This four-sided, pedimented representation is no doubt due to the placement of the theater as a freestanding monument within the open space of the Gendarmenmarkt.

Durand's insistence on fitness and economy as the main causes of beauty was to prove crucial for Schinkel as he tried to establish the monuments of an emerging city-state that was hard-pressed for funds. This is evident from the way in which Durand's museum type informs the parti of Schinkel's Altes Museum, finally realized in the Lustgarden in 1830 (figs. 3.25, 3.26, 3.27). While Schinkel attempted to integrate Durand's utilitarian aesthetic into his theory of architecture, he nonetheless tempered the implicit universalism of the technocratic approach by insisting that architecture should be determined in part by the "customs and requirements of [the] country and the conditions of the region and the site."[17] This insistence on topographic mediation seems to have been the source of his conflict with the more academic Hirt over the use of giant orders for the Lustgarten facade of the Altes Museum, with Hirt denouncing such features as an extravagant and unprecedented impropriety. For Schinkel, as for the younger Gilly and Friedrich Weinbrenner, the land itself was seen as the repository of a primitive identity, and the task of the architect was to adapt his normative typology to the idiosyncrasies of a specific *topos*. Like Herder, Schinkel felt that this synthesis could only be achieved through a fundamental respect for the character of a place and its people. Thus he wrote: "The intrinsic form of a monument of any period must maintain a simple character whose roots reach down into the primitive conditions of human culture while at its peak a sublime flower takes form."[18]

Schinkel's cultural theory derived from Friedrich Wilhelm Joseph von Schelling's identification of the ideal and the real. Thus, Ludwig Mies van der Rohe's twentieth-century aphorism, "God is in the details,"[19] and Schinkel's edict that

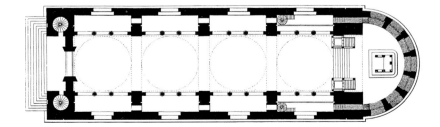

3.22
Karl Friedrich Schinkel, Friedrich Werder
Church, alternative Roman interior.

3.23
Karl Friedrich Schinkel, Schauspielhaus, Berlin, 1821.

3.24
Karl Friedrich Schinkel, Schauspielhaus, side
elevation. Note how the four applied pilasters
in the center allude to the portico on the front
of the building. The underlying modular grid
comes from Durand.

3.25
Karl Friedrich Schinkel, Altes Museum, Berlin, 1830.

3.26
Karl Friedrich Schinkel, Altes Museum. Once again a Durandesque modular grid appears categorically on the rear elevation. The sculpture is by Gottfried Schadow throughout.

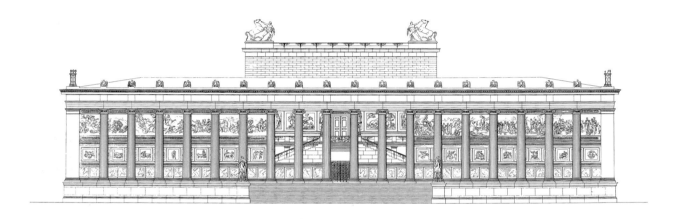

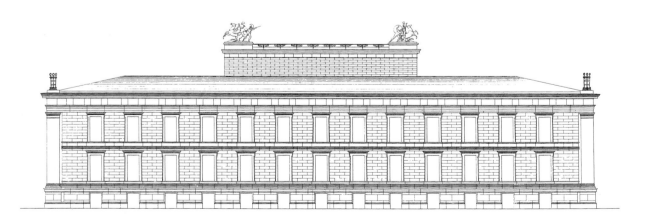

3.27
Karl Friedrich Schinkel, Altes Museum.

"Beauty is the visible proof of the inner intelligence of nature"[20] have much in common. They both reflect Schelling's natural philosophy, his view that the presence of God emanates from every part of the universe. Thus, Schinkel's thought manifests a doubly articulated dualism, that is to say, not only the reconciliation of the ideal and the real but also of the *typos* with the *topos.* Beyond this, Schinkel was to remain indebted to Durand for his way of representing the institutions of the state. In one of his rare theoretical statements, "Das Prinzip der Kunst in der Architektur" (The Principle of Art in Architecture), he wrote:

1. *To build (bauen) is to join different materials into a whole, corresponding to a definite purpose.*

2. *This definition, encompassing a building in both its spiritual and material aspects, clearly demonstrates that purposiveness is the fundamental principle of all building.*

3. *The material edifice, which now presumes a spiritual aspect, is here the subject of my consideration.*

4. *The purposiveness of every building can be considered under three aspects: these are:*
   a) *Purposiveness of spatial distribution or of the plan;*
   b) *Purposiveness of construction or of the joining together of materials appropriate to the plan.*
   c) *Purposiveness of ornament or of the decoration.*[21]

Later in the same theoretical statement he qualifies the criteria of fitness as this applies to construction and ornamentation by stressing the importance of using the best possible material and of revealing not only the quality of the material but also the quality of craftsmanship with which the various components are assembled together. This concern for craft precision and material richness surely derives from Perrault's concept of positive beauty. At the same time, the idea of purposiveness or *Zweckmässigkeit* in Schinkel's work derives in some measure from the philosophy of Kant. As Ikonomou and Mallgrave have written,

Kant advanced the notion of form in a more substantial way in his Kritik der Ur-theilskraft *(Critique of judgment), 1790, which considered the process of how we judge forms to be aesthetically pleasing or beautiful. Parallel to his earlier "forms of intuition" and "forms of thought" . . . Kant now proposed a new principle governing the faculty of aesthetic judgment, one that he hoped would provide it with a measure of universality and at the same time allow it to remain subjective. This principle was the notion of "purposiveness" (Zweckmässig-keit)—for Kant the sense of internal harmony that we presume to exist in the world, the bias, as it were, that we bring to the aesthetic act. Purposiveness is the heuristic rule or standard by which we relate to the forms of nature and art.*[22]

Schinkel would link his interpretation of this concept to hierarchical notions of culture as these are set forth in the writings of Johann Gottlieb Fichte. In his book *Die Bestimmung des Menschen* (The Vocation of Man), published in 1800, Fichte gave primacy to public action and to the cultivation of ethical value. In the light of this, Schinkel insisted that not all buildings were of equal stature and that the presence, location, and choice of ornament should directly express the level of the work. Whereas French influences are detectable here, above all the theories of Cordemoy and Laugier, it is possible to argue that this hierarchical sense of order was latent in the German language, with its capacity to distinguish among *Architektur, Baukunst,* and *Bauen.* Schinkel's ability to discriminate among different levels of building has been remarked on by Kurt Forster in his analysis of the varying syntax employed in the complex that Schinkel built along the banks of the Kupfergraben opening off the Spree in Berlin (fig. 3.28).

Not only the warehouse exhibited such specific characteristics; each one of Schinkel's buildings along the riverfront projected its distinctive role into a panoramic ensemble. The columnar front and acroteria privileged the museum as a monumental building in neo-antique fashion, while the pedimented facade of the customs office reduced its ornamentation and surface treatment to revetted facades. Its twin to the rear, the office block, received only a stuccoed elevation and the exterior of the warehouse was left in unfaced brick. This calibrated sequence of architectural forms and building materials injects into the optical perspective a dimension of rhetorical and historic "depth." Ashlar, revetment, stucco and brick mark rungs on a descending scale of architectural values, each one appropriate—and characteristic—for a particular type of structure. Schinkel differentiated each building stylistically without falling into the trap of purely eclectic justification. The passage from trabeation to arcuation belongs as much to this hierarchy as do the colorist qualities of the different building materials.[23]

Taking as his point of departure the *édifices publiques* of Durand's *Précis des leçons,* Schinkel develops his Neuer Packhof warehouse (see fig. 3.14) as a combination of two types given by Durand, the *halle* and the *maison commune,*

3.28
View of Schinkel's buildings from the Schloss-brücke: Altes Museum in the foreground, the three Packhof buildings behind.

although, as in Friedrich von Gärtner's later *Rundbogenstil* Staatsbibliothek for Munich (1835–1840), there lies behind this synthesis the prototype of the early Florentine palace as we find this, say, in the Palazzo Riccardi dating from the mid-fifteenth century. The warehouse was one of Schinkel's most technostatically articulated works in that the intervals between the five stringcourses of its facade (one for each floor) diminish incrementally as the building rises upward and the cumulative load on the structure reduces. This diminishment is accompanied by a slight batter in the building's load-bearing brick face, which corresponds to a reduction in the thickness of the structural walls. The round-arched window openings also diminish slightly in width as they move upward from floor to floor, inducing a kind of perspectival monumentality, while a line of semicircular openings running above the first stringcourse indicates the presence and the status of the undercroft. Similar indications and technostatic diminishments also occur in the Bauakademie, which likewise is of load-bearing brickwork and derives from mill building typology (see figs. 3.7, 3.8). In this instance, however, the upward diminishment between the first- and second-floor studio windows is in both height and width, while the ground-floor fenestration and triadic basement and attic lights are correspondingly suppressed, thereby indicating their inferior status (see fig. 3.8). This differential is reinforced by further elaboration in the detailing of the first- and second-floor studio lights, framed by mullions and a transom in iron, covered by a flat brick arch and embellished with acroteria and decorative spandrel panels in terra-cotta. Unlike the Packhof warehouse, the interior of the Bauakademie was systematically subdivided into rooms of varying size by load-bearing cross walls, and these structural lines were expressed on the facade as vertical piers,thereby entailing a certain suppression of the stringcourses marking the floors. Despite all this subtle inflection, the British historian James Ferguson, writing at midcentury, would find the building to be misscaled for having been rendered in brick rather than in stone.[24]

Soon after Schinkel's death in 1841, Hirt's neo-Greek theory[25] came to be replaced as the primary ideological text of the Bauakademie by Karl Bötticher's *Die Tektonik der Hellenen* (The Tectonic of the Hellenes), published in three volumes between 1843 and 1852. First attending the Bauakademie as a student in 1827 and thereafter studying with both Beuth and Schinkel, Bötticher became a member of the faculty after his qualification as an architect in 1844. Influenced by Hübsch's structural rationalism and by Hirt's unwavering faith in the symbolic

81

superiority of Greek form, but simultaneously denying both the materialism of the former and the traditionalism of the latter, Bötticher sought to resolve the dichotomy between classicism and romanticism through the specific hieratic procedures exemplified in Schinkel's Neuer Packhof and Bauakademie. Taking Schinkel's *Architektonisches Lehrbuch* as his point of departure, Bötticher sought a synthesis between the ontological status of the structure and the representational role of the ornament. Antithetical to all forms of eclecticism, be it Gothic Revival or neo-Renaissance, and equally susceptible to both the rational (Kant) and the antirational (Herder) lines in Enlightenment thought, Bötticher respectively assimilated the representational to the Greek and the ontological to the Gothic.

Influenced through the writings of Christian Weisse by Arthur Schopenhauer's thesis that architecture could only express its essential form and significance through the dramatic interaction of support and load (*Stütze und Last*),[26] Bötticher insisted on the corporeality of architecture and on the interstitial spatiality of its ligaments at every conceivable scale. Taking his cue in part from Herder's tactile sculptural aesthetic and in part from Schinkel's articulated method, Bötticher maintained that the symbolic revetment of a work must never be allowed to obscure its fundamental, constructional form. Thus as Mitchell Schwarzer has written:

Bötticher's attempt to harmonize the muscular passion of architectural materiality and statics with the objectivity of art was quite different from Kant and Schiller's concept of Architektonik *beauty as the marshalling of the subjective senses towards an objective reality. . . . [Bötticher] proposed that the beauty of architecture was precisely the explanation of mechanical concepts. As much as its artistic demands related to the imagination, the constructive demands of the* Tektonik *argued against the autonomy of architectural from extrinsic ends.*[27]

Bötticher envisaged a kind of reciprocally expressive joint that comes into being through the appropriate interlocking of constructional elements. At once articulate and integrated, these joints were seen as *Körperbilden,* not only permitting constructions to be achieved but also enabling these assemblies to become the symbolic components of an expressive system. In addition to this syntactical/constructional concept, Bötticher, as we have noted, distinguished between the *Kernform* and the *Kunstform,* the latter having the task of representing the constructional and/or institutional status of the former. He wrote: "The concept of each part can be thought of as being realized by two elements: the core-form and the art-form. The core-form of each part is the mechanically necessary and statically functional structure; the art-form, on the other hand, is only the characterization by which the mechanical-statical function is made apparent."[28] According to Bötticher, the shell of the *Kunstform* should be capable of revealing and augmenting the essence of the constructional nucleus. At the same time, he insisted that one must always try to distinguish and express the difference between the constructional form and its enrichment, irrespective of whether this last manifests itself as cladding or ornament. He wrote that the art form "is only a covering and a symbolic attribute of the part—decoration, κοσμος."[29]

Bötticher was as much influenced by Schelling's natural philosophy as was Schinkel, above all by Schelling's view that architecture transcends the mere pragmatism of building by virtue of assuming symbolic significance. For Schelling and Bötticher alike, the inorganic had no symbolic meaning and hence structural form could only acquire symbolic status by virtue of its capacity to engender analogies between tectonic and organic form. Direct imitation of natural form was to be avoided, however, for like Schelling, Bötticher held the view that architecture was an imitative art only to the extent that it imitated itself. Nevertheless, unlike Schinkel, Bötticher tended to distance himself theoretically from an opportunistic borrowing of historical form.

A fuller development of Bötticher's theory came with his 1846 *Schinkelfest* address entitled "The Principles of the Hellenic and Germanic Way of Building," in which, after praising the tradition of the Bauakademie and above all Schinkel as the initiator of "architectural science," Bötticher proceeded to posit, in somewhat Hegelian manner, the future possibility of an unnamed third style capable of engendering a new cultural entity, synthesizing thereby the dual Germanic legacy of the Gothic and the Greek.[30] For Bötticher the true tectonic tradition, what he refers to as the "eclecticism of the spirit," resides not in the appearance of any one style but rather in the essence that lies behind the appearance. While he condones the adaptation of traditional stylistic formats to new situations, he is categorically against any form of arbitrary stylistic selection, such as the *Rundbogenstil* advocated by Hübsch. Bötticher will argue that any new spatial system or future style will have to be brought into being by a new structural principle, and not the other way round. Thus, in a manner that anticipates Viollet-le-Duc, we find him writing:

Our contention that the manner of covering determines every style and its ultimate development is confirmed by the monuments of all styles. Equally evident is the truth that from the earliest and roughest attempts to cover spaces by using stone, to the culmination represented by the Spitzbogen *vault, and down to the present time, all the ways in which stone could possibly be used to span a space have been exploited, and they have completely exhausted the possible structural applications of this material. No longer can stone alone form a new structural system of a higher stage of development. The reactive, as well as relative, strength of stone has been completely exhausted. A new and so far unknown system of covering (which will of course bring in its train a new world of art-forms) can appear only with the adoption of an unknown material, or rather a material that so far has not been used as a guiding principle. It will have to be a material with physical properties that will permit wider spans, with less weight and greater reliability, than are possible when using stone alone. With regard to spatial design and construction, it must be such as will meet any conceivable spatial or planning need. A minimal quantity of material should be needed for the walls, thus rendering the bulky and ponderous buttresses of the* Spitzbogenstil *completely superfluous. The whole weight of the covering system would be confined to vertical pressure, that is, to the reactive strength of walls and supports. Of course, this does not mean that the indirect use of stone vaulting, especially the system of ribbed and stellar vaulting, will be excluded; on the contrary, the latter will be widely used. But it does mean that, for those parts on which the whole system rests, another material will be used, one that makes it possible to transfer their structural function to other parts in which a different principle operates. It makes no difference whether the members to be replaced are buttresses or members that support the ceiling, such as ribs, bands, etc.*

Such a material is iron, which has already been used for this purpose in our century. Further testing and greater knowledge of its structural properties will ensure that iron will become the basis for the covering system of the future and that structurally it will in time come to be as superior to the Hellenic and medieval systems as the arcuated medieval system was to the monolithic trabeated system of antiquity. Disregarding the fragile wooden ceiling (which in any case cannot serve as a comparison) and using mathematical terms, one can say that iron is indeed the material whose principle, yet unutilized, will introduce into architecture the last of the three forces, namely, absolute strength.[31]

As in the later theory of Viollet-le-Duc, Bötticher foresees the essential complementary role to be played by the absolute strength of iron tie rods, thereby enabling the relative strength of stone vaulting to greatly increase its capacity to span. Yet unlike the French structural rationalist, he insists that the tectonic expressivity of such an unprecedented system will have to model its representational form on some kind of reinterpretation of the principles of Hellenic architecture. Through this assertion, based on attributing some measure of symbolic universality to the classical, Bötticher already anticipates the semiotic transformations of the Jugendstil in its crystallizing phase, particularly as one encounters this at the turn of the century in the work of Otto Wagner.[32] Implicitly acknowledging the difficulty of superimposing traditional stereotomic symbolism onto unprecedented lightweight, skeletonal structure, Bötticher looked to the organic as a fundamental form force by which to synthesize the mechanical and the natural and in so doing to reinterpret and transform the received iconography of classic form. Thus he will argue in the 1846 address:

Pictorial art cannot represent an idea as such, but must represent it through a symbol and thus embody it. Architecture follows the same method. It takes its symbols and art-forms only from those natural objects that embody an idea analogous to the one inherent in the members of the architectural system. Therefore, an idea for which no analogue exists in the external world cannot be represented by pictorial art nor for that matter by architecture. The essence of pictorial art and its relation to nature rests in this interaction between concept and object, between invention and imitation.[33]

In 1825, after having studied mathematics in the University of Göttingen, Gottfried Semper appears to have attended architectural classes at the Munich Academy of Fine Arts before fleeing to France in 1826 as the result of a duel. In Paris he studied with Franz Christian Gau, who may have introduced him to the controversy then raging over the original polychromatic rendering of Greek temples.[34] Between 1830 and 1833 Semper traveled in Italy and Greece to see for himself, returning to Germany in 1834 to become architectural director at the Royal Academy in Dresden on Gau's recommendation. His first major commissions following from this appointment were the first Dresden Opera House, completed in 1841, and the Picture Gallery, erected between 1847 and 1854. His participation in the 1848–1849 revolution brought him to exile himself first in France, then in England, where he became part of the Crystal Palace circle around Henry Cole and Richard Redgrave, and then to Zurich where he became head of the Polyteknikum in 1855.

The theoretical elaboration of Semper's *Die vier Elemente der Baukunst* (The Four Elements of Architecture), largely written in 1850, parallels in certain respects some of the arguments advanced by Bötticher in his *Die Tektonik der Hellenen*, the first volume of which Semper did not read until after 1852, following the publication of his *Four Elements* in 1851. The notion of the seminal role played by the internal carpet wall in the evolution of classical architecture seems to have been developed independently by both men. Close to such anthropological insights lay the tectonic theories of Karl Otfried Müller, whose work Semper studied assiduously in 1834 in preparation for his lectures at the Dresden Academy. Another early influence on Semper was the ethnographer Gustav Klemm, who as Royal Librarian was attached to the imperial court at Dresden during the period of Semper's tenure there. That Klemm was seminal for Semper is suggested by his *Allgemeine Kultur-Geschichte des Menschheit* (General Cultural History of Mankind), published in nine volumes between 1843 and 1851, the fourth volume of which accorded particular import to a description of a Pacific Island hut that Klemm had derived from a late eighteenth-century account of a German explorer who had accompanied Captain Cook to the South Seas. Klemm's gloss on this account gave prominence to the same elements as would later make up Semper's model of the primordial dwelling. While Semper would only refer to Klemm on two occasions, he was nonetheless also indebted to him for his theory of cultural transformation in which southern passive races are succeeded by northern nomadic, active, warlike tribes, with the aboriginal dwelling becoming modified according to climate and the racial origin of the nomads as they settle down. As Harry Mallgrave has observed, this pacifying process will give rise to "southern" building types in masonry that, for Semper, formed the historical beginning of architecture, attaining their apotheosis, so to speak, in the dynastic order of Egypt, wherein a warm climate and geographical isolation will allow architecture to develop into a courtyard style of building. The core of the temple complex, for instance, was the hidden *sekos* or tabernacle from which evolved a series of processional yards, formerly open and later covered either with canvas or with a permanent roof. One may see this as similar to the transposition in which a tectonic hut eventually becomes transformed into the stereotomic Greek *megaron* surrounded by columns.[35]

Corroborated by evidence of the Caribbean hut that he saw in the Crystal Palace Exhibition of 1851, Semper's four elements represent a fundamental break with the Vitruvian triad of *utilitas, firmitas, venustas* (fig. 3.29). The empirical fact of this primordial shelter prompted Semper to propose an anthropological counterthesis to Laugier's primitive hut of 1753. In its place, he proposed a more articulated model comprising (1) a hearth, (2) an earthwork, (3) a framework/roof, and (4) an enclosing membrane.

While challenging the authority of Laugier's primitive hut, Semper gave primacy to the tensile frame and its infill as opposed to the compressive earthwork or load-bearing mass. Thus, while Schinkel and Semper made exclusive use of load-bearing masonry in their architecture, they nonetheless conceived of their form as a phenomenally transparent grid, structured about a hierarchical articulation of discrete parts. Nevertheless what Semper added to this hieratic assembly was an emphasis upon the earthwork as a stereotomic, topographic mass upon which the more ephemeral form of the tectonic frame literally took its ground.

This emphasis on the earthwork had a number of consequences. On the one hand, it complemented the universal nomadic textile culture that Semper regarded as the ultimate *Urkunst*; on the other hand, as Rosemarie Bletter has remarked, it gave new importance to a nonspatial element, namely the hearth, which was an inseparable part of the earthwork.[36] For Semper, this last was the

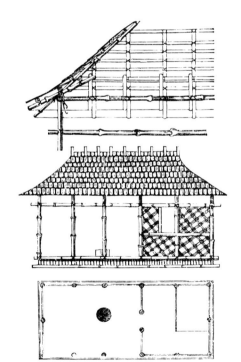

3.29
Gottfried Semper, illustration from *Der Stil in den technischen und tektonischen Künsten*, 1860–1863. The Caribbean hut in the Great Exhibition of 1851.

irreducible *raison d'être* of architecture in that it incorporated in a single element the public and spiritual nexus of the built domain. At the same time, his four elements were possessed of significant etymological ramifications. Thus the Latin term *reredos* was open to a dichotomous reading; on the one hand it signified the back of an altar, on the other the back of a hearth. Meanwhile the term hearth itself carried with it certain civic implications inasmuch as the Latin root *aedificare,* from which the word *edifice* derives, means literally to make a hearth. The institutional connotations of both hearth and edifice are further amplified by the verb *to edify,* which means to educate, strengthen, and instruct. Semper went on to rationalize a great deal of his ethnographic theory on a similar etymological basis. Thus, he would distinguish the massiveness of the fortified wall, as indicated by the word *die Mauer,* from the light, screenlike enclosure signified by the term *die Wand.* Both terms imply enclosure, but the latter is related to the German word for dress, *Gewand,* and to the verb *winden,* which means to embroider. Semper maintained that the earliest basic structural artifact was the knot, from which follows the primary nomadic building culture of the tent and its textile fabric.[37] Here again, one encounters significant etymological connotations of which Semper was fully aware, above all the curious archaic conjunction of *knot* and *joint,* the former being indicated by *der Knoten* and the latter by *die Naht.* In modern German, both words are connected to the concept *die Verbindung,* binding. Thus, for Semper, the most significant basic tectonic element was the joint or the knot (fig. 3.30). As Joseph Rykwert has written,

By a curious use of word-play, Semper foreshadows his later reference to the knot as the essential work of art quite early in the textile chapter, when he considers the term Naht: *the seam, the joining. It is, he says, an expedient, a* Nothbehelf *for the joining of two planes of similar or dissimilar material. But the very juxtaposition of* Noth *and* Naht *suggests a connection.*[38]

Of Semper's characterization of the knot as "the oldest tectonic, cosmogonic symbol," Rykwert notes that

the word-play might have seemed so facile as to be meaningless; though the connection between Naht *and* knot (Knoten, Noeud, nodus) *seemed to him in some way related to the Greek* ἀνακὴ *force, necessity. Presumably he had made himself familiar with the articles* Knoten, Naht *etc. in Jakob and Wilhelm Grimm's German dictionary. However, he found the answer to his problem after he had written this passage in the work on Linguistics by Albert Höfer, a disciple of von Humboldt. Höfer justified the word-play, and pointed out the relation of such words to the Indo-European root* noc, *Latin* nec-o, nexus, necessitas, nectere, νέω *(to spin).*[39]

Semper's emphasis on the joint implies that a fundamental syntactical transition is expressed as one passes from the stereotomic base of a building to its tectonic frame, and that such transitions are of the very essence of architecture.

3.30
Gottfried Semper, typical knot forms used in traditional fabrics, illustrated in the first volume of *Der Still in den technischen und tektonischen Künsten.*

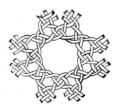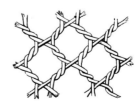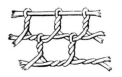

In his later two-volume *Der Stil in den technischen und tektonischen Künsten, oder praktische Aesthetik* (Style in the Technical and Tectonic Arts, or Practical Aesthetics, 1860–1863), Semper assigned certain tectonic crafts to each of the four elements: textiles pertained to the art of enclosure and thus to the side walls and roof, carpentry to the basic structural frame, masonry to the earthwork, and metallurgy and ceramics to the hearth. In the same text, Semper also outlined his *Stoffwechseltheorie,* that is to say his theory of symbolic conservation, in which the mythical-cum-spiritual values attaching to certain structural elements cause them to be translated into petrified compressive forms, even when they were originally of tensile construction. Semper cited sacred Greek architecture as exemplifying the persistence of certain symbolic motifs that had been transformed from a nomadic wooden framework with textile covering to the permanence of stone. According to Semper, this would explain the transposition of textile motifs into the polychromatic ornamental dressings of the triglyphs and metopes in the Doric order. Contrary to the Abbé Laugier, Semper did not feel that such forms arose from the petrification of timber construction, of beam ends and rafters, but rather from features used to tie down the textile fabric covering the roof.

In reference to his own historical period, however, Semper felt that the cheap industrial simulation of one material by another, above all through casting, stamping, and molding, paradoxically undermined the principle of symbolic conservation, largely because these substitutions were expedient and secular and were thus conceptually indifferent to the symbolic continuity essential to the re-creation of tectonic form. The various synthetic substances and processes exhibited at the 1851 Great Exhibition had been an object lesson for Semper, for here he had seen cast iron and gutta-percha employed for the simulation of stone and wood respectively.

In his essay *Wissenschaft, Industrie und Kunst* (Science, Industry, and Art) of 1852, Semper argued that the general crisis of style had arisen out of three different causes, first the alienation of the arts from their original motifs, second the devaluation of material and labor, and third the loss of the ability of the art form to exercise a specific function in relation to the historical moment. Semper sought to counter this degeneration by reasserting the ethnographic origins of the various manufacturing procedures, together with their material references and corresponding forms. In this respect he emphasized the task of the form and the process of fabrication over the specific nature of any given material. Thus, while he regarded clay as the primary molding material or *Urstoff,* this did not prevent him from seeing facing brick or tile as a "dressing," a kind of petrified fabric and hence a transformation of nomadic textile forms into a more permanent material.

Taking something of his taxonomic discourse from the writings of Alexander von Humboldt, Semper, like Hübsch, wanted to transcend the classical paradigm successively advanced by Winckelmann, Hirt, and Bötticher. Like Hübsch he envisaged a return to the "interrupted" style of the Romanesque; to the same style that the American architect H. H. Richardson would assume as his point of departure in 1870. This swerve away from the classical led Semper to ground his theory in the universality of making, placing the burden of tectonic proof on the evolution of the crafts and the industrial arts. As Rykwert has written:

There are, therefore, in Semper's system, two primary archetypes: The hearth and the cloth, the Urherd *and the* Urtuch. *They were the first mark of settlement and the first fabrication; but although they seem to have the same reality for Semper as the* Urpflanze *(original plant) had for Goethe (1788), yet they were not reducible to a single root phenomenon as Goethe would presumably have wanted them, nor do the other root-actions, that of jointing and of heaping, ever merge into each other, but they always, even when they overlap, retain their character, through representation and symbolization.*[40]

For Semper, the ultimate cultural model was linguistic, and in this too, like Bötticher, he was indebted to Wilhelm von Humboldt's insistence that language is not just a description of things but rather a vocalization of action. Linguists of Humboldt's generation saw speech as displaying the will of the people, almost as a Hegelian manifestation of collectivity. In much the same vein, Semper saw artistic culture as an evolving language in which certain root forms and operations are transposed over time.

Semper was a late romantic to the degree that he inherited the epistemological and political project of the *Aufklärung,* and in this regard his participation in the unsuccessful liberal revolution of 1849 is symptomatic. He was Hegelian to the extent that he saw Greek classical architecture as sculptural rather than tectonic in its manner of deploying stone. At the same time he challenged Hegel's triadic scheme of symbolic, classic, and romantic by insisting that the monumental art of architecture derives its formal elaboration from the so-called industrial arts and above all from the craft of textiles, to which Semper would devote the entire first volume of *Der Stil,* according some 480 pages to textiles as opposed to the 200 for ceramics, 132 for carpentry, and 120 for masonry that together make up the second volume. Semper recognized the material and technological ramifications of his four elements by grounding them in different material properties and in correspondingly different crafts. In this vein he would discriminate between the elasticity of textiles, the softness of ceramics, the ductility of carpentry, and the hardness of masonry. Semper saw the articulation of craft capacity in relation to these materials as the evolution of technical skill, in which the hand gradually increases its ability to work a given material to the full extent of its expressive scope.

The emphasis that Semper placed on textiles assumed the form of an obsession, and in one text after another, from his first London lecture of 1853 to his lecture "Über Baustyle" given in Zurich in 1869, he would demonstrate, through anthropological evidence, the symbolic primacy of textile sheathing, as opposed to the corporeality of the form to which it is applied, either as surface decoration or as a shallow, three-dimensional relief. Semper revealed himself a romantic in the Hegelian sense inasmuch as his *Bekleidung* theory became a mode for the progressive dematerialization of architecture, liberating the mind from the stereotomic obtuseness of matter and focusing it instead on a reticulation of surface and thus on a dematerialization that, as in the Crystal Palace, aspired to the dissolution of form into light.[41]

In his "Theorie des Formell-Schönen" (Theory of Formal Beauty) of 1856, he will no longer classify architecture with painting and sculpture as a plastic art but rather with dance and music as a cosmic art, as an ontological, world-making art evocative of nature in action rather than as the static substance of two- and three-dimensional form. Semper regarded the performing arts as cosmic not only because they were symbolic but also because they embodied man's underlying erotic-ludic urge, that is to say the impulse to decorate according to a rhythmic law.

This anthropological insight exposes the conceptual schism running through the entire body of Semperian theory. This split manifests itself, at many different scales, as a representational/ontological division that may be seen as an irreducible aspect of architecture. I am alluding here to the difference between the representational face of a building's surface and the phenomenological (ontic) depth of its space. And while the two may be more easily reconciled in a pantheistic world, this becomes problematic in a secular age, as August Schmarsow was prompt to recognize in his fundamental critique of Semper's *Bekleidung* theory which he saw, in 1893, as having placed an undue emphasis on the representational facade. This stress, for Schmarsow, was at the expense of the experiential body of the building considered as a whole.

Notwithstanding the rationally articulated structural logic of his early work as epitomized in his first Dresden Opera House of 1841, Semper would acknowledge in 1869 that an authentic style of the epoch had failed to emerge and that until such time as it did one would have to make do with the old styles as best one could. It is just this acceptance of eclecticism, made in the name of pragmatic reality and the representation of the bourgeois state, that made him so vulnerable to criticism in the last quarter of the nineteenth century; first from Konrad Fiedler, who saw his architecture as uninspired historicism, overburdened by erudition, second from Otto Wagner, who saw Semper as lacking sufficient courage to push his own tectonic insights to their logical conclusion, namely that a new style must depend of necessity on a new means of construction,[42] and last but not least from Schmarsow, who, however indebted, would regard Semper's architecture as unduly mesmerized by incrusted surface expression and as insufficiently concerned with spatial depth. Semper for his part felt that architecture had lost its cosmic dimension due to secularization and that this loss left his own time with no alternative but to reproduce historical forms, preferably those of the Renaissance that, for him, were symbolic of democracy.

It was left to the next generation of Semperians to pursue the technical and tectonic consequences of his theoretical corpus, together with the legacy of his scientific, architectural realism. Of the many who followed him in this regard, two in particular merit our attention; first the Austrian Otto Wagner, whose work came closest to demonstrating a precise relationship between an articulated skin and the development of a building in depth, and second Georg Heuser, who, in a number of essays written between 1881 and 1894, would assert that architectural realism was more a matter of principle than of style.[43] Heuser believed that architecture could only ultimately evolve through constructive rather than decorative innovation. As if to prove the point, he developed an entire typology of composite, rolled and plated iron supports that according to him could be used for different constructive *and* expressive ends, depending on the situation. While he shared Semper's antipathy to excessive dematerialization, as this had already been demonstrated, so to speak, by the Crystal Palace and by all the ferro-vitreous structures that followed in its wake, he tried to evolve the substance of an iron architecture that had its own corporeal being. To this end he attempted to adduce a strictly tectonic, one might say paleotechnological, equivalent of the classical orders. While Heuser was aware that such built-up elements could only realize their full cultural potential if they were assimilated by the society in everyday practice, he seems to have been among the first to acclaim the riveted steel frame as the new industrial vernacular of the machine age.

If there is a single heir at the turn of the century to the line of Gilly, Schinkel, Bötticher, and Semper, then it is surely Wagner, who, despite the limitations of his practice, attempted to apply the tectonic legacy of the *Aufklärung* to the modernizing realities of the twentieth-century metropolis. This much is already manifest in the pages of his major theoretical text, *Moderne Architektur,* first published in 1896 and later reissued, in slightly modified versions, in 1898, 1902, and 1914. The changed title of the last edition—*Die Baukunst unserer Zeit*—testifies to Wagner's allegiance to the so-called realist approach of such writers as Hermann Muthesius (*Stilarchitektur und Baukunst,* 1902) and Karl Scheffler (*Moderne Baukunst,* 1907). The term *Baukunst* (building art) indicated an approach that was more *sachlich,* in the sense that it responded objectively to the socio-technical building task of everyday life rather than to the ideals of high art. Nevertheless, despite his mature affinity for the real, Wagner never relinquished his aspirations for the ideal, not even at the peak of his career as an engineer/architect in the service of the Viennese *Stadtbahn,* as we may judge from the 1914 edition of *Moderne Architektur,* published some four years before his death in 1918. Here a series of capitalized aphorisms dotted throughout the text highlight the major tenets of his theoretical position, particularly in the seminal fourth chapter dedicated to "Construction" in which we may read the following six apodictic statements:

Every architectural form has risen in construction and has successively become an art-form. It is therefore certain that new purposes must give birth to new methods of construction and by this reasoning also to new forms. The architect always has to develop the art-form, but only the structural calculation and the expense will therefore speak a language unsympathetic to man, while on the other hand, the architect's mode of expression will remain unintelligible if in the creation of the art-form he does not start from construction. Well conceived construction not only is the prerequisite of every architectural work, but also, and this cannot be repeated often enough, provides the modern creative architect with a number of positive ideas for creating new forms—in the fullest meaning of this word. Without the knowledge and experience of construction, the concept "architect" is unthinkable.[44]

While all of this supported Bötticher's thesis that a new *Kunstform* could only arise out of a new *Werkform,*[45] it makes no reference to Semper's *Bekleidung* theory, which Wagner assumed for its capacity to synthesize lightweight panel construction in both stone and metal. At this juncture, Wagner seems to have embraced the metaphor of the mask of which Semper had written in *Der Stil,* with a certain ambiguity: "Masking does not help, however, when *behind* the mask the thing is false."[46] By masking Semper did not intend falsehood, but rather the creation of a tectonic veil through which and by which it would be possible to perceive the spiritual significance of the constructional form, as it lay suspended, as it were, between the pragmatic world of fact and the symbolic world of value. No one has perhaps written more perceptively of Wagner's contribution in this regard than Fritz Neumeyer:

Like the then floating garment that clothes the female body in ancient Greek sculpture, revealing as much beauty as it conceals, Wagner's treatment of the structure and construction exploits a similar kind of delicate, sensuous play that was probably only evident to a connoisseur of a certain age and experience. Exactly this principle gives the interior of the Postsparkasse its quality of silk-like transparency. The glass veil is lifted up on iron stilts that carefully cut into its skin and gently disappear. Semper's theory of "dressing" could find no more ingenious interpretation because here an artist, not a theoretician, generously appealed to it to mask his own interests and obsessions.[47]

Influenced by the *fin-de-siècle* theory of empathy, *Einfühlung,* by which the "form force" of an artwork becomes by association an analogue for corporeal movement and states of bodily being, Wagner found his way back to Bötticher's double articulation of the tectonic, in which the classical legacy of the *Kunstform* would come to be inseminated by the dynamism of the *Werkform* as an inorganically articulated structural invention.[48]

4   Frank Lloyd Wright
and the Text-Tile Tectonic

What, then, could a young radical of the Chicago School learn from the Japanese Imperial exhibit of 1893? Nothing less than a highly provocative clue to a fresh concept of Western architecture: the interplay of solid structure with unprecedented quantities of light and atmosphere. Roofs, walls, and, above all, fenestration could be liberated from bondage to a rigid formalism, could be divorced from their hitherto ambiguous function, in the Western tradition, as boundary lines for preconceived canons of proportion. The Ho-o-den demonstrated that uninterrupted strip fenestration with suppressed sills under eaves restored to their proper place as shades were the means whereby a house could be, so to speak, turned inside out. Given these new directions, the "style" would come naturally—especially to anyone already predisposed. . . . A good house, Wright instinctively realized, must not be rigid; it must consciously acknowledge the earth beneath it and invite the air around it, and yet display its very human need for protection from a nature which is not always benign. In the Ho-o-den, Wright beheld an unfamiliar architectural heritage which approximated the vision in his mind. Here was the germ of continuous plastic fenestration that could be bent around corners, that need recognize no formalistic allegiance to canons of design, that could open the interior to the outdoors anywhere and everywhere, and that would produce by its inherent horizontality and by its awning-like overhangs that level domestic line which Wright intuitively admired and had determined to develop as the main theme of his house architecture.

Within a year of this event, he began to discard the sash window in favor of the casement, to prepare his work for the final change from fenestration in spots to fenestration in strips. Once done, the change automatically obliterated the severity and resistance of wall, fostered the free running treatment of sills and bases, and resulted in the victory of the horizontal as the dominant characteristic of a great style that was, indeed, to make history.
Grant Carpenter Manson, Frank Lloyd Wright to 1910, *1958*

The fact that Frank Lloyd Wright (1867–1959) always referred to Louis Sullivan as his *lieber Meister* testifies to the strong hold that the German culture exercised over Chicago during the last quarter of the nineteenth century. By the time of the Columbian Exposition of 1893, Germans constituted a third of the city's population. In 1898, a survey of distinguished citizens of German origin listed seventeen prominent architects including August Bauer, Frederick Baumann, and Dankmar Adler. It is equally significant that Adler and Sullivan's Schiller Theatre of 1893 would be built for the performance of German plays in the original, just as their canonical Auditorium Building of 1884 was largely devoted to opera, primarily of course to Richard Wagner's musical drama. At this time Chicago published two daily newspapers in German and had numerous German clubs and associations. By 1898 Louis Sullivan had been Adler's design partner for almost a decade. Caught between his Beaux-Arts education and this omnipresent German environment, Sullivan had almost as many German as French books in his library, even if he understood little of the language. Thus, as Barry Bergdoll has written,

While neither Sullivan nor Wright read or understood German they were surrounded by people who did and who took an active interest in redefining the bases of architectural practice. In their own office in the Auditorium tower two of the principals were native Germans, Dankmar Adler and Paul Mueller, the young engineer from Stuttgart who later built many of Wright's most important designs. Sullivan, it should be remembered, had been exposed to German metaphysical philosophy already before joining Adler through his friend, the elusive John Edel-

man, who had spoken German since childhood and according to Sullivan's autobiography reinforced Sullivan's sympathy with American transcendentalist philosophy by long discourses on German Romantic philosophy. In addition the entire office seems to have been interested in Wagner's music, the Auditorium building itself resonant with overtones of the Germanic notion of the Gesamtkunstwerk *and the possibility of dramatic art to lift the spectator to a higher realm of awareness.*[1]

Bergdoll proceeds to show that the influence of the German theorist Gottfried Semper on late nineteenth-century Chicago architecture was as intense as it was diffuse. It entered the architectural discourse from different quarters and was thus subject to varied interpretations. Two architects in particular seem to have been largely responsible for the dissemination of Semper's views. These were the German émigré Frederick Baumann and the American John Wellborn Root.

Baumann would contribute to the development of the Chicago School in different ways. In the first place, he would establish himself as a technician through his formula for constructing isolated pier foundations made available in his pamphlet of 1873, *The Art of Preparing Foundations for All Kinds of Buildings with Particular Illustration of the Method of Isolated Piers.* In the second place, he would play a major public role in the interpretation of German architectural theory in translating Friedrich Adler's *Schinkelfest* address of 1869 and in paraphrasing Semper's theories, the latter in his address "Thoughts on Architecture" presented to the American Institute of Architects convention in 1890 and his lecture "Thoughts on Style" delivered to the AIA convention in 1892. As Roula Geraniotis has remarked:

The reasons why Baumann was so impressed by Semper are obvious: Semper was a profound thinker and a keen architectural critic, who had enjoyed a brilliant career as a designing architect. It is important to note that Semper's influence had reached Baumann directly through one of his former students; from 1869 to 1874 the foreman at the architectural office of Frederick Baumann and Eduard Baumann in Chicago was Carl Maximilian Heinz, who had studied architecture under Gottfried Semper at the Eidgenössisches Polytechnikum (today's ETH) in Zurich. It is known that Semper was literally adored by his students and there is no doubt that Baumann shared fully the fascination that the young Heinz had felt for his master.[2]

Baumann was not the sole figure to introduce Semper to the Chicago architectural scene. In late 1889 and again early in 1890, *Inland Architecture* published John Wellborn Root's translation of Semper's 1869 essay "Über Baustyle." The closeness of theory and practice at this moment is borne out by the fact that Root made the translation in collaboration with his friend, the German émigré Fritz Wagner, who happened to be an architect specializing in terra-cotta facing. It would be hard to imagine more appropriate translators, since terra-cotta was a Semperian material par excellence and it was exactly this material that Root would use in cladding his steel-framed Rand McNally Building, completed in 1890[3] (not to mention Sullivan's acknowledged mastery over this material).

Two aspects of Semper's theory were of special importance for Baumann and for the development of the Chicago School in all its subsequent manifestations: first, Semper's insistence that the archetypal origin of all built form was textile production, with the knot serving as the primordial joint, and second, his contention that the art of building is anthropologically indebted to the applied arts for many of its motifs.[4] These hypotheses led to Semper's theory of *Bekleidung,* wherein clothing is seen as extending itself across time into forms of large-scale enclosure. For Semper, screenlike walls in permanent construction were reminiscent of tented nomadic textile form. As far as he was concerned terra-cotta facing and even brickwork were the tectonic transpositions of woven fabric. While neither Wright nor Sullivan made any reference to Semper, we have every reason to suppose that they were aware of his theory, given that Chicago was so impregnated with German cultural values and ideas. In any event, Sullivan would have heard Baumann's paper delivered to the Illinois State Association of Architects in 1887, wherein he paraphrased Semper's definition of style, namely that "style is the coincidence of a structure with the conditions of its origins."[5]

Among the more fertile encounters in the prehistory of the modern movement is the meeting of the Welshman Owen Jones with Semper's close associate, the young French architect Jules Goury. At the time of their encounter in Athens in 1831, Goury had already traveled with Semper for over a year, the object of their tour being to study the polychromatic decoration in Greek architecture. This concern for documenting aboriginal ornamentation later led Jones and Goury to make a similar study of the Alhambra, their joint results being published in two volumes in 1836 and 1865 under the title *Plans, Elevations, Sections and Details of the Alhambra.*

Following Victor Hugo, Jones and Goury saw the Alhambra as a "palace that the genies have gilded like a dream filled with harmony," and their documentation of this complex helped to further the vision of an exotic heterotopia that ran as a promise of cultural redemption throughout the rest of the century.[6] Jones, Sullivan, and Wright, all anti-establishment figures of Celtic origin, followed each other in this search for an "other" culture with which to overcome the spiritual bankruptcy of the eclectic battle of styles. Jones's *Grammar of Ornament,* published in 1856, served as a polemical guide for the pursuit of this transcultural overcoming; its colonialist sweep through the world of ornament demonstrated by implication the relative inferiority of the European, Greco-Roman-medieval legacy compared to the riches of the Orient, the former being represented by insipid, palely tinted plates, compared to the multicolored illustrations featuring exotic oriental or savage ornament. Over two-thirds of *The Grammar of Ornament* was devoted to these relatively remote cultures, and the plates depicting such ornamental systems were beautifully printed in chromolithography at considerable expense (figs. 4.1, 4.2). Jones's magnum opus led almost directly to Sullivan's own polychromatic ornament—to his richly colored incantatory decor, abstracted from natural form and pattern, that was already fully elaborated by the time of his Chicago Stock Exchange interior of 1894. This efflorescent enrichment reached its apotheosis in the midwestern banks that he designed toward the end of his career between 1906 and 1919. It is significant that almost all of these buildings were faced in rough-cut, tinted, pressed brick, a material that Sullivan regarded as a kind of textile. Thus he wrote in 1910:

Manufacturers, by grinding the clay or shale course and by the use of cutting wires, produced on its face a new and most interesting texture, a texture with a nap-like effect, suggesting somewhat an Anatolian rug. . . . When [tinted bricks are] laid up promiscuously, especially if the surface is large and care is taken to

Owen Jones, Islamic ornament, plate from
The Grammar of Ornament, 1856.

4.2
Owen Jones, Celtic ornament, plate from *The Grammar of Ornament.*

avoid patches of any one color, the general tone suggests that of a very old Oriental rug.[7]

Wright made exactly the same analogy when writing about his textile block system in 1927: "A building for the first time may be lightly fabricated, complete, of mono-material—literally woven into a pattern or design as was the oriental rug."[8] This textile metaphor was present in Wright's thought almost from the beginning; certainly it is already there in his second address to the Architectural League of Chicago delivered in June 1900, entitled simply "The Architect."

Sullivan first came across the work of Jones through the Philadelphia architect Frank Furness. Furness had been influenced by Jones in part through *The Grammar of Ornament,* which he seems to have read first in French translation, and in part through contact with Jacob Gray Mould, who had been apprenticed to Jones.[9] Furness evolved an orientalized Gothicism that was certainly as evocative of Moorish culture as the Alhambresque villas that Jones himself had realized in Kensington Palace Gardens, London, in the late 1840s. Sullivan entered into Furness's employ in 1873 at exactly the moment when the latter's orientalized neo-Gothic attained its maturity in his design for the Pennsylvania Academy of Fine Arts (fig. 4.3). While Sullivan unquestionably used sources other than Jones's *Grammar* as the model and the method for his own ornament, above all his assiduous study of botanical form as this appears in Asa Gray's *Botany,*[10] there is little doubt that many of Sullivan's philosophical ideas find their origin in the various scholarly glosses that accompanied Jones's compendium. Among these one may cite Jones's own recognition of the cultural exhaustion of the West, condemned to the eternal repetition of the same depleted syntax, and his insistence that we need to return to nature as the Egyptians and the Greeks did rather than in the manner adopted by the Chinese and the

Goths.[11] We may also note that passage in Jones's introduction where he follows Semper in insisting on the primacy of tectonic form and urging that one decorate construction rather than construct decoration, a principle that Sullivan did not always adhere to.[12] *The Grammar of Ornament* also contains J. O. Westwood's suggestion that Celtic art had its origin in the East, from which it may have been brought back by Irish missionaries; an incidental fact that must have been extremely stimulating to Sullivan's imagination, given his Irish background.[13] In a chapter dealing with the derivation of ornament from nature, Jones lays out the essence of Sullivan's own ornamental program:

We think it impossible that a student fully impressed with the law of the universal fitness of things in nature, with the wonderful variety of form, yet all arranged around some few fixed laws, the proportionate distributions of areas, the tangential curvature of lines, and the radiation from the parent stem, whatever type he may borrow from nature, if he will dismiss from his mind the desire to imitate it, but will only seek to follow still the path which it so plainly shows him, we doubt

4.3
Frank Furness, Pennsylvania Academy of
Fine Arts, Philadelphia, 1871–1876. Elevation.

4.4
Louis Sullivan, plate from *A System of Architectural Ornament According with a Philosophy of Man's Power,* 1924.

not that new forms of beauty will more readily arise under his hand, than can ever follow from a continuation in the prevailing fashion of vesting only the works of the past for present inspiration.[14]

Sullivan's *A System of Architectural Ornament According with a Philosophy of Man's Powers,* published in 1924, the year of his death, is a complex and subtle demonstration of Owen Jones's hypothetical program, in which Sullivan would further elaborate the procedures outlined by Jones. What Sullivan demonstrated in documenting his method was a series of morphological and geometrical transformations in which the bipolar seed germ (the sycamore pod) was exfoliated into ever more complex organic forms structured about simple Platonic armatures: the square, the circle, the triangle, etc. These basic forms will be further elaborated into complex, inorganic polyhedra (fig. 4.4), eventually to result in the swirling, efflorescent ornamentation that we find on the lower street facade of Sullivan's Schlesinger and Mayer Store of 1904 or in the exuberant elegiac decor of the midwestern banks that brought his career to a close. A form of quasi-scientific nature worship is latent in all of Sullivan's pantheistic ornament, and this serves as a bridge between his Emersonian transcendentalism and the abstract universality of Islamic culture. Sullivan's later ornament may thus be regarded as the incantatory assertion of a cosmological faith, one that impregnates the entire surface of his structures like a magical tattoo, as is evident, say, in the Guaranty Building, Buffalo, of 1895 (fig. 4.5). This underlying intent is suggested by the brief text that accompanies his treatise on ornament.

These simple forms of ancient discovery and use were given esoteric meaning and occult powers by the men of that day in an effort to control, by means of for-

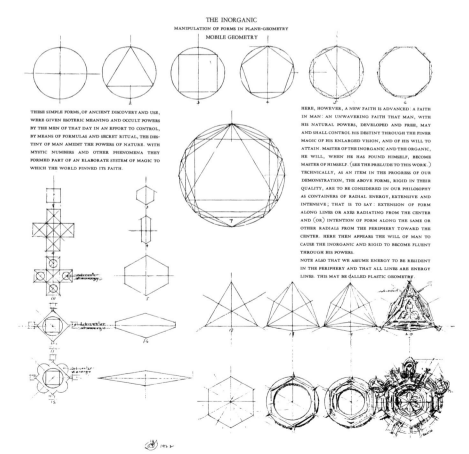

mulas and secret ritual, the destiny of man amidst the powers of nature. With mystic numbers and other phenomena they formed part of an elaborate system of magic to which the world pinned its faith. Here, however, a new faith is advanced; a faith in man: an unswerving faith that man, with his natural powers, developed and free, may and shall control his destiny through the finer magic of his enlarged vision and his will to attain.[15]

That the magical is still implied in this vision of a triumphant democratic future is as consequent as the mystical anthropomorphism that underlay everything Sullivan wrote. Sullivan saw creativity as the giver of both individual and collective identity and as the manifestation of some unnamable divinity. Sullivan and Wright believed in the promise of a modern secular civilization that would be comparable in its spiritual intensity to the great theocracies of the antique world. The implicit metatheology of their work, its tectonic scripture, so to speak, depended for its reticulated surface on the translation and iteration of organic morphological processes and on a conscious fusion of nature with culture. Thus a progressive pantheism came to be inscribed in everything they did, as a kind of cryptic language that invariably took the form of a petrified textile of which we may say that the walls were as much written as they were built.

One is reminded at this juncture of Semper's account of cultural development as a kind of linguistic waxing and waning in which forms emerge and rise to high levels of articulation before degenerating into decadence. Within such a trajectory, Semper imagines primordial form as an idiosyncratic, syntactical craft inflection, from which an entire nonverbal culture might be woven as a kind of rhythmic parallel to poetry or chant. As we have already noted in chapter 3, for Semper, as for Sullivan and Wright, architecture was closer to dance and music than to painting and sculpture.[16] Owen Jones, for his part, would illustrate at length the ornament of non-Eurocentric civilizations, wherein similar iterations could be regarded as a kind of incantatory inscription conducive to hallucination, particularly as this applied to the ornament of India and Islam.[17] Within this broad imperialist view of world culture it is hardly an accident that Wright would be as attracted to pre-Columbian and Japanese civilizations, as Sullivan had been drawn in his own time to Saracenic culture. Moreover, it was already well known that as far as the architecture of such antifigurative civilizations was concerned, the written, the woven, and the tectonic were frequently fused together. Some confirmation of this may be found in Claude Humbert's recent study of Islamic ornament:

4.5
Louis Sullivan, Guaranty Building, Buffalo, 1894–1895. Capital detail.

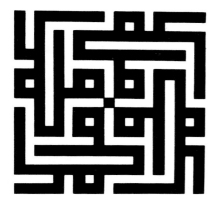

4.6
Calligraphic design incorporating the names of Ali and Mohammed.

Writing, calligraphy and epigraphy are the testimony of a civilization. Not only do the ideas and deeds transcribed and communicated provide content, but the writing and the written page themselves constitute a form that can be analyzed graphically. . . . It is important to consider briefly here this script that forms an integral part of Arab design. Ornamental in itself, it quite naturally comes to be incorporated into other ornaments. . . . From an examination of all the forms of decorative and ornamental Islamic art, two quite distinct types emerge: polygonal ornamentation, characterized by a skilled and critical use of geometry; and plant and floral ornamentation, which, in contrast to polygonal design, are inspired by the natural world.[18]

Humbert cites numerous instances in which Kufic script appears as an ornament that is as much designed as it is written. He gives examples of motifs built up out of permutations of the word Allah or Mohammed or of the phrase "There is no strength but that of God," which assumes in one instance through graphic abstraction the profile of an Islamic city complete with minarets. Alternatively, he cites cases where the names Ali and Mohammed pinwheel about solar crosses (fig. 4.6). It is significant that something akin to a solar cross will serve as Frank Lloyd Wright's square monogram and that this motif will be subjected to a series of Froebel-like permutations in Wright's textile block houses.

While it is unlikely that Wright was ever aware of Semper's *Wissenschaft, Industrie und Kunst* (Science, Industry, and Art) of 1852, certain parallels nonetheless obtain between their respective views of the machine, particularly as Wright's view appears in his seminal address of 1901, "The Art and Craft of the Machine." Unlike his contemporary Adolf Loos, for whom the invention of ornament was an anathema, Wright attempted to derive an authentic ornament from the process of fabrication, irrespective of whether this entailed the mechanized manufacture of basic building blocks or the systematic assembly of prefabricated modular timber elements as they come straight from the mill. Thus while Semper despaired of ever overcoming the newfound capacity of the machine to simulate rich material effects with cheaper material—the problem posed by substitution—Wright optimistically regarded the machine as a phoenix that was destined to arise from the ashes of its current kitsch production to yield a democratic culture of unparalleled quality and extent. After Victor Hugo's famous study of Notre-Dame, Wright saw the rotary press as the sine qua non of the machine. Of the impact of mechanical reproduction on the preliterate text of architecture, Wright wrote:

Thus down to the time of Gutenberg architecture is the principle writing—the universal writing of humanity. In the great granite books of the Orient, continued by Greek and Roman antiquity . . . the Middle Ages wrote the last page. . . . In the fifteenth century everything changes. Human thought discovers a mode of perpetuating itself, not only more resisting than architecture, but still more simple and easy. Architecture is dethroned. Gutenberg's letters of lead are about to supersede Orpheus' letters of stone. The book is about to kill the edifice. The invention of printing was the greatest event in history. It was the first great machine, after the great city. It is human thought stripping off one form and donning another.[19]

While recognizing the inevitable truth of Hugo's famous retrospective prophecy that this (the press) will kill that (architecture)—*ceci tuera cela*—Wright nonetheless argued for the employment of the liberative potential of the machine that

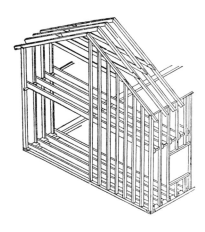

4.7
George E. Woodward, balloon framing, as published in *The Country Gentleman*, 1860.

was lying dormant, so to speak, within the urban, industrialized, middle-class society of the late nineteenth century. As a corollary to this Wright urged the reeducation and reintegration of all the various classes of modern manufacturers from industrialists to craftsmen. He was prompt to recognize, however, that the labor-saving cultural potential of the machine would only come into its own if the machine were allowed to produce according to its own intrinsic order. Thus he wrote:

The machine, by its wonderful cutting, shaping, and smoothing and repetitive capacity, has made it possible to so use it without waste that the poor as well as the rich may enjoy today beautiful surface treatments of clean, strong forms that the branch veneers of Sheraton and Chippendale only hinted at, with dire extravagance, and which the Middle Ages utterly ignored. The machine has emancipated these beauties of nature in wood; made it possible to wipe out the mass of meaningless torture to which wood has been subjected since the world began, for it has been universally abused and maltreated by all peoples but the Japanese.[20]

Since he had yet to visit Japan, Wright was no doubt alluding here to the reassembled Ho-o-den temples that appeared in the Columbian Exposition of 1893. Bergdoll suggests that this work may well have had as great an impact on Wright as the Caribbean hut of the 1851 exhibition had had on Semper. There seems to be a convergence here between Wright's appreciation of the repetitive yet variable order of Japanese domestic architecture and the vastly improved wood-milling capacity that had evolved in part out of the increasing demand for George Washington Snow's balloon frame system of timber construction (fig. 4.7).[21] Thus Wright's early domestic architecture, executed in wood, is invariably conceived and machined according to a repetitive modular order and framed after Snow's invention. Seen in this light, Wright's early wooden architecture seems to be as modular as anything we will encounter in his later textile block construction.

However, vertical members are often suppressed in Wright's eccentric interpretation of the balloon frame, in part to provide a horizontal weatherproof sheathing and in part to unify the surface and to simulate, metaphorically, the coursing of masonry. Thus the horizontal framing members are expressed through cover strips that are secured to the studs through the cladding. This "coursed" expression of the frame was already evident in Wright's Romeo and Juliet Windmill of 1896, where it presented itself as a plaited fabric comprised of timber shingles and horizontal wooden battening (fig. 4.8).[22] Romeo and Juliet inaugurated what Henry-Russell Hitchcock would later characterize as the Forest Period of Wright's architecture, in which he utilized various modes of timber construction that in different ways amounted to simplified versions of the Shingle Style. A number of works exemplify this short-lived phase in Wright's career, ranging from the River Forest Golf Club of 1901 to the Ross House built on Lake Delavan in 1902, together with the Glasner House, completed at Glencoe, Illinois, in 1905. The summer cottages built for the Gerts family in Whitehall, Michigan, in 1902 also belong to this genre (figs. 4.9, 4.10). In each instance a three-foot-square planning module was adopted, together with boarded sheathing, capped by horizontal battens at one-foot intervals.[23] That these battens perform much the same modulating role as stringcourses in rusticated masonry is borne out by the Arthur Heurtley House of 1902, where every fifth brick course is set in advance of the main wall (fig. 4.11). One way or another a plaited approach to architectonic space, derived in some measure perhaps from the Froebel system to which Wright had been exposed as a child, prevailed throughout his long career.[24] Generally speaking, it assumed either a tartan or a quadratic form of varying modular dimension, ranging from the basic three-foot grid of the midwestern Forest Period to the sixteen-inch-square grid of the Californian textile block house period, to the thirteen-inch, recessed horizontal battens that striate the walls of the Usonian houses of the thirties and forties. While this modular order would vary according to local circumstances, in every instance it was as much an economic, democratic, mechanized means of saving labor in construction as it was an architectural concept.

4.8
Frank Lloyd Wright, Romeo and Juliet Windmill, Spring Green, Wisconsin, 1896.

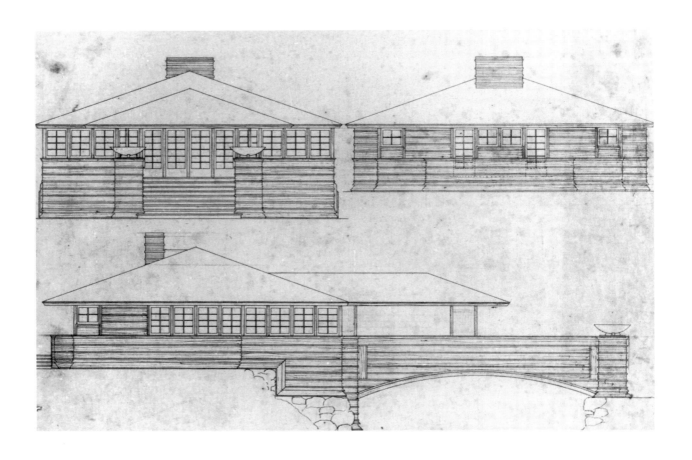

4.9
Frank Lloyd Wright, summer cottage for
George Gerts, Whitehall, Michigan, 1902.
Elevations.

4.10
Frank Lloyd Wright, Gerts Cottage, sections
and details.

4.11
Frank Lloyd Wright, Arthur Heurtley House,
Oak Park, 1902. Elevation.

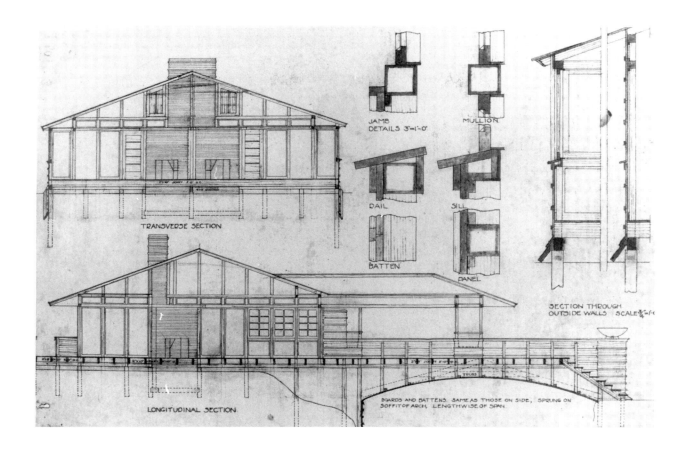

TRANSVERSE SECTION

JAMB DETAILS 3"=1'-0"

MULLION

DAIL

SILL

BATTEN

PANEL

SECTION THROUGH OUTSIDE WALLS SCALE ¾=1'-0"

LONGITUDINAL SECTION

BOARDS AND BATTENS SAME AS THOSE ON SIDE, SPRUNG ON SOFFIT OF ARCH, LENGTHWISE OF SPAN.

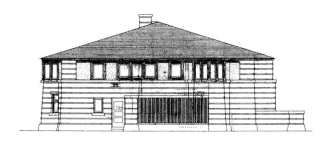

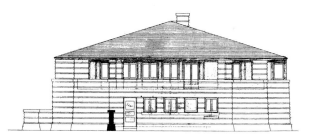

This tectonic method was challenged when Wright had to confront the all-purpose fireproof, durable material of his epoch, namely, monolithic reinforced concrete, cast in situ. This is the material of his Village Bank prototype, projected, ironically enough, for the *Brickbuilder* in 1901 (fig. 4.12), and this same material will constitute the basic fabric of Unity Temple, completed in Oak Park in 1906 (see fig. 8.68). Even here Wright approached the entire design from the standpoint of building production. Thus he wrote of the Temple:

What shape? Well, the answer lay in what material? . . . Why not make the wooden boxes or forms so the concrete could be cast in them as separate blocks and masses, these grouped about an interior space. . . . The wooden forms or molds in which concrete buildings must at that time be cast were always the chief item of expense, so to repeat the use of a single form as often as possible was desirable, even necessary. Therefore a building, all four sides alike, looked like the thing. This, in simplest terms, meant a building square in plan. That would make their temple a cube—a noble form.[25]

However, like the French structural rationalist Anatole de Baudot in his St.-Jean de Montmartre church of 1904 self-consciously constructed of reinforced brickwork or *ciment armé* (see fig. 2.27), Wright realized that monolithic concrete cannot be easily rendered as a convincing tectonic form due to its lack of inherent articulation. This fact is made explicit in his manifesto that appeared in the *Architectural Record* in 1929:

Aesthetically concrete has neither song nor any story. Nor is it easy to see in this conglomerate, in this mud pie, a high aesthetic property, because in itself it is amalgam, aggregate, compound. And cement, the binding medium, is characterless.

Later in the same passage he writes of his invention of the textile block:

I finally had found simple mechanical means to produce a complete building that looks the way the machine made it, as much at least as any fabric need look. Tough, light, but not "thin"; imperishable; plastic; no unnecessary lie about it any-

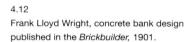

4.12
Frank Lloyd Wright, concrete bank design
published in the *Brickbuilder,* 1901.

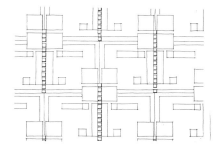

4.13
Frank Lloyd Wright, Harry E. Browne House, Geneseo, Illinois, 1906. Prototypical block construction.

4.14
Frank Lloyd Wright, Avery Coonley House, Riverside, 1908. Ceramic wall ornament inlaid into stucco.

4.15
Frank Lloyd Wright, Midway Gardens, Chicago, 1915. Section.

where and yet machine-made, mechanically perfect. Standardization as the soul of the machine here for the first time may be seen in the hand of the architect, put squarely up to imagination, the limitations of imagination the only limitation of building.[26]

It is interesting to note that Wright made his first attempt to articulate monolithic reinforced concrete in the very year that Unity Temple was completed. This move came with a prefabricated block house designed for Harry E. Browne in 1906 (fig. 4.13). In a later annotation attached to a drawing of this house, Wright claimed it as the first concrete block house, projected some fifteen years before his eventual use of this material in California.[27] Tiled motifs set in plaster in the Avery Coonley House of 1908 (fig. 4.14) and the patterned block capping to the A. D. German Warehouse of 1915 point in the same direction, as do the non-structural concrete blocks applied to Midway Gardens, Chicago, of 1915 (fig. 4.15)[28] and the carved ornamentation in Oya stone that appears in Wright's Imperial Hotel, Tokyo, under construction from 1918 to 1922. Wright finally tackled the idea of wire-reinforced, tessellated block construction (compare de Baudot's wire-reinforced brickwork of 1904) with his 1921 study for a concrete block house for Albert M. Johnson, in Death Valley, California. In terms of both panoramic form and programmatic grandiosity, this somewhat Egyptoid building entertained similar cultural aspirations as the complex that Wright designed for Aline Barnsdall at Olive Hill, Los Angeles, on which he was engaged intermittently from 1916 onward.[29] However, Barnsdall's Hollyhock House was not built in concrete block, so the proof of the potential of a textile block system did not occur until the realization of Alice Millard's canonical La Miniatura, built in Pasadena, California, in 1923 (fig. 4.16).[30] With retrospective aplomb Wright set forth the economic/tectonic advantages of this method in 1932:

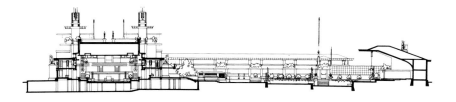

Frank Lloyd Wright

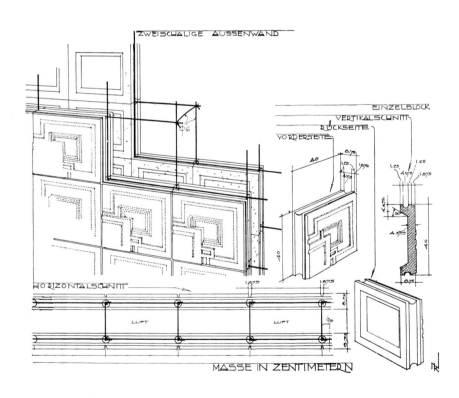

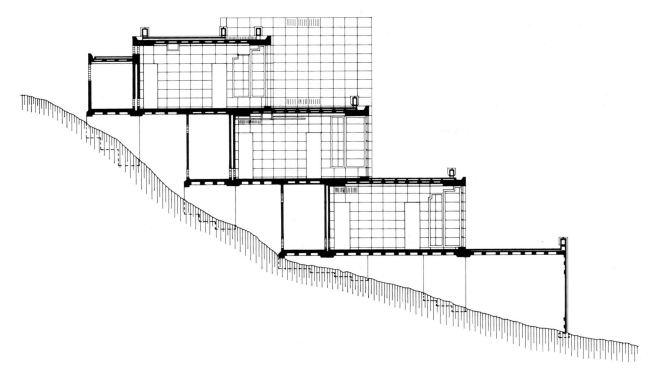

4.16
Frank Lloyd Wright, Alice Millard house, "La Miniatura," Pasadena, California, 1923.

4.17
Frank Lloyd Wright, patent double-wall, light-weight block system.

4.18
Frank Lloyd Wright, San Marcos in the Desert, near Chandler, Arizona, 1927. Section.

We would take that despised outcast of the building industry—the concrete block—out from underfoot or from the gutter—find a hitherto unsuspected soul in it—make it live as a thing of beauty—textured like the trees. Yes, the building would be made of the "blocks" as a kind of tree itself standing at home among the other trees in its own native land. All we would have to do would be to educate the concrete block, refine it and knit it together with steel in the joints and so construct the joints that they could be poured full of concrete after they were set up and a steel strand laid in them. The walls would thus become thin but solid reinforced slabs and yield to any desire for form imaginable. And common labor could do it all. We would make the walls double of course, one wall facing inside and the other wall facing outside, thus getting continuous hollow spaces between, so the house would be cool in summer, warm in winter and dry always [fig. 4.17].[31]

Immediately after this passage Wright referred to himself as the "weaver," thereby stressing, once again, his conception of the textile block as an all-enveloping woven membrane. In practice he suppressed at every turn those latent "unwoven" structural members that contributed to its equilibrium; that is to say, those reinforced concrete beams and columns that were essential to the overall stability of these tessellated walls. This discreet suppression is emphasized by the fact that in almost all of the concrete block houses the floor depths do not coincide with the modular dimension of the system. This displacement is very clear in the Xanadu-like project for San Marcos in the Desert, where the actual floor slab is evidently shallower than the block depth (fig. 4.18).

With its patterned, perforated, glass-filled apertures, La Miniatura already embodied the essential syntax of the textile block system that was employed, with

Frank Lloyd Wright

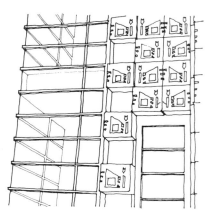

4.19
Frank Lloyd Wright, Samuel Freeman House, Los Angeles, 1924. Sketch of corner.

4.20
Frank Lloyd Wright, National Life Insurance Offices, Chicago, 1920–1925.

subtle variations, in each of the subsequent block houses. With the exception of the Freeman House, Los Angeles, of 1924, where the textile blocks run into open glass corners and where the muntins seem to extend directly from the joints between the blocks (fig. 4.19), Wright's later California block houses, the Ennis and Storer houses, add little to the basic syntax of La Miniatura. The full potential of this singular innovation, the extension, that is, of a tessellated semi-solid membrane into a mitered glass corner, comes into its own with Wright's National Life Insurance Offices, projected for Chicago in 1924, informally dedicated to Sullivan in the year of his demise (fig. 4.20). Conceived nearly thirty years after Wright's Luxfer Prism office project of 1895 but only seven years after Willis Polk had achieved the Hallidie Building, San Francisco, as the first curtain-walled, high-rise structure in the world, Wright elaborated this thirty-one-story skyscraper slab as a woven glass and sheet metal fabric suspended from a concrete core. The exceptional brilliance of this particular synthesis is made clear in Wright's description of 1928.

The exterior walls, as such, disappear—instead are suspended, standardized sheet-copper screens. The walls themselves cease to exist as either weight or thickness. Windows become in this fabrication a matter of a unit in the screen fabric, opening singly or in groups at the will of the occupant. All windows may be cleaned from the inside with neither bother nor risk. The vertical mullions (copper shells filled with non-conducting material), are large and strong enough only to carry from floor to floor and project much or little as shadow on the glass may or may not be wanted. Much projection enriches the shadow. Less projection dispels the shadows and brightens the interior. These protecting blades of copper act in the sun like the blades of a blind.

The unit of two feet both ways is, in this instance, emphasized on every alternate vertical with additional emphasis on every fifth. There is no emphasis on the horizontal units. The edge of the various floors being beveled to the same section as is used between the windows, it appears in the screen as such horizontal division occurring naturally on the two-foot unit lines.

. . . Being likewise fabricated on a perfect unit system, the interior partitions may all be made up in sections, complete with doors, ready to set in place and designed to match the general style of the outer wall screen. These interior partition-units thus fabricated may be stored ready to use, and any changes to suit tenants made over night with no waste of time and material.

The increase of glass area over the usual skyscraper fenestration is only about ten per cent (the margin could be increased or diminished by expanding or contracting the copper members in which it is set), so the expense of heating is not materially increased. Inasmuch as the copper mullions are filled with insulating material and the window openings are tight, being mechanical units in a mechanical screen, this excess of glass is compensated.

The radiators are cast as a railing set in front of the lower glass unit of this outer screen wall, free enough to make cleaning easy.[32]

This entire project can be seen in retrospect as a projection at a mammoth scale of the 1897 patent for the Luxfer Prism electro-glazing process as devised by W. H. Winslow, wherein four-by-four-inch glass lenses, interlaced in two directions with copper filaments, could be fused into glazed panels suitable for the construction of clerestories and roof lights. It is interesting to note that Wright would receive forty-one design patents for decorative patterns to be cast into the Luxfer Prism lenses. Far from this scale, Wright would conceive of the concrete treelike superstructure of his National Life Insurance project as supporting its crystalline envelope in two different ways, first as a composite cantilever about a single support line (fig. 4.21) and second as an independent twin-stem column system, supporting symmetrically cantilevered floors that are linked by a slab of shallower depth spanning between the points of contraflexure (fig. 4.22). In this work Wright moves toward a particularly dense synthesis of ontological and representational tectonic form. The essential continuity and articulation of Wright's late masterwork, his S. C. Johnson Administration Building of 1936, is already anticipated in this dramatic combination of structural and membranous form (fig. 4.23).

As M. F. Hearn has suggested, the National Life Insurance project was particularly significant for the way in which it extended Wright's debt to the Orient to a

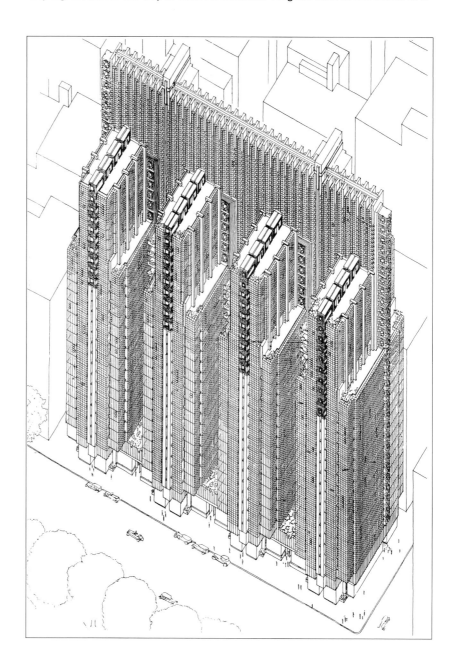

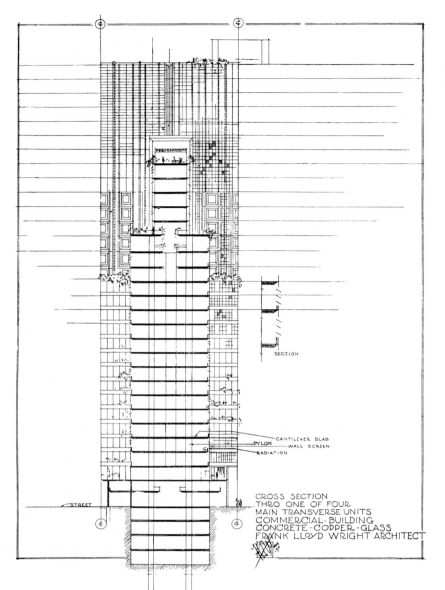

CANTILEVER SLAB
PYLON
WALL SCREEN.
RADIATION

SECTION

STREET

CROSS SECTION
THRO ONE OF FOUR
MAIN TRANSVERSE UNITS
COMMERCIAL · BUILDING
CONCRETE · COPPER · GLASS
FRANK LLOYD WRIGHT ARCHITECT

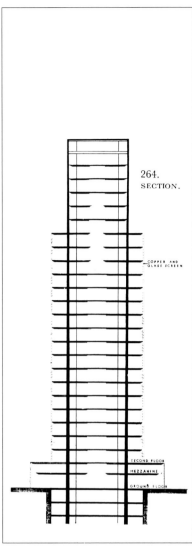

264.
SECTION.

COPPER AND
GLASS SCREEN

SECOND FLOOR
MEZZANINE
GROUND FLOOR

4.21
Frank Lloyd Wright, National Life Insurance
Offices, section.

4.22
Frank Lloyd Wright, National Life Insurance
Offices, section.

4.23
Frank Lloyd Wright, Johnson Wax Administration Building, Racine, 1936–1939. Typical column section.

more structural level. After noting that Wright's previous skyscraper proposal—the twenty-story 1912 San Francisco Call Tower—had been predicated on what by then was already a fairly conventional reinforced concrete frame, Hearn goes on to suggest an oriental prototype for the treelike, high-rise form that he would adopt twelve years later.

Although the Imperial Hotel deeply involved Wright in concern about structural earthquake-proofness, the scheme for that project was unrelated to the one for the insurance company, except that they both employed the cantilever principle. Indeed, the basic idea for each seems to have been transported in different directions across the Pacific Ocean to the opposite shore: the inspiration for the "pincushion" of concrete posts that was poured into the swampy mud in order to ground the foundation platform of the hotel, heretofore not attributed, can be identified in the writings of Wright's hero in architectural theory, Viollet-le-Duc; conversely, the rigid-core skyscraper seems to have been inspired by an indigenous Japanese structure.

As is well known, Wright had espoused a special interest in and regard for the architecture of Japan since seeing the Ho-o-den at the Columbian Exposition in Chicago in 1893. There can be no doubt that, during the years when he resided primarily in Japan (1917–1922), while working on the Imperial Hotel, he was both interested and attentive when he had the opportunity to see something new to him in Japanese architecture. (He acknowledged, for instance, that he got the idea for the heated floors of his Usonian houses from Baron Okuda's "Korean room," with its warm-air ducts beneath the floor.) Therefore, when the occasion for an excursion to major sites of Japanese religious architecture arose, he would certainly have welcomed it. One of the most likely candidates for such an experience would have been the oldest sanctuary in Japan, the Horyu-ji shrine near Nara, preserved from the seventh and eighth centuries. Waiting there for Wright's attention was a feature in the pagoda that had been consciously adopted from China to help the tower withstand the shock of earthquakes: a rigid central member, or "heart pillar," acting as a mast.[33]

The wheel comes full circle when one learns that the pagoda has its ultimate origin in the Indian stupa, the central spine of which was seen as an *axis mundi* or cosmic pillar, identified in Buddhist philosophy as the Tree of Enlightenment.[34] In confirmation of this origin Wright would go on to project his 1946 research tower for Johnson Wax as a "pagoda," complete with a concrete core and cantilevered floors.

Wright's last purpose-made concrete block house, built in 1929 in Tulsa, Oklahoma, for his cousin Richard Lloyd Jones, already appears as a transitional work, since here the hitherto finely woven fabric of the textile block is abandoned in favor of a larger block formation, laid up as piers (figs. 4.24, 4.25). Wright's unrealizable Egyptoid ideal of elevations without windows[35] is relinquished here in favor of an alternating pattern of piers and slots that is as solid as it is void (fig. 4.26). This passage from the sixteen-inch-square block pattern of the Freeman House to the fifteen-by-twenty-inch plain-faced, stack-bonded block pattern of the Lloyd Jones House produces a paradoxical decrease in the apparent mass; the true scale being lost through the suppression of floor heights.[36] Apart from permitting a consistent alignment between block courses and window transoms, the larger block has many advantages, from the saving of labor in laying to the filling of the hollow cores with cement and steel rods to

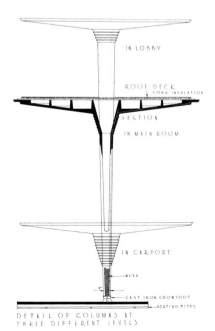

IN LOBBY

ROOF DECK
CORK INSULATION

SECTION

IN MAIN ROOM

IN CARPORT

MESH

CAST IRON CROWFOOT

HEATING PIPES

DETAIL OF COLUMNS AT
THREE DIFFERENT LEVELS

produce an integrated reinforced concrete pier, or the use of similar voids for the purpose of ventilation and other services.

Wright's return to his midwestern roots led to the final phase of his textile tectonic, the self-styled Usonian house that endured in his work as a continuous type right up to his death in 1959. The brick and timber Usonian house emerged as a type in the Malcolm Willey House projected for Minneapolis in 1932, a prototype that was built in modified form two years later. That Wright was aware of the breakthrough that this work represented is borne out by the following passages written in the same year:

Now came clear an entirely new sense of architecture, a higher conception of architecture . . . space enclosed. . . . This interior conception took architecture away from sculpture, away from painting and entirely away from architecture as it had been known in the antique. The building now became a creation of interior space in light. And as this sense of the interior space as the reality of the building began to work, walls as walls fell away.[37]

While this is not the place to enter into the development of the Usonian house, it is nonetheless important to note that once again the prototype was conceived as having woven walls. Double-sided and triple-layered, these walls were of lightweight construction, with timber boards affixed to a continuous plywood core so as to produce horizontal recesses, as opposed to the projecting cover battens of Wright's Forest Style (fig. 4.27). Woven at more than one scale, the Usonian house was also conceived as a three-dimensional gridded cage in which two-foot-by-four-foot and four-foot-square horizontal modular units

4.24
Frank Lloyd Wright, Richard Lloyd Jones House, Tulsa, Oklahoma, 1929. Glazing detailing in relation to concrete block surround.

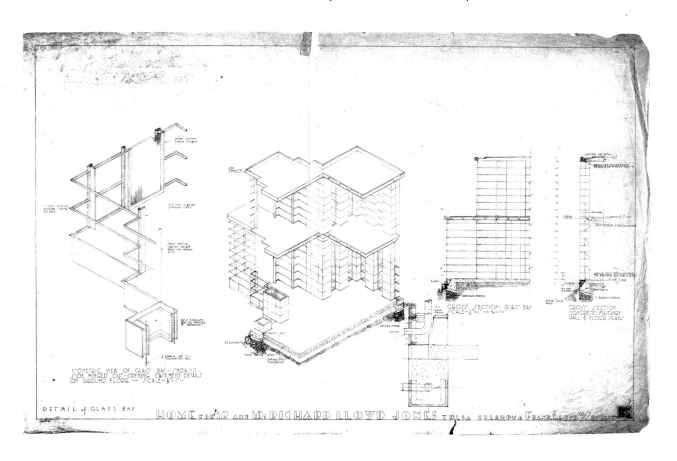

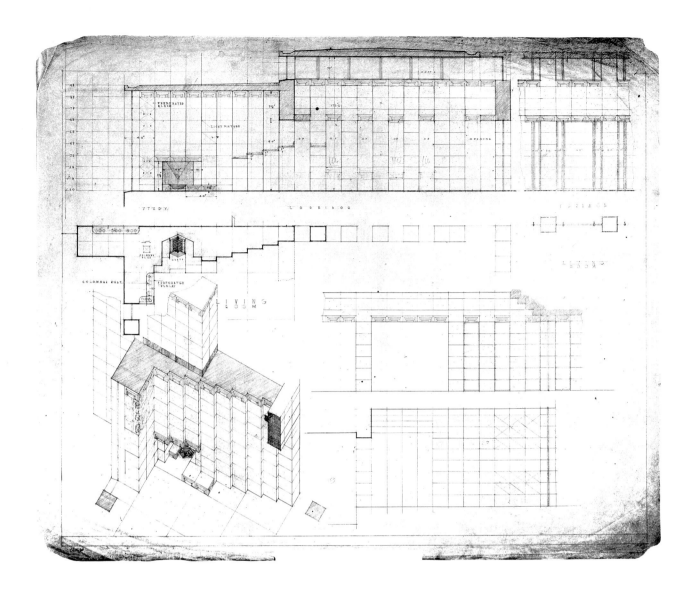

4.25
Frank Lloyd Wright, Richard Lloyd Jones
House, fireplace detail.

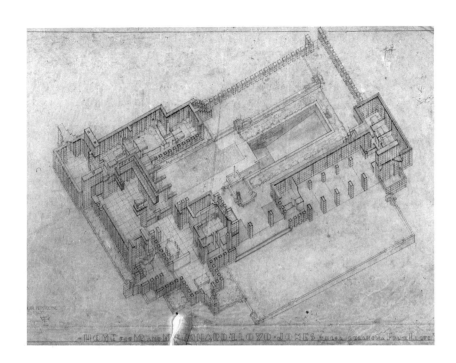

4.26
Frank Lloyd Wright, Richard Lloyd Jones
House, axonometric.

4.27
Frank Lloyd Wright, Usonian house, typical
wall section.

yielded spatial layers that were interwoven with a thirteen-inch vertical interval, governing the module of the horizontal recesses, window transoms, door heights, and built-in furniture. The walls were given a thick warp and woof in which, as Wright put it in the sixth point of his famous *Architectural Forum* manifesto of 1938, "furniture, pictures and bric-a-brac are unnecessary except as the walls can be made to include them or be them."[38] That the typical Usonian dwelling consisted of a three-dimensional matrix made up of interlocking locational fixes and layers is borne out by Wright's provision of three separate plan cuts; one at floor level, one at doorhead or clerestory height, and finally one at roof level. As John Sergeant remarked in his study of the Usonian house, Wright's millwork is interwoven here like basketry.[39]

As far as was feasible, Wright eliminated field labor and reduced wastage in the cutting of timber by adopting a module that corresponded with standard mill dimensions, for example the typical eight-by-four-foot sheet. At the same time, he attempted to exploit the thermal flywheel effect of the in situ concrete slab that tended in any event to be warmer in winter and cooler in summer than the average wooden floor. It is significant that Wright chose to identify this system with the gravity heating systems that he claimed he had first encountered in Japan in 1919. With serpentine, small-bore heating pipes cast into the slab, a typical Usonian dwelling, even when boosted with fire, would be comfortable in the winter rather than overheated, and Wright openly admitted that in severe weather people would simply have to put on more clothes. In high summer the ubiquitous clerestory window system provided ample cross ventilation as did the chimney flues, while the deep overhangs shielded the large areas of full glass from sun penetration in the middle of the day. Many liberative spatial sequences were built into the volume of a typical Usonian house, including ample continuous wall storage (the thick-wall concept), continuous seating, and the close physical and visual proximity of the kitchen to the dining/living area. In the canonical

Herbert Jacobs House, built in Madison, Wisconsin, in 1939, subtle zones of microspace are distributed throughout the house for every conceivable activity (fig. 4.28).

From the beginning Wright conceived of the Usonian system as a kit of parts that had to be assembled according to a particular sequence. His growing recognition of the socioeconomic need for many people to build their own house led him to standardize many of the details in the Usonian system, and these, quite naturally, were repeated with variations from one house to the next. Borrowing its sequence and method of assembly from traditional Japanese house construction, the typical Usonian dwelling was built in a particular order. At each of its stages, this sequence can be seen as incorporating one of Semper's four elements. One would first cast the floor slab and build the masonry chimney and thus arrive at the first two elements of Semper's primordial paradigm, the earthwork and the hearth. This was followed by the Semperian third element, the framework and the roof. The whole was then enclosed through the application of the screenlike fourth element, the infill wall or *Wand.*

Wright will resort to a similar textile metaphor in his master work of the mid-thirties, the S. C. Johnson Administration Building opened at Racine, Wisconsin, in 1939. In this instance the introspective, woven paradigm of the Larkin Building of 1904 will come to be overlaid, as it were, by a gossamer network of glass tubing (fig. 4.29); that is to say, by an interstitial element that will appear throughout as though it were a transformed refractory material, almost on the point of changing into the raked brickwork by which it was borne aloft as a kind of anti-cornice. We are once again close to Semper's *Stoffwechseltheorie,* as where glass is fused into copper sheet as in the National Life Insurance project or where "positive" muntins grow out of the "negative" mortar joints as in the Samuel Freeman house. Housed under a roof composed of 19-foot-diameter three-story-high mushroom columns tied together as a network, this mosquelike workroom, lit from above through tubular glass laylights, is a tectonic tour de force by any standard, as the following account by Jonathan Lipman makes clear.

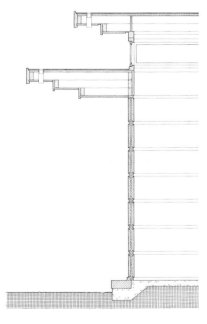

Wright called the columns "dendriform"—tree-shaped—and he borrowed from botany to name three of their four segments, stem, petal and calyx. The base of each column is a seven-inch-high, three-ribbed shoe, which he called a crow's foot. On it rests the shaft, or stem, nine inches wide at the bottom and widening two and a half degrees from the vertical axis. The taller columns are mostly hollow, the walls being only three and a half inches thick. Capping is a wider hollow, ringed band, which Wright referred to as a calyx. On the calyx sits a twelve-and-a-half-inch thick hollow pad Wright called a petal. Two radical concrete rings and continuous concrete struts run through it. Both stem and calyx are reinforced with expanded steel mesh, and the petal is reinforced with both mesh and bars.[40]

Once again, as in Wright's concrete block houses of the twenties, we are presented with the notion of steel rods literally binding the piece together. This concept of the building as a woven fabric is metaphorically reinforced in this instance by hollow glass tubing that in running around the perimeter of the building posits itself almost as the translucent counterthesis to the solid steel rods reinforcing the structure. As Wright was to put it:

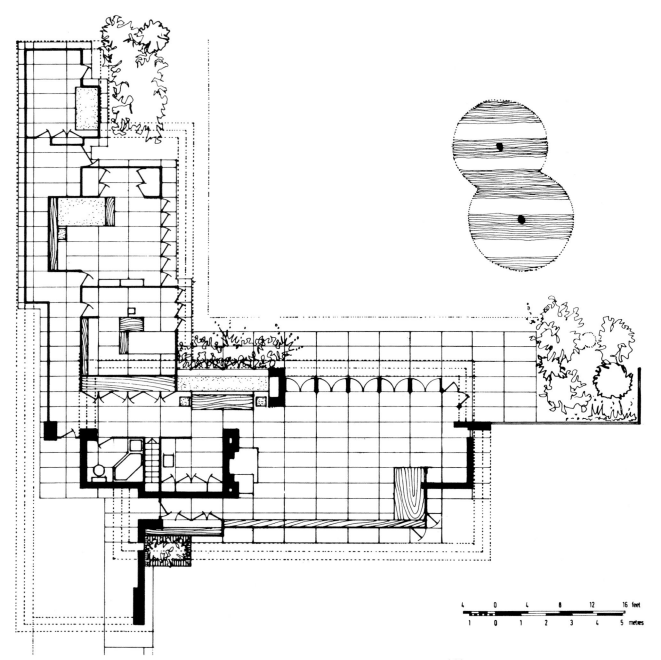

4.28
Frank Lloyd Wright, Herbert Jacobs House,
Madison, Wisconsin, 1936. Plan.

4.29
Frank Lloyd Wright, Johnson Wax Administration Building, glass tubing.

4.30
Frank Lloyd Wright, Johnson Wax Administration Building, prototypical solution to glass
block "anti-cornice"; eventually rejected in
favor of glass tubing.

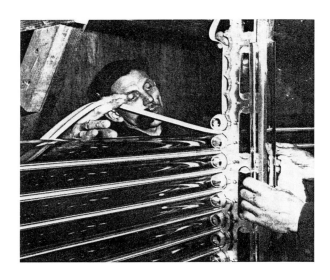

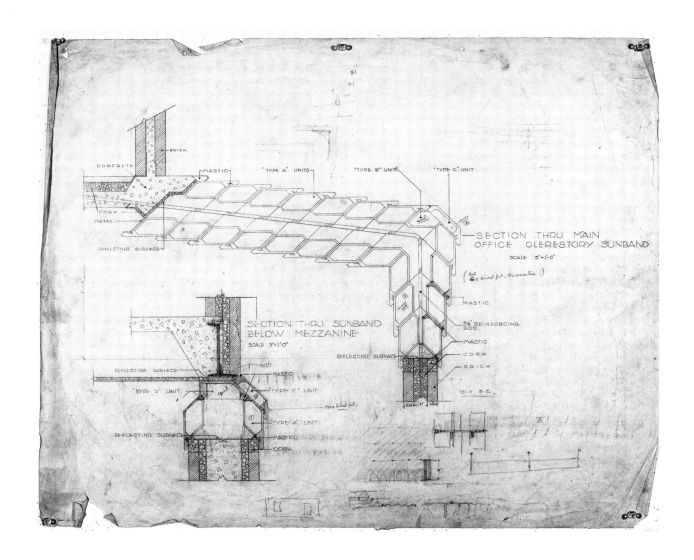

SECTION THRU MAIN
OFFICE CLERESTORY SUNBAND
SCALE 3"=1'0"

SECTION THRU SUNBAND
BELOW MEZZANINE
SCALE 3"=1'0"

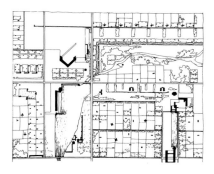

4.31
Frank Lloyd Wright, Broadacre City: sketch plan of the Civic Center surrounded by a "plaid" of farms and Usonian houses.

Glass tubing laid up like bricks in a wall composes all the lighting surfaces. Light enters the building where the cornice used to be. In the interior the box-like structure has vanished completely. The walls carrying the glass ribbing are of hard red brick and red Kasota sandstone. The entire fabric is reinforced concrete, cold-drawn mesh being used for the reinforcement.[41]

An earlier incarnation of this clerestory system assumed the form of interlocking hollow glass blocks that would have provided a more prominent translucent clerestory running around the top of the brick perimeter (fig. 4.30). As realized, the tubular glass hollow anti-cornice, artificially lit at night, effects a magical dematerialization in which solid material becomes void and vice versa, the work being illuminated at night by sweeping, streamlined bands of glowing glass and by equally radiant laylights woven out of the same Pyrex tube.

Apart from his masterworks dating from 1936, Fallingwater and the Johnson Wax Building, Wright's architecture, however structurally consequent, became increasingly arbitrary as the years wore on, even descending, at times, into self-parody bordering on kitsch. Here and there a particular commission, such as the Guggenheim Museum, New York, or the Beth Shalom Synagogue in Philadelphia, achieved a certain tectonic conviction. In the main, however, what remained of Wright's former New World vision was best expressed in the Usonian houses. This Usonian moment in Wright's long career reached its apotheosis during the New Deal in the decade 1934 to 1944, when he realized some twenty-five Usonian dwellings in the course of a decade. Built all over the country, these were not designed for a plutocracy but for an American exurban middle class to whom Wright's message had always been addressed. From the "Small House with Lots of Room in It" of 1901, designed for the *Ladies Home Journal*, to the canonical Herbert Jacobs House of 1936, the underlying liberal vision is always there. Along with the Usonian house went, in theory at least, a similar consciously cultivated and differentiated vision of society as had already been outlined in Peter Kropotkin's *Factories, Fields and Workshops* of 1898. The Usonian house, formulated by Wright when he was already sixty-three, is inseparable from the underlying thesis of his Broadacre City, first broached in his Kahn Lectures given at Princeton University in 1930 and subsequently published as a socioeconomic exurban polemic in *The Disappearing City* of 1932. Broadacre City and the Usonian house shared a similar hypothetical socioeconomic basis in Wright's idealized, egalitarian vision of an acre of ground being reserved for every citizen at birth. The two paradigms, Usonia and Broadacre, were mutually related, since the oversailing horizontal roofs and outriding walls of the typical house would have layered each dwelling into the horizontal land settlement pattern of Wright's motopian plan. Wright's Broadacre City, first exhibited in 1934 (fig. 4.31), may be seen in this light as his ultimate "oriental rug," that is to say as a transcultural, ecological tapestry writ large as an oriental paradise garden woven as a counterpoint to the Cartesian land grid of the North West Ordinance of 1785. This was the Wrightian textile tectonic literally projected over the face of the earth, evoking an Edenic condition in which culture and agriculture would once again be one and the same.

5 Auguste Perret
and Classical Rationalism

The French tradition . . . was based on the correspondence between classical rules and building practice, and through this correspondence they became so automatic as to pass for natural laws. Perret, steeped in this tradition, was naturally led to identify concrete framework (which was a fact of construction) with the framework as it was to appear on the outside of the building, and to transfer to the first the needs and associations of the second. Hence the desire for symmetry and the continued suggestion of the architectural orders, if not as formal presences, at least as terms of comparison. . . . He probably believed that he had discovered the constructional system best suited to the realization of traditional works, since the unity of its elements was real and not apparent, as in the classical orders composed of several blocks of hewn stone. . . . Perret's faith in the universal rules of architecture, although unfounded in our eyes, cannot be discounted as a mere personal quirk, and must be considered within its historical framework. The association between Classicism and the science of building was all the more tenacious in that, after losing its ideological bases in the second half of the eighteenth century, it had been limited to the practical and organizational sphere; the form of the calculations and the habits of the building site still largely reflected the old parallelism, and even the normal terminology used with regard to reinforced concrete—pillar, plinth, architrave, corbel, portal, span—was that of the classical orders.

A whole century of experiment had approved and reinforced this convention from which all advances in modern engineering were born. Perret lived in the midst of it, he was the heir of Durand, of Labrouste, Dutert, Eiffel; his particular merit was to have sensed that this glorious tradition, impoverished by eclecticism, still had a margin of unexplored possibilities to help resolve the problem of our time, and to have developed these possibilities courageously. In doing this, however, he ruined the last chances of structural classicism, and revealed definitively that the path ended in an impasse, because the initial premises were rooted in an outdated mode of thought.
Leonardo Benevolo, Storia dell'architettura moderna, *1960*

As we may judge from the title of the only study of Auguste Perret (1874–1954) in English, *Concrete: The Vision of a New Architecture* published by Peter Collins in 1959, Perret's architectural career was inextricably bound up with the articulation of reinforced concrete frame construction, as though it were the ultimate structural demiurge of the century. While *béton armé* was an unprecedented technique, concrete as such was not, since its use dated from the Roman deployment of *opus caementicum* in foundation work and in the hearting of stone walls. More importantly, plain concrete, combined with brick casing, was used by the Romans to create vaults of considerable span such as the 145-foot-diameter dome of the Pantheon in Rome. Unlike Gothic buildings, such spans depended upon the strength of the monolithic shell itself, rather than on the thrust and counterthrust of arch and buttress. However, with Louis Vicat's perfection of hydraulic cement around 1800, concrete began to be used in a new way, and this led, through the French tradition of constructing low buildings out of rammed earth or *pisé,* to the idea of casting one-off small concrete forms in timber molds, as in Joseph Monier's prefabricated, wire-reinforced flower pots and sewer pipes, put into regular production around 1850. The subsequent Wayss and Freytag monopoly over the Monier system, the patent of which they purchased from him in 1884, did not, in the long run, prevent the French from maintaining their lead in the field, which became decisive with François Hennebique's perfection of reinforced concrete construction in 1897 (fig. 5.1).

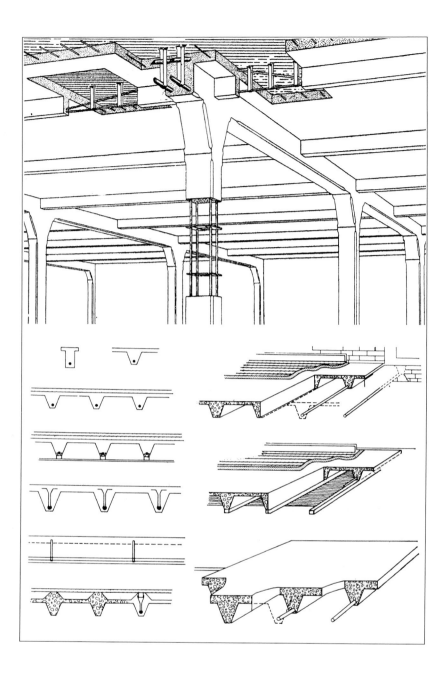

Significantly enough, the contractor Hennebique was to start his building career
as a restorer of Gothic structures, during which time he acquired considerable
archaeological knowledge. In 1880, however, Hennebique familiarized himself
with reinforced concrete in an effort to devise more economical systems of fireproof flooring, made of concrete and steel. It is characteristic of his methodical
and cautious approach that he did not patent his various fireproof concrete
flooring methods until 1892. His real breakthrough, however, came five years
later, with his patent use of iron stirrups for their capacity to resist shear stress
on reinforced concrete beams. Hennebique was to propagate his reinforced concrete system by training contractors in its application under license. Such was
the status of this new technique that to be certified as an "Hennebique con-

tractor" was a mark of great prestige. This is the grounds on which Perret's contractor-father, Claude-Marie Perret, was persuaded, at the urging of his son, to employ the Hennebique system for the framing out of the apartments built at 25 bis rue Franklin, Paris.[1]

Perret's career has its origin in two antithetical experiences: the stimulating and challenging reality of his father's building business and the privileged education that he received in the Ecole des Beaux-Arts, above all from his theory teacher Julien Guadet, whose encyclopedic *Eléments et théories de l'architecture* was published in 1902.[2] This age-old opposition between practice and theory in architectural education was to be decided quite precipitously in Perret's case in favor of practice, for while he dutifully entered the Ecole des Beaux-Arts in 1891 and gained seven *médailles* and the Prix des Architectes Américains during his course of study there, he left abruptly in 1897 without submitting a project for his final diploma.

For Perret, reinforced concrete was the perfect homogeneous system with which to reconcile the two-hundred-year-old schism lying at the very heart of the Greco-Gothic ideal, that is to say, to combine the asperities of Platonic form with the tectonic expressivity of structural rationalism. Three seminal buildings testify to Perret's synthetic approach, as he passes from a brilliant adaptation of the precepts of Viollet-le-Duc to the more idealized forms of classicized rationalism in which he would, nonetheless, remain committed to the primacy of the frame. The three buildings in succession are the Casino at St.-Malo (1899), an apartment block at 25 bis rue Franklin, Paris (1903), and a four-story parking garage completed in the rue Ponthieu, Paris, in 1905.

The general availability of reinforced concrete as a universal technique, which came into being with Paul Christophe's *Le Béton armé et ses applications* of 1902, serves to separate the first of these buildings from the other two, since the casino was built from load-bearing stonework and a timber superstructure. Perret's adoption of reinforced concrete as the primary if not the sole material of his practice would distance him from the more articulate constructed modes of structural rationalism advocated by Viollet-le-Duc. Like Frank Lloyd Wright, who attempted fair-faced, reinforced concrete construction at virtually the same time, Perret knew that this material did not lend itself to the poetic manifestation of construction as an articulate syntax. Nor could its mode of resisting gravity be made precisely expressive, at least not in the Greco-Gothic approach of Perret, who, save for utilitarian work, always chose to dispense with the typical haunched beam of the Hennebique frame, preferring to express his trabeated joints as having a uniform section throughout. This architectonic repression of the moment of maximum stress appeared even when Hennebique himself acted as consultant, as in the rue Franklin apartment; such a formal choice, made surely at the behest of the architect, seems all the more ironic given Hennebique's personal taste for an orientalized Gothic, as is evident from his own house completed in Bourg-la-Reine in 1904, where the haunched brackets of the cantilevered roofs, terraces, and balconies are fairly prominent, as are the fretted precast concrete balconies and the water tower minaret (fig. 5.2).

Where Perret's St.-Malo casino remains a structural rationalist exercise in a manner uncannily close to the work of his American contemporary Frank Furness, 25 bis rue Franklin is a polemical celebration of the reinforced concrete frame,

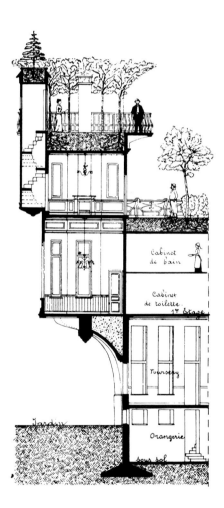

5.2
François Hennebique, his own house in Bourg-la-Reine, 1904. Section.

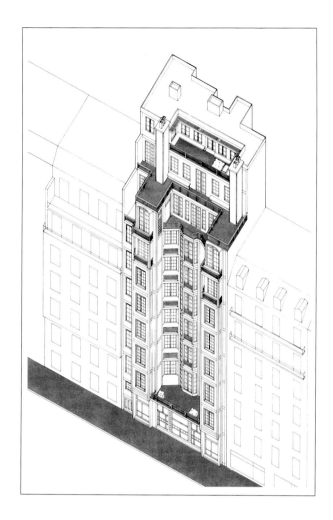

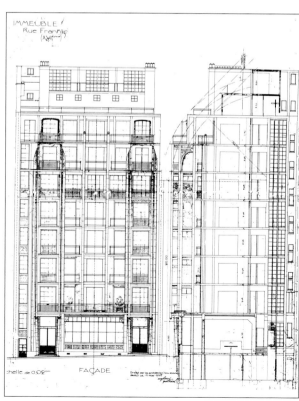

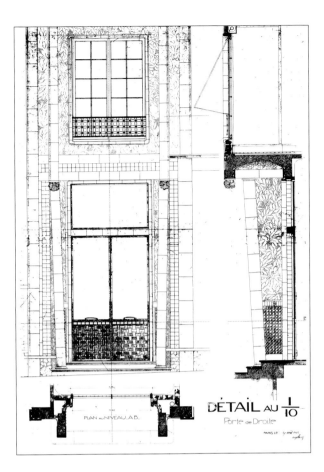

5.3
Auguste Perret, 25 bis rue Franklin, Paris,
1902–1903. Axonometric.

5.4
Auguste Perret, 25 bis rue Franklin, elevation
and sectional setback in relation to 1903 by-
law limits.

5.5
Auguste Perret, 25 bis rue Franklin, sunflower
ceramic infill and terra-cotta cladding to the
framework. Note the carpentry-like boss applied to the cantilever.

for here the frame is *seen* in its entirety, much like a traditional half-timbered
skeleton, rather than being masked under an overriding stone revetment, as
was the standard practice of the period (figs. 5.3, 5.4). Apart from the elimination of the haunch, the frame itself is directly expressed as an assertion of the
basic structure, particularly since a distinction between frame and infill is maintained throughout. However, concrete as such is not apparent since the skeleton is faced throughout with Alexandre Bigot's patent ceramic tiles. Given that
this revetment discriminates between frame and infill (fig. 5.5), we may say that
the overall expression is representational not only because of the articulation of
the frame but also because of a certain referential ambiguity in its detailing. I am
alluding to the decorative newels that terminate the vertical members of the cantilevered bays at the first floor. The carpentry look of these elements encourages
a reading of the frame as though it were made out of wood, an analogical treatment that surely derived in some measure from Auguste Choisy's *Histoire de
l'architecture* of 1899. We need to remark here on Choisy's subscription to the
theory that the classical Greek entablature was a transposition of archaic temple
prototypes in timber, the skeletonal form being retained in order to sustain symbolic continuity (see fig. 2.31).[3] This, together with similar theories advanced by
Guadet, is surely the fundamental basis of Perret's lifelong obsession with the
expression of the skeleton or *charpente*. As he was to put it in his *Contribution à
une théorie de l'architecture* of 1952: "In the beginning architecture is only

125

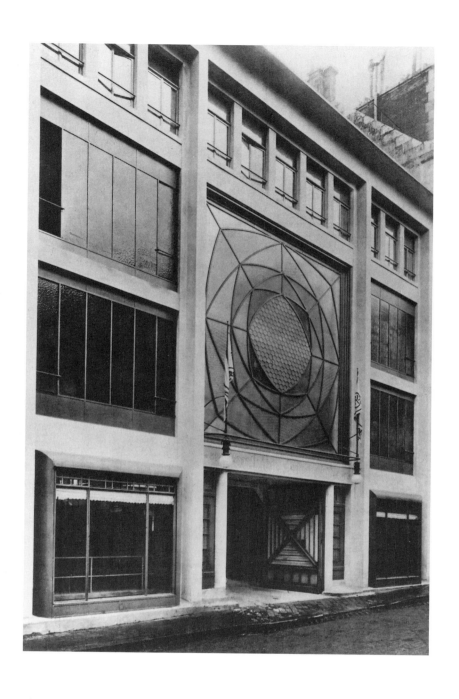

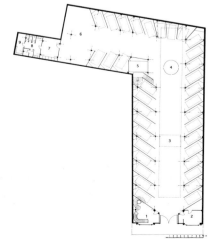

5.6
Auguste Perret, Garage Marboeuf, front facade.

5.7
Auguste Perret, Garage Marboeuf, 51 rue Ponthieu, Paris, 1905. Ground-floor plan.

wooden framework. In order to overcome fire one builds in hard material. And the prestige of the wooden frame is such that one reproduces all the traits, including the heads of the nails."[4] Perret's stress on the *charpente* evokes the same high status accorded to the carpenter or *tekton* as in the antique Greek world.

In spite of the symmetry of its plan, one can hardly interpret 25 bis rue Franklin as a crypto-classical work, for as we have already seen the building would appear to be more Gothic in its affinities than Greek. However, Perret will soon change his attitude in this regard with the rue Ponthieu garage, built by the newly constituted firm of Perret Frères in 1905 (figs. 5.6, 5.7). In this work, the exposed concrete frame is manipulated in such a way as to allude to traditional classical elements; above all, the giant order implied by the two projecting piers situated on either side of the central aisle and the fourth-floor attic clerestory, which, together with its rudimentary projecting cornice, appears to be a conscious simulation of a classical entablature. This Greek feeling is mediated by the neo-Gothic, proto–Art Deco "rose window" that fills the spandrel of the central nave. On balance, however, despite the utilitarian character of the aisles, dedicated to the storage of automobiles, the work makes an overall allusion to the French classical tradition. Peter Collins's acute analysis of the facade tends to confirm this affinity.

The wider spacing of the central bay, the sharp projection of the principal columns, the quickened rhythm of the topmost story and the variations in the depths of beams, have all been introduced or exploited as deliberate aesthetic devices for producing contrasting proportions of a calculated emotional value, whilst the entasis of the main columns and the method of joining the beams to them with intermediate frames or alettes *betokened a regard for the finer subtleties of trabeated articulation seldom seen since the* ancien régime.[5]

Despite the exposed fair-faced concrete and the direct presence of the frame itself, the facade is tectonically manipulated. We need look no further for this than to the orthogonal form of exterior trabeation, as opposed to the haunched column supports carrying the beams of the reinforced concrete skeleton within (fig. 5.8). We may note here that Perret, like Schinkel, introduced hierarchical in-

5.8
Auguste Perret, Garage Marboeuf, interior. Note the haunched beam-column junctions.

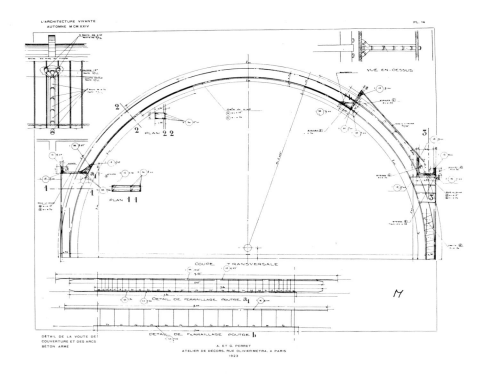

VUE EN DESSUS

COUPE TRANSVERSALE

DÉTAIL DE FERRAILLAGE POUTRE ᴨ

DÉTAIL DE FERRAILLAGE POUTRE ᴫ

DÉTAIL DE LA VOUTE DE
COUVERTURE ET DES ARCS
BÉTON ARMÉ

A. ET G. PERRET
ATELIER DE DÉCORS, RUE OLIVIER-METRA, A PARIS
1923

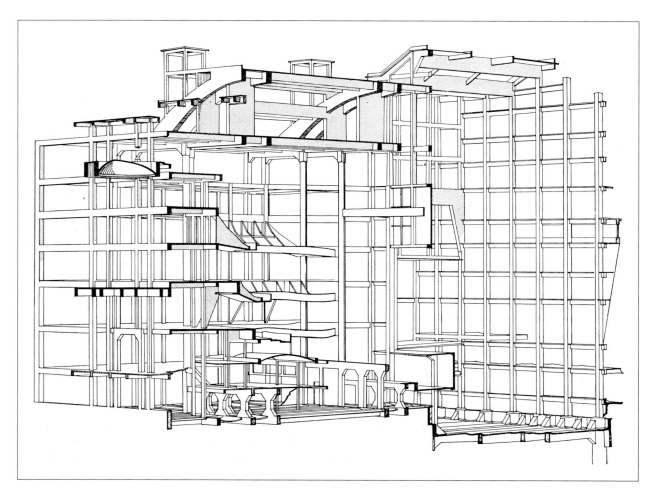

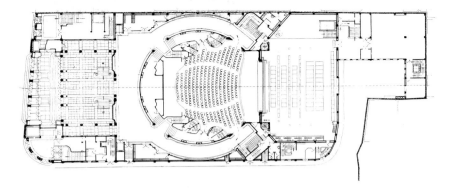

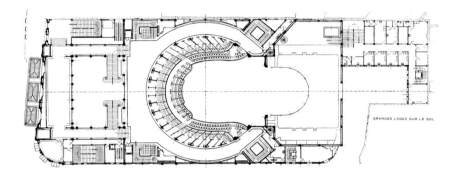

5.9
Auguste Perret, scene painting studios, rue Olivier-Métra, Paris, 1923. Section.

5.10
Auguste Perret, Théâtre des Champs-Elysées, axonometric.

5.11
Auguste Perret, Théâtre des Champs-Elysées, ground floor.

5.12
Auguste Perret, Théâtre des Champs-Elysées, Paris, 1911–1913. Mezzanine level.

flections into his work that varied with the sociocultural status of the institution, this declension at times extending to different parts of the same structure. Thus, in the rue Ponthieu garage, the industrial sash glazing, filled with obscured glass, expresses the utilitarian nature of the galleries on either side of the central aisle, while the rose window, held in place by glazing bars of virtually the same section, represents the honorific space of public appearance; that is to say, the opening through which both pedestrians and automobiles appear. One should note that this kind of differentiation stands in strong contrast to the solely utilitarian work of the firm, where reinforced concrete frames or vaults were simply expressed as such and hence struck straight from timber formwork, as in the vaulted single-story warehouses built at Casablanca in 1915 or the scene painting studio erected in the rue Olivier-Métra, Paris, in 1923 (fig. 5.9). The rue Ponthieu is a transitional work in which Perret's struggle to find a satisfactory expression for a building of this type is suggested by an alternative crypto–Art Nouveau facade, where the main concrete piers are flanked with brick *alettes* and where the spandrels are filled with hexagonal glass blocks, similar in kind to those used by Perret on the rear of the rue Franklin apartment.

Perret's structurally classicist mode is further elaborated in the ABABA Palladian parti adopted for the entrance foyer of the Théâtre des Champs-Elysées, completed in the Avenue Montaigne, Paris, at the end of 1913.[6] This rhythm is extended into the plan in depth, inasmuch as four pairs of columns are used to support the bowstring trusses carrying the roof (fig. 5.10). These columns also serve to carry a series of circumferential galleries opening onto the circular void of the main auditorium (figs. 5.11, 5.12, 5.13). Within the foyer itself, this ABABA

129

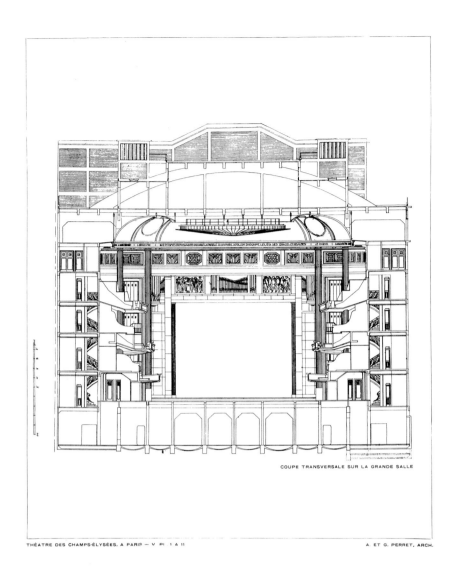

COUPE TRANSVERSALE SUR LA GRANDE SALLE

THÉATRE DES CHAMPS-ÉLYSÉES, A PARIS — V PL 1 A 11   A. ET G. PERRET, ARCH.

bay system generates a peristyle of sixteen columns that orchestrates the space of the entrance hall and thereafter projects its presence onto the front facade in terms of representational pilasters (fig. 5.14). This structural system, represented as a tartan grid on the floor and the ceiling, is articulated all round the perimeter of the space in order to separate the columnar structure from the enclosing walls (fig. 5.13). The resulting slots articulate the full peristyle as an a/ABABA/a scheme, with the facade expressing the diminutive "a" bay as an *alette* and the larger B bay as a coupled pilaster. This syncopated modeling is flanked by two giant, coupled pilasters that, running the full height of the facade, effectively close the composition. Following Henri Labrouste, all these pilasters are terminated by thin golden bands instead of capitals. Otherwise, throughout the facade Perret seems to adhere to the precepts of *modénature* developed by François Mansart. He observes the principles of *vraisemblance,* that is to say, he places his pilasters at the corner in order to *represent* their hypothetical load-bearing capacity, following the model of Mansart's Maisons-Laffitte, Château des Maisons of 1642.

5.13
Auguste Perret, Théâtre des Champs-
Elysées, section through main auditorium.

5.14
Auguste Perret, Théâtre des Champs-
Elysées, front facade.

Once again, as in 25 bis rue Franklin, exposed concrete is not employed for the honorific parts of the structure, the facade and the foyer being veneered in stone and plaster. On the side and end elevations, however, it is left as struck from the timber *coffrage,* the bays being filled in with large expanses of brick-work. Thus, where the corpus of the theater becomes utilitarian, as in the back-stage volume, Perret returns to standard fireproof concrete frame construction, as we find this in the textile mills built by Hennebique in Tourcoing and Lille in 1895 and 1896 respectively.

The final fusion of classical rationalism with the Greco-Gothic ideal comes with the church of Notre-Dame du Raincy, commissioned in 1922 as a memorial to those who were killed in the battle of the Ourcq in the First World War (figs. 5.15, 5.16). With this church, Perret arrived at the essentials of the free plan *avant la lettre,* inasmuch as the building comprised a network of 28 cylindrical concrete columns standing free within a hermetic, non-load-bearing envelope. The columns in question, each 37 feet high, with a longitudinal spacing of 33 feet, tapered upward from a 17-inch base to a 14-inch diameter at the crown. These columns may be read in both ontological and representational terms; first, because of the evident presence of an unfaced concrete support, and second, because of the imprint of the half-round and triangular timber fillets from

FAÇADE PRINCIPALE

THÉÂTRE DES CHAMPS-ELYSÉES. A PARIS ⸱⸱⸱ V. PL. I A II

A. ET G. PERRET, ARCH.

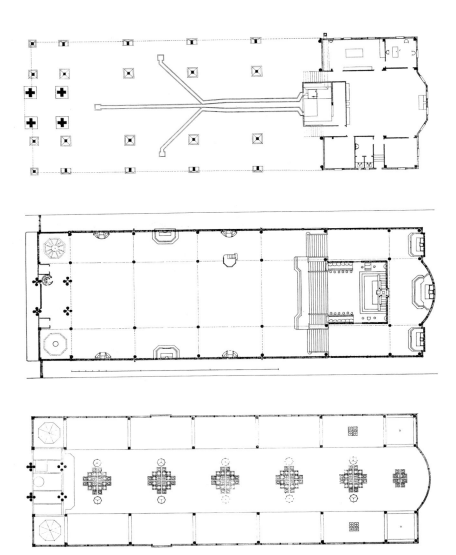

5.15
Auguste Perret, Church of Notre-Dame, Le Raincy, 1922–1924. Basement with heating ducts.

5.16
Auguste Perret, Church of Notre-Dame, Le Raincy, ground floor and reflected ceiling plan.

which the column formwork is constructed. These fillets bestow upon the column an ambiguous profile that may be interpreted as a conscious double reference, first to the tapering flutes of the Doric order and second to the clustering cylindrical forms of a typical Gothic pier. Apart from the Greco-Gothic implications of this double allusion, the freestanding columns within the *Hallenkirche* volume serve to engender that sublime, forest effect so much admired by Cordemoy and Laugier as the crowning attributes of the Gothic cathedral. As Perret himself put it in a letter written to *The American Architect* in 1924:

Ordinarily the exterior row of columns would have been buried in the enclosing walls and each of them indicated by a slight projection. In this building we have entirely isolated these columns from the wall, permitting the walls to pass freely outside of them. By exposing all of the columns free-standing there are four rows of columns seen instead of the usual two rows. This greater number of columns in sight tends greatly to increase the apparent size of the church with a sense of spaciousness and vastness. The small size of the columns, their greater height and lack of distracting detail aid materially in producing this effect.[7]

Perret's aims were patently the same, in this regard, as those displayed by J. N. L. Durand in his economic critique of Soufflot's Ste.-Geneviève, and this, if nothing else, is further evidence of a conceptual link between Notre-Dame du Raincy and Ste.-Geneviève. Vittorio Gregotti has identified this continuity of the Greco-Gothic ideal as a form of classicizing naturalism that permeates French culture from the Enlightenment onward, manifesting itself "as a secular religion of progress and reason and a quest for an unattainable natural objectivity."[8] The continuity with Ste.-Geneviève is further substantiated by the vaulting of Notre-Dame du Raincy, which takes the form of shallow concrete barrel vaults running transversely across the nave and longitudinally down the aisles (fig. 5.17). Moreover, as in Ste.-Geneviève, there is an outer roof that serves to protect the two-inch-thick shell vaults spanning across the aisles and the nave (fig. 5.18). This second membrane consists of a lightweight, tiled, concrete vault system comprised of flat inverted U-sections in the longitudinal section. Surprising as it may seem, this roof section appears to have been capable of spanning clear across the entire width of the church.

The Gothic overtones of Le Raincy were subtly incorporated into the 183-foot-long perimeter curtain wall, assembled out of 2-foot-square precast panels, each one framing rectangular, triangular, or circular apertures filled with clear or colored glass. These concrete panels or *claustra* were laid up as symmetrical geometric grids, arranged in such a way as to produce a large cruciform pattern in the center of each bay. The "pointilliste" colored glass infill of the *claustra,* chromatically varying from one bay to the next in accordance with the natural spectrum, was the work of the symbolist artist Maurice Denis. The *claustra* had first been devised by Perret when he was working for his father on the construction of the cathedral of Oran, begun in 1902 to the designs of Albert Ballu (fig. 5.19). In Le Raincy Perret assures the rhythmic articulation of the curtain wall by treating it as a relief construction in which a number of vertical and horizontal ribs are more pronounced than those produced by the normal jointing between the

5.17
Auguste Perret, Church of Notre-Dame, Le Raincy, sections.

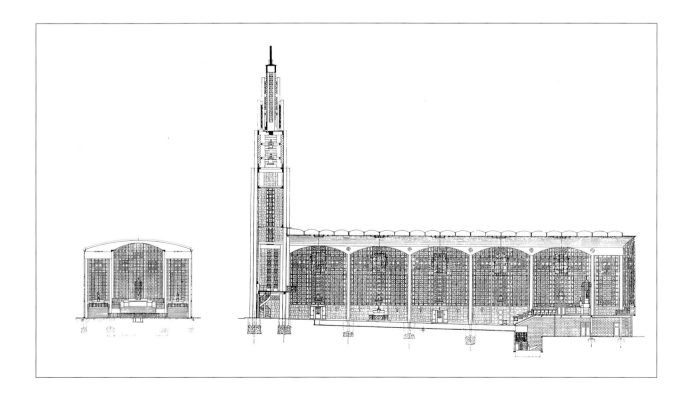

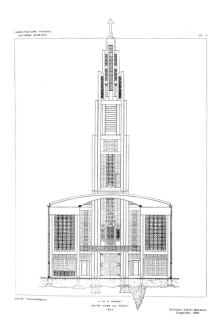

5.18
Auguste Perret, Church of Notre-Dame, Le Raincy, transverse section.

5.19
Auguste Perret and Albert Ballu, Oran cathedral, 1902–1908. Detail of claustra.

5.20
Auguste Perret, Church of Notre-Dame, Le Raincy, details of steeple.

claustra. This hierarchic emphasis served not only to stiffen the membrane but also to establish the border of each cruciform figure. By the permutation of only five different prefabricated *claustra* patterns, set within a bounding square (a cross, a circle, a diamond, a half-square, and a quarter square), Perret was able to avoid the monotony of a regularly reticulated curtain wall, while giving a certain scale to an otherwise uninflected, columnless exterior.

Equally Gothic, of course, was the square-planned, 145-foot-high spire and belfry, comprising, at grade, four cluster piers, each consisting of four 17-inch-diameter columns (fig. 5.20). These composite piers stepped back in three stages as the square plan progressively diminished to the pinnacle. While this arrangement maintained the same proportion and geometry as the rest of the church and served to integrate the hollow volume of the spire and organ loft with the space of the nave, it was somewhat less successful as an external profile. The conformity of the profile with the silhouette of a typical Gothic spire seems somewhat forced, while the stepped, set-back composition suggests by virtue of its apparent weight a stereotomic piling-up rather than a frame. In both Ste.-Geneviève and Le Raincy, the confusion between tectonic and stereotomic form arose out of a similar cause; namely, the presence of hidden reinforcement, which enabled the assembly to perform in a manner that was at variance with its essential nature. This disjunction was accompanied by a repression of the joint as such, which produced the curious telescopic appearance of the pseudo-spire of Le Raincy. It is significant that Perret's syntactical command of the concrete frame fails him exactly at the point where the aim is no longer the tectonic expression of the frame but the simulation of a nostalgic image, that is to say, the point at which the structure becomes pseudo-Gothic rather than a modernized version of the Greco-Gothic.

In two temporary works, designed in 1924 and 1925 respectively, Perret will return to a more straightforward level of tectonic articulation: the Palais de Bois erected in the Bois de Boulogne in 1924 (fig. 5.21), and the Théâtre des Arts Décoratifs, erected for the Exposition des Arts Décoratifs of 1925 (figs. 5.22, 5.23, 5.24).

The former was a tour de force in timber construction, employing standard mill sections in such a way as to construct a hierarchy of *load-bearing* and *load-borne* elements (compare Schopenhauer's *Stütze und Last*). Thus, an exposed boarded roof spans onto standard rafters that in turn take their support from purlins that then rest on deep timber beams, with corbeled brackets and plated timber columns. Light percolating into the structure along the perimeter between the purlins and the rafters imparts a radiance to the work that here and there is augmented by clerestory lights and the occasional top light, let into the roof. It seems in retrospect as though Perret was orchestrating the framework in a consciously "oriental" manner, for it is difficult to look at a photographic record of this work today without being reminded of traditional Japanese construction.

The Théâtre des Arts Décoratifs was a more didactic and ambitious undertaking. In this work Perret tried to transform the syntax of his evolving Greco-Gothic language into the articulate precepts of his later classical rationalism, thereby advancing his nationalistic ambition of evolving a new French order. Seating 900 people, Perret's temporary theater was as much a refinement of a new auditorium type as his Notre-Dame du Raincy had been a reinterpretation

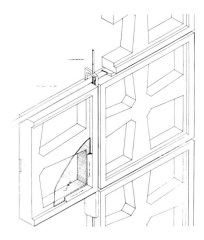

of the traditional *Hallenkirche*. It was in fact based on the shallow tripartite stage as this had been embodied in Henri Van de Velde's Werkbund Theater of 1914 and which had previously appeared in Max Kruger's *Stilbühne* dating from 1912. Directly influenced by the timber tectonic of the Palais de Bois, the syncopated orthogonal order of the theater broke down into an elongated Palladian system. Perret would expand and manipulate the a/ABABA/a peristylar foyer of the Champs-Elysées theater in such a way as it would come to embrace the entire volume of the Théâtre des Arts Décoratifs. Thus, 38 freestanding columns articulating the 180-by-40-foot enclosure would be so arranged as to produce internal columnar rhythms of a/AABAA/a in length and a/ABA/a in width (fig. 5.25). Thus the body of the building was divided into three parts in both directions, with the center being slightly larger in each instance. Disturbed by the lack of structural modulation on the exterior of Notre-Dame du Raincy, Perret arranged for 14 redundant columns to appear as representative orders on the blank exterior of the theater, including two columns set off from each corner in order to terminate the system. (Compare the corner details employed in the steel framing of the various buildings that Mies van der Rohe designed for IIT in Chicago.) Due to the temporary nature of the structure, Perret had to simulate reinforced concrete frame construction. Thus the columns were built up out of square timber

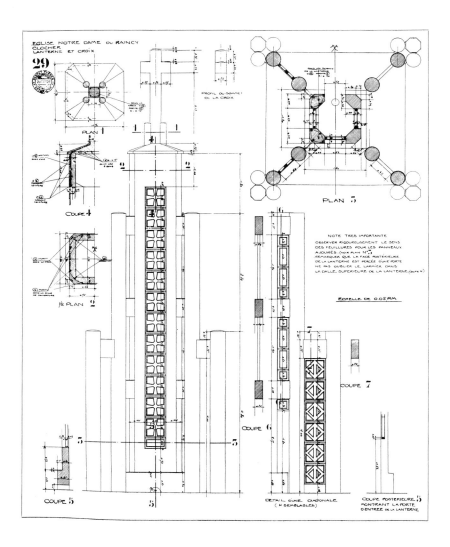

stanchions faced by four fluted quadrants, while the main beams were made out of reinforced, lightweight, clinker concrete. Perret exploited the temporary nature of the building as an occasion for realizing a prismatic crystalline aesthetic having its own intrinsic character. Thus, the entire auditorium was permanently lit during the day through 150 white linen screens that filled the squares of the latticework ceiling and its adjoining celestory lights (fig. 5.26). The weightless vaults covering the reading room of Labrouste's Bibliothèque Nationale may well have been the inspiration for this *velarium,* in that Perret's translucent grid was supported by a light steel armature spanning across the auditorium. The general iridescent effect was amplified through the color scheme of the interior, with side walls finished in matte aluminum paint, prominent features highlighted in shiny aluminum leaf, and seats upholstered in brown-gray fabric. The aura of this dematerialized interior as it responded to different light conditions was surely the opposite to the artificially illuminated interior of Perret's Ecole Normale de Musique of 1929, lined throughout in acoustical plywood panels (figs. 5.27, 5.28). The thin plywood surface of the latter, built out from the walls on timber battens, led the satisfied client, Alfred Corot, to remark, "He told us that he would make us a violin, but he made us a Stradivarius."[9] In both the theater and the concert chamber, Perret sought to establish an introspective tactile interior in which one would feel as though one had entered a world apart.

Two further tectonic attributes need to be noted as evidence of the complexity of the Théâtre des Arts Décoratifs. First, there is the fact that despite the simula-

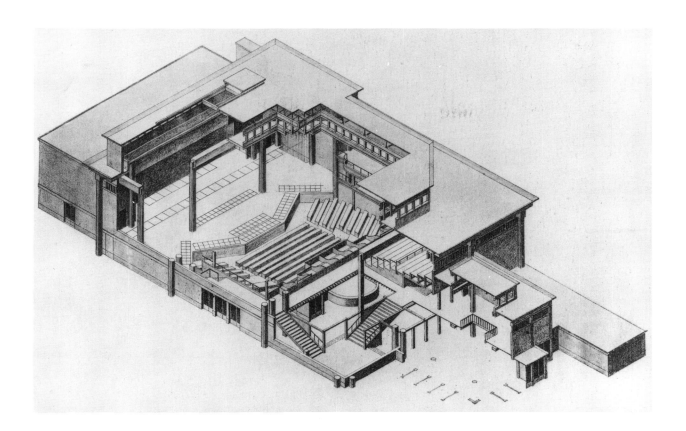

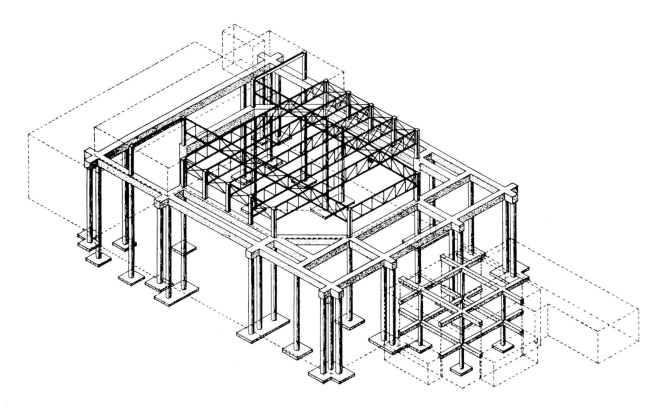

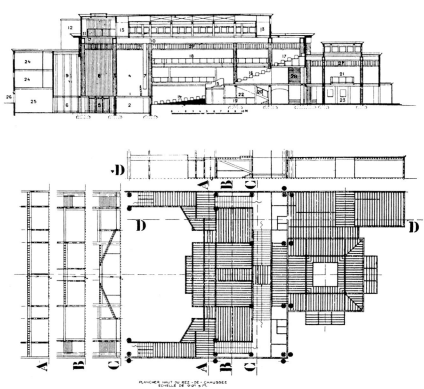

PLANCHER HAUT DU REZ-DE-CHAUSSÉE.

5.24
Auguste Perret, Théâtre de l'Exposition des Arts Décoratifs, section plus "tatami" ceiling.

5.25
Auguste Perret, Théâtre de l'Exposition des Arts Décoratifs, first floor.

5.26
Auguste Perret, Théâtre de l'Exposition des Arts Décoratifs, perspective.

tion of concrete, the interior volume is formed through a highly articulate structure in which, as in the Palais de Bois, the play of the load-bearing against the load-borne evokes the Orient in a double sense, suggesting the culture of Japan by the orthogonal articulation of the structure and recalling one of the key features in Islamic space-making by the pendentive corners of the main auditorium (fig. 5.29). Second, as we have already noted, the building becomes a vehicle for evolving what Perret would regard as a new French classical-rational order. This surely accounts for the regular "fluting" of the columns, and for the ventilation frieze of alternating, half-round pipes running around the perimeter of the building as a vestigial entablature (fig. 5.30). A similar metaphorical frieze, composed of adjustable louvers, would be employed by Perret in the Ecole Normale de Musique.

Like the immediate generations that succeeded him, like Mies, Le Corbusier, and Louis Kahn, Perret sought to establish a systematic and inflected approach

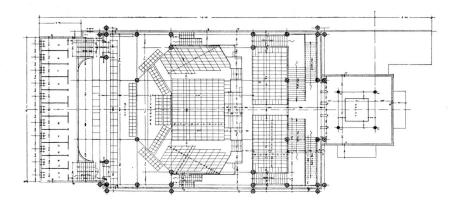

to architecture; one that would allow for different institutions to be given a hierarchically distinct expression. From a normative standpoint, Perret's method and syntax crystallized into a general system in two major works: his own apartment building completed in the rue Raynouard, Paris, in 1932 (figs. 5.31, 5.32), and the Musée des Travaux Publics started in Paris in 1936.

Notwithstanding Perret's perennial emphasis on the *charpente,* his work had already begun to assume a graduated expression depending on its institutional status. Typologically speaking, the expressive range ran from the trabeated frame of the public institution to load-bearing masonry in the private house. Within this representational spectrum lay the syntactical frame and infill of his upper-class villas, the Maison Nubar Bey built at Garches in 1931 being typical in this regard (fig. 5.33). By a similar token, Perret's small domestic works were largely built of unframed, load-bearing masonary, the Palladian Maison Cassandre at Versailles of 1926 being typical (fig. 5.34). At the same time, his apartment buildings implied a higher order of collective expression and hence were invariably framed throughout. Unlike Le Corbusier's general application of *pilotis* (the classic anticlassical trope set in conscious opposition to Perret's classical rationalism), Perret will only allow himself to use a peristyle in an honorific work, such as a public building or a set of monumental sequences like the entrances of the perimeter blocks that make up the inner residential fabric in his rebuilding of Le Havre.

While the plan of rue Raynouard is interesting in itself, what concerns us here is the way in which its status is reflected in the concatenation and refinement of its constructional elements. Here the concrete finish is differentiated in order to distinguish between frame and infill. As Peter Collins writes:

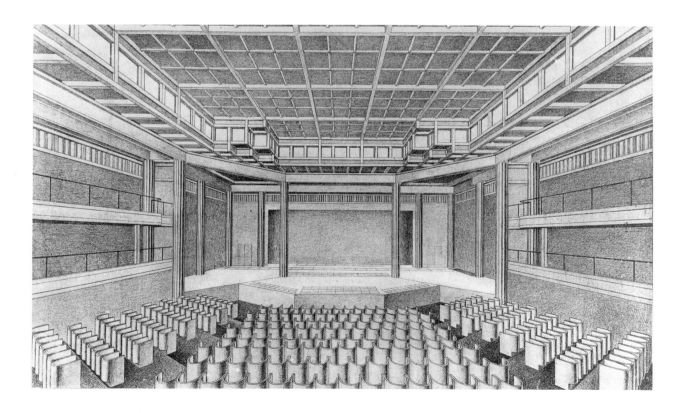

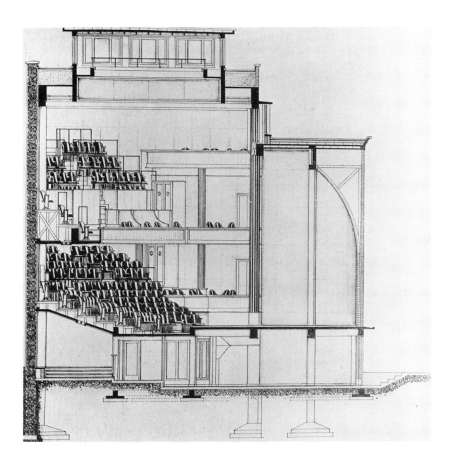

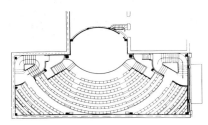

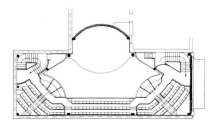

5.27
Auguste Perret, Ecole Normale de Musique,
Paris, 1929. Section.

5.28
Auguste Perret, Ecole Normale de Musique,
orchestra and balcony-level plans.

The general principle of this system, once stated, seems so self-evident that its ingenuity may not be apparent, but it is important to appreciate that until this date, it is doubtful if any architect had seriously considered combining in situ *and pre-cast concrete systematically in the same design, except to make the latter constitute permanent form-work for the former. By suggesting that the structural members should be cast* in situ *as a monolithic frame, and that all non-load-bearing elements should be pre-cast to specific designs on the site itself, rather than in a factory, Perret completely revolutionized one aspect of reinforced concrete building technique at a time when pre-casting was usually thought of as essentially a means of commercial mass-production, and justifiable if carried out by an independent firm which would advertise and distribute each element ready-made.*[10]

Perret was an advocate of rational rather than optimized production, and for him each repeatable piece was a tectonic unit designed as a particular component for a specific job; in this instance, the on-site precasting molds would be discarded once the job was finished. In the rue Raynouard and in subsequent public works, at the scale of the frame the *modénature* of the facade and hence of the body of the building as a whole would derive, in large part, from the hierarchical order built into the sequence of assembly. A sequential modulation was set up between the fixing of the precast concrete window frames and the solid precast infill panels that spanned between the window surround and the in situ

5.29
Auguste Perret, Théâtre de l'Exposition des
Arts Décoratifs, interior.

5.30
Auguste Perret, Théâtre de l'Exposition des
Arts Décoratifs, general view.

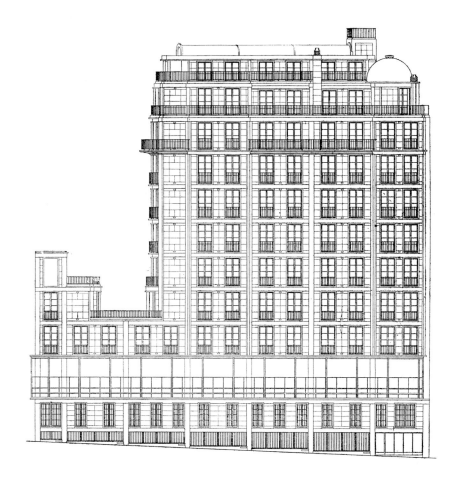

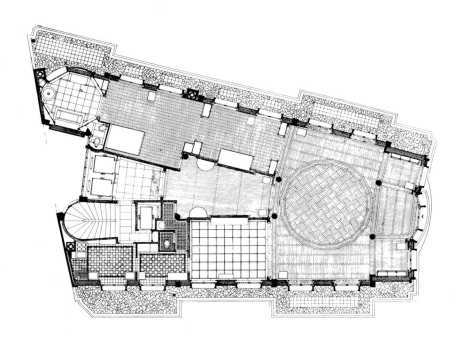

5.31
Auguste Perret, apartment building, 51 rue Raynouard, Paris, 1929–1932. Elevation. Note plate glass fenestration for Perret's professional offices.

5.32
Auguste Perret, apartment building, 51 rue Raynouard, plan of the penthouse.

5.33
Auguste Perret, Maison Nubar Bey, Garches, 1931. Elevation.

skeleton. Modulation in depth was similarly determined by the necessity for rebating joints and providing moldings for weathering purposes. In the case of the window frames themselves, the depth of the unit was determined by the need to accommodate the standard Parisian folding metal shutter (fig. 5.35). The overall rhythm of the surface, once again, reminds one of the modeling of François Mansart, particularly as the French windows, heavily framed in their precast concrete surrounds, were to extend fully between one floor and the next in a manner reminiscent of the so-called "wedged" windows characteristic of seventeenth-century French classicism. At the same time, the distinction that Perret consistently drew between in situ and precast concrete was reminiscent of the play between cast and wrought iron in the work of Viollet-le-Duc.

Perret's move away from *béton brut* toward the bush-hammering of concrete enabled him to discriminate between the exposed aggregate of the in situ skeleton and the latex smoothness of the precast elements. To achieve these effects, he relied on technical processes that had been developed and perfected during the preceding decade, the first consisting of vibrating the concrete for the purpose of achieving maximum consolidation, the second consisting of removing the superficial cement film in order to reveal the stone aggregate beneath. As Collins remarks:

[Perret pioneered] . . . a technique for removing the cement film known as *bouchardage* or *bush hammering. It matters little whether he was the first architect to apply to rough concrete surfaces this masonry technique for cleaning roughly quarried stone. What matters is that for Perret, the visual expression of the structural material was as important as the visual expression of the constructional system. Far from "lacking a sense of detail" he becomes obsessed with the desire to achieve it in profiling and coloration. He obtained the former by modulations in the timber framework. He attained the latter by using aggregates of varying size and color.*[11]

The development of the rue Raynouard apartment building compelled Perret to reassert the canonical status of the traditional French window as opposed to the *fenêtre en longueur* of Le Corbusier. However, Perret was by no means averse to using large areas of undivided plate glass where the particular program demanded unusually high levels of natural light, as in the case of his own drafting studio in rue Raynouard (fig. 5.31). Otherwise he saw the French window as being suffused with a particular cultural significance. As he put it, "la fenêtre en hauteur c'est le cadre de l'homme." For Perret, *la porte-fenêtre*, the French window, with its hinged double doors opening inward, was indicative of the presence of man. Here, a received tectonic element assumes symbolic anthropomorphic dimensions. For Perret the implications of the *porte-fenêtre* went even further, for it not only established the decorum of the bourgeois interior, its rhythm, space, and graduation of light, but it also induced the cadence of human movement within the room. This is particularly evident in 25 bis rue Franklin, where the *porte-fenêtre* serves as an essential punctuation in what is otherwise an *en suite* space. It provides a certain decorum for each action setting and engages in a dialogical play with the opaque subdividing double doors of the interior that serve to interconnect the five-room sequence of smoking, dining, salon, bedroom, and boudoir; the whole providing, as Henri Bresler has observed, a faceted parallel of the civic exterior.*[12]

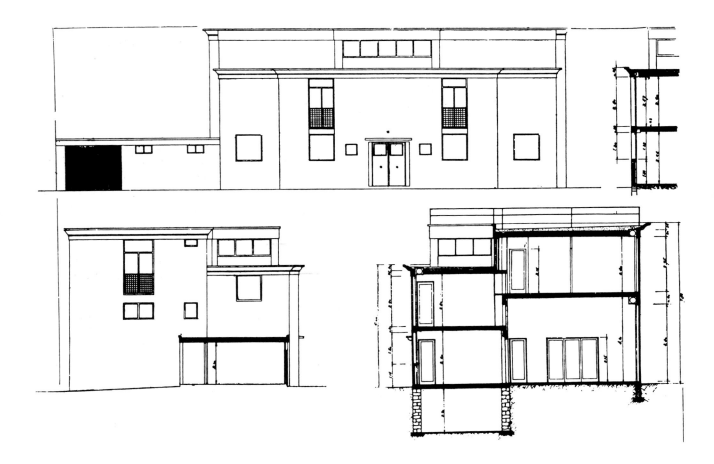

The cinematic effect of the *fenêtre en longueur* was by its very nature totally anti-thetical to this continuous but discretely chambered sequence.[13] That this was one of the most irreconcilable differences between Perret and Le Corbusier is implied by the illustrations of the "Five Points of a New Architecture" (fig. 5.36). For Perret, on the other hand, the French window provided a focused perspectival connection between the interior and the exterior. As Bruno Reichlin has written:

Through the traditional window the interior discloses itself to the outside world; yet at the same time it also defines the locale *and the* sill, *and that amounts to a spatial and emotional "exclusion." Whereas the horizontal window, as Perret declares, "condemns us to the view of an unending panorama," the vertical window stimulates us "by letting us see a complete space* (une espace complete): *street, garden, sky." But above all, these openings may be closed.*[14]

The Musée des Travaux Publics, Paris, largely in place by 1938 but not fully complete until after Perret's death, is without question the most masterly civic monument of Perret's career. Here, as in no other building except the perimeter blocks of Le Havre, which are in his manner but not exclusively by his hand, the structurally classic peristyle asserts itself in its full monumentality (figs. 5.37, 5.38). And yet, this 40-foot-high giant order (Perret's first full attempt at his modern French classical mode) is subject to a series of inflections. In the first place, this order is fabricated out of concrete rather than stone, and Perret goes out of his way to make this difference explicit. Thus both tapering and entasis take place inversely, the column being wider at the capital (with a diameter of 103 centimeters) than at the 80-centimeter-diameter base from whence it rises (fig. 5.39). Through this inversion of the classical entasis Perret is able to express the statical hinge of the column at its base and conversely the condition of monolithic rigidity at its crown. This profile recalls that adopted by Frank Lloyd Wright in his Johnson's Wax administrative building completed at Racine, Wisconsin, in 1939. Both Perret and Wright taper their cylindrical concrete columns upward so as to express zero bending at grade and maximum bending at the point of lateral connection (see fig. 4.23). In other respects the specific profiling of the respective elements assumes quite different connotations, with Wright favoring an organic continuity closer to the precepts of structural rationalism (compare the late projects of Anatole de Baudot) and Perret focusing on the Greco-Gothic ideal and its transformation under the impact of modern technology. One may claim that Perret aspired to an idea of symbolic conservation comparable to that advanced much earlier by Gottfried Semper; that is to say, he emulated the literal petrification of timber in the Greek temple by conserving the features of stereotomic form in his monumental in situ concrete structures. One might even suggest that he attempted to reverse the Hellenistic metamorphosis of timber elements into stone, by rendering cast material in the form of a frame. And yet Perret always stressed the tectonic origin of concrete, namely the timber formwork that was, as it were, the precondition of its existence. In fact, in pursuing his new national order, he will develop an unprecedented capital through the transformation of the traditional Corinthian acanthus leaf into an organic form arising out of a geometric imbrication of timber formwork. Collins gives an account of the raison d'être behind this form as it evolved over a decade from the Musée des Travaux Publics to the capitals employed in the columns of Le Havre.

Little guidance as to the correct means of terminating the shafts of a monolithic frame was offered by historical precedents, whilst even carpentry techniques offered few hints apart from a general indication of what to avoid. In trabeated masonry construction, the problem of transferring the load from a square beam to a circular shaft was solved by separate blocks of stone. . . . In medieval timber construction . . . no termination was considered necessary (apart from carved or applied ornament), since both the posts and beams were usually square in section. Perret never regarded the need for some visible token of translation as absolutely essential, and frequently . . . butted shafts directly against the rectangular beams above, as in the colonnade [in] the interior of the Musée des Travaux Publics. But he felt that if there was in fact some way of creating a transition which would be both structurally logical and aesthetically advantageous, he was under a moral obligation to find it.[15]

This sense of obligation points to a link between tectonic form and the representation of higher values, and this may well explain why Perret reserved his imbricated capital for the external peristyle of the museum while rendering the normative structure of the galleries with simple bead joints, separating the cylindrical column heads from the rectangular beams (fig. 5.40). In all other respects, the inner and outer columns are identical, having the same fluted finish and the same upward-tapering entasis. Collins finds Perret's museum capital too organic and too close to Egyptoid forms, and he clearly prefers the more simply faceted capital adopted in Le Harve. While the capital at Le Havre was cruder it

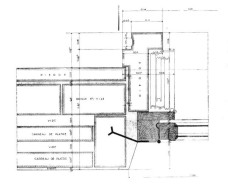

5.34
Auguste Perret, Cassandre House, Versailles, 1926. Elevation.

5.35
Auguste Perret, a typical window reveal with metal shutters.

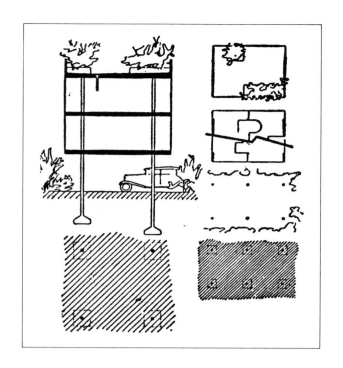

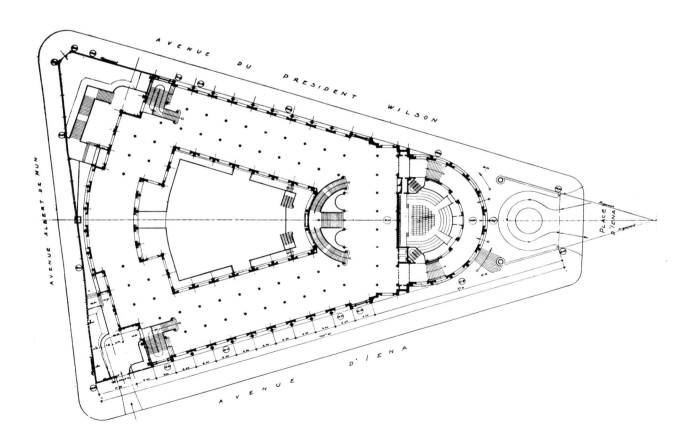

5.36
Le Corbusier, "Five Points of a New Architecture," plate from *La Maison de l'homme,* 1926.

5.37
Auguste Perret, Musée des Travaux Publics, Paris, 1936–1937. Elevation.

5.38
Auguste Perret, Musée des Travaux Publics, ground floor.

5.39
Auguste Perret, Musée des Travaux Publics, facade sections.

A. 3-cm waterproof membrane
B. four layers of volcanic cement
C. 2.5-cm cement screed
D. insulating membrane of porous cement
E. and F. hollow-pot construction
G. reinforced-concrete slab
H. plywood lining
I. 8-cm-thick precast concrete elements
J. cork insulation
K. 3-cm granite floor
L. 2-cm cement screed
M. ceiling panels
N. architrave
O. heating duct
P. incised joint
Q. hot air blower
R. fan
S. hot water pipes
T. and U. cold water feeds
X. hollow bricks
Y. 4-cm air space

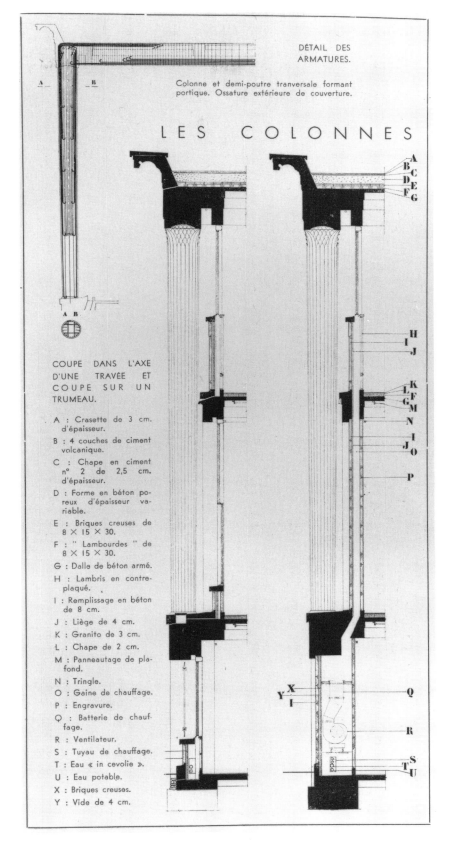

DÉTAIL DES ARMATURES.

Colonne et demi-poutre tranversale formant portique. Ossature extérieure de couverture.

LES COLONNES

COUPE DANS L'AXE D'UNE TRAVÉE ET COUPE SUR UN TRUMEAU.

A : Crasette de 3 cm. d'épaisseur.
B : 4 couches de ciment volcanique.
C : Chape en ciment n° 2 de 2,5 cm. d'épaisseur.
D : Forme en béton poreux d'épaisseur variable.
E : Briques creuses de 8 × 15 × 30.
F : " Lambourdes " de 8 × 15 × 30.
G : Dalla de béton armé.
H : Lambris en contre-plaqué.
I : Remplissage en béton de 8 cm.
J : Liège de 4 cm.
K : Granito de 3 cm.
L : Chape de 2 cm.
M : Panneautage de pla-fond.
N : Tringle.
O : Gaine de chauffage.
P : Engravure.
Q : Batterie de chauf-fage.
R : Ventilateur.
S : Tuyau de chauffage.
T : Eau « in cevolie ».
U : Eau potable.
X : Briques creuses.
Y : Vide de 4 cm.

was nonetheless a geometrically precise transition, composed out of a set of larger intersecting planes (fig. 5.41). Here the points of all the triangles terminate above an arris of the faceted column, employing a generic method that will serve equally well irrespective of the number of faces in the formwork of the shaft, so that "the architect's task is limited to deciding dimensions, as it always was in the past."[16]

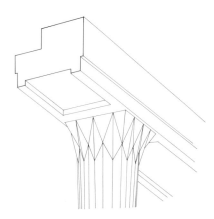

In the Musée des Travaux Publics, Perret brought his concrete syntax to a remarkable level of precision, striking the columns straight from the formwork but bush-hammering all other concrete surfaces in such a way as to expose the aggregate and stress both arrises and seams. This linear accent, running over every surface, created an unexpected atectonic effect, imparting to the aggregate surfaces the paradoxical suggestion that they may not be of a monolithic character (fig. 5.42). At the same time, large unbroken areas of steel-framed plate glass running behind the exterior peristyle interrupted the continuity established by the load-bearing concrete undercroft. This spatial elision helped to express the format of a "building within the building" that was, in fact, the leitmotiv of the entire structure (figs. 5.43, 5.44). At the same time, Perret overcame the redundancy of having to double up the columns around the perimeter of the work as he had been obliged to do in his Théâtre des Arts Décoratifs. In this regard, the museum culminates a dialectical evolution that passes from the thesis of Le Raincy, to the counterthesis of the Théâtre des Arts Décoratifs, and finally to the synthesis of the Musée des Travaux Publics. In terms of the articulation of the

5.40
Auguste Perret, Musée des Travaux Publics,
interior.

5.41
Auguste Perret, City Hall, Le Havre, 1949. Detail of capital.

5.42
Auguste Perret, Musée des Travaux Publics,
perimeter detail.

5.43
Auguste Perret, Musée des Travaux Publics,
axonometric.

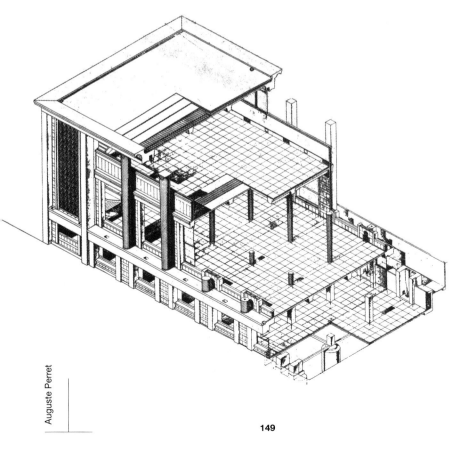

Auguste Perret

149

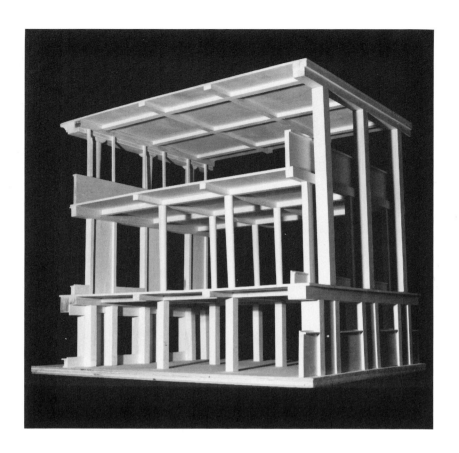

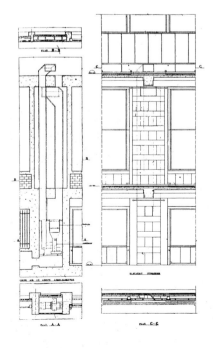

columnar structure in relation to the enclosing generic membrane, Perret went from the column inside to columns on both sides and finally to the column outside.

In the Musée des Travaux Publics, the second order of articulation manifests itself within the recessed body of the work; above all, in the paired pilasters lying on either side of the structural axis behind each column of the peristyle. The voids between these pilasters are filled with plenum duct work (figs. 5.39, 5.45), a provision that prefigures Louis Kahn's later integration of services with structural form. The tectonic unity of the internal volume is assured by bush-hammered, down-stand beams, cast as monolithic elements with the freestanding columns that support them. At the perimeter, these beams are discretely carried by transverse trimmer beams that distribute their load to the twin pilasters, incorporated within the thickness of the wall.

The central circular lantern in the roof over the semicircular auditorium admits natural light, while artificial light is provided by illumination located in the space between the two domes (figs. 5.46, 5.47). There is yet a third lightweight, ferro-cement membrane that, as in Le Raincy, protects the surface of the upper structural dome. Where the lower dome over the amphitheater is made up of stepped rings of glass block set in concrete—what Perret called *béton translucide* (fig. 5.48)—the upper dome is of solid reinforced concrete.

It is characteristic of the mature Perret that the recessed ceiling areas between the beams of the museum are lined with acoustical plywood paneling, which fol-

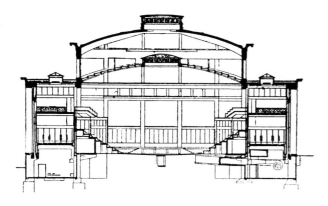

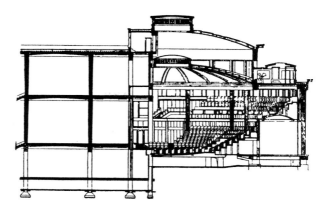

5.44
Auguste Perret, Musée des Travaux Publics, model.

5.45
Auguste Perret, Musée des Travaux Publics, wall elevation and section showing hot air heating system.

5.46
Auguste Perret, Musée des Travaux Publics, sections through the auditorium.

5.47
Auguste Perret, Musée des Travaux Publics, attic space between the two reinforced concrete domes.

lows the treatment devised for the acoustical interior of the Ecole Normale de Musique. For Perret, the acoustics of a volume had an ontological value that went beyond providing appropriate levels of absorption or resonance. Like Le Corbusier after him, he seems to have thought of acoustical tone as being a further manifestation of a building's spatial character. For him, as for the Danish critic Steen Eiler Rasmussen, architecture was to be acoustically apprehended.[17] At the same time, as in the foyer of the Théâtre des Champs-Elysées, the ceiling treatment and the paving pattern were to echo the orthogonal network of the basic skeleton. In the museum, however, Perret was inordinately proud of the fact that not a single square inch of plaster had been used to finish any of the internal surfaces.[18] Every element testified to the material out of which it had been made and to the manner in which it had been wrought. Finally he was able to introduce into the work what he considered to be the fundamental proof of the status of a civilization, namely the spatio-tectonic quality of primary staircases as they rise through space; a value that is made manifest in the freestanding helicoidal stairs that afford public access to the various gallery levels (fig. 5.49).

The main theoretical statement of his life, his *Contribution à une théorie de l'architecture,* was published in book form in 1952, only two years before his death.[19] The style was even more laconic than that adopted in the theoretical

writings of Mies van der Rohe. Perret's credo took the form of a series of aphorisms like Mosaic tablets, classically arranged on the page and composed entirely of capital letters as though each sentence was destined to be carved in stone. At the same time, these aphorisms were arranged so as to succeed each other like the logical steps of an argument, although each one is an independent statement in itself. There are, in effect, sixteen separate statements. Some of them are accompanied by short glosses drawn from other writers. Perret begins:

Technique, permanent homage to nature, essential food for the imagination, authentic source of inspiration, the prayer of everything that is most efficacious, maternal language of every creator, technique, spoken poetically leads us to architecture.

This is followed by a statement that is almost a direct paraphrase of Viollet-le-Duc's own aphorism about structure that appears at the head of his *Dictionnaire raisonné de l'architecture française*. Perret writes, "Architecture is the art of organizing space. It is through construction that it expresses itself." He then goes on to distinguish between fixed and ephemeral form.

Mobile or immobile, all that occupies space belongs to the domain of architecture. Architecture constitutes itself out of space, limits it, closes it, encircles it. It has this privilege of creating magical places, total works of the spirit [l'esprit]. Architecture is of all the artistic expressions the one most subject to material condi-

5.48
Auguste Perret, Musée des Travaux Publics, interior of auditorium.

5.49
Auguste Perret, Musée des Travaux Publics, main staircase.

tions. The permanent conditions are imposed by nature, the transitory conditions are imposed by man. The climate with its temperature changes, the materials and their properties, stability and the laws of statics, optical deformities, the eternal and universal direction of lines and forms, impose conditions that are permanent. He the architect is the one who by virtue of a combination of scientific thought and intuition conceives of a vessel, a portico, a sovereign shelter capable of accommodating within its unity the diversity of organs arising out of functional need.

This passage is an implicit critique of our misguided aspirations for achieving a perfect fit of form and function that can only be of relevance in the most extreme survival situations. Moreover, it also suggests that our modern obsession with comfort is a self-indulgence that, over the last half-century, has only furthered the commodification of architecture. Instead, Perret accords primacy to the space of "human appearance" as this first appeared in the Greek polis, the subject citizen literally emerging from the peristyle much as Hegel had imagined him. Here Perret contrasts the permanence of the civic monument, even as a ruin, to the impermanence of the tangible everyday object. His position, in this regard, is also close to Le Corbusier's observation that the more intimate our relations are to an object, the more it will reflect our anthropomorphic figure; conversely, the more distant, the more it will tend toward abstraction.

Perret then turns his discourse toward the poetic primacy of construction.

Construction is the mother tongue of the architect. The architect is a poet who thinks and speaks in terms of construction. The large buildings of our time presuppose a framework, a framework rendered in steel or reinforced concrete. The framework is to a building what a skeleton is to an animal. Just as the skeleton of an animal is rhythmic, balanced and symmetrical, and contains and supports the most diverse and diversely situated organs, so the framework of a building must be composed, rhythmic, balanced and very symmetrical. It must be able to contain the most diverse and diversely situated organs and services demanded by function and appointment.

Perret places by the side of this aphorism a gloss taken from the writings of Charles Blanc, who was librarian at the Ecole des Beaux-Arts and author of the highly influential *Grammaire des arts de dessin* published in 1867. This gloss reads, "The profound study of ancient monuments reveals this luminous truth, that architecture at its highest level is not so much a construction that is decorated as a decoration that is constructed."

Perret's theoretical position implies a number of other ramifications that require comment here. The first is that he was to remain categorically opposed to the idea of decorative art throughout his life, even though he participated in the 1925 Exposition des Arts Décoratifs. Perret thought that this exhibition represented a regression from the cultural level attained even in the Paris exhibition of 1900. In an interview with Marie Dormoy at the time he states: "Decorative art should be forbidden. I would like to know who stuck these words together: art and decorative. It is a monstrosity. Where there is true art, there is no need for decoration."[20] The second point turns on Perret's opposition to the simulation of tectonic form and structure. There is an interesting footnote in Denis Honegger's "Auguste Perret: doctrine de l'architecture" that touches on this issue. Perret is supposed to have said to him on one occasion:

We no longer know the language of stone. Everything that we make in this material today is only a lie and a trick. We no longer know how to raise a vault and we anchor our stones with iron cramps. The visible lintels are backed up by iron or reinforced concrete beams. I challenge any contemporary architect, no matter who, to reconstruct the nave of Bourges with the same conscience and feeling for material. In our day we are content to make it of reinforced concrete, plaster it over, and paint the joints.[21]

Against such kitsch simulation, Perret continues to assert, like Semper, the primacy of the frame. He extends the anthropological legitimacy that Semper accords to the frame into a natural philosophy of construction. Thus, in his *Contribution à une théorie* he remarks with ethical overtones that remind one of Adolf Loos's polemical essay "Ornament and Crime" of 1908: "He who hides any part of the framework not only deprives architecture of its sole legitimacy but also strips from it its most beautiful ornament. He who hides a column makes a blunder, he who makes a false column commits a crime."[22]

In his aphoristic formulations, Perret will follow both Paul Valéry and Henri Bergson in stressing the fundamental importance of the durability of the framework, that is to say, its fundamental capacity to stand against time.[23] Thus he writes:

It is the framework that furnishes the building with elements and forms imposed by permanent conditions and that, subject to nature, attached to the past, establishes the durability [la durée] of the work. Having satisfied the transitory and permanent conditions, the building, now subject to man and nature, will acquire character; it will have style, it will be harmonious. Character, style, harmony, these are the milestones that lead via truth to beauty.[24]

In his introduction to his play *Histoire d'Amphion,* Valéry would go so far as to equate memory in literate culture with fundamental construction in architecture: "Even in the slightest comparison one must think of duration, that is *memory,* which is to say form, just as the builder of steeples and towers must think of *structure.*"[25]

It is difficult to overestimate the seminal role played by Valéry in the evolution of Perret's thought. Valéry seems first to have met Perret around 1909, some three years before the realization of the Théâtre des Champs-Elysées. Valéry was an *afficionado* of the theater, and apart from his contact with Perret he was on intimate terms with the entire circle that brought the theater into being, including Maurice Denis and Antoine Bourdelle, whose decor and sculptural relief, respectively, graced its interior, and Gabriel Thomas who was the main administrator. Valéry's attitude to architecture as set forth in *Eupalinos ou l'architecte* (1922) is polemically tectonic to the point of being retardataire, since for him true architecture is contingent upon it being made out of hewn stone. In this regard, Valéry makes a precise distinction between (1) simple *bearing* constructions, assembled out of cut stone, (2) *reticulated* construction usually framed out of wood, and (3) *consolidated* constructions cast in reinforced concrete. This differentiation may be seen both as a response to and as a critique of Perret's architectural endeavor in which he sought to combine the tectonic/paratactic configuration of classical architecture and the monolithic organic configuration of reinforced concrete. While Perret made a heroic effort to realize the tectonic potential of the concrete frame, his work was by definition removed from the deeper roots of the tectonic as Valéry had received them from Greek culture.[26]

Valéry would expand upon the purity of this etymological base in a typical Mediterranean fashion by distinguishing between Eupalinos the constructor in stone, who is heir to tradition and in charge of creating a hierarchic human world, and Tridon the builder of ships in wood, who works against and with the unknown to conquer the sea. Here *homo faber* appears in two aspects, the one turned toward the culture and the other toward nature; the first face is that of a world creator, while the second is that of an instrumentalizer.[27]

Perret's use of the terms character and style often seems to be synonymous; it is clear, however, that he associated style with some fundamentally significant inner order, whereas character was merely the outward manifestation of a particular instant. Thus he remarked to Marcel Mayer: "A locomotive merely has character; the Parthenon has both character and style. In a few years, the most beautiful locomotive of today will be merely a mass of scrap metal; the Parthenon will sing forever." "Style," Perret was fond of saying, after Viollet-le-Duc, "is a word that has no plural."[28] Perret's *Contribution à une théorie* closes with an aphorism that is almost a direct paraphrase of Mies's citation from St. Augustine, "Beauty is the splendor of truth," and he goes on to add, paralleling the thesis advanced at the same time in Le Corbusier's *Modulor,* that the enrichment of a structure through proportion is a reflection of man himself.[29] With this last observation, he ends his testament.

The Greco-Gothic ideal was to permeate the work of Perret at every level, and while his use of neo-Platonic form and his particular vision of human destiny were to remain unequivocally Greek, his attitude toward production and his feeling for construction were to be drawn from medieval culture. This double influence brought him to regard the Renaissance with considerable contempt.

The Renaissance was in my opinion a retrospective movement; it was not a "rebirth" but decadence, and one may say that even though, after the end of the Middle Ages, certain men of genius produced monuments that were masterpieces, such as the Val-de-Grâce, the Dome des Invalides and the Palace of Versailles, these edifices are merely magnificent stage decorations. . . . Versailles is badly constructed, and when Time will have exerted its mastery over this palace, we shall not be left with a ruin, but with a mass of unidentifiable rubble. This is not Architecture; Architecture is what makes beautiful ruins.[30]

Inasmuch as he had total control over the means of production, Perret was uniquely privileged to proclaim throughout his career that he was a "constructor" rather than an architect. This eminently tectonic assertion was backed up by a situation in which A & G Perret Constructeurs, the title of his architectural practice up to 1945, were always complemented by the building firm of Perret Frères that was invariably charged with the execution of the work. It was surely this symbiotic conjunction that enabled them to bring their work to such precise levels of resolution, including such delicate adjustments as correcting the "optical" deflection of beam spans. Of this procedure Peter Collins has written:

Whereas in Greek architecture such refinements . . . were the laborious result of sculptural dexterity, in Perret's architecture they derived solely from the natural resilience of wood. The formwork of every beam was planed flat and true by the workmen, and it was only when it was being set in place that these refinements were effected by means of graduated blocks (or scamilli impares *as Vitruvius would have called them) wedged underneath to give the upward curvature desired.*[31]

155

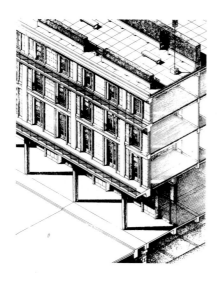

5.50
Auguste Perret, typical apartment blocks for
Le Havre, 1949.

5.51
Antonin Raymond and Ladislav Rado, Reader's Digest Building, Tokyo, 1951. Detail
section.

This capacity to achieve classic refinements with modern constructional means surely contributed to Perret's reputation as an evolutionary realist. However, it was the tectonic dimension of his work that would account for his resignation from the editorial board of *L'Architecture Vivante,* a journal that he had founded in order to further the cause of a modern architecture. Perret's departure from the masthead arose out of a confrontation with the editor, Jean Badovici, turning on the latter's decision to publish Mondrian's polemic "L'Architecture future de néo-plasticisme" in the autumn 1925 issue of the magazine. Perret had founded *L'Architecture Vivante* as an anti-Beaux-Arts publication, but his anti-academicism did not mean that he was willing to abandon the unfolding tradition of tectonic culture. The subsequent distance that he took from the modernist avant-garde and its various ideologies would lead not only to his alienation from the next generation but also to the scant treatment of his work in the received accounts of twentieth-century architecture.

We may say that the particular tectonic line pursued in Perret's work consistently displayed the following attributes: (1) the expression of the structural skeleton as an indispensable ordering principle, (2) the emphasis placed on the joint as a techno-poetic fulcrum, (3) the reinterpretation of traditional features so that they may still express a certain cultural continuity, (4) the resulting emphasis on certain key components, such as the cornice, the French window, and the helicoidal stair, seen as the apotheosis of a tectonic civilization, and (5) an adherence to the rational as a transferable method, dedicated to the continuation and development of a normative culture. This last is surely related to his appraisal of

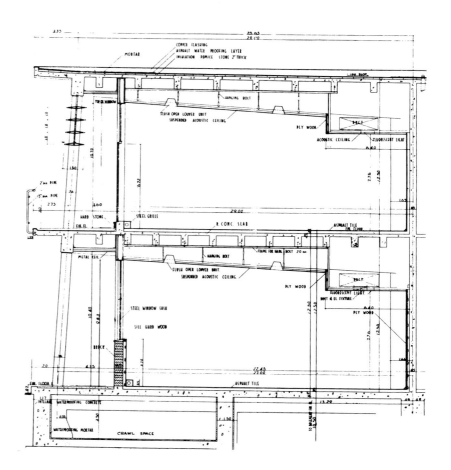

the banal as this appears in his 1945 plan for the reconstruction of Le Havre. In his 1933 address to the Institut d'Art et Architecture, Perret stated:

A country is only old by its monuments, for nature is eternally young. He who, without betraying the modern conditions of a programme, or the use of modern materials, produces a work which seems to have always existed, which, in a word, is banal, can rest satisfied. Astonishment and excitement are shocks which do not endure, they are but contingent and anecdotic sentiments. The true aim of Art is to lead us dialectically from satisfaction to satisfaction, until it surpasses mere admiration to reach delight in its purest form.[32]

Perret's significance today resides in the way in which his work maintained a line of development that, while distanced from the expressivity of the avant-garde, nonetheless avoided the two primary pitfalls of the second half of the twentieth century, pastiche historicism on the one hand and reductive functional-ism on the other. Transcending this double bind, his legacy points toward a future in which tectonic and stereotomic elements may be dialectically combined. The potential for transferring his method to other structural materials is perhaps best indicated in his temporary constructions, above all his Palais de Bois and Théâtre des Arts Décoratifs. These works suggest a richer and freer articulation than that embodied in the "state style" of his late career. Thus both the limitation and promise of his legacy are reflected in the dichotomous nature of his influence. On the one hand then we have his rather academic followers, including Pierre Lambert and Jacques Poirrer, who directly assisted him in the reconstruction of Le Havre (fig. 5.50), and Denis Honegger, whose University of Fribourg, realized in 1939, was already an all too exemplary exercise in the Perret manner veering toward the decorative. On the other, there were his own more modernist pupils such as Erno Goldfinger, Paul Nelson, and Oscar Nitschke, and elsewhere distant followers like the Czech-American Antonin Raymond, whose Tokyo Golf Club of 1930[33] was an adaptation of Perret's structural classicism to Japanese conditions, and even Karl Moser, whose St. Anton's Church, Basel, completed in 1931, may be seen as a transposition of Perret's concrete syntax. Perhaps the very last work to internalize Perret's method, as opposed to his style, was Antonin Raymond and Ladislav Rado's Reader's Digest Building completed in Tokyo in 1951.[34] Everything in this diminutive but sublime piece—from the articulation of structure to the precision of its cast concrete—recalls the tectonic rigor of Perret at his best but without attempting to simulate the idiosyncratic *modénature* of his style.

6 Mies van der Rohe:
Avant-Garde and Continuity

All of Mies's constructions . . . are means by which to resist and to proceed. . . . So they are always capable of conferring meaning, or reorienting the context—always stubborn efforts to imagine existence as true life, always the never-betrayed possibility of an image of salvation.

This is what makes Mies's work solitary in the age of the project, in the age of total forgetfulness of the sense of the polis *(and of the decay of even the sense of the* civitas*), in the age of the formalistic autonomy of beauty, in the age of the complete oblivion of the sense of* kalón*. It is a solitude that is (absolutely) unknown, because it enters into controversy with, and is antagonistic to, individualism. Paradoxically, this solitude affirms the complete meaninglessness of the individual.*
Massimo Cacciari, "Mies's Classics,"*1988*

The career of Ludwig Mies van der Rohe (1886–1969) may be regarded as a constant struggle between three divergent factors: the technological capacity of the epoch, the aesthetics of avant-gardism, and the tectonic legacy of classical romanticism. Mies's lifelong effort to resolve these vectors is revealing in itself, since it enlightens us as to the nature of the avant-garde and indicates the relative incompatibility of abstract space and tectonic form. With this in mind Mies's career may be divided into the following phases: the Schinkelesque period (1911–1915), the G group period (1919–1925), the European transcendental phase (1925–1938), the IIT period (1938–1950), and finally his monumental technocratic practice lasting from 1950 to his death.

During the first stage of his career, ending in 1915, Mies van der Rohe remained immersed in the values of the Berlin *Schinkelschule,* and his most dramatic design of this period, namely, the Kröller-Müller House, projected in 1912 for Otterloo, near Arnheim, was evidently a modernized version of Schinkel's Italianate manner, close to the spirit of Peter Behrens's Wiegand House built in Berlin-Dahlem in the same year. In his second period, 1919–1925, Mies's work is directly affected by avant-gardist art, above all by Expressionism, Neoplasticism, and to some extent Suprematism. When he finally starts to build, however, in 1925, he turns, to the stereotomics of brick construction and then in 1927 to the direct tectonic potential of glass and steel.[1] This middle period is perhaps the most complex of his entire career, since here the conflict between avant-gardism and tradition attains its greatest intensity. After Mies's migration to the States in 1938, he seems to turn back toward normative building, that is to say to *Baukunst* rather than architecture, as we may judge from his earliest projects for the IIT campus in Chicago. As he was to put it in an interview with Christian Norberg-Schulz in 1958: "We do not like the word 'Design.' It means everything and nothing. Many believe they can do everything from designing a comb to planning a railway station—the result is nothing is good. We are only interested in building. We would rather that architects use the word 'building' and the best results would belong to the 'art of building.'"[2]

Mies's work begins to express the full range of this hypothetical hierarchy around 1945 with his monumentalization of the standard steel frame in the Alumni Memorial Hall, and this line of approach increases its hold over his output with the Farnsworth House, Fox River, Plano, Illinois, of 1946 and 860 Lake

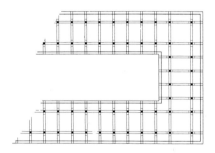

6.1
Mies van der Rohe, project for a reinforced concrete office building, 1922. Perspective.

6.2
Mies van der Rohe, reinforced concrete office building, partial floor plan.

Shore Drive, Chicago, of 1949. During the last two decades of his career Mies enters into a monumentalization of technology, as is evident from Crown Hall, completed at IIT in 1956, the Seagram Building, New York, completed in 1958, and finally the Neue Nationalgalerie, Berlin, under construction from 1962 to 1968.

The second phase of Mies's career, the period 1919 to 1925, yields radical projects of great subtlety, including the famous all-glass skyscrapers of the early twenties and the Concrete Office Building of 1922, first published in 1923 in the inaugural issue of the avant-garde magazine *G* (figs. 6.1, 6.2). This magazine, edited by El Lissitzky and Hans Richter, was of an Elementarist-Constructivist persuasion with Dadaist connections. The text that accompanies the publication of the Concrete Office Building is significant inasmuch as it reveals the ontological emphasis of Mies's thought at the time.

The materials: concrete, steel, glass. Reinforced concrete structures are skeletons by nature. No gingerbread. No fortress. Columns and girders eliminate bearing walls. This is skin and bone construction.

Functional division of the work space determines the width of the building: 16 meters. The most economic system was found to be two rows of columns spanning 8 meters with 4 meters cantilevered on either side. The girders are spaced 5 meters apart. These girders carry the floor slabs, which at the end of the cantilevers, are turned up perpendicularly to form the outer skin of the building. Cabinets are placed against these walls in order to permit free visibility in the center of the rooms. Above the cabinets, which are 2 meters high, runs a continuous band of windows.[3]

The tone and substance of this passage are as laconic and precise as any text by Viollet-le-Duc, so it is hardly surprising that the work should appear as a kind of transhistorical form, suspended outside time; for while there is nothing neoclassical about this proposition, there is nothing Gothic either. At the same time,

by virtue of the starkness of the material employed and the panoptic sequester-
ing of the office workers who cannot see out, the work is suffused with dadais-
tic overtones. Thus, apart from Mies's insistence on the priority of the skeleton
frame, comparable to Perret's insistence on the tectonic importance of the *charpente,* we could not be further from the spirit of Perret's Notre-Dame du Raincy
which happens to be of the same date. As becomes an office building, this
work presents itself as *Bauen* rather than *Baukunst,* and this explains, perhaps,
the conceptual difficulties that Mies encountered in providing a satisfactory entrance. There is little evidence of anything approaching a compositional resolution here except for the almost imperceptible widening of the end bays of the
structure, which would appear to be a hidden vestige of the classical tradition.
For the rest, the building is a polemical demonstration of the *sachlich* principle,
including the heavily textured objectivity of the concrete from which it is made.
It is significant that the representation of this material is achieved with wax cray-
ons, thereby placing a phenomenological stress on the heavily textured cast
surface, and conversely on the smooth, machine tool immateriality of the sash
fenestration. A similar emphasis was also present in Mies's glass skyscraper proposals of two years earlier, also rendered in charcoal and wax. This stress on
the tactility of material, as revealed under light, will recur repeatedly throughout
his career. Indeed, these glass skyscrapers may well be the first instance we
have of Mies treating glass as though it were a kind of transparent stone; a sensibility that will manifest itself even more paradoxically in the revetment of the
Seagram Building. The closeness of this material substitution to both the functionality of the *Neue Sachlichkeit* and the disjunctive use of material in Dadaist
art (cf. Meret Oppenheim's fur-lined cup, her *Objet: déjeuner en fourrure* of
1936), says something about Mies's proximity to the Berlin avant-garde. What
we have here, however, is a tectonic proposition rather than a gratuitous aesthetic speculation; a distinction that is supported by an aphoristic text published
in the second issue of *G* in 1923.

*We refuse to recognize the problems of form, but only problems of building.
Form is not the aim of our work, but only the result.*

Form by itself, does not exist. Form as an aim is formalism; and that we reject.

*Essentially our task is to free the practice of building from the control of the aes-
thetic speculators and restore it to what it should be: building.*[4]

It is difficult to imagine a more categoric declaration than this, and yet what follows in Mies's work is nothing less than an aesthetic proposition, even if the dynamic result is tectonically expressed. Mies's predilection for the determining
power of tectonic form may explain why there are two versions of the country
house that he projected between 1922 and 1924, the one in brick and the other
in concrete (figs. 6.3, 6.4, 6.5). Unlike those of the Dutch Neoplasticist artists, by
whom he was evidently influenced, the system of construction adopted in each
instance is not reduced to some seamless abstraction.[5] Even so, constructional
inconsistencies abound, above all in the concrete version, for unlike the Concrete Office Building, the house is not structured about a frame but rather about
solid concrete walls, save for the symbolic focus of a single column supporting
a cantilevered beam. This potential opposition between abstract aesthetics and
tectonic form is also implied in the masonry version of the country house, where
the Flemish-bonded, load-bearing brickwork is of an entirely different order from
the space form, although this antithesis is partially resolved through the pin-

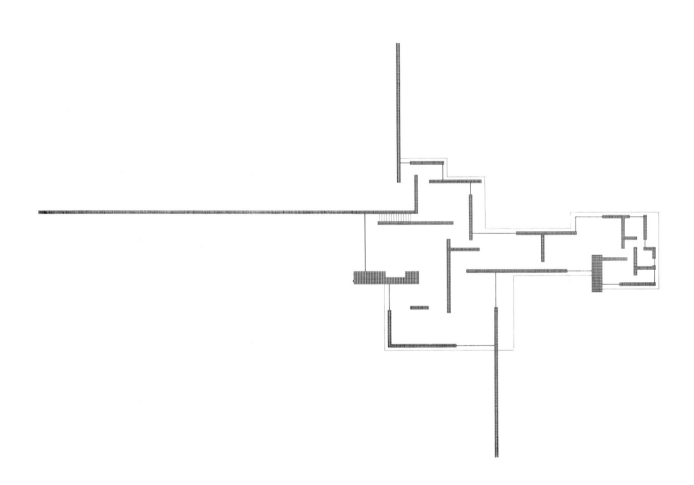

6.3
Mies van der Rohe, Brick Country House, project, 1923. Perspective.

6.4
Mies van der Rohe, Brick Country House, plan. This drawing, by Werner Blaser, is a reconstruction of the brickwork bonding of the walls of the country house.

6.5
Mies van der Rohe, Concrete Country House, project, 1924. Model.

6.6
Mies van der Rohe, Monument to Karl Liebknecht and Rosa Luxemburg, Berlin, 1926. Note the header courses in the atectonic position on the underside of the projecting forms.

wheeling nature of the bonding itself and through the unifying role played by projecting roof slabs. A similar contrast between stereotomic form and planar spatiality appears a few years later in the Berlin monument to Karl Liebknecht and Rosa Luxemburg of 1926 (fig. 6.6) and to some extent in the Wolf House, built in Guben in the same year (fig. 6.7). Particularly significant in this regard is the thoroughly *atectonic* placement of the brick header courses in the Luxemburg-Liebknecht memorial, which are deliberately situated underneath the lowest stretcher course of the projecting planes. The plan of the Wolf House, however, points in another direction, for while the main mass is asymmetrical, an inflection that is stressed through the oversailing concrete roof, rendered in white plaster, the plan is more traditional. It is by no means a free plan in the Neoplasticist sense, however (fig. 6.8), for, like the Hermann Lange and Esters houses, realized in Krefeld in 1928 and 1930 (figs. 6.9, 6.10), the principal rooms of the Wolf House interconnect with each other along a diagonal line. In the Esters House this visual continuity, which cuts across the ground floor of the dwelling, is punctuated by steel-framed, plate glass double doors that separate the smoking, living, and dining rooms (fig. 6.11). At the same time, as Werner Blaser demonstrates in his reconstruction of the masonry bonding for the Brick Country House, the tectonic means adopted in each instance were identical, namely double-sided, fair-faced brickwork, with all the dimensions and proportions worked out on a brick module (fig. 6.12).[6]

It is interesting to note the subtle variations that occur in the detailing of these houses. The Wolf House employs Flemish as opposed to the English bonding

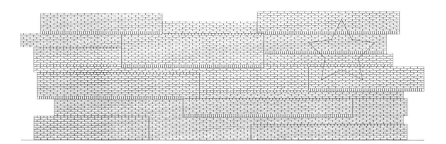

6.7
Mies van der Rohe, Wolf House, Guben,
1926.

6.8
Mies van der Rohe, Wolf House, floor plan.

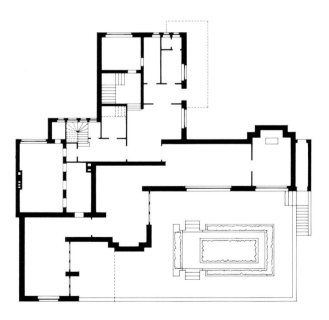

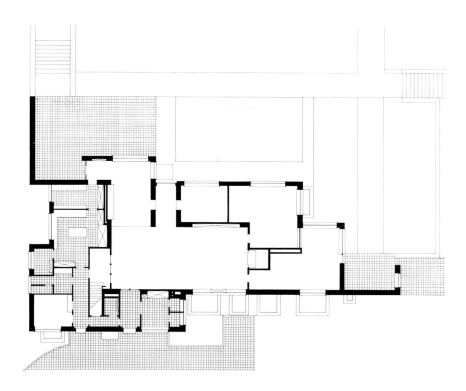

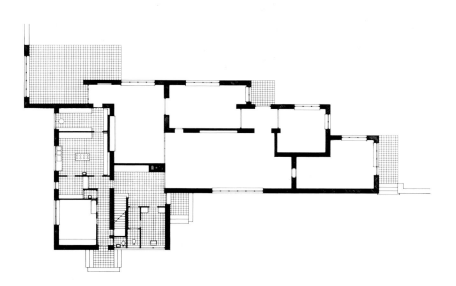

6.9
Mies van der Rohe, Hermann Lange House,
Krefeld, 1928. Floor plan.

6.10
Mies van der Rohe, Josef Esters House, Krefeld, 1930. Floor plan.

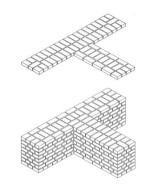

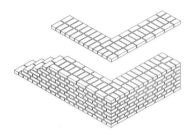

6.11
Mies van der Rohe, Josef Esters House, view through children's room and dining room to entrance.

6.12
Typical brick coursing by Mies (reconstruction by Werner Blaser for the Brick Country House of 1923).

6.13
Mies van der Rohe, Wolf House: reconstruction of original working drawing showing the precision with which the brick coursing was worked out.

that is used in the other two houses (fig. 6.13); header courses are used to cap the upstand walls of the Wolf House, while in the Lange and Esters houses the upstands are crisply terminated with metal copings (fig. 6.14). Moreover, the load-bearing walls of the Wolf House inhibit the incipient spatial dynamism of its plan, in comparison with the later Esters and Lange houses. At the same time, structural logic is variously compromised in all three works, since the steel lintels used in each case to span various horizontal openings remain totally unexpressed. In each instance, joists or trusses are concealed behind brick stretcher courses (fig. 6.15). This was not in any way a minor departure from standard practice, as we may judge from the complex structural devices used to support the masonry in the Lange House (fig. 6.16). Mies's engineer, Ernst Walther, complained at length about the economic and technical problems involved in achieving such large spans in brick openings. In a letter to Mies, he complained of his liberal use of Reiner beams and other elaborate structural devices.[7] However, such spans enabled Mies to provide large picture windows in both the Esters and Lange residences, the latter being equipped with retractable plate glass windows that could be lowered mechanically into the basement. These houses, together with the second Ulrich Lange and Hubbe houses projected in the thirties (figs. 6.17, 6.18), are particularly relevant to our understanding of Mies, since they were as formed by traditional constructional methods as they were influenced by avant-gardist spatial concepts. This possibly accounts for Mies's wistful remark that he would have liked to use more glass in these houses.

While Mies's free plan will finally manifest itself in the Barcelona Pavilion and the Tugendhat House, the only hint of spatial freedom in these early works resides in the ingenuity of the *en suite* planning, in which the living spaces are united with each other by a series of full-height, steel-framed double doors filled with glass (see fig. 6.11). As a result, the walls start to function as screens, producing a discernible contrast between a closed outer volume and a more open interior. This contrast is even more pronounced in the second Ulrich Lange and Hubbe houses projected in 1935 and in the Lemke courtyard house realized in Berlin in 1932 (figs. 6.19, 6.20). In each case, the dynamic space form is contained by bounding courtyard walls, which serve to stabilize the composition. This contrast between avant-gardist space and traditional envelope attains its ultimate articulation in the Tugendhat House, where the main living volume is an open, freely planned spatial continuum and the bedrooms are closed, traditional volumes, illuminated by pierced windows. The capacity of the retractable plate glass wall to transform the living room into an open air belvedere only serves to heighten this contrast.

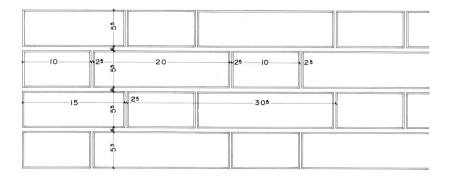

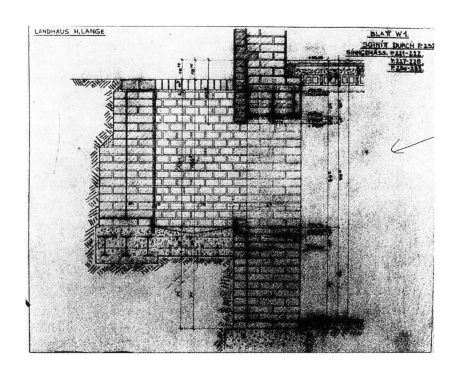

I have focused on Mies's brick houses not only because they remain unfamiliar, but also because they afford a benchmark from which to assess his subsequent achievement. These works are invariably glossed over in most standard monographs, with the unique exception of Philip Johnson's early study.[8] The brick houses are important because they show Mies projecting works that are close in their material expressivity to Hannes Meyer's Trades Union School built in Bernau in 1930; a surprising affinity given the ideological differences that would separate these architects. The use of standard steel sash windows, particularly evident in the Lemke house, is symptomatic in this regard. It is a mode of normative expression that one does not usually associate with the early Mies, although a similar standardizing *sachlich* impulse will determine the continuous industrial glazing applied to the typical floors of his Reichsbank design of 1933.

While there is nothing historicist about these residences, the overwhelming presence of fair-faced, load-bearing brickwork brings them well within the rubric of tradition, even if their walls are deployed as though the overall form was made out of a homogeneous substance. Despite this plasticity, a feeling of sobriety emanates from these works. As Mies was to put it much later in his career: "Architecture is a language having the discipline of a grammar. Language can be used for normal day-to-day purposes as prose. And if you are very good, you can be a poet."[9] Or, as Philip Johnson was to remark of Mies's brick houses: "He calculated all dimensions in brick lengths and occasionally went so far as to separate the under-fired long bricks from the over-fired short ones, using the long in one direction and the short in the other."[10]

It is clear from this and other evidence that the tectonic probity of Mies's work resided in the emphasis he placed on construction and the importance he

6.14
Mies van der Rohe, Josef Esters House, view from the west.

6.15
Mies van der Rohe, Hermann Lange House, cross section showing steel joist reinforcement. Typical working drawing.

6.16
Mies van der Rohe, Hermann Lange House, working drawing showing steel trusswork, suspended ceiling, steel lintels, blind housing, and the system of roof drainage.

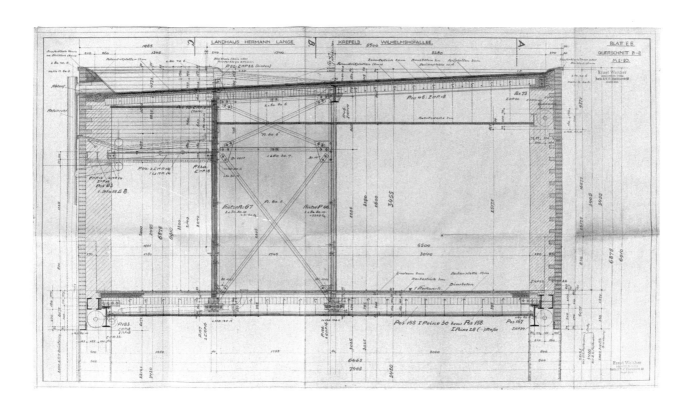

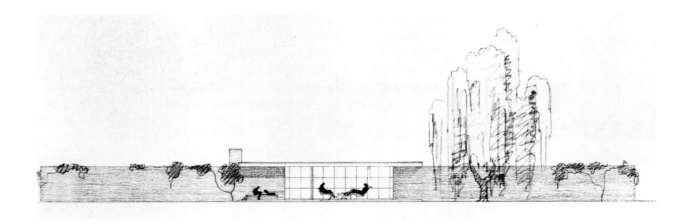

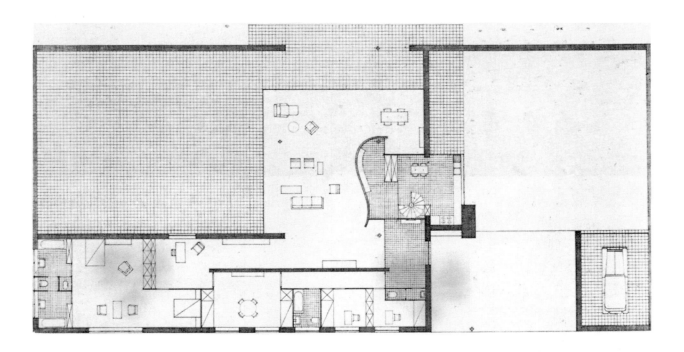

attached to the art of building as an intrinsically poetic act. His famous aphorism that "God is in the details" is indicative of this. The sublime for Mies resided in the quality of the material itself and in the revelation of its essence through careful detailing. His recollection of the way in which he selected the onyx for the core of the Barcelona Pavilion reveals the respect he felt for all material and for the capacity of nature to influence the result.

Since you cannot move marble in from the quarry in winter because it is still wet inside and would easily freeze and break into pieces, we had to find dry material. Eventually, I found an onyx block of certain size and since I only had the possibility of this block, I made the pavilion twice that height and then we developed the plan.[11]

Mies took an equally fastidious attitude toward the selection of brickwork, importing most of his bricks from Holland and visiting the brickyard in order to inspect every firing and choose and match the colors he required.[12]

Between the Wolf House of 1926 and Mies's entry for the Reichsbank competition in 1933, his practice seems to have been grounded in three main considerations; first, in the underlying aesthetic intention, second, in the essence of materials to hand, and third, in the institutional status of the work. I have already touched on the first two in my discussion of the Glass Skyscraper, the Concrete Office Building, and the brick houses. As to the third, it is clear that Mies was

6.17
Mies van der Rohe, Ulrich Lange House (second version), Krefeld, 1935. Elevation and plan.

6.18
Mies van der Rohe, Hubbe House, Magdeburg, 1935. Plan.

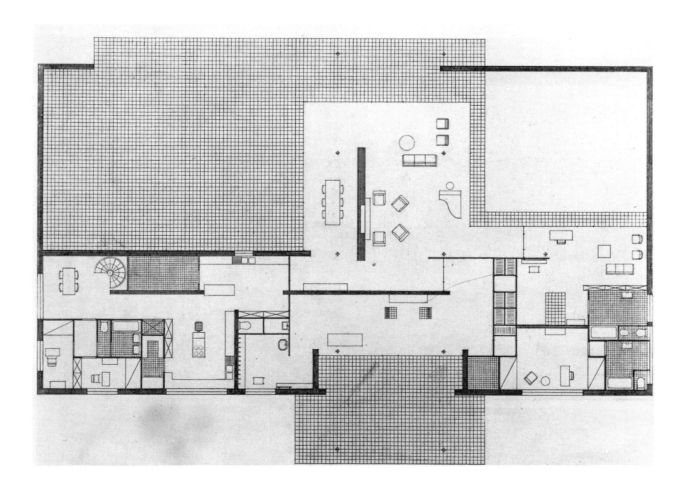

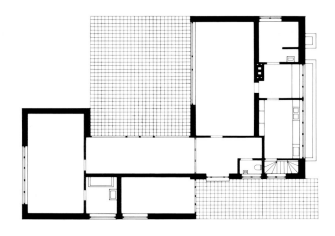

6.19
Mies van der Rohe, Karl Lemke House, Berlin, 1932. Plan.

6.20
Mies van der Rohe, Karl Lemke House, terrace.

acutely aware, throughout his life, of the character that each work ought to possess in relation to its institutional status. As he put it: "Every building has its position in a strata—every building is not a cathedral."[13]

Aside from this, the contrasting qualities of different materials become the terms of a binary opposition in Mies's work, comparable to the distinction that Semper drew between stereotomic mass and skeletonal, tectonic form. This distinction appears in Mies's later German houses as a means for expressing the institutional differences between the public, freely planned status of the living volume and the more private nature of the bedroom, enclosed by load-bearing masonry. In the late twenties there is discernible change in what might be regarded as the prime material of Mies's architecture, as one passes from the load-bearing brick of the Krefeld houses to the seminal exhibitions that Mies designed with Lilly Reich in 1927, the glass industry exhibit staged at the Werkbund Ausstellung in Stuttgart (figs. 6.21, 6.22) and the silk exhibition, the so-called Exposition de la Mode, mounted in Berlin in the same year (fig. 6.23).[14]

This shift from heavy opacity to light translucence had both tectonic and aesthetic ramifications. In the first place, glass implied, indeed demanded, a skeleton frame and hence a strictly tectonic system in order to sustain itself against gravity. It is significant that the ephemeral semitransparent screens of the Exposition de la Mode were, in fact, textiles, thereby returning Mies quite literally to the Semperian wall hanging as the symbolic representational form of built enclosure. In the second place, this very material, silk, when set against plate glass, yielded a dematerialized aesthetic plus a constant mirroring of the interplay between the transparent and the translucent. Hence, it displayed an affinity for the spatial paradigms that preoccupied avant-garde artists at the end of the First World War. I am referring, in particular, to the ineffable vision of the suprematist painter Kazimir Malevich. Despite Mies's insistence that the Russian avant-garde had no impact on his work ("I was very strongly opposed even to Malevich," he was to tell Peter Blake in 1962), there remains an uncanny parallel between his dematerialized works and the visionary projects of the neo-Suprematist architect Ivan Leonidov.[15] We need only read Johnson's account of the materials employed in the Stuttgart exhibition to sense the closeness of this Miesian aesthetic to Malevich's famous *White Square on White* painting of 1918: "chairs, white chamois and black cowhide; table, rosewood; floor, black and white linoleum; walls etched clear and grey opaque glass."[16]

Mies's glass and silk exhibitions present us with a paradox; on the one hand, the necessity for a frame to support the freestanding silk or glass screens, on the other hand, the ineffable, free-floating, even illusory volumes that these screens engender. These exhibits already embody that quality of *beinahe nichts* or "almost nothing" with which he will attempt to reconcile the palpable rigor of tectonic order with the spatial figuration of avant-gardist form. Aside from the play of tinted and opaque glass in the Barcelona Pavilion and the somewhat Russian color scheme adopted in the Exposition de la Mode, namely black, orange, red, gold, silver, and lemon yellow, a number of other exhibitions designed by Mies in the late twenties point in a comparable direction; above all, the various German industrial exhibits mounted in Barcelona in 1929. Largely designed by Lilly Reich, these three exhibits for silk, industrial products, and electrical equipment were modeled after the Stuttgart glass industry exhibition. This was especially true of the silk industry section, where silk was mounted against freestanding planes of etched and tinted glass—once again stressing, by associa-

tion, the translucent nature of both materials (fig. 6.24). The close conjunction of all these exhibits suggests Mies's affinity for German industry at the time and the way in which he aspired to inherit the mantle of Peter Behrens as the norma-tive form-giver of the German industrial state. This aspiration is even implied in his use of the so-called *Skeletschrift* typeface; a lean, mechanical-looking type had been expressly devised for the occasion by Mies's assistant, Sergius Ruegenberg. Aside from his concern for the normative, Mies saw glass as em-bodying a new challenge, as it were, to the fundamental tectonic elements of the wall, the floor, and the ceiling. He was to state as much in his contribution to a prospectus written for the Union of German Plate Glass Manufacturers in 1933 wherein he stressed the symbiotic impact of glass on modern form.

What would concrete be, what steel without plate glass? The ability of both to transform space would be limited, even lost altogether, it would remain only a vague promise. Only a glass skin and glass walls can reveal the simple structural form of the skeletal frame and ensure its architectonic possibilities. And this is true not only of large utilitarian buildings. To be sure, it was with them that a line of development based on function (Zweck) and necessity began that needs no further justification; it will not end there, however, but will find its fulfillment in the realm of residential building. Only here, in a field offering greater freedom, one not so bound by narrower objectives, can the architectural potential of these technical methods be fully realized. These are truly architectural elements form-ing the basis for a new art of building. They permit us a degree of freedom in the creation of space that we will no longer deny ourselves. Only now can we give shape to space, open it, and link it to the landscape. It now becomes clear once more just what walls and openings are, and floors and ceilings. Simplicity of con-struction, clarity of tectonic means, and purity of materials have about them the glow of pristine beauty.[17]

Such a programmatic view of modern transparency was surely already evident in the Barcelona Pavilion of 1929, where tectonic value is unequivocally as-serted in the eight freestanding cruciform columns, and where the space field is framed by the freestanding planes that bypass these supports (fig. 6.25). Aside from this patent opposition between columnar and planar form, it is possible to break down the Barcelona Pavilion into a series of polarities; tectonic versus stereotomic, still versus agitated, open versus closed, and above all, perhaps, traditional material versus space endlessness. The first dyad is tectonically self-evident, the second and third are related to the surfaces and the contents of the open and enclosed pools, while the last is evident in the opposition between the marble-faced pinwheeling planes and the symmetrical placement of the eight columns in relation to the roof. This pinwheel organization may also be read as a planimetric allusion to the Arts and Crafts asymmetrical plan form and hence to *building,* while the columnar peristyle recalls classical *architecture.* This last, rein-forced by the particular treatment of the column casings, is further evidence of Mies's capacity to integrate tectonic meaning with abstract form.

Mies's Barcelona column is a dematerialized cruciform point support, and yet at the same time it is altogether more planar than the half-round cruciform column casings employed in the later Tugendhat House. The planar character of the Barcelona column derives from the orthogonal profile adopted by the bent, chromium-plated, sheet steel case covering the built-up steel core (fig. 6.26). Like Le Corbusier's *pilotis* in his Purist *plan libre,* this column has neither base

6.23
Mies van der Rohe in collaboration with Lilly Reich, silk exhibition, Exposition de la Mode, Berlin, 1927. Materials and colors: black, orange, and red velvet; gold, silver, black, and lemon-yellow silk.

6.24
Mies van der Rohe in collaboration with Lilly Reich, silk exhibition, German section, International Exposition, Barcelona, 1929.

6.25
Mies van der Rohe, German Pavilion, International Exposition, Barcelona, 1929. View toward small pool.

6.26
Mies van der Rohe, German Pavilion, International Exposition, Barcelona, plan of column.

nor capital. Both column types are, in fact, abstractions of the idea of support, since, due to the fact that no beams are expressed in either instance, a somewhat insubstantial act of bearing is conveyed by the form. In both instances the ceiling is treated as a flat, continuous plane. Here we see how modern, beamless construction favors the suppression of the frame; that is to say, it eliminates the very trabeation that for Perret was a prerequisite of tectonic culture. In this regard, both the Villa Savoye and the Barcelona Pavilion may be seen as atectonic, although they are by no means as extreme in this regard as Josef Hoffmann's Stoclet House of 1911. In drawing our attention to Hoffmann's atectonic propensity, Eduard Sekler will stress the dematerializing effect that the edge cable molding would exert on the facades of Hoffmann's building, and a similar judgment may also be applied to the treatment of its internal structure.[18] While columnar support is patently a key element in the structuring of the Barcelona Pavilion both technically and phenomenologically, the ontological interaction between support and burden (Schopenhauer's *Stütze* and *Last*) is patently absent. One may argue that this absence is more categoric than in the Villa Savoye, since in the latter the monolithic appearance of the reinforced concrete structure permits the perception of a certain fixity between column and soffit, particularly since both are monolithically expressed by being plastered and painted white throughout. In Barcelona, on the other hand, the riveted steel frame supports a faired-out, plastered soffit that appears to float independently of the chromium columns. This illusion of levitation is strengthened by the uninterrupted planar continuity of the ceiling and the floor, white plaster above and travertine below; an effect that is partially countered by the free assembly of pinwheeling planes and screens rendered in heavier material, in *vert antique* marble, in onyx, and in various kinds of glass of a translucent or transparent nature, set in chromium-plated frames (fig. 6.27). These last also tend to make any sense of fixity uncertain due to their proliferation of highlights and reflections. No one has perhaps written more perceptively of the illusory, empty character of this spatial field than the Catalan critic José Quetglas.[19]

177

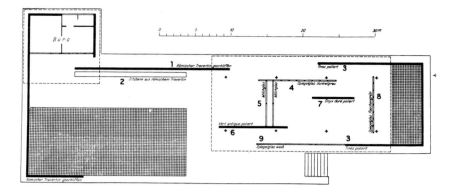

All of these vertiginous effects are emphasized, as Robin Evans would later observe, by the vertical mirroring of the volume about a horizon that happens to coincide not only with eye height but also with the central horizontal seam in the onyx plane, thereby suggesting a potential inversion of floor and ceiling that is paradoxically heightened rather than diminished by the differences in finish. As Evans remarks, since the floor reflects light and the ceiling receives it, the perceptual differences in the planar tone would have been greater had they been of the same material. Thus Mies would use "material asymmetry to create optical symmetry, rebounding the natural light to make the ceiling more sky-like and the ambience more expansive."[20] Traces of traditional value still remain, however, above all in the jointing of the travertine which tends not only to stress the tactility of the stone, as paving, but also to assert the presence of a *stereotomic* earthwork. Some vestige of the tectonic also remains in the columns, first, because the eight-column grid is perceivable as a peristyle, despite the asymmetrical freestanding planes, and second, because the reiterated highlights on the profiles of the casings effect a reference to classical fluting. Thus while the essential quality of chromium is its modernity, the form that it assumes in this instance also evokes a subtle traditional resonance.

The hallucinatory character of this synthesis is mediated in the Tugendhat House in Brno (Brünn) of the following year, where the bedrooms are excluded from the free plan and where the cruciform chromium-plated column casings are rounded (fig. 6.28). Here, with the single exception of the frosted glass in the entrance hall, the glazing is transparent and restricted to the perimeter of a simple rectangular envelope. This rather pragmatic attitude will inform the various row and courtyard houses that Mies designed between 1930 and 1935, beginning with the Gericke House projected for Wannsee in 1930 (fig. 6.29) and the Lemke House built in Berlin two years later, and continuing with such projects as the courtyard house with garage of 1934 and the Hubbe House and the first and second versions of the Ulrich Lange House projected for Krefeld of 1935. Despite this sobriety, the Tugendhat House (fig. 6.30) is in some respects more complex than the Barcelona Pavilion, for in addition to the opposites expressed in the pavilion, values of a more explicitly mythic and metaphorical nature find themselves incorporated into the Brno villa. Thus, the narrow winter garden, flanking the shorter side of the living volume, may be read as a third term between the petrified nature of the freestanding onyx plane subdividing the internal space and the living nature of the garden beyond. Here, as in the later Farnsworth House, the decorative manifests itself as an oscillating play between verdure as it is and verdure transformed either by reflection or by petrification. As in Adolf Loos's ironic use of heavily veined and matched marble, organic ornament appears here either as an intrinsic part of the material finish or as an optical effect, rather than through formal invention. At another level entirely, one may argue that the onyx dorée plane, separating the living room from the library, asserts, through its honorific character, the worldly cerebral status of the spaces on either side (fig. 6.31), while by a similar token the macassar ebony veneer to the semicircular dining alcove evokes through its material warmth the domestic, corporeal ritual of dining.

As in the large fenestration of the Lange House, the tectonic attains its most direct expression here in the *detailing* of the 80-foot-long plate glass window that, when withdrawn into the basement, converts the living space into a belvedere. Much as in the Krefeld houses, this intricate window section incorporates a retractable sun blind and a surface-mounted curtain track, plus a chromium balustrade and a series of chromium-plated heating tubes poised just above the floor. Once again, as in the Barcelona Pavilion, the suppression of the tectonic in the planar space-endlessness of the interior finds its countervailing reification

6.28
Mies van der Rohe, Tugendhat House, Brno, 1928–1930. Plans, section, and details. The entire plate glass wall of the living room may be slid into the basement in good weather.

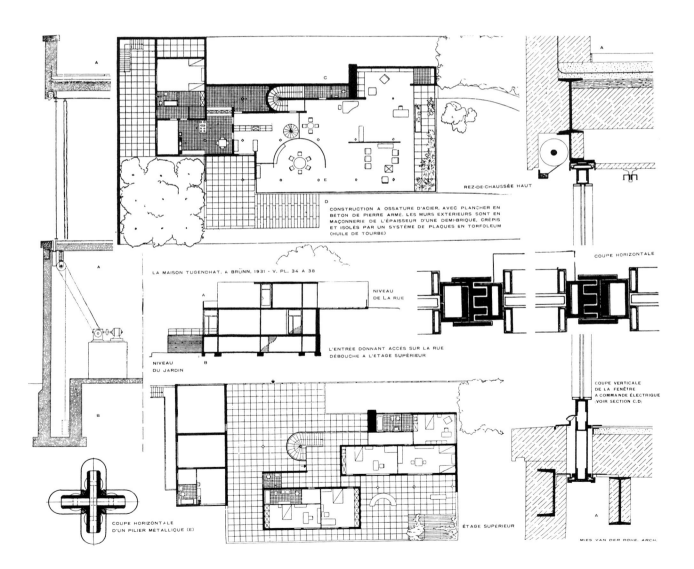

through the careful placement of material and the precision of small-scale detail (fig. 6.30). Again Lilly Reich enabled Mies to engage in an all but suprematist palette through the dissonant but rich furnishings employed throughout: the use of full-height curtains in black raw silk and black velvet on the winter garden wall and beige raw silk on the south wall, and the upholstery of the Tugendhat and Bruno chairs in emerald green leather and in ruby-red velvet and white vellum. All of this radiated out across a white linoleum floor, against separate sheets of retractable plate glass each some fifteen feet in length. That Mies intended a transcendental Baudelairean sense of *luxus* is borne out by Walter Riezler's contemporary appraisal of the house:

No one can deny the impression . . . of a particular spirituality of high degree dominating these spaces, a spirituality, to be sure, of a quite new kind. It is very much "tied to the present," and is therefore utterly different from the spirit dominating spaces of any earlier epoch. It is already the "spirit of technology"—not in the sense of that narrow-minded practicality that is so frequently deplored, but in the sense of a new freedom in living. . . . This is not to say that precisely this present project, namely the creation of a single residence for a high-spirited personality, is the very project that can best demonstrate the new spiritual ideas. Possibly, on the contrary, this project has been still somewhat determined by the sense of the epoch now approaching its end. But that is less important than the proof it provides that it is indeed possible to elevate oneself above the purely rational and functional thinking that has characterized modern architecture heretofore and into the realm of the spiritual.[21]

6.29
Mies van der Rohe, Gericke House, Wannsee, Berlin, 1930. Model.

6.30
Mies van der Rohe, Tugendhat House, view from dining room toward living room. The belvedere living room with a section of the glass wall removed. Here the tectonic quality of the work depends exclusively on the detailing, mostly carried out in polished chromium steel.

6.31
Mies van der Rohe, Tugendhat House, view toward library and living room.

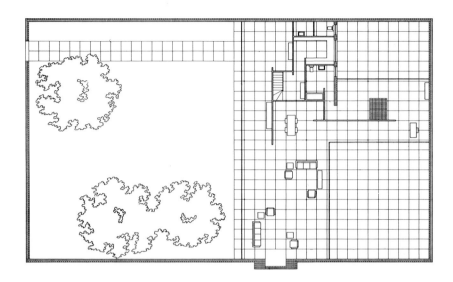

6.32
Mies van der Rohe, House with Three Courts, project, 1934. Elevation.

6.33
Mies van der Rohe, House with Three Courts, plan. Note the way the glass line does *not* coincide with the modular grid of the paving.

The unrealized House with Three Courts project of 1934 is in many respects the most generic of Mies's courtyard houses (figs. 6.32, 6.33). The delimiting boundary of this house is a brick perimeter wall that is interrupted three times; first for the entrance, then for the service core, and finally for the chimney. The floor of the courtyard itself is divided into two planes, the one being paved in square slabs of travertine and the other being lawn. The paved area is treated as a continuous domestic domain which in turn contains two subcourts, one for sleeping, one for living. The positioning of the plate glass enclosure outside the modular grid suggests that these courts are to be read as outdoor rooms. At the same time, the paving grid establishes the centers of the eight cruciform columns supporting the roof; a six-by-six modular spacing, as per the paving pattern. Within this overall frame the house breaks down into two elements: a *stereotomic* domain comprising the bounding wall together with the travertine paving, and a dematerialized *tectonic* domain, that is, the plate glass enclosure with its marble-veneered walls and chromium-plated columns (fig. 6.34).

The two successive projects for the Ulrich Lange House and the Hubbe House, all of 1935, elaborate a series of permutations derived from this three-court formula. Some of these variations depart from the generic type, such as the totally enclosed volumes of the first Ulrich Lange House (fig. 6.35), the subdivided double court of the second Ulrich Lange House, or the freestanding brick planes at the center of the Hubbe House, projected for Magdeburg (see fig. 6.18). As in the Barcelona Pavilion, the sublime interplay between natural form and sculpture evokes the spirit of romantic classicism. The picturesque lakeside vista, punctuated by trees and projected beyond the interior of the Hubbe House, is equally romantic, as are the wisteria-bedecked elevations of the first Ulrich Lange House (fig. 6.36). This is the picturesque as we find it in Schinkel, although the way in which these vistas are framed depends upon the presence of abstract space.

As Fritz Neumeyer has shown in his 1986 study *Das kunstlose Wort* (The Artless Word), Mies belonged to that generation of German intellectuals who were traumatized by the apocalypse of modernization that Germany had undergone throughout the second half of the nineteenth century. Like the Jesuit philosopher and theologian Romano Guardini by whom, as we now know, he was strongly influenced, Mies felt that the human intellect and spirit had no choice but to accept the radical transformations of the technological millennium as a fate that cannot be escaped. As Guardini put it in his 1927 *Briefe vom Comer See:*

We belong to the future. We must put ourselves into it, each one at his station. We must not plant ourselves against the new and attempt to retain a beautiful world, one that must perish. Nor must we try to build, with creative fantasy, a new one that claims to be immune to the ravages of becoming. We have to formulate the nascent. But that we can only do if we honestly say yes to it; yet with incorruptible heart we have to retain our awareness of all that is destructive and inhuman in it. Our time is given to us as a soil on which we stand, as a task that we have to master.[22]

Mies would respond quickly and directly to this challenge three years later in an essay entitled "Die neue Zeit" (The New Era):

Let us not give undue importance to mechanization and standardization. Let us accept changed economic and social conditions as a fact. All these take their blind and fateful course.

One thing will be decisive: the way we assert ourselves in the face of circumstance. Here the problem of the spirit begins. The important question to ask is not "what" but "how." What goods we produce or what tools we use are not questions of spiritual value.

How the question of skyscrapers versus low buildings is settled, whether we build of steel and glass are unimportant questions from the point of view of the spirit. . . .

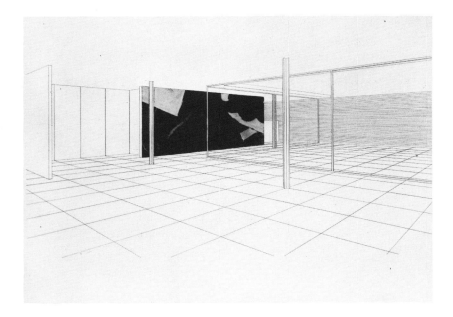

6.34
Mies van der Rohe, House with Three Courts, collage with composition by Georges Braque.

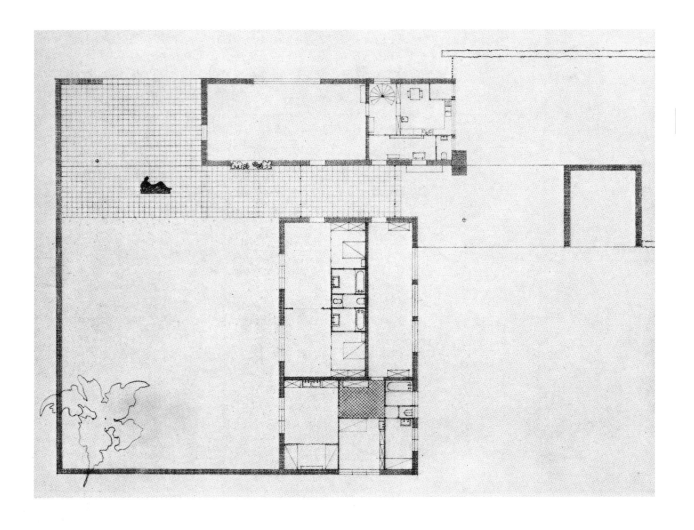

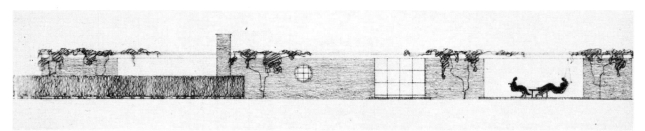

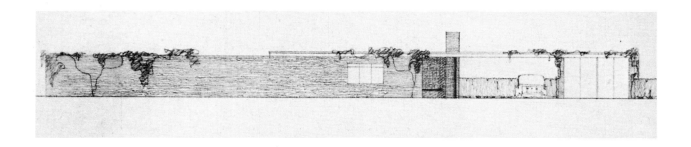

6.35
Mies van der Rohe, Ulrich Lange House (first version), Krefeld, 1935. Plan.

6.36
Mies van der Rohe, Ulrich Lange House (first version), elevations.

Yet it is just the question of value that is decisive. We must set up new values, fix our ultimate goals so that we may establish standards. For what is right and significant for any era—including the new era—is this: to give the spirit the opportunity for existence.[23]

This spirit of resignation and resistance was hardly new to Mies, for he had long since been preoccupied with the demise of craft culture and the positive potential of rationalized machine production. As he wrote in an essay entitled "Baukunst und Zeitwille" (Building Art and the Will of the Epoch) of 1924:

As I was born into an old family of stone masons, I am very familiar with hand craftsmanship, and not only as an aesthetic onlooker. My receptiveness to the beauty of handwork does not prevent me from recognizing that handicrafts as a form of economic production are lost. The few real craftsmen still alive in Germany are rarities whose work can be acquired only by very rich people. What really matters is something totally different. Our needs have assumed such proportions that they can no longer be met with methods of craftsmanship. . . . The need for even a single machine abolishes handicraft as an economic form. . . . Since we stand only in the beginning phase of industrial development, we cannot compare the initial imperfections and hesitancies to a highly mature culture of craftsmanship. . . . Old contents and forms, old means and work methods have for us only historical value. Life confronts us daily with new challenges: they are more important than the entire historical rubbish. . . . Each task represents a new challenge and leads to new results. We do not solve formal problems, but building problems, and the form is not the goal but the result of our work. That is the essence of our striving; and this viewpoint still separates us from many. Even from most of the modern building masters. But it unites us with all the disciplines of modern life. Much as the concept of building is, for you, not tied to old contents and forms, so it is also not connected to specific materials. We are very familiar with the charm of stones and bricks. But that does not prevent us nowadays from taking glass and concrete, glass and metal, into consideration as fully equivalent materials. In many cases, these materials correspond best to present day purposes.[24]

Fourteen years later, in his inaugural address at IIT, he would elaborate further on the same theme: "Thus, each material has its specific characteristics which we must understand if we want to use it. This is no less true of steel and concrete. We must remember that everything depends on how we use the material, not on the material itself."[25]

According to Werner Blaser, Mies regarded the perennial invention of arbitrary form as both trivial and absurd. He saw the discipline of construction as the sole guarantee of quality in architecture.[26] In 1961, in an issue of *Architectural Design* devoted to Mies, Peter Carter records him as saying:

Berlage was a man of great seriousness who would not accept anything that was fake and it was he who had said that nothing should be built that is not clearly constructed. And Berlage did exactly that. And he did it to such an extent that his famous building in Amsterdam, the Beurs, had a mediaeval character without being mediaeval. He used brick in the way the mediaeval people did. The idea of a clear construction came to me there, as one of the fundamentals we should accept. We can talk about that easily but to do it is not easy. It is very difficult to stick to this fundamental construction, and then to elevate to a structure. I must make it clear that in the English language you call everything structure. In Europe we don't. We call a shack, a shack, and not a structure. By structure, we have a philosophical idea. The structure is the whole, from top to bottom, to the last detail—with the same ideas. That is what we call structure.[27]

This passage is remarkable not only for its evocation of structural rationalism but also for its indirect allusion to medieval scholasticism. And yet, at the same time, Mies's preoccupation with progressive form remained as technological as it was aesthetic. This we may glean from a 1950 IIT address:

Technology is far more than a method. It is a world in itself. As a method it is superior in almost every respect. But only where it is left to itself, as in gigantic structures of engineering, there technology reveals its true nature. There it is evident that it is not only a useful means but that it is something that has a meaning and a powerful form—so powerful in fact, that it is not easy to name it. . . . Where technology reaches its real fulfillment it transcends into architecture.[28]

On the other hand, he seems to have been fully aware of the split in his work between the conservative nature of his tectonic structure and the radical stance of his spatial aesthetics. Thus, in an essay on the IIT curriculum, he wrote:

It is radical and conservative at once. It is radical in accepting the scientific and technological driving and sustaining forces of our time. It has a scientific character, but it is not science. It uses technological means but it is not technology. It is conservative as it is not only concerned with a purpose but also with a meaning, as it is not only concerned with a function but also with an expression. It is conservative as it is based on the eternal laws of architecture: Order, Space, Proportion.[29]

It would be hard to imagine something more overtly classical than this last triad, and yet Mies continues to differentiate between *Bauen* and *Baukunst,* between building and architecture, particularly after his Reichsbank competition entry of 1933. Indeed, this project implied a declension from a higher to a lower tectonic status *within* a single structure. This is evident in the differentiation between the gridded industrial glazing of the typical floor and the double-height, representative plate glass facade of the bank at street level (fig. 6.37). While the free plan is still in evidence, inasmuch as the curtain wall is projected in front of the column line throughout, Mies's previous preoccupation with the avant-gardist space form is relaxed somewhat, presumably because the public status of the institution demanded a more normative and symmetrical approach. At the same time the *sachlich* curtain wall of the repetitive floors is rendered even more normative, for as Ludwig Glaeser has remarked, Mies's model for the brick and glass banded perimeter of the Reichsbank was derived from the German industrial vernacular of *Fachwerkbauten* in which exposed steel framing was combined with brick and glass infill. This building system derived in its turn from traditional, timber-framed *Fachwerkbauten,* and by the second half of the nineteenth century this modified "steel frame" vernacular was already a common model for inexpensive factory sheds, to which countless industrial buildings erected throughout Europe adequately testify.[30] Despite this vernacular presence, Mies's Reichsbank, like his initial scheme for the Illinois Institute of Technology of 1939, features a continuous curtain wall rather than a frame and infill system, and it is this sense of dematerialized continuity that will be decisive in the formation of his American career.

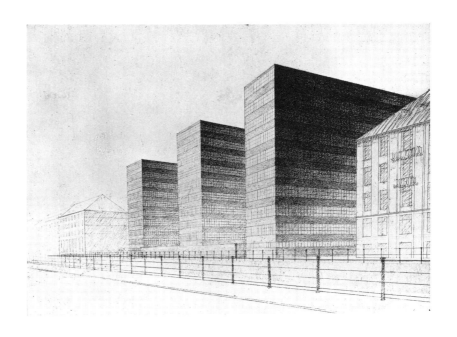

6.37
Mies van der Rohe, Reichsbank, Berlin, 1933.
The Reichsbank as *Fachbauwerk*.

6.38
Mies van der Rohe, Promontory Apartments,
Chicago, 1949.

6.39
Mies van der Rohe, Promontory Apartments,
partial section and plan. Note the articulation
of the reinforced concrete structure both in
plan and in section.

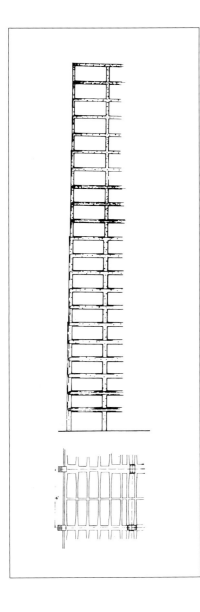

Despite their varying status, the very first building projected for the IIT campus, the Minerals and Metals Research Building of 1943, should be construed as an example of *Baukunst* rather than *Architektur,* and a similar objective restraint can be sensed in the Promontory Apartments built in Chicago between 1946 and 1949 (figs. 6.38, 6.39). The stepped rectangular reinforced concrete column employed in this last—the cross section of which diminishes as it rises due to a reduction in compressive load—may be regarded as a structurally rationalist element. A similar feature will be deployed by Mies in his IIT faculty apartments of 1951 (fig. 6.40), and a comparable level of constructional directness, indicative again of building rather than architecture, will appear in the infill panels of the Promontory Apartments (figs. 6.41, 6.42). An even more laconic version of the same infill comprising brick spandrels and standard steel sash will govern the character of the IIT apartments.

While the Resor House projected for Wyoming in 1938 still employs the cruciform column, Mies will shortly abandon this element, along with the free plan. From now on, the tectonic focus shifts to the exposed steel frame with brick and glass infill. No one has written more cogently of the spatial consequences of this tectonic metamorphosis than Colin Rowe.

Mies's characteristic German column was circular or cruciform; but his new column became H-shaped, became that I-beam which is now almost a personal signature. Typically, his German column had been clearly distinguished from walls and windows, isolated from them in space; and typically, his new column became an element integral with the envelope of the building where it came to function as a kind of mullion or residue of wall. Thus the column section was not without some drastic effects on the entire space of the building. The circular or cruciform section had tended to push partitions away from the column. The new tectonic tended to drag them towards it. The old column had offered a minimum of obstruction to a horizontal movement of space; but the new column presents a distinctly more substantial stop. The old column had tended to cause space to gyrate around it, had been central to a rather tentatively defined volume; but the new column instead acts as the enclosure or the external definition of a major volume of space. The spatial functions of the two are thus completely differentiated. . . . As an International Style element, the column put in its last appearance in the museum project of 1942; while in the Library and Administration Building project of 1944, the effects of the H-shaped column are already apparent and are clearly exhibited in the published drawings of its plans. From these drawings it is evident that the column is no longer to be allowed to float ambiguously beneath a slab. It is now—apparently for the first time—tied to a network of beams, and these beams have appointed definite positions for the screens, and for the most part the screens have already leapt into these positions—in fact only the extra-thick walls around the lavatories seem to have been able to resist the new attraction.[31]

As Rowe indicates, this change is of an epistemic nature, not only because the integration of frame and partition transforms the character of the space, but also because the revelation of the joint between column and beam represents a shift back toward the tectonic tradition, first manifest at IIT in the Minerals and Metals Building. Mies's general focus now begins to shift away from universal modernist space to the primacy of the frame and its joint. This change is fundamental, for it means that the opposition between modernity and tradition will

189

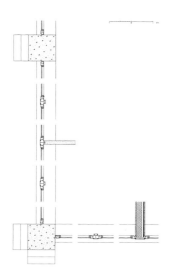

now no longer be mediated by an elision between columnar support and the system of spatial enclosure. At the same time, the suspended ceiling will be retained as a normative element, irrespective of the program, dispersing the tectonic energy of Mies's later work toward the perimeter of the space. The moment of this transition is already evident in the earliest buildings for the IIT campus, where the steel frame was only partially fireproofed, as in the project for the Library and Administration Building (figs. 6.43, 6.44) and in the Minerals and Metals Research Building (fig. 6.45). In the library project an exposed H-section is the main tectonic element (fig. 6.46), while in the research building an elongated version of an H-section appears at the reentrant corner columns. This is complemented by a normative composite column comprising two reversed channel sections, welded together to form a square box. This box column is set flush with the fair-faced infill brickwork on both sides (fig. 6.47). In each case, we are justified in speaking of a tectonic that is partially ontological and partially representational, although in the Minerals and Metals Building the deep steel sections facing the concrete downstand beams, as permanent formwork, are evidently a representation of the fireproofed steelwork within the concrete (fig. 6.48). In the library, the steel roof beams are shown partially concealed by a suspended ceiling (fig. 6.43). This "cutaway" solution was adopted in order to facilitate the servicing of the interstitial space while revealing the tectonic probity of the structural frame.[32] This expression is in strong contrast to the Minerals and Metals Building, where the steel roof beams are directly expressed on the interior. This difference in attitude toward the ceiling may perhaps be explained by the differ-

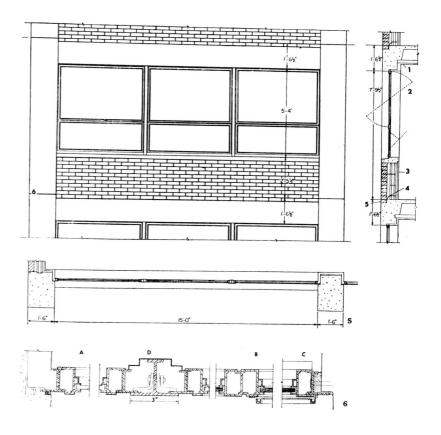

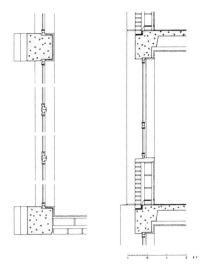

6.40
Mies van der Rohe, Carman Hall, Illinois Institute of Technology, Chicago, 1953. Horizontal detail, showing decreasing column section.

6.41
Mies van der Rohe, Promontory Apartments, plan, section, elevation, and detail of brick and aluminum window infill.

6.42
Mies van der Rohe, Promontory Apartments, plan and section of infill, showing decreasing column section.

ent status of the works involved; for where in the first instance the building is a public institution, in the second it merely accommodates a utilitarian volume.

With the IIT Alumni Memorial Hall of 1945, Mies's expression becomes more monumental, in part because the steel frame had to be fireproofed throughout and in part because this was the most honorific building erected on the campus to date. Here, the primary tectonic elements break down into the *Kuntsform* of the representative steel profiles and the *Kernform* of the fireproofed steel within (fig. 6.49). The H-columns, encased in square concrete piers, are now set behind the skin, thereby permitting a more symmetrical treatment of the reentrant corners. These corners were compounded in part out of steel facing and angles, representing the column, and in part out of I-sections that formed the receiving frame for the 9-inch-brick solid infill walls spanning between the uprights of the framework. This corner treatment recalls the neoclassical corner favored by Schinkel, particularly in his Altes Museum and Schauspielhaus.

Three works projected in the mid-forties are seminal to Mies's subsequent career. These are the Farnsworth House, initially designed in 1946, the unrealized Hi-Way Restaurant of the same year, and the twin apartment towers known as 860 Lake Shore Drive, Chicago, designed in 1948.

The Farnsworth House returns us to the avant-gardist spatial paradigm but now in the form of a virtual volume suspended between the pure planar surfaces of a floor and a ceiling (figs. 6.50, 6.51). Where on the one hand Farnsworth asserts itself as a skeleton frame, on the other it amounts to an asymmetrical assembly comprising a prism and a platform, the one sliding past the other in a manner that is reminiscent of Schinkel's Italianate compositions. To some extent this house may be analyzed in terms of Semper's *Four Elements,* particularly with regard to its separation into stereotomic and tectonic elements; the former being embodied in the travertine paving of the twin platforms, while the latter assumed the form of the steel skeleton and its infill. The structural details are reduced to a minimal expression, from the open-jointed paving, laid absolutely flat, on top of the gravel-filled drain pans made of welded steel, to the eight face-mounted, full-height H-section columns carrying the steel-framed floor and roof (figs. 6.52, 6.53). The architectonic purity of this welded steel frame is heightened by grinding the welds flat and by finishing the steel in white paint. Here, once again, we seem to encounter a passing reference to Malevich's famous white-on-white paintings of the period 1917–1920. At the same time, the elision between the terrace and the house is reinforced by an overlap between the eight full-height columns of the house and the four stub columns of the terrace.

From a tectonic standpoint, there is an affinity between 860 Lake Shore Drive (1948–1951) (fig. 6.54) and the IIT Alumni Memorial Hall. In both instances, the steel frame is totally fireproofed in concrete and the columns and beams are represented by plated steel surfaces implanted on the outside of the fireproofed structure (fig. 6.55). In 860 the secondary framing system of the mullions, carrying the fenestration, is mounted on these steel plates, thereby rendering the overall assembly as a continuous curtain wall (fig. 6.56). It is important to note that the assembly of this wall depended upon the welding of these mullions, together with the steel spandrels and column plates, into a continuous floor-height frame, and on the lowering of this prefabricated bay into its final position from a

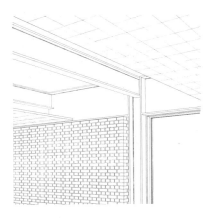

6.43
Mies van der Rohe, Library and Administration Building, Illinois Institute of Technology, Chicago, 1944.

6.44
Mies van der Rohe, Library and Administration Building, corner detail.

tower crane mounted on the roof. The syncopated rhythms obtaining between the structural frame, the mullions, the face plates, and the glazing has been perceptively analyzed by Peter Carter in the following terms:

Mies's introduction of projecting steel mullions at the quarter points of each bay and on the column surfaces engenders a new and unexpected quality from the separate identities of the elements involved. The structural frame and its glass infill become architecturally fused, each losing a part of its particular identity in establishing the new architectural reality. The mullion has acted as a kind of catalyst for this change.

The columns and mullions determine window width. The two central windows are, therefore, wider than those adjacent to the column. These variants produce visual cadences of expanding and contracting intervals: column—narrow window—wide window, *then reversing,* wide window—narrow window—column, *and so on, of an extraordinarily subtle richness. And to this is added the alternating opacity of the steel and reflectivity of the glass caused by the blinker quality of the mullions en masse. . . . Before Mies's "860" solution, there were two clear basic possibilities for the enclosure of skeleton frame buildings. Either the skin acted as an infill between the structure or hung in front of it. . . . While acceptable on their own pragmatic terms, these solutions have, with the exception of the Seagram Building, rarely been touched by the magic of great architecture. At*

6.45
Mies van der Rohe, Minerals and Metals Research Building, Illinois Institute of Technology, Chicago, 1943. Laboratory.

6.46
Mies van der Rohe, Library and Administration Building, vertical and horizontal details.

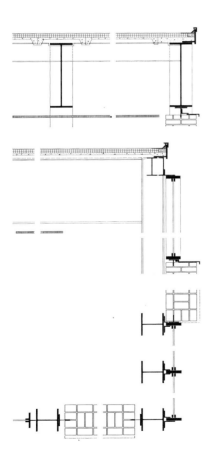

"860" the solution has come directly out of the problem of finding a single architectural expression which would embrace both skin and structure. At "860" the structure and the skin retain much of their individual identities but the application of the mullion has caused a philosophical transformation from pluralistic to a monotheistic character.[33]

Mies's neo-Suprematist sensibility assumes a perceptually dynamic character in the foreshortening of the mullioned facades of 860 Lake Shore Drive, where the mutual positioning of the two slabs is such as to engender a constantly changing three-quarters view of either the one or the other facade (fig. 6.57). As one moves around this rotational composition, the projecting mullions either open out to reveal the full extent of the infill glazing or close up to present the illusion of being a twenty-six-story relief construction in opaque steel. Viewed from a distance, the building appears as an assembly of virtual volumes and planes in space, whereas when approached frontally each slab and structural bay assumes the format of a symmetrical composition.

This generic curtain wall changes markedly in its tectonic attributes as Mies passes from one high rise building to the next. No two treatments are perhaps more contrasting in this regard than 860 Lake Shore Drive and the Seagram Building. In 860, the concrete fireproofed structural floors and columns are covered in steel plates onto which the mullions are face-welded, whereas in the Seagram the fireproofed frame is set back from the curtain wall, with the result that the floors are suppressed behind a continuous skin of brown-tinted glass, with the mullions running uninterruptedly across glazed spandrel panels (fig. 6.58). Equally hybrid, given the perceptual fusion of bronze anodized fenestration with brown glass, are the reentrant corners of the service shaft to the rear of the Seagram Building, where very dark green marble sheeting is used to give the im-

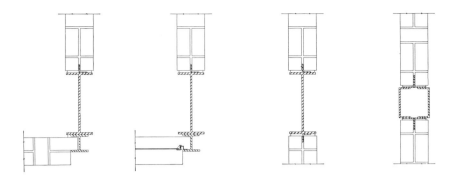

6.47
Mies van der Rohe, Minerals and Metals Research Building, horizontal details.

6.48
Mies van der Rohe, Minerals and Metals Research Building, vertical exterior details.

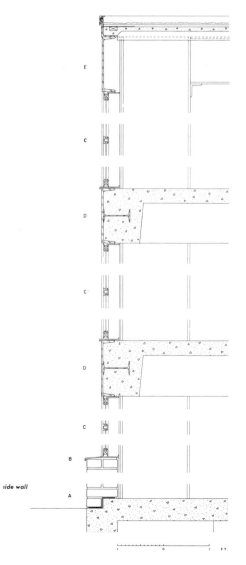

pression of a vertically striated, monolithic metal box. From this point of view we may claim that Seagram is the more membranous of the two works, substituting the steel-plated representation of the structural frame in 860 Lake Shore Drive with a plate glass curtain wall that does no more than represent its own tectonic autonomy.

The unrealized Hi-Way drive-in restaurant, designed for Joseph Cantor of Indianapolis in 1946, introduces the long-span trussed structure that Mies will explore, in various ways, during the remainder of his career. The roof of the Hi-Way Restaurant was to have been hung from the underside of two exposed lattice trusses, each spanning 150 feet. This format appears in two subsequent works, first in the Mannheim Theater proposal of 1952 (figs. 6.59, 6.60) and then in Crown Hall, built at IIT in 1956 (fig. 6.61). In the first instance, 15-foot-deep exposed lattice trusses are projected across 266 feet, while in the second, two-foot-deep stiffened steel beams span 150 feet. Within the glass cage of the former, Mies intended to suspend two theaters, set back to back and surrounded by a continuous foyer. Of these three works, Crown Hall is perhaps the most canonical, not only because it was the only one to be realized, but also because it combined the sectional schema of the Farnsworth House with the mullion-framing system of 860 Lake Shore Drive (figs. 6.62, 6.63). At the same time, in being analogously structured about a *corps de logis,* Crown Hall makes a distant allusion to Schinkel's Altes Museum, however much this axial order is mediated by the general diffusion of space throughout its interior. As Colin Rowe has written:

Like the characteristic Palladian composition, Crown Hall is a symmetrical and, probably, a mathematically regulated volume. But, unlike the characteristic Palladian composition, it is not an hierarchically ordered organization which projects its centralized theme vertically in the form of a pyramidal roof or dome. Unlike the Villa Rotonda, but like so many of the compositions of the twenties, Crown Hall is provided with no effective central area within which the observer can stand and comprehend the whole. The observer may understand a good deal of the interior while he is external to it (although even this Mies is disposed to disallow by planting a screen of trees across the front); but, once inside, rather than any spatial climax, the building offers a central solid, not energetically stated it is true, but still an insulated core around which the space travels laterally with the enclosing windows. Also, the flat slab of the roof induces a certain outward pull; and for this reason, in spite of the centralizing activity of the entrance vestibule, the space still remains, though in very much simplified form, the rotary peripheric organization of the twenties, rather than the predominantly centralized composition of the true Palladian or classical plan.[34]

The other long-span type favored by Mies comprised a two-way, space frame roof carried on perimeter point supports, set in from the corners. This type was first broached in his Fifty by Fifty House, projected in 1950, the name deriving from the fact that the house was roofed by a 50-by-50-foot space frame carried on four central columns, each being set at the midpoint of one side (figs. 6.64, 6.65). Mies was to project a similar cantilevered space frame roof on four subsequent occasions. The first of these was his 1953 project for a convention hall for Chicago, accommodating 79,000 people and measuring 720 feet along each of its sides. There followed three more modest variations on the same theme: the Bacardi Office Building, Santiago, Cuba, of 1957 (figs. 6.66, 6.67), the Georg Schäfer Museum proposal of 1960, and finally, the Neue Nationalgalerie in Berlin dating from 1962.

Like Viollet-le-Duc, Mies saw the "great space" as the ultimate proof of the stature of a civilization; a proof that in this century was more likely to be found in civil engineering than in architecture. Two projects from Mies's American career testify to the symbolic import that he would attach to the achievement of such a span and volume, and it is significant that he would employ the ultramodernist technique of photomontage in the representation of both of them. While the first of these is a project for an auditorium dating from 1942 (fig. 6.68), the second is

6.49
Mies van der Rohe, Alumni Memorial Hall, Illinois Institute of Technology, Chicago, 1945. Horizontal and vertical details.

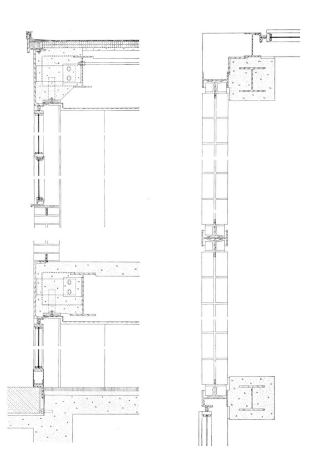

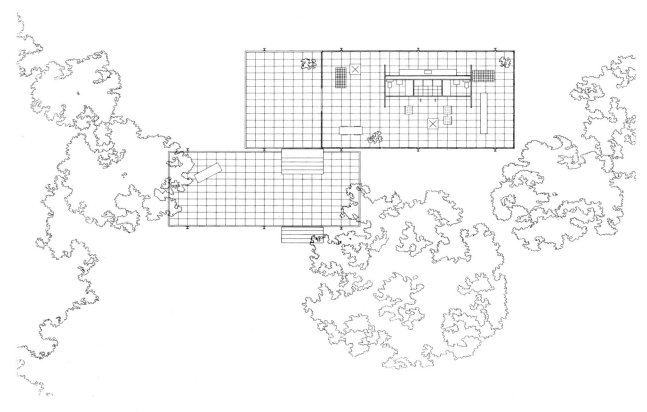

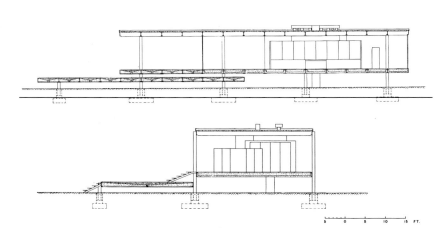

6.50
Mies van der Rohe, Farnsworth House, Plano,
Illinois, 1950. Plan.

6.51
Mies van der Rohe, Farnsworth House, longitudinal and transverse sections.

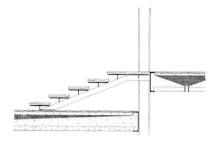

6.52
Mies van der Rohe, Farnsworth House, exterior stair detail.

6.53
Mies van der Rohe, Farnsworth House, exterior horizontal details.

the convention hall projected for Chicago in 1953 (figs. 6.69, 6.70). Where the former is rendered as a wood veneer and metal collage laid over a photograph of one of Albert Kahn's aircraft factories, the latter uses marbled paper to represent the stone-clad walls of a vast column-free hall. The structural roof of this 720-foot-square, steel space frame was projected as 30 feet deep, while the overall height of the structure would have risen to 110 feet. The sides of the hall would have been carried on two 60-foot corner cantilevers and five 120-foot-wide structural bays. The roof was projected as resting on lattice supports that in their turn took their bearing off hinge joints mounted on stub columns (fig. 6.71).

The last realized work of his life, the Neue Nationalgalerie in Berlin (fig. 6.72), was a homecoming for Mies in more ways than one, since in this final work he was able to reconcile the conflicting poles about which his work had been divided: namely, the infinite continuum of avant-gardist space and the constructional logic of tectonic form. These values were never more at variance with each other than in the main volume of Crown Hall, where the uninterrupted ceiling plane obscures the tectonic articulation of the peripheral structure. Despite their precise termination in a steel cornice that caps the roof line, the mullions at Crown Hall, when seen from the inside, appear to be totally unintegrated, since they extend beyond the suspended ceiling into a slot running around the perimeter of the loft space (fig. 6.73).

This aporia of the suspended ceiling, which occurs in various forms throughout Mies's late career, first approaches resolution in the concrete space frame of the Bacardi Building, which he projected in 1957. The ceiling plane is now the lower chord of a space frame supported on eight columns set in from the corners of a square plan (see fig. 6.66). This paradigm, translated into steel for the Georg Schäfer Museum, will become the parti for the square pavilion of the Neue Nationalgalerie. Although the space frame appears here as an infinite plane in space, it nonetheless establishes its tectonic presence through the intersecting grid of its rolled-steel chords (fig. 6.74). This egg crate grid, divided into sixteen square modules in both directions, receives columnar support four modules in from its extremities, on each of its sides. Furthermore, the chords of the space frame are spaced so as to coincide with the column heads of the eight supports.

With this reinterpretation of the Suprematist space field as a space frame structure carried on cruciform supports, Mies returns to the neoclassical resonance that is detectable throughout his work, even in his freely planned houses of the

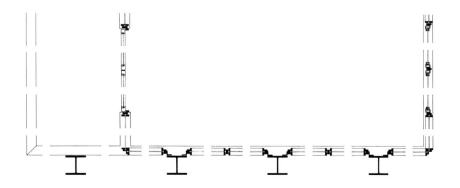

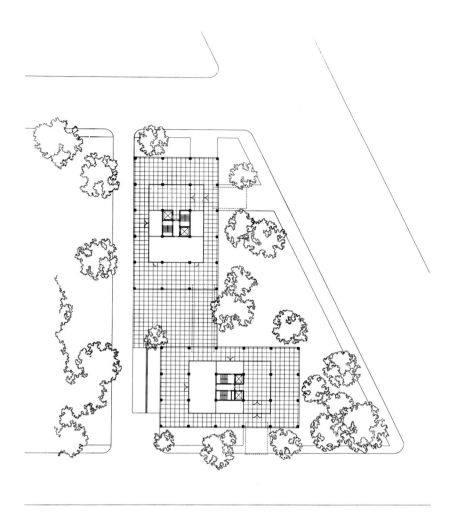

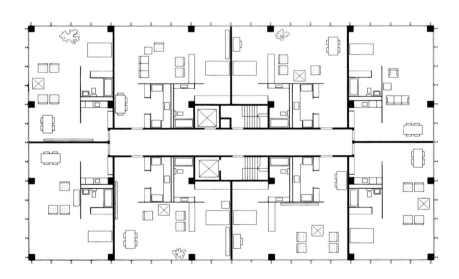

6.54
Mies van der Rohe, 860 and 880 Lake Shore
Drive Apartments, Chicago, 1951. Typical
floor plan as proposed by Mies; site plan.

6.55
Mies van der Rohe, 860 and 880 Lake Shore
Drive Apartments, vertical details.

6.56
Mies van der Rohe, 860 and 880 Lake Shore
Drive Apartments, horizontal details.

thirties. While these welded steel cruciforms, like their freestanding predecessors, serve as metaphors for the classical order of the antique world, they are, at the same time, removed both from classical precedent and from the dematerialized chromium plate supports of Mies's middle period. For now, the chromium-plated allusion to classical fluting has been replaced by the four T-sections welded into a cruciform about a central point (fig. 6.75). Thus the column of the Neue Nationalgalerie is capable of asserting its own structural and mythical character within the context of structural rationalism. In this instance its ontological authority is reinforced by the hinged column head, which, as a metaphorical capital, inverts the position and significance of the steel hinged joint as this had appeared in Peter Behrens's turbine factory of 1909. The hinge now appears as part of a surrogate entablature rather than the echinus of a stylobate. In their mode of support, the column and its hinge reinterpret the tectonic tradition of the Occident, while the egg crate roof, painted dark gray bordering on matte black, depends for its reading on the play of planes, situated at different spatial depths, so that the intersecting lower flanges of the space frame seem to hover as a slightly lighter grid below the dark inner soffit of the roof. Here Mies's black-on-black aesthetic, recalling Ad Reinhardt's minimalism,[35] becomes legible through the play of reflected light. By virtue of variations in luminosity it alludes through the uncertain depth of the space frame to the tradition of the avant-garde, and thus we pass in his last work from a highly accomplished tectonic solution to an intangible, almost mystical assertion of the sublime in the form of a universal plane suspended in space.

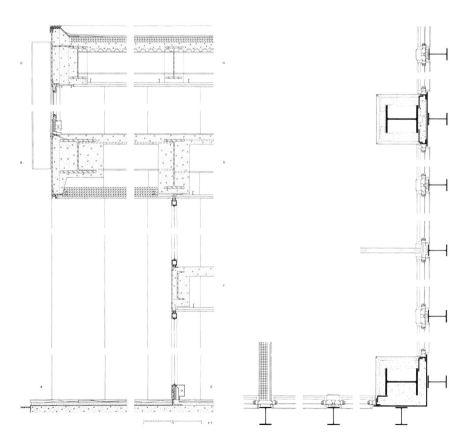

6.57
Mies van der Rohe, 860 and 880 Lake Shore
Drive Apartments.

6.58
Mies van der Rohe, 860 and 880 Lake Shore
Drive Apartments and Seagram Building, New
York, 1958: curtain wall details.

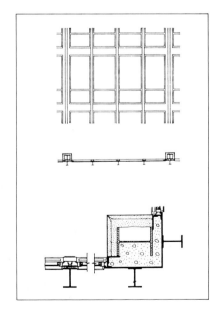

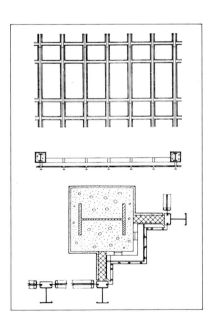

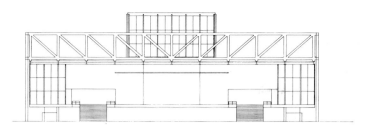

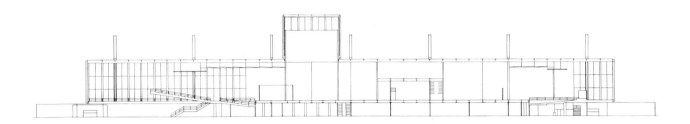

6.59
Mies van der Rohe, National Theater, Mannheim, 1952. Section.

6.60
Mies van der Rohe, National Theater, Mannheim, transverse section.

6.61
Mies van der Rohe, Crown Hall, Illinois Institute of Technology, 1956. Elevation and plan.

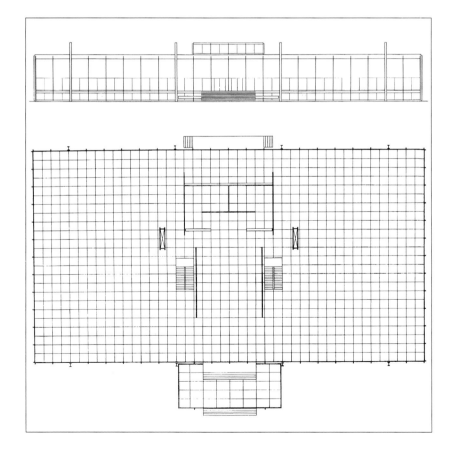

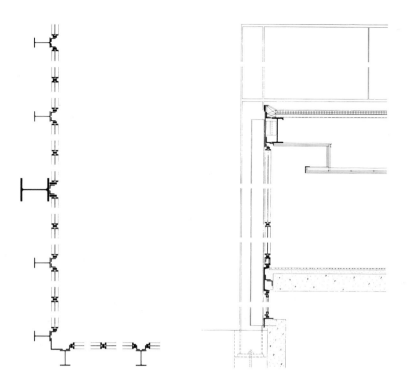

6.62
Mies van der Rohe, Crown Hall, horizontal details.

6.63
Mies van der Rohe, Crown Hall, vertical details.

From the Barcelona Pavilion onward, the picturesque placement of sculpture in Mies's work invites analysis, particularly in the light of the role played by elementarist avant-gardist art in the formation of his spatial ideas. This combination of classical sculpture with universal planar space draws one's attention to the complementary roles played by figurative and abstract elements in Mies's work. As far as the figurative is concerned, Mies's view was conservative from the beginning, and his taste in sculpture, while touched by Expressionism, was not far removed from the romantic classical ethos that informed the close collaboration of Schinkel with his sculptor Gottfried Schadow. While Mies's favorite contemporary sculptor was Lehmbruck (the Georg Kolbe figure in Barcelona being a last-minute substitution), the figurative for Mies invariably entailed some allusion to Greece. His habit of populating his architectural renderings with sculptural figures rather than people inadvertently evokes the didactic role assumed by the figure in the perspectives of Schinkel. The reified human figure, as sculpture, is clearly intended in Mies's collages to animate and humanize the otherwise silent planar extensions of his abstract space (fig. 6.76). As far as abstract art is concerned, he seems to have countenanced two different attitudes toward its cryptic expressivity. The first of these finds reflection in his personal collection of paintings by Paul Klee, for here he seems to have favored hieroglyphic, hermetic pieces that could be adapted to his architectural vision of free-floating planes in space; that is to say, they could be made to double as symbolic surfaces to be read against other, more material freestanding space dividers. The second attitude, deriving directly from abstract art at its most ethereal, is surely neo-Suprematist, in that Mies seems to have favored the dematerialization of the picture plane and the diffusion of any vestigial figuration into the dynamics of avant-gardist space. Hence, perhaps, the highly diffused

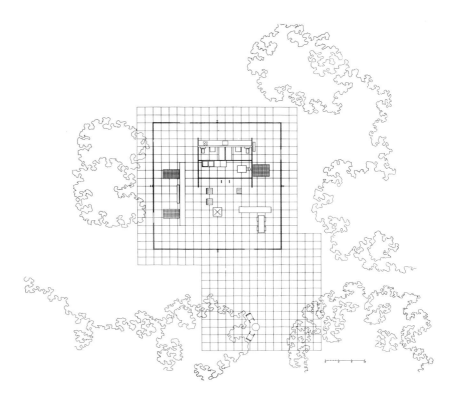

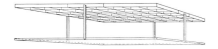

6.64
Mies van der Rohe, Fifty by Fifty House, project, 1950. Plan.

6.65
Mies van der Rohe, Fifty by Fifty House, axonometric.

character of the human figure in his perspectives. We may perhaps relate this last, however coincidentally, to Giorgio Grassi's strictures as to the role to be played by abstract figuration in the constitution of architectural form. As we have seen, Mies's version of the Suprematist sensibility comes close at times to the transrational mysticism of Kazimir Malevich's nonobjective world. All in all, Mies's *beinahe nichts* or "almost nothing" seems, in retrospect, to have been a fusion of two equally ineffable visions: the misty light of Caspar David Friedrich's landscapes and the ethereal expanse of Malevich's "environment reality stimulating to a Suprematist."[36] The way in which this synthetic vision was to qualify Mies's reinterpretation of the *Schinkelschule* tradition is perhaps most evident in the chromium-plated columns of his freely planned houses. A more condensed metaphor in the history of modern culture would be hard to find, since these columns evidently reduced into a single tectonic icon a wide range of cultural allusions. This preoccupation with dematerialization runs throughout Mies's career, as though modern machine tool production, with its value-free objectivity, was the last demiurge of the sublime. The Nordic origin of this obsession was never more touchingly evoked than when Mies remarked toward the end of his life: "I remember the first time I ever went to Italy. The sun and the blue skies were so bright, I thought I'd go crazy! I couldn't wait to go back to the north, where everything was gray and subtle."[37]

Mies's work always involved a reintegration of countermanding principles in both an ideological and a phenomenological sense. The model for such a synthesis was Schinkel, inasmuch as Schinkel strove in all of his buildings to combine rationalistic order with the *poesis* of construction and to bring these two together in the service of a mythically didactic urbanism. This romantic synthe-

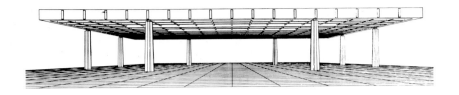

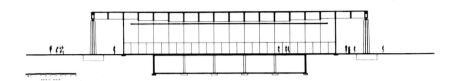

6.66
Mies van der Rohe, Bacardi Office Building, Santiago de Cuba, 1957. Note how the concrete space frame structure progressively increases in depth from the perimeter cornice as it moves to the center of the long span.

6.67
Mies van der Rohe, Bacardi Office Building, section.

6.68
Mies van der Rohe, Concert Hall, project, 1942. A collage made over a photo of the interior of Albert Kahn's Glen L. Martin factory, Baltimore.

sis was facilitated by the precise articulation of the components out of which his work was made. A similar elementarism is detectable in the work of Mies, and he was to acknowledge his debt to Schinkel in this regard when he remarked in 1959: "In the Altes Museum he [Schinkel] *separated* the elements, the columns and the walls and the ceiling, and I think that this is still visible in my later buildings."[38] This principle of *separation* seems to have enabled Mies to articulate quite different components whose conjunction would otherwise have been impacted.

With the exception of his furniture and his large-span structures, Mies tended to underemphasize the connectivity of the joint and its fabrication; a technical silence that attains its apotheosis perhaps in the flat welds of the Farnsworth House. Thus despite his appreciation of Viollet-le-Duc, Mies did not fully embrace the structurally rationalist principle of revealing the transmission of load or the Kahnian penchant for maintaining the marks of the assembly process as a form of ornament. Hence his recourse to welded steelwork in order to render the junctions as invisible as possible, and hence, also, the "separating" role played by his suspended ceilings that were an anathema to architects of a more structurally rationalist persuasion, such as Perret, Kahn, and Utzon.

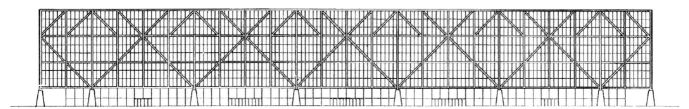

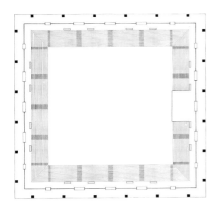

6.69
Mies van der Rohe, Convention Hall, project,
Chicago, 1953. Elevation and plan.

6.70
Mies van der Rohe, Convention Hall project,
interior perspective.

6.71
Mies van der Rohe, Convention Hall project:
alternate structural systems with concrete
(left) and steel (right) piers.

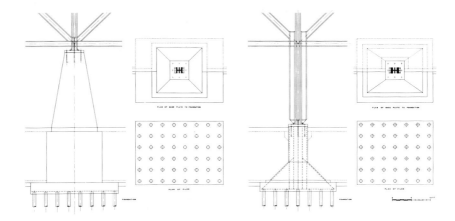

Mies attempted to express the technoscientific civilization of his time as a fac-
tual given, as though this "almost nothing" was the only authentic form that civilization could now attain. In assuming this Hegelian stance he came to regard
modern technology as the manifestation of transcendental reason, comparable
in its objectivity to the anonymity of building culture in the Middle Ages. And
while tectonic value is constantly evident in his work, this is displaced at times
by an autonomous drive toward dematerialization that is at variance with his

6.72
Mies van der Rohe, Neue Nationalgalerie, Berlin, 1968. Elevation and plan.

6.73
Mies van der Rohe, Neue Nationalgalerie, interior.

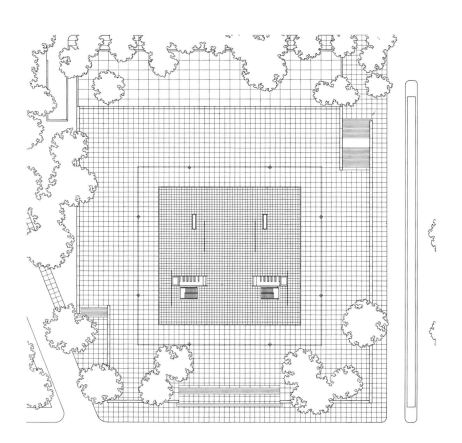

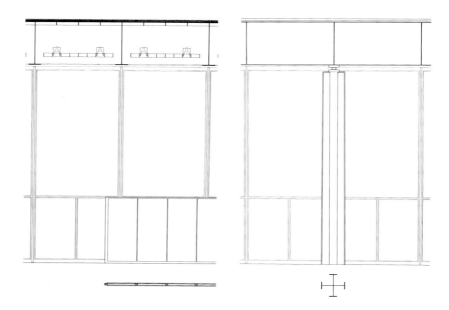

6.74
Mies van der Rohe, Neue Nationalgalerie, typical section.

6.75
Mies van der Rohe, Neue Nationalgalerie, column elevation and plan.

6.76
Mies van der Rohe, Museum for a Small City, project, 1943.

concern for cultural continuity and the permanence of material. The continuous travertine floor in the Farnsworth House is a case in point, for while it covers the entire floor, including the bathroom, it is countered in its materiality by the abstract immateriality of the suspended ceiling. At the same time Mies, like Louis Kahn, was drawn to the sublime, not only in terms of light and space but also in a temporal sense, so that, after the *Schinkelschule* by which he was influenced, his works aspired to a state of eventual ruination. This romantic prospect already finds reflection in the habitual planting of ivy against the pristine elevations of his buildings. Thus his concern for the precision of tectonic form was always tempered, not only by the infinite space field of the avant-garde and the dematerialized membrane but also by the ever-changing fateful forces of technology and time. By accepting the triumph of universal technology and by concentrating as a result on the "how" of technique rather than the "what" of institutional form, Mies strove to liberate the subject from the pathos of its insignificance when set against the flood tide of modernization. Like others of his generation, like Max Weber, Ernst Jünger, and Martin Heidegger and above all like the church architect Rudolf Schwarz, by whom he was directly influenced, Mies recognized modern technology as a dichotomous destiny that was at once both destroyer and provider. He saw it as the apocalyptic demiurge of the new era and as the inescapable matrix of the modern world. It was this that prompted him to shift the focus of architecture toward technique and away from type and space form, always assuming that the latter would be spontaneously fulfilled, either through the limitless freedom of the open plan or through the changing subdivision of cellular space. Within these parameters, the art of building for Mies meant the embodiment of the spirit in the banality of the real; the spiritualization of technique through tectonic form.

7 Louis Kahn:
Modernization and the New Monumentality,
1944–1972

In reality the arches, squares, cylinders, skylights, exedrae and symmetrical axes which spring from this architecture in ever richer and more complex ways, give rise, once they are realized, to fragile and powerful simulacra of the discontinuous and the non-homogeneous, of what is ours and at the same time what is not. The clean-cut surfaces of the walls are slim diaphragms, the flexible and unconventional use of which creates a continuous interplay of light and shade,—highly refined and complex filters of the energy field of light; but the light relayed from these surfaces is an unreal light, une lumière 'autre'. The more intelligent and pertinent the use of Design and appropriate the choice of materials, perfect the technique of execution and detail, meticulous the expression of all the static forces involved, the more the measurable enters the realm of the immeasurable, and from what is physically and tangibly present, from surfaces, cracks, holes, and pools of light, it blows like a metaphysical, weightless breeze—without the weight of earthly gravity I mean, but in return, laden with allusions to mnemonic depth and dimension and to everything that this architecture, in its fragile, contingent, physical and almost miraculous equilibrium "is not". . . . In this sense, and almost reversing the terms of the problem, Kahn's architecture recovers the sense of history and re-proposes the basic theme of Sullivan's aesthetics: that of the impact and weight of the language, of its dangerous and inescapable semantic burden, with which all creative projects must struggle. But in Sullivan, who had also been strongly attracted towards what "is not" the sense of history and the surrender to the infinite represented only a necessary counterweight, an alternate phase of what "is" and what comes to light; just as the seed must lie in the darkness of the earth before it flowers and vegetates, so the artist must plunge into the depths of life and language before creating something new. . . . But in Kahn, the finite-infinite dichotomy has another meaning which in no way implicates Sullivan's vital dynamism towards a formal-formative end. He, on the contrary, proposes modern cognitive space, in which (after filtering through European rationalism) the subjective and individual can be realized only by limiting, denying, decentralizing itself; but in which, on the other hand, the assumption of subjective finitude with its incessant self questioning as to the myth of the Beginning, in a vital and problematic way brings up for examination once more the synchronous and logical classifications of rationalism, pointing from behind its fragile, immobile, and provisional screen, at the dark and blind forces of change in progress and the inevitable erosion of time.
Maria Bottero, "Organic and Rational Morphology in Louis Kahn," 1967

Modernization and monumentality may be seen as the dialogical theme running throughout the later career of Louis Kahn (1901–1974); the former being the singular processal character of the modern world with which he will struggle throughout his life, the latter being the institutional referent that will form the fundamental focus of his architectural system. Kahn's unique contribution in this regard stems from his conviction that tectonic structure, rather than mass form or type, must be pursued as the first condition of monumental form. To predicate the monument on architectonic expressivity was to take an entirely different approach from the sociopolitical attitude assumed by Sigfried Giedion, José Luis Sert, and Fernand Léger in their seminal and highly influential *Nine Points on Monumentality*, written in America in 1943.[1] Shortly after this revisionist manifesto was first issued, the idea of a new monumentality was generally in the air, and within a year a symposium largely devoted to this theme was staged by Paul Zucker at Columbia University under the somewhat misleading title "The New Architecture and City Planning."[2] Kahn's contribution to this symposium was to establish the basic thematic of his work. It was also one of the most revealing statements he ever made with regard to his conception of monumental form. Kahn approached the issue of monumentality in an unusual way, emphasizing the character of the tectonic element above all other considerations.

Neither the finest material nor the most advanced technology need enter a work of monumental character for the same reason that the finest ink was not required to draw up the Magna-Carta. . . . In Greek architecture engineering concerned itself fundamentally with materials in compression. Each stone or part forming the structural members was made to bear with accuracy on each other to avoid the tensile action which stone is incapable of enduring. The great cathedral builders regarded the members of the structural skeleton with the same love of perfection and search for clarity of purpose. Out of periods of inexperience and fear when they erected over-massive, core-filled veneered walls, grew a courageous theory of a stone over stone vault skeleton producing a downward and outward thrust, which forces were conducted to a column or a wall provided with the added characteristic of the buttress. . . . The buttress allowed lighter walls between the thrust points and these curtain walls were logically developed for the use of large glass windows. This structural concept, derived from earlier and cruder theories, gave birth to magnificent variations in the attempts to attain loftier heights and greater spans creating a spiritually emotional environment unsurpassed.

The influence of the Roman vault, the dome, the arch, has etched itself in deep furrows across the pages of architectural history. Through Romanesque, Gothic, Renaissance and today, its basic forms and structural ideas have been felt. They will continue to reappear but with added powers made possible by our technology and engineering skill.[3]

This passage is revealing, for reading between the lines, it is possible to discern not only the specific nature of Kahn's formation, as a student at the University of Pennsylvania under the Beaux-Arts tutelage of Paul Cret, but also the terms in which he was to conceive his own architectural agenda. It says something for his French education that his own point of departure was to recall the long debate surrounding the evolution of the Greco-Gothic idea. This may explain why he would adopt a totally different attitude toward the steel frame than that assumed by Mies van der Rohe, for where Mies readily accepted the rolled steel joist as the structural norm of twentieth-century architecture, Kahn began his thesis on monumentality with an elaborate critique of this universal building element.

The I-beam is an engineering accomplishment deriving its shape from an analysis of the stresses involved in its use. It is designed so that the greater proportion of the area of cross-section is concentrated as far as possible from the center of gravity. The shape adapted itself to ease of rolling and under test it was found that even the fillets, an aid in the rolling process, helped convey the stresses from one section to another in continuity. Safety factors were adopted to cover possible inconsistencies in the composition of the material of manufacture. Large scale machinery and equipment needed in its fabrication lead to standardization.

The combination of safety factors (ignorance factor as one engineer termed it) and standardization narrowed the practice of engineering to the selection of members from handbooks, recommending sections much heavier than calculations would require and further limited the field of engineering expression stifling the creation of the more graceful forms which the stress diagrams indicated.[4]

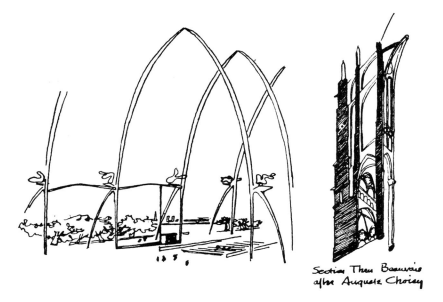

Section Thru Beauvais
after Auguste Choisy

7.1
Louis I. Kahn, esquisse for a modern cathedral in welded tubular steel, 1944. The accompanying section through Beauvais cathedral is taken from Auguste Choisy's *Histoire de l'architecture*.

Kahn would follow this critique of standard engineering practice with a rather general advocacy of welded tubular steel construction.

Joint construction in common practice treats every joint as a hinge which makes connections to columns and other members complex and ugly. To attain greater strength with economy, a finer expression in the structural solution of the principle of concentrating the area of cross-section away from the center of gravity is the tubular form, since the greater the moment of inertia, the greater the strength. A bar of a certain area of cross-section rolled into a tube of the same area of cross-section (consequently of a larger diameter) would possess a strength enormously greater than the bar.

The tubular member is not new, but its wide use has been retarded by technological limitations in the construction of joints. Up until very recently, welding has been outlawed by the building codes. In some cases, where it was permitted, it was required to make loading tests for every joint.[5]

The above passages surely testify to the underlying influence of Viollet-le-Duc; above all, the reference to oversectioned members that do not reflect the stress variations to which they are subject and the double allusion to both graceless joints and a failure to consider the frame as a total system. Kahn is critical of the inorganic trabeated rigidity of the standard steel frame and so favors the more organic, one may even say neo-Gothic, potential of welded tubular steel. Kahn was to clarify his position with a number of sketches that illustrate the essay. The first of these is an esquisse for a modern cathedral in welded tubular construction (fig. 7.1). This is directly related, as the drawing indicates, to Auguste Choisy's axonometric of the structure of Beauvais cathedral as this appears in his *Histoire de l'architecture* of 1899. Of this, Kahn wrote:

Beauvais cathedral needed the steel we have. It needed the knowledge we have. Glass would have revealed the sky and become a part of the enclosed space framed by an interplay of exposed tubular ribs, plates and columns of a stainless metal formed true and faired into a continuous flow of lines expressive of their stress patterns. Each member would have been welded to the next to create a

211

7.2
Robert Maillart, storage shed for S. A. Magazzini Generali, Chiasso, 1924. Section and partial elevation.

7.3
Louis I. Kahn, proposal for a welded tubular steel structure projected for Philadelphia, 1944.

continuous structural unity worthy of being exposed because its engineering gives no resistance to the laws of beauty having its own aesthetic life.[6]

The structural rationalist nature of this argument is self-evident, as is its relation to the production and statical limits of the materials involved. It is easy to see, for example, that Kahn's hopes for the future of welded tubular steel are not unlike those that he will later entertain toward reinforced concrete, and this, in turn, will be close to the attitude assumed by Auguste Perret with respect to the same material. It was patently evident to Kahn and Perret alike that reinforced concrete structural members could be easily modified in section in order to accommodate and reflect variations in stress. In this regard, the organic potential of the material had already been amply demonstrated by Eugène Freyssinet in his bowstring factory roofs and by Robert Maillart in the storage shed that he erected in Chiasso in 1924 (fig. 7.2).[7] One should also mention Pier Luigi Nervi in this connection, to whom Anne Tyng showed the City Tower project that she had designed with Kahn in 1953.[8]

That Kahn did not immediately fix on reinforced concrete as the material of the new monumentality testifies to Kahn's regard for the structural elegance of metal construction. He advocated welded tubular steel largely because of its lightweight modern industrial nature and the apparent ease with which it could be fabricated. In comparison to welded steel, reinforced concrete displayed a number of disadvantages. In the first place, there was the inelegance of having to build one structure in order to cast another; in the second, it possessed a tectonically ambiguous nature inasmuch as it was a "conglomerate": while it appeared to be compressive, it invariably concealed a tensile component. Welded tubular steel came close to Kahn's ideal building material, of which he spoke in later life to the effect that "I dream of space full of wonder. Spaces that rise and envelop flowingly without beginning, without end, of a jointless material white and gold. When I place the first line on paper to capture the dream, the dream becomes less (fig. 7.3).[9]

Although the oriental tone of this vision should not go unnoticed, it is clear that the paradigm evoked has much in common with the Gothic cathedral. The great

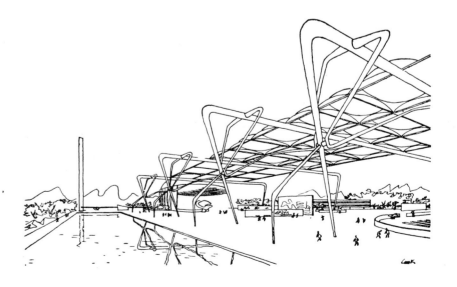

advantage of welded tubular steel lay in its potential for achieving an ontological tectonic comparable in its expressive substance to the self-evident continuity of Gothic stonework. What Kahn had in mind was the continuous flow of force that seemingly passes from vault to rib to pier in one and the same material. While this modulated continuity could be achieved in reinforced concrete, as Perret had already demonstrated, concrete lacked for Kahn the intrinsic lightness and clarity of welded tubular steel and was in this sense less modern. Furthermore, it could not be erected as a constructional continuity, since the process of construction did not allow its respective components, above all the steel rods, to *appear* in their final and appointed place.[10] The fact that it was a casting operation rather than an assembly made it categorically inimical to the precepts of structural rationalism.

The shortcomings of reinforced concrete from a tectonic standpoint had long been perceived by Viollet-le-Duc's prime pupil Anatole de Baudot, above all in his church St.-Jean de Montmartre, under construction in Paris from 1894 to 1904. As we have already seen, de Baudot, educated by both Henri Labrouste and Viollet-le-Duc, carried the legacy of structural rationalism into the twentieth century. St.-Jean de Montmartre (figs. 2.27, 2.28), completed when de Baudot was seventy, was the most significant work of his life. No two works, ostensibly both deriving from the precepts of Viollet-le-Duc, could be more opposed than Perret's 25 bis rue Franklin apartments and de Baudot's church in Montmartre. Where the one embraced the Hennebique system, the other categorically rejected it, not only because, unlike Gothic architecture, it failed to reveal the patterns of stress induced in its structural members, but also because it was incapable of generating an architectonic syntax arising out of the constructional process. As we have seen, it was for this reason that de Baudot's church was built out of a unique system of reinforced brick and concrete construction, developed in collaboration with the engineer Paul Cottancin and proposed under the name of *ciment armé,* in order to distinguish it from Hennebique's *béton armé.* To this end, de Baudot and Cottancin deployed cement-reinforced, perforated-brick arches, walls, and piers. These lean components were held in place by reinforcing wires that were painstakingly inserted into the perforated masonry; the interstices were thereafter charged with cement (fig. 7.4). Here Semper's textile revetment became transposed, as it were, into the substance of the building rather than its cladding. De Baudot employed a building system that resulted in a monolithic but articulate assembly, compounded of structurally taut and expressive elements comparable to those of Gothic architecture. These elements could be perceived as being determined to an equal degree by both gravity and the act of construction.

While Kahn never alluded to de Baudot, it is almost certain that he would have been aware of his work through his teacher, Paul Cret. Cret gave his own public assessment of de Baudot in his famous and influential essay "The Architect as Collaborator of the Engineer," published in 1927, three years after Kahn's graduation.[11] Although Cret takes pains in this essay to distance himself from de Baudot and to reassert the primacy of imitative form, structural rationalism nonetheless remained an important and seminal reference for him, and from this standpoint de Baudot may be adduced as a possible influence on Kahn. The case is further strengthened by the space-framed, vaulted roof structure in *ciment armé* that de Baudot projected during the last decade of his life. Kahn's tubular-steel-framed exhibition pavilion, with which he illustrated his 1944 essay on monumentality (fig. 7.3), is indicative of his structural naivete in that, unlike cast-iron tubing, it is impossible to extrude steel tubing with a continuously diminishing diameter. Nevertheless, the didactic intent of the proposal is obvious. The tapered components recall the tapered cast-iron members of Viollet-le-Duc's great hall featured in the *Entretiens,* where similar hypothetical variations in stress were to find reflection in the comparable varying diameter of the cast-iron tubular cross section.[12] Moreover, Kahn's account of space frame construction leaves one in no doubt as to his feeling for the difference between the *stereotomics* of the earthwork and the *tectonics* of the frame. More importantly, perhaps, this essay, dedicated to monumentality, concludes with an inventory of modern materials that reads, paradoxically enough, as though it had been compiled by a prewar functionalist.[13]

7.4
Anatole de Baudot, St.-Jean de Montmartre, Paris, 1894–1904. Construction details. This drawing shows the positioning of the reinforcing rods passing through the reinforced brickwork.

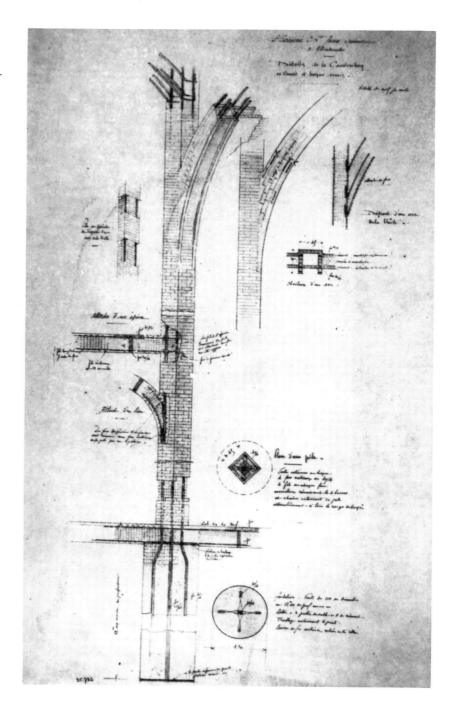

Steel, the lighter metals, concrete, glass, laminated woods, asbestos, rubber, and plastics, are emerging as the prime building materials of today. Riveting is being replaced by welding, reinforced concrete is emerging from infancy with pre-stressed reinforced concrete, vibration and controlled mixing, promising to aid in its ultimate refinement. Laminated wood is rapidly replacing lumber and is equally friendly to the eye, and plastics are so vast in their potentialities that already numerous journals and periodicals devoted solely to their many outlets are read with interest and hope. The untested characteristics of these materials are being analyzed, old formulas are being discarded. New alloys of steel, shatter proof and thermal glass and synthetics of innumerable types, together with the materials already mentioned, make up the new palette of the designer. . . . Standardization, pre-fabrication, controlled experiments . . . are not monsters to be avoided by the delicate sensitiveness of the artist. They are merely the modern means of controlling vast potentialities of materials for living, by chemistry, physics, engineering, production and assembly, which lead to the necessary knowledge the artist must have to expel fear in their use, broaden his creative instinct, give him new courage and thereby lead him to the adventures of unexplored places. His work will then be part of his age and will afford delight and service for his contemporaries. [14]

It is remarkable that Kahn's first theoretical statement would turn on a hypothetical synthesis between structural form and modern material technique, although he was to insist in conclusion that he did not wish to imply that monumentality could be attained scientifically or that it could be simply derived from the application of engineering methods. Viollet-le-Duc was nonetheless an influence on the remarkable space frame tower structure that Kahn and Anne Tyng were to project for Philadelphia in a number of different versions between 1952 and 1957 (figs. 7.5, 7.6, 7.7). The architects would describe the first version of their proposal in terms that the French master of structural rationalism would have appreciated.

In Gothic times, architects built in solid stones. Now we can build with hollow stones. The spaces defined by the members of a structure are as important as the members. These spaces range in scale from the voids of an insulation panel, voids for air, lighting and heat to circulate, to spaces big enough to walk through or live in. The desire to express voids positively in the design of structure is evidenced by the growing interest and work in the development of space frames. The forms being experimented with come from a closer knowledge of nature and the outgrowth of the constant search for order. Design habits leading to the concealment of structure have no place in this implied order. . . . I believe that in architecture, as in all art, the artist instinctively keep the marks which reveal how a thing was done. . . . Structures should be devised which can harbor the mechanical needs of rooms and spaces. . . . It would follow that the pasting over of the construction, of lighting and acoustical material, the burying of tortured, unwanted ducts, conduits, and pipe lines, would become intolerable. The desire to express how it is done would filter through the entire society of building, to architect, engineer, builder and craftsman. [15]

The influence of structural rationalism is revealed by the first sentence, while the degree of Kahn's involvement with modernization is indicated by his unprecedented attitude toward mechanical services. He becomes preoccupied at this juncture with the idea that services should be accorded the same tectonic sta-

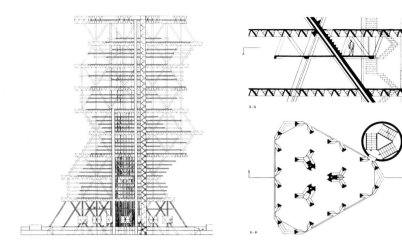

7.5
Louis I. Kahn, City Tower project ("Tomorrow's City Hall"), Philadelphia, 1957. Section through tower. Kahn's caption reads: "The concrete struts forming the triangulated frame come to a point every 66′ with 9 of these sections occurring in a total height of 616′. The column capitals at these intersections, 11′ deep, are spaces for service needs."

7.6
Louis I. Kahn, City Tower, detail plan and section.

tus as structural form. It is hard to overestimate the radical nature of this concern, for prior to Kahn's formulation of the theoretical opposition of "servant and served," contemporary architecture had failed to address the problems posed by the increase in the amount of services being installed in buildings in the second half of the twentieth century. Centralized air-conditioning imposed a quantum leap in this regard, but, unlike Mies, Kahn could not accept the suspended ceiling as a normative method for the accommodation of ducts in the servicing of open floor space, largely because a false ceiling inevitably conceals the basic floor structure. As far as Kahn was concerned, the fundamental structure of a building had to be made manifest both inside and out.

A transcendental strain is detectable in Kahn's thought at this juncture, a mode of beholding in which he appears to have become preoccupied with the latent order of nature as this had been revealed through scientific research. This is partly what he has in mind when he writes in 1944 of the purity of engineering form which has "no resistance to the laws of beauty having its own aesthetic life,"[16] or in 1952 of forms that "come from a closer knowledge of nature."

Tyng (who first worked with Kahn in 1945, in the office of Stonorov and Kahn, and then, after 1947, in Kahn's own practice) clearly exercised a major influence on Kahn's development, introducing him to D'Arcy Thompson's *On Growth and Form* in 1952. Between 1951 and 1953, Tyng designed two independent works employing octatetrahedron geometry, a prototypical school and a house for her parents realized on the eastern Maryland shore in 1953. This triangulated space frame building, left open for habitation, was of the same order as Kahn's Yale University Art Gallery design of virtually the same date, although by now Kahn was also familiar with the work of Richard Buckminster Fuller, whom he had met while teaching in the architectural school at Yale. While Tyng played a major role in initiating the City Tower project, both Kahn and Tyng were influenced by the then recent realization that certain molecular structures were ordered according to tetrahedral geometry and by Fuller's development of the Octet (octahedron/tetrahedron) truss principle, a demonstration version of which was erected in 1959.[17] The tripartite tetrahedral ordering principle of the final version of the tower was thus imagined by Kahn and Tyng as a Transcendental construction, all but identical in its form with natural crystalline structure. Kahn would first employ this geometry in combination with the interstitial mechanical services in his Yale Art Gallery, under construction in New Haven between 1951 and 1953. In the final version of the City Tower, the term "servant space" would apply not only to the volume within the triagrid floors and the tetrahedral capitals, used for the accommodation of lavatories, but also to the provision of catwalks for the purpose of maintenance and for the horizontal transfer of ducts and pipes (fig. 7.6). At this point, the structuralist principle of giving primacy to the joint and the transmission of stress is no longer solely a matter of careful detailing but is further amplified through geometry to include the provision of hierarchic space as well. In this way a clear separation was maintained between the secondary "servant" spaces, such as the elevators, service cores, lavatories, etc., and primary "served" volumes. As Kahn put it later, with regard to his penchant for interstitial servicing elements, "I do not like ducts; I do not like pipes. I hate them really thoroughly, but because I hate them so thoroughly, I feel they have to be given their place. If I just hated them and took no care, I think they would invade the building and completely destroy it." [18]

Unlike either Perret or Viollet-le-Duc, Kahn will repudiate any direct relation to historical form, be it Classic or Gothic. And yet while he will distance himself from historicism he will nonetheless gravitate toward a transhistorical evocation that is modern without being utopian and referential without becoming eclectic. Thus certain analogical allusions abound in Kahn's work, evoking Roman, Romanesque, neoclassical, and above all Gothic paradigms, particularly with his advocacy of "keeping the marks which reveal how the thing was done." Equally Gothic in the City Tower proposal are the 11-foot-deep tetrahedral capitals or nodes provided not only to absorb the shear stress but also to accommodate services, lavatories, etc. This light yet monumental tetrahedral frame is conceptually dematerialized in contrast to the heavy treatment of its podium and masonry undercroft, with its massive cylindrical light wells and circular ramps. The Roman allusions in this instance are obvious, and yet Kahn's description of the sun control system projected for the surface of its crystalline curtain wall makes his commitment to modern technology equally evident.

7.7
Louis I. Kahn, City Tower, plaza-level plan.

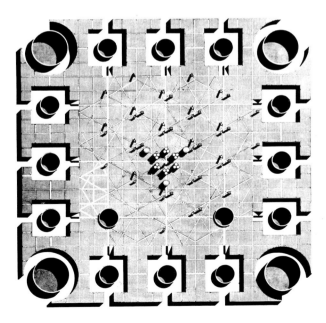

To shade the building from the sun and to hold its panels of glass, a permanent scaffolding of aluminum is planned to cover the entire exterior. From a distance windows per se, would not be apparent. A lacey network of metal reflecting the color of the light and its complementary color of shadow would be seen by the passer-by.[19]

Inasmuch as this project established an opposition between the tectonic of the skeleton frame and its skin and the stereotomic base of the earthwork, it may be seen as exemplifying Semper's *Four Elements of Architecture* of 1851. Close to a feeling for the Gothic, as this was embodied in Bruno Taut's concept of the city crown in his book *Die Stadtkrone* of 1919, we may interpret Kahn's City Tower as a dematerialized crystal set above an all-material base.[20]

Although tubular steel gave way to concrete in all of the versions of the City Tower and indeed in all of his work thereafter, the precept of a hollow structural form would remain a perennial theme throughout his career. This, plus the tactile presence of subordinate components such as the generic arch, window, and door would become irreducible elements for Kahn, because he saw them as deriving from the geometrical essences of archetypal, universal forms. For him they would stand as the ultimate morphemes of building culture without which one cannot create anything. And yet Kahn's overall notion of tectonic authenticity went beyond this necessary articulation and inflection of components to consider the experiential impact of the work on the subject. This much is implied in a statement that he made about the tactility of the Yale Art Gallery. He clearly saw the pseudo-Brutalist interior of this work as embodying a kind of psycho-ethical challenge. Thus he wrote: "One might feel that only persons who are in flight from themselves, who need plaster and wallpaper for their emotional security, can be uncomfortable in this building."[21] Despite this rather patronizing, all but trivial attitude, Kahn is nonetheless close in this work to the principles embodied in Perret's plaster-free Musée des Travaux Publics and to Perret's equally tectonic concern for the integration of services into the hollow interstitial structure of the building.

The way in which Kahn comes to terms with orthogonal geometry in the Yale Art Gallery will be decisive for the rest of his development (fig. 7.8), as will the manner in which its reinforced concrete skeleton is both revealed and concealed by the continuity and discontinuity of its cladding. The solution adopted recalls the tectonic/stereotomic interplay in Kahn's City Tower proposal, for here, in contrast to the homogeneity of the principal street elevation in brick, the return curtain wall in glass is subdivided so as to read as a tessellated, translucent skin. In order to express the common hermetic nature of both, Kahn alternates the manner of the structural expression between the northern and southern faces, so that where the curtain-walled facade, on the northwest and northeast elevations, serves to conceal the concrete floor and to reveal the columns, the converse applies on the main Chapel Street front, where the columns are suppressed except at the returns and where the floors read continuously throughout. These last are represented by horizontal stringcourses in stone, which are made of the same depth as the concrete ribs projecting from the tetrahedral floors. These stringcourses are of a similar tectonic order as the metal facing plates that cover and represent the floors in the fully glazed facades.

Within this play, the triagrid floor functions both as a structural network and as a distributive membrane, with tubular air ducts and electrical raceways running

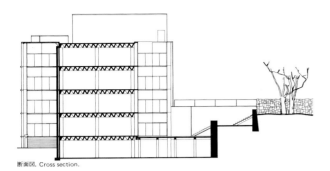

断面図. Cross section.

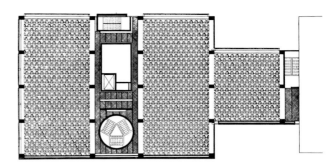

7.8
Louis I. Kahn, Yale University Art Gallery, New Haven, 1951–1953. Cross section and reflected ceiling plan.

in the interstitial space of the monolithic but hollow concrete tetrahedrons that make up the three-foot floor depth (figs. 7.9, 7.10). The fact that these triagrid floors had, in the end, to be calculated as inclined structural beams, due to the kind of calculations required by the city building code, hardly discredits the inventiveness and inherent probity of the design. One needs to note in this regard that each octahedron space within the tetrahedron network is four times greater in volume than the space of the tetrahedron itself. The ontological character of this geometry no doubt accounts for the autocritical sketch that Kahn made after the completion of the museum. As in the space frame proposed for the floor and roof of the Adath Jeshurun Synagogue projected for Elkins Park, Pennsylvania, in 1954–1955, this post-facto sketch proposes to support the tetrahedral floors of the gallery on a number of inclined tetrahedral pylons (fig. 7.11). This hypothetical idealized gallery appears in two versions, first as a square and then as an octagonal plan, fed in each instance by freestanding cylindrical services cores. Against this sketch, Kahn would append the note, "a tetrahedral concrete floor asks for a column of the same structure."[22] This may be read as a direct indication of the way in which his tectonic preconceptions would be at variance, at times, with the spatial and structural requirements of the work in hand.

Kahn's sketch of an alternative tetrahedral structure for the Yale Art Gallery may derive from the fact that the floor as built was about 60 percent heavier than what would have been required for a normal 40-foot span, and while the finished ceiling possessed all the ethical and aesthetic attributes that Kahn desired, the revealed structure was not, as we have noted, designed as initially envisaged. The tetrahedral unit, as designed by Kahn and the engineer H. A. Pfisterer, was to have been a two-foot-high pyramid having 3½-inch-thick sides, cast integrally with a 4-inch concrete floor. While this made for a heavy floor, the overall ingenuity of the concept lay in the integration of the mechanical services running within the depth of the tetrahedrons.

Kahn's "servant versus served" theme is further articulated particularly where the floor of the middle servant bay is distinguished from the honorific volumes it serves by being made of flat concrete plank construction rather than being cast in the form of the triagrid floors. This narrower structural bay accommodates at the next level of detail three servant elements: a cylindrical tripartite stair, an elevator/bathroom core, and a standard dogleg escape stair. Of these, the first is the main public stair, and this accounts for its honorific format comprising an equilateral triangular stair housed in a cylinder, as previously employed by Kahn

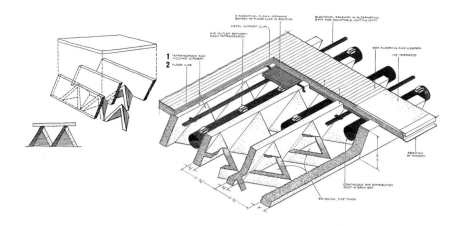

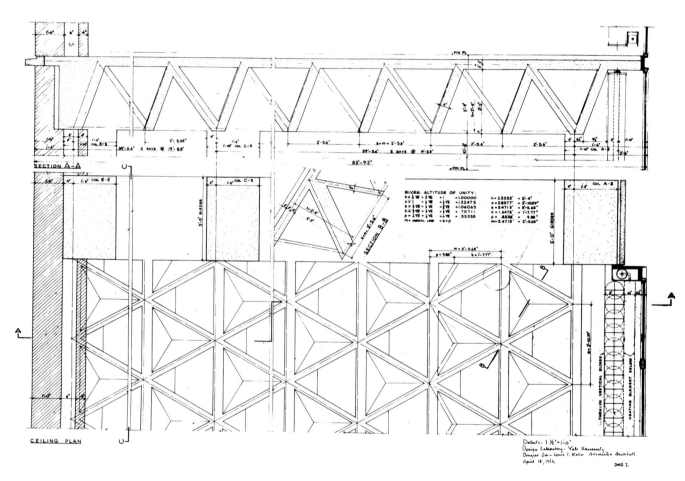

SECTION A-A

CEILING PLAN

Details - 1½"=1'-0"
Design Laboratory - Yale University
Douglas Orr - Louis I. Kahn Associated Architects
April 18, 1952

DWG 1

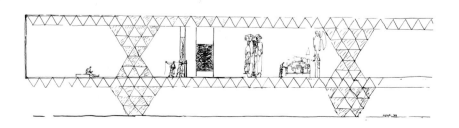

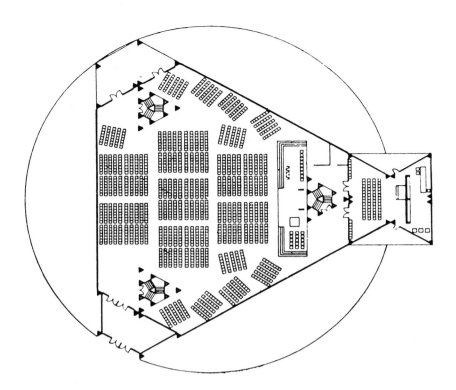

7.9

opposite, top

Louis I. Kahn, Yale University Art Gallery, isometric drawing showing integration of structural and air distribution systems.

7.10

opposite, center

Louis I. Kahn, Yale University Art Gallery, detail plan and section of floor structure.

7.11

opposite, bottom

Louis I. Kahn, Yale University Art Gallery, section sketch made after completion of the building (1954). Appended caption reads: "A tetrahedral concrete floor asks for a column of the same structure."

7.12

Louis I. Kahn, project for Adath Jeshurun Synagogue, Elkins Park, Pennsylvania, 1954. Second-floor plan.

Louis Kahn

in the City Tower design. The same honorific stair will appear in the plan for the Adath Jeshurun Synagogue projected for Elkins Park in 1954 (fig. 7.12). Meanwhile at Yale a second servant bay, accommodating another escape stair adjacent to the existing neo-Gothic Weir Hall, will also be simply rendered in concrete plank construction.

That Kahn was always concerned with the specific appearance of the constructional elements employed is evident from the care with which the Yale Art Gallery was detailed. This is confirmed by William Huff's memoir dealing with the construction of the gallery, particularly in the light of Kahn's concern for the quality of microtectonic elements.

In addition to his innovative handling of the basic concrete structural system, into which he deftly integrated the mechanical systems, and to the concrete's consequent exposure as one of the primary architectural finishes at the Yale Gallery addition, other major materials, such as the gallery floors and special concrete block, both of which played against the rugged concrete, evidenced his innate urge for the sensual. Other architects were using polished brick pavers or rubber tile or something like that for their floors. But in his free-searching survey of an inventory of imaginable, albeit viable, products, Lou stumbled upon the gymnasium floor, made up of carefully matched end-grain maple-strips—a wonderfully rich, as well as wonderfully comfortable and durable, material. And, saying that nothing looked more like a concrete block than the common 8 × 16 block, he had special 4 × 5 blocks manufactured, whose dimensions and proportions gave the walls wonderful scale and texture.[23]

Elsewhere, in the same memoir, Huff remarks on the recessed shadow joint adopted in the paneling of all of Kahn's interior cabinetwork: "Lou's detailing of doors and wood wall panels was strictly out of the Elizabethan age; but he had his own profiles. It allows the breathing of the wood so that the wood doesn't crack or check. Lou's panel doors were uniquely his 'look', but they acknowledged and incorporated the basic principles."[24]

Kahn's consciously archaic but critical and radical approach finds reflection in his intense awareness of the ontological distinction between column and wall, his Albertian preference for the primordial separation of the two, by virtue of light penetrating into the opaque impassivity of wall and thereby liberating the freestanding column from within its mass. This poetic intuition linked Kahn to the principle of structural articulation in Mies but at the same time distanced him from the Miesian free plan. In a 1957 interview given to the *Architectural Forum* he said: "You should never invade the space between columns with partition walls. It is like sleeping with your head in one room and feet in another. That I will never do."[25]

This tension between modernization and monumentality will assume a particularly dramatic form in Kahn's speculations about future urban development, and above all in the various plans that he projected for Philadelphia between 1952 and 1962. Kahn was to remain preoccupied with the myth and reality of Philadelphia throughout his life. For him, it could not be entered via the high-speed osmosis of the airport and the freeway; that is to say, by the experiential alienation picturesquely justified as a necessary, universal condition in the 1963 study *View from the Road* by Donald Appleyard, Kevin Lynch, and Jack Myer.[26] As far as Kahn was concerned, Philadelphia had to be approached through that which had graced all cities since time immemorial, an honorific gateway, which in the case of Philadelphia was the monumental Beaux-Arts peristyle of 30th Street Station. Something of Kahn's sense for the institutional and political continuity that is to be found in urban foundations may be gleaned from a text he wrote in the early sixties (fig. 7.13):

The city, from a simple settlement, became the place of the assembled institutions. Before, the institution was the natural agreement—the sense of commonality. . . . The measure of greatness of a place to live must come from the

7.13
Louis I. Kahn, "The City from a simple settlement . . . ," 1971.

The City from a simple settlement
became the place of the assembled Institutions
Before the Institution was natural agreement – the sense
of commonality. The constant play of circumstances, from
moment to moment unpredictable distort Inspiring beginnings
of natural agreement.
The measure of the greatness of a place to live must come
from the character of its Institutions sanctioned thru how
sensitive they are to renewed, and Desire for new agreement

character of its institutions, sanctioned through how sensitive they are to re-newed agreement and desire for new agreement, not through need, because it comes from what already is.[27]

By this date, twenty years after his initial essay on monumentality, the manifest destiny of monumental form had become amplified, that is to say it had evolved from an initial focus on the tectonic expressivity of built form to include within its scope the seminal character of the civic institution. Kahn was well aware that all traditional institutions were threatened by the processal aspects of late metropolitan development. Thus, his concern for the continuity of the city as an assembly of institutions is paralleled by his efforts to accommodate and overcome the contrary demands being made upon the traditional city by the ever-changing dynamics of modern locomotion. This much is clear from the way he was to conceive of the automobile in relation to the city. Thus, we find him writing in 1961:

The circumstantial demands of the car, of parking and so forth, will eat away all the spaces that exist now and pretty soon you have no identifying traces of what I call loyalties—the landmarks. Remember, when you think of your city, you think immediately of certain places which identify the city, as you enter it. If they're gone, your feeling for the city is lost and gone. . . . If because of the demands of the motorcar, we stiffen and harden the city—omitting water, omitting the green world—the city will be destroyed. Therefore the car, because of its destructive value, must start us rethinking the city in terms of the green world, in terms of the world of water, and of air, and of locomotion.[28]

From the scale of the tectonic element to the scale of mega-urban form, Kahn constantly attempted to introduce into the fundamental structure both the essential services and the character of the served place-form in order to neutralize the destructive aspects of twentieth-century technology. Thus, his efforts to interpret modern space frame construction in the light of principles derived from structural rationalism were to be paralleled by attempts to transform the elevated freeway into a new form of civic architecture. This preoccupation lay behind Kahn's paradoxical aphorism that "the street wants to become a building" and his later projection of what he disingenuously referred to as "viaduct architecture."[29] This was also the primary impulse behind his 1957 plan for midtown Philadelphia (fig. 7.14), above all his so-called Civic Center Forum, surrounded by parking silos, of which he wrote:

This strategic positioning around the city center would present a logical image of protection against the destruction of the city by the motor car. In a sense the problem of the car and the city is war, and the planning for the new growth of cities is not a complacent act but an act of emergency. The distinction between the two architectures, the architecture of the viaduct and the architecture of the acts of man's activities, could bring about a logic of growth and a sound positioning of enterprise.[30]

The ambivalent tension in Kahn's work between modernization and monumentality is perhaps never more evident than in the evolution of the cylindrical parking towers by which the city center was to have been surrounded (fig. 7.15). In his first version of these "wound-up streets" it is clear that Kahn cannot quite decide as to whether they should be treated as monuments or utilitarian semiotic elements. Thus, we find him writing in 1953:

The tower entrances and interchanges, wound-up parking terminals, suggest a new stimulus to unity in urban architecture, one which would find expression from the order of movement. The location and design of these entrances are an integral part of the design of the expressway. . . . At night we know these towers by their illumination in color. These yellow, red, green, blue and white towers tell us the sector we are entering, and along the approach, light is used to see by and give us direction in ideas of lighting in rhythm with our speed. From these entrances a system of canals or interior streets feed the various activities of center city life.[31]

Apart from the reference to "canals," this reads like a prescription for identifying urban sectors according to a color code. However this seemingly semiotic approach to the ordering of urban space is immediately followed by a typical Kahnian metaphor in which the proposed access system breaks down into rivers, harbors, canals, and docks, that is to say into an all but mythical, analogical world, wherein expressways are seen as "rivers," streets as "canals," parking towers as "harbors," and the cul-de-sacs as "docks"; these last finally giving onto building entrances and car-free pedestrian zones. The provision by which some vehicles would park in harbor towers while others would penetrate into canals and cul-de-sacs is never made fully explicit in any of Kahn's Philadelphia studies. The familiar "stop and go" street plan does not seem to account for the fine-grain distribution of the traffic. Moreover, in all of his Philadelphia plans the parking silos are invariably seen as the equivalent of bastions, while the bounding freeway is regarded as a twentieth-century version of the medieval city wall. Of this last Kahn would write:

Carcassonne was designed from an order of defense. A modern city will renew itself from its order concept of movement which is a defense against its destruction by the automobile. . . . Great vehicular harbors or municipal entrance towers

7.14
Louis I. Kahn, plan for midtown Philadelphia, 1957. Perspective; north view from Spruce Street. The existing City Hall is shown on the extreme left.

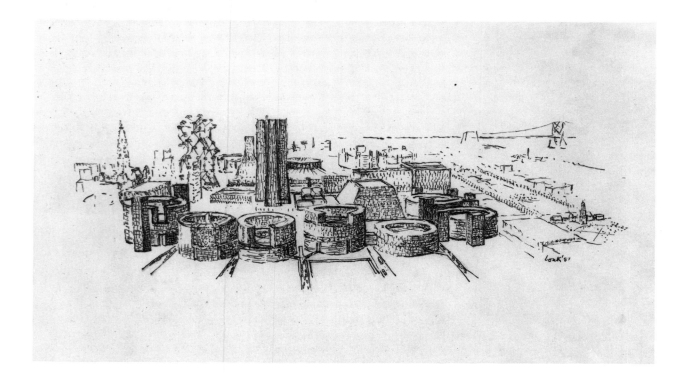

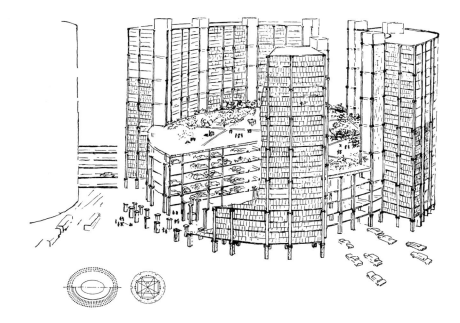

*will surround the innermost center of the city. They will be the gateways, the land-
marks, the first images that greet the visitor. . . . The main body of the tower gateways between the outer perimeter and the inner core will be the wound-up
street of vehicular arrival and stopping.*[32]

Kahn's preoccupation with the idea of a hollow structure—"now we can build
with hollow stones"—was to unify his thinking at both an architectural and an urban level. And where the former announced itself, in various ways, in the triagrid
floors of the Yale Art Gallery, in the Vierendeel trusses projected for the Trenton
Jewish Community Center (1954–1959) (fig. 7.16), and finally in the hollow floor
beams of the Richards Medical Research Building of 1957, the latter was to
manifest itself as a viaduct architecture of his last urban proposal for Philadelphia, dating from 1962. Of this last, Alexandra Tyng has written:

Viaduct *literally means a "carrying street." Kahn extended its original Roman
meaning to signify a complex consisting of levels for pedestrian traffic, automobile traffic, mass transportation systems, and rooms under the street for piped
services, which could then be repaired without interruption of traffic. The viaduct
is actually a hollow column turned on its side, channelling the energy flow of the
city.*[33]

If on one level the monumental for Kahn was contingent upon the institution and
the city, on another, as we have already seen, it turned upon the structure and
the joint. These two poles were related to each other by natural light, that is to
say, by the way in which light, as revealed by structure, was capable of imparting a specific character to a given institution or a civic element. Kahn would
even see light as a divine transforming essence, as something that could make
solid structures translucent, even transparent in their material consistency, as is
suggested in his famous sketch of Albi cathedral (fig. 7.17).

As Kahn's career advanced, he became increasingly antithetical to open-
planned, loft space and more concerned with the irreducible character of the

room *in se.* For him, the quality of light made manifest through its interaction with a specific structural volume was the essential determinant of its character (fig. 7.18). Hence, he would write:

Architecture comes from the Making of a Room. . . . The Room is the place of the mind. In a small room one does not say what one would in a large room. In a room with only one other person . . . the vectors of each meet. A room is not a room without natural light. Natural light gives the time of day and [allows] the mood of the seasons to enter.[34]

In a similar vein, Kahn wrote of the penetration of light into the multilevel freeway viaducts that he proposed for midtown Philadelphia in the early 1960s in terms of allowing a sliver of light to enter into the darkest room; to penetrate even into a cinema in order to reveal how dark it is.[35] The windowless, climate-controlled box was a total anathema to Kahn, as was the indifferently assembled, underdetailed modern building so often found in commercial architecture. Thus, as far as he was concerned, the joint, as revealed by light, was the tangible proof of the constructional probity of the work in much the same way as it had been the touchstone of tectonic form in the writings of Viollet-le-Duc and Semper.

Kahn's emphasis on the joint naturally leads to a comparison with Mies van der Rohe and to the drawing of certain parallels between their respective achievements. This is particularly true of their mature work, and above all of their comparable essays in reinforced concrete construction. Thus, one may compare

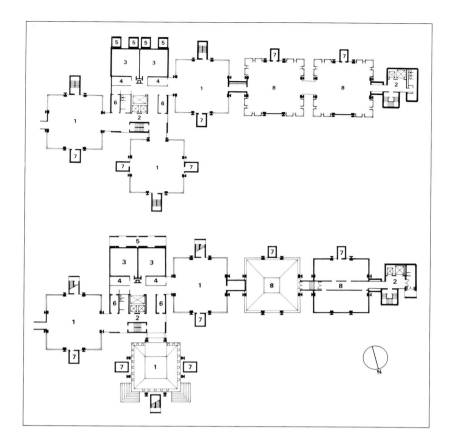

7.17
Louis I. Kahn, sketch of St. Cécile cathedral, Albi, France, 1959. Note the representing of the cylindrical elements as "wind-up" forms.

7.18
Louis I. Kahn, "Architecture comes from the Making of a Room . . . ," 1971.

7.19
Louis I. Kahn, Richards Medical Research Laboratories, University of Pennsylvania, Philadelphia, 1957–1961. Typical floor plan (above) and first-floor plan (below):
1. studio towers
2. elevators and stairways
3. animal quarters
4. animal service rooms
5. fresh air intake stacks
6. air distribution shafts
7. fume and exhaust stacks
8. biology building towers

Mies's Promontory Apartments of 1949 to Kahn's cylindrical parking/office silos, first published in 1953 as part of the midtown Philadelphia plan. An exposed trabeated reinforced concrete frame is the primary expressive element in each instance. Moreover, the structural frame is similarly articulated in each case; that is to say, the perimeter concrete columns, carrying the spandrels, diminish in section as they rise upward due to a decrease in compressive stress. Aside from this singular case, however, their preferred generic columns could hardly have been more different, with Mies favoring a standard rolled steel stanchion and Kahn preferring a hollow or solid concrete pier.

Kahn's preoccupation with hollow structure reaches its apotheosis with the Richards Medical Laboratories realized for the University of Pennsylvania between 1957 and 1961 (fig. 7.19). As others have remarked, this building synthesizes for the first time the multifarious aspects of his tectonic approach: the use of hollow structure at every conceivable scale, the articulation of servant and served spaces, the full integration of mechanical services, and not least the dialogical "gravitational/levitational" expression of static weight and gaseous exhaust. From this point onward, Kahn treats the structure as the potential generator of space, that is, as a hollow diaphragm from which the volume itself emerges by extension. At the same time, the articulation of the joint assumes an organic character; thus he was to write:

A building is like a human. An architect has the opportunity of creating life. It's like a human body—like your hand. The way the knuckles and joints come to-

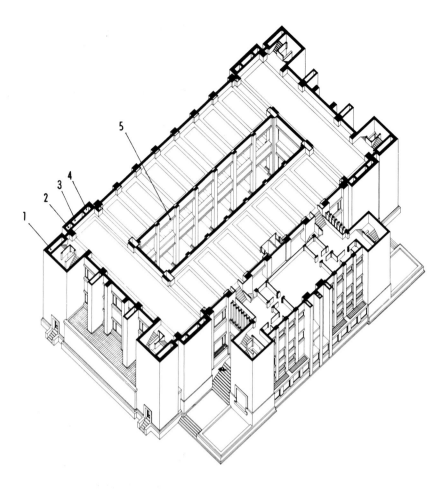

7.20
Frank Lloyd Wright, Larkin Building, Buffalo, 1904. Axonometric at third-floor level. Note the service ducts built into the walls of the stair shafts. Numbers indicate built-in services according to the following key:
1. fresh air intake
2. utilities
3. foul air exhaust
4. miscellaneous ducts and services
5. tempered air outlets under balcony fronts and ceiling beams

7.21
Louis I. Kahn, Richards Medical Research Laboratories, perspective sketch from the southwest, 1957 version showing cantilevered and ribbed exhaust stacks.

7.22
Louis I. Kahn, Richards Medical Research Laboratories, early plan.

gether make each hand interesting and beautiful. In a building these details should not be put in a mitten and hidden. You should make the most of them. Space is architectural when the evidence of how it is made is seen and comprehended.[36]

This anthropomorphic conception of the joint is to be given a more tectonic rendering in his homage to Carlo Scarpa, made shortly before his own death:

*Design consults Nature
to give presence to the elements.
A work of art makes manifest the wholeness of 'Form',
the symphony of the selected shapes of the elements.
In the elements
the joint inspires ornament, its celebration.
The detail is the adoration of nature.*[37]

This feeling for the organic surely derives in large measure from Frank Lloyd Wright. Wright is, in any event, still an insufficiently acknowledged influence on Kahn, not only in the Richards Medical Laboratories but throughout his career. And while many earlier twentieth-century architects were inspired by Wright's domestic architecture, including, of course, Hendrik Petrus Berlage and Ludwig Mies van der Rohe, few if any were able to develop the introspective concatenations of hierarchic form that characterized Wright's public buildings. In a roundabout way, this legacy fell to Kahn. The totally blank exterior of the hollow service towers in the Richards Laboratories and the division of the parti into servant and served spaces are all surely incipient in Wright's Larkin Building, Buffalo, of 1904 (fig. 7.20), and a similar relationship clearly obtains between the Richards Laboratories and the S. C. Johnson Administration complex built at Racine, Wisconsin, in 1937. It is significant that Wright's own 1945 description of the S. C. Johnson Building has much about it that could have been from the hand of Kahn:

Laid out upon a horizontal unit system twenty feet on centers both ways, rising into the air on a vertical unity system of three and half inches: one especially large brick course. Glass was not used as bricks in this structure. Bricks were bricks. The building itself became—by way of long glass tubing—crystal where crystal either transparent or translucent was felt to be most appropriate. In order to make the structure monolithic, the exterior enclosing wall material appeared inside wherever it was sensible.[38]

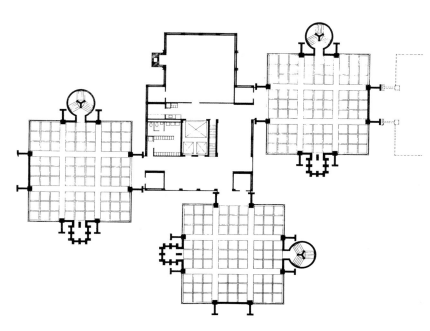

7.23

Louis I. Kahn, Richards Medical Research Laboratories, plan and elevation sketches of service towers, 1957 version.

In much the same spirit Kahn wrote of his laboratories as being "conceived in recognition of the realization that science laboratories are studios and that the air to breathe should be away from the air to throw away."[39] Here once again the hollow column comes into play, particularly in the initial sketches for the exhaust and air intake towers (figs. 7.21, 7.22, 7.23) against which Kahn would jot down the following notes: "The air supply gets smaller as it rises . . . the air return gets larger as it returns. The fumehood exhaust accumulates on its ascent. The column gets smaller as it rises. From this comes the design of the area around the column."[40] These ventilation manifolds, built out of corbeled masonry and dialectically conceived as opposing the ascent of gas to the descent

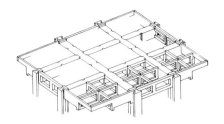

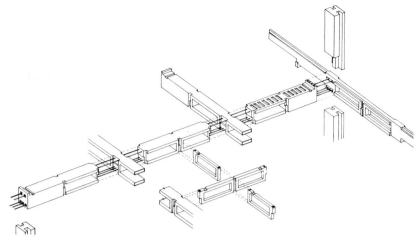

7.24
Louis I. Kahn, Richards Medical Research Laboratories, isometric drawing of precast concrete floor system.

7.25
Louis I. Kahn, project for Washington University Library, St. Louis, 1956.

of gravitational force, had eventually to be abandoned in favor of simpler boxlike sections for the process of air intake and foul exhaust. Nevertheless, as in the original sketches, a clear division was maintained between the stereotomics of the ventilation system built in brick and the tectonics of the columnar structure cast in concrete. As in the Yale Art Gallery, Kahn was able to integrate the horizontal distribution of services within the post-tensioned diagrid, two-way cantilevering floors of the laboratories, the structural depth being reduced toward the corners as the bending stress diminished. It is to the great credit of Kahn's engineer August Kommendant, with whom he would work continuously from 1956 to the end of his career, that this cantilevered Vierendeel was executed entirely of prefabricated concrete (fig. 7.24). Unlike the dialectic between ascendant air and descendant gravity, this horizontal interweaving of the services into the "space frame" of the flow structure was maintained throughout.

In one design after another, Kahn constantly strove to reveal the structural skeleton, together with its cross-sectional reduction in area as the load diminished. However, Kahn's project for the Washington University Library of 1956 (fig. 7.25) was his last didactically tectonic essay in this regard, for thereafter masonry would play a more decisive role in his work, either rendered as a screen wall or treated as a kind of stressed-skin construction, as in the calculated load-bearing concrete blockwork of the Tribune Review newspaper building erected in Greensburg, Pennsylvania, in 1961 (fig. 7.26). Where the masonry was not structural it was handled as though it were a representative shell or "ruin," that is to say, as though it were a screen running outside the structural and institu-

tional substance of the building (cf. Schinkel's Friedrich Werder Church, Berlin, of 1830). The interior face of this screen was invariably treated as a "space between," wherein the play of light could reveal the difference between the inner substance of a building and the outer surface of its appearance. This masonry encasement is first unequivocally adopted by Kahn in his project for a U.S. Consulate in Luanda, Angola, dating from 1959, wherein the outer envelope of the structure is partially covered by screens for the purpose of sun control (fig. 7.27). Of this provision Kahn would write:

I came to the realization that every window should have a free wall to face. This wall receiving the light of day would have a bold opening to the sky. The glare is modified by the lighted wall and the view is not shut off. In this way the contrast made by separated patterns of glare, which skylight grilles close to the window make, is avoided. Another realization came from the effectiveness of the use of breeze for insulation by the making of a loose sun roof independently supported and separated from the rainroof by a head room of 6 feet. Notice also that the piers that hold the main girders for the sun roof are completely independent of the rain roof. The rain roof is never pierced.[41]

This tectonic response to extreme climatic conditions had, however, its representational aspect, for both the cut-out frontal screen and the tessellated sun canopy on the roof evidently served to represent the honorific status of the building. Kahn was fully aware of this fact: "Considering the type of building it is, one should have the feeling of entrance and reception *not* by way of a sign but by its very character."[42] Kahn seems to have posited the idea of structure at two interlocking levels, first a general spatial structuring to be effected by the octatetrahedral system that, like Buckminster Fuller, he identified with the basic molecular order of the universe, and second a detailed structural order that employed the time-honored tropes of building culture: the cantilever, the catenary, the arch, the vault, the buttress, and the bridge. On occasion these primary and secondary levels—the spatial and the structural—would be conflated into one, as in the towers of the Richards Laboratories or the pseudo-vaults of the Kimbell Art Museum or the octagonal staggered cellular units initially envisaged for the structure of Eleanor Donnelly Erdman Hall at Bryn Mawr College in 1960. In all these instances, the resulting cellular space demonstrated his belated rediscovery that "a bay system is a room system," as he wrote in his notebook of 1955, in a passing reference to the Palladian plan.[43] This short pronouncement about the spatial implications of the generic structural bay was the main way in which Kahn distanced himself from the free plan or *plan libre* of the prewar European avant-garde. Influenced by Rudolf Wittkower's 1949 reappraisal of Palladianism, in which rooms were to be designated by their proportion and not according to their use, Kahn invariably projected clearly defined spaces, open to varying modes of appropriation. As we have already noted, he would eventually impose over structure and space a third corporeal order that we may identify as

7.26
Louis I. Kahn, Tribune Review Building, Greensburg, Pennsylvania, 1958–1961.

7.27
Louis I. Kahn, project for U.S. Consulate, Luanda, Angola, 1959–1961. Detail section, elevation, and isometric.

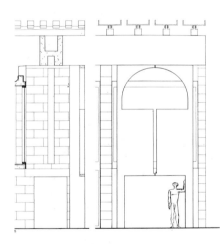

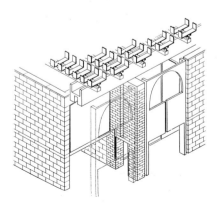

encasement, after the masonry-encased metal armatures to be found in the work of Labrouste and Viollet-le-Duc. While this third order was first justified by Kahn as a means of shielding the core of the building from glare, in his late monumental works such as the posthumously realized Bangladesh Parliament, the Sher-e-Bangla Nagar completed in Dacca in 1982, these three levels of structuring—the cellular, the structural, and the encasement—become fused, in certain sequences, into a single in situ concrete fabric engendering an all but infinite concatenation of interstitial space. In this instance it is significant, from a Semperian standpoint, that Kahn would elect to represent the concrete case of the building as a woven screen, the concrete being subdivided vertically by inlaid bands of stone. Within his entire oeuvre, Exeter Library (1967–1972) appears as the sole work in which the three levels of structuring become so compounded as to cancel each other out. Thus the brick piers sustaining the perimeter carrel wall running around all four sides of the library are totally at variance with the reinforced concrete column system holding up the book stacks. At the same time this overstructuring of the building has nothing whatever to do with the masklike facade that exploits its stepped-back brick piers, diminishing toward the top, to make a nostalgic allusion to the warehouse and mill vernacular of the eighteenth and nineteenth centuries, while the structure within has little to do with this tectonic tradition. Nothing could be further, one might note, from the tectonic fidelity of Schinkel's Bauakademie in this regard.

Kahn felt that the processes of modernization had a debilitating effect on received architectural forms, and even more importantly on the sociocultural essence of the institutions they once housed. As a result, he felt that modern institutions could no longer be predicated on historically derived types. For Kahn, these forms had either to be assembled piece by piece out of structurally articulate components, developed from the interaction of construction, gravity, ventilation, services, and light, or they had to be evoked as institutions, through employing geometrically determined forms or Platonic solids, that is to say, through the use of absolute plan forms derived from circles, triangles, squares, or other regular polygons. Kahn's intuition in this regard linked him to the rational Cartesian doubt that had dominated French thought since the end of the seventeenth century. As Marcello Angrisani has shown in his 1965 essay "Louis Kahn and History,"[44] Kahn welcomed the reappearance of the arbitrary architectural paradigms of the French Enlightenment, the massive, largely blank cubes, spheres, and pyramids and their various intersecting permutations that make up the visionary repertoire of Claude-Nicolas Ledoux and Étienne Boullée. At the end of the eighteenth century these architects were already to suggest a way for accommodating and representing the utopian (not to say apocalyptic) institutions of the unprecedented bourgeois, industrial world. In this regard Emil Kaufman's Three Revolutionary Architects: Boullée, Ledoux and Lequeu, published in Philadelphia in 1952, had a certain influence on Kahn, as is suggested by the Yale Art Gallery, the Trenton Bath House (fig. 7.28), and the Elkins Park synagogue, all dating from this period. Unlike Boulée and Ledoux, however, Kahn rarely used the primary forms in isolation, but always as the elemental parts of more complex assemblies.

In the Rochester Unitarian Church of 1959, Kahn will make his first didactic demonstration in this vein, that is to say the representation of the *what* of the institution, as opposed to the articulation of the *how* of its structure. As in the equilateral triangular plan adopted for the Elkins Park synagogue but never fully

233

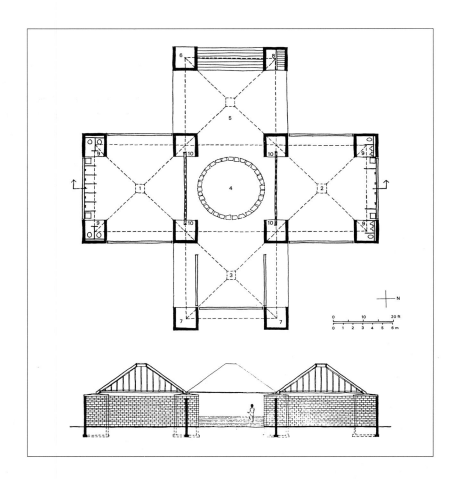

7.28
Louis I. Kahn, Jewish Community Center,
Bath House, Trenton, 1955–1956. First-floor
plan and section through dressing rooms:
1. women's dressing room
2. men's dressing room
3. basket room
4. atrium
5. entry
6. pool director's kiosk
7. storage
8. entrance to chlorinating equipment
9. toilets
10. wall baffled entrances

7.29
Louis I. Kahn, Unitarian Church, Rochester,
1959–1967. First-floor plan, 1959 version.

7.30
Louis I. Kahn, Unitarian Church, Rochester:
model, 1959 version.

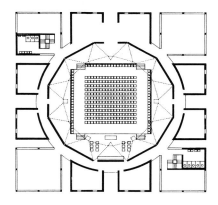

postulated as a mass form, Kahn will assume a regular polygon for the body of the church. This is first projected as a structural octagon set within a square inside a decahedron that in its turn is further inscribed within a circle and an outer square (figs. 7.29, 7.30). An earlier version shows the church as a freestanding octagonal structure, with its roof held in place by buttress-like, reinforced concrete members running in pairs around the periphery (fig. 7.31). The fact that the Rochester church would finally be realized as an empirical, additive form, due to programmatic demands, in no way detracts from Kahn's institutional concerns, as we may judge from the symbolic symmetry of the inner sanctum with its four corner monitor lights and shell concrete roof. The full spirituality of this church as an institution is expressed in the roof section, from which a mysterious light enters into the four cubic corners of the meeting room, highlighting the flying tie beams that serve to sustain the stability of its quadripartite shell form (fig. 7.32). As Kahn was to put it: "It's very Gothic isn't it? Does that bother you? I like it myself."[45]

7.31
Louis I. Kahn, Unitarian Church, Rochester, plan and elevation sketches, 1959 version.

7.32
Louis I. Kahn, Unitarian Church, Rochester, longitudinal section and first-floor plan, final (fifth) version.

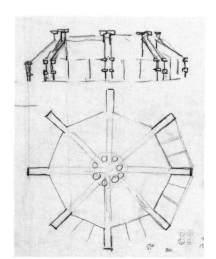

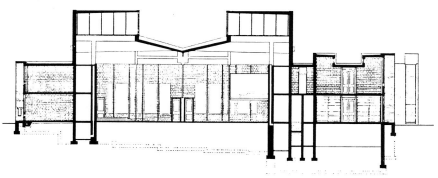

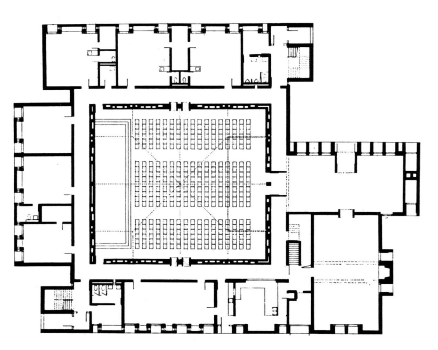

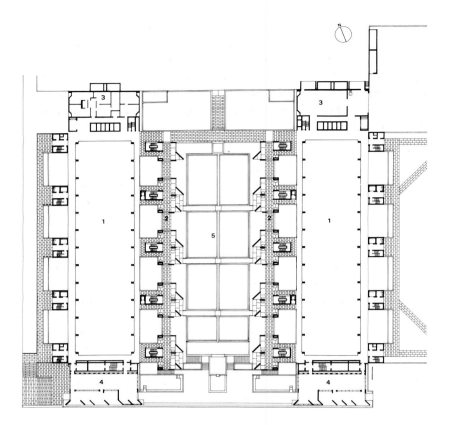

Kahn's penchant for embodying institutions in arbitrarily geometric plan forms had its limits, however, as is event from the Richards Medical building where it became clear that a biological laboratory was something more processal than Kahn's overly idealistic conception of a "science studio." And indeed he took this lesson to heart in the design of the Salk Institute Laboratories at La Jolla, California, first projected in 1959 and finally completed in 1965 (fig. 7.33). He was able to persuade his client, Dr. Jonas Salk, that it was necessary to provide separate physical environments for the conceptual realm of the intellect and the processal realm of empirical research, the former being housed in well-appointed study cells facing onto a common internal court, the latter being accommodated in well-serviced loft space. Kahn still attempted to render the clear span over this last in accordance with the precepts of structural rationalism, with interstitial man-height service spaces being integrated within the depth of the 100-foot box-truss girders. This triangular-sectioned space would occupy the depth of 50-foot prestressed folded plates spanning the opposite dimension. While this arrangement would have yielded a folded-plate ceiling running between the box trusses for the entire length of the laboratory (figs. 7.34, 7.35),

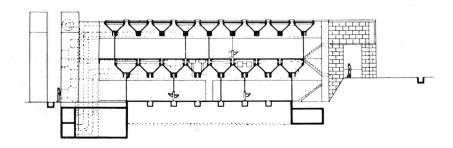

it seems that this provision was eventually rejected in the interests of lowering costs and shortening the construction time.[46] It was thus decided to achieve the transverse span with inverted post-tensioned concrete Vierendeel trusses occupying the full depth of the interstitial space, with a 10-inch concrete slab above and a suspended, 8-inch hollow core slab beneath. Permanent slots were cast at frequent intervals in the lower slab so as to allow the services to be dropped through at virtually any location above the loft laboratory space (fig. 7.36).

Salk is the first occasion on which Kahn integrates the undercroft of the building into the overall domain of the site; indeed one might say that he "builds the site" in Mario Botta's sense, for its symmetrical form, comprising two laboratory wings flanked by study cells facing onto a central court, is raised clear of the undulating clifftop site by the use of a concrete substructure. This earthwork is rendered as a kind of templum, clad throughout in travertine, in which every upstand edge or reveal accommodates in one way or another a point of access or a joint; an iron-framed gateway here, a shallow flight of steps there, or simply a recessed seam between the vertical face of the building and its undercroft. Many of these narrower seams are treated as stormwater gulleys, as though the entire stereotomic foundation was subject to seasonal flooding. This metaphorical opposition between explicit earthwork and implicit waterwork is finally consummated, so to speak, by a shallow water channel running down the central axis of the podium toward the sea. It is surely not without some transcultural significance that the Mexican architect Luis Barragán would play a decisive role in determining the final form of the space, deeming it to be a civic plaza rather

7.35
Louis I. Kahn, Salk Institute Laboratories, views of laboratory study model.

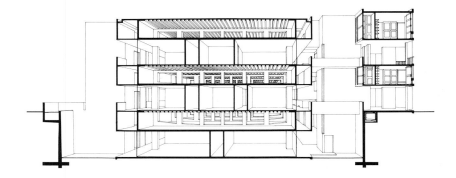

7.36
Louis I. Kahn, Salk Institute Laboratories, section through laboratory wing, final version as built.

than a garden court and thus suggesting that it should be left without any planting whatsoever. Kahn's account of the way this decision was made reveals a great deal about the spirit in which the entire work was achieved.

I asked Barragan to come to La Jolla and help me in the choice of the planting for the garden to the studies of the Salk Laboratory. When he entered the space he went to the concrete walls and touched them and expressed his love for them, and then said as he looked across the space and towards the sea, "I would not put a tree or blade of grass in this space. This should be a plaza of stone, not a garden." I looked at Dr. Salk and he at me and we both felt this was deeply right. Feeling our approval, he added joyously, "If you make this a plaza, you will gain a facade—a facade to the sky." [47]

Aside from the overall Mozarabic character of this provision, the specific nature of its detailing is Kahnian throughout. This much is evident from the way in which the watercourse is handled as a reciprocally symbolic system, with fountainhead and gargoyle rendered as the alpha and the omega of a self-contained microcosmos. The fountain is contained within an upstand cube, faced in travertine, in which three slots, set around three sides of a square basin, discharge their flow across shallow weirs, thereby forming a perfectly mitered, three-part trajectory of water cascading into the channel beneath. The symbolic and geometrical counterform to this source is the equally cubic gargoyle that, faced in the same travertine, discharges its flow into a monumental stone cistern set below the surface of the podium, in front of the sea. Since the rate of discharge requires a certain hydraulic pressure, the flow from the source is allowed to accumulate in two holding tanks, each one paralleled by a stone bench, before finally discharging into the cistern below. This entire assembly, court, water, and cistern, is held conjointly in a state of suspension before the undulating contours of a clifftop panorama, while the whole is preceded by an irregular grove of eucalyptus trees that deftly screen the court and the view of the ocean from the landward side. [48]

These primordial elements, as offset by the interplay between tectonic form and changing light, were to be integrated in an equally sublime way in the Kimbell Art Museum at Fort Worth, Texas, first projected by Kahn in 1966 and finally completed in 1972, two years before his death (fig. 7.37). The Kimbell may be seen as the apotheosis of his career, above all for the way in which one dominant tectonic element, namely a barrel vault, determines the overall character of the piece. The other determining factor is once again a stereotomic earthwork, here the manifest integration of the building into its site. And where the former, the split and articulated structure of a pseudo-vault, is the provider of light, the

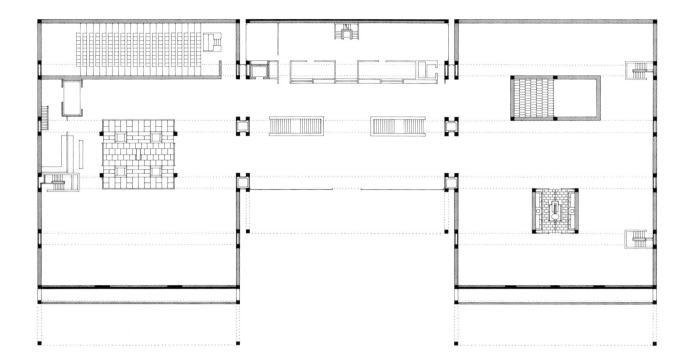

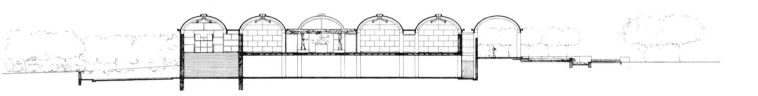

7.37
Louis I. Kahn, Kimbell Art Museum, Fort Worth, 1966–1972. Upper-floor plan and cross section.

latter is to evoke the presence of nature in a more telluric aspect. Thus while light is the ubiquitous natural element par excellence, Kahn was to inscribe the Kimbell into its site in such a way as to establish a categoric "clearing" and to endow the resultant precinct with a particular presence. In this respect, the Kimbell seems to demonstrate the importance that Martin Heidegger would attach to the boundary in his seminal essay "Building, Dwelling, Thinking" of 1954: "A boundary (*peras*) is not that at which something stops but, as the Greeks recognized, the boundary is that from which something begins its presenting."[49] Thus the implantation of the Kimbell amounted to the establishment of an earthwork in every conceivable sense, from the travertine revetment of its elevated podium to the acoustics of its graveled forecourt, from the solemnity of the Yaupon holly grove that crowns the entrance from the park to the more distant, low-slung deciduous planting of the park itself (fig. 7.38).

In the laconic remarks that accompany the presentation of the Kimbell, Kahn reveals, as nowhere else, the cosmological intent of his entire approach. Thus, of light he was to write: "We were born of light. The seasons are felt through light. We only know the world as it is evoked by light. To me, natural light is the only light because it has mood—it provides a ground of common agreement for

239

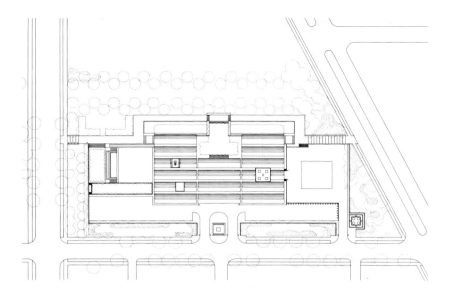

man—it puts us in touch with the eternal."[50] Elsewhere of the vaulted, top-lit galleries (figs. 7.39, 7.40) he wrote:

By the nature of the vault-like structure, you have the play of loft rooms with a space between each vault which has a ceiling at the level of the spring of the vault . . . the dimension of its light from above is manifest without partitions because the vaults defy division. Even when partitioned, the room remains a room. You might say that the nature of a room is that it always has the character of completeness.[51]

While Kahn goes on to speak about the paradoxical flexibility of these galleries, he also refers to those place-forms within the overall matrix that do not change, the three open courts that are let into the continuous vaulted roof. He will write of these incidental elements in terms that evoke the Mediterraneanism of Le Corbusier.

Added to the skylight from the slit over the exhibit rooms, I cut across the vaults, at a right angle, a counterpoint of courts, open to the sky, of calculated dimensions and character, marking them Green Court, Yellow Court, Blue Court, named for the kind of light that I anticipate their proportions, their foliation, or their sky reflections on surfaces or on water will give.[52]

Kahn causes us to focus on the precise nature of the joint at Kimbell and to discriminate, as Perret or Labrouste had done before him, between ornament and decoration. "I put the glass between the structure members and the members which are not of structure because the joint is the beginning of ornament. And

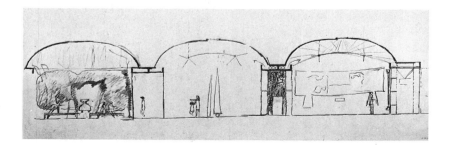

that must be distinguished from decoration which is simply applied. Ornament is the adoration of the joint." [53]

Kahn's habit of emphasizing the aggregate yet cast character of concrete, as opposed to the archaic, fossilized and glyptic character of travertine, made itself manifest at the Kimbell in a particular juxtaposition of these two materials. Of this particular aspect of Kahn's tectonic syntax, William Huff has written:

The only trouble with concrete, he told us, was that it looks awful when it's wet. Otherwise, it's a fantastic material. One way to counteract that, is to have in-sets of travertine or other marbles to take your eye off the concrete when the water streaks it. Lou knew how to do that. He knew how to integrate a travertine handrail with a concrete stair—the cool blue concrete against the warm yellow travertine; the porous rough concrete and the porous polished travertine trim. [54]

Of this paradoxical sameness and difference between concrete and travertine, Kahn wrote, with particular reference to the Kimbell:

Concrete does the work of structure, of holding things up. The columns are apart from each other. The space between must be filled. Therefore the travertine. . . . Travertine and concrete belong beautifully together because concrete must be taken for whatever irregularities or accidents in the pointing reveal themselves. Travertine is very much like concrete—its character is such that they look like the same material. That makes the whole building again monolithic and it doesn't separate things. [55]

Of Kahn's capacity to transform the quality of in situ concrete by virtue of its precision formwork, Huff goes on to remark:

Retrievable metal screw-ties are used both to hold in place and to separate at the specified distances two parallel sheets of plywood, between which concrete is poured to form a wall. Holes, carefully patterned, were left in the poured wall by wood plugs which are located at both ends of the ties. Instead of being "buttered in", as is common practice, these holes were plugged with lead, held ¼" back from the surface. Furthermore, where two sheets of plywood, in the same

plane, but, there is invariably bleeding of the concrete at the junctures. Here, vertical and horizontal projecting vee joints were formed by controlled tolerances, which allowed the bleeding to be molded into relief elements. The central vertical joint is an indented, poured joint, also plugged with lead.[56]

At the Kimbell, as in the Salk Laboratories, Kahn introduced a certain amount of volcanic ash or *pozzolana* into the concrete mix in order to give the concrete when cast and cured a brownish hue. As it happens, the *pozzolana* had the effect of reducing the expansion of the concrete in casting, although it produced dust and made a high finish more difficult to obtain. As at Salk, the tie cones for the formwork at the Kimbell were plugged with lead after the removal of the molds, and the gaps between the panels produced thin upstand seams on the surface of the finished concrete.[57]

Mention must be made of the way in which services are integrated into the galleries at Kimbell, not only the reflecting light baffles and lighting consoles below the crown of the vault, but also the service channels that run between the downstand beams under the springing (fig. 7.41). These metal service boxes, together with the moving partitions that are bracketed off longitudinal tracks let into their form, enabled Kahn to orient the space of the museum into two countervailing and ideologically distinct directions; on the one hand, the traditional gallery as a discrete room, running in the same direction as the vault, on the other, the lateral expanse of space running across the vault, capable of providing a flexible, open floor area appropriate to a wide range of exhibition formats.

The Kimbell Art Museum is a work that has been subjected to a great deal of controversy on both tectonic and technical grounds, not the least of which has been the character of the 104-foot-by-23-foot "false" vaults by which the building is covered. The roof of the museum reiterates in many ways the dilemma and the aspirations of the Greco-Gothic ideal, for in its evolution two conflicting impulses can be identified. On the one hand, there is the folded-plate, factory-like, concrete roof that Kahn projected in his spring 1967 design for the mu-

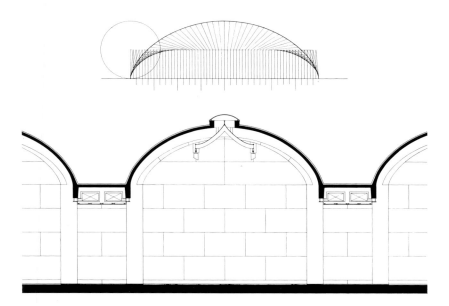

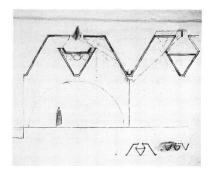

7.41
Louis I. Kahn, Kimbell Art Museum, section of cycloid, final version.

7.42
Louis I. Kahn, Kimbell Art Museum, early sketch of folded-plate roof structure.

seum (fig. 7.42), a design that clearly anticipated the folded-plate structure to be used in the final work. On the other hand, there are the semicircular, purely vaulted galleries projected by Kahn and his assistant Marshall Meyers in autumn of 1967, when Kahn proposed vaults having a 12-foot radius, set on top of a 12-foot-high beam line supported by columns at 24-foot centers. Nothing surely could have been more Platonic and monumental than this double-square gallery section, and this seems to have been why it was rejected by the client, namely, for being too magisterial, since the director Richard Brown wanted a villa for his museum rather than a palace. This pertinent critique was answered, so to speak, by the cycloid vault section that Meyers happened upon in Fred Anger-er's book *Surface Structures in Architecture* (1961). The introduction of the cy-cloid and the decision to pierce its apex with a continuous light slot brought the structure back to its original folded plate form, even if lateral ties were intro-duced across the slot, in order to permit the structure to act in both directions. The root of *vault* in the Latin verb *volvere*—meaning literally to revolve across— is particularly apt in the case of the cycloid vault, since the profile arises out of the rotation of a point on the circumference of a circle rolling along a line. There is a further incidental analogy between the roll of the vault and the curvature of the fountain flow that parallels the vaulted porticoes on either side of the main entry. To this cycloid section August Kommendant imparted certain engineering refinements: the deepening of the upstand beams around the slot, the thick-ening of the cycloid wall toward its base, in order to facilitate pouring, the cast-ing of the cycloid as a second pour above the downstand beams, and finally the post-tensioning of the cycloids in the long direction in order to attain a clear span of 104 feet (figs. 7.43, 7.44). This hidden catenary cable network gave an uplift to the cycloid beams so as to counteract their inevitable deflection. Kom-mandant needed a diaphragm of a certain depth at the return ends of the vaults, and this led to a circumferential light slot of varying depth, let into the end wall of the section (fig. 7.45). In the final development of this form one might say that Kahn was neo-Gothic to the degree that he followed the pre-cepts of Viollet-le-Duc and Greco-Gothic to the degree that he strove for the pu-rity of the form, once the empirical engineering requirements were satisfied.

Doug Suisman's critical appraisal of the Kimbell highlights once again Kahn's fa-miliar ambivalence toward the automobile, for by the time Kahn turned to the Kimbell he had already been struggling to integrate the automobile into his work for well over two decades (fig. 7.46). By this date we may say that the fundamen-tal dilemma posed by the car had defeated him, and in this of course he was by no means alone. The fundamental hostility of the automobile to architecture and to urban civilization as a whole is surely a treatise that is waiting to be written. In any event, there is no doubt whatsoever that the conception of the Kimbell is ba-sically antithetical to the car, or to put it conversely, the ideal way to enter this museum is hardly from its parking lot. Thus, as Suisman writes:

The first impression of the Kimbell parking lot facade is its blankness—no recog-nizable windows, unbroken panels of concrete and travertine, a dark horizontal gash for an entryway. . . . Passing into the recess of the entry your eyes have no time to adjust before entering the lobby, so your initial impression of the interior is a gloomy one indeed.

The ideal entrance is by way of the pedestrian approach from the park, but this is relatively unused:

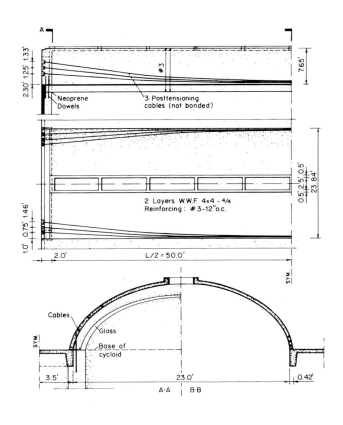

A

2.30' 1.25' 1.33'

#3

7.65'

Neoprene Dowels

3 Posttensioning cables (not bonded)

0.5' 2.5' 0.5'
23.84'

2 Layers W.W.F. 4x4 - 4/4
Reinforcing : #3-12"o.c.

1.0' 0.75' 1.46'

2.0'

L/2 = 50.0'

SYM.

SYM.

Cables

Glass

Base of cycloid

3.5'

23.0'

0.42'

A-A | B-B

7.43

Louis I. Kahn, Kimbell Art Museum: side elevation of shells with post-tensioning cables; plan, post-tensioning cables, and skylight; cross section of shell-end arch, with glass separation between end arch and walls.

7.44

Louis I. Kahn, Kimbell Art Museum, isometric drawing of the elements of construction.

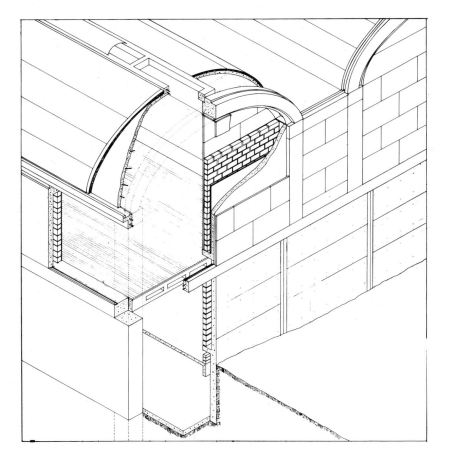

7.45
Kahn in the Kimbell auditorium.

7.46
Louis I. Kahn, Kimbell Art Museum, view of entrance.

It's only later that you learn that a mere 15 per cent of all museum visitors actually enter through this so-called entrance where Kahn expected them; the other 85 per cent arrive by car, park in the lot, and enter through the basement. Could Kahn's reported failure to obtain a driver's license possibly explain this flagrant miscalculation of suburban habits?[58]

It is nonetheless clear that the traditional occidental monument, together with the institution it embodies, demands that one should arrive on foot and enter via a threshold in order to undergo an appropriate rite of passage between the representational portico of the monument and its internal space of public appearance, the very transition that is compromised everywhere today by the universal aporia of the automobile. For Kahn this was particularly distressing inasmuch as he had striven throughout his life for the full integration of modern technology with the substance of institutional form. As we have remarked, this rite of passage is ideally achieved at Kimbell in the approach from the park, where, passing under the foreground canopy of trees, one crosses a stepped threshold between the cascading fountains before entering the museum proper via a graveled forecourt and a grove of diminutive trees. Once upon this axis, one finds oneself in a green labyrinth, where the gravel underfoot is destabilizing and where the corresponding sound of one's footfall is overlaid by the continual rush of the water. In such a setting, perhaps more fitting for a temple than a museum, we find ourselves returned to the tactility of the tectonic in all its aspects; to a meeting between the essence of things and the existence of beings, to that pre-Socratic moment, lying outside time, that is at once both modern and antique.

8 Jørn Utzon:
Transcultural Form and the Tectonic Metaphor

Jørn Utzon's work prefigured the third generation's conversion to an organic conception of environmental order which displaced the first generation's rational bias. The inapplicability of the first generation's rigid rationalistic and extrinsic formulae as templates for structuring the environment forced architects among Utzon's generation to investigate relatively freer, intrinsic systems of order. Almost without exception—Roche and Stirling—the third generation acquired an organic outlook which involved taking instructions from the environment instead of enforcing preconceived rationalistic structures upon it. Wright's architecture is usually understood as a romantic nineteenth-century liaison with nature. At the heart of his understanding of the organic was the insistence that the designer listen to the environment. Utzon followed his understudy of Gunnar Asplund and Alvar Aalto (1945) with a visit to Taliesin West and Taliesin East where he spent a short time with Frank Lloyd Wright (1949). He thus learned to work with nature. Unselfconscious architecture was the route taken by the European mind in reestablishing contact with the organic domain of environmental structure. A visit to Morocco in 1948 supplied Utzon with a model of molecular form generation of "additive architecture." . . . The implementation of the concept of system-generating systems enabled Utzon to resolve the conflicting demands of standardization for repetitive production without sacrificing the flexibility essential for negotiating the indeterminate terrain of human functions. . . . Utzon substituted the anonymous expression of collective consciousness and symbiosis with landscape in place of rampant individual expression. . . . The physical tension induced by Utzon's opposition of hovering roofs and strong earth-hugging platforms defines the architectural space. . . . The edges of the platform and underside of the roofs mark the transition from architecture to landscape. The omission of vertical structure from Utzon's esquisses evokes a trance-like quality of ascension and cosmic awareness.
Philip Drew, The Third Generation, *1972*

Surely the most singular aspect of Jørn Utzon's contribution is his particular concern for the expressivity of structure and construction. Like the Norwegian architect Sverre Fehn, with whom he has collaborated on several occasions, Utzon's work is grounded in the tectonic line of the modern movement. In this regard he may be seen as part of a continuous development extending from Auguste Perret to Carlo Scarpa. As we have seen, this line has its origins in the nineteenth century in the practice of such architects as Henri Labrouste and in the writings of Eugène Viollet-le-Duc, who argued that truth in architecture had to be determined about the twin axes of the program and the construction. Within this tradition, for Utzon, as for Louis Kahn, "what the building wants to be" has depended upon the embodiment of an institutional form within an expressive structure.

A prominent element in Utzon's architecture is his transcultural intention, his tendency to seek inspiration outside the Eurocentric domain. This critical, cross-cultural stance informs almost all of his architecture, and in this he has much in common with Frank Lloyd Wright, whom he met in 1949 and by whom he was to be profoundly influenced. Utzon's point of departure in this regard is set forth in one of his few didactic texts, his essay "Platforms and Plateaus: The Ideas of a Danish Architect" that appeared in the Italian periodical *Zodiac* in 1962. This essay makes a number of intercultural comparisons that are experiential rather than visual in character.

The floor in a traditional Japanese house is a delicate bridge-like platform. This Japanese platform is like a table top. It is a piece of furniture. The floor here at-

tracts you as the wall does in a European house. You want to sit close to the wall in a European house, and here in Japan, you want to sit on the floor and not walk on it. All life in Japanese houses is expressed in sitting, lying or crawling movements. Contrary to the Mexican rock-like feeling of the plateau, here you have a feeling similar to the one you have when standing on a small wooden bridge, dimensioned just to take your weight and nothing more. A refined addition to the expression of the platform in the Japanese house is the horizontal emphasis provided by the movements of the sliding doors and screens, and the black pattern made by the edges of the floor mats that accentuate the surface.[1]

Utzon rightly perceives such tactile oriental forms as having a corporeal impact on the subject. Clearly, by platform he intends the lightweight timber floor of traditional Japanese domestic construction (fig. 1.8). He contrasts the flexion of such a floor to the inertia felt by the body as it stands on a pre-Columbian pyramid, where gravity braces the subject against an immobile mass beneath. This opposition between the culture of the light and the culture of the heavy will manifest itself to different degrees in different cultures, with certain societies tending to be either exclusively stereotomic or exclusively tectonic in character, as in, say, the pyramids of Mesoamerica in the first instance or the timber building cultures of Southeast Asia in the second. In many cultures, including that of China, one will find a typical opposition between a heavyweight masonry podium and a lightweight timber roof floating over it, as in Utzon's generic sketch of the podium/pagoda paradigm (fig. 8.1). We will encounter this formula in one Utzon scheme after another, where it invariably assumes the form of a shell roof or a folded slab structure suspended over a terraced earthwork. Elsewhere in his *Zodiac* essay Utzon remarks that our bodily posture is also culturally conditioned. "In the West," he writes, "one gravitates towards the wall, in the East one gravitates towards the floor."[2] The transcultural domestic equivalent of the oriental podium/pagoda paradigm can be found in Utzon's characteristic patio house, invariably rendered as an L-shaped cell enclosing the semipublic space of the atrium within its form. Covered by a lightweight monopitched roof, this courtyard house is a synthesis of many cultural strands, in part Islamic, in part Chinese, in part an antique type of Mediterranean or African origin.

We have already noted that for Viollet-le-Duc the achievement of a great span was the touchstone, so to speak, of a great civilization. And in this regard, despite the technological prowess of the nineteenth century he saw the tectonic culture of the Occident as having attained its apotheosis in the medieval cathedral. While one can hardly claim that Utzon has been obsessed with large spans, he has nonetheless consistently displayed a preference for column-free public volumes covered by folded slabs or shell roofs, that is to say, for works in which the basic character derives from structural articulation of the sectional form. In as much as he has favored organically profiled clear-span structures, his work may be assimilated to the tradition of the North, that is, to a particularly Baltic ethos that is manifest in different ways in the work of Alvar Aalto and Hans Scharoun. All these figures share a common impulse that surely draws some of its inspiration from Paul Scheerbart's prose-poem *Glasarchitektur* of 1914, or even with greater likelihood from the anarcho-socialist, mystical vision of Bruno Taut. I have in mind Taut's seminal text *Die Stadtkrone* of 1919, wherein he posits the "city crown" as being essential not only to the spiritual well-being of society but also to the sociocultural constitution of civic life. This concept was cross-cultural to the extent that Taut regarded the *Stadtkrone* as a

8.1
Jørn Utzon, sketch of Chinese temple; roof and platform.

8.2
P. V. Jensen-Klint, Grundtvig Church, Copenhagen, 1920–1940. West elevation.

8.3
P. V. Jensen-Klint, Grundtvig Church, plan.

universal phenomenon, assuming different forms in different places and at different times, whether a Greek temple, a Gothic cathedral, an Indian stupa, or a Chinese pagoda. Thus out of some sixty images that illustrate *Die Stadtkrone,* thirty are Gothic or Romanesque in origin, seven are Islamic, and ten are pagodas of various kinds.[3] While Utzon may not have read Taut's essay, he would surely have known of its existence through Steen Eiler Rasmussen, who was his prime theory teacher at the Royal Danish Academy in Copenhagen. In any event, such a city crown was under construction in Utzon's home town during the early years of his life; namely, P. V. Jensen-Klint's Grundtvig Church that, together with its surrounding residential enclave, was not finally complete until 1940 (figs. 8.2, 8.3). We know that this building was a fundamental point of reference for Rasmussen, notably for the precision of its craftsmanship and its use of uncut fair-faced brickwork throughout.

In his book *Experiencing Architecture* of 1959, Rasmussen cites Jensen-Klint to the effect that one should consciously cultivate the art of brickwork and above all use a minimum of shaped or cut bricks. In this regard, the Grundtvig Church may be seen as a prime source of Utzon's tectonic principles, not only for its craft precision and ingenuity but also for its exclusive use of a single modular material.[4] That the work of the younger Klint was also an influence on Utzon is borne out not only by the tectonic furniture that Kaare Klint designed for the Grundtvig Church but also, somewhat incidentally, through a particular plaque that he designed in 1930 as a commemorative tablet for Thomas Bredsdorf and his wife (fig. 8.4). Bredsdorf had been director of the Flensberg Dockyards in Copenhagen, and appropriately enough this plaque depicts a hull under construction, in both plan and section. This image recalls Utzon's own shipbuilding background, his marine architect father, and the similarity that obtains between the framing of a wooden boat and the construction of a Scandinavian stave church. This traditional affinity between boat building and church building, which was put forward as a seminal key to classical culture in Paul Valéry's *Eupalinos* of 1922, is also remarked on by Sverre Fehn who would characterize the church as an inverted boat; an association that would appear to be supported by a curious etymological connection in which the Latin word for ship, *navis,* is also commonly applied to the principal volume of a church.[5]

The extent to which Utzon is a product of the Klint School has perhaps been insufficiently recognized, for Jensen-Klint imparted to his followers an attitude

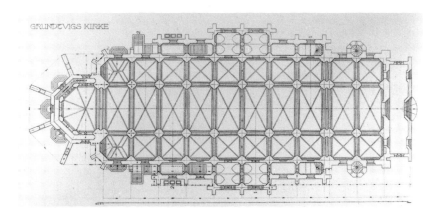

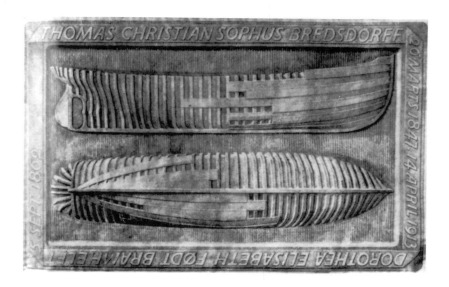

8.4
Kaare Klint, tombstone for his parents-in-law,
Thomas Bredsdorff and his wife, 1930.
Bredsdorff was a director of Flensborg
Dockyards.

that went beyond the tectonic purity of his heroic church. Jensen-Klint's Grundt-
vigian (Christian Socialist) feeling for rooted vernacular was incorporated into
the pedagogy of the Royal Academy through his architect son Kaare, who was
still on the faculty there when Utzon was a student. The extent to which Utzon
was influenced by the Klintian line is suggested by Lisbeth Balslev Jørgensen's
account of Jensen-Klint's philosophy. The anti-academic, anticlassical elder
Klint thought that architectural students should be trained to build rather than
design and that the student "should study the landscape of dolmens, churches,
manors, and farms, and when all these architectural manifestations of his ancestors have become part of him, he can give them back reborn without copying,
because then he gives himself." Jørgensen goes on to characterize Jensen-
Klint's first house, the Villa Holm of 1896, as having "an organic nature, growing
according to the laws of nature." Thereafter she remarks on Jensen-Klint's
polemical use of the term building, his preferring to style himself as a master
mason (*bygmester*) and to allude to his craft as "building culture" rather than
architecture.[6]

This profound feeling for an inflected landscape shaped by topography, climate,
time, material, and craft, and hence for an architecture engendered in large measure by natural forces, is a fundamental principle of Utzon's architecture. In his
1981 thesis, "Jørn Utzon: His Work and Ideas," Robert Bartholomew cites numerous instances that testify to Utzon's personal rapport with nature, let alone
his complimentary feeling for craft production that stemmed, in large part, from
his father and from the shipyards of Helsingør, which shaped his earliest experiences as a child.[7] As to the inspiration that Utzon derived from nature, we may
cite Kjeld Helm-Petersen's appreciation of Utzon's Kingo housing to the effect
that "[for] this artist there is no essential difference between a city organism and
a plant organism. He deduces living truths from the construction of nature and
reshapes them quickly into rough drafts for houses for human beings. . . . His
houses grow, like organisms, they reflect the form of nature's growth, they are
not theoretical frameworks for human life but live their own life because they are
structured according to the same physical laws that govern their inhabitants."[8]

To this we may add Utzon's lifelong love of sailing and the sea and go on to cite the testimony of a former assistant, Michael Tomaszewski, to the effect that "boat building would have given him a much freer geometric approach . . . he was not tied to a set-square and T-square like so many trained architects. He would have seen from a small child his father using the hundreds of French curves that they use in boat design."[9]

It is symptomatic of Utzon's background that, like Jensen-Klint, he would seek to escape from both formalism and academic functionalism by turning to nature and by returning to vernacular craft as though this too was ultimately a manifestation of nature. In this respect Utzon's architecture would seem to have been governed by two interrelated principles: the constructional logic of tectonic form and the syntactical logic of geometry. These two precepts were fused into a remarkable synthesis in the Sydney Opera House, where many of the parts were determined by solid geometry, thereafter to be reproduced wholesale through procedures that guaranteed acceptable levels of both quality control and dimensional tolerance. In this way, in 1961, after almost four years of constant search, Utzon hit upon the idea of deriving all the shell segments of Sydney from the surface of a sphere. This ingenious move not only testified to his early training in solid geometry but also, once again, to the influence of his shipyard youth.

The German occupation of Denmark coincided with Utzon's graduation from the Academy in 1942, and thereafter he left immediately for Sweden where he enlisted in the Danish brigade.[10] Toward the end of hostilities he worked for Paul Hedquist in Stockholm, then went to Helsinki to serve a brief apprenticeship with Aalto. On returning to Denmark early in 1945, he set up his first partnership with the architect and architectural historian Tobias Faber.[11] This short-lived but fruitful association led to a number of seminal projects, including their remarkable entry for the London Crystal Palace competition of 1947, designed in collaboration with Morgens Irming (fig. 8.5). Terraced podia and shell roofs were already as evident in this project as they had been in Utzon's earlier design for a crematorium. More important, however, was their joint manifesto of the same date entitled "Trends in Contemporary Architecture," wherein they took an independent stand against the nightmare of history that, for them, already included the ruined history of the "modern."[12] They recognized how welfare state functionalism, that is to say the *funkis* ideology and practice of the Swedish functionalist *Acceptera* declaration of 1930, had been undermined as a progressive cultural development by the advent of the war and its aftermath.[13] They acknowledged that the postwar world was as distanced from the social democratic utopian vision of Gunnar Asplund's 1930 Stockholm exhibition as it was from the neoclassical liberalism of Hack Kampmann's Copenhagen Police Headquarters of 1918 or from the Christian Socialist, neo-Gothic ideology of the Klint School. Thus they wrote:

Looking back on the development of architecture, up to the turn of the century architects worked in a tradition that was as in step with the slow evolution of technology as it was with the slowly evolving style of life. In the thirties, architects had a solid functionalist program, which arose from the fantastic technical development and from their love for it and from a radically changed lifestyle. The forties, however, are largely bereft of handholds. Our period has still not found its expression, neither in technique nor in art nor in lifestyle, because development continues unabated; and in contrast to the thirties, it has not found a clear direction, but rather it continues to aspire to unanticipated possibilities.

In opposition to this uncertainty, many are again sustaining themselves with tradition, with those forms with which there had been a break well before functionalism. In favorable circumstances this tradition becomes refined but in bad ones it merely reverts to functionalism. Others try to carry functionalism further but are unable to do so without ending up with formalistic results. One might call them motivists, in that they assemble the form of their architecture out of motives torn loose from their origins; motives with which they are infatuated. Their architecture becomes unclear, just like a language without a grammar.

Finally, there are architects who are in complete contact with today's lifestyle and who come from a school of thought that holds that architecture should embody the framework for this lifestyle—that first and foremost one has to live in it. They base their work on the people's fundamental feeling for architecture; a feeling which through the ages has always been the foundation of a true architecture. The notion of architectural feeling is employed here in a dual sense; that is, the feeling that allows us both to experience architecture and to make it.[14]

8.5
Jørn Utzon and Tobias Faber, competition entry for the London Crystal Palace, 1947. Site plan.

8.6
D'Arcy Thompson, illustration from *On Growth and Form,* showing how the *trabeculae* in a human femur (right) follow the stress patterns produced in the head of a crane (left).

8.7
Jørn Utzon, project for a paper factory in Morocco, 1947. Section showing the gravity feed of the production process.

8.8
Jørn Utzon, project for housing in Morocco, 1947. Schematic plan and elevation.

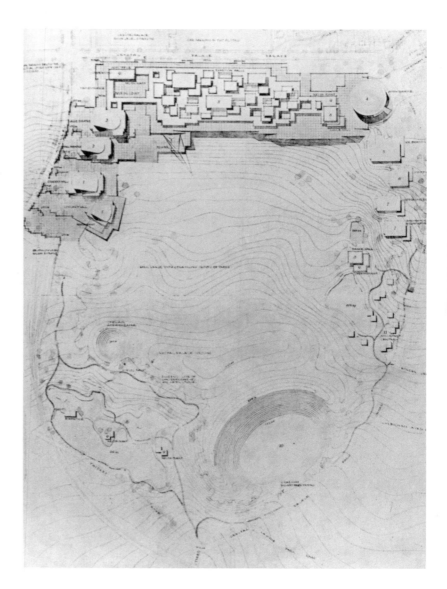

Following the thesis advanced by D'Arcy Thompson in his book *On Growth and Form* of 1917 (fig. 8.6),[15] the Faber-Utzon team attempted to derive their architecture from nature and vernacular form rather than from elite culture. The didactic illustrations that accompanied their 1947 manifesto were indicative in this regard; out of twenty-eight images, eleven were of natural forms (fungi, crystals, landscapes, etc.), nine were vernacular, and five were drawn from the so-called organic architecture of Wright and Aalto. In fact, both Utzon and Faber were interested in anonymous architecture long before the publication of Bernard Rudolfsky's book *Architecture without Architects*.[16] They sought to model their additive assemblies on natural forms of accretion and growth. It is significant that the very last illustration was of an iceberg set in a mountainous landscape; an image that returns us to Taut's alpine utopias as set forth in his book *Alpine Architektur* of 1919, not to mention Hans Scharoun's preoccupation with the image of icebergs floating in the Baltic.[17]

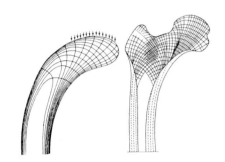

Utzon's short stay in Morocco in 1948 was already indicative of his affinity for the Orient. There he became involved with designs for a gravity-fed paper mill (fig. 8.7) and a stepped housing scheme (fig. 8.8), both being inspired by indigenous prototypes. What impressed Utzon about the Moroccan vernacular was "the unity of village and landscape, brought about by their identical material— earth."[18] The following year he received a travel scholarship for North America, and during this study tour he not only made contact with Wright in Taliesin West but also had occasion to meet Mies van der Rohe in Chicago. While Wright was to exercise an obvious influence on Utzon, the impact of Mies was equally decisive, despite the latter's distance from the ideology of organicism. Mies's early IIT work seems to have made an impression on Utzon at a number of fundamental levels. In the first instance there was Mies's susceptibility to the intrinsic quality of material; in the second, his concern for precision detailing, combined with rational, modular assembly. Finally there was also his application of standard

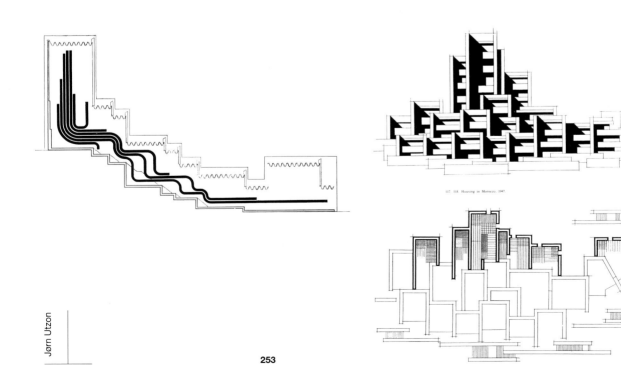

117. 118. Housing in Morocco, 1947

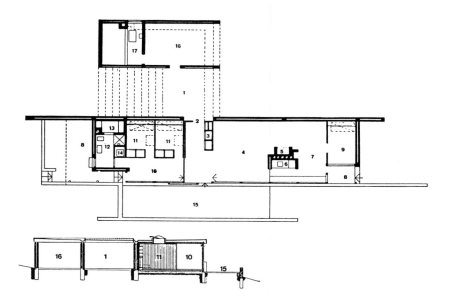

rolled steel sections that demonstrated the productive logic that Utzon would apply to the creation of three-dimensional, curved form. Of Mies's tectonic consistency, Utzon wrote: "Mies once mentioned to me, once a design was established and finalized, he made every effort to ensure that this design was emphasized in the design of secondary elements, such as doors, windows, non-load bearing walls and so on." [19]

Utzon's own house, built in Hellebaek, North Zealand, in 1952, was in many ways a synthesis of the principles he had absorbed from both Wright and Mies (fig. 8.9). This is evident from the low lines of the oversailing flat roof and horizontal window wall that jointly recall Wright's Usonian houses and from the contrapuntal, pinwheeling nature of the composition that recalls Mies's Brick Country House project of 1923 (figs. 6.3, 6.4). Shades of Mies's Farnsworth House (1947) are also present, most notably in the freestanding service core, but the whole is strongly affected by Wright's Usonian period and by the asperities of Danish brick and timber traditions. Nevertheless Mies's abstract aesthetic is still detectable in the vertical pine board lining of the interior, where full-height doors are rendered in such a way as to be indistinguishable from the planar walls and where the timber siding stops short of the soffit so as to separate, visually, the ceiling from the walls and induce the sense of an infinite space field.

Utzon's 1949 American tour gave him the opportunity to visit Mexico, and his initial experience of the Maya ruins of Chichén Itzá and Uxmal had a lasting im-

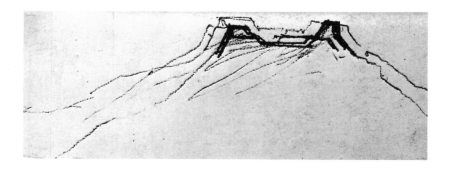

pact on his work and thought (fig. 8.10). Here, amid the stepped pyramid forms of the Yucatán jungle, he was to experience a different view of the horizon that would remind him not only of the sea but also of seasonal changes in the Scandinavian climate. In "Platforms and Plateaus" he wrote:

By introducing the platform with its level at the same height as the jungle top, these people had suddenly obtained a new dimension of life, worthy of their devotion to their gods. On these high platforms—many of them as long as 100 meters—they built their temples. They had from here the sky, the clouds and the breeze, and suddenly the jungle roof had been converted into a great open plain. By this architectural trick they had completely changed the landscape and supplied their visual life with a greatness corresponding to the greatness of their gods.

Today you can still experience this wonderful variation of feeling from the closeness in the jungle to the vast openness of the platform top. It is parallel to the relief you feel here in Scandinavia when after weeks of rain, clouds and darkness, you suddenly come through all this, out into the sunshine again.[20]

On his return to Denmark, Utzon projected his audacious, neo-Wrightian Langelinie Pavilion (1953) and then went on to enter a number of Swedish competitions in collaboration with the Swedish architects Erik and Henny Anderson. This was the period during which he also associated with the Norwegian architects Arne Kosmo and Sverre Fehn. Out of the Anderson-Utzon collaboration came one realized work, the Svaneke Seamark watertower built on Bornholm Island in the Baltic in 1955, together with a remarkable high-rise housing complex and town center projected for Elineberg, Hälsingborg, Sweden, in 1954 (fig. 8.11). This last, a neighborhood unit comprising a school, a shopping center, and high-rise bachelor housing, was, in effect, a more sophisticated version of the housing that Utzon had previously projected for Morocco. The Elineberg scheme is seminal at a number of levels; first, because of the way in which six fourteen-story cluster towers are united as a single form by a podium containing parking; second, because these towers are made up of combinations of the same megaron unit; and third, because the upper floors of the smaller units step down in section from back to front, that is to say from their northern core walls down to their south-facing window walls (fig. 8.12). Of this ingenious inflection Utzon wrote:

The section shows clearly an attempt to see more than the grey Nordic sky from the flats. . . . The grey Nordic sky is namely what you see when you have the normal windowsill and balcony balustrade. Here the floors are terraced—the higher, the steeper the steps—so you can stand on the 14th floor and see the beautiful ocean 2 kilometers away. The windowsill and the balcony balustrade are at the same level as your feet. The facade with balconies in these concrete (slip-form) houses, with their rather closed northern, eastern and western fronts, is constructed of vibrated concrete elements, like sticks woven together, as seen on the elevation. . . . The dizzy feeling on the top floor has been reduced by protecting vertical elements and greenery will grow on them.[21]

Since these trellises increase their density across the facade the higher they go, thereby compensating for their distance from the ground by a greater sense of enclosure, the overall tower section may be seen as pursuing a similar notion of incremental form to what we will find in Louis Kahn's initial proposal for the Richards Laboratories (1959). In both instances, the aerial elements increase their

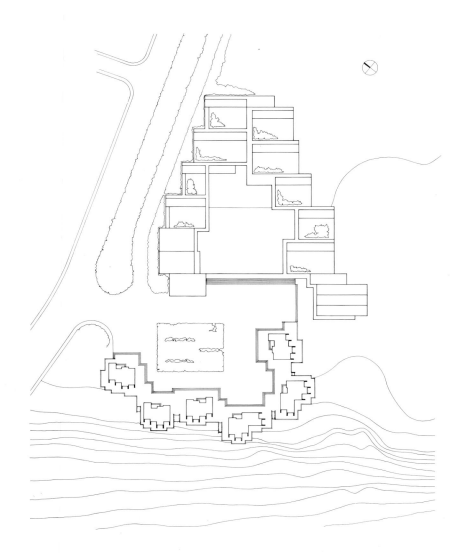

8.11
Jørn Utzon, housing complex and town center, Elineberg, Hälsingborg, Sweden, 1954. Site plan. Housing towers are stacked on a parking podium; a shopping center is located to the northeast of the housing cluster.

8.12
Jørn Utzon, Elineberg, section, plan, and elevation of housing tower. The sectional displacement of the floors increases on the upper levels of the building.

density as they rise upward—trellises in Elineberg and ventilating shafts in Philadelphia—while conversely the telluric elements increase their density as they descend, the exterior terraces and cross walls in Elineberg and cantilevering beam sections in Philadelphia. Of equal import, however, is Utzon's proposition to grow vines on the trellises so as to transform the cluster towers into cliffs of cascading greenery; a provision that would tend, as in much of Utzon's work, to attenuate the boundary separating culture from nature. One may even see this incremental trelliswork as an effort to compensate for the disappearance of ornament; to make up for that lack remarked on by Adolf Loos in "Ornament und Verbrechen" (Ornament and Crime) in 1908:

What makes our period so important is that it is incapable of producing new ornament. We have outgrown ornament and struggled through to a state without ornament. . . . The lack of ornament is a sign of intellectual power. Modern man uses the ornament of past and foreign cultures at his discretion. His own inventions are concentrated on other things.[22]

Loos capped this conclusion two years later by the following observation about the cultural disinheritance of the modern world.

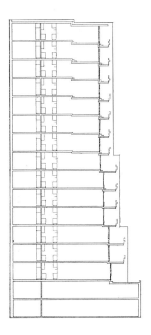

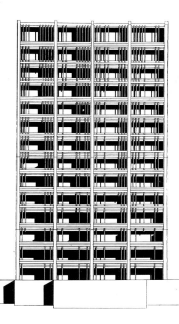

Mankind's history has not yet had to record a period without culture. The creation of such a period was reserved for the urban dweller during the second half of the nineteenth century. Until then the development of our culture has remained in a state of flux. One obeyed the commands of the hour and did not look forwards or backwards.[23]

Loos's own use of natural form as a surrogate ornament is most evident in his internal application of thin marble revetment. Loos used the stone as a thin screen, however, as a mask that he referred to ironically as inexpensive wallpaper; and this proto-Dadaist stance could hardly be further removed from the benevolent organicism underlying Utzon's work.

Utzon's involvement with China dates from 1959, when he went to the Far East to study traditional Chinese building methods. There he came across the twelfth-century Chinese building manual *Yingzao fashi,*[24] a document that prior to the twentieth century had served as the basic Chinese building code. Utzon found this text exemplary, largely because it demonstrated how a timber syntax, compiled out of interlocking standard components, could be used to create an extremely varied range of building types (fig. 8.13). What intrigued him about the system was the way in which the typical roof truss was not triangulated as it is in the West, but made up of stacked beams stepping up toward the apex. This trabeated additive structure, comprising straight beams plus elaborate cantilevered brackets, assured the expressive flexibility of the system (fig. 8.14). Without such a stepped approach the characteristic curve of the Chinese roof could never have been achieved (fig. 8.15). This additive method had a great impact on Utzon, but of even greater consequence was the fact that the same kit of parts could be used to assemble quite different roof forms, the type being modified according to local climatic conditions throughout China. Moreover, the system had inherent antiseismic properties inasmuch as the weight of the roof and the friction points between the joints had the capacity to dampen and absorb the shock waves. According to the Australian architect Peter Myers, Utzon kept a copy of the *Yingzao fashi* in his Sydney office and used it as his *vade mecum,* applying its fundamental principles to the development of the Sydney Opera House, which had been won in competition in 1957.[25] On his way back from China Utzon visited Japan, where he encountered a different and more delicate inflection of the original Chinese architecture as this appeared in the traditional Japanese architectural syntax of standard partitions, shutters, and modular floor panels, respectively the *shoji, amado,* and *tatami* of the Japanese house (see figs. 1.20, 1.21). In the following year, Utzon widened his experience of the Orient by visiting India, Nepal, and Tibet.

Utzon's Langelinie tower restaurant proposal of 1953 is effectively a reinterpreted pagoda form that owes a great deal to Wright's Johnson Wax research tower, built in Racine, Wisconsin, in 1947 (figs. 8.16, 8.17). In Langelinie, as in Racine, the basic structure comprises a cylindrical hollow service core, from which cantilevered platforms extend to embody the floors of the building (fig. 8.18). Where the floors in Wright's tower are of constant width and merely alternate between square and circular plan shapes, Utzon's circular platforms not only alternate between large and small but also progressively diminish in diameter as they rise toward the top, in a manner that simulates the traditional pagoda profile. The hollow concrete structure of the platforms, the use of voids within the structural diaphragm as air-conditioning ducts, the gently stepped section of

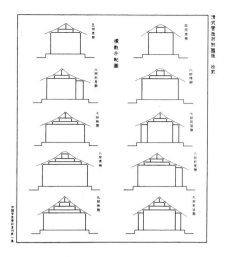

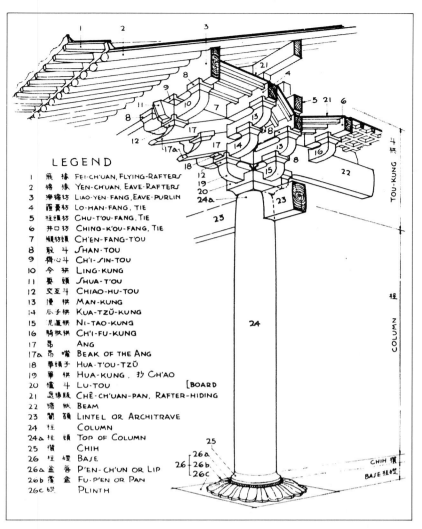

LEGEND

1 飛 椽 Fei-ch'uan, Flying-Rafters
2 橑 椽 Yen-ch'uan, Eave-Rafters
3 撩檐枋 Liao-yen-fang, Eave-Purlin
4 羅漢枋 Lo-han-fang, Tie
5 柱頭枋 Chu-t'ou-fang, Tie
6 井口枋 Ching-k'ou-fang, Tie
7 襯枋頭 Ch'en-fang-t'ou
8 散 斗 Shan-tou
9 齊心斗 Ch'i-sin-tou
10 令 栱 Ling-kung
11 耍 頭 Shua-t'ou
12 交互斗 Chiao-hu-tou
13 慢 栱 Man-kung
14 瓜子栱 Kua-tzŭ-kung
15 泥道栱 Ni-tao-kung
16 騎栿栱 Ch'i-fu-kung
17 昂 Ang
17a 昂 嘴 Beak of the Ang
18 華頭子 Hua-t'ou-tzŭ
19 華 栱 Hua-kung, 抄 Ch'ao
20 櫨 斗 Lu-tou   [Board
21 遮椽版 Chê-ch'uan-pan, Rafter-hiding
22 榑 栿 Beam
23 闌 額 Lintel or Architrave
24 柱 Column
24a 柱 頭 Top of Column
25 櫍 Chih
26 柱 礎 Base
26a 盆 脣 P'en-ch'un or Lip
26b 覆 盆 Fu-p'en or Pan
26c 磉 Plinth

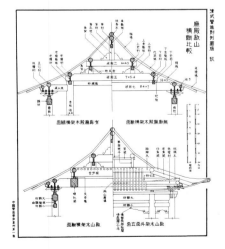

8.13
Plate from a Chinese building manual of the Ch'ing dynasty (1644–1911).

8.14
Chinese bracketing: the *tou kung* system.

8.15
Plate from a Chinese building manual of the Ch'ing dynasty.

8.16
Jørn Utzon, Langelinie Pavilion project, Copenhagen, 1953.

8.17
Frank Lloyd Wright, S. C. Johnson and Son Research Center, Racine, Wisconsin, 1947. Section.

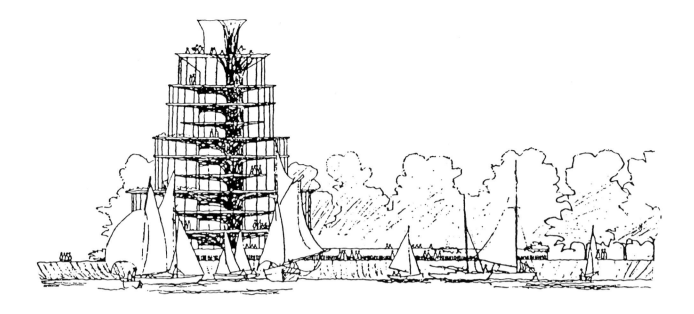

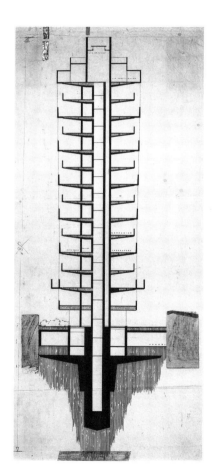

the dining levels, inflected so as to afford panoramic views to every table, the integrated structural core comprising lavatories, dumb-waiters, and elevators, the stepped tiers of the suspended glazing, all of these features testify to the power of Utzon's tectonic imagination and to his capacity to adapt a Wrightian paradigm to a different program.

It is hard to overestimate the influence of Wright on Utzon, for while there is nothing that is stylistically Wrightian about Utzon's work, Wright's tectonic concerns are evident in one form or another throughout the Danish architect's career. This influence is at its most explicit perhaps in the Langelinie Pavilion and in the Silkeborg Museum, designed in 1962 as a sculptural gallery for the Norwegian artist Asger Jørn, who had been a founder of the international Cobra group. The fact that the Cobra movement was equally non-Eurocentric in its cultural affinities is surely significant, given Utzon's own disposition.[26]

The parti of Silkeborg derived from Utzon's personal experience in China, stemming directly from his visit to the Tatung caves where he saw a collection of Buddhist sculptures cradled in the fissures of the earth. Utzon's radical transformation of this image into an underground museum was peculiarly appropriate to the *art brut* primitivism of the Cobra circle. Not withstanding this, the concentrically ramped galleries of the Silkeborg scheme (fig. 8.19) also came from a transposition of Wright's Guggenheim Museum (fig. 8.20), which had in its turn been derived from the inversion of an Assyrian ziggurat. In this development, Wright's first ziggurat project, the upward-spiraling Gordon Strong Automobile Objective and Planetarium of 1924 (fig. 8.21), becomes the inverted, hollowed-out, downward-spiraling Guggenheim Museum.[27] Typologically speaking, we pass via the Guggenheim, from the monumental but dematerializing thrust of the Gordon Strong spiral to the bowel-like, earthbound materiality of Utzon's Silkeborg. In this trajectory it was the inspiration of the oriental form that was a constant for both Wright and Utzon.

Shaped like two large intersecting double cisterns and equipped with interlocking circuits of circular ramps and an ingenious system of gridded roof lights, Silkeborg has to be counted among the more unique of Utzon's early inventions, and surely if one had the choice of realizing only one of his unbuilt works, this would be a preference. An earthwork by definition, Silkeborg can be seen as the categoric antithesis to the Langelinie Pavilion; the cavernous *mundus*[28] versus the aerial pagoda. However, we need to note two other important aspects of the work; first, the way in which Wright's metaphorical transposition of the generic car ramp in the Guggenheim Museum (transposed from the Gordon Strong proposal) reappears in the swirling concentric trajectories of the passerelles conducting visitors down into the bowels of Utzon's museum (fig. 8.22), and second, the way in which the concentric organic geometry of the galleries is ingeniously offset by translucent roof lights having a corrugated structural section, capable of spanning the lower volumes at ground level (cf. Sverre Fehn's Nordic Pavilion for the Venice Biennale of 1967). A similarly ribbed and striated structure reappears in the inverted vaults supporting the floor of the mezzanines situated between the ground and the subterranean cisterns.

As I have already remarked, Utzon's architecture may be read in terms of the Semperian formula of the earthwork versus the roofwork. This countervailing but complementary opposition generally appears in his work through the spectrum of three different type forms of increasing hierarchical complexity, each type being largely determined by a variation in the roof. Thus we advance from the

8.18
Jørn Utzon, Langelinie Pavilion, detail plan and section.

8.19
Jørn Utzon, Silkeborg Museum, 1962. Gallery floor plan and section.

8.20
Frank Lloyd Wright, Solomon R. Guggenheim Museum, New York, 1946–1959. Section.

8.21
Frank Lloyd Wright, Automobile Objective and Planetarium for Gordon Strong, Sugarloaf Mountain, Maryland, 1924.

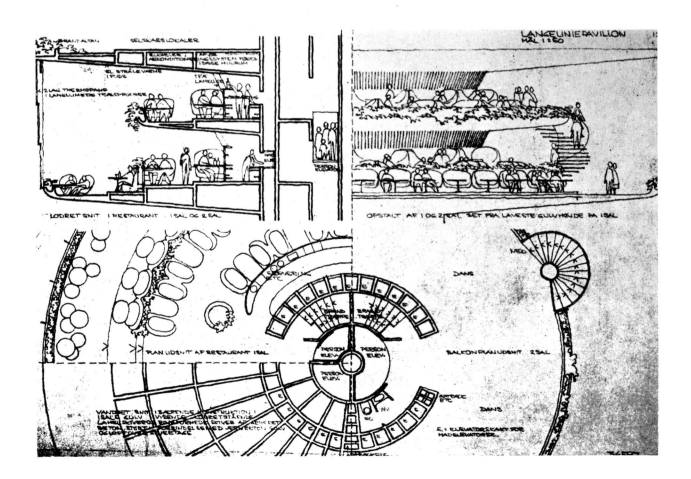

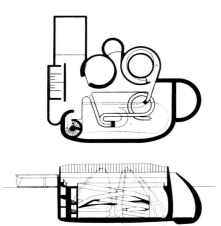

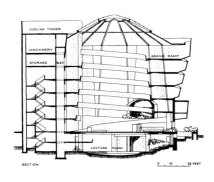

monopitch roof of Utzon's domestic atrium, to the folded slab roof of his typical concourse space, to his use of the shell-pagoda form for a larger assembly space. In each instance, significant differences occur in the nature of the wall spanning between earthwork and roofwork. In the first type, the main wall element is a load-bearing boundary that encloses both house and atrium, although this is paralleled by a lightweight screen wall running around the interior of the court. In this type the podium is reduced to a shallow platform accommodating the slope. In the second type the roofwork consists of a folded concrete slab suspended above the elevated earthwork, while in the third type the roofwork is a shell form set above a stepped podium. While these last two types are invariably bounded by screen walls, the Silkeborg Museum is something of an exception since it comprises an earthwork that is sunken into the ground and roofed by a mixture of folded-slab and shell form construction.

The first of these types, the atrium, appears in two related housing schemes realized early in Utzon's career, the Kingo and Fredensborg residential settlements of 1958 and 1963 respectively. The same typology also appears in a project for a new quarter designed for the town of Odense in 1963. The second paradigm, the folded slab roof, manifests itself in two different versions, the domestic and the civic. In the first instance, it shows up in Utzon's own house projected for Bayview, Sydney, between 1964 and 1965; in the second it crowns the parti for both the Helsingør school and the Zurich Opera House projects of 1963. Meanwhile the third type, the shell-pagoda suspended above the podium, recurs repeatedly throughout the first fifteen years of Utzon's practice, attaining its fullest expression in the Sydney Opera House.

If some kind of pagoda is a recurrent theme in Utzon's civic architecture, its domestic complement is the atrium house, with its potential to accommodate itself to any kind of topography. This is a primordial dwelling in which the roofwork

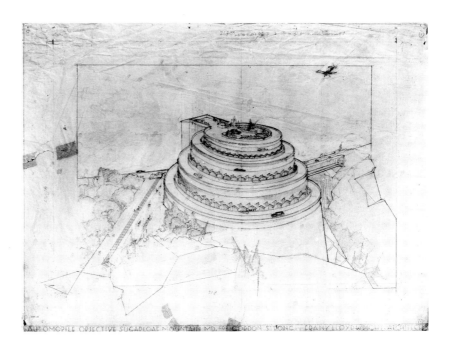

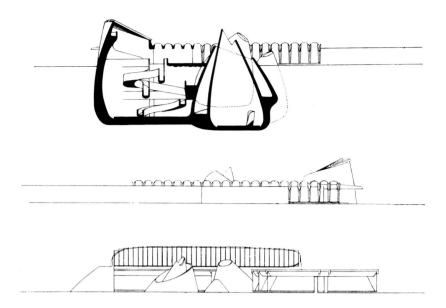

and the earthwork are linked by a perimeter wall that gives shape to the morphology of the settlement. With the exception of its latent presence in his own house in Hellebaek, this wall first appears in his expandable *skånske hustyper* designed for towns in Skåne, southern Sweden, in 1953.[29] The same concept will be returned to in his Kingo housing scheme of 1956 in Helsingør (Elsinore), comprising some 63 single-story, square atrium houses, arranged in eleven contiguous clusters of varying size on a rather irregular site (fig. 8.23). All the courtyards face south, southwest, or southeast, while the walled-in northern elevations serve to link the garages and entries that line the perimeter of the development. This neo-Radburn approach to the site plan allows the residents to wander at liberty over an inner greensward that is loosely defined by the perimeter and by two fingers of patio housing that break up the inner domain.

Unlike his later Fredensborg settlement of 1962–1963 (fig. 8.24), Kingo comprises a much looser house form, in which the first line of demarcation is the courtyard itself. Utzon projected a number of alternative plans for Kingo and even suggested that, as in the Skåne type, the units may grow across time within the confines of the bounding wall (figs. 8.25, 8.26, 8.27). The different plans proposed by Utzon amount to a series of permutations on a standard three-bedroom L-shaped unit. At times the continuity of the L-form is only carried by the roof, with the living volume breaking down into a separate study or a semidetached room for an elderly person. In all the different versions, the carport is variously accommodated beneath the roof and the garden is treated in a variety of ways. In one instance the house is equipped with a conservatory, in another with a playroom, in yet another with a boatyard. As I have already noted, Wright's Usonian house is unquestionably an influence on the Utzon atrium dwelling as this appears in both Kingo and Fredensborg, the debt being acknowledged, as it were, by the use of the Wrightian cherokee red as a finish for the timber fenestration of Fredensborg. However, the Usonian house is not the only model to which these housing schemes are indebted. Thus, we find the use of tile-capped Chinese walls in both schemes and chimneys profiled after

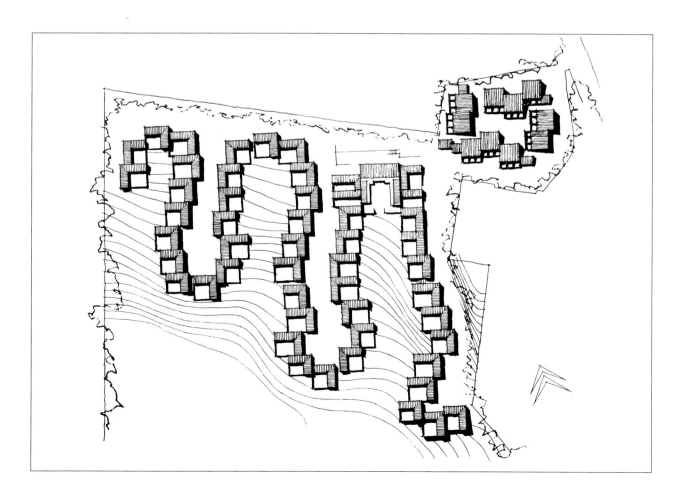

the shape of Middle Eastern ventilation shafts, a reference surely to the wind towers of Iran reinterpreted in Danish brickwork (cf. the Bad-Ghir of Yazd) (figs. 8.28, 8.29). Iberian culture is also evoked through the use of Spanish tiles and in the timber-battened grillwork to the pierced window openings. In his retrospective essay on the Fredensborg settlement Tobias Faber also cites a particular type of courtyard farm complex to be found in the Vaucluse area of southern France, and mentions the general influence of the Austrian architect Roland Rainer on Utzon.[30] Japanese rock gardens and Scandinavian dolmens are also surely evoked by Utzon's random placement of rocks in the surrounding greensward.

In the plan for Odense, Utzon assembles his carpet housing paradigm into a larger urban whole (fig. 8.30). In this instance, some two hundred patio dwellings are shown radiating out, Radburn style, from a "city crown," thereby positing a categorical opposition between the private fabric of the patio and the public realm of the city hall, roofed by a concrete shell. Utzon orchestrated this assembly in such a way as to resemble a traditional Islamic city, where each individual courtyard house is bonded to the next as part of a continuous fabric. This modular/morphological approach is present in all of Utzon's urban studies, irrespective of whether the basic unit is an atrium or a cross-walled megaron, as in the Elineberg or Birkehøj town plans respectively, dating from 1945 and 1960. In

8.25
Jørn Utzon, Kingo housing, alternative rectangular and square prototypes, allowing for growth.

8.26
Jørn Utzon, Kingo housing, house plan, one variation.

8.27
Jørn Utzon, southern Swedish house types competition, 1950, First Prize. Axonometric. This type will be reworked in the Kingo housing scheme of 1956.

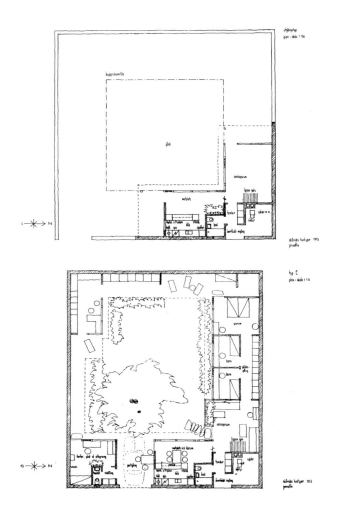

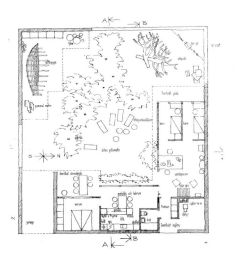

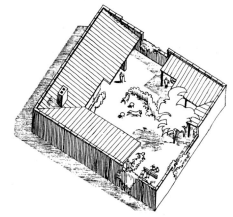

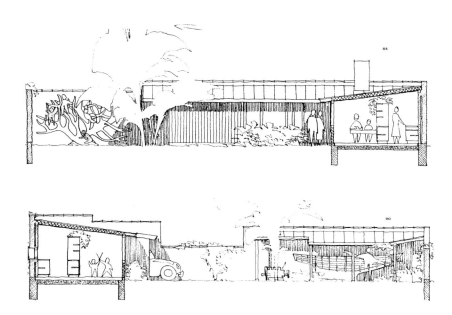

these plans, tripartite clusters of towers and terrace houses are respectively employed as the basic units from which the urban fabric is compounded (fig. 8.31).
Inspired by Aalto's Kauttua housing (1937) (fig. 8.32), and by his radical terrace
housing for Sunila (1936) (fig. 8.33), Utzon's terraced Birkehøj dwelling units fan
out across the contours in groups of three, reminiscent of the adobe housing of
the American Southwest. Of this arrangement he wrote:

*The small square on top of the hill surrounded by houses with small flats for old
people will create an environment with a peaceful protected atmosphere in a relatively open landscape, not unlike the feeling in small Italian villages. Great care
has been taken to follow the landscape and to utilize its values. The standardized
building elements will be combined in such a way . . . in the flats and in the
single houses themselves to get a combination without the awful stiffness well-
known from many modern housing schemes. There are many ways to arrange
the same books in a book-shelf. I can hardly see any reason for repetition of the*

8.28
Jørn Utzon, Fredensborg housing, sections.

8.29
Jørn Utzon, Fredensborg housing.

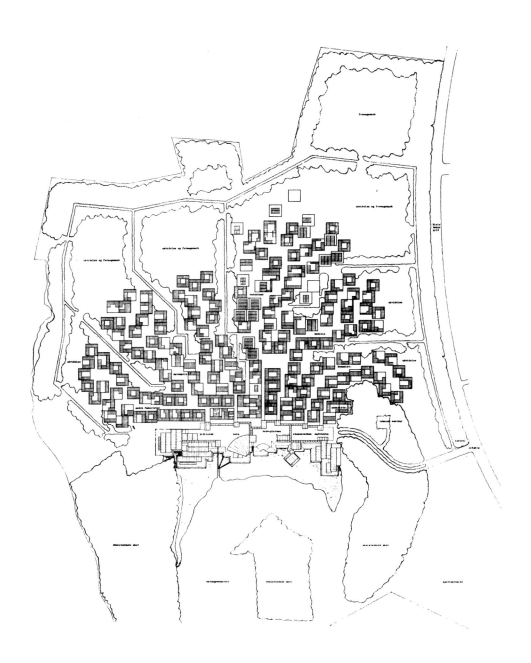

8.30
Jørn Utzon, project for Odense, 1967. Site
plan; section and plan of public buildings.

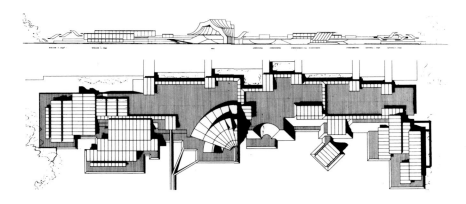

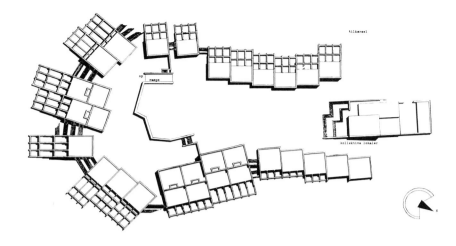

same face on different flats beside each other and over each other in these sad modern housing schemes. [31]

As Sigfried Giedion and others have remarked, Utzon's work displays that rare capacity of combining *organic* with *geometric* form and of creating the former out of the latter. Nowhere is this more evident than in his Kingo and Fredensborg settlements and in his plans for Odense and Birkehøj. A comparable, if less cellular, version of the same approach may be found in a heroic megastructural scheme that he designed for Elviria, Spain, in 1960.

Like Wright, Utzon has engaged structural form in ways that few architects have had the will or the capacity for; for while architects invariably employ engineers to help them achieve large spans, few have elected to ground their primary expression in the spanning capacity of folded-slab construction. I refer here not only to Utzon's involvement with reinforced concrete shell construction, as is evi-

8.31
Jørn Utzon, housing at Birkehøj, North Zealand, 1960. Site plan of the town.

8.32
Alvar Aalto, housing at Kauttua, Finland, 1937–1940. Site plan.

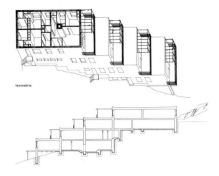

Isometrie

denced by the Sydney Opera House, but also his folded-slab roofs projected as post-tensioned long-span structures in reinforced concrete. This particular form, rarely employed outside the engineering work of Eugène Freyssinet and Pier Luigi Nervi, first appears in the wide-span folded-plate roofs that Utzon proposed for his World Exhibition Center designed for Copenhagen in 1960 (fig. 8.34). Here we find both cantilevered and clear spans in folded-slab construction, varying from 80 feet in the first instance to 240 feet in the second. These audacious spans were being projected at a time when among the largest folded-plate structures in concrete was the 164-foot span employed by Nervi for the lecture hall that he built in 1956 for the UNESCO headquarters in Paris, as designed by Marcel Breuer and Bernard Zehrfuss (fig. 8.35).

A more moderate application of an all-encompassing folded-plate roof appears in Utzon's main entry for the Højstrup High School, projected for the Danish Trades Union as a college for further education to be built at Helsingør in 1958 (fig. 8.36).[32] Although no basement plans have been published for this work, one may assume that the undercroft was allocated to parking while its upper surface was terraced in such a way as to evoke a city in miniature, recalling in its orthogonal geometry and rhythmic scale those classic Maya sites that Utzon had visited nine years before (fig. 8.37). Instead of temples, the podium projected for Helsingør supported a series of classrooms arranged around a central sunken court or "agora." We may think of these classrooms, roofed by folded slabs, as surrogate city fabric and of the shell-roofed assembly hall as the civic center, the equivalent of a church or a city hall. This combination of shell form with folded-plate structure is offset here by a high-rise residential tower, modeled on the fourteen-story Elineberg tower of 1954 (fig. 8.38). However disjunctive this last may seem in the context of a low-rise school, it patently serves to reinforce a reading of the complex as a mini-city. A similar use of folded plates appears in Utzon's design for a shopping center projected at virtually the same time. In this instance the V-shaped concrete roof sections span 120 feet over the principal shopping hall with cantilevered end spans of 40 feet each (fig. 8.39).

The folded-plate concept will reappear at a totally different scale in Utzon's designs for his own house at Bayview, Sydney, worked on intermittently between 1961 and 1965. Designed for a sloping site overlooking Pittwater, this house went through four separate versions before it was finally accepted by the local authorities. Conceptually related to the Silkeborg Museum, the Bayview project clearly breaks down, once again, into an earthwork and a roofwork. Like many of Wright's houses, the house establishes the character of the site by extending its domain horizontally through outriding boundary walls (figs. 8.40, 8.41). This

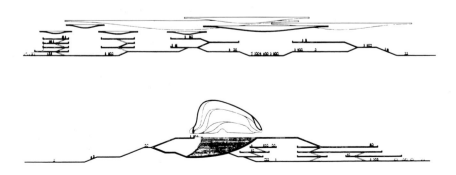

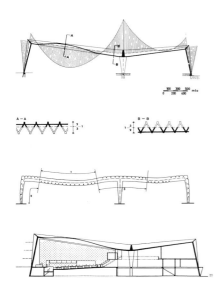

8.35
Pier Luigi Nervi, Marcel Breuer, and Bernard Zehrfuss, UNESCO Headquarters, Paris, 1953–1956. Structural diagrams (moment, tension, compression, and deflection) and building section of lecture hall.

8.36
Jørn Utzon, Højstrup Danish Trades Union High School for Further Education, Helsingør, Denmark, 1958. Roof plan.

not only increases the apparent size of the house but also establishes the territory of the dwelling within the topography rather than merely meeting the required area in a freestanding object. Like the Silkeborg Museum, the Bayview house is rendered as a kind of mirage on the horizon that announces itself largely through the skyline profile of its folded roof. It is significant that Utzon first projected this roof as a leaflike skeleton spanning some 50 feet across an earthwork compounded of terraced levels and stepped walls (fig. 8.42). An early sketch of this proposal carries the caption:

The roof can be hanging above, it can be spanning across or jumping over you in one big leap or in many small ones. The problem is to master the waterproofing, the structural requirements and the heat insulation in one mass-produced element, which in combination with itself can give various roof-forms, a nice problem to be solved. This platform courtyard-house shows a vivid roof-grouping formed by such an element-composition.[33]

Unlike his previous folded roofs, the Bayview roof structure is made out of U-shaped, hot-pressed plywood sections that are stacked side by side, and capped by a narrower plywood piece in the form of an inverted U, made waterproof through a bonded aluminum skin. These plywood sections span onto hollow-cored, concrete plank walls, the planks and roof being tied back to the in situ concrete footings by wire cables. The unity of the earthwork is assured through employing the same precast concrete planks for both the walls and the ground floor. Needless to say the plywood roofwork and the concrete earthwork were intended to be self-finishing forms inside and out, and Utzon would pursue this constructional ethic subsequently in his own Can Lis house, built in Porto Petro, Majorca, in 1974. Comprised of three separate units from the outset—main house, guest house, and studio—the fourth and final version of the Bayview house eliminates the freestanding guest wing and breaks up the main house into separate living and sleeping units cranked across the contours of

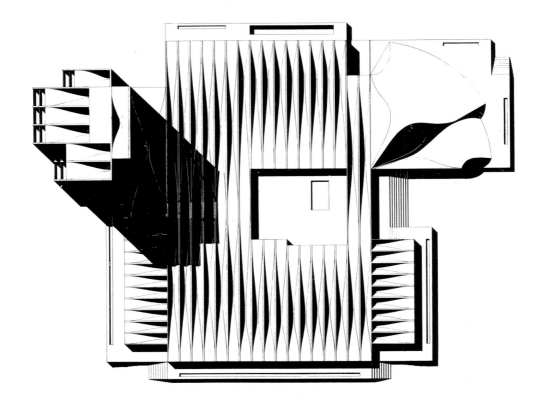

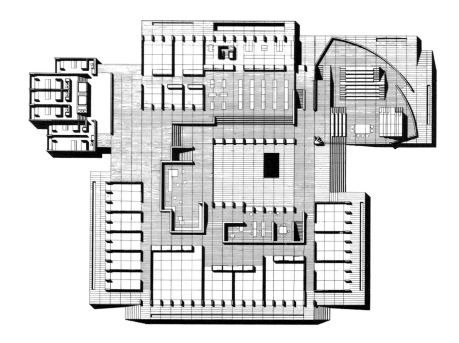

8.37
Jørn Utzon, Højstrup School, plan. The
school is conceived as a *res publica* with
classrooms grouped around a public courtyard and parking beneath.

8.38
Jørn Utzon, Højstrup School, section.

8.39
Jørn Utzon, scheme for a shopping center,
1959. Section.

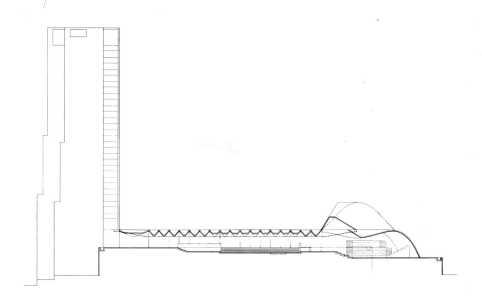

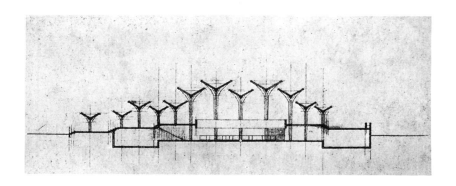

the site; a form that anticipates the parti of Porto Petro. While shallow concrete vaults will substitute for the plywood roof units devised for Sydney, Can Lis will realize many of the themes first broached by Utzon at Bayview (figs. 8.43, 8.44, 8.45, 8.46, 8.47).

Folded-slab construction plays an equally seminal role in Utzon's winning design for the Zurich Opera House of 1964 (figs. 8.48, 8.49). In this work the folded-plate roof covers not only the main auditorium but also the side and back stages, together with such ancillary facilities as a restaurant, a bar, foyers, etc. In this work Utzon will combine the undulating canoe-shaped vault developed for the Helsingør school with a subtle shift in the point of columnar support, which is now positioned either at midspan or at the prow of the vault. Similar support variations occur under the folded roof surrounding the forecourt, where the folded roof cantilevers out toward the open space. In the Zurich opera, as in the Helsingør school, this undulating roof is combined with the podium in such a way as to evoke a city in miniature, recalling here such equally microcosmic works as the Palais Royale, Paris, of 1785 or Wright's Midway Gardens, Chicago, of 1914. The discreet, introspective quality of the Zurich proposal stems from the fact that it is a theatrical precinct rather than a monumental, freestanding institution (figs. 8.50, 8.51). This typological referent is echoed inside the principal volume, where the main auditorium assumes an amphitheatral form instead of the classical proscenium stage.

Double walls occur throughout this project, and the resultant interstitial spaces, of varying thickness, function as "servant" spaces accommodating a wide range of subsidiary elements, including air-conditioning ducts, heating chambers,

8.40
Jørn Utzon, house for his family, Bayview, Sydney, Australia, 1961–1965. Northeast (top) and northwest (bottom) elevations. Bent plywood units laid over cross walls.

8.41
Jørn Utzon, house in Bayview, plan.

8.42
Jørn Utzon, house in Bayview, conceptual drawing: earthwork and roofwork.

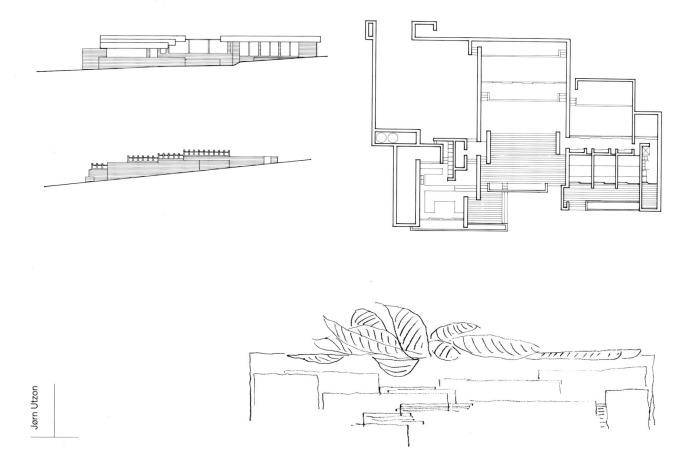

8.43
Jørn Utzon, house in Bayview, scheme four
(June 1965), roof plan.

8.44
Jørn Utzon, house in Bayview, scheme four,
plan of living and bedroom wings:
1. living room
2. terrace
3. court
4. dining
5. kitchen
6. storage
7. entry
8. WC
9. hall
10. enclosed link
11. garden court
12. drying court
13. bedrooms
14. bathrooms
15. laundry

8.45
Jørn Utzon, house for his family, Porto Petro,
Majorca, 1974. Plan:
1. entrance
2. covered outdoor area
3. atrium court
4. pantry
5. kitchen
6. dining area
7. living room
8. bedroom
9. bath

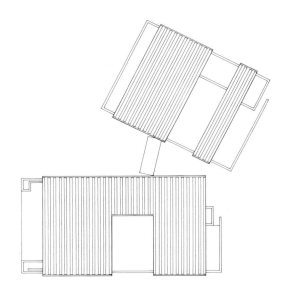

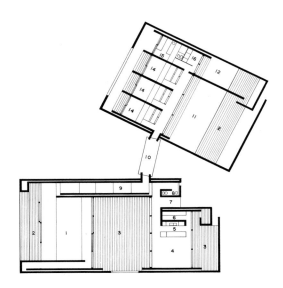

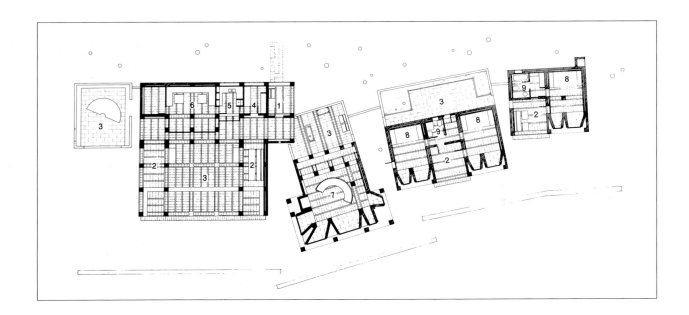

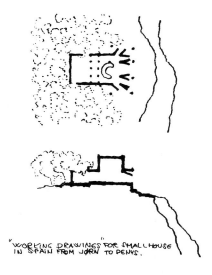

"WORKING DRAWINGS" FOR SMALL HOUSE IN SPAIN FROM JØRN TO PENYS.

8.46
Jørn Utzon, Porto Petro house, conceptual sketches.

8.47
Jørn Utzon, Porto Petro house, section.

bars, kitchens, control rooms, lavatories, serveries, etc. A plate glass wall serves to separate the auditorium foyer from the exterior, and within this volume the audience would have had equally free access to the 1,200-seat amphitheater and the adjacent 400-seat experimental stage. Part Greek, part pre-Columbian, the main arena is let into the podium, while elsewhere, on the perimeter, the earthwork serves to house support services and an underground car park that is fed from a *porte-cochère* entry situated to one side (fig. 8.52). Utzon's Zurich proposal was sensitively related to the urban fabric, and the decision not to realize this work was surely a loss for both the city and the culture of this century.[34]

Throughout Utzon's work, shell roofs appear as public, symbolic elements that are readily distinguished from their attendant folded-plate roofs or from the podia upon which they are raised. The most complete realization of this last type is surely the Sydney Opera House, first projected by Utzon in 1957 as an entry to an international competition. It was eventually completed, without his supervision, sixteen years later in 1973 (figs. 8.53, 8.54). Of the twin forms from which Sydney is composed the earthwork/podium was the easiest to resolve (fig. 8.55). Indeed, its form changed little from the competition entry to the realized design. The shell roofs, on the other hand, were to prove intractable both conceptually and statically, let alone the technical difficulties that attended their erection. As initially projected, the shells were gestural rather than generational in character, and Utzon would be occupied with their unresolved geometrical structure for almost four years before he finally happened on a solution that would allow him to produce arched segments of varying curvature from the same range of precast modular units (fig. 8.56). The concrete shells of Sydney were finally generated by cutting a three-sided segment out of a sphere and by deriving regularly modulated curved surfaces from this solid (fig. 8.57). Utzon's Sydney proves the point that a tectonic concept and a structurally rational work may not necessarily coincide; a disfunction that recalls Damisch's critique of Viollet-le-Duc, that there is always some inescapable gap between the constructional means and the architectonic result (see chapter 2).

Within the history of European building, there are two moments when this aporia seems to arrive at the threshold of almost total closure. The first of these occurs during the high Gothic period, while the second arises in the second half of the nineteenth century with the perfection of ferro-vitreous construction. Even in these instances, however, discrepancies are to be found between the statical logic of the structure and the formal or constructional logic of its physical form. We know that the Gothic cathedral was largely built on an intuitive structural

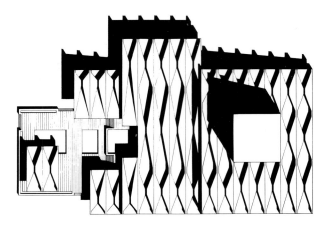

8.48
Jørn Utzon, Zurich Opera House, 1964. Roof plan.

8.49
Jørn Utzon, Zurich Opera House, plans and sections. Lower floor:
 1. garage exit
 2. garage entrance
 3. entry court
 4. upper-level entry
 5. box office
 6. foyer
 7. stairs to cloakroom and WCs
 8. office
 9. staff entrance
 10. stage manager
 11. wood shop
 12. gallery
 13. side stage
 14. main stage
 15. rear stage
 16. scene painting
 17. storage
 18. experimental theater
Upper floor:
 1. *Kunsthaus*
 2. entry court
 3. foyer
 4. buffet
 5. service space
 6. canteen
 7. office
 8. library and archive
 9. caretaker's dwelling
 10. wood shop
 11. gallery
 12. side stage
 13. main stage
 14. rear stage
 15. scene painting
 16. storage
 17. experimental stage
 18. auditorium

8.50
Jørn Utzon, Zurich Opera House, model.

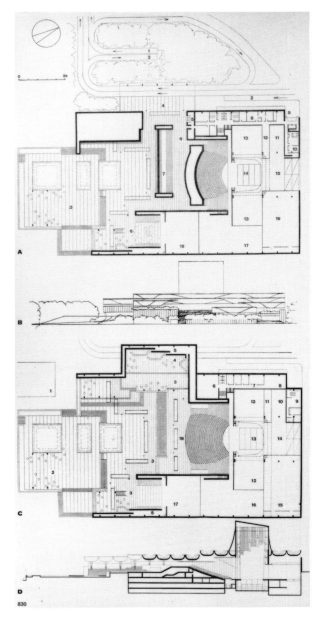

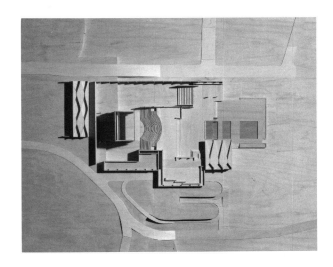

basis backed by generations of experience and that, as Pol Abraham demonstrated in 1933, certain ribs in a typical cross vault are structurally redundant.[35] They exist partly to assist in the erection of the vault and partly to complete its symmetrical order. In ferro-vitreous construction such discrepancies are less in evidence, although even in the Crystal Palace of 1851 we may find certain discrepancies between the varying loads carried by the hollow iron columns and the need to maintain a standard column diameter in order to facilitate assembly. In the genesis of the Sydney Opera House a comparable split occurs between the stresses set up at the springing of the arcuated vaults and the nature of their constructional form. This noncorrespondence was compounded by the magnitude of the dimensions involved, the main hall rising for some 179 feet above the podium to top out 29 feet higher than the roadbed of Sydney Harbour Bridge. At the same time, the shells had to span over large areas; the main hall being 400 feet long and 176 feet wide while the small hall was 352 feet long and 128 feet in width.

Utzon's idea of "building the site" at Bennelong Point was a direct response to a number of contextual features, including the city, the harbor, and the profile and size of the Sydney Harbour Bridge, with its twin masonry towers and its 1,650-foot riveted steel bowstring span. Utzon responded to this challenge with a profound sense of what was required to both *form* the building and *transform* its site and to combine the two adjacent megastructures into a panoramic unity. However, he would justify the particular character of the shells in terms of the ambient light.

Sydney is a dark harbour. The colours of the waterfront are dull and the homes are of red brick. There is no white to take away the sun and make it dazzle the eyes—not like in the Mediterranean countries or South America and other sunlit countries. So I had white in mind when I designed the opera house. And the roof, like sails, white in the strong day, the whole thing slowly coming to life as the sun shone from the east and lifted overhead. In the hot sun of the day it will be a beautiful, white, shimmering thing—as alive to the eyes as architecture can make anything, set in the blue-green waters of the harbour. At night the floodlit shells will be equally vibrant but in a softer more majestic way. . . . The final effect will at times resemble what we call Alpenglochen (Alpineglow)—*the colour you get on snowcapped mountains when the sun is setting—the beautiful pink and violet reflections from the combination of matt snow and shining ice. This*

8.51
Jørn Utzon, Zurich Opera House, model.

8.52
Jørn Utzon, Zurich Opera House, model.

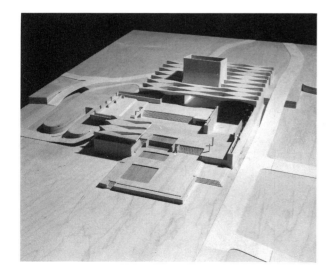

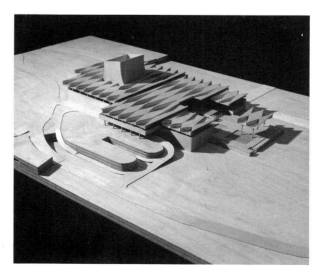

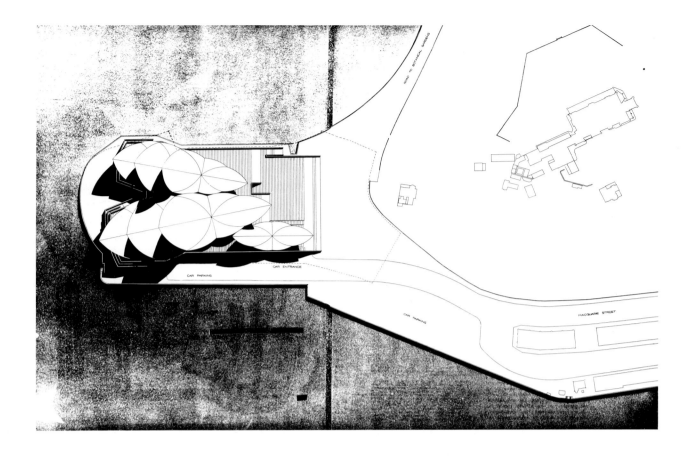

8.53
Jørn Utzon, Sydney Opera House, 1957–1973. Site plan.

8.54
Jørn Utzon, Sydney Opera House, view from the harbor with Sydney Harbour Bridge beyond.

8.55
Jørn Utzon, Sydney Opera House, west elevation.

8.56
Jørn Utzon, Sydney Opera House: west elevation of the major auditorium, indicating the final version of the structural arrangement all to be covered, as shown, with precast concrete lids faced with Höganäs tiles.

roof will be very sensitive. Unlike a building which has only light and shade, it will be a very live sort of thing, changing all day long.[36]

The London-based Danish engineer Ove Arup was fully appreciative of this vision when he wrote in 1965 of the difficulties of realizing Sydney, arguing that these problems stemmed as much from the unfortunate narrowness of Bennelong Point as from the boldness of Utzon's conception.[37] By placing the twin auditoria side by side and by having the audience enter from behind the stage, Utzon was able to reconcile the countervailing vectors of the site; that is to say, the waterfront of the city on the one hand and the promontory and harbor on the other (fig. 8.58). At the same time, he was able to combine the belvedere panorama of the prominent foyer/restaurant spaces with the necessary upward thrust of the auditorium roof as a striking sculptural form with which to respond to the parabolic arch of the adjacent bridge. Utzon's overriding sculptural intent in Sydney reminds one of the affinity he felt for the French sculptor Henri Laurens, and more specifically perhaps of a tomb for an aviator that Laurens had designed for the cemetery of Montparnasse in 1924 (fig. 8.59).

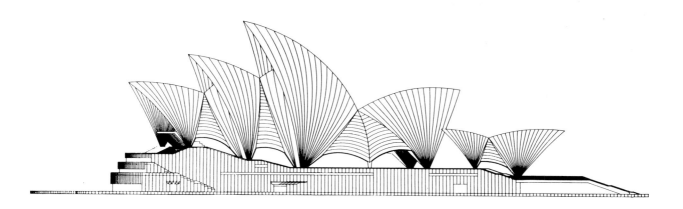

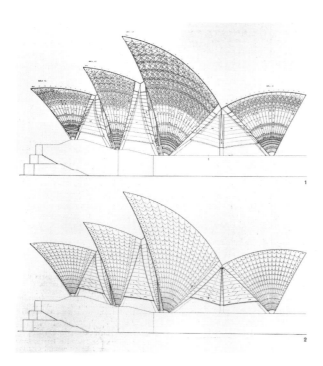

8.57
Jørn Utzon, Sydney Opera House, spherical model from which all shells are derived.

Aside from that of reconciling the sculptural and structural logic of the shell roofs spanning the auditoria, the overall arrangement brought with it other difficulties. In the first instance the unavoidable elimination of side stages, due to the mode of access and the narrowness of the site, necessitated the introduction of hydraulic stages within the basement of the podium; in the second, the structural-cum-sculptural profile of the shell roofs proved to be unstable from a statical point of view and neither architect nor engineer was able to reconcile the rib cage form of the shell with the statical instability of its overall shape. Statically speaking each shell needed four feet to stand on rather than two, and this shortcoming was compounded by Utzon's determination to build the shells out of precast concrete modular segments. These segments may be seen as the precast concrete equivalent of the cast-iron components of the Crystal Palace writ large, only this time in accordance with totally different technical and tectonic constraints. Utzon's preference for a building realized as an additive structure, comparable to Jensen-Klint's Grundtvig Church, did more than delay the resolution of the forms, for as Arup was to suggest, it would have made more statical sense to have conceived the shells as hybrid structures, combining a parabolic steel substructure with a precast concrete eggshell skin. It is worth quoting from Arup at length since one can hardly improve on the clarity of his exposition:

Utzon's design for the roof of each of the halls consisted of four pairs of triangular shells supported on one point of the triangle and each of the two symmetrical shells in a pair leaning against each other, like a pair of hands or fans. The shape of the gothic arch formed between the two supports in each pair did thus not follow the line of thrust—it should not have been pointed at the top—so that the deadload would induce heavy moments. If we counted on the shells being fixed at the supports we were up against the fact that just where the greatest strength is needed, the width of the shell is reduced to a minimum. Moreover, each pair of shells is not balanced longitudinally, but transmits a force to the next pair of shells. Longitudinal stability can therefore only be obtained by considering the whole system of four pairs of shells as one. These shell-pairs are connected by eight side-shells spanning like vaults between the sides of two adjoining pairs of shells, and by louvre walls, which are cross-walls closing the opening between the two shells of a pair—in a rather unsatisfactory fashion, structurally.

It soon became clear that any alteration to the cross-section which would eliminate some of the heavy moments induced by self-weight would completely destroy the architectural character, the crispness and the soaring sail-like quality of the structure. To replace the sails with rabbit-ears would be disastrous. And to make a domelike structure over the whole of each hall or both halls, which would probably have been easier, was of course out. So in the end Utzon and I decided that the scheme had to go forward as designed by Utzon, more or less. It is one of those not infrequent cases where the best architectural form and the best structural form are not the same.

If we had known at that time what we let ourselves in for, we might well have hesitated. We underestimated the effect of the scale of the structure. The trouble is that the thing escalates—the moments require more material, more material induces more moments, and so on. As you all know, one has to be very careful about transferring a statical system from one scale to another. We knew that, of course—but we realized that there would be a hidden strength in the longitudi-

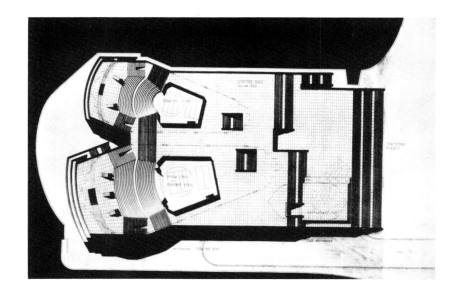

nal continuity and that we could utilize the louvre walls and perhaps combine stage towers and roof in some ways. And we had to say to the clients whether the scheme was feasible, and if we had hesitated on that score, it would probably have given the opponents of the scheme the upper hand. And we liked the scheme and the architect and the clients, and we knew we could do it somehow—so we went ahead. . . . Some time during 1961 it was clear that a slight inclination of the shells—which until then had risen vertically from their supports, would be very desirable and also the louvre walls assumed a much greater importance for the stability. And to reduce the weight we were also veering towards a solution with structural steel ribs, with concrete slabs inside and outside—required by the acoustical experts anyway—but this was heartily disliked by Utzon and I did not really like the idea either. I now almost think that it might have been easier, if not better.[38]

Utzon's shells began to assume their final shape in 1961 when he realized that one could derive all the shells from a single 246-foot-diameter sphere. This meant that all the ribs were identical, although compounded of different lengths

8.58
Jørn Utzon, Sydney Opera House, plan.

8.59
Henri Laurens, Aviator's Tomb projected for Montparnasse Cemetery, Paris, 1924.

and set at different angles to the axis of each shell. Inspired by the Chinese ceramic tradition, Utzon decided to face the shells in off-white, Swedish Höganäs tiles, employing a gloss finish for the main surface and matte for the seams. Utzon realized that the only way to get this textile cover perfectly in place would be to integrate the tiles with the precast concrete segments. In the event, the tiles were cast into precast concrete lids that were subsequently bonded onto the ribbed superstructure of the shells. Over one million Höganäs tiles were laid up in this way (fig. 8.60). The rationale behind this two-stage roofing process has been well accounted for by Utzon's top assistant on the site, the Australian architect Bill Wheatland.

Jørn had some tests made to see whether the tile cladding he was already visualizing could be efficiently laid by tilers working up in the air on scaffolding on the sides of the roof. Jørn decided that there was no chance of getting workmanship to the standard he wanted if the workmen had to climb hundreds of feet into the air and lay tiles while they clung to planks. Also, there was the risk of getting poor workmanship from tile-layer with a hangover or a headache who said: 'The hell with it today—I'll slap this lot on anyhow.' Jørn decided we must adopt the European technique wherein tiles are laid on panels on the ground. So the Opera House tiles were laid on the ground on big concrete trays (we call them lids) and the lids were hoisted to their places on the roof ribs, where they were attached with brackets and bolts. Jørn always says that the human eye is so keen that it can detect flaws in repetitive workmanship even on walls high up in the air and apart from any question of cheapness or speed, he looked on prefabricated building as a way to obtain first-grade workmanship.[39]

Getting all the heavy rib components into position, some 200 feet above the ground, was no mean feat, as Arup makes clear (figs. 8.61, 8.62):

When a unit weighing ten tons is placed a hundred feet up in the air and has to be supported temporarily on an adjustable steel erection arch and the last completed rib, which is not yet firmly attached to the rest of the shell, then all sorts of complicated things happen. The arch gives, the rib moves, the temporary prestress causes strains, temperature variations make their contribution—and we must know what happens. The whole structure acts as a mechanism with sliding joints and adjustable bolts and what not.[40]

8.60
Jørn Utzon, Sydney Opera House, details of arch ribs and precast lid elements. The drawing shows the system of tile revetment in relation to the precast concrete ribs that make up the shell. The dark "feathering" lines on the shell elevation indicate the differentiation between the matte tiles of the seams and the shiny tiles covering the main surface.

8.61
Jørn Utzon, Sydney Opera House, construction photograph.

8.62
Jørn Utzon, Sydney Opera House, axonometric showing the tower crane system of structural assembly.

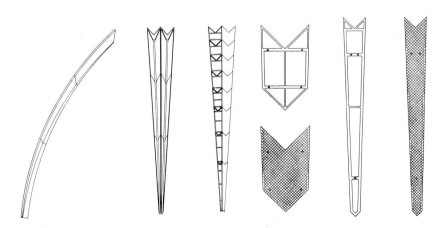

Utzon's penchant for folded-slab construction reemerged in Sydney in the design of the podium, where Utzon and Arup jointly decided to use such a section to achieve the 164-foot clear span of the podium deck.[41] This section ran across the site for almost the full width of Bennelong Point, some 280 feet (figs. 8.63, 8.64). Utzon insisted that this vast podium *porte-cochère* be kept column-free, not only to liberate the turning circles of buses and cars that would enter the opera undercroft at this point but also to create a monumental entry volume. As in Helsingør and Zurich the roof over this space would assume the form of a concrete folded slab, cast in situ, with the bulk of the structural concrete section

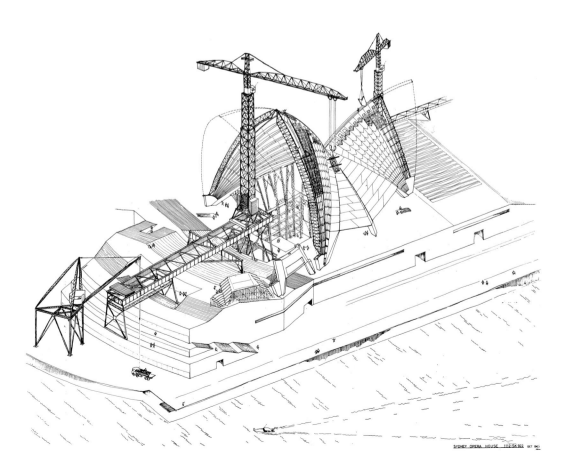

SYDNEY OPERA HOUSE   1112-SK 922 OCT 1963

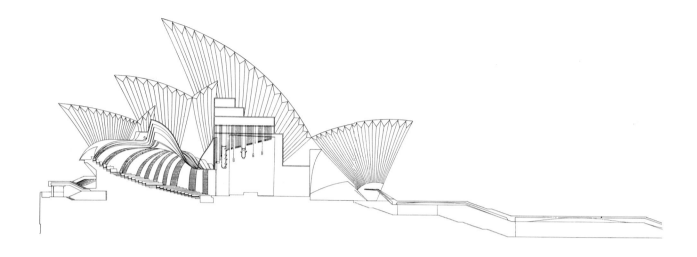

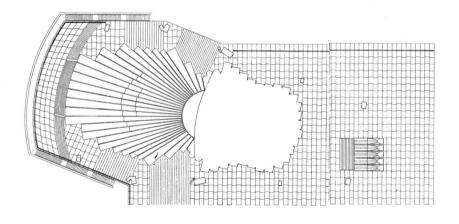

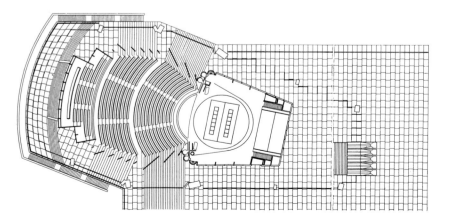

8.64
Jørn Utzon, Sydney Opera House, variable sections of the folded-slab roof that make up the deck of the podium.

shifting from the bottom to the top as the effective bending moment shifted from positive to negative (fig. 8.62). Serving as a cranked profile for the concourse steps, this slab also acted partially as an arch.

Utzon's insistence on constructing the shells out of modular precast concrete elements is ultimately neo-Gothic in feeling, so it is hardly surprising to find him justifying the overall form in Gothic terms.

If you think of a Gothic church, you are close to what I have been aiming at. Looking at a Gothic church, you will never get tired. You will never finish looking at it. When you pass around it, or see it against the sky, it is as if something new goes on all the time. This is important—with the sun, the light and the clouds, it makes a living thing.[42]

While Utzon's Sydney breaks down all too readily into a Semperian earthwork and roofwork, it also has a Semperian screen wall spanning between the earthwork of the podium and the roofwork of the shells (fig. 8.65). Utzon would be prevented from bringing this element to its ultimate resolution largely because the political furor surrounding the opera house brought him to resign the commission before all the profiles and details of this curtain wall could be resolved. Prior to his resignation, however, he had already determined the basic principle of this membrane.[43] Attached to the leading edges of the shell roofs, the vertical hangers supporting the glass were to have been assembled out of segments of varying length and section so that the three-dimensional profile of the curtain wall could vary progressively from one deep mullion to the next. Glass would have been affixed to these hangers like the planar scales of a fish, while the hangers themselves were to have been formed of hot-pressed plywood, reinforced by an aluminum core and externally faced in bronze. It is difficult to imagine the full-faceted effect of this imbricated screen had it been realized. The greenhouse glazing built in its stead is obviously a much more economical version of Utzon's original concept. As far as Utzon was concerned, the coordinating role of this screen was to relate the podium paving grid to the three-dimensional curvature of the shells. At the same time he wanted to avoid vertical panes of glass, since such surfaces have the tendency to make glass read as a load-bearing element (fig. 8.66). Some measure of the complexity of this whole concept may be gleamed from Bartholomew's description of the final resolution.

In Utzon's final solution each basic mullion component is comprised of three molded plywood 'U' shaped pieces. These form the basic hollow structural system with a skin of hot-bonded bronze laminated to the exterior surface. These 'U' shaped channel pieces are produced in three sizes corresponding to the three planes of inclination in the wall created by the sweep of the mullion.

Vertically, the surface was built up to a sweep by varying inclinations. This tendency was most pronounced in the southern glass walls of the two foyers due to the delivering axes of the shells and the plane of the mullions governed by the four foot paving module of the podium (the mullions carry the four foot building grid vertically through to the shells). In the southern walls the glass is staggered horizontally in plan in response to the relationship between the mullion plan and the shell axis, and the vertical projection from the shell rib of each consecutive glass band. In the northern walls the mullions and shell axes are instead, parallel.

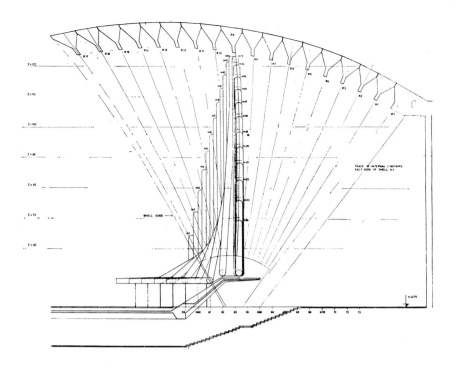

Tremendous flexibility was accommodated in the assembly of the elements. The mullion case was built up of five basic fins in 1/2 inch plywood, with two extra layers being added each time there was a bend. This sandwich system of fins could slip past each other to accommodate large variations in folds, staggering of glass panels and other adjustment tolerances. To these basic center layers were added 'U' shaped channel pieces each with sides of different lengths so that each adjacent mullion in the built wall could overlap allowing the glass to be fitted between this overlap, always having its top and bottom edges parallel to the cross grid of the podium paving geometry.[44]

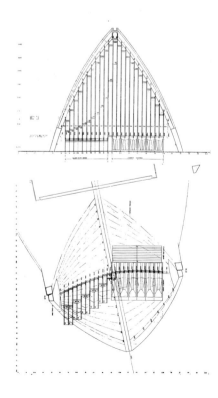

In many respects this unrealized screen wall is a condensation of the tectonic vision permeating the entire building (fig. 8.67). Profoundly influenced by Wright, Utzon attempted to develop the opera house design in such a way as to extend the scope of Wright's organic architecture. Structural repetition was a key to everything that Utzon attempted at Sydney, and in this respect the curtain wall projected for the opera harked back to the suspended glazing proposed for the Langelinie Pavilion and thus to the textile-like, tubular glass fenestration employed by Wright in his Johnson Wax Administration Building of 1936 (fig. 4.29).

Apart from Sydney, Bagsvaerd Church, completed in a suburb of Copenhagen in 1977, represents the built apotheosis of Utzon's tectonic vision to date. As such it stands at the convergence of many different strands. On the one hand it may be seen as an extension of the Nordic Gothic Revival, that is to say, of the line that came to fruition in Jensen-Klint's masterly Grundtvig Church; on the other, the building patently derives in section from Utzon's preoccupation with the pagoda form. Interwoven with this fusion of occidental and oriental paradigms we find, once again, the perennial inspiration of Wright, recalling, in this instance, the parti of Wright's Unity Temple of 1904 (fig. 8.68). Thus, as if by happenstance, the bipartite, longitudinal plan of Bagsvaerd Church seems to paral-

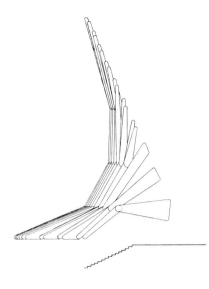

8.65
Jørn Utzon, Sydney Opera House, section
showing system of plywood hangers carrying
the curtain wall.

8.66
Jørn Utzon, Sydney Opera House. Top: elevation showing system of plywood hangars carrying the curtain wall. Bottom: plan showing
geometrical intersection between entrance
canopy and curtain wall hangars.

8.67
Jørn Utzon, Sydney Opera House, plywood
mullions to the shells, showing varying
curvature.

lel only too nicely the plan form of Unity Temple. Aside from certain liturgical
similarities, deriving no doubt from a common Protestant base (Unitarianism in
one instance and a rather free interpretation of Lutheranism in the other), both
buildings were to combine sacred and secular spaces within one continuous corpus. Both architects also chose to accommodate their ecclesiastical space in a
squarish centralized volume. Moreover both buildings depend for their intrinsic
organization on tartan-like systems of spatial subdivision and on thick-wall perimeter volumes that serve in both instances as vestigial aisles. In Unity Temple
these shallow spatial bands provide for access stairs and also serve to accommodate shallow balconies, whereas in Bagsvaerd, aside from housing the organ
loft, they double in the main as both light slots and corridors (fig. 8.69). However, in alignment, width, and general disposition Utzon's narrow aisles are
closer perhaps to traditional church aisles than to the "thick wall" device used
by Wright. Aside from these similarities and differences, the form of each work
is inflected by an alien culture; by the evocation of Mesoamerica in the case of
Wright and by Chinese culture in the case of Utzon. Tectonically speaking,
Bagsvaerd is the more articulate work; a judgment that Wright would perhaps
have been willing to endorse, given his ambivalence about the nature of reinforced concrete as a material having an unfortunate conglomerate nature. In this
regard the rational-constructive logic of Bagsvaerd is closer to Wright's textile
block work of the 1920s than to the ethos of his earlier Prairie period.

Like the traditional Nordic timber stave church to which it is related, Bagsvaerd
is a framed structure despite the fact that it makes extensive use of monolithic,
reinforced concrete. In this particular regard Bagsvaerd recalls Auguste Perret's
transposition of trabeated timber construction into a reinforced concrete framework. In different ways both Perret and Utzon recall Semper's *Stoffwechseltheorie,* wherein a given material and structural method preserve their original
tectonic character in a different constitutional format. Since Bagsvaerd is only
partially framed, the level of tectonic transposition from one material to another
varies, and by virtue of this variation the structural articulation of the church acquires its symbolic character. I have in mind, in this respect, the point at which
the skeleton frame of the concrete structure gives way to shell vaulting while being cast of the same monolithic material throughout. Bagsvaerd is framed from
the outside in as it were, so that the four parallel lines of 30-centimeter-square
reinforced concrete columns change their character and function as they pass,
on each flank, from the external to the internal column line. In each instance the
external columns are articulated as vertical framing members throughout their
height while the internal columns merge above the gallery level into a concrete
diaphragm, cast integrally with the columns. This change from articulate frame
to monolithic diaphragm provides the necessary abutment and support for the
reinforced concrete shell vaults covering the 18-meter span over the nave. The
shells or vaults at Bagsvaerd were built by spraying special concrete onto
wire mesh reinforcement, the whole being sustained during casting by rough-
boarded formwork, the imprint of which is clearly visible on the finished shell
vaults. Given that, as in the case of Sydney, this span might have been achieved
more economically in metal trusswork, this transition, depending on the continuity of the material, seems to derive from a particular symbolic intent; namely to
represent the passage from the semisecular status of the aisles to the sacred
character of the nave.

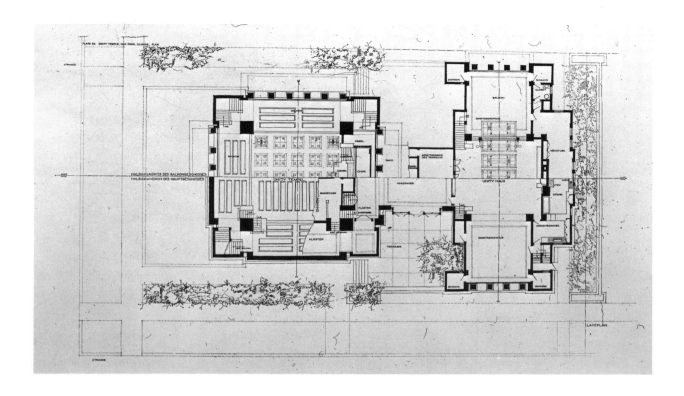

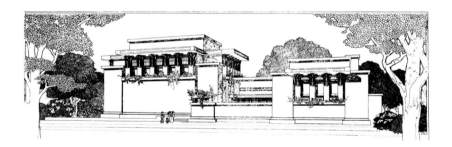

8.68
Frank Lloyd Wright, Unity Temple, Oak Park, Illinois, 1906. Plan and perspective.

Aside from this differentiation, we can have little doubt as to the symbolism of the shell form; the fact that it makes the traditional allusion to the celestial vault and thereby to all the innumerable vaulted spaces of the Christian tradition. The two preliminary sketches that Utzon issued with respect to Bagsvaerd confirm this intention, for the first of these depicts a Cartesian view of the earth lying flat beneath undulating cumulus (fig. 8.70). This perspectival, rationalistic flatness lies in absolute contrast to the evanescent, light-giving arch of the heavens. Both are implicated in the infinite, but where the one is a regular, man-made order, the other is an amorphous arching expanse of indeterminate form and immeasurable depth; the vault of the heavens versus the rationalized horizon of the mortal earth. In this we seem to encounter an unconscious reference to the Heideggerian *Geviert* or "foursome"; to the Earth, the Sky, Divinities, and Mortals.[45] In the second sketch these two planes are shown as encompassing the house of God (fig. 8.71). The clouds have been transformed into longitudinal vaults running across the perspectival axis of the nave, while on the foreshortening plane beneath, people are shown spontaneously gathering themselves into an assembly. The very idea of the church as a social condenser shines through this rendering and gives resonance to the etymology of the Greek word *ecclesia,* meaning "house of assembly." The superimposed cross that emerges like a mirage on the surface of the second sketch aligns its horizontal bar with the span of the vault and its vertical axis with the central perspective axis. The fact that this duality assumes a more complex and obscure form in the church as built is due to a number of factors, not the least of which is the transcultural character of Utzon's pagoda-vault that extends the idea of the sacred beyond any narrow Eurocentric focus on Christendom alone.

Thus the longitudinal cut through the multiple shell sections that span the nave at Bagsvaerd assumes the profile of a pseudo-pagoda, and while this all but imperceptible profile is hardly a direct reference to the Orient, it nonetheless endows the space with an atmosphere and a quality of light that seems extraneous to the Christian tradition. This transcultural trace, so to speak, seems to be echoed in the stepped longitudinal elevations, since such an eaves profile is as much Chinese as it is Hanseatic, as we may judge from the stepped gabled architecture of the Anhui, Zhejiang, and Jiangsu provinces.[46] Like the *fin-de-siècle* fascination with the East, the deeper impulses lying behind such hidden, possibly unconscious references are as elusive as they are complex. One thinks of Louis Sullivan's recourse to Saracenic form and ornament or of Wright's deep admiration for Japanese culture; one thinks of Bruno Taut's preoccupation with China or of Hans Poelzig's affinity for the tectonic iterations of Islamic architecture. This constantly recurring oriental tendency in modern architecture leads by extension to the non-Eurocentric, anthropological references underlying the structuralist work of Aldo van Eyck and Herman Hertzberger, architects who are close to Utzon's generation in terms of their age and cultural affinity. A Spenglerian awareness of spiritual decline is surely the common reflex lying behind many of these manifestations, and this impulse acquires a greater cogency

8.69
Jørn Utzon, Bagsvaerd Church, Copenhagen, 1976. Section and plan. Plan key:
1. entrance
2. church
3. sacristy
4. waiting room
5. office
6. candidate's room
7. parish hall
8. meeting rooms
9. kitchen
10. atrium garden
11. chapel

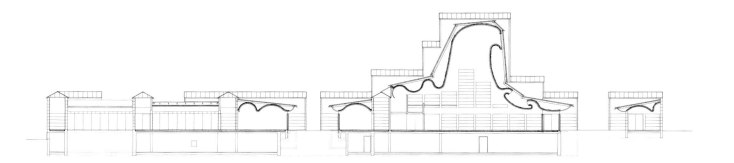

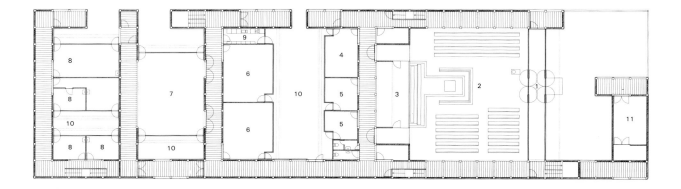

when the commission under consideration is a church. The nature of this dilemma is diachronic rather than synchronic, and the context within which this church has been realized is rather decisive in this respect. Thus, where Jensen-Klint could depend on the spiritual conviction of the Christian Socialist group of which he was a member, Utzon has had to build against the more skeptical ethos of our largely secular, consumerist society.

Reminiscent of a pagoda but tectonically removed from traditional Chinese roof construction, the vaults at Bagsvaerd have a Baroque aura about them, particularly with regard to the way in which they modulate light. As in Le Corbusier's Ronchamp chapel, light diffuses across the *béton brut* surface of the vaults in a constantly changing manner, producing luminous, chiaroscuro effects within the nave, depending on the time of day, the condition of the weather, and the season of the year. Equally Baroque is the fact that, for various reasons, the vaults are not allowed to register their presence on the exterior (fig. 8.72). Nevertheless the sectional organization is implied on the exterior through the pattern of the precast concrete elements, which introduce a stepped seam that approximates to the undulating vault as the cladding changes from plank to block units within the external infill wall. In order to differentiate front from back, this undulating rectilinear seam varies very slightly in its profile as one passes from the northern to the southern elevation.

As in Perret's Notre-Dame du Raincy of 1923, to which it may be compared, the main volume at Bagsvaerd is roofed by a double shell, in the first instance by the vaults themselves and in the second by a lightweight, waterproof, inclined shed form constructed out of corrugated asbestos siding. However, unlike Baroque outer domes that usually echo the volume within, this outer membrane conceals, as in Perret's church, the dynamic shape of the vaults spanning the interior. Thus the shed at Bagsvaerd is far from decorated. Indeed its extremely utilitarian form suggests an ordinary agricultural building rather than a semisacred, public structure. This reading is almost guaranteed by the use of asbestos

8.70
Jørn Utzon, Bagsvaerd Church, conceptual sketch.

8.71
Jørn Utzon, Bagsvaerd Church, conceptual sketch.

cement sheathing and the deployment of standard greenhouse glazing. Aside from providing economical roofing, the expressive motives lying behind this use of agricultural elements would appear to be threefold: first, to make an indirect allusion to the sacred barn that is encoded, so to speak, in the traditional barn-like form of the stave church (fig. 8.73); second, to represent an archetypal religious institution without resorting to the kitsch of pseudo-Gothic form; and third, to confront a suburban community with the authenticity of its preindustrial past; that is, to evoke a more ecologically stable moment in history when agriculture was the dominant mode of production and when the value crisis brought about by industrialization and the demise of faith had yet to occur.

This cryptic agrarian metaphor is reinforced by a subtle modification of the surrounding landscape. As in Fredensborg, rock forms have been randomly disposed about the surrounding greensward[47] in order to extend the building into the landscape, while birch saplings have been planted so as to frame the overall mass of the church and to provide enclosing cover for two adjacent parking lots (fig. 8.74). The fact that these stands of saplings have been planted with a view to their eventual maturity testifies to Utzon's faith in the durability of architectural form.[48] Thus Bagsvaerd does not yet fully exist and indeed will not come into its own until the surrounding trees have grown to their full height. This feeling for the long *durée* is quintessentially Nordic and close to both the elegiac sensibility of Gunnar Asplund's Woodland Cemetery Chapel (1923) and the civic deportment of Alvar Aalto's Säynätsalo City Hall (1949).[49] Thus Utzon would confirm in an interview with Per Jensen: "Well, we are not . . . really interested in how things will be in 25 years, whatever we build. Actually, what we are interested in is that if in 2000 years some people dig down, they will find something from a period with a certain strength and purity belonging to that period."[50]

Lit almost exclusively from above, Bagsvaerd Church, like Unity Temple, maintains an all but totally hermetic facade, despite the articulate distinction between frame and infill. The coursework of this last, together with its undulating seam representing the vaults within, imparts a textile character to this plaited, screenlike envelope. At the same time it assures that a simple "agrarian" mode of construction will be the dominant character of the work. This laconic principle of systematic assembly is reinforced by the asbestos cement sheeting and by the application of standard glazing to the light slots over the aisles. An ethic of constructional economy and precision prevails throughout, from the timber grills that enclose the entrance foyer to the built-in, bleached timber furnishings of the interior. And yet despite the consistent use of precast concrete elements

8.72
Jørn Utzon, Bagsvaerd Church, north elevation. Note the way in which the change in the size of the infill elements suggests the profile of the shell vault within.

8.73
Norwegian stave church, section.

inside and out, there seems to be nothing that is unduly utilitarian about Bagsvaerd. The subtle change in tone, as one enters, derives in part from the bleached purity of the woodwork and in part from the varying levels of luminosity emanating from the vaults over the nave and from the lanterns above the aisles. The fusion of light with structure is as crucial here as it is in the work of Louis Kahn.

One is tempted at this juncture to draw a number of parallels between Utzon, Kahn, and Perret. In all three there is the same insistence on the ontological probity of tectonic form. In Bagsvaerd as in Kahn's Tribune Newspaper Building of 1959, an equally meticulous distinction is maintained between the in situ concrete frame and the precast concrete infill; a distinction depending as much on surface quality as on a tectonic differentiation between tessellated and monolithic construction. The delicate contrast obtaining between concrete and travertine in Kahn's Kimbell Art Museum finds its parallel in Bagsvaerd in an equally subtle differentiation between the whitened, latex surface of the precast concrete and the white light that emanates from the bleached joinery, further offset by the open, earthenware altar screen, built in a triangular pattern out of Flensborg bricks set edgewise and painted white. This paradoxical play between sameness and difference sustains the homogeneity of the work while articulating its parts. We are close here to Jensen-Klint, to a building made of one material inside and out. The interior of Bagsvaerd is open to as many readings as its exterior. Thus while the precast concrete and the wooden furnishings of the interior attain a high level of precision and refinement, consciously recalling perhaps the purity of Shaker or even Shinto building, there remains, at the same time, a certain theatricality. This manifests itself in the perforated screen backing the altar, reminiscent of Perret not only for its cellular patterning but also for its evocation of the tripartite stage (fig. 8.75). This closeness to Perret is reinforced by the fact that Bagsvaerd eschews the uses of plaster, just as Perret tended to eliminate rendering from his public interiors.

Other devices strengthen the character of the church as a liturgical space, ranging from the theatrical lighting battens that flank the aisles on either side of the nave to the church raiments designed by Lin Utzon, the dominant color of which is rotated according to the season of the year. No less ritualistic and tectonic in

8.74
Jørn Utzon, Bagsvaerd Church, site plan showing the containment of the church by a screen of trees.

8.75
Jørn Utzon, Bagsvaerd Church, altar screen.

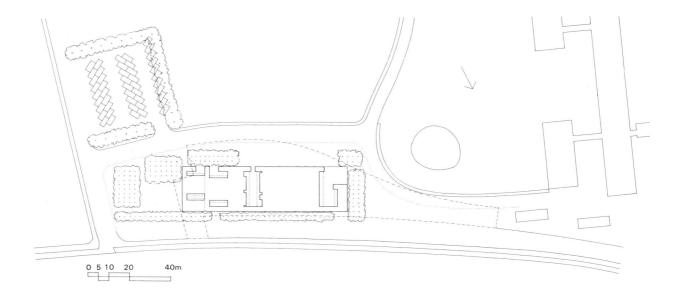

0 5 10 20   40m

their associations are the exposed white-metal organ pipes, together with their timber encasement (fig. 8.76). This muted, decorative enrichment has no doubt proved essential to the popular acceptance of the church as a religious space. Nonetheless Utzon's allegiance to a Klintian tectonic rigor prevails throughout, above all in the joinery, where even nail heads are allowed to protrude ever so slightly above the surface of the wood.

Like all of Utzon's civic work Bagsvaerd lends itself to being analyzed in Semperian terms, for, despite the absence of a podium as such, the body of the building breaks down into the quadripartite form of earthwork, hearth (altar), roofwork, and infill wall. Although the main floor is virtually at grade, Utzon has explicitly rendered it as an earthwork: first by building it out of precast concrete planks set on top of the reinforced concrete basement and second by assembling the dais and pulpit out of precast hollow concrete slabs similar to the planking used for the floor. The problematic Semperian screen wall, as was encountered in Sydney and Zurich, is resolved in Bagsvaerd through the continuity of the framework with the monolithic diaphragm of the shell. Since the frame is present as a rhythmic continuity throughout, the screen wall is readily integrated with both the roof and the frame. Elsewhere, as in the symbolic west front, gridded wooden fenestration runs continuously beneath the outriding eaves of the lowest horizontal vault. These transverse screen walls impart a further oriental inflection to the church in that the density of the mullions together with the wood-to-glass ratio and the counterpoint of the transoms seem to be derived from

Chinese prototypes, as does the ribbed precast guttering above the protruding vaults. The circular geometry governing the sectional profile of these last is related to the cross-sectioning of the sphere employed in generating the shells of the Sydney Opera House. In each instance a rhythmic, generative geometry is used to modulate the overall composition through its structure (fig. 8.77).

Bagsvaerd Church is the last realized public work over which Utzon has been able to exercise total control. Thus the structure not only represents a maturation of his thought but also the literal homecoming of his transcultural vision. Utzon's insistence on rational economic construction permeates every part of its fabric, displaying a mastery over prefabrication in which he is able to exploit a modular productive system as a source of inspiration rather than as a limitation. Like Wright, Utzon believes that the poetics of built form must derive in large measure from the totality of its tectonic presence and that it is this, plus an essential critical reflection on the status of the work in hand, that constitutes the mainspring of architectural form. Moreover, despite the Danish dimensions that are detectable in his work—the affinity for the Gothic, the strong feeling for craftsmanship, and a particular responsiveness to both climate and context— Utzon remains committed to the ideal of an emerging world culture that, while springing from local conditions, transcends them at the same time, thereby reintegrating and revitalizing different traditions through a kind of cultural transmigration.[51]

8.76
Jørn Utzon, Bagsvaerd Church, interior.

8.77
Jørn Utzon, Bagsvaerd Church, geometrical section.

8.78
Jørn Utzon, Farum Town Center, Farum, Denmark, 1966. First stage. Covered street formed out of standard precast concrete elements. The plan drawings on the right illustrate various forms of flexible combinations.

8.79
Jørn Utzon, Jeddah Stadium, 1969. Section, elevation, and plans of the precast structural system for the large stadium with combined football pitch.

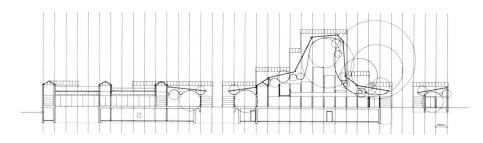

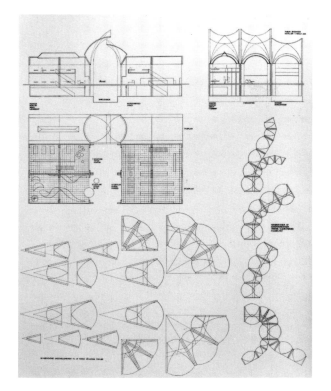

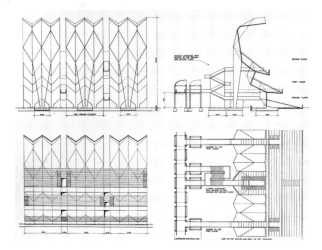

Utzon's preoccupation with the idea of an additive architecture dates from his design for Farum Town Center in 1966, where an extensive urban matrix was projected on the basis of the repetition of a single spatial unit derived from a series of precast concrete modules (fig. 8.78). Two different transcultural paradigms seem to be brought together in this work: the Middle Eastern bazaar as a homogeneous and introspective city-in-miniature and the Chinese tradition in which built form is assembled out of a limited number of parts. Utzon's synthesis of these rather different concepts within a repetitive precast system risks the reiteration of units at an inappropriate scale, for it is one thing to employ the standard brick or block as a basic module and quite another to select a full-height space cell as the primary repetitive unit. Nonetheless the fertility of this proposition is evident from Utzon's account of the additive principle, as set forth in the Danish magazine *Arkitektur* in 1970.

A consistent utilization of industrially produced building components can only be achieved if these components can be added to the buildings without having to be cut to measure or be adapted in any way.

Such a purely additive principle results in a new architectural form with the same expression . . . [by] adding more trees to a forest, more deer to a herd, more stones to a beach, more wagons to a marshalling yard; it all depends on how many different components are added in this game. Like a glove fits a hand, this game matches the demands of our age for more freedom in the design of buildings and a strong desire for getting away from the box-type house. . . .

When working with the additive principle, one is able—without difficulty—to respect and honour all the demands made on design and layout, as well as all the

Jørn Utzon

293

requirements for extensions and modifications. This is just because the architecture or perhaps rather the character of the building is that of the sum total of the components and not that of composition or that dictated by the facades. . . . The drawings are not a thing in se with meaningless and dimension-less module lines; the module lines represent wall thicknesses and the lines on paper form the contours of the finished thing. The projects show the degree of freedom that can be achieved with the additive principle. . . . They also demonstrate the vital problems associated with the design of units or components, and provide some indication (e.g. in the stadium project) of the advantages in respect of production control, costs and erection time that can be achieved in comparison with a group of buildings constructed in a purely artisan fashion.[52]

While much of this argument cites the familiar and, in some measure, proven advantages of rationalized, quasi-industrial production, it also implies the tectonic character that should be incorporated into the components and their interconnection from the beginning. That Utzon's joints are intrinsically morphological serves to distinguish them from such mechanical assemblies as Paxton's Crystal Palace or Max Bill's Swiss Landesausstellung exhibition building of 1963. Utzon's aim is to exploit the productive logic of the construction for tectonic ends rather than to celebrate the purely processal and economic elegance of a technological system.

That the repetitive, domed, cross-wall module of the traditional oriental bazaar should become the canonical prototype of Utzon's additive architecture is hardly an accident. We have already dwelt on Utzon's lifelong involvement with non-Eurocentric form, and to this we may add his Gothic preference for the vaulted cell as a volumetric unit, comparable as a building block to the role played by the atrium in his earlier housing schemes. Thus we should not be surprised if the more convincing applications of his additive principle should be encountered in projects destined for the Middle East: the Jeddah Stadium project of 1969 and above all his parliament building realized for the State of Kuwait in 1982. In his Jeddah proposal, Utzon was to combine, in different permutations, five generic structural units, each one being conceived in terms of its connective and constitutive role. These include a two-story bazaar module, a cylindrical roof element, a cylindrical vault suitable for covering restaurants, changing rooms, etc., and a stadium grandstand component, provided as a series of bents. In addition to its supporting function this unit also provides for a faceted

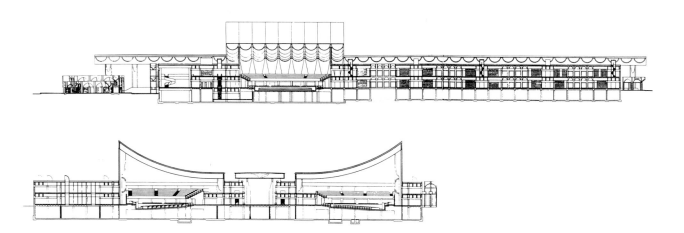

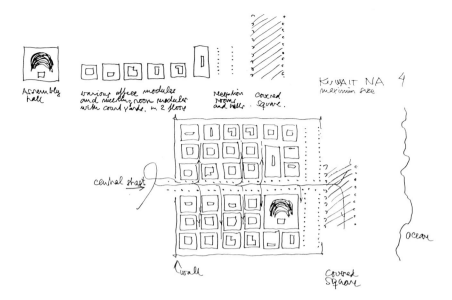

8.81
Jørn Utzon, National Assembly Building, conceptual drawing of the parliament as a city in miniature.

brise-soleil (fig. 8.79). A variation on this last element (structural unit no. 5) is intended to roof over long-span sports facilities. It is interesting to note that the folded-slab structural principle is present in almost all of these elements.

In the Kuwait parliament building Utzon combines the prefabricated additive principle with monolithic construction, the one complementing the other (figs. 8.80, 8.81). Where Farum Town Center was a small city core treated as though it were a medieval labyrinth, the Kuwait Parliament is a major state institution treated as a city-in-miniature, the *souk* being the common Middle Eastern paradigm in both instances. Thus we will find Utzon writing of his parliament building in the following terms.

The construction of the National Assembly also reflects the purity of Islamic construction. The building is a prefabricated concrete structure in which all elements are structurally designed to express the load they are carrying, the space they are covering—there are different elements for different spaces. They are all meant to be left visible—contrary to the constructions of the "cardboard architecture" of most modern office and administration buildings where hidden structures, lowered ceilings and gypsum walls give you an impression of being in a cardboard box.

In the National Assembly complex you see very clearly, what is carrying and what is being carried. You get the secure feeling of something built—not just designed.

The demand for very busy intercommunication between the various departments has led to the decision to arrange the complex as a two-storey building. This provides an easy orientation inside the building in contrast to the abrupt disorientated feeling you may experience in buildings with many floors with intercommunication depending on elevators.

When you enter the central street, you can see all the entrances to the various departments. The orientation is as simple as the orientation you get when you open a book on the first page with its table of contents presenting the headings of all the chapters. The central street leads toward the ocean into a great open hall which gives shade to a big open square, where the people can meet their ruler. In Arab countries there is a tradition for very direct and close contact between the ruler and his people.

The dangerously strong sunshine in Kuwait makes it necessary to protect yourself in the shade—the shade is vital for your existence—and this hall which provides shade for the public meetings could perhaps be considered symbolic for the protection a ruler extends to his people. There is an Arab saying: "When a ruler dies, his shadow is lost."

This big open hall, the covered square, between the compact closed building and the sea, has grown out of this very special situation in quite a natural way—caused by the building's position directly on the beach. This big open hall connects the complex completely to the site and creates a feeling that the building is an inseparable part of the landscape, a feeling that it has always been there. The hall is just as much part of the openness of the ocean as it is part of the compact building and its structure. The hall seems born by the meeting between the ocean and the building in the same natural way as the surf is born by the meeting of the ocean and the beach—an inseparable part of both.[53]

Unlike Farum and Jeddah, the additive order of Kuwait is unified by the two monumental shell roofs respectively covering the open ocean square and the assembly itself (figs. 8.82, 8.83, 8.84).[54] Kuwait and Jeddah prove as it were the strength and weakness of the additive principle, for without such unifying vaulted forms there is a tendency for the aggregation to become a scaleless iteration of small units rather than the manifestation of a hierarchical order.

When one looks back on Utzon's achievement one is struck by the key role played by the Sydney Opera House, not only in regard to his own career but also with respect to the representation and accommodation of Australian cultural life. Whatever the travails suffered in the realization of this work, and however much it may fall short of Utzon's initial vision, the opera house has nonetheless become what he imagined it would be, a "door" through which a young continent would be able to realize its full potential, would be able to create, to quote Utzon, "an individual face for Australia in the world of art."

8.82
Jørn Utzon, National Assembly Building, preliminary plan; the mosque by the main entrance and one of the two meeting halls were later eliminated.

8.83
Jørn Utzon, National Assembly Building, model.

8.84
Jørn Utzon, National Assembly Building.

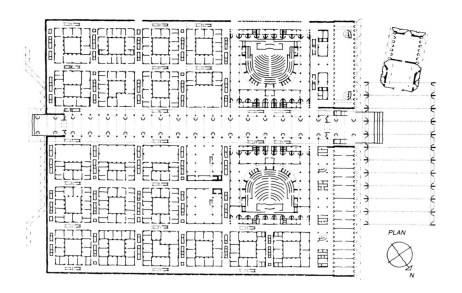

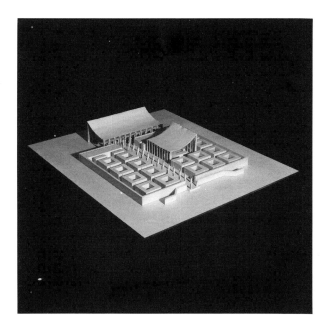

But the consequence of its achievement as a tectonic work goes even deeper, for with this remarkable pagoda form Utzon not only realized a specific site but also created an image for the nation. Thus just as the Eiffel Tower became a symbol of France, so has the Sydney Opera House become the icon of the Australian continent. While there may be many reasons for this, among them we must count the strong topographic relationship obtaining between the building and its site; like Kronborg Castle in Helsingør or, more to the point, Santa Maria della Salute in Venice, the opera house is a city crown poised on a promontory in the midst of a busy harbor, and the strength of its image stems from the ever-changing dynamism of its relationship to the surrounding panorama. Thus while it is firmly rooted on its podium, the double metaphor of the shell clusters is readily decipherable: on the one hand, the allusion to the spinnaker of a yacht under full sail; on the other, a city crown, radiant in the ever-changing Sydney light, that adds its essential rhythm to the historical accretion of the site, the islands, the lighthouse, the harbor and the bridge and all the vessels that ply their way in the archipelago.

9 Carlo Scarpa
and the Adoration of the Joint

These are only some of the thoughts evoked by bringing together philosophy and architecture under the sign of interpretation, and I realize that they are only hints, sparse suggestions. It may be necessary to take something else into account: namely, that edification has two principal meanings—to build and to be morally uplifting. Both are quite closely tied in today's rather vertiginous coming and going between architecture and philosophy, insofar as one can individuate even remote similarities between the two. That is, edification must be ethical, entailing communication of value choices. In the present situation of thought on the one hand and architectonic experience on the other (we shall consider this a provisional and limited conclusion), the only possibility of edifying in the sense of building is to edify in the sense of "rendering ethical," that is, to encourage an ethical life: to work with the recollection of traditions, with the traces of the past, with the expectations of meaning for the future, since there can no longer be absolute rational deductions. There follows then edification as a fostering of emotions, of ethical presentability, which can probably serve as the basis for an architecture which is determined not by the whole but by the parts.
Gianni Vattimo, 1987

The work of Carlo Scarpa (1906–1978) may be seen as a watershed in the evolution of twentieth-century architecture, not only for the emphasis that he placed upon the joint but also for his particular use of montage as a strategy for integrating heterogeneous elements. Throughout his work, the joint is treated as a kind of tectonic condensation; as an intersection embodying the whole in the part, irrespective of whether the connection in question is an articulation or a bearing or even an altogether larger linking component such as a stair or a bridge. All of this is immediately apparent in Scarpa's first work of consequence, the renovation and reorganization of the Fondazione Querini Stampalia in Venice, completed in 1963. In this instance, a stereotomic earthwork, laid into the undercroft of a sixteenth-century palace, is accessed by a lightweight bridge that acts as a kind of fixed hinge between the terra firma of the campo and the transformed shell of the palazzo (fig. 9.1).

In contrast to this lightweight, flat arch resting on stone abutments, Scarpa renders the earthwork as a monolithic concrete tray (fig. 9.2). Separated from the existing walls, this tray serves not only to contain but also to represent the seasonal flooding of the city. This shallow concrete walkway, paved with tiles, embodies the traditions of Venice in more ways than one, first by containing the *acqua alta* and second by affording direct gondola access through the existing *portego*.[1] The ceremonial nature of this last is implied by a winding stair descending to the canal and by openwork ornamental gates, dressed in metal, that fill the twin-arched openings of the portico (fig. 9.3). In this way, Scarpa arranges for two complementary entries: an everyday passage from the campo via a delicately articulated bridge, and a more honorific approach from the water; an approach that in its symbolic obsolescence is an elaborate reminder of the original mode of entering the palace. As Maria Antonietta Crippa has remarked, the whole of this sequence is treated as a kind of three-dimensional inlay.

The small entrance hall—its mosaic floor reminiscent of a design by Joseph Albers that Scarpa had originally intended to reproduce—gives onto a marble-dressed staircase leading to the library and also onto a gangway above the

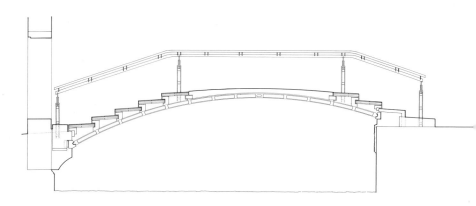

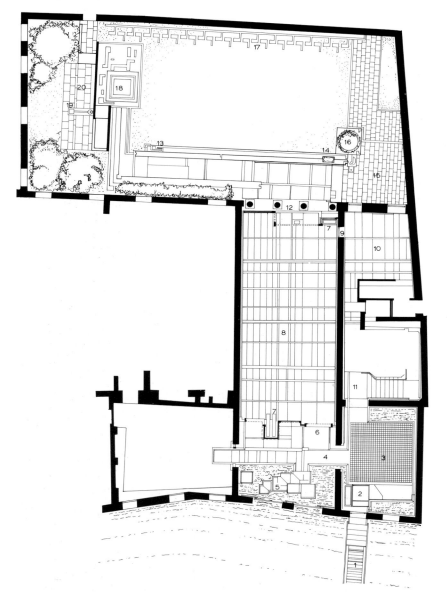

9.1
Carlo Scarpa, Fondazione Querini Stampalia,
Venice, 1963. Bridge.

9.2
Carlo Scarpa, Fondazione Querini Stampalia,
ground-floor plan:
  1. wooden bridge
  2. entry
  3. foyer
  4. concrete causeway
  5. steps down to canal entry
  6. gallery entrance
  7. radiators
  8. main gallery
  9. secret door
  10. small gallery
  11. stair to library
  12. garden portico
  13. fountain
  14. stone lion
  15. sump
  16. old well
  17. stepping stones
  18. lily pond
  19. outflow
  20. porter's court
  21. garden court

9.3
Carlo Scarpa, Fondazione Querini Stampalia,
ornamental gates.

9.4
Carlo Scarpa, Fondazione Querini Stampalia,
main exhibit hall.

entrance area that leads into the great hall on the ground floor opposite the portego. The stone gangway crossing the portego is almost like a bridge overlooking the lagoon; from it one can see the ebb and flow of water playing into the cisterns placed on various levels. A sheet of glass separates this gangway from the great hall. The radiators in the great hall are concealed within a parallelepiped with golden lines and glass panels fitting into each other, which has a geometric similarity to the mosaic in the entrance hall. Seventeenth century mouldings and remnants of walls, clearly distinct from modern additions, are visible throughout.[2]

Scarpa's characteristic use of revetment makes itself evident here in the travertine lining to the walls of the great hall, where, apart from the traditional use of stone cladding, there is the suggestion of a metonymic exchange between wood and masonry; between wood as it is employed in the deck and handrail of the bridge and travertine as it is laid up against the walls of the exhibition space (fig. 9.4). Stone thus appears in two aspects; in the first simply as cladding and in the second as a kind of "wood," where it is incised, inlaid, and hinged as

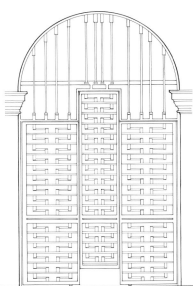

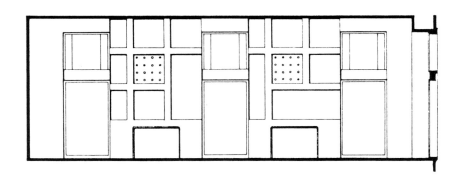

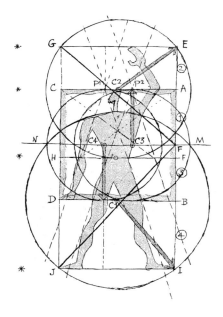

9.5
Theo van Doesburg, Café Aubette, Strasbourg, 1926–1928. Elevation of cabaret wall.

9.6
Le Corbusier, Modulor system, 1946.

though it were petrified cabinetwork. Such a reading is implied by a slotted brass rail, let into the stone cladding to form a horizontal groove at eye height, for the purposes of hanging pictures. This material interplay is enhanced by 10-centimeter-wide, ground-glass panels set flush with the travertine revetment. As translucent covers to neon tubes, these luminous accents run across the wall like a descant, echoing a similar modulation in the concrete floor that is subdivided by strips of Istrian stone of the same width. These translucent cover plates constitute a series of vertical accents that double up in pairs as they run down the depth of the space. Scarpa may have derived this syncopated arrangement in part from the Neoplasticist wall relief that Theo van Doesburg designed for the Café Aubette in 1926 (fig. 9.5) and in part from Le Corbusier's proportional system, as published in his book *Le Modulor* twenty years later (fig. 9.6).

Stone treated as cabinetwork is also evident in the hinged door to the side gallery, made out of a single sheet of travertine, that is cut out on its front and carved on its retroface (fig. 9.7). Throughout, brass is the key for this metonymic transposition between stone and wood, since the inlaid picture rail, running around the gallery, recalls a similar use of brass connectors in the bridge handrail. Such accoutrements allude both to marine detailing and to the kind of fittings found in eighteenth-century gentleman's furniture (fig. 9.8).

Like all of Scarpa's bridges, the Querini Stampalia *passerelle* is structured about the themes of bearing and transition, which may explain one of the least-noticed features of this bridge, namely its contrived asymmetry, particularly since the datum on either side is almost the same (see fig. 9.1).[3] It seems that this asymmetry arose out of the need to meet two different conditions: on one hand the bridge had to be high enough to permit gondolas to pass close to the campo; on the other hand it had to come down lower and more gradually in order to clear the lintel of the building entry. All of this is effected by displacing the bearings of the layered superstructure so that the point of the hinged support is 70 centimeters higher on the landward side. Thus, one steps up from abutments in Istrian stone before crossing two oak treads onto the curved oak deck of the bridge itself. The descent, on the other hand, is effected by five similar treads, the last of which lies flush with the stone threshold to the palace. Of the seven wooden treads, three are set flush with the surfaces to which they give access. This redundancy, together with the subdivision of the oak decking, makes the distinction between threshold and span ambiguous. The deck functions as a kind of tectonic elision that simultaneously both extends and curtails one's experience of crossing. This inflection finds its correspondence in the balustrading,

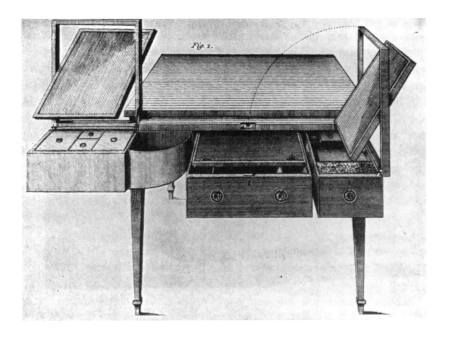

9.7
Carlo Scarpa, Fondazione Querini Stampalia, door to gallery annex.

9.8
Reflecting dressing table or Rudd's table, 1788.

which is shortened on the landward side and extended toward the building. The unequal spacing of uprights that results from this asymmetry necessitates a twin-rail balustrade, since an unbraced handrail would be insufficient for the long span. In this combination, a lower structural rail in tubular steel and an upper handrail in teak, we find that synthesis of structural economy and ergonomic form that is so characteristic of Scarpa's work.

The highest point of the *acqua alta,* indicated by the height of the concrete upstand in the entry, finds reflection in the surface treatment of the main exhibition space, where the travertine stops short at the same datum and the exposed aggregate concrete floor is taken up to meet it. The strips of Istrian stone subdividing this relatively inexpressive floor amount to a kind of basketwork that bonds the concrete tanking into a unity. These bands are irregularly modulated, thereby echoing but not following the syncopation of the wall revetment (see fig. 9.2). In addition to this modulation, these courses seem to be subtly aligned so as to correspond with an existing splay in the plan form of the building. Thus, while the first three transverse Istrian strips on entering the gallery are set at right angles to the walls of the exhibition space, the remaining strips, nine in all (five singles and two doubles), appear to be normal to the walls of the stair hall.[4] This subtle adjustment in alignment is accompanied by a diagonal inflection through

9.9
Carlo Scarpa, Fondazione Querini Stampalia, glass doors to garden.

9.10
Carlo Scarpa, Fondazione Querini Stampalia, water channel in garden, sump to the left, fountain to the right.

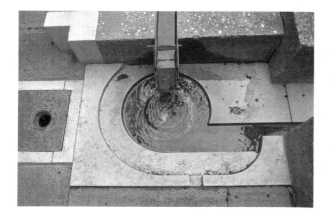 

the space that passes from left to right toward the garden court. This movement is underlined by the placement of iron radiators; a vertical, encased stack at the entry and a single, freestanding horizontal radiator bracketed off the floor to one side of the glazed opening to the garden. The concrete stanchions supporting the armored plate glass garden doors are also treated as elements in a Neoplasticist composition, so that where the axis of one lies parallel to the cross axis of the hall the other is rotated ninety degrees; each being inscribed with a gilded bar on its face (fig. 9.9). This rotation is subtly reflected in the treatment of the glass itself, so that a 10-centimeter, ground-glass light panel planted on one of the stanchions is balanced by two 5-centimeter safety strips etched into the plate glass. A similar asymmetrical translucent light panel and safety strip are also incorporated into the glazed screen wall separating the exhibition hall from the initial foyer.

A parallel play with asymmetrical elements appears in the water channel running across the garden court, in which two different spirals, a rectilinear fountain in Apuan marble and a circular concrete drain, are the beginning and the end of a flow running from east to west, passing beneath a Venetian stone lion by which the channel is surmounted (fig. 9.10). This Islamic reference seems doubly significant in that the flow from the east not only serves to evoke the dependency of Venice on the Orient but also Scarpa's own genealogy; his self-characterization as "a man of Byzantium, who came to Venice by way of Greece." At the same time this fountain may be read as a metaphor for the life cycle. As Giuseppe Zambonini has written:

Water is used as a counterpoint to the treatment of the ground floor of the Palazzo. Its source is a small labyrinth carved in marble which suggests the pain of its forced birth. It is then channeled through a long trough, parallel to the Rio (Santa Maria Formosa) which extends almost the entire length of the garden. It then passes beneath a stone lion that faces the source and finally disappears into the drain which is magnificently expressive of the idea of vortex. [5]

The influence of China in Scarpa's work can hardly be overestimated, particularly when it comes to the walled gardens of both the Querini Stampalia and the Brion Cemetery in San Vito d'Altivole.[6] In both instances a frieze of enameled tiles, as an artificial horizon, is inlaid into certain sections of the perimeter walls. In Venice this is matched by the tiled lining of a lily pond laid out to the designs

of the painter Mario de Luigi (fig. 9.11). As Albertini and Bagnoli have suggested, these tiled ornaments in Murano glass initiate and enrich the promenade through the court.

The garden forms a rectangle roughly corresponding to two squares, each 12 m per side, cut by a concrete dividing wall. It is largely laid out with lawn and shrubs. A square copper container for papyrus plants is inset in a larger pond riveted with mosaic tesserae; here water collects before rechanneling. Isolated from this, a small basin (75 × 33.5 × 4.5–6 cm), formed of Apuan marble of a purplish hue, collects the water dripping into it from a small pipe and channels it into a miniature maze, where it fills a series of shallow concavities before flowing into a long, deep water course in which water lilies flourish. At the end opposite the small basin, serving as a bird bath for the winged inhabitants of the garden, a low cascade lends impetus to the flow of water, carrying it into proximity with an ancient and now dry wellhead. A short path with a number of steps completes the garden layout, branching off from the glazed wall of the portico to lead the visitor either toward the papyrus pool or in the direction of the wellhead.[7]

In Scarpa's work everything turns on the joint to such an extent that, to paraphrase Le Corbusier, the joint is the generator rather than the plan, not only in respect of the whole but also with regard to alternative solutions lying latent, as it were, within any particular part (fig. 9.12). These alternatives arise spontaneously from Scarpa's method, his habit of drawing in relief, wherein an initial charcoal sketch on card, one of his famous *cartoni,* becomes progressively elaborated and overlaid by traces, washes, and even white-out to be followed by further delineations, entering into a cyclical process of erasure and redesign respect of a given junction, without ever fully abandoning the first incarnation of the solution. In this way, as Marco Frascari has remarked, Scarpa's *cartoni* serve as an archaeology of the project: "In Scarpa's architectural production relationships between the whole and the parts, and the relationship between craftsmanship and draftsmanship, allow a direct substantiation *in corpore vili* of the identity of the process of perception and production, that is, the union of the construction with the construing."[8]

This observation stresses two essential aspects of Scarpa's method, first the gestural impulse passing almost without a break from the act of drafting to the act of making, and second a reciprocity obtaining between what Frascari characterizes as the *techne of logos* and the *logos of techne;* that is to say, between construing a particular form and constructing its realization (and then, later in the cycle, the moment in which the user construes the significance of the construction). We are close here to Giambattista Vico's anti-Cartesian idea of corporeal imagination. Scarpa would directly acknowledge this affinity on succeeding to the deanship of the Istituto Universitario di Architettura di Venezia by superimposing the Viconian motto *Verum Ipsum Factum* on the school's diploma and, later, by inscribing the same legend into his design for the school portal, thereby literally dedicating architects to the Viconian pursuit of "truth through making."

While Scarpa may have become familiar with Vico's thought by reading Benedetto Croce's *Aesthetica* of 1909, another source would have been the eighteenth-century Venetian architect Carlo Lodoli who was a contemporary and a promoter of Vico's ideas.[9] Vico's *Verum Ipsum Factum* would have been

9.11
Carlo Scarpa, Fondazione Querini Stampalia, lily pond.

9.12
Carlo Scarpa, Brion tomb, San Vito d'Altivole, 1969. Map of details.

important for Scarpa at two levels; first in confirming the cognitive aspect of his own activity and second in providing a philosophy of education. According to Vico, knowledge was to be acquired not through passive acceptance but through its active formulation—for only then can the subject take possession of it. For Scarpa, as for other architects, the first intervention in this process was the delineation of the thing to be constructed, while the second was the on-site process of its realization. As Hubert Damisch has remarked,

The essential goal therefore lies in the purpose of verification, if not actually experimentation, which Scarpa assigns to the drawing, which has to embody all necessary misgivings. For instance, a perspective image of a staircase does not allow sufficient accuracy in identifying the number of steps and their height, let alone the details of their jointing—jointing being a link-up with Cézanne's doubt.

A critical position of this kind acquires special significance at a time like the present, characterized by an attempt to reduce architectural thought to the single dimension of an image, to the detriment of its symbolical and real dimensions. In this there is no paradox; the man who revealed the full potential of museum architecture also uttered the most stringent criticisms of the ever-recurring error of confusing architecture with its image or any kind of scenography.[10]

A more precise analysis of the various levels involved in Scarpa's delineatory method has been provided by Sergio Los, who distinguishes between three kinds of drawings. The first is the *cartone,* Scarpa's initial drawing on stiff ochre card that would then be overlaid with variants of the same detail on tracing paper; if found to be sufficiently stable, these versions would be incorporated into the basic drawing on card. In this way the specific outline of the work would be developed, with incidental markings in pencil and in dilute black and red India ink. This evolutionary manner, so to speak, assured an indestructible record of the design process with regard to the initial schema. This procedure would be sustained, as we have seen, by detailed drawings on tracing paper in pencil, with colored crayon being employed to identify different layers and levels in both plan and section. In the end, of course, the final whole was traced over at the very last minute to produce a reliable construction document.[11]

Scarpa had such respect for craftsmanship that on occasion he would detail in such a way as to suit its procedural needs. This much is evident from his habit of forming L-shaped brackets out of steel plate, cut in such a way as to facilitate the meeting of two cuts at right angles to each other. Scarpa drilled a small hole at the crossing point so that the saw would change tone when it hit the intersection and thus produce a clean cut with no overrun. To finish this produc-

9.13
Carlo Scarpa, design for layout and display of Roman relics, Feltre, 1975–1978. Section.

9.14
Carlo Scarpa, Museo di Castelvecchio, Verona, 1953–1965. Section through entrance room.

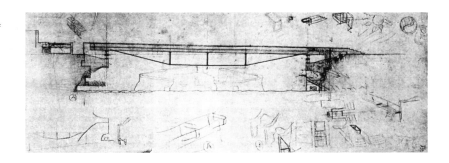

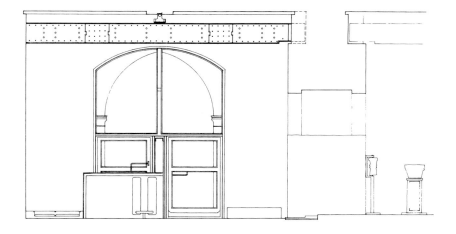

tive detail, Scarpa inserted a small brass washer at the point of the intersection.[12]

Scarpa's affinity for the archaic made itself manifest not only in the sculptural simplicity of his form but also in the hieratic elaboration of his joints. As we have already seen, rather than simply juxtapose the support and the load (*Stütze und Last*), Scarpa would "postpone" the final moment of support, as is evident from his 1975 project for a bridge over the archaeological remains at Feltre (fig. 9.13) or in the various capitals he would invent in his later years. A similar protraction is evident in the ground floor of the Museo di Castelvecchio in Verona, where intersecting concrete floor beams are carried at midpoint by built-up, riveted steel beams (fig. 9.14). the postponement of the bearing in this instance derived, as Scarpa himself would reveal, from the spatial continuity of the ground-floor enfilade subdivided into five cubic volumes. In each cube a transverse steel beam was introduced running along the east-west axis of the sequence and thereby unifying it. As he put it:

I wanted to preserve the originality of each room, but I didn't want to use the earlier beams of the restoration. Since the rooms were square, I set a paired steel beam to support the point where the two reinforced concrete beams crossed, so indicating the main lines of the building's formal structure. Where they crossed the importance of that square was emphasized because the crossing of the two beams in the centre implies the pillar which helps define the whole space. This is the visual logic I wanted to use as a frame of reference. The way the beams are made also brings out the visual logic but only in the details. I could have used the steel profiles already on the market.[13]

By establishing the point of the absent column, the cylindrical hinged joint between the concrete and steel, ostensibly introduced in order to allow for differential movement, was as crucial to the articulation of the space as the built-up character of the steel joist. This obsession with the elaboration of bearing would also be remarked on by Albertini and Bagnoli in their description of the attic colonnade in the Banca Popolare di Verona of 1978 (fig. 9.15).

A quite complex architectural system is applied to the top story of the Banca Popolare di Verona—almost a modern interpretation of an ancient order: supports

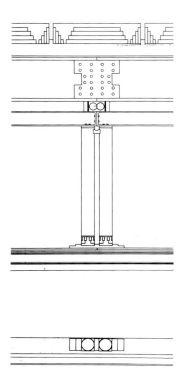

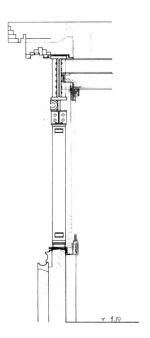

9.15
Carlo Scarpa, Banca Popolare di Verona,
1973–1981. Colonnade.

and architrave in metal, frieze in colored mosaic, and cornice in white Botticino stone. The long ribbon of the architrave, formed of two plate girders of differing dimensions (the larger 600 mm high, the smaller 180 mm high) joined by riveting plates, is supported at regular intervals by pairs of coupled colonettes in tubular iron (166 mm in diameter), replacing the metal sections of an earlier version.

The colonettes are fitted with muntzmetal collars, acting as linking elements to the architrave above and the base beneath. This is formed of deep flats, cut and milled, riveted to a flat (22 mm deep) laid on the masonry. The tall columns on the court front have a more elaborate muntzmetal link at the base: a motif frequently used by Scarpa and typical of Indian architecture, by means of which a square plan becomes, by successive divisions, first octagonal, then a sixteen-sided polygonal figure, ending up as a circle. A small block of muntzmetal, recessed to form the symbol of two intersecting rings, gleams against the dark iron above each pair of colonettes. Connectors of the same metal are used as the head and base of the columns to create a single support: these are small elements, distancers, screwed to the tubular shafts, articulating the proportions of the whole.[14]

Scarpa's excessively articulated joints may be read as a critical commentary on the economic expediency of our utilitarian age or, alternatively, as a heroic attempt to compensate for our inability to equal the poetic authority of classical form. Of this last he wrote:

Modern language should have its own words and grammar just as this happened in the case of classical forms. Modern shapes and structures should be used following a classical order. . . . I should like that a critic could discover in my works certain intentions that I have always had, namely an enormous desire to stay within tradition but without building capitals and columns, because these can no

310

longer be built. Not even a God today could invent an Attic base, which is the only beautiful one; all the others are only slags. From this point of view even those designed by Palladio are awful. As regards columns and entablatures only the Greeks were able to reach the apex of pride. Only in the Parthenon do the shapes live like music.[15]

With the *factum* of Venetian craft at his side,[16] Scarpa steered an uneasy course between the legacy of Art Nouveau—one thinks of Hermann Obrist's Egyptoid column (fig. 9.16), or Perret's new concrete capital devised for the Musée des Travaux Publics (fig. 5.42)—and a more objective elaboration of the hinged joint in steel construction as this appears, say, in Peter Behrens's turbine factory of 1909 (fig. 9.17) or in Mies van der Rohe's Neue Nationalgalerie of 1968 (fig. 9.18). Scarpa evolved his joints not only as functional connections but also as fetishized celebrations of craft as an end in itself. This sense of "nearness," to evoke Heidegger's term, was not only expressed through Scarpa's elaboration of the joint but also through the patina and color of delicate surface finishes, demanding highly specialized techniques. I am alluding in particular to Scarpa's revival of *stucco lucido,* that traditional rendering technique in which colored pigment and marble dust are combined with lime plaster and other materials to yield highly polished surfaces reminiscent of dressed stone or lacquer.[17] Like the tempera technique in painting, the color in polished plaster appears to emanate from the interior of the rendering. A similar synthesis of luminosity and texture crops up in other aspects of Scarpa's palette, from the use of Murano glass tes-

9.16
Hermann Obrist, *Monument to the Pillar,* 1898.

9.17
Peter Behrens, AEG turbine factory, Berlin, 1909. Detail.

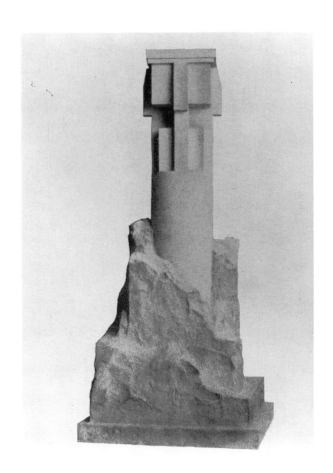

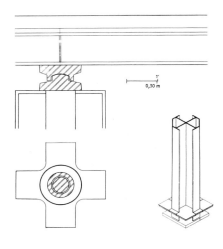

9.18
Mies van der Rohe, Neue Nationalgalerie, Berlin, 1968. Column details.

9.19
Carlo Scarpa, Olivetti shop, Piazza San Marco, Venice, 1957–1958. Ground-floor plan.

9.20
Carlo Scarpa, Olivetti shop, Piazza San Marco, section.

serae for the floor of his Olivetti store on the Piazza San Marco of 1966, to the constant interplay among tile, marble, metal, and wood that is so evident in the multiple finishes in which his work abounds.

Apart from the canonical joint and its attendant membrane, Scarpa often consolidated his work about iconic foci; about pivotal sculptural pieces such as Alberto Viani's abstract metal sculpture, poised above a sheet of black water, that plays such a prominent role in the spatial organization of the Piazza San Marco store (figs. 9.19, 9.20) or the fulcrum provided by the Cangrande statue in the Museo di Castelvecchio (fig. 9.21)[18] or the ubiquitous double circle motif that occurs at different scales throughout his work. While Scarpa's obsession with this motif has been attributed to many different sources, one of the more likely origins is the mystical ideogram known as *vesica piscis* (from *vesica,* bladder, and *piscis,* fish).[19] While the interlocking version of this icon is reminiscent of the oriental yin-yang symbol, it also represents the opposition between solar universality and lunar empiricism (fig. 9.22). Even if, as legend has it, Scarpa first encountered this symbol on a packet of Chinese cigarettes, he would surely have become aware of its place in the European tradition and of its latent cosmic attributes. He later became cognizant of the role played by this figure in the generation of certain church plans, such as Bernini's Sant'Andrea al Quirinale in Rome (fig. 9.23),[20] and from this he would also have known how such a construction may be used to proliferate a whole series of equilateral triangles deriving from a single side (fig. 9.24).

Whatever its attributes, it is somehow fitting that Scarpa would employ this figure as a definitive symbol in his last work, which, as it happened, would also be his own resting place: the Brion Cemetery, completed posthumously in 1979. Irrespective of the ultimate dialogical attributes of the *vesica piscis,* whether sun/

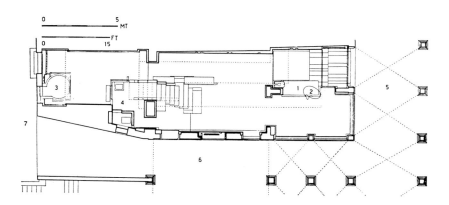

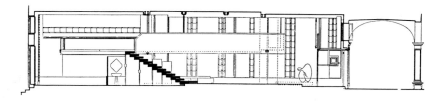

moon, male/female, Eros/Thantos, its three-dimensional rendering in pink and blue tiles may also have alluded to more modern sources, to the cosmological values of the primary colors in Dutch Neoplasticism or to the red and blue proportional series of Le Corbusier's *Modulor*.[21] However, the fact that Scarpa once employed the figure of the squared circle suggests a deeper familiarity with hermetic lore (fig. 9.25). I have in mind the "oculi" that he incorporated into the upper level of the Olivetti store, each one bisected by sliding teak and palisander screens that, reminiscent of Japanese *shoji,* serve metaphorically to open and close each eye (fig. 9.26).[22] In one form or another the *vesica piscis* will manifest itself in much of Scarpa's architecture as a kind of tectonic icon, from its first use in the Gavina shopfront realized in Bologna in 1963 (fig. 9.27) to its last in the Banca Popolare di Verona, completed after Scarpa's death, where it appears at different scales (fig. 9.28).

While Scarpa seems to have made little use of the root-three rectangle contained within the *vesica,* he nonetheless used an 11-centimeter module whenever possible, and this figure may be related to the inherent duality of the *vesica,* particularly when its multiple use yields the double numbers 22, 33, 44, and even 5.5 centimeters as a half-module. Of Scarpa's obsession with this double number pattern and its roots in traditional measure Frascari has written:

In China eleven is the number of the Tao, but it is not often taken in the quantitative sense of ten plus one; it signifies the unity of the decade in its wholeness.

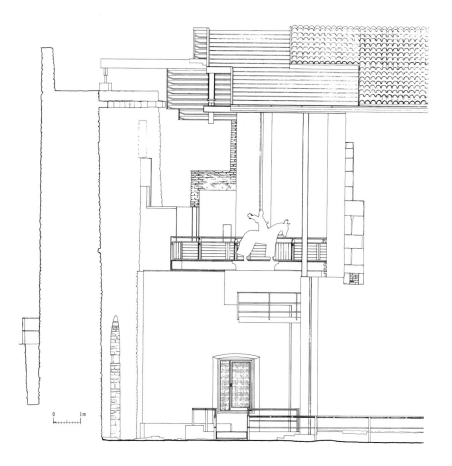

9.21
Carlo Scarpa, Museo di Castelvecchio, partial section, looking north through Cangrande space.

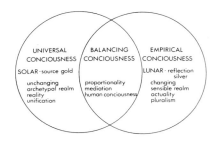

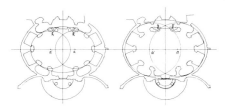

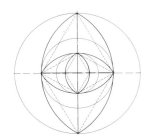

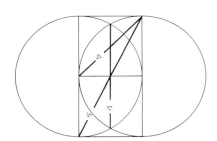

Eleven appears as a factor, and a multiple, though not by itself, in the Imperial system of measuring: 5 1/2 yards are one rod, pole or perch, 4 perches make 22 yards which are a chain, 220 yards a furlong and 1760 (11 × 160) yards makes a mile. . . .

The understanding of the peculiarity of the usage of eleven in Scarpa's architecture must begin with the consideration of two Byzantine occurrences. On the one hand, there is the bizarre fact that a total of eleven letters composes the name . . . Carlo Scarpa. On the other hand, in the Italian tradition of construction, the thickness of a standard hollow tile partition wall is approximately 11 cm, although the nominal dimension is 10 cm (9 cm of the tile and 1/2 cm of plaster on both sides), [but] in the reality of construction, tiles are never assembled following a perfect plumb-line and the reoccurring mistake is corrected in the thickness of the plaster, thus bringing the total width of the partition wall closer to the real dimension of 11 cm.[23]

A preoccupation with duality is evident, in any event, throughout Scarpa's career, particularly in his funerary architecture, from his Capovilla monument built in the San Michele Cemetery, Venice, in 1944 to the Galli tomb realized in Genoa in 1978, and this dualism will surface again in the Brion Cemetery. Assuming the form of an elevated (fig. 9.29), L-shaped temenos, this final funerary work divides on entry into two distinct zones; a division that is axially reinforced on approach by a *vesica piscis* let into the courtyard wall, the blue ring favoring the reflecting pool to the right and the red circle inflecting toward the left and the greensward that covers the rest of the open compound (fig. 9.30). These two colors also recall the twin colors of the alchemical ouroboros, the snake eating its own tail that has a red head signifying fire and a green tail representing water.[24]

Scarpa, following the example of Lodoli, was committed to the idea of analogy at every level in his work, that is to say, to a deductive argumentation that does not proceed from the whole to the part but rather moves homologically from part to part. This analogous principle is perhaps never more evident than in the ambiguous role played by water in the Brion Cemetery: on the surface, as slow-moving water, it symbolizes life, as opposed to its containment in a long sump or channel covered by precast paving slabs. In this morbid form, as it were, it leads us away from the threshold of the Brion Cemetery toward the meditation

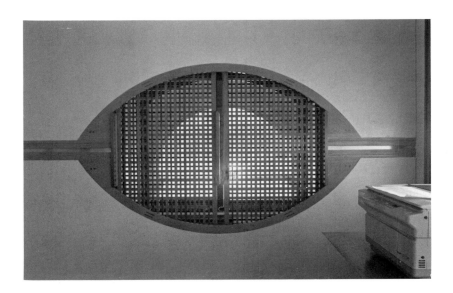

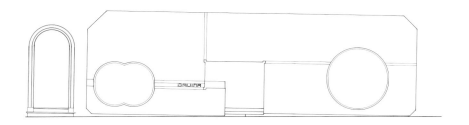

pool. As Guido Pietropoli informs us, this passageway (fig. 9.31) resonating with our footsteps, as we move toward a transparent but hermetic glass door, is intended to evoke in our minds the passage of Orpheus into the underworld, thereby evoking the Orphic myth about which the entire cemetery seems to be organized.[25]

To a typical Venetian play between waterwork and earthwork Scarpa thus imparts an ambivalent reading, emphasizing the fact that water implies both regeneration and death. Thus, while a water channel extends from the reflecting pool

opposite page:
9.22
Vesica piscis.

9.23
Gianlorenzo Bernini, Sant'Andrea al Quirinale, Rome, 1658–1670. Plan.

9.24
Vesica piscis. The relationship of the smaller axis to the large axis of the *vesica piscis* in progressive growth visually demonstrates a geometric progression: axis 1 / axis 2 : axis 2 / axis 3 : axis 3 / axis 4 = $1/\sqrt{3}$: $\sqrt{3}/3$: $3/(3\sqrt{3})$.

9.25
The circle and the square, in the art of self-division, give rise to the 3 "sacred" proportional relationships of $\sqrt{2}$, $\sqrt{3}$, and $\sqrt{5}$.

9.26
Carlo Scarpa, Olivetti shop, Piazza San Marco, interior shutter.

this page:
9.27
Carlo Scarpa, Gavina store, Bologna, 1961–1963. Elevation.

9.28
Carlo Scarpa, Banca Popolare di Verona, stairhall.

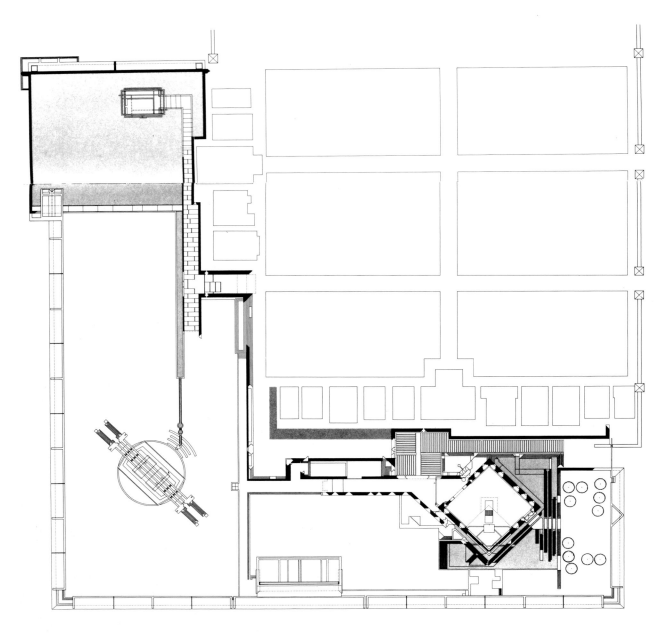

9.29
Carlo Scarpa, Brion Cemetery, San Vito d'Altivole, Treviso, plan, 1969–1978.

9.30
Carlo Scarpa, Brion Cemetery, entrance.

to irrigate, as it were, the sunken tumulus of the tomb, the only way of gaining access to the domain of the pool is via a glass guillotine door. This dichotomy seems to be reinforced by the water itself, which appears to be divided between the water lilies that lie suspended on the surface of the meditation pool and the submerged world of an inundated civilization implied by Scarpa's ziggurat profiles that lose themselves in its depths.

Two further details serve to emphasize the ambiguity of the pool: a wire barrier (fig. 9.32) that suggests its forbidden nature, and second the counterweight mechanism of the guillotine door that seems to represent the mechanism of time from which there is no escape. This last metaphor is reinforced by the guillotine itself, which operates like a kind of metaphysical sluice gate that can only be opened by lowering it into the sump, or conversely closed by raising it with the assistance of a counterweight regulated by a system of pulleys (fig. 9.33). This Duchampian device[26] seems to be suspended between mortality and immortality, for when the glass door is in the one element, the water, it is withdrawn from the other, the air, and vice versa. There is the further vague implication that this alchemical device is a kind of pump that draws the water from the arcosolium into the meditation pool (fig. 9.34).[27] In a remarkably perceptive essay, Paolo Portoghesi expands upon the parallel meanings embodied in the arcosolium itself:

Arch, bridge, roof, boat, each of these connotations, these words, projects a symbolic value onto the place, symbols of death, in that they are symbols of life, since death isn't given except dialectically as life which bears within itself its negation and the negation of its negation. . . . Scarpa prefers periphrasis to direct evocation, the round of words that avoids the use of the repeated archaic term.

The difference, it could be said—referring to Deleuze—doesn't come from repetition but from the initial removal compensated for by an endless reproaching.[28]

With its elevated superstructure and its inundated undercroft, the Brion Cemetery seems, in many ways, to be an oriental reflection on the acceptance of mortality, and it would be hard to find another contemporary commemorative work that is so removed from the morbidity commonly associated with death in the West. Instead, Scarpa sought a transcultural, ecumenical expression that would transcend the Christian preoccupation with guilt and redemption. The idea of death as a joyous (re)union, indissolubly linked to the erotic, is subtly confirmed in this instance by Scarpa's cunning use of the Chinese character "double happiness"—a character traditionally employed on the occasion of a wedding—that is ingeniously incorporated into the form of the concrete lattice window cast into the only open corner of the cemetery compound.[29]

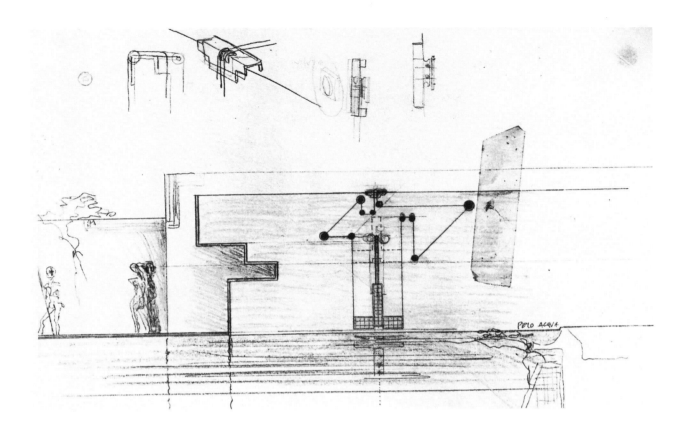

9.31
Carlo Scarpa, Brion Cemetery, corridor.

9.32
Carlo Scarpa, Brion Cemetery, symbolic triple-strand wire barrier.

9.33
Carlo Scarpa, Brion Cemetery, mechanism operating the plate glass door.

The principle of enigmatic displacement is ever present in Scarpa's architecture and never more so than in the Brion Cemetery, where ostensibly light and heavy modes of construction are mixed in ways that often seem perverse, as in the steel doors that serve respectively to close the openings to the chapel and an adjacent storeroom. Where the one is filled with white lacquered plasterwork, the other is loaded up with the ballast of concrete panels, cast in situ. Where the first finish is surely appropriate to a formal entrance, the second is the improbable paneling of a utilitarian opening. Since the reference in both instances is to lightweight Japanese walling, the one seems appropriately light and dematerialized, while the other is inexplicably heavy and opaque. One can hardly help being reminded at this juncture of Semper's *Stoffwechseltheorie,* although here the shift from light to heavy has little to do with the preservation of symbolic form. A similar enigmatic allusion is evident in the treatment of the large horizontal, concrete walls that serve to separate the existing cemetery from the Brion compound. These *béton brut* planes are filled with beige-colored plaster panels that occupy the best part of the available surface. However, since these panels do not run uninterruptedly for the full height of the wall, they are in effect treated as blank friezes, where the tectonic allusion would end were it not for the cryptic application of ornamental metal disks at the four corners of each panel, implying that the panels are some kind of *petrified* Semperian fabric stretched across the surface of the concrete.[30]

Boundary, datum, measure, and ornament, these are the themes that come to mind in experiencing Scarpa's architecture, and never more so than in the two penultimate works of his life, the Brion Cemetery and the Banca Popolare di Verona. Thus, in the cemetery, as in the Querini garden, the raising of the general datum is the principal device by which the space is guaranteed its remoteness, its sense of being apart (fig. 9.35). In each instance, from a midaxial approach people in the garden are perceived as elevated figures who are at once remote and paradoxically accessible. As Francesco Dal Co has remarked of the Brion Cemetery, the elevated eye level finds itself at a new datum removed from the ordinary world.

The sloping wall with its dummy buttresses serves to mark out the difference in level between the flat surrounding countryside and the lawn which the built structures of the tomb either rise above or sink beneath. To a viewer on the outside the wall forms a barrier. On its skyline stand out the coping of the chapel and the silhouette of the cypresses, while from the inside the wall appears as a slender line merely denoting a drop in the level of the ground.[31]

Thus we come to realize that a ground floor for Scarpa was never merely a serviceable covering laid over an abstract plane, but rather it was an elevated artificial datum to be read as a tactile palimpsest (fig. 9.36). At the same time, as Dal Co remarks, measure itself, far from being an expedient and arbitrary delimitation of size, is in fact inseparable from the coming into being of form. After Coomaraswamy, Dal Co observes that, according to its etymology, the Sanskrit word *matra* means both "measure" and "matter."[32] Thus, making matter manifest, one might say, is the prime function of measure, that is to say, the creation of artificial order from natural chaos through the presence of geometry and the constructional joint. The act of realization is thus a reciprocal process in which measure simultaneously reveals both the material and itself. A very similar argument is to be found in Heino Engel's study of the Japanese house:

9.34
Carlo Scarpa, Brion Cemetery, sarcophagi.

9.35
Carlo Scarpa, Brion Cemetery, corner detail of boundary wall.

Measure in building precedes construction. Before man could build, he had to conceive of measuring. Measuring is one of man's first intellectual achievements; it distinguishes man's house from the animal's den. . . . Measure . . . then, is the instrument by which man masters the basic fabric of the building. Thus, it is his "measure" to organize the elements of building into an entirety.[33]

The French word *encadrement* is suggestive in this regard, since its etymology indicates how framing, far from being dispensable, is an essential boundary that arises out of material through measurement. Thus, again, as Dal Co remarks, "The forms of order cannot be manifested or described without indicating their measure, i.e., without individualizing their ornaments."[34] And yet, despite Scarpa's preoccupation with constructed ornament, he was by no means indifferent to function. On the contrary, functional purpose was a requirement that would always be given priority in his work. Thus, his tectonic expression oscillated constantly between the instrumentality of function and the sensuality of ornament, so that, as in Pierre Chareau's Maison de Verre of 1932, one could no longer tell where the one began and the other ended.[35]

Both Marco Frascari and Manfredo Tafuri have stressed the fragmentary nature of Scarpa's architecture—the former by comparing it to the Beaux-Arts exercise of the *analytique* wherein the overall composition and its details are unified at different scales within the format of a single drawing,[36] the latter by seeing it as "a perverse dialectic between the celebration of the form and the scattering of its parts." Scarpa's work may also be perceived in a more cognitive and critical discursive light. This is surely never more evident than in the restoration and adaptation of the Museo di Castelvecchio in Verona, which he would work on intermittently between 1953 and 1965. Scarpa elected to treat the building as a continuously unfolding promenade that would mark its progress through space by the discrete articulation of different elements. Here his constructional poetic becomes manifest over a wide range, from the all but imperceptible movement of water in the ornamental pools of the forecourt, their surfaces gently agitated by submerged outflows, to the deft deployment of freestanding radiators that, as in the Querini Stampalia, are used to quicken and deflect the circulation through the space (fig. 9.37).

In Castelvecchio the changing character of the interior arises from a constant play between the worked surfaces of different materials and the articulation of contingent seams, steps, borders, and reveals that serve to advance or check the overall progression. Against this constant yet changing beat are set all the accents that arise out of the necessary orchestration of various spans, supports, joints, and hinges, irrespective of the scale at which they emerge. The revelation of engineered form is repeatedly assumed by Scarpa as a syntactical key from which all other junctions should take their cue, whether the joint is a hinge, a pivot, a pedestal, or a fixed bracket. These are particularly evident in the various forms of mountings used to display the archaeological exhibits on the ground floor, each mounting being conceived as a tectonic complement to the piece in question (fig. 9.38). The work of the Romanian sculptor Constantin Brancusi was surely an inspiration here for the way in which sculpture and base were regarded as integral parts of the same plastic unity.

Scarpa's repertoire runs across a wide spectrum in this regard, from pivoting statues whose planimetric position may be spontaneously adjusted according to the light, to heavy monumental pieces that are supported in such a way as

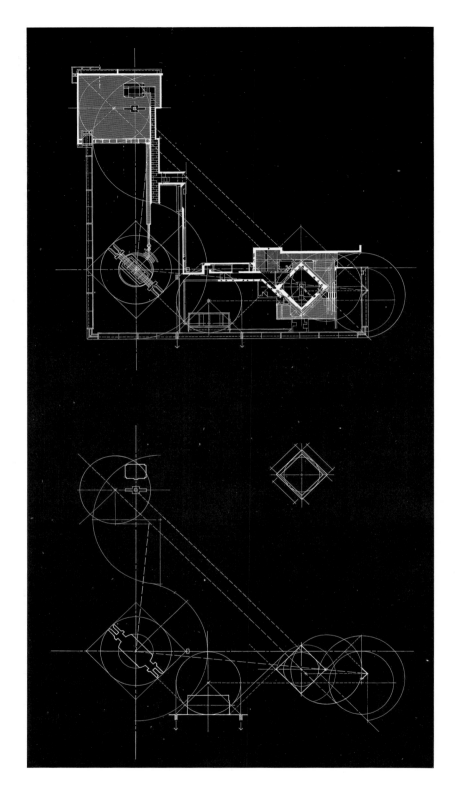

9.36
Carlo Scarpa, Brion Cemetery, analysis of
plan geometry.

to echo their figurative rhythm in the modulated shape of their base (fig. 9.39). However, as Sergio Los has observed, Scarpa's concern for the setting of a *topic* into a suitable *topos* went well beyond its appropriate mounting, to embrace its sequential and reciprocal placement within the overall narration of the space. In this way he tried to accord the uprooted fragment something of its lost aura. This surely accounts for the mounting of certain paintings on easels, so as to remind the viewer of their craft origin, as opposed to presenting such works always as fetishized, wall-hung images (fig. 9.40). One may possibly regard these stratagems as subtle ways of achieving a *Verfremdung* effect, that is to say, as a means for overcoming our habitually distracted way of beholding art. Nothing surely could be more tectonic than this return to "thingness" that, in Scarpa's case, is as evident in the framing of an object as in the fabric of the building in which it is housed. Here as elsewhere in his architecture, it is the working of the material itself that carries the semantic charge. We are presented with a tactile syntax that is grounded in difference, turning, that is, on evident transitions from rough to smooth, from polished to matte, from worked to unworked (fig. 9.41). Hence the differential reciprocity set up between the exposed concrete cross beams spanning over the ground-floor gallery—supported at midpoint by composite steel beams—and the in situ concrete slabs used to pave the gallery floor (figs. 9.42, 9.43). In the first instance we are confronted with an undressed *béton brut* finish that may be read as the petrification of the timber formwork, whereas in the second the tamped finish of the concrete floor—a technique traditionally reserved for the laying of *pastellone veneziano*—imparts to the top surface of the in situ slab a striation reminiscent of the grain to be found in stone. This association is reinforced by subdividing the concrete pours with bands of Istrian stone. What is intended in both instances, of course, is an allusion to another material rather than a simulation. This same

9.37
Carlo Scarpa, Museo di Castelvecchio, plan:
1. parallel hedges
2. lawn: great courtyard
3. entrance to Sala Boggian
4. entrance room
5. library
6. northeast tower
7. sculpture galleries
8. Cangrande space and statue

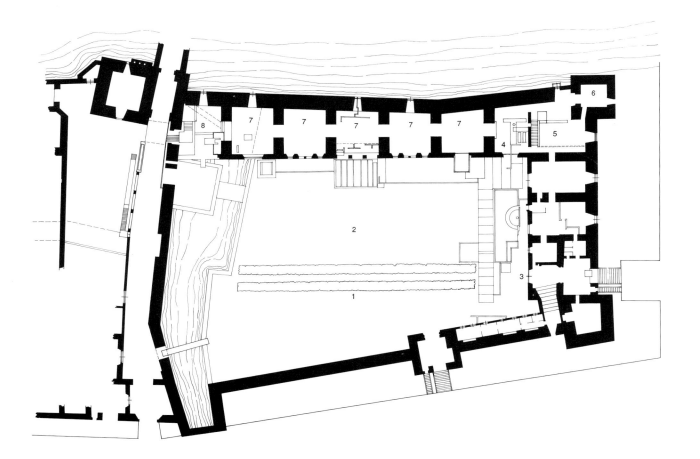

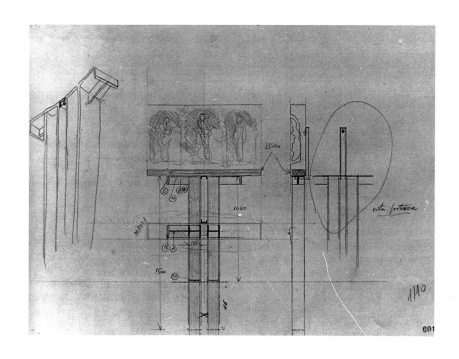

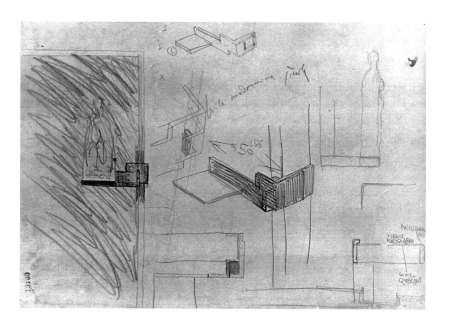

9.38
Carlo Scarpa, Museo di Castelvecchio, sculpture stand.

9.39
Carlo Scarpa, Museo di Castelvecchio, sculpture bracket.

concrete flooring is separated from the rough-plastered *spaca di cava* walls of the perimeter by a shallow recess that serves to establish the floor as a raised datum. We are returned here, as in Querini Stampalia, to a traditional Venetian earthwork complete with a perimeter channel in which to accommodate the surplus water of the *acqua alta*. At the same time, as Franco Fonatti has remarked, the subdivision of the concrete ground floor recalls the paving of the Piazza San Marco.[37]

Scarpa's penchant for the rhetorical joint reaches its apotheosis in the Banca Popolare di Verona, the penultimate work of his life, started in 1973 and posthumously completed by his assistant, Arrigo Rudi, three years after his death, in 1981 (figs. 9.44, 9.45). Within this complex and compact organization, Scarpa's denticulate molding is applied as a device by which to determine both the cornice of the loggia that crowns the building and the upper limits of its rusticated base. Within this earthwork the castellated profile reveals the massivity of the stone window surrounds and the stereotomic order of their joints (fig. 9.46). Elsewhere, it functions as a means to elevate and modulate the proportion of the facade. In this regard, the measure of its rhythm is inseparable from the syncopated order of the overall composition, as Albertini and Bagnoli have attempted to show.

The first axis of symmetry is picked up in the center line of the first span of the loggia, coinciding with the center line of the inverted molding on the cornice, an alignment that, as the eye travels down, takes in the center lines of the two stiffeners of the wing of the big girder, the round window and its dripstone, tying into the left-hand molding of the rectangular window beneath. The second axis starts in the next span, runs down through the center line of the small balcony to coincide with those of the projecting window and the window beneath. The third, instead, is that of the third base of the colonettes, which falls between two stones of the cornice, coincides with the axis of the girder riveting plate, that of the gilded-spheres motif, and ties in once more with that of the round window, its dripstone, and the rectangular window.

Moving to the right, the fifth span mirrors the situation of the first. In direct succession, the axis of the next pair of colonettes states itself forcefully between the two bay windows.

9.40
Carlo Scarpa, Museo di Castelvecchio, picture support and frame.

9.41
Carlo Scarpa, Museo di Castelvecchio, detail of the Sacello exterior, of local Prun stone.

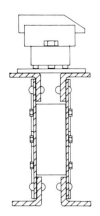

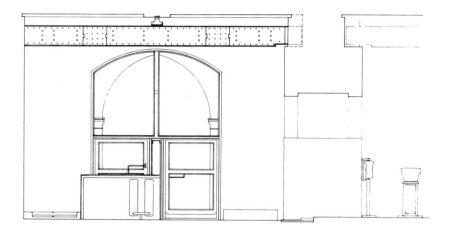

9.42
Carlo Scarpa, Museo di Castelvecchio, details of concrete and steel cross beam at ground-floor gallery.

9.43
Carlo Scarpa, Museo di Castelvecchio, ground-floor slab showing perimeter channel and the relation to the rendered wall.

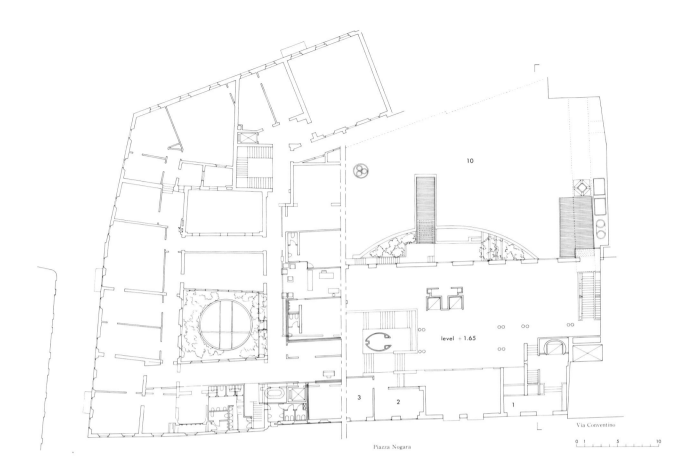

9.44
Carlo Scarpa, Banca Popolare di Verona,
ground-floor plan and second-floor plan:

1. entrance from Via Conventino
2. director
3. secretary
4. exchange
5. vice-director
6. reception
7. central corridor
8. staircase
9. terrace
10. courtyard

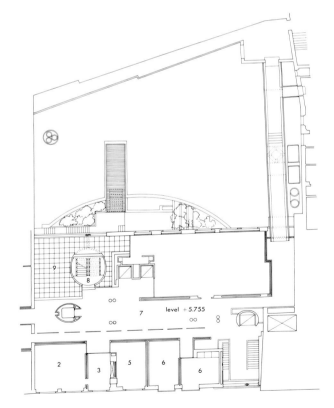

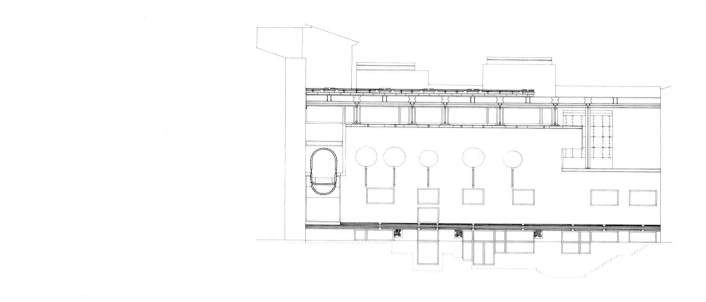

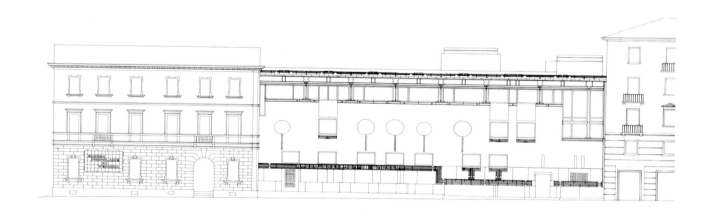

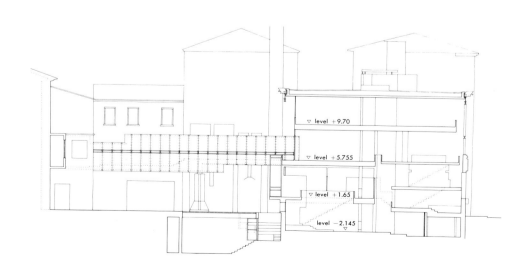

▽ level +9.70

▽ level +5.755

▽ level +1.65

level −2.145

The principal facade of the Banca Popolare (fig. 9.47) appears to be articulated according to Semper's four elements, so that we are presented with an earthwork in stone, a screen wall in plaster, and a steel framed loggia at the top of the building. The ziggurat molding serves to divide up the body of the building into these specific elements. Thus, the three dematerialized plate glass windows are countered by the contrasting weight of the ziggurat corbels arranged in T-formation beneath. A very similar figure is used to stress the massivity of the marble surround to the staff entrance on the Piazza Nogara. The powerful sculptural presence of this last is due in large measure to the revealed thickness of the marble, to the rupture of its surround by horizontal rustication, and last but not least to the presence of a single chamfered gun slit above the lintel (fig. 9.48). Once again one is reminded of Brancusi; this time perhaps of *The Gate of the Kiss* erected at Targu-Jiu in Romania in 1937. The phenomenological intensity of this facade is also due to the contrast between the rough finish of the *cocciopesto* plastered wall and the dressed surface of the Botticino marble.

This difference not only separates the rendering from the rustication but also distinguishes between the plaster and the polished stone surrounds of the seemingly circular window openings, assembled out of five separate pieces. Situated on axis beneath these surrounds are thin vertical grooves of red Veronese marble receiving the downpipes of the rainwater gulleys that drain the inner leaf of the double-layered facade. These lines not only accommodate the weathering of the facade but also emphasize the watermark from the very beginning, thereby anticipating the inevitable transformation of the building over time (figs. 9.49, 9.50). To the rear of this frontal screen, square wooden window frames are let into the inner leaf of the wall, thereby establishing an oriental interplay be-

9.45
Carlo Scarpa, Banca Popolare di Verona, courtyard elevation, front elevation, and section.

9.46
Carlo Scarpa, Banca Popolare di Verona, constructional details of cornice and axonometric of denticulate cornice.

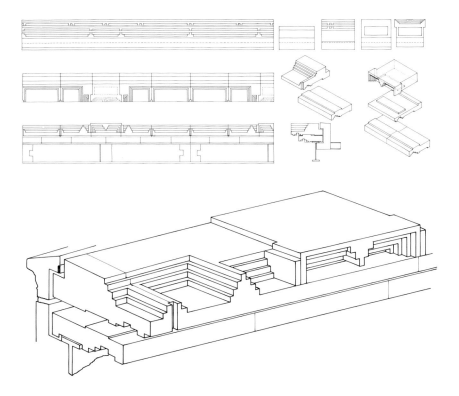

9.47
Carlo Scarpa, Banca Popolare di Verona,
front facade.

9.48
Carlo Scarpa, Banca Popolare di Verona,
entrance on Piazza Nogara.

9.49
Carlo Scarpa, Banca Popolare di Verona,
window details.

9.50
Carlo Scarpa, Banca Popolare di Verona, analytique of ornamental system.

tween the orthogonal timber fenestration and the circular oculi of the surface aperture (fig. 9.51).[39]

Aside from a characteristically rich spectrum of finishes, ranging from various tones of *stucco lucido* to panels of translucent onyx, the most striking aspect of the banking halls from a tectonic standpoint is the way in which a suspended ceiling is provided without compromising the probity of the structure, since the soffits of the concrete beams and their concrete columnar supports are left exposed, as cast from faceted formwork, except for a 1.5-meter-high sheath in steel that surrounds the base of each column (fig. 9.52). The suspended nature of the plaster ceiling is made manifest through its subdivision into fairly large areas by seams that not only impart scale to the expanse of the overall soffit, but also return the eye to the salient points at which the concrete column heads come through the plaster to lie flush with the ceiling.[40]

Excessively enriched, the tops of the twin columns are ornamented by incised gold bands set some 27.5 centimeters below the ceiling; close to the point of bearing itself, we again encounter a diminutive, gilded version of the *vesica piscis,* cast into a Muntz metal fitting that is wedged between the column heads (fig. 9.53). As in the Castelvecchio, the giant tatami-like panels of the suspended ceiling are rhythmically modulated so as to achieve an effect that is reminiscent of neoplasticism. This seems to induce a pinwheeling dynamic that is focused about certain elements, such as the onyx stair hall, the red elevator shaft, and a glazed cylindrical, metal-framed stair that rises to the top of the building (fig. 9.54). As Pier Luigi Nicolin has remarked, all of this elaboration was made with little regard for the conventional status of the building.

In his relation to institutional space, Scarpa's attitude is one of conscious indifference. As far as the bank is concerned, he limits himself to celebrating its wealth in the luxury of the materials used in the furnishings. There is no sign of rhetorically emphasizing the institution in the Louis Kahn manner, no indulgence in the requirement to interpret company philosophy in a "corporate image"; nor does this sophisticated and complex building seem to want to underpin the complex patterns of human interaction in the manner of Van Eyck.

The spatial complexity of the building, frequently underscored, is developed with a sort of private language and pleasure which hovers enjoyably about the web

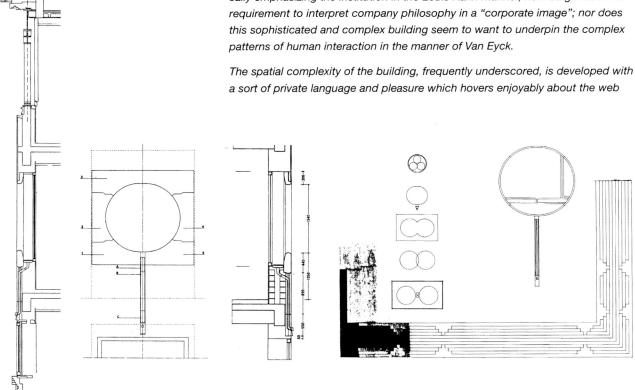

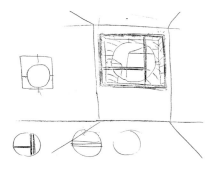

9.51
Carlo Scarpa, Banca Popolare di Verona, sketch of circular window.

9.52
Carlo Scarpa, Banca Popolare di Verona, second-floor hall.

9.53
Carlo Scarpa, Banca Popolare di Verona, column-ceiling joint.

9.54
Carlo Scarpa, Banca Popolare di Verona, exterior staircase.

of its functions, as if lingering over the effort made to render them feasible. This achieved freedom can only express itself in a space of "transparencies" in which materials, mechanisms, links, finishings, all share in this virtuosity of execution: its felicity troubled only by melancholy over the unrepeatability of the achievement.[41]

Scarpa's concern for the expressive probity of a building's basic structure would parallel that of Louis Kahn, as is evident from another late work, the Fondazione Masieri on the Grand Canal in Venice where an exposed concrete floor evidently rests on an unpainted steel framework. Set flush with the soffit of the in situ *béton brut* floor, the steel joists are supported at intervals by twin cylindrical columns, also made of steel, the steelwork being clear-sealed throughout in order to retard oxidation.

It is difficult to write about Scarpa's work in a systematic manner, for in the last analysis his achievement can only be comprehended as a continuum. It is this, perhaps more than anything else, that served to set him apart from the mainstream, for in his case there was never the intention of an ideal whole in either a humanist or an organic sense. There was only the "nearness of things" and their unfolding progression from part to part and joint to joint. Spatial interpenetration is largely absent in his work. Place is there, but only as a momentary location that is constantly modified by movement and the fluctuation of light. It is above all a disquisition on time, on the paradoxical durability and fragility of things; an all but cinematic sensibility, permeated by an ineradicable melancholy. Beyond this, Scarpa's work serves not only as a demonstration of tectonic authenticity but also as a critique of the two main utopias of our time; the organic utopia of Wright and the technological utopia of modern functionalism. That this was so, despite Scarpa's lifelong attachment to Wright and his affinity for industrial design, says much for Scarpa's sense of limit and for his capacity to offset the assumption of any particular criteria with a discreet sense of irony. Antiutopian to the core, he always addressed the specific terms of the brief and the boundaries of the site; yet despite this responsiveness, he never allowed his imagination to be stifled by precedent.

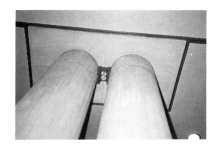

Like Alvar Aalto, Scarpa knew that the poor man cannot be saved by architecture, let alone by all the well-meaning exertions of the welfare state. Instead, he offered an architecture of disjunctive narrative in which what is is always accompanied by what has been and what might have been. The development of local craft was a key element in this undertaking, even if he refused any a priori typological approach to the generation of form. Thus, while constantly exigent about craft and dimensional precision, he rarely yielded to the systematization of modular production. Influenced by the ethical impulse of the Viennese Krausian circle and above all by the writings of Karl Kraus and Adolf Loos, Scarpa strove against Loos's renunciation of ornament for an ornament that was a kind of impenetrable writing. In this way, he lay, on his own confession, closer to Loos's other, Josef Hoffmann. At once critical and celebratory, Scarpa saw such cryptic, microtectonic inscriptions as somehow capable of transcending the ruinations of time. In this regard we may think of his work as an enchanted disenchantment.

10 Postscriptum:
   The Tectonic Trajectory,
   1903–1994

Good architecture starts always with efficient construction. Without construction there is no architecture. Construction embodies material and its use according to its properties, that is to say, stone imposes a different method of construction from iron or concrete.

I believe we can create contemporary architecture with all materials—with any material as long as we use it correctly according to its properties. In areas where we can find nothing but stone, we shall build with that stone, that is the local stone. We shall create contemporary architecture as we would have done with any other material (iron, concrete, wood) which we would have found in another area, because the leading ideas are the spirit of construction and the flexibility of our outlook and not the constructional whim foreign to the site. . . . The finite location; the climate, the topography and the materials available in each area determine the constructional method, the functional disposition, and finally the form. Architecture cannot exist without landscape, climate, soil, and manners and customs. This is the reason why we sometimes see old buildings looking contemporary and for the same reason we build today contemporary buildings which could have been built in the past. Since man from time immemorial to this day has always lived, moved about and breathed in the same way, since in our way of life perhaps nothing has changed basically . . . I can build with the most modern materials (iron, concrete, and with the ARTIFICIAL materials of contemporary building construction) a building which will be related harmoniously with the character of the landscape. I shall do this frequently in order to challenge my architectural inventiveness, and this I must do in order to be able to prove that true architecture can be created in any place with any material. But I cannot ignore a sentimental factor, which we must reveal in our construction, otherwise we shall be stagnant and inhuman . . . , then we shall choose our material not only according to the standards of economy and pure science but with the spirit of emotional freedom and artistic imagination. Hence architecture finally stands beyond pure purpose; higher than the achievements of logic and cold calculation.
Aris Konstantinidis, Architecture, *1964*

Although, as Konstantinidis insists, the tectonic must by its nature transcend the logic of calculation, the fact remains that any account of modern building culture must acknowledge the crucial role played by structural engineering. This much is surely self-evident from the seminal contributions made across the century by such distinguished engineers as Othmar Ammann, Ove Arup, Santiago Calatrava, Felix Candela, Eladio Dieste, Eugène Freyssinet, François Hennebique, Albert Kahn, August Kommendant, Fritz Leonhardt, Robert Maillart, Christian Menn, Ricardo Morandi, Pier Luigi Nervi, Félix Samuely, Eduardo Torroja, and E. Owen Williams. This is obviously nothing more than a rather random listing of a number of prominent structural engineers who have either been primary form-makers in their own right, as in the case of say Calatrava and Candela (fig. 10.1), or, as in the instance of Arup, Kommendant, and Samuely, have conceived their finest work in collaboration with architects. Between these two alternative modes of practice lie such unique figures as Robert Le Ricolais, Frei Otto, and Vladimir Suchov, who have worked mainly in the field of network suspension structures, and a number of idiosyncratic craftsman-constructors such as Konrad Wachsmann, Richard Buckminster Fuller, and Jean Prouvé. Within this broad spectrum the career of Owen Williams has been particularly remarkable for the concept and realization of a number of exceptionally brilliant reinforced concrete works between 1930 and 1954. Certainly his structurally plastic inventions bear comparison to those of an architect like Auguste Perret, who worked in the same material over the same period. Of mushroom column, in situ con-

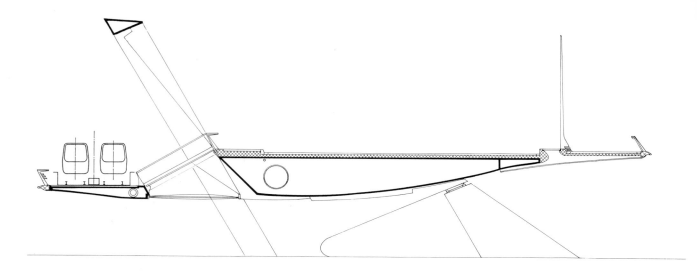

10.1
Santiago Calatrava, Project for Gentil Bridge,
Paris, 1988.

10.2
Owen Williams, Boots pharmaceutical plant,
Nottingham, 1932.

crete construction, Williams's pharmaceutical plant, built in Nottingham for Boots in 1932, remains, for all its indifference to the classical tradition, of equal stature to the finest work of Perret (fig. 10.2).

Of all these engineers none perhaps has been more sensitive to the tectonic potential of structural form than Nervi, and it says much for Nervi's exceptional sensibility that he would regard the closely spaced columns of the Egyptian temple as the consequence of a tectonic intention rather than as the outcome of a certain structural limitation. Moreover, no modern engineer has expressed himself more lucidly as to the necessary relations that must obtain between structural analysis and constructional form. As he was to put it toward the end of his career, in 1961:

The experience acquired in almost fifty years of direct contact with activities in various fields of design and construction have led me to an optimistic conclusion: the unlimited possibilities of design offered by scientific theories of construction, the executions made possible by new building materials and current techniques, and the architectural themes growing ever greater and more complex as dictated by our social and economic developments, open horizons of unprecedented possibilities of construction as compared to what humanity has achieved from prehistoric times to the present.

Nevertheless these marvelous possibilities cannot be fully developed if the three fundamental factors of any construction—the architectural concept, the structural analysis . . . and the correct solution to the problems of execution—do not proceed in close collaboration having as its aim the sole and unique goal of arriving at a proposed result combining functionality, solidity, and beauty.[1]

Of the many omissions in this account of the evolution of tectonic culture none is perhaps more glaring than that of the Dutch architect Hendrik Petrus Berlage, who fell directly under Semper's influence by virtue of being an early graduate of the Polytechnikum, now the ETH, the school that Semper founded in Zurich in 1855. This was not the only tectonic tradition to which Berlage was heir, however, for a major influence in the Netherlands in the 1880s was the structural rationalist P. J. H. Cuypers, the designer of the Rijksmuseum (1885) and the Central Station in Amsterdam (1889). Cuypers was profoundly influenced by Viollet-le-Duc, and this is the credo that he passed on to the younger generation, including K. P. C. de Bazel, J. C. M. Lauweriks, and Berlage himself. As a result of this double formation Berlage can be seen as achieving a unique synthesis between the French and German traditions. This much is evinced by his masterwork, the Stock Exchange completed in Amsterdam in 1903 that was obviously a realization of one of the didactic illustrations to be found in Viollet-le-Duc's *Entretiens* of 1872. From the same source came his use of an overall proportional grid based on the isosceles triangle (the so-called Egyptian triangle) as a device for establishing the position and size of every element, no matter how small, not only in the Stock Exchange but in much of his subsequent work. Elsewhere, and above all in the interior of the main hall, patterned insets of multicolored brickwork and the hanging, castellated curtain relief of the enclosing walls, particularly in the upper reaches of the space, point to the influence of Semper's *Bekleidungstheorie* (fig. 10.3). That Berlage was fully aware of his indebtedness to Semper, not only for his theory of cladding but also for his broad socioanthropological and political views, is borne out in his writing.[2]

Like Louis Kahn after him, Berlage was to envision the walls of the environment as literally embodying the space of society; as being the matrix within which and by which the society is formed. In this regard his Stock Exchange building assumed the existence of a social community or *Gemeinschaft,* both within and without its volume. Thus the contingent street space around the structure is as

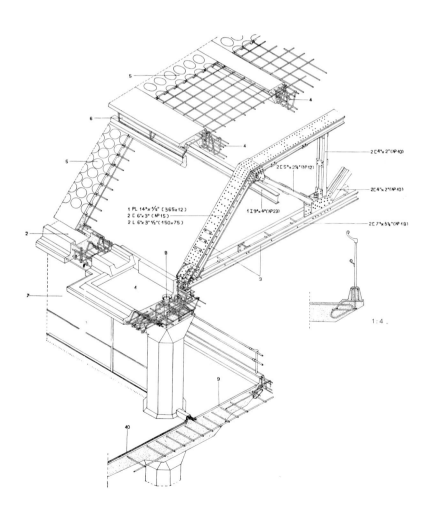

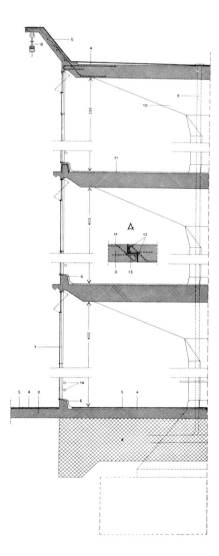

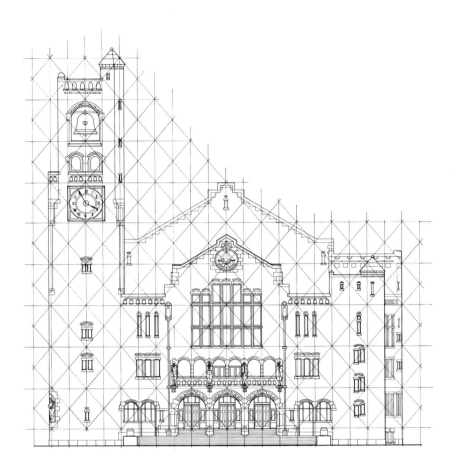

metrically modulated and defined by the building's face as its trading halls are influenced by the nature of their enclosing brick walls and glass roofs. Aside from displaying the hierarchical sequence of its construction, Berlage's masonry, stiffened and enriched by brick piers and by heavy stone dressings, seems to evoke the guild and burgher values that, even in the late nineteenth century, could still be experienced in the Netherlands as the continuation of a *modus vivendi* going back to the Middle Ages. For Berlage, both the art of diamond cutting and the intricate fair-faced brickwork of his Diamond Workers' Union Building of 1903 derived equally from a time-honored Dutch capacity for high-quality craftsmanship (fig. 10.4). For all that Berlage's socialism should appear to be a revolutionary daydream to his Marxist contemporaries, the fact that it should also be so eminently realizable (as opposed to the utopianism of William Morris) may have been due to the vestiges of a preindustrial culture that continued amid the industrialization of the Netherlands—to the persistence, that is, of rooted communal ideals that derived, in part, from the techno-agrarianism of the dike upon which the survival of the country depended. In terms of his tectonic development, Berlage came to adopt the technology of reinforced concrete only in the last decade of his career, beginning with the office building that he built in The Hague between 1920 and 1927 for the leading insurance company De Nederlanden van 1845. With its vaguely oriental syntax, corbeled-out in form but not in fact due to the homogeneity of the material, this work was almost the only occasion on which Berlage would employ fair-faced reinforced concrete (fig. 10.5). Similar to the late work of Perret, the concrete in this instance is of bush-hammered skeletonal construction, with brick and glass infill. Thus both architects attempted to treat concrete as though it were synthetic stone. With the single exception of a diminutive glass and concrete flower kiosk with inset lenses realized in The Hague in 1925 (fig. 10.6), Berlage would not attempt to use the material in its fair-faced form again. The assimilation and transformation of concrete in Berlage's work between 1925 and his death in 1934 is significant for the evolution of tectonic form in Dutch architecture, since the final work of his career, the Gemeentemuseum erected in The Hague between 1927 and 1935, is structured about a reinforced concrete frame that is faced on the outside in brick and on the inside is left fair-faced. Where the brick effectively covers the frame, tile appears in the interior as a form of infill cladding. Three particular inflections determine the tectonic character of this work. In the first instance, there is the frame itself, which, expressed as an armature throughout, is covered externally in a non-load-bearing brick skin. In the second, there are the internal partition walls, which are faced in ceramic tile so as to express their screenlike character. Finally there is the contrapuntal form of the brick skin, the bay windows, and the pitched-roof skylights that are alternately advanced and recessed in a fugal fashion, so as to express the changing spatial differential of the volumes within the gallery enfilade. As Chris Burrows has written:

For Berlage, the "clothing" is the obligatory brick. To overcome the material's traditional association as a load bearing element, . . . it is bonded in such a way as to suggest its role as a skin. Double courses of stretchers alternate with single courses of headers to convey a decidedly non-structural quality and even metaphorically to evoke the weave of Semper's space-defining mats. Furthermore,

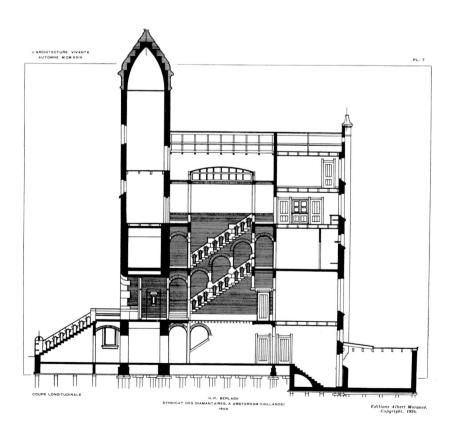

10.3
H. P. Berlage, Stock Exchange, Amsterdam, 1897–1903. South elevation with the system of proportions (1898 drawing).

10.4
H. P. Berlage, Diamond Workers' Union, Amsterdam, 1896–1903. Longitudinal section.

10.5
H. P. Berlage, office building for De Nederlanden van 1845, The Hague, 1920–1927.

10.6
H. P. Berlage, flower kiosk, The Hague, 1925.

structural elements characteristic of load-bearing masonry such as quoins are notably absent.

Internally, Berlage discovers the space-generating properties of the monolithic frame. Its orthogonal constituents imply the space which they delineate rather than positively enclosing it in the manner of the load-bearing wall. Adjacent spaces are individual at the same time as being part of one great space flowing through the entire building. This concept and use of space is in marked contrast to the distinct compartmentalization inherent in cellular masonry construction as illustrated by the spatial relationship in the Stock Exchange.[3]

This subtle tectonic differentiation will lie dormant in Dutch architecture for some thirty years before resurfacing in the work of Herman Hertzberger, where the interplay between the framework and volume will come to be simultaneously expressed both inside and out, in an equally rigorous manner.[4]

The other important architect largely omitted from this study is the Austrian Otto Wagner, although, unlike Berlage's, his architecture may be seen as a constant oscillation between the tectonic of the structure and the largely atectonic veil of the skin. This tension is immediately evident in his urban masterwork, the Postsparkassenamt, built in Vienna between 1904 and 1912 (fig. 10.7). While Semper's *Bekleidungstheorie* is again an influence, one may also detect the theoretical presence of Karl Bötticher, above all Bötticher's distinction between core form and art form that seems to manifest itself here as a constantly interpenetrating exchange between the underlying structural core and the outer membrane, this last making itself manifest in the Sterzing marble revetment, held in place by iron bolts covered with a sheet of lead and an aluminum cap. While these bolts are not the sole means of securing the masonry, they nonetheless perform the double function of both assisting the adhesion and representing the sheathing as a form of textile. In this regard they may be read as the links in a coat of chain mail or as knots in a knitted garment. Moreover, the fact that these studs are of metal makes them of the same order as the light metal, semistructural furnishings used elsewhere, from the horizontal metal balustrading of the *piano nobile* to the metal entry doors and ferro-vitreous canopy that together serve to articulate the entrance.

10.7
Otto Wagner, Postsparkassenamt, Vienna,
1904–1912.

10.8
Otto Wagner, St. Leopold, Steinhof, Vienna,
1907. Longitudinal section.

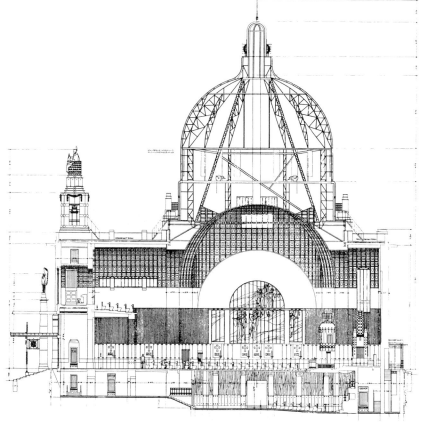

As in Mies van der Rohe's Seagram Building of 1958, there is a noticeable tendency to transfer the character of one material to the next. Thus we may compare the metalization of the glass in the Seagram Building, brought about by an elision between brown tinted glass and bronze anodized fenestration, to the metalization of stone in the case of Wagner's Postsparkassenamt or his St. Leopold Church at the Steinhof Sanatorium dating from 1907 (fig. 10.8). Both of these works convey the impression of being sheathed in metallic stone, an effect that achieves its greatest intensity in the interior of the church where the entire surface seems to consist of a stone membrane impregnated with metal. One recalls by way of contrast the tectonic work of Henri Labrouste, where the ferrovitreous cage remains totally differentiated from its stone encasement. Here, on the contrary, the light steel trusswork supporting the dome is erected into position and then concealed. At the same time, small-scale, microstructural armatures are present as tectonic metaphors throughout the fabric, from the surrogate dome of the suspended baldachino to the various ornaments of the altar, the cross, and the candelabra (fig. 10.9). Paradoxical as it may seem, these devices reinforce the impression that the entire corpus is permeated by an interstitial metal network, not only by virtue of the repetitive stud pattern that covers the internal stone sheathing but also in terms of the railings, doors, reliefs, and light fittings that effectively articulate the space.

This synthetic contrast between the compressive crystalline nature of stone and the ductile character of metal is equally evident in Wagner's engineering work, above all in his *Stadtbahn* viaducts, where metal is used not only for the structural span but also for the wreaths that embellish the stone pylons on either side of the typical crossing, as in his Zeile Viaduct of 1898. In this case, dressed masonry confers its traditional status on the supporting pylons, which represent themselves as the supporting pillars of the benevolent state. Thus both metal and stone serve in this instance as symbolic elements. Elsewhere there is an explicit differentiation between *monument* and *instrument* as these two aspects play out their respective roles in Wagner's Nussdorf and Kaiserbad dams in the new Danube regulation works, under construction between 1894 and 1907 (figs. 10.10, 10.11). While the antithetical values of *Kunstform* and *Werkform* are

10.9
Otto Wagner, St. Leopold, Steinhof, altar detail.

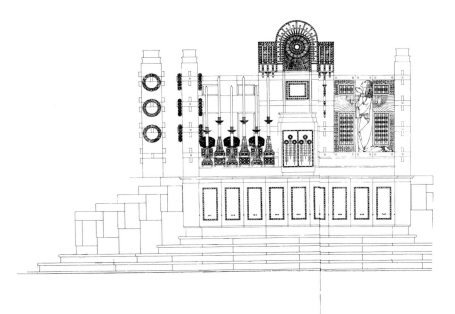

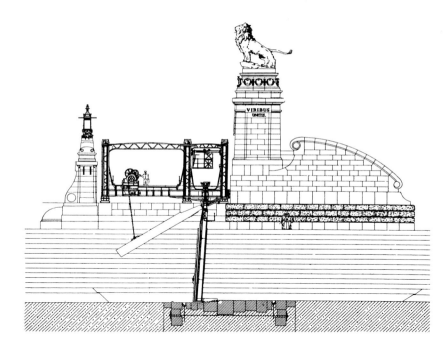

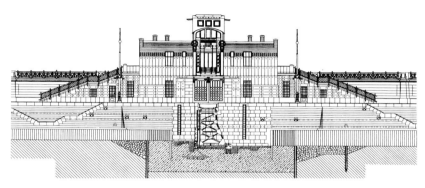

10.10
Otto Wagner, Nussdorf Dam, Vienna, 1894–1898. Section showing one of the abutments.

10.11
Otto Wagner, Kaiserbad Dam, Vienna, 1904–1907. Section of the sluice gate showing control building as seen from the canal.

clearly separated from each other in the Nussdorf dam, in the Kaiserbad installation a retractable sluice is housed in a sheet metal cabin. It is thereafter embellished with metal wreaths in such a way as to mediate between the instrumentality of the crane and the monumentality of its masonry emplacement.

In the history of twentieth-century architecture perhaps nothing is more unacknowledged than the emergence of tectonic form in the work of Le Corbusier. This is particularly evident after his atectonic Purist villas of the late twenties and his curtain-walled, machinist works of the next decade, which appear in retrospect to be technologically "productivist." While certain tectonic features are clearly expressed in the machinist works built between 1932 and 1935, the curtain wall facade of the Maison Clarté, Geneva, and the steel-framed, glass block front of the Porte Molitor apartments in Paris, constructional syntax will only begin to play a primary poetic role in Le Corbusier's work with his Maison Week-End of 1935 (fig. 10.12). This small house will be accompanied by the realization of three other works in which tectonic articulation will greatly determine the overall character of the architecture, the Mandrot House, near Toulon (1931), a

343

10.12
Le Corbusier, Maison Week-End, St.-Cloud, near Paris, 1934–1935. Axonometric.

10.13
Le Corbusier, vacation house, Mathes, 1935. West and east elevations.

10.14
Le Corbusier, reconstruction of the Hebrew Temple, from *Vers une architecture,* 1923.

house at Mathes (1935) (fig. 10.13), and a seminal tented structure erected for the Paris World Exhibition in 1937.

Le Corbusier's Maison Week-End, built at St.-Cloud near Paris, announces a totally fresh departure, one that was to be as much at variance with the ideology of Purism as with the functionalism of the *Neue Sachlichkeit.* For while this house employed eminently modern techniques, such as reinforced concrete, steel-framed plate glass, glass lenses, plywood paneling, and industrial tiles, it also made abundant use of archaic building methods, evident in the rubble stone cross walls that carried the reinforced concrete vaults. It surely says something about the Mediterranean vernacular origin of the form that these roofs were of a rise and span that could easily have been achieved with Roussillon or Catalan vaulting. If the internal top-lit, ferro-vitreous banking hall of Wagner's Postsparkassenamt can be seen in retrospect as aspiring to a tectonic that will attain its apotheosis in the *Produktform* of the so-called High-Tech architects of the 1970s (one thinks of such architects as Norman Foster and Renzo Piano), then Le Corbusier's canonical weekend house may be seen as demonstrating the opposite thesis, namely a conscious move away from modernization and its faith in the inevitable benevolence of modern technology.

The Maison Week-End evokes a kind of eternal return in which neither the archaic nor the modern predominate. We may think of this house as a Nietzschean embodiment of vanquished historical states, as an aspiration for some transhistorical condition, removed from the nightmare of maximization and accelerating obsolescence. It is hardly an accident that this house, partially buried beneath the earth, should evoke a going-to-ground, as though it were a kind of archaeological manifestation, a troglodyte *objet trouvé* that while contaminated by modern technique remains irredeemably archaic. Le Corbusier's *Voyage d'Orient* (1912) and his later experiences in North Africa were both influential in this regard, for, as the shallow vaults of the house indicate, it may be seen as a piece of Cycladic fabric into which modern technology had been quite surreptitiously inserted.

Thus the Maison Week-End is a tectonic montage in which we pass from the white-washed, rubble-walled interior, with vaults lined in plywood sheet, to a full-height, plate-glass window, framed in steel, that, filling an entire bay, gives onto a freestanding concrete vault removed from the house. This last appears as an *al fresco* primitive hut, consisting of a thin-shell vault spanning onto equally thin concrete piers. This idealized tectonic form will be overwhelmed and absorbed by the coarse tectonic capacity of primitive building technique that, instead of allowing this vault to function as a unifying structural module, will render its effete piers redundant and thus replaceable by load-bearing rubble stone cross walls. Despite this conscious dissolution of an underlying structural grid, expressive detailing was to be of primary importance to the expressivity of the form. Thus as Le Corbusier wrote:

The designing of such a house demanded extreme care since the elements of construction were the only architectonic means. The architectural theme was established about a typical bay whose influence extended as far as the little pavilion in the garden. Here one was confronted by exposed stonework, natural on the outside, while on the interior, wood on the walls and ceiling and a chimney out of rough brickwork, with white ceramic tiles on the floor. Nevada glass block walls and a table of Cippolino marble.[5]

Where the Maison Week-End returned to the Mediterranean megaron, the Pavillon des Temps Nouveaux (1937) evoked the tent as the primordial nomadic form, the roof of which is simultaneously both cladding and structure since the stability of the whole depends upon the tensile surface of the fabric. This particular evocation of the eternal present had already been intimated by Le Corbusier in the pages of *Vers une architecture* (1923), above all in the reconstruction of the Hebrew temple in the wilderness that was depicted as a gridded temenos (fig. 10.14). The tectonic significance of the modular order in this instance resided in the fact that structure, cladding, and proportion were all integrated into

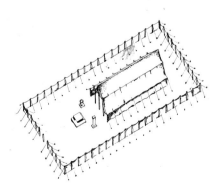

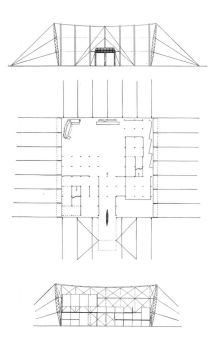

10.15
Le Corbusier, Pavillon des Temps Nouveaux, Paris, 1937. Main elevation, ground-floor plan, and cross section.

10.16
Le Corbusier, Pavillon des Temps Nouveaux, construction details.

a tensile membrane. Following this Judaic model, the modular order of the Pavillon des Temps Nouveaux coincides with the guy lines supporting its tented form.

Sustained by an "exoskeletonal" structure, the Pavillon des Temps Nouveaux was ordered about a grid that comprised six modules in one direction and seven in another (fig. 10.15). This adaptation of a nomadic paradigm entailed a typical Corbusian inversion in which the struts would be exterior to the tent and the tent itself would fall inward as a catenary rather than outward as a pitch. Like the Maison Week-End it was a synthesis of the archaic with the modern, the whole being stabilized by a system of wire cables and by steel latticework that jointly resembled the inverted superstructure of a dirigible (fig. 10.16). At the same time the Pavillon des Temps Nouveaux was an antithesis of the Maison Week-End, for where the one was permanent and heavy, the other was impermanent and light; where the one was roofed by rigid vaults, the other was covered by a pliable skin. Moreover, these different structural paradigms implied different institutional types, for where the house was an earthbound megaron, the tent, furnished with both altar and pulpit, rose up toward the light like an archetypal *templum.* This sacred tectonic/typological synthesis will be reinterpreted twenty years later in Le Corbusier's Ronchamp chapel (1956), where the tent/temple of the chapel will stand in opposition to the megaron form of the Maison du Gardien and the Maison des Pelerins, which will be built as attendant, load-bearing cross-wall structures comparable to the Maison Week-End (fig. 10.17).

The Philips Pavilion, built for the Brussels World's Fair of 1958 and designed in collaboration with the composer/architect Iannis Xenakis, may be regarded as the end of a tectonic trajectory in which Le Corbusier will finally reconcile both tent and vault into one complex hyperbolic, cable-stayed volume (fig. 10.18). The cladding of this folded volume in a chain mail of tesselated metal sheet takes us back, however inadvertently, to Wagner and Semper, and testifies to a tectonic continuity that passes from the saddleback section of the Pavillon des Temps Nouveaux through to the convoluted Möbius form of the Philips Pavilion, embracing en route not only Ronchamp but also the canopied exhibition stands that Le Corbusier projected for Liège and San Francisco in 1939 (fig. 10.19). In terms of built works, this trajectory will culminate for Le Corbusier in the yin/yang, steel plate roof structure of his Heide Weber Pavilion, posthumously completed in Zurich in 1967.

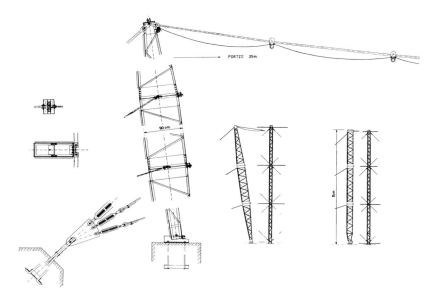

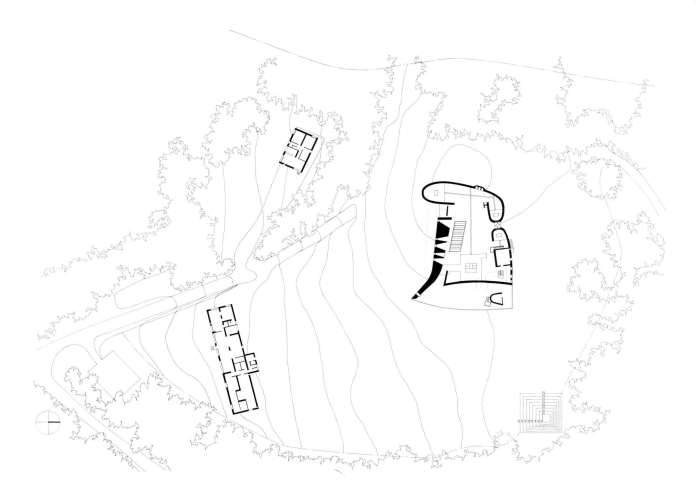

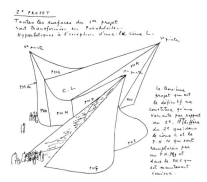

10.17
Le Corbusier, Chapel of Notre-Dame du Haut,
Ronchamp, 1950–1956. Site plan.

10.18
Le Corbusier with Iannis Xenakis, Philips Pavilion, Brussels World's Fair, 1957–1958.

While the first fourteen years of Le Corbusier's Parisian career took him away from the tectonic, his return to expressive structure is perhaps not so surprising, particularly when one recalls that the Five Points of a New Architecture of 1925 amounted to a repudiation of the Greco-Gothic tradition. Inspired by the plasticity of reinforced concrete construction, Le Corbusier will progressively transpose the neoclassicism of his Purist period into a kind of archaism in which the purely cylindrical peristyle becomes the Egyptoid *pilotis*[6] and so on. This shift toward the primordial enabled him to transcend both the avant-gardism of the Purist line and the *idées reçues* of the Greco-Gothic.

To the extent that the tectonic in the second half of this century has been involved with the reiteration of vaulted spatial units, the Dutch architect Aldo van Eyck would also play a seminal role in the midcentury recovery of preclassical form, in the first place through his anthropological approach to the primitive building cultures of North Africa, and in the second through his didactic adaptation of these non-Eurocentric cultures to the orphanage that he built in Amsterdam in 1960. Deriving from his concept of "labyrinthine clarity," this residential school building depended upon the repetitive, hierarchical combination of two kinds of shallow concrete domes, each one springing from a square cell of different dimensions. While he initially eschewed van Eyck's domes, a similar although more pyramidal aggregational approach is evident in the early work of Louis Kahn; above all in his Trenton Bath House and Community Center projects dating from 1954.

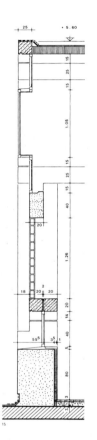

A more tectonic elaboration of van Eyck's space-making principle will wait upon the career of his most prolific pupil, the Dutch architect Herman Hertzberger, who will combine the anthropological insights of van Eyck with a structurally rationalist line inherited from the legacy of Berlage and Johannes Duiker. Hertzberger's first attempt at such a synthesis appears in the industrial laundry that he built in Amsterdam-Sloterdijk in 1964. The tectonic density of this work derives in part from the mutual articulation of its structure and fenestration (fig. 10.20) and in part from the successive, partially prefabricated assembly of its structural cells (fig. 10.21). In this regard it may be compared to the insurance company offices, De Nederlanden van 1845, that Berlage built in The Hague in 1927 (see fig. 10.5), since the exterior expression stems in each instance from the articulation of a concrete frame and from the concatenation of a number of discrete infill elements precisely articulated in respect of each other. Hertzberger's emphasis on microtectonic elements such as terraces, benches, sills, balustrades, and thresholds also owes much to Berlage, as we may judge from the *saku*[7] that plays such a prominent role in the main entry to the Montessori School that Hertzberger realized in Delft in 1966, for this feature seems to be a diminutive version of the monumental granite balustrade with which Berlage announced the entry to the Stock Exchange (fig. 10.22).

Hertzberger's original Montessori School is significant for the way in which it broadens the scope of his tectonic syntax, extending it into microspace and giving it an implicit sociocultural meaning. This is at once evident from the plan and section of the typical classroom (fig. 10.23), where the expressive structure of the building breaks down into a series of sequential components that both em-

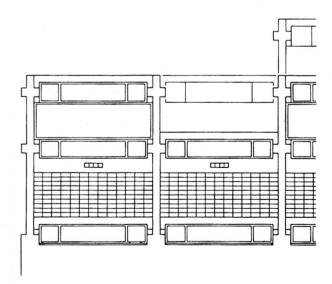

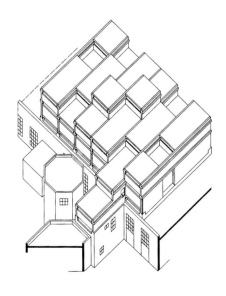

body and express the spatial progression; hence the orchestrated sequence of coat alcove, threshold, wet room, dry room, window, and terrace, together with the multiplicity of transitional, microspatial episodes, comprising sills, ledges, recesses, and shelves, with which each classroom abounds. As far as Hertzberger is concerned, tectonic elements become meaningful through being appropriated by the subject, so that in a limited sense the ultimate meaning of a work is contingent upon the uses to which it is put. This idea of a work being transformed through appropriation is made explicit in the sitting pit incorporated into a 1970 extension to the same school (fig. 10.24). Of the sixteen hollow wooden cubes packed flush into this square recess set in the floor of the principal foyer, Hertzberger would write:

10.19

opposite, top

Le Corbusier, project for an exhibition pavilion for Liège or San Francisco, 1939.

10.20

opposite, center and lower left

Herman Hertzberger, laundry addition, Amsterdam-Sloterdijk, 1962–1964. Detail elevation and detail section.

10.21

opposite, lower right

Herman Hertzberger, laundry addition, Amsterdam-Sloterdijk.

10.22

Herman Hertzberger, Montessori School, Delft, 1966, main entry.

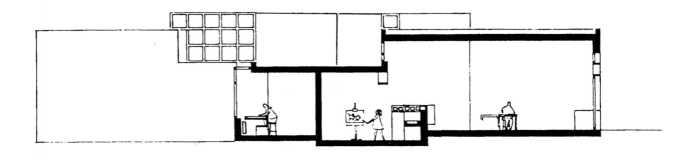

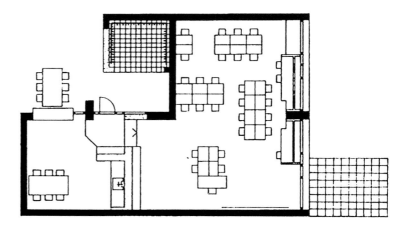

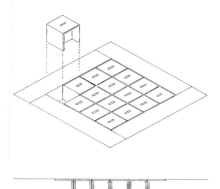

10.23
Herman Hertzberger, Montessori School,
Delft, plan and section of classroom.

10.24
Herman Hertzberger, Montessori School,
Delft, sunken sitting area.

When these are removed one has a square sunken sitting area. The scale of the hole is such that a whole class can fit into it to form a talking circle, or for story-telling. The hole is in many respects the negative form of the stone podium block [installed into the first phase of the school]. Where the block evokes images associated with mountain and viewpoint, the hole gives a feeling of protection, of a place one can retreat to, and evokes images connoting valley and hollow. The podium is an island in the sea, the hollow is a pond, which the children make into a swimming pool by adding a plank for walking over.[8]

Hertzberger's preoccupation with the corporeal appropriation of articulated structural form is first realized on a more public scale in his Centraal Beheer office building, completed in Apeldoorn in 1973. However inadvertently, this work may be seen as the synthesis of a number of different strands that lead from Semper and Viollet-le-Duc to culminate in a building that is as much indebted to Wright's Larkin Building of 1904 as it is to the tradition of Berlage. The fact that every precast beam, slab, upstand, concrete block, glass lens, and window bar has its rhythmic place within the orchestration of Centraal Beheer is immediately evident from the detailed sections (fig. 10.25). At the same time this complex structural assembly also establishes an explicit division between the earthwork of the parking, sustained by massive mushroom columns, and the framework of the offices above. The fact that the assembly system employed in Kahn's Richards Laboratories was partially repeated in the construction of this building testi-

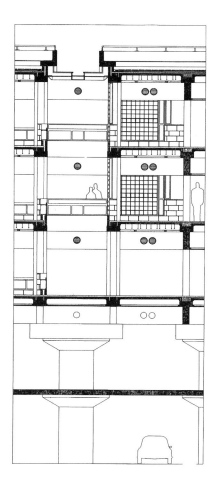

10.25
Herman Hertzberger, Centraal Beheer, Apeldoorn, 1970–1973. Section.

fies to the way in which all these works are part of the same tectonic tradition. As in Kahn's laboratories, the typical office platform, in the shape of a square, is carried on eight columns set in from the corners. The tartan circulation grid established by these structural coordinates serves to subdivide the basic square into four corner squares, which may then be variously arranged according to the changing requirements of the user (fig. 10.26). Of the appropriation of the resultant space Hertzberger writes:

The character of such an area will depend to a large extent on who determines the furnishing and decoration of the space, who is in charge, who takes care of it and who is or feels responsible for it. . . . The form of the space itself must have the competence to offer such opportunities, including the ability to accommodate basic fixtures, fittings, etc., and allow the users to fill in the spaces according to their personal needs and desires.[9]

The socio-anarchic nature of all this is obvious. What is less readily perceived, however, is the way in which this provision is integral to the overall woven character of the volume, together with the way in which this spatial warp and woof is a reworking of Wright's textile tectonic as this was already present in the Larkin Building. Kahn's Richards Laboratories are also a part of this legacy, not only because of their structural articulation but also because their internal subdivision breaks down into servant and served spaces, with the servant units carrying the mechanical services and stairs. A similar servant/served dyad articulates Centraal Beheer, and this affinity is paralleled by a system of modular assembly that assumes a comparable role in both works (fig. 10.27). Despite these Kahnian affinities, Dutch Structuralism remains a regional or even a national movement, not only in terms of its tectonic expressivity but also with regard to its sociocultural reception. Indeed, one may argue that despite his relative indifference to mass form, Hertzberger has remained inadvertently close to Berlage throughout his career; a proximity that has increased as he has become more concerned with the unifying boundary of the whole work, as in a school extension that he realized in Aerdenhout in 1990.

It is hard to imagine a building that is more removed from the Centraal Beheer than the three-story, glass-walled Willis Faber and Dumas insurance offices built at Ipswich, England, in 1974 to the designs of Foster Associates (fig. 10.28). In marked contrast to the Hertzberger building, the emphasis here is on the elegance and economy of the productive system; that is to say, on what the Swiss architect Max Bill once called the *Produktform*.[10] Foster indicated his affinity in this regard when he specifically acknowledged his debt to Bill's reinterpretation of the Crystal Palace in his Swiss National Exhibition Pavilion built in Lausanne in 1963 (fig. 10.29).[11] Unlike the Centraal Beheer, where the tectonic concept opens out toward a social appropriation of its volume, a typical Foster assembly invariably focuses on two equally dematerializing factors: in the first instance, on the spatially generative structure, be it a clear span or a repetitive framework, and in the second, on the production of a hermetic membrane that encases the structure in a gasketed or caulked skin. This combination has perhaps attained its most didactic synthesis to date in the Sainsbury Centre for the Visual Arts, built at the University of Norwich, England, in 1977 (fig. 10.30).[12] To the extent that the cross section of this structure divides into servant and served spaces, that is to say, into the thick but hollow lightweight servant wall, packed with me-

351

chanical services, and the served volume of the hangar space itself, Kahn may once again be cited as a prime influence. However, as buildings equally dedicated to the exhibition of art, it is hard to imagine two works more unlike than Foster's Sainsbury Centre and Kahn's Kimbell Art Museum. The differences between them are instructive, for they point toward opposed cultural intentions that are latent, as it were, in one line of tectonic discourse rather than another. Everything turns, in the last analysis, on the intrinsic nature of the technology adopted and on the degree to which the resultant space is mediated by the superimposition of more traditional institutional values.

While both Sainsbury and Kimbell come into being, rather paradoxically, through standard forms of long-span industrial construction, the one being dependent on a repeated space truss and the other on a folded-plate system, the monumental expression is distinctly different, for where the former is approached along an elevated *passerelle* that, at one point, penetrates rather arbitrarily into the hermetic volume of the hangar, the folded-plate pseudo-vaults of the latter are displaced in plan in such a way as to provide an honorific entrance flanked by porticos. Comparable differences in value can be found throughout; from the relatively random distribution of art objects, set against movable screens, within the *Bürolandschaft* space of Sainsbury, to the volumetric accommodation of the art within the cycloid vaults of the Kimbell; from the industrial production of the skin in Sainsbury, to the tectonic interplay of concrete and travertine in the Kimbell. Where the one is partly a product of the aircraft industry and is, as such, essentially indistinguishable from the hermetic cladding of pressurized aircraft, the other turns on the difference between the mass character of its concrete earth-

10.26
Herman Hertzberger, Centraal Beheer, partial floor plan and ceiling plan.

10.27
Herman Hertzberger, Centraal Beheer, structural diagrams.

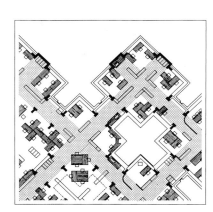

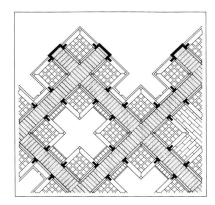

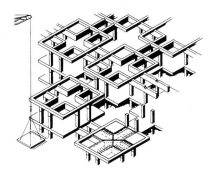

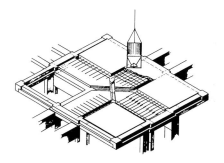

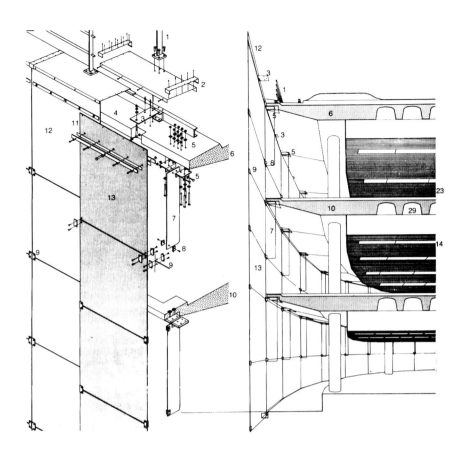

10.28
Foster Associates, Willis Faber and Dumas offices, Ipswich, England, 1974. Glass wall details and section.

work and the skeletonal nature of its concrete frame, and even further on the separation between the frame and its block infill that in this instance is covered with travertine.

As one can see from this comparison, the body of a building and its capacity for modulation are crucial qualities that arise almost spontaneously from the nature of the construction and above all from the values latent in one structural technique rather than another. I have in mind, of course, the open-ended spatial connotations of space frame construction versus the traditional closed volumes that are implicit in the repetition of cellular form; or, say, the difference between a reinforced concrete, intercolumnar spatial system and traditional cross-wall construction, or, at the level of cladding, the phenomenological difference that separates the sheer face of a gasketed curtain wall from the woven continuity of fair-faced brickwork.

The interplay among technology, tectonic syntax, and mass form assumes particular relevance in the work of both Hertzberger and Foster. This is perhaps most noticeable in their insurance office buildings of the mid-seventies, the mass form of the building being equally problematic in both instances, for different reasons, while the expressive syntax in each case stems not only from different technologies but also from different tectonic intentions. At the same time, their common anti-urban character would seem to derive from the fact that, like Wright's Larkin Building, to which they are mutually related, they are both introspective office buildings and hence their civic potential lies within rather than

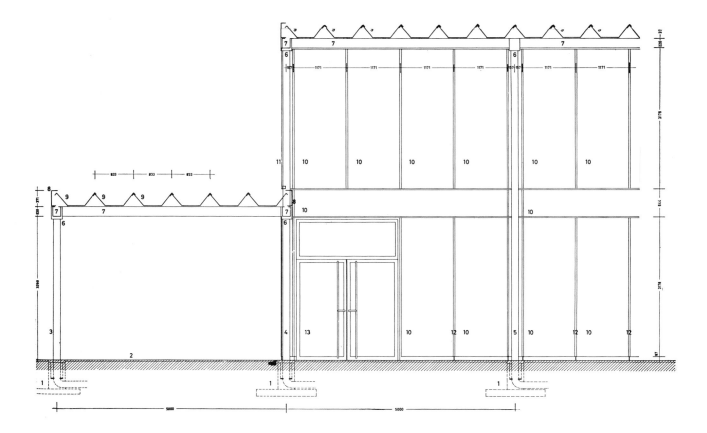

10.29
Max Bill, Swiss National Exhibition Pavilion,
Lausanne, 1963.
1. foundation
2. asphalt on gravel floor
3 and 5. tubular steel column with supporting head
4. tubular steel column with two supporting heads
6. supporting head
7. channel support
8. asbestos cement eaves element
9. asbestos cement roof element
10. wall element of white polyvinyl sheet
11. transparent polyester elements
12. chromium nickel section
13. double-winged door element

without; that is to say within the interstitial space, however it is constituted, rather than in an implicit interaction with the surrounding environment. Despite this similarity, the ideological base of each work could hardly be more divergent, for where Willis Faber reduces its exterior to the silence of a gasketed plate glass wall, hung like chain mail without mullions from the concealed cornice of its undulating perimeter, Centraal Beheer consolidates its mass form as a castellated pyramid, within which the repeated structural unit plays a reiteratively expressive role. Thus, where the one is a well-serviced package, symbolic of technological perfection, the other posits a concatenation of tactile form. In both, curiously enough, the main entrance can only be identified with difficulty, this perceptual shortcoming deriving in each instance from the uninflectable nature of the syntax employed.

This expressive inadequacy is already evident in the Crystal Palace of 1851, and a similar limitation will arise much later in the technocratic proposals of Fuller and Wachsmann, in which productive and geometrical means rather than institutional ends will be the prime movers of the form. Moreover while Carlo Scarpa and Konrad Wachsmann were equally preoccupied with the nature of the joint, Wachsmann could not have been further removed from Scarpa's cultural concerns, particularly when he described his prototypical aircraft hangar of 1959 (fig. 10.31) as a dematerialized structure and space "determined by the use of one type of connector, distributed and rhythmically repeated within a three-dimensional modular order."[13]

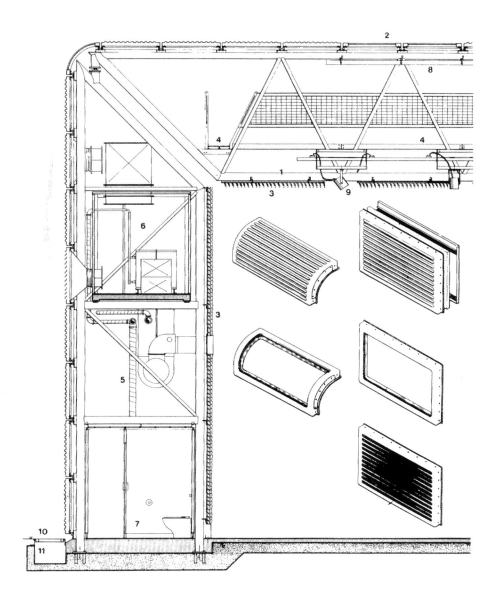

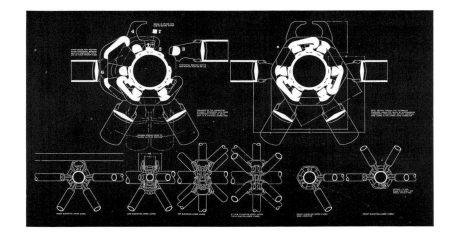

10.30
Foster Associates, Sainsbury Centre for the Visual Arts, University of Norwich, England, 1977. Wall section.

10.31
Konrad Wachsmann, aircraft hangar, 1959. Details.

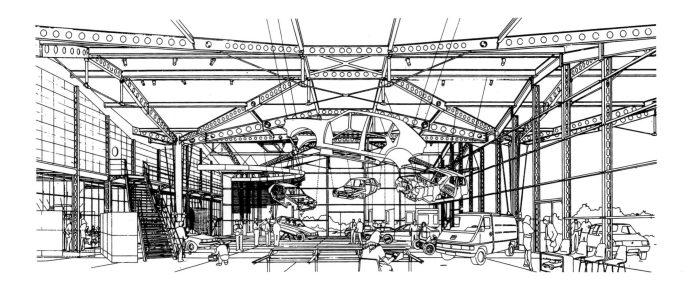

In recent years both Foster and Hertzberger have tended to modify the exclusively productive character of their earlier work. Thus where Foster has abandoned the anonymity of the *undecorated* shed in favor of a series of buildings in
which the basic structure plays a more expressive role, as in the Renault Centre,
completed just outside Swindon in 1983 (fig. 10.32), or the Hong Kong and
Shanghai Bank of 1985 (fig. 10.33), Hertzberger has increased the scale and
spatiality of his modular units, as is evident, say, in his Ministry of Social Affairs
completed in The Hague in 1990 (fig. 10.34). At the same time in his recent public work, such as the Ambonplein School, Amsterdam (1983–1986), he has employed a non-load-bearing perimeter wall held in front of the frame as a means
of unifying the mass of the building.

While a more comprehensive study along these lines would include many other
architects, I have elected to treat here only those works in which a *poetic of construction* is patently manifest or, as in the case of Le Corbusier, where the emergence of a tectonic expressivity constitutes a decisive moment within a more
general development. Even with such exclusive criteria there remain many other
architects whose work has been markedly affected by tectonic considerations.
This is particularly true in Scandinavia, where two architects who have so far
been absent from this account deserve particular mention, the Finnish master
Alvar Aalto and the Norwegian Sverre Fehn. While tectonic form, as a consistently repetitive articulation, manifests itself rather sporadically in Aalto's architecture, it is only too present in his furniture and makes an equally decisive
appearance in his all-wooden structures, such as the Finnish Pavilion built for
the 1937 Paris Exhibition or the sports hall built at Otaniemi, Finland, in 1952
(fig. 10.35). Aalto would also exhibit marked tectonic sensibility in smaller utilitarian works, such as the warehouse that he built for the Karhula glass company in
1949 where composite timber roof trusses are bracketed off concrete pillars
that divide the interior volume into three parallel bays (fig. 10.36). Here Aalto in-
dulged in a particularly ingenious device as a means of inflecting the roof form
in a particular direction. Thus while the trusses divide the space into three equal
bays, the subsequent division of each truss into three segments would allow
him to modulate the roof so as to yield one major and one minor monitor pitch.

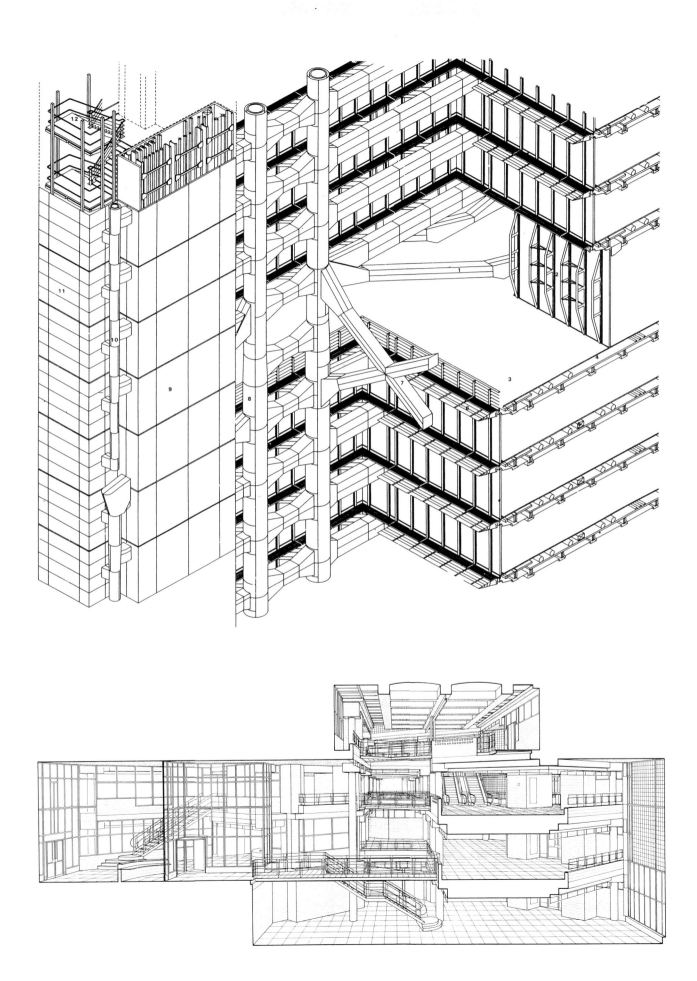

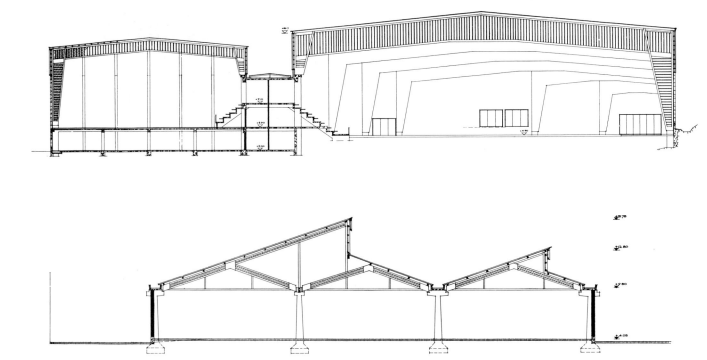

10.35
Alvar Aalto, gymnasium, Otaniemi, 1949–1952. Section. The construction is of nailed timber trusses assembled on the site and lifted into position.

10.36
Alvar Aalto, warehouse for Ahlström, Karhula, 1949.

A more plastic inflection of an equally directional character will be made at a much larger scale in the catenary roof of the large sports hall that he projected for Vienna in 1953. In general, Aalto displays a marked tendency to impart a topographic character to tectonic form. This impulse is evident in all of his work, so that the site is as much made by the building as the building is formed by the site. This last is the basis of the geological metaphor in Aalto's architecture; the tendency, that is, for the earthwork to appear as part of the building and for the roof to appear, at times, as though it were an extension of the landform. This phenomenon is particularly evident in his auditoria, where blank walls, in brick or in stone, rise from the ground in the form of escarpments.

Fehn, on the other hand, has often emphasized tectonic form as a large structural motif that encompasses the entire building, from his brilliant Nordic Pavilion built for the Venice Biennale in 1962 (fig. 10.37) to his municipal library projected for Trondheim in 1978 (fig. 10.38). He also seems to have felt an affinity for the joint as this appears in the work of Scarpa, as is particularly evident in his exhibition layouts for the Oslo Ethnographic Museum (1980). That construction has played a phenomenological role in all of Fehn's architecture is suggested by the theoretical position advanced in his book *The Thought of Construction,* written with Per Fjeld and published in 1983. In the title chapter we find the following reflection on the expressive range of constructional form:

The use of a given material should never happen by choice or calculation, but only through intuition and desire. The construction accords the material, in its opening towards light, a means of expressing its inherent color. However, a material is never a color without a construction. While stone has form, as a material it is defined by its shape, just as the keystone is defined by its precision. When stone is placed upon stone, its form resides in the joint.

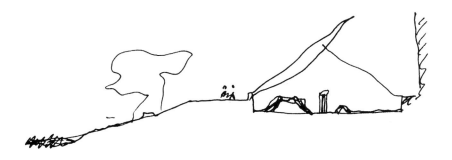

*. . . The calculated column expresses nothing more than a particular num-
ber. . . . No words are spoken and the alphabet remains unwritten. This is the
world of silence. The calculated number celebrates the victory of the void, a fertile poverty. . . . In a world that is determined by calculation, material loses all capacity for the expression of constructive thought.*

*For the young architect each material is a measurement of strength. To apply the
material to its ultimate capacity is natural for youth. The expression of this inherent force complements a natural vitality. The material's sensation carries its conviction and the energy of youth attains a structural perfection. With time certain
architects will accept age as a tiredness which has a beauty of its own, allowing
raw material a dimension of life and wisdom. The acquiescence of age is a recognition of maturity, a sign of personal growth. It is a generosity transcended
through simplicity.*[14]

This penetrating reflection alludes in part to his Venice pavilion, realized as a tectonic tour de force in long-span concrete construction when he was only 28.
The structural *Gestalt* of this work consists of a single mega-beam spanning 25
meters that splits into two as it cantilevers out over a V-shaped column in order

to avoid a large tree. This dynamic gesture is complemented by a double-layered concrete latticework roof, with a fiberglass gutter system suspended above. Spanning in one direction, this last is a translucent membrane that, in its suspended U-form in section, recalls the roof that Jørn Utzon proposed for his Sydney Bayview house at virtually the same time. Profoundly influenced by Scarpa's reading of Venice, this pavilion alludes to the lagoon on which the city has depended for its life.

The pavilion carries the ingredients of Venice. The city belongs to the water from which came its inspiration. The areas of green contrast with the water. The park with its landscape of grass and trees is very precious and scarce. Every existing tree grows unhindered inside the building, finding a total freedom through the roof. The main tree is honored, as the dominant structure gives room for its participation; this is the place where the unity between nature and building is at its maximum.

The transparent channels covering the roof pay homage to the rain. It is directed much like the water of the city and thereby provides sustenance for plants both inside and out, linking the pavilion with the cycle of the park. The leaves turn towards the sun and inflect the building according to the seasons. This honoring of sun and rain, framed in a place of the non-rational, is the beginning of a search for a higher order of architecture.[15]

There is a discernible if marginal return to tectonic values throughout the 1950s and 1960s, as one may judge not only from Fehn's Nordic Pavilion but also from the emergence of such architects as Amancio Williams in Argentina, Dolf Schnebli in Switzerland, and Sigurd Lewerentz in Sweden, as well as from the various strands of regionally inflected Italian modernism that became evident during this period. I am thinking in particular of the work of Ernesto Rogers, Angelo Mangiarotti, Franco Albini, and Gino Valle.[16] While the term "New Brutalism" was specifically coined by Alison and Peter Smithson, it became a convenient rubric by which to characterize much of this development, as we may judge from Reyner Banham's critical survey *The New Brutalism* of 1966. There will be a discernible return in these years to the expressive potential of structure, construction, and services, and in this regard we may cite not only the neo-Miesian Hunstanton School, built in Norfolk in 1954 to the designs of Alison and Peter Smithson, but also Williams's Maillart-like bridge house realized in Mar del Plata some nine years before.[17]

In a similar way a certain stereotomic expressivity may be seen as uniting works as diverse as Le Corbusier's Maison Jaoul, Paris (1956), Stirling and Gowan's Ham Common Housing, London (1958), Schnebli's Castioli House at Campione d'Italia (1960), and Lewerentz's St. Mark's Church completed near Stockholm in the same year.[18] In each of these works, load-bearing, fair-faced brickwork aspires to a common telluric sensibility; a testament to the existential authenticity of brick that in almost every instance is complemented by brick vaulting. Lewerentz's longstanding commitment to tectonic form warrants special comment, particularly for his load-bearing brick cemetery chapels completed in Malmö in 1945 (fig. 10.39). Lewerentz's entry into tectonic brickwork begins with these chapels and goes on to assume a more brutal, load-bearing form in his St. Mark's Church. This roughly coursed, warehouse aesthetic would be raised to a higher level in his St. Peter's Church, completed at Klippan in 1966. Here a varie-

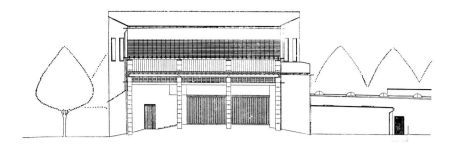

gated, flat canopy of brick vaults, resting on a network of low-riding steel girders, encapsulates the entire church in a catacomb-like space, of which Colin St.
John Wilson has written the following appraisal.

*A square plan seems simple enough; but let the floor as it slopes down to the
altar swell into a shallow mound and burst open to reveal a well for the baptismal
shell; and let a raw steel column crowned with a cross-beam stand like a crucifix
off-center of that space to vie with pulpit and altar as a center of focus, and a certain drama enters in.*

*The column itself is not what it at first appears to be: split in two from top to bot-
tom, its twin cross-trees—which are not symmetrical—carry at their extremities
yet further beams which are also split into pairs. Upon these beams stand steel
struts to support the metal ribs that support the brick vaults at both springing
and ridgelines alternately. Then again, these ribs to the vaults are neither horizontal nor do they run parallel but expand and contract as they run from wall to
wall. Lewerentz speaks of the vaults as a recall of the ancient symbol of the heavens, but here his treatment of them is strangely moving and insinuates into the
mind a closer analogy to the rhythm of breathing—the rise and fall, the interlocking of expansion and contraction. Lewerentz (who was qualified as an engineer) worked closely with the project engineer and himself proposed the use of
smaller steel sections, paired, rather than larger single sections so that light
could shine through the middle of the structural assembly. To what extent these
shifts and discontinuities are brought about for visual reasons or in compensa-
tion for the difference in physical performance between steel section and brick
vault I do not know; the fact is that a technical requirement is transformed into a
mystery and how this transformation is brought about is unfathomable.*[19]

Equally compelling but totally different constructional approaches are evident in
Italy during this period, first in the intimate work of Scarpa, who will evolve his
montage manner outside the mainstream, and second in the more structurally didactic work of Albini and Franca Helg, not to mention Rogers's Torre Velasca
erected in Milan in 1958. Close to the microtectonics of Scarpa, particularly in
an exhibition that he designed for the Palazzo Bianco in Genoa (1951), Albini will
come to the fore at a more public and comprehensive scale in the department
store that he designed with Helg and realized in Rome in 1961 (fig. 10.40). This
structure returns us to the plaited discourse of Wagner's Postsparkassenamt,
the skin being interwoven in this instance not only with the structure but also
with the perimeter ductwork. Some idea of the complexity of the result may be
gleaned from the following description.

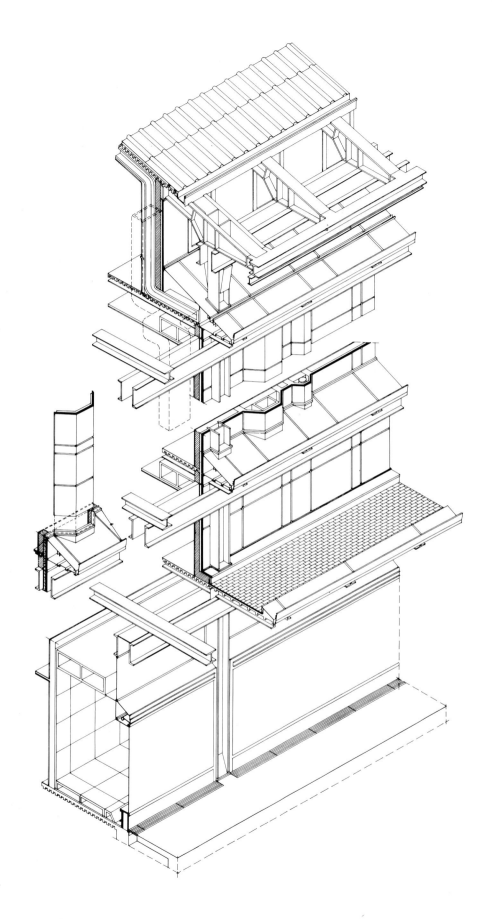

10.40
Franco Albini with Franca Helg, La Rinascente, Piazza Fiume, Rome, 1957–1961. Axonometric section.

10.41
Angelo Mangiarotti and B. Morasutti, Baranzate Church, Milan-Vialba, 1959.

The structural composition of the La Rinascente building derives from the combination of formal and technological factors in its design. The building is marked by certain bare decisions: locating the vertical service mains on the outside, modifying the shape of the curtain wall panels in line with the direction of the ducts; leaving the external metal structure exposed and using the parametrical cornice girders for the horizontal service mains, also leaving the heads of the secondary girders exposed; using the rail on the top floor as a device for outlining the top of the building, interrupting it at the corner with the Via Aniene. The corrugated design of the panels, although influenced by the technical needs of air-conditioning pipes, complies with aesthetic criteria and has been used to recall surface features typical of Roman architecture. . . . [The contrast] between the main structure and the curtain walls lies in the use of color and plastic treatment. The external wall was constructed of panels prefabricated from a crushed mix of cement, granite powder, and red marble; each panel is divided perpendicularly into four parts, the third from the bottom being narrower and in a light ivory color. The same contrast is to be found in the compositional method, since the panels, which contain main ducts, bulge more or less as bow windows do to create a surface that changes constantly according to the strength of the light.[20]

Influenced by the spectacular concrete structures designed by Nervi and Morandi, certain Italian architects began to move toward precisely articulated structural assemblies in reinforced concrete. This tendency led at times to a kind of tectonic minimalism, as is evident say in Mangiarotti and Morasutti's Baranzate Church, realized near Milan in 1959 (fig. 10.41). Conceived as a *Hallenkirche* and

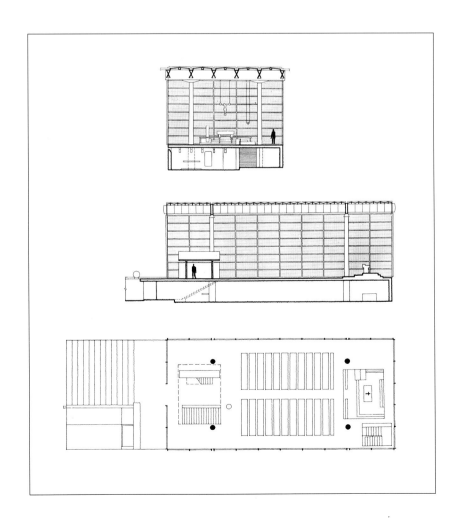

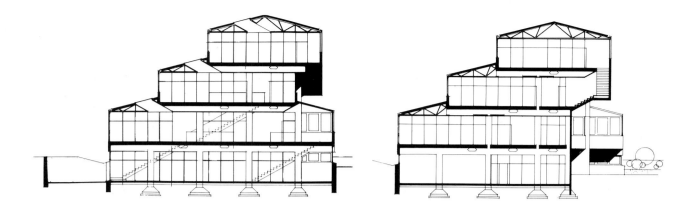

10.42
Gino Valle, factory for Zanussi Rex, Pordenone, 1961.

built entirely of concrete, the quadripartite structure of its nave comprises a diagrid roof carried on six longitudinal beams, two transverse girders, and four cylindrical columns. Clad throughout in a double-glazed, translucent envelope, this work may be seen as a midcentury interpretation of Perret's Notre-Dame du Raincy.

Gino and Nani Valle would pursue equally tectonic themes but with an inflection that was more evidently regional. This is particularly noticeable in their early work; in their bank at Latisana of 1956 and their Casa Quaglia built at Sutrio, near Udine, in 1953–1954. In structural terms both the bank and the house seem to be predicated on a Kahnian application of load-bearing brick piers, square in plan and eight in number, carrying a 15-by-23-meter lenticular metal roof in the case of the bank and a heavy traditional timber 15-by-15-meter truss system in the house (cf. Louis Kahn's Adler House project of 1954). In both instances, the main expression stems from a play between load-bearing and load borne, and this will persist as a theme in almost all of Valle's work, even if he will never again attain quite the same level of expressive simplicity. Valle's masterwork of this period is unquestionably his Zanussi Rex offices built at Pordenone in 1961 (fig. 10.42).[21] This work is particularly distinguished for its rhythmic use of a tiered and cantilevered concrete armature with concrete upstands, over which is suspended a stepped and pitched light trussed metal roofwork, clad in asbestos cement sheeting.

Among Italian architects of the past forty years who have made a consistent contribution to *Baukunst* in the Miesian sense, one must certainly include Vittorio Gregotti, who in both theory and practice has been consistent in his articulation of constructional form, most notably in his early housing built for Novara and Milan in 1962 and in his later institutional work executed for the universities of Palermo (1969) and Calabria (1973) and more recently, perhaps, in a number of stadia, including the main arena for the 1992 Barcelona Olympics (fig. 10.43). In all this work, recognition must also be accorded to the Japanese architect Hiromichi Matsui, who played a salient role in the office of Gregotti Associati in the second half of the 1960s and the early 1970s.

The British Brutalist movement will be brought to a close with the Economist Building completed in 1964 to designs of Alison and Peter Smithson (figs. 10.44, 10.45). This built fragment of the Smithsons' Berlin Hauptstadt proposal (1958) was a diminutive reinterpretation of American high-rise construction; one that attempted to reintegrate the romantic classicism of the *Schinkelschule* with its Gothic origins. However, where Mies will represent the fireproof steel frame through an application of steel facings (cf. 860 Lake Shore Drive), the Smithsons will face their concrete frame in roach-bed Portland stone, with gray aluminum trim running down the structural piers, along the sills, and up into the spandrels to form an aluminum-fenestrated curtain wall, anodized gray. The Gothicism of the resultant profile is emphasized through setting back the stone-faced structural mullions as they rise upward, a device evidently taken from Mies's Promontory Apartments. The Economist Building emerges today as that rare example of a modern building that has withstood the "flow of time," where the quality of the work has improved rather than the reverse.[22] In retrospect this structure would seem to come closest to Peter Smithson's archaeological ideal of a building that could, in some future time, be reconstructed from its ruined fragments. Close to the Semperian *Stoffwechseltheorie,* Smithson first advanced this thesis in 1966 in a remarkably insightful essay in which he compared the transformed timber

10.43
Gregotti Associates, main arena for 1992 Olympic Games, Barcelona, 1983.

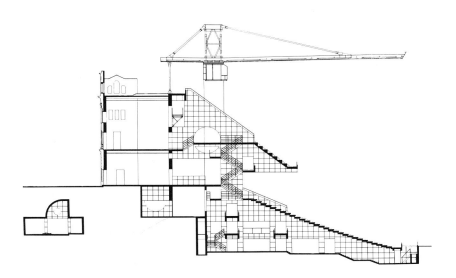

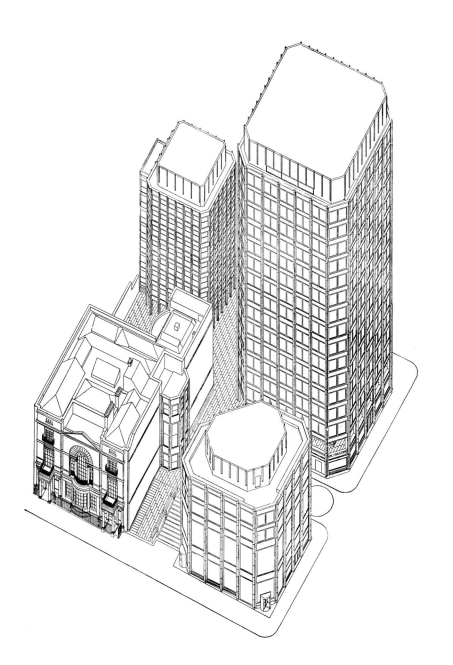

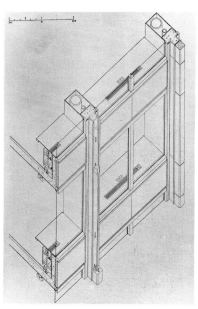

10.44
Peter and Alison Smithson, The Economist Group, St. James Street, London, 1964. Axonometric.

10.45
Peter and Alison Smithson, The Economist Group, axonometric showing perimeter construction.

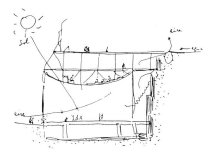

10.46
Alejandro de la Sota, Maravillas School gymnasium, Madrid, 1962.

character of the Greek classical Doric order to the comparable Japanese timber order of the Naiku and Geku sanctuaries at Ise.

The essence of the Doric is rectangularity of platform and an unusually densely formulated language. This "density" is not a question of internal consistency— but that it is capable of doing a lot of internal explaining, of telling us what to expect; for example, and most obviously (but withheld from me for 25 years) the angle of slope of the underside of the soffit of the cornice lets us know, without it being necessary for us to move away from the flank of the temple, the slope of the pediment. A wall with an incised line, or tiny projection tells us to expect a column around the corner. Even the pitching of the floor lets us sense where the outside is—for we know without thought that water most sensibly flows to the outside—the curvature is telling our feet, before our eyes, of the building's structuring. It is no exaggeration to say that one only needs a fragment of a temple to be put in touch with the building's whole form through eyes, feet, skin-sensation. Totally. And this is not a metaphysical nonsense, one is actually told about dimensions, angles, proportions of the whole in the fragment. That fragment is not an absolute part in the Renaissance sense, *it is an* explaining part in the primitive sense. *This is what makes the parallel with the Ise shrines so extraordinary, for at Ise not only is one told of the whole by the fragment, by a stretch of fence for example, but one experiences the same sense of affront—of loss of meaning, of sacrilege almost, when the Order drifts away from its real structure explanatory-metaphor role. . . . It is tempting to generalize and say all architecture is metaphor of structure—that the Modern Architecture of the Heroic Period is a metaphor for a not-yet-existing, machine-built structure, that Romanesque and Gothic are metaphors for their actual structures, etc. . . . Kahn's Philadelphia Laboratory is such a metaphor. It is an architecture of pre-cast concrete.*[23]

With the completion of the Economist Building, the British tectonic line passed to the so-called High-Tech architects, not only to Foster Associates, whose work has already been cited, but also to the Richard Rogers Partnership whose work would make an equally seminal contribution to the field, above all in their megastructural office complex, completed in London in 1984, as the new premises of Lloyds.

Spanish architectural practice has been one of the most tectonically consistent to be found anywhere in recent years. The most influential Spanish architect in this regard has been Alejandro de la Sota, whose laconic but flexible neoconstructivist approach dates from his Maravillas gymnasium, completed in the center of Madrid in 1962 (fig. 10.46). De la Sota took advantage of a natural cliff face to add to an existing school complex. Employing an exposed steel frame, a normative curtain wall, and a wire mesh fence enclosing a playground on the roof, and housing the whole beneath an inverted, suspended steel truss, de la Sota was able to create an expressive structure that was at once modular, well-detailed, and subtly inflected. It was an exemplary demonstration of an architecture that exploited both repetitive production and lightweight technology without compromising the tectonic expressivity of the work.

Among the many Spanish architects who have been partially influenced by de la Sota over the past thirty years, one thinks of Corrales and Molezun, whose Spanish Pavilion for the Brussels World's Fair of 1958 presaged the rebirth of Spanish architecture. Equally touched in various ways by de la Sota one may

367

cite the work of Rafael Moneo, the Sevillian architects Cruz and Ortiz, and the Catalan architect Josep Llinas, with whom de la Sota has recently collaborated.[24] The Catalan architects Esteve Bonell and Francesc Rius have been able to continue the Iberian tectonic tradition in two remarkable stadia: a velodrome built in the Vall d'Hebron district of Barcelona in 1985 (fig. 10.47), and a basketball arena realized in 1991 in the nearby suburb of Badalona (figs. 10.48, 10.49, 10.50). In the case of the velodrome the architects strove to achieve a structure that in tectonic terms would be as laconic as possible.

A building having two scales, due to two [views], a distant one and a close one. On the other hand we wanted a building with a clear image, with a unitary architectural definition, one that would be capable of organizing the immediate environment . . . if we had to define the velodrome in a few words we would say that it possesses a certain classicism, [one that is] at the same time an elaborated modernism. Classicism because of the way in which it sets itself on the landscape and because of the rotundity of its conception. Modernism because of its pragmatic and realistic appearance, because of its simplicity and the way in which construction is coherent with the materials used.[25]

Reminiscent of the opposition between ideal and empirical form as we find this in the work of Le Corbusier, the elliptical, banked cycle track is enclosed by a circular ring that accommodates a variety of services around its perimeter, ranging from the main entrance to toilets, bars, and stairs. The monumental character of this work is assured by its scale and proportion and by the hierarchical interplay between the concrete undercroft containing services and the in situ concrete framed superstructure. This last is filled with bricks and the cement blocks set within the concrete blade walls that support the circular concrete canopy above. The feathering of this canopy on its inner and outer edges amounts to a kind of vestigial cornice that, together with the elegant artificial lighting masts in tubular steel, complete the skyline of the composition. Between the outer ring and the banked, elliptical seating surrounding the track lies a paved concourse for the accommodation of spectators during intermissions. The architects were to account for their constructive approach to the overall design in the following rather pragmatic terms:

Because of the short time available both for the design and its realization, which had to be carried out in ten months, materials and building techniques were chosen in order to avoid any particular difficulty. The structure of the external ring, the locker room's covering and the support of the seats are made of panels, pylons, pilasters or walls in reinforced concrete. The seat tiers, also in reinforced concrete, are the only pre-fabricated parts of the whole building.[26]

Like the Vall d'Hebron velodrome, the Badalona sports hall was also conceived as a modern variation on an ancient amphitheater, structured about the traditional format of the arena above with services below. In this case, however, the architects were to interpret the type as though it were a surrogate cathedral or "social condenser."[27] To this end the cigar-shaped mass form is set at an angle to the principal street so as to assert its independence from the surrounding urban fabric. The columnar structure of this 13,000-seat elliptical arena is extended above the last tier of seats in order to support a concrete ring beam from which a light-metal, sawtooth monitor roof is suspended. The cable-stayed trusses supporting these monitor lights are carried at midspan by a 2-meter-

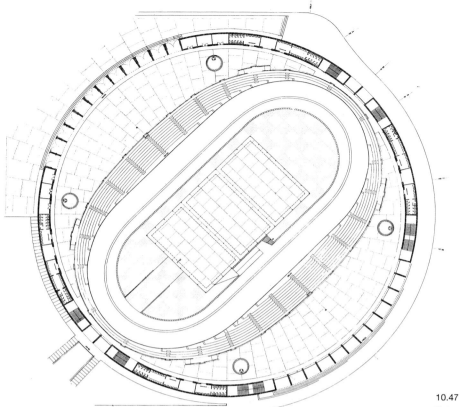

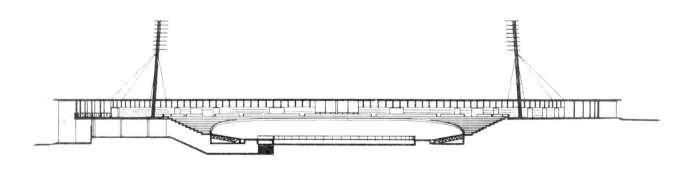

10.47
Esteve Bonell and Francesc Rius, velodrome,
Vall d'Hebron, Barcelona, 1985.

 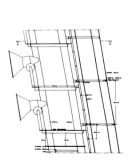 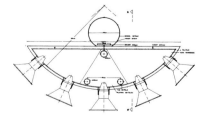

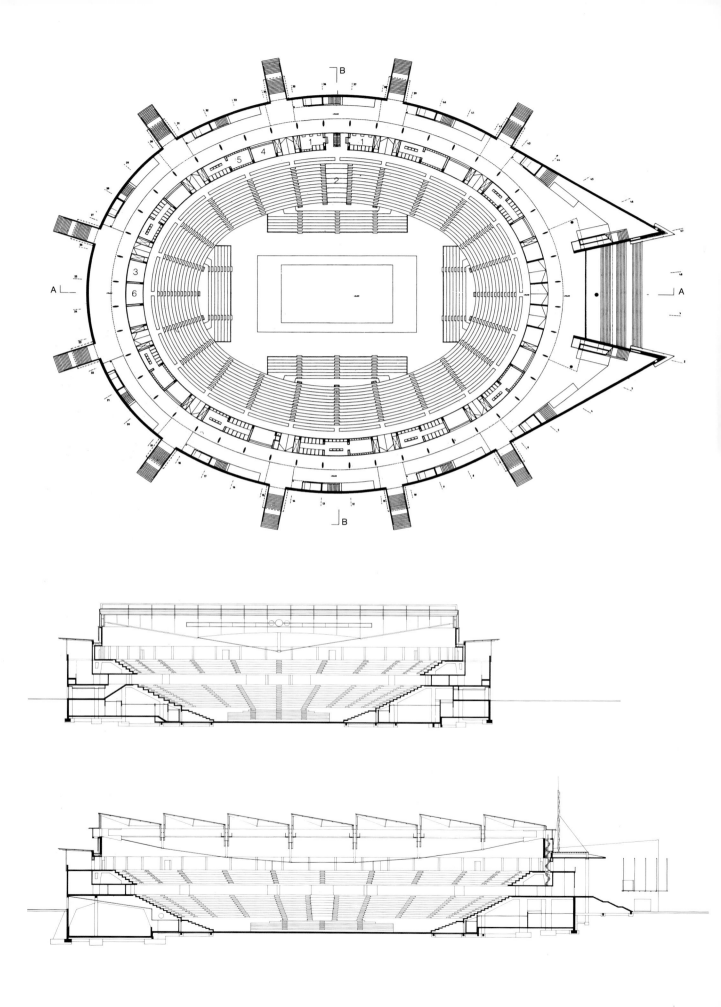

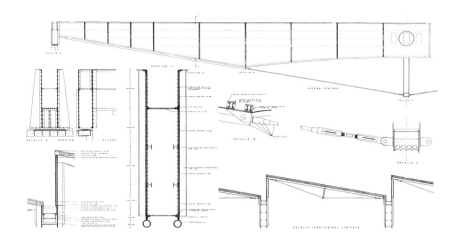

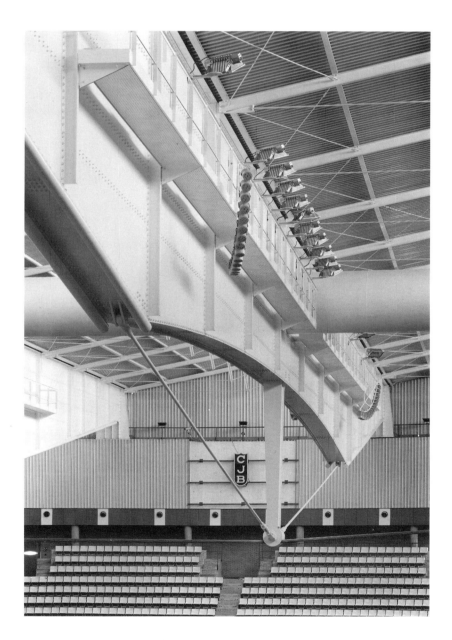

10.48
Esteve Bonell and Francesc Rius, sports hall,
Badalona, 1991. Plan and sections.

10.49
Bonell and Rius, sports hall, Badalona,
details.

10.50
Bonell and Rius, sports hall, Badalona,
interior.

diameter tubular beam, running down the central axis of the arena for its 120-meter span. The elegance of this steel-plated assembly, designed in collaboration with the engineers Robert Brufan and Agusti Obiol, recalls pioneer tubular steel construction of the previous century.[28]

Finally one should mention the Ticino school that has exhibited a strong feeling for the poetics of structure ever since Rino Tami's neo-Wrightian *autostrada* bridges of the early 1960s. I have in mind of course not only Mario Botta's earliest pieces in which he would display his prowess as a craftsman, but also his altogether more mannered Ransila offices built in Lugano in 1985; a work exemplary for its use of brick as an expressive cladding form (fig. 10.51). At a different end of the spectrum, and more comprehensively tectonic in its overall expression, one must acknowledge Livio Vacchini's early masterwork designed with Alberto Tibiletti, the so-called Macconi Building realized in Lugano a decade earlier. This is surely one of the finest exposed-steel-frame structures built in the last quarter of this century, rivaling the best of Mies's *Fachbauwerk* (fig. 10.52). Evocative as much of Otto Wagner as of Mies, however, this structure, filled with glass, glass brick, and blockwork and faced in dressed stone, also subtly recalls the trabeated *modénature* of Perret.

I would like to conclude this brief survey of the tectonic tradition in the second half of the twentieth century by returning to the gloss at the head of this chap-

10.51
Mario Botta, offices for Ransila, Lugano, 1981–1985. Details of exterior wall and windows.

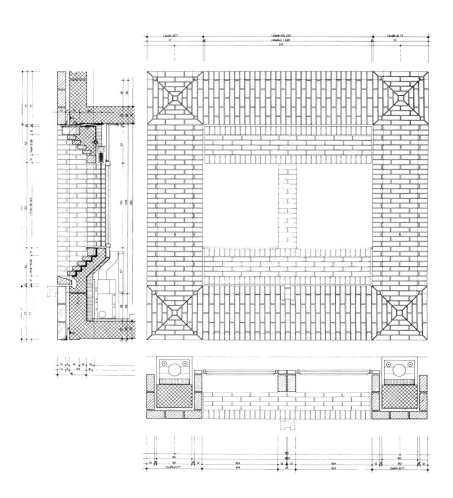

ter, for Aris Konstantinidis remains the only Greek of his generation besides Dimitris Pikionis who has been so singularly susceptible to the Greek landscape, and hence committed to the creation of a critical modern architecture that would remain appropriate to the time and place in which it is built. Just such an architecture is surely manifest in the small stone house with which he began his career in Eleusis in 1938, and in a similar but altogether more sophisticated house that he erected out of local stone in Sikia in 1951 (fig. 10.53). An equally compelling rapport at a topographic level is also achieved in the reinforced concrete hotel structure that he built near the mountains of Meteora, at Kalambaka, in 1959 (fig. 10.54).

Toward the end of his professional career, in 1975, Konstantinidis would publish an elegiac evocation of the Greek vernacular in which he was able to demonstrate its close ties to the landscape from which it stems and within which it remains embedded. Here in his *Elements for Self-Knowledge,* compounded of photographs, sketches, notes, and aphorisms, Konstantinidis sets forth the ontological limits of all architectural form. For Konstantinidis the vernacular lies forever beyond time because nobody can determine its age. Such a work may still be encountered, even now, in the rock walls of Andros or the terraces of Sifnos, both equally timeless in that they illustrate all too precisely the words of Fernand Léger: "Architecture is not art, it is a natural function. It grows out of the ground,

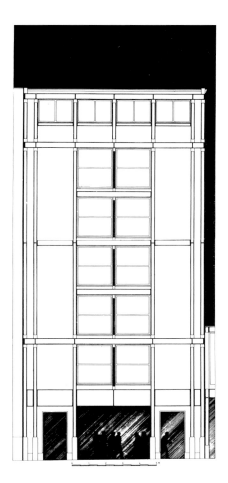

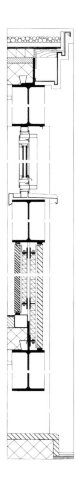

10.52
Livio Vacchini and Alberto Tibiletti, Macconi Building, Lugano, 1975.

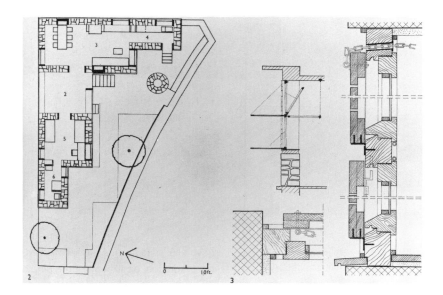

like animals and plants."[29] In contrast to this condition in which culture and life are not yet separated, Konstanidis writes of the spurious character of the new when it is pursued as an end in itself.

As for the efforts of a so-called "new" architecture to produce something unprecedented and advanced (admittedly, the modern age has discovered some "new" truths—in fact, it has discovered many, so many that Matisse once felt compelled to cry out: "No more new truths!"), let us accept once and for all that a truly unprecedented and advanced work is not that which uses superficial brilliance to make a temporary and sensational impact, or that which seeks to take one by surprise by means of ostentatious, acrobatic contortions, based on momentary "finds," but only that which is justified by a continuing, living tradition, that which endures because it is put to the test again and again, within each new context, so that it expresses afresh inner experiences, secretly nurtured disciplines, forms that have truly been handled over and over again. What we may accept as reality cannot possibly be what we see ready-made around us, but much more what we attempt to visualize in a dream, all of us together and each one of us separately, the dream of a new—truly new—life, shaped like a poem.[30]

10.53
Aris Konstantinidis, house, Sikia, 1951. Plan and details.

10.54
Aris Konstantinidis, hotel, Kalambaka, 1959.

10.55
Enric Miralles and Carme Pinós, Olympic archery training range, Barcelona, 1989–1990.

It is undeniable that over the course of this past century the tectonic has assumed many different forms, and it is equally clear that its significance has varied greatly from one situation to the next. Yet one thing persists throughout this entire trajectory, namely, that the presentation and representation of the built as a constructed thing has invariably proved essential to the phenomenological presence of an architectural work and its literal embodiment in form. It is this perhaps more than anything else that grounds architecture in a cultural tradition that is collective rather than individual; that anchors it, so to speak, in a way of building and place-making that is inseparable from our material history. The fact that this century has wantonly destroyed so much of its cultural and ecological heritage through the rapacity of industrial and postindustrial development in no way denies the validity of this profound truth. It is significant that the progressive loss of the vernacular throughout the last two centuries has largely stemmed directly from the elimination of the traditional agricultural base that gave rise to its form. A similar demise may now be observed in respect of the urban, industrial civilization of the nineteenth century with which our awareness of the tectonic value first came into being.

One may argue that the tectonic resists and has always resisted the fungibility of the world. Its tradition is such that it has constantly sought, at one and the same time, both to create the new and to reinterpret the old. Notwithstanding the idiosyncrasies of any particular architect, it is, in its essence, anti-individualistic, for unlike painting and sculpture it is not given to the subjective creation of images. In this sense the figurative is denied to architecture both subjectively and objectively; and while architecture inevitably possesses sculptural qualities, in and of itself it is not sculpture. It is exactly this that makes the architecture of Enric Miralles and Carme Pinós so ambiguous, since, as with much later modern work, it oscillates uneasily between the sculptural and the architectural. Thus it is at its best where the work is incised into the ground, as in their Olympic archery building or their cemetery at Igualada, both dating from 1992. Here the architecture both cuts into the earth and rises athletically above it, particularly in the archery structure where it counters the stereotomic form of the earthwork with the articulated counterpoint of propped folded plates in concrete, of which the shifting complexity of the shell roof is composed. As subject to tradition as to innovation, it returns us to the tectonic as Antoni Gaudí would have understood it, and thus via Gaudí to a line of thought that runs straight back to Viollet-le-Duc. By a similar token Igualada returns us to Louis Kahn's

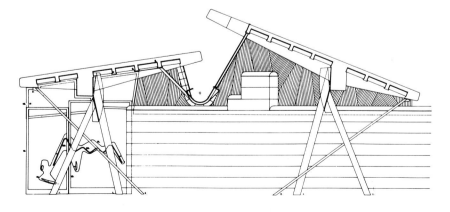

concept of "hollow stones." In this instance they assume the form of prefabricated concrete sarcophagi, from which the retaining walls of the necropolis are systematically constructed. Here they serve to transform a disused quarry by lining its sides with deep, hollow, prefabricated units keyed together in much the same way as prefabricated interlocking concrete plates are now used to stabilize autoroute embankments. The resulting tectonic is as much gravitational as it is engineered. However, once the work of Miralles and Pinos is no longer rendered as either a rampart or a cutting, the architecture tends to degenerate into structural exhibitionism as it flies only too free of the ground to aggregate into irreconcilable cacophonic figures, as in the civic center for Hostalets of 1992 or the sports hall for Huesca of 1994.

Here then as elsewhere, we are confronted with the time-honored challenge that Paul Ricoeur once formulated as "how to become modern and return to sources,"[31] or, to put it in other terms, how to maintain the tectonic trajectory in the face of a postindustrial civilization that seeks nothing less than the reduction of the entire world to one vast commodity.

The Owl of Minerva:
An Epilogue

It is indeed unfortunate that human society should encounter such burning problems just when it has become materially impossible to make heard the least objection to the language of commodity; just when power—quite rightly because it is shielded by the spectacle from any response to its piecemeal and delirious decisions and justifications—believes that it no longer needs to think; and indeed can no longer think.

It is sometimes said that science today is subservient to the imperatives of profit, but that is nothing new. What is new is the way the economy has now come to declare open war on humanity, attacking not only our possibilities for living, but our chances of survival. It is here that science—renouncing the opposition to slavery that formed a significant part of its own history—has chosen to put itself at the service of spectacular domination. . . .

What is false creates taste, and reinforces itself by knowingly eliminating any possible reference to the authentic. And what is genuine is reconstructed *as quickly as possible, to resemble the false. . . .*

Feuerbach's judgement on the fact that his time preferred "the sign of the thing to the thing signified, the copy to the original, fancy to reality," has been thoroughly vindicated by the century of spectacle, and in several spheres where the nineteenth century preferred to keep its distance from what was already its fundamental nature: industrial capitalism. Thus it was that the bourgeoisie had widely disseminated the rigorous mentality of the museum, the original object, precise historical criticism, the authentic document. Today, however, the tendency to replace the real with the artificial is ubiquitous. In this regard it is fortuitous that traffic pollution has necessitated the replacement of the Marly Horses in the Place de La Concorde, or the Roman Statues in the doorway of Saint-Trophime in Arles, by plastic replicas. Everything will be more beautiful than before, for the tourist's cameras."
Guy Debord, *Commentaires sur la société du spectacle, 1988*

For all of its marginality, tectonic culture still possesses a vestigially resistant core, particularly as this is manifest in its proclivity for the tactile. This dimension resists the maximizing thrust of capitalism, determined now, as never before, on the process of global commodification. In this context it is regrettable that the European Community should simultaneously both patronize architecture[1] and engender its demise, as is evident from its ruthless pursuit of a unified market, irrespective of the cultural cost. An unforeseen consequence of this economic impulse has been the recent attempts on the part of various member states to undermine the authority of the architect, and with it, one should note, the capacity of the profession to be effective in the design of civic form. In this regard, EC policy seems to be moving beyond the provisions of the U.S. antitrust laws of the seventies, when the American Institute of Architects lost its right to maintain a fixed scale of fees. This destabilization of the profession has been indirectly effected through EC pressure on its community members, which in their turn have introduced national legislation that seeks to deregulate the profession by challenging its legal status. To date this stratagem has emerged to varying degrees in Spain, Britain, and Austria.[2] One assumes that other EC countries will soon be pressured into following suit.

The impact of such a reductive strategy in Spain is particularly marked for a number of reasons; first, because Spain has produced a particularly high general level of architectural culture over the past twenty years; second, because Spanish architects have enjoyed a correspondingly higher social status than in any other European country; and third, because to date the Spanish profession has been better organized than any other comparable national body. As with other Spanish liberal professions, every major city has its own *collegio de arquitectos,* whose powers have now been summarily curtailed by legislation promulgated by the Spanish parliament in October 1992, in the name of opening the country to foreign architects under the terms of the EC agreement. The fact that there were other ways by which this policy could have been effected suggests that a broader economic strategy lies behind the form that this legislation has assumed. There can be little doubt that such measures will have a deleterious effect on the overall quality of Spanish architecture, since the *collegio* served as a local "guild" that not only maintained a standard of quality but also preserved a certain sense of regional identity. This it achieved mainly through its mandate over building permissions, since until recently all plans had to be approved not only by the municipality but also by the *collegio.* Moreover, since the *collegio* was the initial recipient of the fees on behalf of the architect, from which it deducted a small percentage for its services, it also acted to prevent any undercutting of the fee structure, while at the same time insuring the architect against exploitation by unscrupulous clients who might otherwise refuse to settle their final accounts. This fiscal power also enabled the *collegio* to function as an independent cultural institution, staging exhibitions, organizing lectures, and subsidizing magazines and other publications. Whether it will be possible to maintain such activities in the future remains to be seen.

As a further consequence of its federalist policies, the EC has been attempting to restructure and shorten European architectural education. And while this may be justified as nothing more than the necessary provision of a common European curriculum for the training of architects and thus as being of the same order as pursuing a common European policy with regard to human rights, this rationalization masks a subtly reductive approach to educational reform that, in my view, is also being unduly influenced by maximizing interests. I am not thinking so much of the understandable emphasis now being placed on computer-aided design (although this too has its reductive aspects) but rather of the move to discontinue more reflective, critical methods of instruction, plus the current tendency of studio teaching to oscillate between the simplistic application of technique and the generation of fashionable images. There is, at the same time, a tendency to privilege technology as though this were an essential but totally acultural discourse.[3] The ambivalent role played by the culture industry in late modern society also emerges here in that, as I have already intimated, architecture is no more immune to the impact of the media than any other field. Hence the stress placed on photographic representation in current practice; one that often includes within its purview, however unconsciously, an entirely photogenic preconception of architectural form. And yet unlike the other plastic arts, architecture cannot even be nominally represented by a single photographic image, although this is often the mode in which it is disseminated for professional and lay public alike. Seen in this light building appears to be imagistic and perspectival rather than tactile and spatial.

In July 1993, the Spanish architect Rafael de la Hoz made the following public assessment of the restructuring then being introduced into architectural education in Spain and other European countries, as part of an EC strategy for shortening the length of architectural education with the ostensible intent of improving its efficiency and reducing its cost, a draconian transformation being carried out with precious little regard for the time it takes a student to mature or for the most appropriate way in which the knowledge of the field should be conveyed.

Trapped in the impossible situation of adapting the syllabus to the now insufficient teaching time available, faculties today are divided between "humanists" and "technologists," with each group endeavoring to exclude the other. . . . "When I am to choose between A or B," Lyautey is supposed to have said, "I assuredly should choose A + B." In any event there is no such dilemma if the time allocated for correct instruction is sufficient. However, the situation, far from being resolved, is worsening, particularly after the arrival of that other powerful coterie, favoring, the "massification" of the profession; that is today, those technocrats who want to consider architecture as just another commodity. For them, it is imperative to reduce the duration of our studies even further in order to cause a demographic explosion and increase the number of architects beyond market capacity, thereby making supply exceed demand and reducing the price for architectural services. . . . For the first time in history generations of architects are coming out of European universities that are worse prepared than their forebears. . . . Paradoxically, by trying to create more competitive architects, only less competent ones are being produced.[4]

As de la Hoz suggests, much of this restructuring may be attributed to a global policy that favors monetarist economics and the increased privatization of the public sphere, not to mention the obvious interest of maximizing builder-developers in limiting the authority of the architect. At the same time, the consolidation of the construction industry favors ever larger units of production, and this plus the increased fluidity of international capital creates a climate that is generally inimical to the critical cultivation of architectural form. This has long since been evident in the practice of the "package deal," where architectural and engineering services are provided within the industry itself. However, it has to be admitted that this integration of design and production has, on occasion, been able to produce works of outstanding quality. This is particularly true in the case of Japan, where large contracting firms have been able to produce works of exceptional refinement.

Despite this corporatization of the industry, the independent architect still continues to practice, particularly at the small and intermediate scale, not only as a designer but also, at times, as a general contractor and project manager.[5] This is especially the case in Switzerland, where the architect has traditionally organized the building process into its respective stages and further controlled the operation not only through strict site supervision but also through the direct selection of subcontractors. In all this, the architect is dependent on the competence of specialized fabricators and above all on his own capacity for integrating the various trades and components. This skill has also been displayed by highly disciplined, so-called "high-tech" architectural practices, which have often gone outside the traditional building industry to find components of an otherwise unattainable finish and performance.[6]

These different procedures both professionally and productively seem to correspond to two rival tendencies in late modern economy: on the one hand, a vestigial Fordism[7] entailing guaranteed markets and rather large amounts of investment; on the other, a more hybrid approach to production fed by a more flexible accumulation of both capital and resources. In general, we may say that where the former tends to directly satisfy the market demand that arises "spontaneously," as it were, out of the convergence of consumerism with bureaucratic norms, the latter strives to transcend such limitations and in so doing to respond in a more articulated and reflective way to specific requirements and local conditions. Moreover, where the one seeks a relatively prompt return on the investment and hence is only marginally concerned about the durability of the product, the other displays the tendency to make a more fundamental commitment to the permanence of the work and to its appropriate maturation over time.[8] In other words, where the one optimizes commodification, the other tends to resist it.

One needs to set these alternatives in a larger historical context, one that recognizes not only the general parameters of the postmodern condition but also the way in which the generic building process has radically changed in the last century and a half. In so doing one has to acknowledge the extent to which the second half of this century has seen the erosion of almost every fundamental reference, even to the extent of eclipsing the utopian tradition of the "new." Not least among the consequences of this process has been the decline of the welfare state and the emergence of multinational capitalism. These transformations are perhaps only symptoms of a profounder value crisis, covering a wide range of experience. One recalls in this context such reactionary formations as the rise of fundamentalist religion and the proliferation of small regional conflicts having an arcane and brutal character. All of this transpires in a climate in which the idea of progress is by no means as assured as it was in the first quarter of the present century. The perpetual amelioration of the human condition is a vision that is difficult to sustain in a world in which the rate of technological change has escalated beyond our capacity to assimilate it. This is most evident, perhaps, from the way in which nature is being ravaged by technology to such an extent that, for the first time, the survival of the species is called into question. Thus while the escalating process of modernization continues unabated, the concept of modernity as an ideal has lost its conviction. Mallarmé's slogan "Il faut être absolument moderne" carries little assurance as a call to arms in an age in which the *novum* is no longer new in the same euphoric sense. Moreover, despite the advances of technoscience as these may be discretely applied for the benefit of human life, one remains apprehensive about the tendency of technology to become a new nature covering the entire globe. Against this tendency, the phenomenon of uneven development is a redeeming influence in that building, like agriculture, tends to be grounded in time-honored processes that are essentially anachronistic.

At the same time one has nonetheless to recognize the critical impact that countless technical innovations have had upon the character of the built environment; innovations that since the end of the eighteenth century have brought about the progressive dematerialization of built form, together with the all too literal mechanization and electrification of its fabric. This penetration of electromechanical technique into tectonic form has been accompanied by many now familiar improvements in the construction and equipment of buildings, ranging from devices as singular as the invention of the balloon frame in 1834 to a more comprehensive incorporation of electromechanical technique, including plumbing, central heating, electric lighting, air-conditioning, and of late a whole range of increasingly exotic communicational devices. As R. Gregory Turner indicates in his study *Construction Economics and Building Design: A Historical Approach,* these innovations together with the major changes wrought by the introduction of steel and reinforced concrete construction have had the effect of shifting the focus away from the relatively undifferentiated mass of traditional stereotomic construction to the articulation of built form into the Semperian categories of podium, "hearth," frame, and envelope. Turner shows that in the past thirty-five years each of these components has grown increasingly independent and has developed its own economic criteria. As he puts it: "Separate design professionals, consultants, craftsmen and code officials each focus on one component and are occasionally contracted with individually by clients. Design now consists of an architect devising an envelope and infill that will conceal the work of structural, mechanical, electrical, and plumbing engineers."[9]

Irrespective of Turner's indifference to the cultural consequences of this ever-proliferating division of labor, there is no denying that while load-bearing masonry was one of the main means of enclosing space from archaic times to the Baroque, it thereafter tended to become greatly reduced in thickness and eventually became transposed into a thin lightweight membrane that either enveloped or subdivided the basic volume. We already sense a recognition of this change in Paxton's characterization of the Crystal Palace as a table covered with a tablecloth, while Edward Ford has described this development as an abandonment of the monolithic in favor of a layered fabric, particularly during the last quarter of the nineteenth century and first two decades of the twentieth.[10]

This dematerialization of building has since been taken further by the development of gypsum, dry-wall construction, the introduction of glass-reinforced fiber products, and the advent of high-strength glues and sealants that facilitate the application of a wide variety of veneers, ranging from plywood to thin layers of machine-cut stone. Turner proceeds to show that while the cost of the earthwork/podium has remained relatively stable at about 12½ percent of the budget of a building, mechanical services have risen to consume some 35 percent since the late nineteenth century. At the same time with the transition from load-bearing wall to skeleton frame construction, the amount devoted to the basic structure has dropped from around 80 percent in former times to some 20 percent today. Conversely the amount allocated to lightweight partitioning has risen from 3 to 20 percent, thereby leaving around 12½ percent to be devoted to the building envelope. That we spend more today on building services than on any other single item is surely indicative of the importance we now attach to environmental control. This maximization of comfort, verging on gratuitous consumption, leads, as D. Andrew Vernooy has argued, to a phenomenological and cultural devaluation of the tectonic and to a state affairs in which *simulation* rather than *presentation* and *representation* becomes the main expressive mode.

The seminal achievements of heroic Modernism, which used the structural system as the syntactic basis of configuration, are now difficult to duplicate in the context of current ordinance and performance. . . . For the most part, the envelope has been relieved of the burden of structural clarity. . . . Faced with the need to reconsider the plastic responsibility of the exterior wall, one asks to what end or ends should the craft of architecture be directed? The exterior wall of the thin-walled building is composed of several layers that are internally expressive, but concealed in such a manner that they remain externally mute about the condition of their configuration. These layers are covered by machine-produced veneers which are fashioned to imply forms developed honestly by earlier methods of construction. Thus, the material investment of the architectural image has been devalued for the sake of expediency and performance. This dislocation of material meaning is an understandable concomitant of a media society that accepts readily devalued imagery of all types. It is no longer necessary, for example, to rely on heavy stone construction to denote permanence. The formal allusion is adequate. Here, the metaphysical implications of material and detail investment are reduced to gestures which imply, but do not denote; they express ideas which represent architecture's customary functions—the registration of built form with its physical and cultural context—but they are phenomenally weak. This has further confused the role of figuration in architecture because it now has less to do with anchoring spatial experience through a fundamental response to material (which must be grounded in the traditions of its manufacture, use and configuration) and more to do with the associative qualities of the shape selected. The envelope has ceased to be a reflection of cultural operations that include evidence of the production of material and the production of device. It has become instead a reflection of cultural fashion.[11]

Architects are confronted today by a crisis of value comparable to that experienced by Gottfried Semper in 1851, when he first realized the cultural depreciation that had already been effected through machine production and the substitution of materials, as this was then manifest in such processes as casting, molding, pressing, and electroplating.[12] Over the last century and a half this cultural devaluation has greatly increased its scope, and its main effect has now shifted to the "spectacular" side of the economic cycle.

As privatization extends its inroads into the public realm, the institutional legacy of the bourgeois world becomes increasingly undermined by technological change and the all-pervasive thrust of the media and the market. Victor Hugo's *ceci tuera cela,* "this will kill that," said of the printed word in respect of architecture, now assumes a disturbing cast under the emerging hegemony of cybernetics, telemarketing, and the general spectacle of electromedia manipulation. One should note that none of the received types of the nineteenth-century city are immune to the effects of this deinstitutionalization. Not even a law court or a museum can save itself today from the impact of commodification, particularly as rationalized through the politics of populism. And what is true of the civic is even more the case for the processal institution, the factory, the department store, the railway station, or even the airport,[13] all of which are destabilized not only through the devaluations wrought by the culture industry, but also through their direct superannuation through changes in production and the consumptive cycle. To embrace the purportedly subversive culture of a deconstructive architecture seems to be a paradoxical form of speculative aestheticism in an age in which the environment is constantly being eroded by the forces of modernization. One is witness to a curious *trahison des clercs* in which architects proceed to exacerbate their marginalization by embracing a quixotic intellectuality totally removed from any kind of responsible practice.[14]

If this assessment is essentially correct, then two critical holding strategies suggest themselves. In the first instance the manifest necessity for architects to maintain their command over the art of building as a spatial and tectonic discipline; in the second, the equally pressing demand to educate and sensitize their potential clientele, for as is obvious from the "spectacular" nature of late capitalism, little of cultural significance will be achieved in the future without the presence of an enlightened client. This quixotic aspiration recalls Donald Schon's concept of reflective practice; that is to say, a form of practice that is critically discursive in its rapport with the client. However, as Alvaro Siza has remarked, this discourse may become on occasion very conflicted, in which case the architect has two choices: he can simply acquiesce to the client's ill-informed criteria and desires, or he can attempt to arrive at a resolution by challenging the client's prejudices every step of the way. [15]

There is perhaps no architect who better demonstrates the full potential for a reflective practice today than Renzo Piano, as the recent achievements of his Building Workshop amply testify. It is hardly surprising to find that such an approach depends for its success on a self-consciously collaborative team effort, both within and without the office. Of the character of this effort Piano was to write in 1992:

Unless an architect is able to listen to people and understand them, he may simply become someone who creates architecture for his own fame and self-glorification, instead of doing the real work he has to do. . . . An architect must be a craftsman. Of course any tools will do. These days, the tools might include a computer, an experimental model, and mathematics. However, it is still craftsmanship—the work of someone who does not separate the work of the mind from the work of the hand. It involves a circular process that draws you from an idea to a drawing, from a drawing to an experiment, from an experiment to a construction, and from construction back to an idea again. For me this cycle is fundamental to creative work. Unfortunately many have come to accept each of these steps as independent. . . . Teamwork is essential if creative projects are to come about. Teamwork requires an ability to listen and engage in a dialogue.[16]

Apart from Piano's remarkably rapid realization of the gargantuan Kansai International Airport, three equally exceptional works stand out as exemplifying the achievements of the Building Workshop over the past decade. These are the Lowara Office Building, completed in Montecchio Maggiore, near Vicenza, in 1985 (fig. 11.1), the San Nicola Football Stadium erected outside Bari in 1990 (fig. 11.2), and most recently a segment of infill housing built in the rue de Meaux, Paris, in 1991 (figs. 11.3, 11.4). What is of importance is that while they are each the outcome of the same developmental method and constructional discipline, they are each carefully inflected not only with regard to the context in which they are situated but also with regard to their societal status. And while they may be said to be similarly expressive from a tectonic standpoint, the technical means adopted in each instance is quite different and the overall character is distinct as a result. Thus, covered by a parabolic, sheet-steel catenary roof hung over a rectangular open office space, the Lowara office building is an undecorated shed par excellence. This new administrative building for an existing factory may be seen as a carefully oriented light modulator. Poised on top of V-shaped steel struts, the corrugated metal roof is, in fact, an enormous sun

11.1
Renzo Piano Building Workshop, Lowara Office Building, Vicenza, 1984–1985.

shade the surface temperature of which can be thermostatically controlled through the activation of an automatic roof spray. At the same time it displays a superbly articulated catenary profile of exceptional elegance.

In terms of weight, constructional method, and material, nothing could be more removed from the well-serviced anonymity of Lowara than the San Nicola Stadium that, with its capacity of 60,000 spectators, crowns a natural mound in the suburbs of Bari like the momentary presence of a gigantic spaceship. One doesn't know which to admire most, the ingenuity of its partially prefabricated assembly of large concrete elements or the dramatic contrast between the kite-like teflon sun screens and the heavyweight cantilever of the tribune. One is equally impressed by the way in which the architect has elected to surround the mound with a contoured parking parterre in such a way as to create a topographic counterform to the stadium.

At a totally different scale, the infill housing inserted into the rue de Meaux is an equally impressive exercise in prefabricated modular production. Here the fabric of the building is greatly enriched through a subtle interplay between different components set within a 90-centimeter grid. Naturally where light is required this module is filled with glass, shielded where required by glass-fiber-reinforced cement (GRC) louvers. However, the most innovative aspect by far is the cladding of the opaque walls. In this instance, the 90-by-90-centimeter coffered reinforced GRC panels, cast from steel molds, are faced with six 20-by-42-centimeter terra-cotta tiles that are quite literally hung onto lugs cast integrally with the back of the panel. This incidental Semperian treatment, in which a building is faced with large, loose tiles (a literal *Bekleidung* in fact), seems to me to exemplify exactly a realistic but subtle metaphorical approach, whereby rationalized modular production comes to be inflected in such a way as to be both popularly accessible and profoundly evocative of tradition.

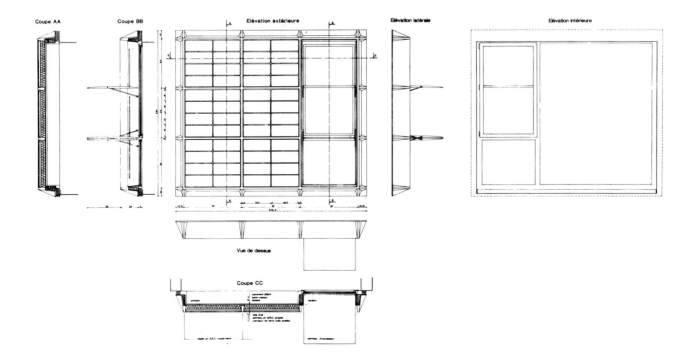

What all of these works demonstrate in different ways is a mastery over the means of production and an ability to break down the construction of a building into its constituent parts and to use this articulation as a stratagem bestowing an appropriate character on the work in hand. This regionally inflected but universal approach highlights the crossroads at which the profession stands, for the fact is that either architects will maintain their control over the *métier* of building design, irrespective of the scale at which it occurs, or the profession as we know it will cease to exist. We may say that the profession will either rise to the occasion by coming to terms with the transformed techno-economic character of building or it will be overwhelmed by the thrust of development, by escalating rate of change, and by all the special interests, large and small, that these combined forces bring in their wake. Whether architects will be able to reposition themselves with sufficient pertinence and rigor as to be able to resist or mediate these forces remains to be seen. In any event, indicators suggest that they will only be able to do so in a sporadic and interstitial way since late capitalism displays an indifference toward tectonic culture at many different levels, from its disdain for the physical and historical continuity of civic form to its latent disregard for the wholesale entropy of the built environment as it presently exists. One thing seems certain, that except for relatively small or prestigious commissions, the architect will have little prospect of maintaining control over every single aspect of the fabric. As we have seen, this is in part due to the increased technological character of building that today has attained such a complexity that no single practitioner can master all the processes involved. Thus it will be increasingly incumbent upon the architect to direct the different sectors of the industry to design their respective components in support of an overriding tectonic paradigm, and then to refine the combined result through a process of careful coordination. Even now, this is the only means by which large constructions can be orchestrated in a responsible way. Through such methodical stratagems architects are enabled to reinstate their authority and to overcome, as it were, the redundancy of the somewhat circular working drawing–shop drawing procedure as it presently exists. Such operational refinements will increasingly depend on the coordinating capacity of the computer and on the ability of architects to understand the constraints and tolerances of the procedures involved. Surely no one has foreseen the cultural potential of this cybernetic approach with greater optimism than Piano's prime collaborator, the engineer Peter Rice, who wrote of his role in the design of the Centre Pompidou in the following way:

By using the castings as the main building joints, the shapes and form were liberated from the standard industrial language. The public could see the individual design preference. Modern computers and analysis techniques and modern testing methods made this possible. We were back to the freedom of our Victorian forefathers. The individual details were exploited to give a personal design philosophy full rein. The final design was of course the work of more than one person. Many architects, engineers and craftsmen at the foundry contributed to the actual shape of each piece. And each piece was subject to the rigors of detailed structural analysis to ensure that it was fit for its purpose in every way and this too influenced the shape and final configuration. But this does not matter. The pieces are indeed better for all the different expertise which went into their make-up. They are more logical, more self-evidently correct in their form. What matters is that they are free of the industrial tyranny. They require people to look and perceive so that they may understand. This brings to mind another myth about technology. The feeling that technological choice is always the result of a predetermined logic. The feeling that there is a correct solution to a technical question is very common. But a technical solution like any other decision is a moment in time. It is not definitive. The decision is the result of a complex process where a lot of information is analyzed and examined and choices made on the evidence. It is a moment in time and place where the people, their background and their talent is paramount. What is often missing is the evidence of human intervention, the black box syndrome. So by looking at new materials, or at old materials in a new way we change the rules. People become visible again. [17]

For all that Rice's tone is technocratic, he patently alludes to a poetic formal dimension that is capable of transcending instrumentality as an end in itself. He is thus concerned with the revelation of the human spirit, through the specific manner in which a work comes to be collectively developed and realized. As an engineer he understood only too well that a technological device is a cultural choice and not simply a matter of reductive logic. This surely is the stand of the critical intellect against the mindless optimizing process of our "spectacular" bureaucracies, against the current tendency to maximize any one single value irrespective of the costs involved, whether environmental or otherwise. Truth, as Le Corbusier wrote, does not now lie in extremes; it lies, as he put it with self-deprecating irony, in a constant struggle to maintain a state of equilibrium whatever one's metier. Hence the wider ideological implications of his beautiful metaphor of the architect as acrobat. "Nobody asked him to do this. Nobody owes him any thanks. He lives in the extraordinary world of the acrobat." [18]

But are we not all in the last analysis acrobats, that is to say, is not the species as a whole caught on its technological high wire from which if it finally falls it will be impossible to recover? In the meantime the culture of the tectonic still persists as a testament to the spirit: the poetics of construction. All the rest, including our much-vaunted manipulation of space, is mixed up with the lifeworld, and in this it belongs as much to society as to ourselves.

Notes

Foreword

1
Phillip Lopate, *The Rug Merchant* (New York: Penguin, 1988).

1   Introduction: Reflections on the Scope of the Tectonic

Epigraph: Manfredo Tafuri and Francesco Dal Co, *Modern Architecture* (New York: Abrams, 1979), p. 9. (First published as *L'architettura contemporanea,* Milan: Electa Editrice, 1976.)

1
See Eugène-Emmanuel Viollet-le-Duc, *Discourses on Architecture,* 2 vols., trans. Benjamin Bucknall (New York: Grove Press, 1959; reprint of first American edition of 1889). While Viollet-le-Duc alludes to the experience of perspectival foreshortening in depth (Lecture VIII, p. 334 and following) and to space as necessary volume, there is no notion of modern space in his writing, save perhaps for his advocacy of liberating the ground floor through use of glazed partitions and freestanding pillars (Lecture XVIII, p. 320).

2
This was Schmarsow's inaugural lecture as professor of art history at the University of Leipzig in 1893. This lecture, like Konrad Fiedler's of fifteen years earlier, was a critique and an expansion of Semper's *Bekleidung* theory. Schmarsow was opposed to the stress that Semper gave to architecture as an art of "dressing," since he felt that this reduced architecture to a triviality. To counter this aesthetic from without, Schmarsow proposed an aesthetic from within, an aesthetic of interior space form versus the exterior "form feeling" championed by Heinrich Wölfflin. While an affinity clearly obtained between Schmarsow's spatial concept and Robert Vischer's idea of empathy, Schmarsow would distinguish in an interesting way between *Raumwissenschaft,* or the mathematical science of space, and *Raumkunst,* the architectural art of space. Later, in 1905, he would also discriminate among the arts of sculpture, painting, and architecture.

3
As far as the evolution of our modern space consciousness is concerned, 1893 can be considered the *annus mirabilis* since it saw the all but simultaneous publication of three seminal works: Schmarsow's *Das Wesen der architektonischen Schöpfung,* Theodor Lipps's "Ranästhetik und geometrisch-optische Täuschungen" in the collection of the *Gesellschaft für psychologische Forschungsschriften* (second collection, vol. IX–X, Leipzig), and last but not least Adolf von Hildebrand's *Das Problem der Form in der bildenden Kunst,* published in Leipzig in 1893 and translated into English as *The Problem of Form in Painting and Sculpture* in 1907. For further details on the evolution of modern spatiality in the work of these theorists see Cornelis van de Ven, *Space in Architecture* (Assen, The Netherlands: Van Gorcum, 1978).

While phenomenological spatial perception was first developed by Schmarsow, an awareness of space as a transformational continuum in architecture had emerged in the last half of the seventeenth century. This new consciousness was in part due to the geometrical methods that had been devised for the cutting and setting-out of vaulted stonework as these were compiled in Abraham Bosse's treatise of 1643, *La Practique du train à preuves de Mr Desargues Lyonnois, pour la coupe des pierres en l'architecture.* In the second half of the century the emerging science of stereotomy was to arouse the interest of architects and mathematicians alike, beginning with Girard Desargues, whose work on the planar intersections of a cone, published in 1639, led to the transformational space forms of Guarino Guarini.

It is no accident perhaps that in the second decade of this present century Sigfried Giedion should become preoccupied with transformational space of a somewhat different kind in his doctoral thesis under Heinrich Wölfflin, *Spätbarocker und romantischer Klassizismus,* published in Munich in 1922.

4

In his seminal *Space, Time and Architecture* (Cambridge, Mass.: Harvard University Press, 1941, with subsequent revised editions), Sigfried Giedion discusses the parallel development of Cubist aesthetics and modern theoretical physics. As Giedion notes, Renaissance space was literally contained by three-dimensional perspective and hence already oriented toward the abstraction of spatial infinity—the paradox of the vanishing point. Giedion is particularly impressed by the relationship in the Baroque between architecture and mathematics. He argues that both Guarini's San Lorenzo in Turin and Balthasar Neumann's Vierzehnheiligen in Bavaria employ three-dimensional curves that could not have been imagined without calculus. About 1830, Giedion notes, mathematics developed geometries of more than three dimensions, thereby preparing the ground for both the "simultaneity" of Cubist painting and Einstein's general theory of relativity, as developed in 1905.

In his "Cubist Aesthetic Theories" (Ph.D. dissertation, Harvard University, 1951), Christopher Gray shows that the Cubists were indeed interested in modern mathematical ideas of space, even though they possessed only a superficial understanding of these ideas. Gleizes and Metzinger wrote in *Du cubisme* of 1921 that geometry in Cubist painting should be referred to non-Euclidean geometries, particularly of the kind that was proposed by the German mathematician Georg Riemann. Such geometries emerged when mathematicians began to question Euclid's basic assumptions. Particularly important was the work of the Russian mathematician Nikolai Ivanovich Lobachevsky, who challenged Euclid's fundamental axiom that parallel lines never meet. Drawing from visual experience and assuming that the surface of the lines would meet at infinity, as was assumed in the development of perspective through qualitative rather than algorithmic analysis, Riemann proposed a notion of curved space not contained in other space, in which the curvature would be an internal feature of the space and not a result of surrounding conditions. Riemann's geometry was not concerned with time in the sense of the "fourth dimension," as was commonly supposed by the Cubists. His geometry is significant, nonetheless, because it became the framework within which Einstein developed his general theory of relativity. For further elaboration of this complex issue, see Linda Dalrymple Henderson, *The Fourth Dimension and Non-Euclidean Geometry in Modern Art* (Princeton: Princeton University Press, 1983).

5

See Le Corbusier, *Towards a New Architecture*, trans. Frederick Etchells (London: John Rodker, 1931). The "Three Reminders" follow immediately after the significant first chapter postulating a tectonic opposition between the Engineer's Aesthetic and Architecture. After the initial formulation under the rubric of the Engineer's Aesthetic, structure and construction are taken for granted by Le Corbusier and are quite literally overtaken by form in his early Purist period.

6

Giorgio Grassi, "Avant Garde and Continuity," *Oppositions* 21 (1980), pp. 26–27.

7

Ignasí de Sola Morales, "Critical Discipline; Review of Giorgio Grassi, 'L'architettura come mestiere,'" *Oppositions* 23 (1981), p. 146.

8

I am indebted for this etymological information to Professor Alexander Tzonis, Technische Universiteit Delft, The Netherlands.

9

Adolf Heinrich Borbein, "Tektonik, zur Geschichte eines Begriffs der Archäologie," *Archiv für Begriffsgeschichte* 26, no. 1 (1982).

10

Karl Otfried Müller, *Ancient Art and Its Remains, or a Manual of the Archaeology of Art*, trans. J. Leitch (London, 1847), p. 7.

11

For the full text of *The Four Elements of Architecture* in English translation, see Harry Mallgrave and Wolfgang Herrmann, *The Four Elements of Architecture and Other Writings by Gottfried Semper* (Cambridge: Cambridge University Press, 1989). The universality of the earthwork as an essential element in all building is evident in many different cultures, from early Japanese pit dwellings to the semi-buried timber buildings of Iceland. See Gisli Sigurdson, "Maison d'Islande et génie du lieu," *Le Carré Bleu* (1984, no. 3), pp. 10–21.

12

As we shall see in chapter 3, Semper will also remark on the etymological link between *die Wand,* the wall, and *das Gewand,* the dress.

13

Karl Gruber, *Die Gestalt der deutschen Stadt* (Leipzig: Bibliographischen Institut in Leipzig, 1937; reissued in an expanded version by the Verlag Callwey, Munich, in 1952). See in particular the reconstructed views of Büdingen and Worms. In each instance there is a contrast between the *Fachwerk* (wattle and daub screen walling) as applied to the residential fabric and the heavy coursed stonework of the castle, the cathedral, and the fortifications. The Germanic etymological distinction between *die Mauer* and *die Wand* is paralleled in Spanish by a differentiation between *pared* and *perrete*.

14

See the various forms of bonding commonly used in northern European brickwork, the so-called English, Flemish, stretcher, header, and monk bonds. In Roman building culture this finds a parallel in various kinds of coursed masonry such as *opus siliceum* (large polygonal blocks of hard stone laid dry), *opus quadratum* (rectangular stone blocks), *opus latericum* (brick walling), *opus caementicum* (a mixture of mortar with various fragments of stone and terra-cotta), and *opus reticulatum* (small roughly squared blocks laid up in diamond formation and backed by a cement core). See Martino Ghermandi, "I moderni e gli antichi Romani," *Costruire*, no. 58 (June 1988), pp. 90–93.

15

It is interesting to note that the Japanese were able to improve on the durability of exposed timber by the use of planing knives (*yari-ganna*) that were capable of providing a waterproof finish without the application of either lacquer or varnish. See William H. Coaldrake, *The Way of the Carpenter* (New York and Tokyo: Weatherhill, 1990), pp. 87, 88.

16

Vittorio Gregotti, address to the New York Architectural League, October 1982, published in *Section A* 1, no. 1 (February/March 1983), p. 8. The marking of ground with megaliths (literally "great stones" in Greek), that is to say with earthworks, dolmens, and menhirs, seems to have been due to different cosmogonic motives, from the creation of astronomical clocks as in Carnac to the channeling of earth's "energy" as in Stonehenge. This last would appear to be similar to the practice of geomancy in China, where apotropaic adjustments known as *feng shui* (wind and water) are still practiced today. See Alastair Service and Jean Bradbery, *Megaliths and Their Mysteries* (London: Weidenfeld & Nicholson, 1979).

17

See Liane Lefaivre and Alexander Tzonis, "The Grid and the Pathway," *Architecture in Greece,* no. 15 (1981), p. 176.

18

Dimitris Pikionis, "A Sentimental Topography," *The Third Eye* (Athens, November–December 1933), pp. 13–17.

19

Steen Eiler Rasmussen, *Experiencing Architecture* (Cambridge, Mass.: MIT Press, 1949), pp. 224–225.

20

Ulrich Conrads and Bernhard Leitner, "Audible Space: Experiences and Conjunctures," *Daidalos,* no. 17 (Berlin, 1985), pp. 28–45.

21

Michael Mooney, *Vico in the Tradition of Rhetoric* (Princeton: Princeton University Press, 1985), p. 214. See also Donald Phillip Venene, "Vico's Philosophy of Imagination," in *Vico and Contemporary Thought,* ed. Giorgio Tagliacozzo et al. (Atlantic Highlands, N.J.: Humanities Press, 1976).

22

Adrian Stokes, "The Stones of Rimini," in *The Critical Writings of Adrian Stokes,* vol. 1 (London: Thames & Hudson, 1978), p. 183. Stokes's aesthetic writings are suffused by a constant critique of industrial civilization. This critique ranges across a wide spectrum, from an appreciation of the self-reflexive corporeality of pagan civilization characterized "by a respect for the body of an intensity we do not find paramount in ourselves for long, by an awed identification of being with bodily being" (vol. 2, p. 253), to Stokes's omnipresent tactile perception of reality as is manifest in the following passage: "The roof tiles bring another quality of illuminated roughness: light and dark, differing planes, assert their difference in a marked equality beneath the sky, like an object of varied texture that is grasped and completely encompassed by the hand. . . . In employing smooth and rough as generic terms of architectural dichotomy, I am better able to preserve both the oral and tactile notions that underlie the visual" (vol. 2, p. 243). Stokes tends to regard all modifications of the earth's surface in corporeal, even maternal terms, evoking in different ways the archaic idea of the "earth mother." Thus we read "quarried stone, rock carved thoughtfully and indeed the quarry itself are as love compared with the hatefulness, the wastefulness and robbery that could be attributed to mining" (vol. 2, p. 248), and elsewhere in the same text, "Whereas ploughing roughens and freshens the progenitor earth, raking smooths it for the seed that will produce our food" (vol. 2, p. 241). *Smooth and Rough,* from which all the above quotations were taken, was written in Ascona in 1949. Toward the end of this study Stokes cites a certain Dr. Hans Sachs for the psychoanalytical insight that "the Ancient World overlooked the invention of machines not through stupidity nor through superficiality. It turned them into playthings in order to avoid repugnance." (See Sachs's *The Creative Unconscious,* Cambridge, Mass.: Sci-Art Publishers, 1942.)

23
Scott Gartner, unpublished manuscript of a lecture presented to the Association of Collegiate Schools of Architecture conference held at Washington in 1990.

24
Mark Johnson, *The Body in the Mind* (Chicago: University of Chicago Press, 1987), p. 15.

25
Tadao Ando, "Shintai and Space," in *Architecture and Body* (New York: Rizzoli, 1988). Unpaginated publication, edited by students of the Graduate School of Architecture, Planning and Preservation, Columbia University, New York.

26
See Merleau-Ponty's classic *Phenomenology of Perception,* first published in 1962. The citations here are from Colin Smith's 1962 translation (New York: Humanities Press), pp. 130–142:

Movement is not thought about movement and bodily space is not space thought of or represented. . . . In the action of the hand which is raised towards an object is contained a reference to the object, not as an object represented, but as that highly specific thing towards which we project ourselves. . . . We must therefore avoid saying that our body is in space or in time. It inhabits space and time. . . . Mobility is the primary sphere in which initially the meaning of all significances (der Sinn aller Signifikation) is engendered in the domain of represented space.

Elsewhere Merleau-Ponty writes of an organist playing an unfamiliar instrument. "There is no place for any 'memory' of the position of the stops and it is not in objective space that the organist in fact is playing. In reality his movements during rehearsal are consecratory gestures; they draw effective vectors, discover emotional sources, and create a space of expressiveness as the movements of the augur delimit the *templum.*"

It is interesting to note that Sigfried Giedion would also address the significatory role of the body, not only the body of the building but also the body by which the building is lived. See Sokratis Geogiadis, "Giedion, il simbolo e il corpo," *Casabella,* no. 599 (March 1993), pp. 48–51.

27
"Let us imagine a square, vertical pillar which is sharply defined by right angles. This pillar without base rests on the horizontal blocks which form the floor. It creates an impression of stability, of power to resist. A body approaches the pillar; from the contrast between the movement of this body and the tranquil immobility of the pillar a sensation of expressive life is born, which neither the body without the pillar,

nor the pillar without the body, would have been able to evoke. Moreover, the sinuous and rounded lines of the body differ essentially from the plane surfaces and angles of the pillar, and this contrast is in itself expressive. Now the body touches the pillar, whose immobility offers it solid support; the pillar resists; it is active. Opposition has thus created life in the inanimate form; space has become living." Adolphe Appia, as cited in Walter René Fuerst and Samuel J. Hume, *Twentieth Century Stage Decoration* (New York: Dover, 1967), vol. 1, p. 27.

28
Gottfried Semper, Prolegomenon to *Style in the Technical and Tectonic Arts,* in Semper, *The Four Elements of Architecture and Other Writings,* p. 196.

29
Pierre Bourdieu, "The Berber House or the World Reversed," *Social Science Information* 9, no. 2 (1969), p. 152. See also *Exchanges et communications: Mélanges offerts à Claude Lévi-Strauss à l'occasion de son 60 anniversaire* (Paris and The Hague: Mouton, 1970).

30
Gunter Nitschke, "Shime: Binding/Unbinding," *Architectural Design* 44 (1974), pp. 747–791. Etymologically *shime* means sign, hence the term *shime-nawa,* meaning "sign-rope." The term *musubu* means literally to bind, and *musubi* is the term for knot. Nitschke writes: "The name for this central mark of occupation, the *Shime,* was transferred and used for the occupied land, the *shima,* on the one hand and on the other for the rope of demarcation, *Shime-nawa.* And later, so we argue, this same term *Shima* was used for an island, a piece of land gained from the sea. . . . We face an amazing parallel process of human significance in the family of German words, *Mark, Marke* and *Marken;* originally mark did not stand for the boundary of a piece of land but for the way its occupation was marked" (p. 756). See also by the same author "Shime: Building, Binding and Occupying," *Daidalos,* no. 29 (September 1988), pp. 104–116.

31
See J. Drummond Robertson, *The Evolution of Clockwork* (London: Cassell, 1931), In particular chapter 3 on Japanese clocks, pp. 217–287. After the introduction of Western mechanical clocks into Japan at the beginning of the seventeenth century, the Japanese began to make mechanical clocks of their own that were capable of keeping variable time. The length of the day and night varied in Japan as elsewhere according to the seasons, a problem that the Japanese met in mechanical terms by the provision of a double balance and escapement that through adjustment mutually compensated for variations in the respective lengths of the days and nights. This meant of course that the increment of one hour was not constant throughout the seasonal cycle.

32
For a detailed description of these methods see Heino Engel, *Measure and Construction of the Japanese House* (Rutland, Vermont, and Tokyo: Tuttle, 1985), pp. 36–42.

33
Harry Mallgrave, introduction to Semper, *The Four Elements of Architecture and Other Writings,* p. 42.

34
See Adolf Loos, *Spoken into the Void: Collected Essays 1897–1900* (Cambridge, Mass.: MIT Press, 1982), pp. 66–69.

35
See Robert Schmutzler, *Art Nouveau* (New York: Abrams, 1962), pp. 273, 274: "In late Art Nouveau, biological life and dynamism give way to rigid calm. The proportions are still directly related to those of High Art Nouveau and the rudimentary forms of the older curve are equally present everywhere. But we might well wonder whether, between geometrical rigid late Art Nouveau and organically animated High Art Nouveau, a profounder relationship had not been expressed in a common nostalgia for the primitive state. The feeling of discomfort that culture produced in Freud, the lure of music and of decoration developed into music, the attraction of chaos created by the general fusion of the forces of life—might not the rigor of late Art Nouveau be understood as a necessary final phase of all this secret nostalgia, in fact as an 'urge in all animated life to return to a more primitive condition,' even to that of inanimate matter, of the crystalline stone?"

36
See Gyorgy Kepes, ed., *Structure in Art and in Science* (New York: Braziller, 1965), pp. 89–95. See also Sekler's "Structure, Construction and Tectonics," *Connection: Visual Arts at Harvard* (March 1965), pp. 3–11. For further references to the *tectonic* in American critical scholarship see Stanford Anderson, "Modern Architecture and Industry: Peter Behrens, the AEG and Industrial Design," *Oppositions,* no. 21 (Summer 1980), p. 83. Of Karl Bötticher's *Die Tektonik der Hellenen* Anderson remarks that the tectonic referred "not just to the activity of making the materially requisite construction that answers certain needs, but rather to the activity that raises this construction to an art form." In this formulation the "functionally adequate form must be adapted so as to give expression to its function. The sense of bearing provided by the entasis of Greek columns became the touchstone of the concept *Tektonik.*"

37
Eduard F. Sekler, "The Stoclet House by Josef Hoffmann," in *Essays in the History of Architecture Presented to Rudolf Wittkower* (London: Phaidon Press, 1967), pp. 230–231.

38
For Junger's concept of total mobilization, see his essay "Die totale Mobilmachung," 1930. For a detailed discussion of this see Michael E. Zimmermann, *Heidegger's Confrontation with Modernity* (Bloomington: Indiana University Press, 1990). Zimmermann writes (p. 55): "The elitist Junger asserted that in the nihilistic technological era, the ordinary worker either would learn to participate willingly as a mere cog in the technological order—or would perish. Only the higher types, the heroic worker-soldiers, would be capable of appreciating fully the world-creating, world-destroying technological, industrial fire-storm. He coined the term 'total mobilization' to describe the totalizing process of modern technology. . . . [Junger] believed that humanity would be saved and elevated only if it submitted to the nihilistic claim of the technological Will to Power."

Of Junger's and Heidegger's ideologically fascist affinities both before and after the Third Reich there can be little doubt, but this does not in itself discredit their pessimistic insights into the intrinsic character of modern technology. This difficult question has been taken up with great precision by Richard J. Bernstein in his book *The New Constellation: The Ethical-Political Horizons of Modernity/Postmodernity* (Cambridge, Mass.: MIT Press, 1991), pp. 79–141. In his critique of Heidegger Bernstein shows, after Hannah Arendt and Hans Georg Gadamer, that technology may be mediated not only by *poetic* revealing but also by political *praxis.*

39
In his recent book entitled *The Transparent Society* (Baltimore: Johns Hopkins University Press, 1992), Gianni Vattimo writes (pp. 52–53): "For if the 'founding' role art plays in relation to the world is overstated, one ends up with a view heavily laden with romanticism. . . . Yet Heidegger's concern, and this comes to the light in many passages of the 1936 essay ['The Original of the Work of Art'] . . . is not to give a positive definition of the world that poetry opens and founds, but rather to determine the significance of the 'unfounding' which is always an inseparable part of poetry. Foundation and unfounding are the meaning of the two features Heidegger identifies as constitutive of the work of art, the setting up (*Aufstellung*) of the worlds and the setting forth (*Herstellung*) of the earth. . . . Earth is not a world. It is not a system of signifying connections: it is the other, the nothing . . . the work is a foundation only in so far as it produces an ongoing disorientation that can never be recuperated in a final *Geborenheit.*"

40
Martin Heidegger, "Building, Dwelling, Thinking," in *Poetry, Language, Thought* (New York: Harper & Row, 1971), pp. 154–155. For the original presentation of this text in German see *Mensch und Raum: Das darmstädter Gesprach,* 1951 (reprinted Braunschweig: Vieweg, 1991).

41
Martin Heidegger, "On the Origin of the Work of Art," in *Poetry, Language, Thought,* p. 26.

42
Ibid., p. 46.

43
Ibid., p. 41.

44
One commentator who has seen Heidegger in these terms is George Steiner, *Martin Heidegger* (New York: Viking Press, 1979), esp. pp. 136–148. The concept of eco-philosophy or ecological humanism has been developed by Henryk Skolimowski, with a particular reference to architecture, in his book *Eco-Philosophy: Designing New Tactics for Living,* (Boston: Boyars, 1981). Despite the idiosyncratic nature of his thought, Skolimowski is surely correct when he identifies the overdetermined role played by building regulations as technological. With his slogan "form follows culture" Skolimowski argues that universal bureaucracy reproduces and facilitates the domination of a global technology and that the overall telos of this technology tends to be quantitative rather than qualitative in nature. See in particular pp. 92–93.

45
For a discussion of the origin of "weak thought" in Italian philosophy see Giovanna Borradori, "Weak Thought and Postmodernism: The Italian Departure from Deconstruction," *Social Text,* no. 18 (Winter 1987/88), pp. 39–49. As Borradori puts it at the end of her article: "In the age of the 'loss of the referent,' be it historical, social, political, cultural or even ontological, the attempt of philosophy, as weak thought suggests, should make available *new spaces of referentiality* in which art and particularly knowledge can operate." For the theoretical application of "weak thought" to architecture see Ignasí de Sola Morales, "Weak Architecture," *Ottagono,* no. 92, pp. 88–117.

46
See Charles Correa, *The New Landscape—Bombay* (Bombay: Book Society of India, 1985), p. 10. It is estimated that by the year 2000 there will be 50 conurbations in the world each with populations of 15,000,000, of which 40 will be located in the Third World.

47
Hans Georg Gadamer's concept of the "fusion of horizons" is an essential part of hermeneutical understanding. See Georgia Warnke, *Gadamer: Hermeneutics, Tradition and Reason* (Stanford: Stanford University Press, 1987), p. 69. Warnke writes: "For this reason, Gadamer finds something suspect in the attempt to restore the authenticity of works of art by placing them in their original settings; on his view this attempt to retrieve an original meaning simply obscures any meaning works of art have as fusions of horizons. Understanding does not involve re-experiencing an original understanding but rather the capacity to listen to a work of art and allow it to speak to one in one's present circumstances." See also p. 82.

48
Ibid., p. 170.

49
Ibid., p. 39.

50
Siza's aphorism throws into question the whole issue as to the nature of invention and originality. In this regard one might do well to recall Picasso's saying "I do not seek, I find." Thus one enters into a prospect in which one happens upon an "original formulation" through an empirical, circular process of design that is not rational in any linear, causal sense. Siza's aphorism implies that formal originality should not be pursued as an end in itself; that it should be allowed to arise spontaneously from out of a responsive transformation of the given circumstances. This notion finds invention having an inevitable and fertile dependency on the unfolding of an unpredictable *event.* This has been well characterized by Sylvianne Agacinski in her thesis about the decisive character of the *event:* "A work of art is fostered by invention, which itself is the result of a multiplicity of decisions. And I would contend that each decision is an 'event', i.e. something which, far from simply falling in the province of necessity, happens to the architect along with that share of contingency typical of artistic and technical work. . . . That share of event in invention is precisely what undermines invention's autonomy. . . . Now, the relationship between invention and event, the share of the empirical in invention, is exactly what metaphysics recoils from thinking about." See Sylvianne Agacinski, "Shares of Invention," a lecture given to the Afterwords Conference. See *D: Columbia Documents of Architecture and Theory* 1 (1992), pp. 53–68.

51
Gianni Vattimo, *The End of Modernity* (Cambridge, England: Polity Press, 1988), p. 104.

52

For Gadamer's concept of the "bad infinite" see Warnke, *Gadamer,* p. 170. For Gehlen's concept of *post-histoire* see his book *Man in the Age of Technology* (New York: Columbia University Press, 1980). See also his 1967 essay "Die Säkularisierung des Fortschritts," in volume 7 of his collected works entitled *Einblicke,* ed. K. S. Rehberg (Frankfurt: Klochtermann, 1978). Gehlen argues that technoscientific progress as economic routine, linked to continuous late capitalist development but otherwise divorced from basic vital needs and even opposed to them, discharges the responsibility for the ideology of the new onto the arts, a burden that they can no more sustain than the atomized multiplicity of the various subsets of technoscience. Gehlen writes: "The overall project [of the new] fans out in divergent processes that develop their own internal legality ever further, and slowly progress . . . [and] is displaced towards the periphery of facts and consciousness, and there is totally emptied out." See Vattimo, *The End of Modernity,* p. 102.

53

Gianni Vattimo, "Project and Legitimization," proceedings of a conference held on June 6, 1985, under the auspices of the Centro Culturale Polifunzionale at Bra, p. 124. See also "Dialoghi fra Carlo Olmo e Gianni Vattimo," translated into English as "Philosophy of the City," *Eupalino,* no. 6 (1986), pp. 4, 5.

54

See Jürgen Habermas, *Towards a Rational Society* (New York: Beacon Press, 1970), pp. 118–119:

Above all, it becomes clear against this background that two concepts of rationalization must be distinguished. At the level of the subsystems of purposive-rational action, scientific-technical progress has already compelled the reorganization of social institutions and sectors, and necessitates it on an even larger scale than heretofore. But this process of the development of the productive forces can be a potential for liberation if and only if it does not replace rationalization on another level.

Rationalization at the level of the institutional framework can only occur in the medium of symbolic interaction itself, that is through removing restrictions on all communication. Public, unrestricted discussion, free from domination, of the suitability and desirability of action-orientating principles and norms in the light of the socio-cultural repercussions of developing subsystems of purposive-rational action—such as communication at all levels of political and repoliticized decision-making processes—is the only medium in which anything like "rationalization" is possible.

55

See Hannah Arendt, *The Human Condition* (Chicago: University of Chicago Press, 1958). For Arendt the term "space of appearance" signifies the paradigmatic political space of the Greek *polis* (pp. 201, 204).

56

Vittorio Gregotti, "The Obsession with History," *Casabella,* no. 478 (March 1982), p. 41.

57

See Vittorio Gregotti, *Il territorio dell'architettura* (Milan: Feltrinelli, 1966).

58

See Serge Chermayeff and Christopher Alexander, *Community and Privacy: Toward a New Architecture of Humanism* (Garden City: Doubleday, 1963). More than 30 years ago, this text proposed a rational system of dense low-rise suburban land settlement served by automobiles, one that unfortunately has no influence on current development practice. The forces of land speculation, aided and abetted by the universal distribution of the automotive infrastructure, have effectively inhibited the adoption of more ecologically responsible patterns of land settlement.

59

Vittorio Gregotti, "Clues," *Casabella,* no. 484 (October 1982), p. 13.

60

Gregotti, "The Obsession with History," p. 41: "So what is the answer? There is no answer except the reverting to the uncertainty of reality, maintaining 'a total lack of illusions about one's age, yet supporting it relentlessly.' How to revert to 'enduring reality' is, undoubtedly, a very complex theoretical and ideal matter; this becomes apparent as soon as one goes beyond reality's empirical, tangible surface and defines it in terms of deliberate choices and projects, as a 'concrete utopia,' a 'principle of hope,' to borrow Ernst Bloch's beautiful expression (today such terms are so much out of fashion as to appear either naive or self-interested). But it is also a *constructive effort, a problem concerning the choice of tools and methods.*" (Emphasis added.)

61

Ibid.

62

Arendt, *The Human Condition,* p. 204. Arendt contrasts the light of the *res publica* to the intimate darkness of the private dwelling—the *megaron.*

63

For the distance between graphic immediacy and the permanence of construction see Rafael Moneo, "The Solitude of Buildings," Kenzo Tange lecture, March 9, 1985, Graduate School of Design, Harvard University:

Many architects today invent processes or master drawing techniques without concern for the reality of buildings. The tyranny of drawings is evident in many buildings when the builder tries to follow the drawing literally. The reality belongs to the drawing and not to the building. . . . The buildings refer so directly to the architect's definition and are so unconnected with the operation of building that the only reference is the drawing. But a truly architectural drawing should imply above all the knowledge of construction. Today many architects ignore issues about how a work is going to be built. . . . The term that best characterizes the most distinctive feature of academic architecture today is "immediateness." Architecture tries to be direct, immediate, the simple, dimensional extension of drawings. Architects want to keep the flavor of their drawings. And if this is their most desirable goal, in so wishing architects reduce architecture to a private, personal domain. It follows that this immediateness transforms the intentions of the architect, and turns what should be presumed as general into a personal expressionist statement. . . . I do not think that we can justify as architecture the attempts of some artists who, confusing our discipline with any three-dimensional experience, create unknown objects that at times relate to natural mimesis and other times allude to unusable machines. . . . The construction of a building entails an enormous amount of effort and investment. Architecture in principle, almost by economic principle, should be durable. . . . Today's architecture has lost contact with its genuine supports, and immediateness is the natural consequence of this critical change.

64

Cited in Clive Bamford Smith, *Builders in the Sun* (New York: Architecture Book Publishing Company, 1967), p. 54.

2 Greco-Gothic and Neo-Gothic: The Anglo-French Origins of Tectonic Form

Epigraph: Francesco Dal Co, *Figures of Architecture and Thought: German Architecture Culture, 1880–1920* (New York: Rizzoli, 1990), p. 282.

1

Robin Middleton, "The Abbé de Cordemoy and the Graeco-Gothic Ideal: A Prelude to Romantic Classicism," *Journal of the Warburg and Courtauld Institutes* 25 (1962), p. 238; 26 (1963), pp. 90–123.

2

Marc-Antoine Laugier, *Essai sur l'architecture,* trans. Wolfgang and Anni Herrmann as *An Essay on Architecture* (Los Angeles: Hennessey & Ingalls, 1977), pp. 103–104.

3

For details of the relationship between Laugier and Soufflot and the building of Ste.-Geneviève see Joseph Rykwert, *The First Moderns: The Architects of the Eighteenth Century* (Cambridge, Mass.: MIT Press, 1980), pp. 430–470.

4

Werner Oechslin, "Soufflot, Jacques-Germain," *Macmillan Encyclopedia of Architects* (New York: Free Press, 1982), vol. 4, pp. 109–113.

5

See Nikolaus Pevsner's *Some Architectural Writers of the Nineteenth Century* (Oxford: Clarendon Press, 1972). Willis may be seen as close to both Pugin and Viollet-le-Duc in that he took much from Frézier's *La Théorie et la pratique de la coupe des pierres,* of 1737, for his seminal essay read before the newly formed Institute of British Architects in 1842. Gothic in England never became fully extinct since the Renaissance arrived late at the end of the sixteenth century and was acclimatized slowly. As Kenneth Clark remarked in his study *The Gothic Revival* of 1928, vestiges of Gothic construction still survived in England at the end of the eighteenth century when Gothic became the subject of antiquarian inquiry. In less than seventy years, one passed from the picturesque Gothic of Horace Walpole's Strawberry Hill (1753) to wholesale church building under the auspices of the state with the Church Building Act of 1818. This act led to a complex debate, couched in archaeological, liturgical, and tectonic terms, as to what was the true Gothic mode, as utilitarian Protestantism came to be challenged by Anglo-Catholicism.

6

It was exactly this form of construction that served as a positive model for Karl Friedrich Schinkel's Bauakademie, erected in Berlin between 1831 and 1836.

7

A. W. N. Pugin, *The True Principles of Pointed or Christian Architecture* (London: John Weale, 1841; reprint, London: Academy Editions, 1973), p. 1.

8

Ibid., p. 3.

9

A. W. N. Pugin, article published in the *Dublin Review* (May 1841), quoted in Phoebe Stanton, "Pugin, Augustus Welby Northmore," *Macmillan Encyclopedia of Architects,* vol. 3, pp. 489–490.

10

Phoebe Stanton, *Pugin* (New York: Viking, 1972), p. 194.

11

David T. Van Zanten, "Labrouste, Henri," *Macmillan Encyclopedia of Architects,* vol. 2, p. 594.

12

See Herman Hertzberger, "Henri Labrouste, la réalisation de l'art," *Technique et Architecture,* no. 375 (1987–1988). Hertzberger's appreciation of this building is worth quoting at some length:

The long-drawn reading room of the Bibliothèque Sainte-Geneviève, though enclosed by heavy neo-Renaissance outer walls, has a surprisingly fragile internal canopy with two longitudinally parallel barrel vaults. The thin steelwork is as an addition of another era onto the heavy remains of the past. Though one still finds classical motifs on the columns, thin as stems, these motifs are proportionally transformed into mere superficial decorations. And when you come to think of it: the floral forms in the open-web semicircular trusses hardly cover up their structural character of diagonal bars; this is Art Nouveau avant la lettre!

The banded roofs go around the corner instead of coming to a dead end at the end facade, and though they are related to barrel vaults, they don't divide the space into two parallel strips; it stays one whole. The row of columns in the middle doesn't continue along the total length either, but keeps a distance from the ends without dividing the floor or interfering with the view through the reading room.

. . . Labrouste, however, didn't work with semicircular but quarter-circular truss elements. He not only connects them to make semicircles but also to make corners of 90 degrees, and what's more he connects them to the ridge beams, which he uses as complementary elements.

13

Peter McCleary, "The Role of Technology in Architecture," The Rowlett Report 86, Proceedings of Rowlett Lecture/Symposium, Texas A&M University, April 1986, pp. 14–21. See also McCleary's essay "Structure and Intuition" in the *AIA Journal* (October 1980), pp. 59, 60. He writes:

As is often the case in the building industry, new materials and their fabricated elements replace or 'substitute' for the old materials and elements whose performances are found inadequate. As is also often the case, the form of the new copies the form of the old. Arch bridges in stone are replaced by arch bridges in cast iron. Banded barrel vaults in stone are replaced by banded barrel vaults in cast iron, i.e., Labrouste's library of St. Genevieve, Paris (1838–1850). The details of Labrouste's arches clearly indicate "casting" and the joints differentiate for us what was made off-site from that which was connected on-site. The availability of cheap puddled wrought iron separates his first library from his design for the national library (1854–75). In this later building, the arches, which combine to support and define the domes, have a completely different expression. The parts are clearly rolled or hammered and riveted together. The manufacturing process and the new engineering expertise are evident. The ornamentation comes from the geometry of the parts and there is no cast foliage as in St. Genevieve. The column remains cast iron, fluted and with an Ionic capital—or, one might say, it remains inhibited by the tradition of stone. However, a new expression and a new structuring is made possible and is realized by Labrouste.

14

Robin Middleton, "Viollet-le-Duc, Eugène-Emmanuel," *Macmillan Encyclopedia of Architects,* vol. 4, p. 327.

15

Eugène-Emmanuel Viollet-le-Duc, *Discourses on Architecture,* trans. Benjamin Bucknall (New York: Grove Press, 1959), Lecture IX, p. 422.

16

Ibid., Lecture XX, pp. 385–386.

17

Ibid., Lecture XII, pp. 58, 61.

18

Ibid., Lecture XII, p. 89.

19

Ibid., Lecture XII, p. 86.

20

Ibid., Lecture XII, pp. 84–85.

21

Hubert Damisch, "The Space Between: A Structuralist Approach to the Dictionnaire," *Architectural Design* 50, nos. 3/4 (1980), pp. 88–89 (Architectural Design Profile 27).

22

The influence of Viollet-le-Duc on late nineteenth-century practice is of course very extensive, as I have tried to show in chapter 4, part II, of my study *Modern Architecture: A Critical History* (London: Thames & Hudson, 1980). The entire Art Nouveau was indebted to Viollet-le-Duc in one form or another, particularly the French and Belgian adherents of this movement; above all, Hector Guimard, Victor Horta, Henri Sauvage, and Franz Jourdain. Clearly the Catalan *modernismo* school comprising Antoni Gaudí i Cornet, Lluis Domenech i Montaner, and Josep Puig i Cadafalch also owes much to Viollet-le-Duc. Outside of this, the two masters of the proto-modern movement, Berlage and Auguste Perret, are also strongly indebted to the founder of structural rationalism.

23

See J. B. Ache, "Anatole de Baudot," *Les Monuments historiques de la France,* pp. 103–121; he gives the date of 1890 for Cottancin's patent on the system of *ciment armé.*

24

The intrinsically Gothic approach of Cottancin is evident from his design for an apartment building in the Boulevard Diderot. See Albert W. Buel, *Reinforced Concrete* (New York, 1906), pp. 205–206.

25

See "A French Method of Cement Construction," *Architectural Record* (1902), pp. 375–393.

26

Quoted in Franco Borsi and Ezio Godoli, *Paris 1900* (New York: Rizzoli, 1978), p. 16.

27
See Auguste Choisy, *Histoire de l'architecture* (1899). It is obvious that certain buildings were more easily represented by Choisy's isometric method than others. The famous illustrations taken from Choisy in Le Corbusier's *Vers une architecture* of 1923 are a case in point, for here the method is at its iconographic best. It is clear, however, given the small format and the encyclopedic scope of his study, that Choisy was unable to represent timber trusswork in a sufficiently comprehensive way, as we may judge from his treatment of the roof structures used to protect Gothic vaults (pp. 257–263).

28
Choisy, *Histoire de l'architecture,* vol. I, pp. 216–266.

29
Cornelis van de Ven, *Space in Architecture* (Assen, The Netherlands: Van Gorcum, 1978).

3 The Rise of the Tectonic: Core Form and Art Form in the German Enlightenment, 1750–1870

Epigraph: Kurt W. Forster, "Schinkel's Panoramic Planning of Central Berlin," *Modulus* 16 (Charlottesville, 1983), p. 65.

1
E. M. Butler, *The Tyranny of Greece over Germany* (Boston: Beacon Press, 1958), pp. 178–179. The quotation is from Friedrich Schiller's *On the Art of Tragedy* of 1792.

2
Published by his students in 1835.

3
Hugh Honor, *Neo-Classicism* (London: Penguin, 1968), p. 59.

4
See Charles Taylor, *Hegel and Modern Society* (Cambridge: Cambridge University Press, 1979), p. 1, p. 158, and p. 160. Taylor's use of the term *expressivist* derives from Isaiah Berlin's "expressionism," as this appears in Berlin's essay "Herder and the Enlightenment," 1965.

5
See Nikolaus Pevsner, "Goethe and Architecture," in *Studies in Art, Architecture and Design* (New York: Walker & Co., 1968), vol. 1, pp. 165–173.

6
See W. T. Stace, *The Philosophy of Hegel* (New York: Dover, 1955), pp. 465–466.

7
Ibid., p. 470.

8
Friedrich Gilly would anticipate the tectonic theory of Karl Friedrich Schinkel and Carl Bötticher in his essay "Einige Gedanken über die Notwendigkeit die verschiedenen Theile der Baukunst, in wissenschaftlicher und praktischer Hinsicht, möglichst zu vereinigen," in *Gilly: Wiederburt der Architektur,* ed. Alfred Rietdorf (Berlin, 1940).

9
Hermann G. Pundt, *Schinkel's Berlin* (Cambridge: Harvard University Press, 1972), p. 42.

10
See *In What Style Should We Build? The German Debate on Architectural Style,* introduction and translation by Wolfgang Herrmann (Santa Monica: Getty Center for the History of Art and the Humanities, 1991).

11
See Herrmann, *In What Style Should We Build,* pp. 10, 11.

12
The Berlin Bauschule was reorganized as the Bauakademie in 1799. Sometime in the 1840s or the 1850s the name changed again, but later reverted back to Bauakademie. In 1806 Schinkel obtained a position at the academy teaching geometry and perspective. In 1811 he became a member of the academy and in 1820 he was appointed professor of building. However, his involvement and duties remained somewhat minimal.

Beuth first went to England in 1822 as a member of the Prussian state council. He wrote to Schinkel from Manchester about the eight- and nine-story factories of the city, full of windows that he found to be among "the marvels of our recent time."

13
The publication of this book was of far-reaching significance. It was first issued as single engravings and afterward collected into two portfolios. In 1821 Beuth founded the Gewerbeverein or Association for the Encouragement of Trade and Industry in Prussia. See Michael Snodin, *Karl Friedrich Schinkel: A Universal Man* (New Haven: Yale University Press, 1991), pp. 61, 62.

14
In contrast to Pugin's lifelong ambivalence toward cast iron, Schinkel would deploy the material to great effect from the very beginning of his practice as an architect, as we may judge from the monuments that he realized in iron for Queen Luise at Gransee in 1811 and for the dead of the Wars of Liberation at Spandau in 1816 and at Grassheeren in 1817, not to mention the elegant simplicity of the iron cross, designed in 1813 as the highest Prussian military honor on the eve of the liberation war against the French. See Barry Bergdoll, *Karl Friedrich Schinkel: An Architecture for Prussia* (New York: Rizzoli, 1994), pp. 38, 43. See also Snodin, ed., *Karl Schinkel: A Universal Man,* p. 103.

15
See Nikolaus Pevsner, *Some Architectural Writers of the Nineteenth Century* (Oxford: Clarendon Press, 1972), p. 622. "Schinkel, before designing the most beautiful Neo-Grecian buildings in Europe and long before becoming Prussian *Oberbaudirektor* in 1831, had been a passionate Gothicist, though in drawings and paintings rather than buildings. In 1810 he wrote, 'Antique architecture has its effects, scale and solidity in its material masses, Gothic architecture affects us by its spirit . . .' Later Schinkel wrote in the opposite vein, 'To build Greek is to build right . . . The principle of Greek architecture is to render construction beautiful and this must remain the principle of its continuation.'"

16
See Martin Goalen, "Schinkel and Durand: The Case of the Altes Museum," in Snodin, ed., *Karl Friedrich Schinkel: A Universal Man,* pp. 27–35. According to Goalen, Schinkel's rendering of the Altes Museum as an Ionic temple, reminiscent of the temple of Apollo at Didyma, compelled him to depart in certain points from the mechanistic method of Durand.

17
Edward R. De Zurko, *Origins of Functionalist Theory* (New York: Columbia University Press, 1957), p. 196. Quotation from August Grisebach, *Karl Friedrich Schinkel* (Leipzig: Im Insel Verlag, 1924).

18
Ibid., p. 196. De Zurko is quoting from Wolzogen's study "Schinkel als Architekt, Maler and Kunstphilosoph," *Zeitschrift für Bauwesen* 14, nos. 1–2 (1864), col. 253.

19
Aby Warburg is apparently the first person to have used this phrase: "Der Liebe Gott steckt in Detail."

20
De Zurko, *Origins of Functionalist Theory,* p. 197, quoting from Wolzogen, col. 250.

21
This translation is by Harry Mallgrave. It is taken from *Aus Schinkel's Nachlass,* book II, section 208. See also De Zurko, *Origins of Functionalist Theory,* pp. 197, 198.

22
Eleftherios Ikonomou and Harry Francis Mallgrave, introduction to *Empathy, Form, and Space: Problems in German Aesthetics, 1873–1893* (Santa Monica: Getty Center for the History of Art and the Humanities, 1994), pp. 9–10.

Schinkel's total immersion in the philosophical discourse of the *Aufklärung* has led various interpreters to assert different influences on his thought. Thus where Bergdoll stresses the primacy given to architecture by Schinkel's close associate, the philosopher Karl W. F. Solger,

Caroline van Eck shows how Schinkel's concern for the reconciliation of intellectual freedom with natural law may be traced back to Schlegel's *Kunstlehre* of 1801–1802. See Bergdoll, *Karl Friedrich Schinkel*, p. 48, and Caroline van Eck, *Organicism in Nineteenth Century Architecture: An Inquiry into Its Theoretical and Philosophical Background* (Amsterdam: Architectura and Natura Press, 1994), pp. 114–124.

23
Kurt W. Forster, "Schinkel's Panoramic Planning of Central Berlin," p. 74.

24
In his *History of the Modern Styles of Architecture* of 1862, James Ferguson wrote of the Bauakademie: "The ornamentation depends wholly on the construction, consisting only of piers between the windows, string-cornices marking the floors, a slight cornice, and the dressings of the windows and doors. All of these are elegant, and so far nothing can be more truthful or appropriate, the whole being of brick, which is visible everywhere. Notwithstanding all this, the Bauschule cannot be considered as entirely successful, in consequence of its architect not taking sufficiently into consideration the nature of the material he was about to employ in deciding on its general characteristics. Its simple outline would have been admirably suited to a Florentine or Roman palace built of large blocks of stone, or to a granite edifice anywhere; but it was a mistake to adopt so severe an outline in an edifice to be constructed of such small materials as bricks. Had Schinkel brought forward the angles of his building and made them more solid in appearance, he would have improved it to a great extent."

25
Schinkel, while appreciative of Hirt's erudition, did not approve of his academicism, and this led to a widening gulf between them culminating in Hirt's pedantic criticism of the Altes Museum.

26
See Arthur Schopenhauer, *Die Welt als Wille und Vorstellung* (The World as Will and Idea, 1819), English translation in *The Works of Schopenhauer*, ed. Will Durant (New York: Ungar, 1955), pp. 131–133:

For just because each part bears just as much as it conveniently can, and each is supported just where it requires to be and just to the necessary extent, this opposition unfolds itself, this conflict between rigidity and gravity, which constitutes the life, the manifestation of will, in the stone, becomes completely visible, and these lowest grades of the objectivity of will reveal themselves distinctly. In the same way the form of each part must not be determined arbitrarily, but by its end, and its relation to the whole. The column is the simplest form of support, determined simply by its end. . . . All this proves that architecture does not affect us mathematically, but also dynamically, and that what speaks to us through it is not mere form and symmetry, but rather those fundamental forces of nature, those first Ideas, those lowest grades of the objectivity of will. The regularity of the building and its parts is partly produced by the direct adaptation of each member to the stability of the whole, partly it serves to facilitate the survey and comprehension of the whole, and finally, regular figures to some extent enhance the beauty because they reveal the constitution of space as such. But all this is of subordinate value and necessity, and by no means the chief concern; indeed symmetry is not invariably demanded, as ruins are still beautiful.

27
See Mitchell Schwarzer, "Ontology and Representation in Karl Bötticher's Theory of Tectonics," *Journal of the Society of Architectural Historians* 52 (September 1993), p. 276.

28
Wolfgang Herrmann, *Gottfried Semper: In Search of Architecture* (Cambridge, Mass.: MIT Press, 1984), p. 141. Herrmann is quoting from Karl Bötticher's *Die Tektonik der Hellenen*, 2 vols. (Potsdam, 1852), vol. 1, p. xv.

29
Herrmann, *Gottfried Semper*, p. 141.

30
There is a difference between the position adopted in *Die Tektonik der Hellenen* and the 1846 essay. In the former the fusion of Hellenic and Germanic styles is style solely as a matter of cultural synthesis; in the later text it is made dependent on the new material, iron.

31
Karl Bötticher, "The Principles of the Hellenic and Germanic Way of Building," trans. Wolfgang Herrmann in *In What Style Should We Build*, p. 158.

32
Ibid., p. 159.

33
Ibid., p. 163.

34
The issue of polychromy in antique Greek sculpture had first been raised by the publication of Quatremère de Quincy's text "Le Jupiter Olympien" in 1816. However, Quatremère resisted the idea of polychromy in architecture except insofar as it arose out of the natural color of the materials themselves. The possibility that the Greeks painted their temples was advanced again by Leo von Klenze's colored reconstruction of the temple at Aegina in Hittorf's *L'Architecture polychrome chez les Grecs* of 1827 and by Henri Labrouste's *envoi* from the French Academy in Rome in 1828 consisting of his reconstruction of the Greek temples at Paestum.

35
Harry Francis Mallgrave, "Gustave Klemm and Gottfried Semper," *Res* (Spring 1985), p. 76.

36
Rosemarie Haag Bletter, "On Martin Fröhlich's Gottfried Semper," *Oppositions* 4 (October 1974), p. 148.

37
In *De l'architecture égyptienne*, his 1803 rewriting of his 1785 entry to the competition of the Académie Royale des Inscriptions et Belles-Lettres, Quatremère de Quincy posited a triadic origin to all building: the tent, the cave, and the hut.

38
Joseph Rykwert, "Semper and the Conception of Style," in *Gottfried Semper und die Mitte des 19. Jahrhunderts* (Basel and Stuttgart: Birkhäuser, 1976), pp. 77–78.

39
Ibid., p. 72.

40
Ibid.

41
However, as for Ruskin and Pugin, the Crystal Palace was a traumatic form for Semper. He saw it as a vacuum enclosed by glass and thereafter thought it essential that the use of iron should be tempered by the deployment of masonry forms.

42
In his 1987 essay "Gottfried Semper, architetto e teorico," Benedetto Gravagnuolo cites those various fragmented passages in *Moderne Architektur* in which Wagner criticizes Semper for not having insisted sufficiently that architecture always derives from the principle of construction and that new constructional means must eventually produce new constructional forms: "In his way Otto Wagner is correct in maintaining that Semper didn't push himself to the extreme consequence of the modern project. His architecture remains arrested before the problematic threshold of the symbolic status of building. . . . In his discourse about building there was a kernel of inertia . . . that remained opposed to taking an integral and a critical view about the triumph of hegemonic modernization over the collective values of civilization and the ethnological culture to which it belongs. The modern theory that new form necessarily arises from new techniques is absent from his discourse. Style for Semper must not follow function but must represent through architecture the feeling of an epoch." See *Gottfried Semper: architettura, arte e scienza* (Naples, 1987), p. 34.

43
See James Duncan Berry, "The Legacy of Gottfried Semper: Studies in Späthistoricismus," Ph.D. dissertation, in the History of Art and Archi-

tecture, Brown University, 1989. I am totally indebted to Duncan Barry for his study of Georg Heuser.

44
See Otto Wagner, *Modern Architecture,* trans. Harry Mallgrave (Santa Monica: Getty Center for the History of Art and the Humanities, 1988), pp. 91–99. The text is from the 1902 edition, but for these passages the 1914 version is virtually the same.

45
I am indebted to Mitchell Schwarzer for drawing my attention to Bötticher's later use of the term *Werkform* to refer to technically innovative constructional form. Schwarzer, "Ontology and Representation," pp. 278–280.

46
Gottfried Semper, "Style in the Technical and Tectonic Arts or Practical Aesthetics," in Harry Mallgrave and Wolfgang Herrmann, eds., *Gottfried Semper: The Four Elements and Other Writings* (Cambridge: Cambridge University Press, 1989), pp. 257–258.

47
Fritz Neumeyer, "Iron and Stone: The Architecture of the Grossstadt," in Harry Mallgrave, ed., *Otto Wagner: Reflections on the Raiment of Modernity,* (Santa Monica: Getty Center for the History of Art and the Humanities, 1993), p. 135.

48
See Schwarzer, "Ontology and Representation," p. 280. Of the part played by *Einfühlung* implicitly in Wagner and by anticipation, so to speak, in the case of Bötticher, Schwarzer writes, with regard to Richard Streiter's critique of Bötticher's *Tektonik* in 1896: "Bötticher's theory represents an ideological bridge between the speculative aesthetics of Sulzer, Moritz and Schelling and the ideas of projective visuality and *Einfühlung* (empathy) that later appeared in the writings of Conrad Fiedler, Adolf Hildebrand and Theodor Lipps."

4 Frank Lloyd Wright and the Text-Tile Tectonic

Epigraph: Grant Carpenter Manson, *Frank Lloyd Wright to 1910: The First Golden Age* (New York: Reinhold, 1958), pp. 38–39.

1
Barry Bergdoll, "Primordial Fires: Frank Lloyd Wright, Gottfried Semper and the Chicago School" (paper delivered at Buell Center Symposium on Fallingwater, Columbia University, 8 November 1986), p. 4.

2
Roula Geraniotis, "Gottfried Semper and the Chicago School" (paper delivered at Buell Center Symposium on the German influence on American architects, Columbia University, 1988) p. 5.

3
Donald Hoffman, *The Architecture of John Wellborn Root* (Baltimore and London: Johns Hopkins University Press, 1973), p. 91. See also J. A. Chewing's entry on Root in *Macmillan Encyclopedia of Architects* (New York: Free Press, 1982), vol. 3, p. 606.

4
Geraniotis, "Gottfried Semper," p. 5.

5
Ibid., p. 11.

6
David Van Zanten, entry on Owen Jones in *Macmillan Encyclopedia of Architects,* vol. 2, p. 514.

7
Louis Sullivan, "Suggestions in Artistic Brickwork" (1910), reprint, *Prairie School Review* 4 (Second Quarter, 1967), p. 24.

8
Frank Lloyd Wright, "In the Cause of Architecture IV," *Architectural Record,* October 1927; reprinted in *In the Cause of Architecture: Essays by Frank Lloyd Wright for Architectural Record, 1908–1952,* ed. Frederick Gutheim (New York: McGraw-Hill, 1975), p. 146.

9
James F. O'Gorman, *The Architecture of Frank Furness* (Philadelphia: Philadelphia Museum of Art, 1973), pp. 33, 37.

10
Narciso Menocal, *Architecture as Nature: The Transcendentalist Idea of Louis Sullivan* (Madison: University of Wisconsin Press, 1981), pp. 7, 31.

11
Owen Jones, *The Grammar of Ornament* (1856; reprint, New York: Portland House, 1987), p. 154.

12
Ibid., p. 5.

13
Ibid., p. 95.

14
Ibid., p. 156.

15
Louis Sullivan, *A System of Architectural Ornament According with a Philosophy of Man's Power* (1924; reprint, New York: Eakins Press, 1966), text accompanying plate 3.

16
Gottfried Semper, *The Four Elements of Architecture and Other Writings,* trans. Harry Mallgrave and Wolfgang Herrmann (New York: Cambridge University Press, 1989). See in particular the prolegomena to "Style in the Technical and Tectonic Arts" (1860), p. 196.

17
Rudolf Gelpke, "Art and Sacred Drugs in the Orient," *World Cultures and Modern Art* (Munich: Bruckman, 1972), pp. 18–21. Gelpke argues after Georg Jacob and Henri Michaux that the culture of Islam has a mystical hallucinatory origin.

18
Claude Humbert, *Islamic Ornamental Design* (New York: Hastings House, 1980), pp. 13, 16, 17.

19
Frank Lloyd Wright, *Frank Lloyd Wright: Writings and Buildings,* ed. Edgar Kaufman and Ben Raeburn (New York: Horizon Press, 1960), pp. 57–58.

20
Ibid., pp. 65–66.

21
Sigfried Giedion, *Space, Time and Architecture,* 15th ed. (Cambridge, Mass.: Harvard University Press, 1967), pp. 353–354. See also p. 347 for an illustration of St. Mary's Church, Chicago, of 1833, the first all-balloon-frame building.

22
Romeo and Juliet was refaced in board and batten in 1939.

23
Kenneth Martin Kao, "Frank Lloyd Wright: Experiments in the Art of Building," *Modulus* 22 (University of Virginia, 1993), p. 77. Kao shows the wood-siding details for six successive houses, including the Gerts Double Cottage of 1902.

24
G. C. Manson, "Wright in the Nursery: The Influence of Froebel Education on the Work of Frank Lloyd Wright," *Architectural Review,* June 1953, pp. 349–351. Of the 20 Froebel "gifts," numbers 14, 15, and 17 are of particular importance since they directly involve the art of weaving. It is also interesting to note, with regard to the importance that Semper attached to music and dance, that the more advanced Froebel exercises also entail music and dance wherein the geometric-relationship "gifts" would be acted out three-dimensionally.

25
Frank Lloyd Wright, "On Building Unity Temple," in *Frank Lloyd Wright: Writings and Buildings,* p. 76.

26
Wright, *Frank Lloyd Wright: Writings and Buildings,* p. 225.

27

It is generally accepted that Wright's post facto dating of some of his early projects was not always reliable.

28

David A. Hanks, *The Decorative Designs of Frank Lloyd Wright* (New York: Dutton, 1979), p. 120. It is interesting to note that these blocks had green and red flushed glass laid into their perforations.

29

Wright was working on the Barnsdall House from 1916 to 1918 prior to the final establishment of the Olive Hill site. Subject to a tight budget, Wright elected to build the house out of brick and lath and plaster on concrete foundations. The finials, lintels, sills, and copings of the house were out of precast concrete, so-called "art-stone." See Kathryn Smith, *Frank Lloyd Wright: Hollyhock House and Olive Hill* (New York: Rizzoli, 1992), pp. 119–120.

30

It has come to light that the Millard House was not built with Wright's patent hollow-walled textile block system of 1923. In this pioneering work, the two leaves of the block were closely interlocked. See Robert L. Sweeney, *Wright in Hollywood* (Cambridge: MIT Press, 1994), pp. 20–21.

31

Wright, *Frank Lloyd Wright: Writings and Buildings,* pp. 215–216.

32

Frank Lloyd Wright, "In the Cause of Architecture. VIII. Sheet Metal and a Modern Instance," *Architectural Record,* October 1928; reprinted in *In the Cause of Architecture,* pp. 217–219.

33

M. F. Hearn, "A Japanese Inspiration for Frank Lloyd Wright's Rigid-Core High-Rise Structures," *Journal of the Society of Architectural Historians* (March 1991), p. 70.

34

Ibid. Reference to D. Seckel, *The Art of Buddhism* (New York: Crown, 1963), pp. 121–122.

35

Kathryn Smith, *Frank Lloyd Wright: Hollyhock House and Olive Hill,* relates this goal to the practice of using decorative grillage in Islamic architecture known by the term *mashrabiya*.

36

For details of these blocks, see Sweeney, *Frank Lloyd Wright in Hollywood,* pp. 189–191.

37

Frank Lloyd Wright, *An American Architecture* (New York: Horizon, 1955), p. 218.

38

See the entire issue dedicated to the work of Wright, *Architectural Forum,* January 1938, p. 79.

39

John Sergeant, *Frank Lloyd Wright's Usonian Houses* (New York: Whitney Library of Design, 1976), p. 19.

40

Jonathan Lipman, *Frank Lloyd Wright and the Johnson Wax Buildings* (New York: Rizzoli, 1986), pp. 8–12.

41

Frank Lloyd Wright, *An Autobiography* (London: Faber & Faber, 1945), p. 472.

5 Auguste Perret and Classical Rationalism

Epigraph: Leonardo Benevolo, *Storia dell'architettura moderna* (Cambridge, Mass.: MIT Press, 1971), pp. 327–331. English translation of a two-volume Italian history first published in 1960.

1

See Peter Collins, *Concrete: The Vision of a New Architecture* (London: Faber & Faber, 1959), pp. 174, 175. The otherwise impeccably consistent text is contradictory on this point. Collins insists on Claude-Marie Perret's antipathy to concrete, claiming that no works of the firm could be carried out in this material until after his death in 1905, and yet he knew only too well that 25 bis rue Franklin was executed in this material.

2

For Julien Guadet see Reyner Banham, *Theory and Design in the First Machine* (New York: Praeger, 1960).

3

See Banham, *Theory and Design in the First Machine Age,* p. 30. Of Choisy's influence on Perret, Banham writes of "Auguste Perret's transposition of wood-framing technique on to reinforced construction, [as] a procedure which he, apparently, held to be warranted by Choisy. . . . But Perret's structural methods owe a further debt than this to Choisy, and to his views on Gothic structure in particular. Gothic, as has been said, was one of Choisy's two preferred styles, because it constitutes in his eyes, the culmination of logical method in structure." Here Banham quotes Choisy to the effect that "the [Gothic] structure is the triumph of logic in art; the building becomes an organized being whose every part constitutes a living member, its form governed not by traditional models but by its function, and only its function." Later Banham continues, in the chapter dealing with the French protomodern academic succession: "The three pre-1914 buildings [25 bis rue Franklin, the rue Ponthieu garage, and the Théâtre des Champs-Elysées] depend, as Perret himself admitted, on a Choisyesque transposition of reinforced concrete into the forms and usages of wooden construction—a rectangular trabeated grid of posts and beams. This procedure which makes little use of the monolithic qualities and less of the plastic ones of the material, the assertions of Perret's followers notwithstanding, appears to have a complicated derivation" (p. 38).

4

Auguste Perret, *Contribution à une théorie de l'architecture* (Paris: Cercle d'études architecturales André Wahl, 1952), unpaginated. (First published in *Das Werk* 34–35 [February 1947]).

5

Collins, *Concrete,* p. 186.

6

For the most exhaustive recent treatment of the complex history behind the building of this theater see Dossiers du Musée d'Orsay no. 15, *1913 Le Théatre des Champs-Elysées* (Paris: Editions de la Réunion des Musées Nationaux, 1987), pp. 4–72. Particular attention should be given to Claude Loupiac's essay "Le Ballet des architectes" in which he shows how four architects were commissioned in succession: first Henri Fivax in 1906, then Roger Bouvard between 1908 and 1910, and then Henri Van de Velde and Bouvard together in 1911. Auguste Perret was asked to collaborate with Van de Velde in May of that year and shortly after was able to gain complete control over the work, following Van de Velde's resignation in July.

7

Ibid., p. 242.

8

Vittorio Gregotti, "Auguste Perret, 1874–1974: Classicism and Rationalism in Perret," *Domus,* no. 534 (May 1974), p. 19.

9

Collins, *Concrete,* p. 254.

10

Ibid., p. 217.

11

Peter Collins, "Perret, Auguste," *Macmillan Encyclopaedia of Architects* (New York: Free Press, 1982), vol. 3, p. 394.

12

Henri Bressler, "Windows on the Court," *Rassegna* 28 (1979).

13

See Bressler, "Windows on the Court." The English translation in this unpaginated appendix describes the dichotomous character of the interior space at 25 bis rue Franklin: in the following terms:

From the entrance hall the triptych doors give onto three main rooms like a miniature of the stage of the Teatro Olimpico. In the center, the room is lit by a large bow-window, which corresponds symmetrically to the entrance niche where a console stands and is (potentially) surmounted by a mirror. On the sides, the rooms split, offering oblique visual axes which reveal the apartment's largest perceptible dimensions. In the center of the main hall it appears as if there were only one large room which regresses to infinity thanks to the many mirrors laid out face to face on the small fireplaces of the dining and main rooms. In truth, here all elements are part of this spatial explosion: the diagonal position of the partitions, of doors and windows, the transparency and reflections of the double glass doors and the light channeled into the splay of the loggias which are reflected in the mirrors. Thus we stand, plunged into an almost magic, marvelous box, despite its limited size. . . . It is certainly true, however, that such a device able to multiply doors and double doors at will (there are seven double doors in the entrance gallery) turns out to be rather difficult to furnish. A few consoles, chests of drawers or clothes closets can be set against the remaining free wall spaces. . . . To ensure that this arrangement, which opens as an integral unit, might rediscover the virtues of a true apartment, Perret cut the walls back until they seem like panels, he redesigned the door springers and underscored the ensemble with the figures of the different rooms: stylobates, moldings, vegetation-motif frames; he manages to somehow reuse the entire catalogue of definitions of the traditional lodging. In short, he in no way attempted to violate the boundaries of lifestyles and their social codes of behavior: the apartment must lend itself fully to the reception ritual; it appears that even the Baroness of Staffe in person might be received in this apartment.

Once within the main hall, guests may cross through the double glass doors in proper order, with arms linked, and enter the dining room. After dinner, the gentlemen can retire to the fumoir, *while the ladies reach the "gynaeceum" of the lady-of-the-house, and, the most intimate among them, the boudoir. All present may then meet again in the main hall to delight in some sort of merry-making. The main rooms lend themselves to the reception device. All is offered to sight, multiplied by the effects of light and mirrors. Nothing keeps the guests from believing that the hall doors—access to facilities and bathrooms—do not lead to bedrooms.*

If you seek, instead, some place amenable to intimacy, suffice to close the doors and pull a curtain or two; each room, with the exception of the fumoir *(whose access runs oblique to the dining room), is completely autonomous.*

In my view this dichotomous arrangement, so precisely described by Bressler, anticipates the ambivalent but equally illusionistic devices that Louis Kahn will employ, seventy years later, in the Kimbell Art Museum at Fort Worth, Texas, when he will attempt to combine the traditional gallery of discrete rooms with open flexible loft space.

14
Bruno Reichlin, "The Pros and Cons of the Horizontal Window: The Perret-Le Corbusier Controversy," *Daidalos* 13 (September 1984), pp. 71–82.

15
Collins, *Concrete*, pp. 206–207.

16
Ibid., p. 208.

17
See Steen Eiler Rasmussen, *Experiencing Architecture* (Cambridge: MIT Press, 1964), chapter 10, "Hearing Architecture."

18
It is interesting to note that even in repetitive domestic work, as in the apartments designed for Le Havre, Perret attempted unsuccessfully to eliminate plasterwork and suspended ceilings. See Collins, *Concrete*, p. 275.

19
The following excerpts are from Perret, *Contribution à une théorie de l'architecture* (unpaginated).

20
Marie Dormoy, "Interview d'Auguste Perret sur l'Exposition internationale des arts décoratifs," *L'Amour de l'Art*, May 1925, p. 174.

21
Denis Honegger, "Auguste Perret: doctrine de l'architecture," *Techniques & Architecture* 9, nos. 1–2 (1949), p. 111.

22
Perret, *Contribution à une théorie de l'architecture.*

23
One is reminded in this of the German word for object, *Gegenstand*, meaning literally to "stand against."

24
Perret, *Contribution à une théorie de l'architecture.*

25
Paul Valéry, "The History of Amphion," in *The Collected Works of Paul Valéry*, ed. Jackson Mathews, vol. 3 (Princeton: Princeton University Press, 1960), p. 215. Valéry published *Eupalinos ou l'architecte* in 1921. In an unpublished analysis of this text (1985), Georgios I. Simeoforidis has written: "This is an important text that has not yet found its acknowledgement from and within architectural culture. Valéry's interest in architecture was a product of his own *durée* . . . architecture was Valéry's first love, an *amour* for the construction of both ships and building. Valéry was very interested in naval architecture following his other love, his *amour* for the sea, the Mediterranean sea. His philosophical . . . thought is a liaison between *construction* and *knowing*, a liaison that he finds in the architect, but also in the poet and the thinker. All are concerned with a process that has two moments: analysis and synthesis, repetition and composition. The poet is an architect of poems, the architect is a poet of buildings; both 'construct' through mental work. Valéry gives to construction a specific quality, as making and doing, *faire*. . . . It is ultimately this idea of *poiein, faire*, that could be extremely significant in architecture, especially if we understand the word construction, in the physical and mental range of its manifestation, as an act that has to have a form and a memory."

26
I am indebted for much of this to an unpublished essay on Paul Valéry by Georgios Simeoforidis, particularly for his reference to the work of the Greek architect and theoretician Panayiotis Michelis and his distinction between the tectonic/paratactic order of classicism and the monolithic/organic order of concrete. Clearly Michelis's *The Aesthetics of Concrete Architecture* deserves to be translated from the Greek and hence to be better known. Among Simeoforidis's sources it is worth mentioning *Paul Valéry Méditerranéen* by Gabriel Fauré (Paris: Les Horizons de France, 1954).

27
With the term *homo faber* (man the maker), I am alluding to the profound insights to be found in Hannah Arendt's *The Human Condition* (Chicago: University of Chicago Press, 1958), pp. 158–174. She writes: "If one permits the standards of *homo faber* to rule the finished world . . . then *homo faber* will eventually help himself to everything as though it belongs to the class of *chremata*, of use objects, so that to follow Plato's example, the wind will no longer be understood in its own right as a natural force but will be considered exclusively in accordance with human needs for warmth or refreshment—which, of course, means that the wind as something objectively given has been eliminated from human experience." Later she writes (p. 173): "If the *animal laborans* needs the help of *homo faber* to ease his labor and remove his pain and if mortals need his help to erect a home on earth, acting and speaking men need the help of *homo faber* in his highest capacity, that is, the help of the artist, of poets and historiographers, of monument-builders or writers, because without them, the only product of their activity, the story they enact and tell, would not survive at all."

28
Collins, *Concrete*, pp. 157, 158.

29
Perret, *Contribution à une théorie de l'architecture.*

30
Collins, *Concrete*, p. 163. It is ironic to say the least that this argument would come so close to paraphrasing the so called Law of Ruins promulgated by Albert Speer under the Third Reich. For Speer, however, it was reinforced concrete that was seen as the nemesis, since as far as he was concerned this material was incapable of producing sublime

ruins; hence it was forbidden to use this material in realizing the high representative buildings of the National Socialist state. The current sorry state of Le Raincy tends to mock Perret's thesis, but it fails to disprove it at a deeper level.

31
Ibid., p. 221.

32
Ibid., p. 223.

33
It is of interest that Raymond's top assistant on the Tokyo Golf Club was the Czech architect Bedrich Feuerstain, who had worked for Perret in Paris on the design of the Théâtre des Arts Décoratifs. Feuerstain also served as job captain on Raymond's Rising Sun Petroleum Company Building of 1927.

34
For details of the design and construction of this building, in collaboration with Raymond's postwar partner Ladislav Rado and the engineer Paul Weidlinger, see Antonin Raymond, *An Autobiography* (Rutland, Vermont: Charles E. Tuttle Company, 1973), pp. 211–221.

6 Mies van der Rohe: Avant-Garde and Continuity

Epigraph: Massimo Cacciari, "Mies's Classics," *Res* 16 (Autumn 1988), pp. 13, 14.

1
Cornelis van de Ven, *Space in Architecture* (Assen, The Netherlands: Van Gorcum, 1978), p. 77. Following the theories of Semper, van de Ven deals in a very instructive way with this distinction between tectonics and stereotomics: "Tectonic form embodies all skeletal frameworks, such as post and lintel construction, whereas stereotomic form refers to cases where wall and ceiling form one homogeneous mass. . . . With stereotomic Semper meant, above all, a constructive method of assembling mass in such a manner that the total plasticity was moulded in one undivided dynamic unity, such as the formal relation of arch and pier without interruption, unlike the segregate post and lintel assemblage of the tectonic method."

2
Interview with Christian Norberg-Schulz, *Architecture d'Aujourd'hui*, no. 79 (September 1958), p. 100. The priority given to the term "building" in this passage recalls the similar ideological emphasis that Hannes Meyer gave it in his Bauhaus address "Bauen" of 1928.

3
Reprinted in Philip C. Johnson, *Mies van der Rohe* (New York: Museum of Modern Art, 1947), p. 183.

4
Ibid., p. 184.

5
See Wolf Tegethoff, *Mies van der Rohe: The Villas and Country Houses* (New York: Museum of Modern Art, 1985), p. 65.

6
Werner Blaser, *Mies van der Rohe: The Art of Structure* (New York: Praeger, 1965), pp. 20–24. This seems to have been the standard adopted, even though the interior walls were plastered.

7
The full text of this letter is given in Wolf Tegethoff, *Mies van der Rohe: The Villas and Country Houses* (New York: Museum of Modern Art, 1985), p. 61.

8
Johnson, *Mies van der Rohe*, pp. 38–41.

9
Walter F. Wagner, Jr., "Ludwig Mies van der Rohe: 1886–1969," *Architectural Record* 146 (September 1969), p. 9.

10
Johnson, *Mies van der Rohe*, p. 35.

11
Peter Carter, "Mies van der Rohe: An Appreciation on the Occasion, This Month, of His 75th Birthday," *Architectural Design* 31, no. 3 (March 1961), p. 100.

12
"Mies van der Rohe: European Works," special issue of *Architectural Design* edited by Sandra Honey (London, 1986), p. 56.

13
Ibid., p. 104.

14
See Kenneth Frampton, "Modernism and Tradition in the Work of Mies van der Rohe, 1920–1968," in John Zukowsky, ed., *Mies Reconsidered: His Career, Legacy, and Disciples* (Chicago: Art Institute of Chicago, 1986), p. 45. The importance of Lilly Reich in Mies's overall development can hardly be overestimated since she seems to have brought to a dematerializing sensibility an extremely refined sense of material finish. Her presence is surely evident even in the furnishing of the Tugendhat House, which, as Franz Schulze informs us, was curtained with black raw silk and black velvet on the winter garden wall and with beige raw silk on the south wall. See Franz Schulze, *Mies van der Rohe: A Critical Biography* (Chicago and London: University of Chicago Press, 1985), p. 169.

15
Peter Blake, "A Conversation with Mies," in Richard Miller, ed., *Four Great Makers of Modern Architecture* (New York: Columbia University, 1963). Leonidov was surely as preoccupied with dematerialization as Mies; see his student thesis project for the Lenin Institute (1927) and above all his proposal for a Palace of Culture (1930), both of which feature glazed buildings that are as minimalist in their conception as Mies's glazed prisms and R. Buckminster Fuller's geodesic domes.

16
Johnson, *Mies van der Rohe,* p. 51.

17
L. Mies van der Rohe, "Address to the Union of German Plate Glass Manufacturers, March 13, 1933." This text appears in English translation in Tegethoff, *Mies van der Rohe: The Villas and Country Houses,* p. 66.

18
Eduard F. Sekler, "The Stoclet House by Josef Hoffmann," in Howard Hibbard, Henry Millon, and Milton Levine, eds., *Essays in the History of Architecture Presented to Rudolf Wittkower* (London: Phaidon, 1967), pp. 228–294.

19
See José Quetglas, "Fear of Glass: The Barcelona Pavilion," in *Architectureproduction,* ed. Joan Ockman and Beatriz Colomina (New York: Princeton Architectural Press, 1988), p. 144. Quetglas cites in the same essay one of the only firsthand critical accounts of the original pavilion, in *Cahiers d'Art* 8–9 (1929) by the Catalan critic N. M. Rubio Tuduri.

20
Robin Evans, "Mies van der Rohe's Paradoxical Symmetries," *AA Files,* no. 19 (Spring 1990), p. 113.

21
Quoted in Tegethoff, *Mies van der Rohe: The Villas and Country Houses,* p. 96. Walter Riezler's article, "Das Haus Tugendhat in Brünn," was originally published in *Die Form* 6, no. 9 (September 15, 1931), pp. 321–332.

22
Romano Guardini, as cited in Fritz Neumeyer, *The Artless Word* (Cambridge: MIT Press, 1991), p. 199. With this study, first published by Siedler Verlag, Berlin, in 1986 under the title *Mies van der Rohe: Das kunstlose Wort. Gedanken zur Baukunst,* Neumeyer totally revolutionizes our knowledge of Mies's ideological roots. Through painstaking research into archival material held in the Museum of Modern Art, New York, in the Library of Congress in Washington, and in the Special Collections department of the University of Illinois, Chicago, he has been able to show how Mies's reading was far more extensive than had

been thought hitherto and the way in which he was influenced by two thinkers in particular: by Raoul Francé, whose 1908 protoecological "plasmatic" view of universal harmony was an overt attack upon the Promethean, hyperindustrializing thrust of Wilhelmine Germany, and by the Bauhäusler Siegfried Ebeling, whose book *Der Raum als Membran* (Space as Membrane) was published in Dessau in 1926. This last, affiliated with anthroposophical cosmology, argued for a dematerialized organic, biological architecture, anticipatory in certain respects of R. Buckminster Fuller's Dymaxion philosophy. To these writers must be added two interrelated and even more influential figures as far as Mies was concerned, the philosopher-theologian Romano Guardini and the architect Rudolf Schwarz, both of whom were Catholic intellectuals involved in the Quickborn Catholic youth movement which had its meeting place at the Castle Rothenfels, near Frankfurt. These two men edited the magazine *Die Schildgenossen* (Comrades-in-Arms) to which Mies would make a contribution.

23
See Philip Johnson, *Mies van der Rohe*, 3d ed. (New York: Museum of Modern Art and New York Graphic Society, 1978), p. 195. Johnson gives the entire text of "Die neue Zeit," a speech Mies delivered to the Viennese Werkbund in 1930 and published in *Die Form* in 1932. Mies first became acquainted with the thinking of Guardini and Schwarz through Schwarz's essays in this periodical. Of the latter Neumeyer writes: "The position Schwarz assumed in respect to the 'new things' of his times resolved those very contradictions that Mies had been unable to reconcile theoretically in his unilaterally expressed manifestos. Schwarz did not deny that the 'new world' with its technical potential had its own sort of magnitude, but he professed 'a great fear of things to come,' particularly the tendency of the times to 'become abstract'; this, in his eyes, made 'grace, charm, playfulness, love, and humility' impossible. The word 'rationalization' seemed to him 'one of the most stupid slogans of our time' because it conveys only a mechanical, not a spiritual message. Mies, who had expressed similar notions, albeit in milder terms, could here only have found encouragement." (*The Artless Word*, p. 164.)

In order to appreciate the closeness of these three men one need only remark on Guardini's warm appraisal of Rudolf Schwarz's Corpus Christi church completed in Mies's home town of Aachen in 1930. On this occasion Guardini wrote: "The properly formed emptiness of space and plane is not merely a negation of pictorial representation but rather its antipode. It relates to it as silence relates to the word. Once man has opened himself up to it, he experiences a strange presence." (Quoted in ibid., p. 165.)

In 1958 Mies would write the introduction to Rudolf Schwarz's book *The Church Incarnate,* which had first appeared in German, with an introduction by Guardini, in 1938. Mies and Schwarz publicly acknowledged their mutual respect at a later date when Schwarz gave a birthday address to Mies, "An Mies van der Rohe," in 1961 and Mies made a contribution two years later to the Schwarz memorial catalogue published by the Akademie der Künste, Berlin.

24
See the translation of this text in Neumeyer, *The Artless Word*, pp. 246–247.

25
The original text of Mies's Inaugural Address as Director of Architecture at Armour Institute of Technology (1938) is given in Johnson, *Mies van der Rohe* (1947), pp. 191–195.

26
Blaser, *Mies van der Rohe: The Art of Structure*, p. 10.

27
Peter Carter, "Mies van der Rohe: An Appreciation," p. 97.

28
Reprinted in Johnson, *Mies van der Rohe* (1947), p. 203.

29
Peter Carter, "Mies van der Rohe: An Appreciation," p. 106.

30
For a discussion of Mies's choice of the German vernacular and its relation to the traditional *Fachwerkbauten,* see "Epilogue: Thirty Years After," in Johnson, *Mies van der Rohe* (1947), pp. 205–211.

31
Colin Rowe, "Neoclassicism and Modern Architecture," Part II, *Oppositions* 1 (September 1973), p. 18.

32
One cannot help being reminded here of Heinrich Hübsch's St. Cyriacus Church, Bülach, of 1837 where exposed tectonic brickwork in wall, arch, and vault occupies the upper part of the volume while the lower walls are finished in plaster, although Mies was surely not influenced by this example of partial repression and expression.

33
Peter Carter, "Mies van der Rohe: An Appreciation," p. 108.

34
Colin Rowe, "Neoclassicism and Modern Architecture," p. 21.

35
For a comprehensive treatment of the work of Ad Reinhardt see Lucy R. Lippard, *Ad Reinhardt* (New York: Abrams, 1981). For a summation of his theoretical position see *Art-as-Art: The Selected Writings of Ad Reinhardt,* ed. Barbara Rose (New York: Viking Press, 1975). A perceptive introduction to Reinhardt's spirituality is given in the following gloss by the editor: Reinhardt's writings on religion are both ambiguous and provocative. They reflect the difficulty the modern artist experienced in finding a "spiritual" subject in a secular age. Raised a Lutheran, Reinhardt disclaimed the many religious epithets attributed to his ascetic stance, although he must have been influenced by Protestant iconoclasm. Undoubtedly one of the attractions Eastern art held for him was that much of it, such as Islamic decoration and tantric mandalas, was both abstract and concretely spiritual. For in Islamic and Buddhist cultures, the art object is not only an object of contemplation but an aid to meditation. In these cultures, the purpose of art is still religious and spiritual, although art need not glorify any specific deity or his image. That art might serve as an abstract imageless icon, an aid to the cultivation of a state of consciousness simultaneously self-conscious and detached from worldly concerns, was an idea Reinhardt began to develop through his contact with non-Western art. Eventually he posited his conception of an art renewed in "spirituality" in its rigorous discipline and unchanging form against the demands of the market for a decorative art and of the media for a sensational art. The black square paintings are thus like the changeless Buddha image Reinhardt studied: static, lifeless, timeless—a form of the Absolute. The search for the timeless and the absolute, begun with Plato and the various modern forms of neo-Platonic idealism from Kant to Mondrian, ended for Reinhardt with the abstract, black "mandala." As for his use of the Greek cross in the square black paintings, Reinhardt disclaimed any specific religious imagery. In an interview with Walter Gaudnek, he discounted symbolism as his reason for adopting the cross image. "I never had . . . the cross as a symbol in mind in my paintings. . . . I want to give it no meaning."

Reinhardt's reading in Oriental religions took him from the monism of Judeo-Christian traditions to the polarities of Eastern thought, in which an idea cannot be conceived without immediately calling up its opposite. In this context, the cross became an ideal image for expressing the polarities of horizontal and vertical.

Reinhardt was uncomfortable with the notion that an artist should hire himself to decorate the chapels of a religion in which he did not believe, and felt that such commissions were part of the general corruption that had entered the art world when patronage (in this case religious) became a possibility for the avant-garde artist.

If one can draw conclusions regarding Reinhardt's fragmentary writing on the subject, it appears that he preferred the academy or the "monastery" of art to the museum or the "temple" of art, since he considered art a discipline and not a religion.

36
See Kazimir Malevich, *The Non-Objective World* (Chicago: Paul Theobald & Co., 1959), p. 25. This was translated from the German by Howard Dearstyne with an introduction by Ludwig Hilberseiner; one hardly needs more proof of Mies's Suprematist affinities than the association of Dearstyne and Hilberseimer with this publication.

37
Peter Blake, *The Master Builders* (New York: Knopf, 1960), p. 207.

38

Graeme Shankland, "Architect of the 'Clear and Reasonable': Mies van der Rohe," *The Listener,* 15 October 1959, pp. 620–622.

7 Louis Kahn: Modernization and the New Monumentality, 1944–1972

Epigraph: Maria Bottero, "Organic and Rational Morphology in the Architecture of Louis Kahn," *Zooiac* 17 (1967), pp. 244, 245.

1

Sigfried Giedion, José Luis Sert, and Fernand Léger, "Nine Points on Monumentality," in Sigfried Giedion, *Architecture, You and Me* (Cambridge: Harvard University Press, 1958), pp. 48–52.

2

See Paul Zucker, ed., *The New Architecture and City Planning* (New York: Philosophical Library, 1944).

3

Louis I. Kahn, "Monumentality," in Zucker, ed., *The New Architecture and City Planning,* pp. 578–579.

4

Ibid., pp. 579–580.

5

Ibid., p. 580.

6

Ibid., pp. 581–582. However, as Pol Abraham was to observe, the cross ribs of a Gothic vault are at times structurally redundant and are deployed for formal reasons and to facilitate assembly. See Pol Abraham, *Viollet-le-Duc et le rationalisme médiéval* (Paris: Vincent Fréal, 1934).

7

For details of this construction see David P. Billington, *Robert Maillart and the Art of Reinforced Concrete* (Cambridge, Mass.: Architectural History Foundation and MIT Press, 1990), pp. 28–29.

8

Information given by Anne Griswold Tyng to the author in February 1993. When Tyng was in Rome in the fall of 1953 she showed the City Tower project to Nervi, who regarded the proposed structure as a three-dimensional version of his two-dimensional "folded" and triangulated concrete structures.

9

Louis Kahn, "Form and Design," *Architectural Design* 31, no. 4 (April 1961), pp. 145–148. Kahn's distinction between form and design was to reverse in many respects the emphasis that Mies van der Rohe placed upon the "how" of architecture rather than the "what." That the "what" was of more importance to Kahn was largely due to his profound commitment to the institution, or what he called an "availability" in a civic and spiritual sense. In "Form and Design" he would write: "Form is 'what', Design is 'how'. Form is impersonal. Design belongs to the Designer. Design is a circumstantial act, how much money there is available, the site, the client, the extent of knowledge. Form has nothing to do with circumstantial conditions. In architecture it characterizes a harmony of spaces good for a certain activity of man."

To these distinctions Maria Bottero would add the following illuminating gloss in her essay "Organic and Rational Morphology in the Architecture of Louis Kahn": "The Psyche is the source of what a thing wants to be . . . he means that life (or the drive towards *being*) runs through us but does not belong to us individually, so that man finds himself curiously decentralized with respect to his own work: which as Kahn himself says, is an achievement all the greater, the less it pertains to *Design* (i.e. the contingent, measurable, and subjective) and the more it belongs to *Form* (i.e. the transcendental, immeasurable, and universal). Between *Form* and *Design,* the creative process takes place as an indefinitely repeated shuttling process, and by this the plot of the work is laboriously woven; a plot which is a strip stretched across the non-homogeneous, the non-continuous, or in the end—the unconscious."

10

Anne Tyng manifests that this expressive dilemma was overcome to some extent by the invention of post-tensioned, reinforced concrete in which the steel rods, inserted into tubes cast in situ, effectively articulated the tensile reinforcement in relation to the compressive concrete. In this instance the tectonically expressive potential depends on the necessity of leaving the restraining plates and tensioning bolts exposed during the course of construction.

11

For this essay see Theo. B. White, ed., *Paul Philippe Cret: Architect and Teacher* (Philadelphia: Art Alliance Press, 1973), pp. 61–65.

12

In fact there is no change in the compressive stress in Viollet-le-Duc's support, and the tapering in this instance has two functions; first to express the idea of the statical force, and second to facilitate constructional joints and bearing.

13

See Hannes Meyer's inaugural address as the director of the Bauhaus in 1928, given under the title "Bauen" (Building), in which he itemized a whole range of explicitly modern, nontraditional man-made materials such as ferro-concrete, wire, glass, aluminum, asbestos, plywood, ripolin, silicon steel, cold glue, casein, cork, rolled glass, and synthetic rubber, leather, resin, horn, and wood. See Claude Schnaidt, *Hannes Meyer: Buildings, Writings and Projects* (London: Tiranti, 1965), p. 95.

14

Kahn, "Monumentality," p. 587. Kahn's interest in pioneering new materials was to continue throughout his life. See in particular his use of "pewter finish" stainless steel cladding for the Yale Center for British Art, posthumously completed by Pellecchia & Meyers, Architects. This dull, variable surface is produced by omitting final baths in the fabricating process. That the revetment is a skin, a *Bekleidung* in the Semperian sense, is indicated by the weathering details employed throughout.

15

Louis Kahn, "Toward a Plan for Midtown Philadelphia," *Perspecta* 2 (1953), p. 23.

16

Kahn, "Monumentality," pp. 581–582.

17

As Konrad Wachsmann shows in his book *The Turning Point of Building* (New York: Reinhold, 1961), this form of tetrahedral spatial geometry had first been explored by Alexander Graham Bell in his trussed kites of the turn of the century (see pp. 29, 30) and in the 80-foot tetrahedral space frame tower erected on Bell's estate in Canada in 1907. According to Robert Mark and Fuller himself (see *The Dymaxion World of Buckminster Fuller* [New York: Anchor/Doubleday, 1973], p. 57), Fuller first load-tested a tetrahedron/octahedron truss at the University of Michigan in 1953. Fuller patented this combination as the Octet truss and a demonstration truss 100 feet long, 35 feet wide, and 4 feet deep was exhibited at the Museum of Modern Art, New York, in 1959. The exceptional structural efficiency of this device is borne out by the following description: "In Fuller's three-way-grid Octet Truss system, loads applied to any one point are distributed radially outward in six directions and are immediately frustrated by the finite hexagonal circles entirely enclosing the six-way distributed load." One should also note that this truss was composed of struts alone without any special hub joints.

Kahn's relationship to R. Buckminster Fuller was complex. Both men were teaching at Yale University in the early fifties. Despite Tyng's patent interest in Fuller at the time, Kahn justly wanted to distance himself from Fuller's position in retrospect, as he was to make clear in his 1972 interview with John Cook and Heinrich Klotz, when referring to the Yale Art Gallery he pointed out that Fuller's structural concepts were incapable of producing a flat ceiling. See John W. Cook and Heinrich Klotz, *Conversations with Architects* (New York: Praeger, 1973), p. 212.

18

See Richard Saul Wurman and Eugene Feldman, *The Notebooks and Drawings of Louis I. Kahn* (Cambridge: MIT Press, 1973), unpaginated.

19
Louis Kahn, "Order in Architecture," *Perspecta* 4 (1957), p. 64. In a 1957 brochure, published by the Universal Atlas Cement Company, which was the sponsor of the main version of the City Tower proposal, we learn that the tower was projected as rising to a height of 616 feet, with principal floor levels at every 66 feet, and standing on a podium measuring 700 by 700 feet. This last comprised three levels, an elevated pedestrian plaza, a shopping concourse at grade, and a service/parking level beneath. The main tetrahedral floor slabs were 3 feet deep with spans up to 60 feet from one diagonal strut to the next. In a descriptive text Kahn and Tyng would write: "The skin of a tower is usually regarded as an enclosure playing no part in the structural concept of the building. . . . This is rationalized into an acceptance of the skin as only skin. . . . Instead this intermediary element between the building and the outside forces should be conceived as the beginning of a structural reaction against these forces. In this tower the many positioned sun louvres, related to the growth of the building, act an initial break-up of sun, wind and temperature change . . . out of this purposeful design comes a beautiful tracery texture with everchanging light and shade."

20
See Bruno Taut's *Die Stadtkrone* (Jena: Eugen Diederichs, 1919).

21
Kahn, "Order in Architecture," p. 69. The reference to "Brutalist" in the previous sentence refers of course to the British New Brutalist movement, to which the art gallery was related by such critics as Reyner Banham. See Banham, *The New Brutalism* (New York: Reinhold, 1966); also his "The New Brutalism," *The Architectural Review,* December 1955, pp. 355–362. Important not only for Banham's critique of Kahn but also for his neo-Palladian analysis of the work of Peter and Alison Smithson.

22
Kahn, "Order in Architecture," p. 67.

23
William Huff, "Louis Kahn: Sorted Reflections and Lapses in Familiarities," *Little Journal* (Society of Architectural Historians, New York Chapter) 5, no. 1 (September 1981), p. 15.

24
Ibid., p. 12.

25
See Walter McQuade, "Architect Louis Kahn and His Strong-Boned Structures," *Architectural Forum* 107, no. 4 (October 1957), pp. 134–143. William Huff comments on the typical Kahnian use of the term "invade" in this comment. Clearly Kahn had in mind the column and (screen) wall arrangements in Mies's Barcelona Pavilion. See Huff's memoir in the *Little Journal* above.

26
Donald Appleyard, Kevin Lynch, and John R. Myer, *The View from the Road* (Cambridge: MIT, 1964).

27
In Romaldo Giurgola and Jaimini Mehta, *Louis I. Kahn* (Boulder, Colorado: Westview Press, 1975), p. 224.

28
Louis Kahn, "The Animal World," *Canadian Art* 19, no. 1 (January/February 1962), p. 51.

29
Heinz Ronner, Sharad Jhaveri, and Alessandro Vasella, *Louis I. Kahn: Complete Works, 1935–74* (Boulder, Colorado: Westview Press, 1977), pp. 31, 29.

30
Ibid., p. 29.

31
Kahn, "Toward a Plan for Midtown Philadelphia," p. 17.

32
Kahn, "Order in Architecture," p. 61.

33
Alexandra Tyng, *Beginnings: Louis I. Kahn's Philosophy of Architecture* (New York: Wiley & Sons, 1984), p. 79.

34
Giurgola and Mehta, *Louis I. Kahn,* p. 187.

35
Nell E. Johnson, ed., *Light Is the Theme: Louis I. Kahn and the Kimbell Art Museum* (Fort Worth, Texas, 1975), p. 38.

36
Architectural Forum, October 1957, quoted in McQuade, "Architect Louis Kahn and His Strong-Boned Structures," p. 142.

37
Louis Kahn, foreword to *Carlo Scarpa architetto poeta* (London: Royal Institute of British Architects, Heinz Gallery, 1974).

38
Frank Lloyd Wright, *An Autobiography* (London: Faber & Faber, 1945), pp. 409–410.

39
Kahn, "Form and Design," p. 151.

40
Ronner, Jhaveri, and Vasella, *Louis I. Kahn: Complete Works,* p. 111.

41
Ibid., p. 140.

42
Louis Kahn, "Louis Kahn," *Perspecta* 7 (1961), p. 11.

43
It is likely that this entry was made after receiving from Colin Rowe Rudolf Wittkower's book *Architectural Principles in the Age of Humanism* (1949). See David De Long, "The Mind Opens to Realizations," in *Louis I. Kahn: In the Realm of Architecture* (Los Angeles: Museum of Contemporary Art; New York: Rizzoli, 1991), p. 59.

44
Marcello Angrisani, "Louis Kahn e la storia," *Edilizia Moderna,* no. 86 (1965), pp. 83–93.

45
Kahn, "Louis Kahn," p. 18.

46
See August E. Kommendant, *18 Years with Architect Louis I. Kahn* (Englewood, N.J.: Aloray, 1975), pp. 41–73. It would seem that Kommendant played a major role in the evolution of the first section for the Salk labs, devising the 100-foot-span, prefabricated, prestressed, box-truss girders carrying 50-foot-span prestressed folded plates over the laboratories in the other direction. These trusses were 9 feet deep, as was the upper floor.

47
Alexandra Tyng, *Beginnings,* p. 171.

48
This original relationship to the landscape has recently become compromised by a rather bulky addition to the campus.

49
Martin Heidegger, "Building, Dwelling, Thinking," in *Poetry, Language, Thought* (New York: Harper & Row, 1971), p. 154. For an exposition on the relation between Kahn's architecture and Heidegger's thought see Christian Norberg-Schulz, "Kahn, Heidegger and the Language of Architecture," *Oppositions* 18 (1979), pp. 29–47.

50
Ronner, Jhaveri, and Vasella, *Louis I. Kahn: Complete Works,* p. 345.

51
Johnson, ed., *Light Is the Theme,* p. 34.

52
Ibid., p. 22.

53
Ibid., p. 22.

54

Huff, "Louis Kahn," p. 16. Kahn was particularly sensitive to the weathering of wall surfaces in his work. Thus in defending the blank brick facade to the Yale Art Gallery, he was to tell Klotz and Cook, "A wall is a wall. I considered rain as important to the wall, so I introduced those ledges to the wall at intervals. I could have left the wall bare just for monumentality." See Cook and Klotz, *Conversations with Architects,* p. 179.

55

Johnson, ed., *Light Is the Theme,* p. 44.

56

Huff, "Louis Kahn," p. 29.

57

See Patricia Cummings Loud, *The Art Museums of Louis I. Kahn* (Durham: Duke University Press, 1989), pp. 135–150.

58

Doug Suisman, "The Design of the Kimbell: Variations on a Sublime Archetype," *Design Book Review,* Winter 1987, p. 38.

8 Jørn Utzon: Transcultural Form and the Tectonic Metaphor

Epigraph: Philip Drew, *The Third Generation: The Changing Meaning of Architecture* (New York: Praeger, 1972), pp. 44–46.

1

Jørn Utzon, "Platforms and Plateaus: The Ideas of a Danish Architect," *Zodiac* 10 (1962), p. 116. It is interesting to note in this regard the early influence of the Danish painter Carl Kylberg on Utzon and the fact that Kylberg was involved with Indian philosophy. See Henrik Sten Møller's "Jørn Utzon on Architecture," *Living Architecture* (Copenhagen) no. 8 (1989), ed. Per Nagel. This being a conversation between Sten Møller and the architect. In this interview Utzon also reveals his strong affinity for the architecture of Luis Barragán.

2

Utzon, "Platforms and Plateaus," p. 116.

3

Bruno Taut, *Die Stadtkrone* (Jena: Eugen Diederichs, 1919).

4

Steen Eiler Rasmussen, *Experiencing Architecture* (London: Chapman and Hall, 1959), p. 169. "Use few or no shaped bricks. Do not copy details, make them yourself from the material . . . the style is created by the material, the subject, the time and the man."

5

Sverre Fehn and Per Feld, *The Thought of Construction* (New York: Rizzoli, 1983), pp. 36–43.

6

See Lisbeth Balslev Jørgensen's entry on P. V. Jensen-Klint in *Macmillan Encyclopedia of Architects,* vol. 2 (New York: Free Press, 1982), p. 497.

7

Robert Bartholomew, "Jørn Utzon: His Work and Ideas" (unpublished thesis, University of New South Wales, Australia, 1981), p. 92. See also Jørn Utzon, Royal Gold Medal address, *RIBA Journal,* October 1978, p. 427.

8

Kjeld Helm-Petersen, "Jørn Utzon: A New Personality," *Zodiac* 5 (1959), pp. 70–105.

9

Bartholomew, "Jørn Utzon," p. 92: Michael Tomaszewski in an interview with Robert Bartholomew. See also the interview with Richard Le Plastrier in the same text, p. 93: "If you look at the beams in the Opera House over the concourse and see the change in section you start to understand that they are like the hulls of the boats."

10

Utzon was in Stockholm from 1942 to 1945, where he encountered Osvald Sirén's books on Chinese architecture. See Tobias Faber's essay in *Jørn Utzon: Houses in Fredensborg* (Berlin: Ernst & Sohn, 1991), p. 7.

11

Ibid. Faber cites two early housing schemes that he designed together with Utzon in 1945 and 1948 respectively; one for Bellahøj in Copenhagen and the other for Boras in Sweden.

12

Jørn Utzon and Tobias Faber, "Tendenze: Notidens Arkitektur," *Arkitekten* (Copenhagen, 1947), pp. 63–69.

13

Acceptera (Stockholm: Tidem, 1931; reprinted 1980). This was an anonymously authored polemical statement arising out of the 1930 Stockholm exhibition. Written by E. G. Asplund, Gregor Paulson, et al., it was in fact a series of militant position papers in relation to an emerging welfare state policy on architecture and design.

14

Utzon and Faber, "Tendenze."

15

D'Arcy Wentworth Thompson, *On Growth and Form,* ed. J. T. Bonner (Cambridge: Cambridge University Press, 1971). First published in 1917, the book was expanded and revised in 1942.

16

Bernard Rudolfsky, *Architecture without Architects* (New York: Museum of Modern Art, 1965).

17

See Margit Staber, "Hans Scharoun: ein Beitrag zum organischen Bauen," *Zodiac* 10 (1963). Scharoun was born and brought up in Bremen. While icebergs are not cited in this piece, Scharoun nonetheless refers to his Philharmonie in Berlin as his "Nordic" theater.

18

Bartholomew, "Jørn Utzon," p. 8.

19

Jørn Utzon, "Own Home at Hellebaek, Denmark," *Byggekunst* 5 (1952), p. 83. "When some clients of Mies objected to the doors continuing to the ceiling, on the grounds of their warping, Mies retorted, 'Then I won't build.' Here, an essential principle of the structure had been put into question and in such a case he wouldn't budge." Utzon, as cited in Bartholomew, "Jørn Utzon."

20

Utzon, "Platforms and Plateaus," p. 114.

21

Jørn Utzon, "Elineberg," *Zodiac* 5 (1959), p. 86.

22

Adolf Loos, "Ornament and Crime" (1908), in *The Architecture of Adolf Loos* (London: Arts Council of Great Britain, 1985), p. 100.

23

Adolf Loos, "Architecture" (1910), in *The Architecture of Adolf Loos.*

24

See Else Glahn, "Chinese Building Standards in the 12th Century," *Scientific American,* May 1981, pp. 162–173. See also by the same author, "Yingzao Fashi: Chinese Building Standards in the Song Dynasty," in Paula Behrens and Anthony Fisher, eds., *The Building of Architecture,* Via, no. 7 (Philadelphia: University of Pennsylvania; Cambridge: MIT Press, 1984), pp. 89–101.

25

Peter Meyers, in Bartholomew, "Jørn Utzon," p. 112. Utzon was introduced to the *Yingzao fashi* by Professor Liang, whom he met in the Danish Academy in Peking (Utzon, interview with Robert Bartholomew, ibid., p. 44).

26

Cobra, founded in 1948, saw itself as a continuation of the prewar international Surrealist movement. As such it rejected rational Western culture, which it associated with the nightmare of the Second World War. Led by Dutch and Danish artists, the movement drew participants from Belgium, France, England, Germany, and Sweden. While the name Cobra was derived from the first letters of the capital cities in which its major members lived and worked, Copenhagen, Brussels, and Amsterdam, the acronym Cobra had other connotations, to wit the reference to a snake that was both deadly and holy. As Willemijn Stokvis has written in his 1987 study of Cobra, *An International Movement in Art after the Second World War:* "Wishing to reach the very source of human creativity, they took their examples from those forms of art which appeared not to have been tainted with the rules and conventions of the Western World: from, for example, primitive peoples with their totems and their magic signs, from Eastern calligraphy, from prehistoric art and from the art of the Middle Ages." Intimations of this interest and work can be found in the prewar work of the Danish sculptor Ejer Bille, such as his *Mask Fortegn* (Mask, Sign) of 1936. Aside from Jørn, the Danes Henry Heerup and Carl-Henning Pederson played major roles in this movement. A number of architects were, as it were, on the fringes, including Thone and Erik Ahlsen of Sweden and the Dutch architect Aldo van Eyck. See also *Cobra 1948–51,* ed. Christian Dotremont (Paris: Jean-Michel Place, 1980).

27
One of Wright's early sectional sketches for the Guggenheim Museum is inscribed with the title ziggurat. On one drawing, however, Wright will also employ the term Taruggiz, to indicate that the form had indeed been derived from an inversion of a ziggurat.

28
See Mircea Eliade's *The Sacred and the Profane* (New York: Harcourt, Brace & World, 1959). Eliade illustrates the concept of the *axis mundi* with the sacred pole of the Kwakiutl tribe of British Columbia, for whom the *axis mundi* is "the trunk of a cedar tree, thirty to thirty-five feet high, over half of which projects through the roof. This pillar plays a primary part in the ceremonies; it confers a cosmic structure on the house" (p. 36). Elsewhere he writes, "The historian of religion encounters other homologies that presuppose more developed symbolism . . . such, for example, is the assimilation of the belly on the womb to a cave, of the intestines to a labyrinth, of breathing to weaving, of veins and arteries to the sun and moon, of the backbone to the *axis mundi*" (p. 169). See also Joseph Rykwert, *The Idea of a Town* (Cambridge: MIT Press, 1988).

29
See Faber's essay in *Jørn Utzon: Houses in Fredensborg,* p. 6.

30
Ibid., p. 7.

31
Utzon, "Elineberg," p. 90.

32
One should note that the Danish engineer Pove Ahm of the Ove Arup Partnership served as the structural consultant on the Højstrup High School and also on the Bank Melli and to some extent even the Sydney Opera House. Ahm was also a close personal friend of Utzon.

33
Utzon, "Platforms and Plateaus," p. 131.

34
Utzon will return to his parti for the Zurich Opera House in his 1965 entry for the Wolfsburg Theater competition.

35
Pol Abraham, *Viollet-le-Duc et le rationalisme médiéval* (Paris: Vincent Fréal & Cie., 1934).

36
See Bartholomew, "Jørn Utzon," p. 168. See also Pat Westcott, *The Sydney Opera House* (Sydney: Ure Smith, 1968), p. 132.

37
Robin Boyd, "A Night at the Opera House," *Architecture Plus,* August 1973, pp. 49–54. This text, written just before Boyd's untimely death in 1972, reasserts the argument that the point was too narrow to place the two halls side by side.

38
Ove Arup, "Sydney Opera House," in *Architectural Design,* March 1965, p. 140. Between 1959 and 1965 the shell structure of the opera house went through ten different versions. See *Sydney Opera House* (Sydney: Sydney Opera House Trust, 1988), a reprint of the technical report by Ove Arup & Partners that first appeared in *The Structural Engineer* in March 1969.

39
John Yeomans, *The Other Taj Mahal* (London, 1968), p. 58. See also Shelly Indyk and Susan Rich, "The Sydney Opera House as Envisaged by Jørn Utzon," unpublished thesis.

40
Arup, "Sydney Opera House," p. 142.

41
Ove Arup & Partners clearly played a major role in the design and realization of the entire structure, not only Arup himself but also such serious engineers as Pove Ahm, Jack Zunz, and the then tyro engineer Peter Rice. In a letter to the author (October 3, 1990) Sir Jack Zunz of the Ove Arup partnership writes: "Utzon was a most inspiring man to work with. He was probably the most inspirational architect I have met. Walking down a street with him was like seeing the world anew. His visual perception and sensitivity is unique and astounding. He always joked about his shortcomings in the use of the English language, yet he used words to conjure up visual images in the most inventive and evocative ways. While my admiration for his gifts are unbounded, there are *buts.* . . . "

As far as Zunz is concerned, Utzon, contrary to his claims, never solved the problem of converting a 3,000-seat concert hall into a 2,000-seat opera house, and his overingenious unrealized curtain wall devised for the space beneath the shell vaults would remain for Zunz unbuildable. For a more generous assessment of Zunz's experience of working on Sydney, see his "Sydney Opera House Revisited," a lecture given at the Royal College of Art, London, in 1988.

42
Jørn Utzon, "The Sydney Opera House," *Zodiac* 14 (1965), p. 49.

43
It is important to note, as Alex Popov does in a letter to the author (May 25, 1992), that Utzon's "retreat" from Sydney was accompanied by an intensity of output in the tectonic sense not seen since Nervi. To prove his point Popov cites the Kuwait parliament, Farum Town Center, Bagsvaerd Church, the Zurich Opera, and the project for a theater in Beirut. He writes: "I think that after the opera house debacle an intensely feverish period of creative activity ensued which was to reveal that he really did have all the solutions to the opera house, contrary to commonly held opinion in Sydney that he did not know how to solve the acoustics or the glass or that he was naive in structure."

44
Bartholomew, "Jørn Utzon," p. 207.

45
For a detailed gloss of Heidegger's concept of the Fourfold see Vincent Vycinas, *Earth and Gods: An Introduction to the Philosophy of Martin Heidegger* (The Hague: Martinus Nijhoff, 1969), in particular pp. 224–237. Vycinas writes: "The foursome (Geviert) is the interplay of earth, sky, god and men as mortals. In this interplay the world as openness is stirred up in the sense of being opened. World is not something which is dynamic, but is dynamism itself. This dynamism is the coming-forward from concealment into revelation—it is an event of truth. Event, again, indicated not merely a taking place in time, but the becoming what one is, the entering into one's own self. In German 'eigen' is 'our' and 'Er-eignis' is not only an 'event' but also the 'entering-into-one's-own-self' by gathering oneself into unity of self-possession."

46
The author is indebted to Shun-Xun Nan of Beijing University for this information. In a letter to the author (February 10, 1993) he writes: "The stepped gable wall and pitched roof of the Bagsvaerd Church and its wall/opening relationship is reminiscent of those in South China. . . . These are popular in Anhui, Zhejiang and Jiangsu provinces. . . . The grand open shed of the National Assembly building in Kuwait reminds me of the open shed or pavilion type of open hall which is the center of the house in the South, where ancestral worship takes place and where the elders meet friends and the younger generation."

47
It is interesting to note in this context the mythical role played by boating in Viking society, reflected in the archaic stone ships staked out in rocks in various parts of Denmark, at Lindholm Hoje near Nørresundby, at Hojlyngen near Ehesbjerg, and at Glarendrup in North Funen. See P. V. Glob, *Denmark: An Archaeological History from the Stone Age to the Vikings* (Ithaca: Cornell University Press, 1971).

48
These saplings were in fact planted by Utzon himself at his own personal expense.

49
Mention should also be made in this regard of Sigurd Lewerentz's Malmö Cemetery chapel, completed in 1945. A very comparable, dryly constructed tectonic is evident in this work, with its tiled monopitched roofs and trabeated portico. See G. E. Kidder Smith's *Sweden Builds: Its Modern Architecture and Land Policy: Background, Development and Contribution* (New York: A. Bonnier, 1950), pp. 174–175, and Janne Ahlin's *Sigurd Lewerentz, Architect* (Cambridge: MIT Press, 1987).

50
See Bartholomew, "Jørn Utzon," p. 422. See also Svend Simonsen, *Bagsvaerd Church* (Bagsvaerd Parochial Church Council, 1978). This pamphlet, edited by the pastor of the church, carries an interview between Jørn Utzon and Per Jensen in which Utzon makes a number of revealing statements about his approach to the design, including the following: "We discussed back and forth whether to place our altar in the middle of the floor, and we got afraid of that—[of] people looking in each other's eyes, while centering their thoughts on, for example, a funeral. We gave that up. We chose a certain broad angle toward a place which is not so stagelike, but where what's going on happens lengthwise. That's why we ended up with a broad room."

This text also gives certain dimensions and technical details. The concrete frames vary in height from 4.5 to 7.56 meters while the aisles between them are 2.45 meters wide. The shell vaults, spanning 17.35 meters, are made of special concrete sprayed onto wire mesh yielding a thickness that varies from 80 to 100 millimeters. These rough-cast, timber-boarded shells are asphalted on the outside and covered with rock wool insulation. The earthwork and altar flagstones are of precast white concrete, while the altar screen is made of Flensborg bricks placed edgewise in a triangular pattern so as to symbolize the Trinity.

51
Of Utzon's direct influence mention needs to be made of Rafael Moneo, who assisted Utzon on the initial designs for the Sydney Opera House. Others of a slightly younger generation include Rick Le Plastrier, who aside from practicing on his own account now teaches at the University of Hobart in Tasmania, and Alex Popov, Utzon's direct pupil and one time son-in-law who now works for himself in Sydney. Popov worked on the detailing of Bagsvaerd when he was in Utzon's office. His most recent work, a house built in the Walter Burley Griffin suburb of Castlecrag, displays something of Utzon's influence. See *Vogue Living,* April 1990. For Le Plastrier's work as a "tectonic" teacher see Rory Spence, "Constructive Education," *The Architectural Review,* July 1989, pp. 27–33.

52
Jørn Utzon, "Additive Arkitektur," *Arkitektur* (Copenhagen) 14, no. 1. (1970).

53
Jørn Utzon, "The Importance of Architects," in Denys Lasdun, *Architecture in an Age of Skepticism* (New York: Oxford University Press, 1984), p. 222.

54
There is an uncanny resemblance between the roof of the Kuwait National Assembly (1980) and Boris Podrecca's Kika supermarket built in Wiener Neustadt, Vienna, in 1985. See *Parametro,* March 1987, pp. 44–47.

9   Carlo Scarpa and the Adoration of the Joint

Epigraph: Gianni Vattimo, Turin Conference with Pietro di Rossi, c. 1987.

1
For the parameters of Scarpa's brief, given to him by Giuseppe Mazzariol who was then the director of the foundation, see Giuseppe Mazzariol, "A Work of Carlo Scarpa: The Restoration of an Ancient Venetian Palace," *Zodiac* 13 (1964), pp. 218–219. The relevant passage reads: "The ground floor of the seventeenth-century Querini Stampalia palace had been devastated in the last century by a vaguely neoclassic scenic arrangement with ornamental colonnades which completely spoiled the fundamental and original passages of the buildings. The first research work carried out by Scarpa aimed at discovering the location of the old foundations through tests, so as to restore to their original sites a few works which had been dug up and placed elsewhere for purely ornamental reasons. The result of this first and fundamental rearrangement was the shape of the 'portego' (portico). With the reconstruction of this central nucleus—the only one which could be recovered with some iconological legitimacy—there began the work of general rearrangement which, paying due attention to certain very precise functional needs, has been articulated into four fundamental themes: the bridge accessible by way of the small square; the entrance with the embankment against high tides; the 'portego' hall; and the garden. . . . [The *acqua alta*] ruined the practicability of the land-zone of the palace, where a big public library, a famous gallery, and an important state institute were housed. The remedy to this limited access would be a direct entrance from the square, as a substitute for the entrance used since the end of the century, a doorway situated in a poorly lit and not easily accessible side lane. The client also commissioned two halls, for meetings and exhibits; one situated inside, the other outside, in the area of an abandoned and impracticable rear courtyard. The artist was then faced with two associated problems: 1) the elevation of the whole pavement area of the zone overlooking the canal to a level corresponding to the highest levels reached by the high tides in the last ten years, and 2) a system for lining ceilings and walls so as to offset the effects of humidity. In fact, the absorption of humidity very quickly corrodes any plaster or marble facing. To eliminate this serious drawback, Scarpa used panels fastened with wall clamps so as to ensure the complete and continuous ventilation of all the walling."

2
Maria Antonietta Crippa, *Carlo Scarpa* (Cambridge: MIT Press, 1986), p. 157.

3
Here as elsewhere I am indebted to the recent work of Richard Murphy, who points out that there is in fact a difference in level despite the fact that one of Scarpa's drawings suggests the two levels are virtually the same. See Richard Murphy's analytical essay in *Querini Stampalia Foundation/Carlo Scarpa,* Architecture in Detail Series (London: Phaidon, 1993).

4
A similar distortion occurs in the planning of the Banca Popolare di Verona, where a seemingly orthogonal plan is actually out of rectangular alignment by 1.5 degrees in order to conform to the inclination of the party walls in the adjacent buildings.

5
Giuseppe Zambonini, "Process and Theme in the Work of Carlo Scarpa," *Perspecta* 20 (1983), p. 31. One should note, after Richard Murphy (see note 3 above), that this water channel is stocked with fish and that Scarpa had apparently once remarked, "Let's have some trout here!"

6
A number of books on Chinese gardening were held in Scarpa's library including Osvald Sirén, *Gardens of China* (New York: Ronald Press, 1949), and Henry Inn, ed., *Chinese Houses and Gardens* (New York, 1940).

7
Bianca Albertini and Sandro Bagnoli, *Carlo Scarpa* (Cambridge: MIT Press, 1988), p. 221. It is interesting to note that, as Murphy points

out, the papyrus basin had been previously used in Scarpa's Turin pavilion of 1961.

8
Marco Frascari, "The Tell-the-Tale Detail," in Paula Behrens and Anthony Fisher, eds., *The Building of Architecture,* Via, no. 7 (Philadelphia: University of Pennsylvania; Cambridge: MIT Press, 1984), p. 24. Frascari has written a whole series of insightful articles on the work of Scarpa including "A Heroic and Admirable Machine: The Theatre of the Architecture of Carlo Scarpa, Architetto Veneto," *Poetics Today* 10 (Spring 1989), pp. 103–124; and "Italian Facadism and Carlo Scarpa," *Daidalos* 6 (December 1982), pp. 37–46.

9
Lodoli entertained very similar anti-Cartesian views to Vico's. In his essay "Lodoli on Function and Representation," from his anthology *The Necessity of Artifice* (New York: Rizzoli, 1982), pp. 115–122, Joseph Rykwert writes that Lodoli was closely related to "Giambattista Vico, the Neapolitan philosopher, lawyer and rhetorician, to whom the *verum* and *factum* of Baconian experimental philosophy had an important corollary: that the touchstone of the verifiable or knowable was what we and our like had made. And that therefore historical and not geometrical knowledge could provide us with the only real certitude. . . . Moreover Lodoli taught his pupils the independence of Italic and Etruscan institutions of Greek precept—an idea to which Vico had given great force in his book *On the Ancient Wisdom of the Italians* and which he was to refine through the various editions of his major work, the *New Science.*"

10
See Hubert Damisch, "The Drawings of Carlo Scarpa," in Francesco Dal Co and Giuseppe Mazzariol, eds., *Carlo Scarpa: The Complete Works* (Milan: Electa; New York: Rizzoli, 1985), pp. 209, 212. Damisch writes: "Scarpa's approach was completely dominated by the problem of *realization*. From this viewpoint, it seems that the Venetian architect's attitude has curious similarity to Cézanne. Scarpa harbored the same doubt as Cézanne, if we believe what Merleau-Ponty tells us. And it is this doubt, clearly methodological, which gives his work, seemingly so modest, a historical incisiveness that some consider extraordinary. Now this doubt can be grasped best of all by examining his practice as a draftsman." Damisch is alluding here to Maurice Merleau-Ponty's essay "Le Doute de Cézanne," first published in 1945 and translated into English in *Sense and Non-sense* (Evanston: Northwestern University Press, 1964). Merleau-Ponty wrote that "the work itself completed and understood, is proof that there was *something* rather than *nothing* to be said" (p. 19).

In their essay dealing with the life of Carlo Scarpa in *Carlo Scarpa: The Complete Works,* Giuseppe Mazzariol and Giuseppe Barbieri note that for Scarpa the drafting materials were of the utmost importance; hence a given pencil, ink, and paper were recognized in every case as being capable only of certain tasks, just as the results produced with specific building materials differ one from another. They also quote Mamolio Brusatin to the effect that "every object manipulated and laid open by his draftsmanship is virtually a geological record, a convincing explanation that the objects and appurtenances of the city are not just remote reproductions of the present and of the things of today, but also tell us everything about their having really lived and having really died."

11
See Sergio Los, "The Design for the Central Pavilion of the Biennale," in Dal Co and Mazzariol, eds., *Carlo Scarpa: The Complete Works,* pp. 164, 165. See also Los's essay "Carlo Scarpa, Architect," in *Carlo Scarpa* (Cologne: Taschen, 1993), pp. 44, 48.

12
See Stephen Groak, *The Idea of Building* (London: Spon, 1992), pp. 151, 152.

13
Cited in Richard Murphy, *Carlo Scarpa and the Castelvecchio* (London: Butterworth, 1990), p. 56. Murphy's detailed analysis and documentation of the Castelvecchio is without parallel.

14
Albertini and Bagnoli, *Carlo Scarpa,* p. 205.

15
Sergio Los, *Carlo Scarpa: architetto poeta* (Venice: Edizioni Cluva, 1967). At the end of this text Los gives a brief account of his posthumous realization of Scarpa's gate for the school of architecture in Venice. A somewhat different version of the same text is given in the transcript of a lecture that Scarpa delivered in Madrid in 1978. See Carlo Scarpa, "A Thousand Cypresses" in Dal Co and Mazzariol, eds., *Carlo Scarpa: The Complete Works,* p. 287.

16
In his study of the Querini Stampalia, Richard Murphy records the names of leading members of Scarpa's regular production team who traveled with him, much as Frank Lloyd Wright had developed such a team for the realization of his Prairie Style. Murphy lists Servevio Anfodillo (joinery), Paolo Zanon (steel), Silvio Fassio (concrete), Eugenio de Luigi (stucco), as well as the engineer Maschietto and the draftsman Luciano Zinatto. We are close here to Ruskin's culture of craftsmen.

17
Scarpa was perhaps more familiar with the lore of Italian plaster finishes than any other Italian architect of his generation, and the revival and popularity of polished plaster is due in no small measure to his efforts. Some sense of the degree to which this technique has been elaborated in Italy may be gleaned from the fact that traditional Roman plastering comprises seven successive layers of plaster finish. Something of the scope of this technique with all its regional variations, may be gleaned from a study commissioned by the Comune di Verona. See Giorgio Forte, *Antiche ricette di pittura murale* (Venice: Noale, 1984). I am indebted to Sergio Los for providing me with this information.

18
As Licisco Magagnato has informed us, it took Scarpa five years to finally resolve the positioning of the Cangrande statue that was the ultimate symbolic "joint" of the museum.

See Licisco Magagnato, "The Castelvecchio Museum," in Dal Co and Mazzariol, eds., *Carlo Scarpa: The Complete Works,* p. 160.

19
See Robert Lawlor, *Sacred Geometry* (London: Thames and Hudson, 1982), p. 31.

20
See Guido Pietropoli, "L'invitation au voyage," *Spazio e Società,* June 1990, pp. 90–98. Pietropoli confirms that Scarpa was also well aware of the use of the *vesica piscis* figure by Borromini, but only after he had already built the intersecting circles at Brion. He writes: "It was obvious that he wasn't so much upset about the aesthetic effect of his design, but more because Borromini's geometric construction was more accurate, more true, from a strictly symbolic point of view. According to the strict law of analogy ruling the relationship and harmony between material form and spiritual significance, all possible harmonies within a symbolic theme must be highlighted. Borromini's design adds the so-called 'AURA' or 'MANDOLA' to the eros expressed by the two intersecting circles. The 'Mandola' consists of two facing equilateral triangles which, metaphorically, refer to King Soloman's seal. In my opinion this is one of the symbols of the 'Mandola' which can also be interpreted as the expression of balance acquired between lay and sacred love."

21
Le Corbusier, *The Modulor* (1950; first English edition 1954). It is interesting to note that Le Corbusier's choice of his standard height of 2.20 meters (the height of a man with his arms upraised) should correspond to Scarpa's modular system based on permutations of the number 11. Le Corbusier would also entertain the double-circular theme, particularly in the regulating lines used to control the composition of the enameled doors in Ronchamp. See Le Corbusier, *The Chapel at Ronchamp* (New York: Praeger, 1957), pp. 124–125. See note 23.

22
Japanese culture was as omnipresent in Scarpa's work as the art and architecture of China. What is less well known perhaps was the way in which his architecture was appreciated by contemporary Japanese practitioners. Typical in this regard is Fumihiko Maki's insightful comment about the *suki* aspect of Scarpa's work: "A generalization that might be made about superior architectural works whether past or

present, East or West, is that they reveal at a stroke 'something' that many architects and non-architects of the time had unconsciously wanted to express. Architectural creation is not invention but discovery; it is not a pursuit of something beyond the imagination of an age. These few works of Scarpa are attractive in that they also respond in this sense to the latent desire we share. However, unlike Mies's Barcelona Pavilion or Le Corbusier's Savoye, they do not represent the prototypes of the 'age'. Although they belong to the impregnative world of the same period, Scarpa's works have been developed in the still imagination of a private world. Scarpa believed only in seeing and created so that the creation could be seen. The ability to choose and reconstruct, based on a superior power of appreciation and a still, private hedonism—this is truly the art of *suki*, and in this I sense the true value and limitations of the designs of Carlo Scarpa." Cited by Gianpiero Destro Bisol in "L'antimetodo di Carlo Scarpa," *Ricerca Progretto* (Bulletin of the Department of Architecture and Urbanism in the University of Rome), no. 15 (July 1991), pp. 6–12.

23
Marco Frascari, "A Deciphering of a Wonderful Cipher: Eleven in the Architecture of Carlo Scarpa," *Oz* 13 (1991). One may add to Frascari's list of somewhat arcane dimensions the equally odd fact that there are 22 books in the Old Testament, 22 generations from Adam to Jacob, and that God is supposed to have made 22 works. Frascari's account of this numerical obsession parallels almost to the letter that given by Scarpa himself in "A Thousand Cypresses," p. 286. In both instances, however, we are confronted with a description of a system that fails to account for its origin. The esoteric character of this obsession with the double numbers leads one to wonder whether Scarpa was familiar with René Schwaller de Lubicz's alchemical study *The Temple in Man* that first appeared in French in 1949. In a parallel text published in 1957, Schwaller de Lubicz writes: "In considering the esoteric meaning of Number, we must avoid the following mistake: Two is not One and One; it is not a *composite*. It is the multiplying *Work*; it is the notion of the plus in relation to the minus; it is sexuality; it is a new *Unity*; it is the origin of Nature, *Physis*, the *Neter* Two." See Robert Lawlor's introduction to the *The Temple in Man* (Rochester, Vermont, 1981), p. 10.

Other elements in Scarpa's work suggest familiarity with the writings of Schwaller de Lubicz. This is particularly true of chapter 4 in *The Temple in Man* where Schwaller de Lubicz describes the rebuilding of temples on preexisting foundations as symbolizing "water, that is to say the mud of the waters." He also remarks on the fact that the Egyptians (like Scarpa) were in the habit of introducing subtle distortions of the orthogonal into their plan forms, so that, as he puts it, "certain chambers apparently square or rectangular in plan will be slightly rhomboidal or trapezoidal. One need only examine, in their angles, the cut of the stones to establish that for this distortion, an exceptional effort was required to give these angles a few degrees more or less than a right angle" (*The Temple in Man*, pp. 69, 71).

24
It is more than likely that Scarpa was cognizant of the alchemical wheels of Ezekiel that resemble the *vesica pisci*. A similar duality also appears in the icon of the philosopher's egg from which a double-headed eagle is hatched wearing spiritual and temporal crowns. Moreover Scarpa's identification of himself as a man of Byzantium who came to Venice by way of Greece may be seen as an allusion to the two great alchemical traditions; the Pythagorean school of South Italy that sought to structure the world in terms of number and the Ionian school that sought the secret of reality in the analysis and synthesis of substances. See Jack Lindsay, *The Origins of Alchemy in Greco-Roman Egypt* (London: Muller, 1970). The dragon or snake biting its own tail is of alchemical and Gnostic origin. In some versions, it is shown as half light and half dark and in this respect resembles the Chinese yang-yin principle, depicting the continual transition of one value into its opposite. Assimilated to Mercury, the ouroboros is symbolic of self-fecundation, of the primitive idea of a self-sufficient nature that continually returns to its own beginning. See J. E. Cirlot, *A Dictionary of Symbols* (New York: 1962), p. 235.

25
Pietropoli, "L'invitation en voyage," p. 12. Of the latent Orphic mythology in the Brion assembly, Pietropoli writes (p. 12):

On the other side of the cemetery, permanently against the light except during the semi-darkness of dawn and dusk, there is a large pond of black water, the lake of our hearts. In order to reach the island we must turn right going through the tunnel/Orphic flute; our footsteps are noisy and heavy because the ground is hollow and water flows underneath; to enter we must use all our strength and body weight to lower a glass door; in doing this we have to bend over, like a kind of dive and a return to the fetal position. When we have passed through the opening, if we glance back we can see our image reflected in the glass pane as it swings upward. In front of us there is only a concrete wall with a line of mosaic tiles and a sign to turn left, once again toward the heart, and bowing our heads we can enter the water pavilion.

This is a strange rectangular building supported on four iron pillars placed in the form of a vortex. The upper part is made with fir-wood planks, which have turned silver-grey in the sun, arranged so as to give the impression of a pathway with a labyrinth-like perspective, evoking the idea of convolutions of the brain; coverings of green marine plywood patterned with copper nails stoop downward allowing us to see only the pond.

A series of hastily drawn designs, time had almost run out (we were about to leave for Sendai in Japan where Scarpa died on November 28, 1978), show four virtual areas, a sort of disassembling of the "lake of my heart" into atriums and ventricles: the poet (the pavilion), and the ancient fairy tales (the cross with the water jet and the hibiscus, the desert rose), the man (the pond with the bamboo canes) and, once again, the interlocking circles (the eros).

In the center of the pavilion a vertical crack with a deliberate viewpoint allows us to see only the "arco solio" with the tombs of the father and mother: this is the only link with society that, even in our self-conceit, we cannot deny.

26
This whole "alchemical" contraption recalls Marcel Duchamp's Large Glass or Bachelor Machine, *La Mariée mise à nu par ses célibataires mêmes*. It is thus a double metaphor; on the one hand, a heart, that is to say a pump; on the other, it appears to be the related act of coitus.

27
With a certain artistic license, Francesco Dal Co writes: "Significantly, the water flows towards the great basin, gushing out from the very spot where the 'arks' rest, under the protection of the 'arcosolium.' Springing out from the place of death, it flows around the 'isle of meditation' on which stands the pavilion that Scarpa designed while imagining it haunted by the full-bodied forms of youthful women." See Dal Co, "The Architecture of Carlo Scarpa," in Dal Co and Mazzariol, eds., *Carlo Scarpa: The Complete Works*, p. 68.

28
See Paolo Portoghesi, "The Brion Cemetery by Carlo Scarpa," *Global Architecture*, no. 50 (1979): *Carlo Scarpa Cemetery Brion-Vega, S. Vito, Treviso, Italy 1970–72*. Portoghesi writes first of Scarpa's alchemical understanding of Venice and then of the arcosolium that constitutes the fulcrum of the Brion Cemetery. Thus we read: "For Scarpa, then, Venice was a way of seeing and using, a way of connecting things in function of the values of light, texture, color, capable of being grasped only by an eye used to observing . . . water, glass, together with stones and bricks exposed to an inclement atmosphere which doesn't allow the material to hide its structure, but continually forces it to discover, by consuming itself, its most hidden qualities." Later of the double tomb we read: "It could be said that Scarpa reflected at length on the word *arca* (in Italian *arca* means both ark and sarcophagus) and its historical meanings, on the Latin origin which defines its sense, close to that of coffin or monumental sarcophagus, on the transformations undergone in the Christian world. . . . From the arch of the catacomb niches we pass to the Romanesque and Gothic tomb which in the Po area assumes the form of an architectural casket, a shrine in scale. . . . The tomb of the Brion family is thus contemporaneously 'arch', 'bridge', 'roof', 'overturned boat' . . . each of these connotations, these words, projects a symbolic value onto the place, symbols of death in that they are symbols of life, since death isn't given except dialectically, as life which bears within itself its negation and the negation of its negation."

29

Needless to say it also refers to Scarpa's obsession with the "double" throughout his work.

30

Sergio Los arrives at parallel Semperian interpretations of Scarpa's work through Konrad Fiedler's "Essay on Architecture," with which Scarpa was apparently familiar. See Sergio Los, "Carlo Scarpa Architect," p. 38.

31

Francesco Dal Co, "The Architecture of Carlo Scarpa," p. 63.

32

See A. K. Coomaraswamy, "Ornament" (1939), in *Selected Papers,* ed. R. Lipsey, vol. 1 (Princeton: Princeton University Press, 1977), pp. 32–33. For Coomaraswamy the articulation of order out of chaos requires the appearance of decoration as a way of both measuring and joining at the same time.

33

Heino Engel, *The Japanese House* (Rutland/Tokyo: Tuttle, 1964), p. 48. The importance of measure and the intimate relation between craft dimension and proportion has been commented on by P. H. Schofield in his study of proportional systems in architecture: "Architecture, much more than painting, pottery or sculpture, is a co-operative art, the work of many men. In order that men can co-operate in this art, in order, for instance, that the joiner can make a window frame to fill the opening left by the mason, and that both can work to the design of the architect, they need a language of size, a system of measures. Logically only one measure is required, such as a foot or a meter, used in conjunction with an effective system of numeration. This, however, presupposes the existence of simple methods of arithmetical calculation, and on the other hand of a reasonably high general level of mathematical education. To the Egyptian, burdened by a clumsy method of arithmetic and a low standard of mathematical literacy, outside the priestly class, such a method would be impracticable."

The earliest tendency would be to develop a system of many measures, each one with a name of its own. And, as Vitruvius points out, such a system was ready to hand in the measures of the human body. "Making a large number of not very widely separated measures commensurable would automatically lead to the repeated use of rather small whole numbers. It would in fact lead quite automatically to the establishment in some degree of a pattern of proportional relationships between the measures." See P. H. Schofield, *The Theory of Proportion in Architecture* (Cambridge: Cambridge University Press, 1958), pp. 27–28.

34

Dal Co, "The Architecture of Carlo Scarpa," p. 56.

35

Portoghesi, "The Brion Cemetery by Carlo Scarpa": "If decoration can be talked about with regard to Scarpa, it is still in the utopia of 'organic decoration', born from things instead of superimposing itself on them. The crystallographic decoration of the Brion cemetery seems to be a result of the 'natural' flaking of the crystalline blocks, of the revelation of a hypothetical structure of every prismatic block or of every slab, considered as products of successive crystalline layers sedimented around an ideal geometric matrix, a translation in 'mineral' terms of the system of growth through the concentric wind typical of the vegetal trunk."

36

Marco Frascari, "The Tell-the-Tale Detail," p. 24. Sergio Los employs the terms *hypotactic* and *paratatic* to distinguish between Scarpa's notion of an underlying whole as determined by the geometry or the "enfilade" and the *paratactic* type forms in which it was invariably broken down. Los, "Carlo Scarpa Architect," p. 46.

37

Franco Fonatti, *Elemente des Bauens bei Carlo Scarpa* (Vienna: Wiener Akademiereihe, 1988), p. 59.

38

Albertini and Bagnoli, *Carlo Scarpa,* pp. 21–22.

39

Scarpa was exceptionally sensitive to the size and deportment of any window and the light that must of necessity emanate from its form. Thus as Carlo Bertelli has written: "The range of solutions explored, discarded, and finally adopted is one of the most exciting testimonies to Scarpa's approach to architectural design. They reveal, first of all, that no window is the same as any other not only because the orientation is different, but also because its age and the size and the shape of the room it illuminates vary. Second, the various systems of grilles and the asymmetrical combinations of vertical and horizontal elements are all ways of designing with light and turning it into an event." Carlo Bertelli, "Light and Design," in Dal Co and Mazzariol, eds., *Carlo Scarpa: The Complete Works.*

40

A similar treatment of the suspending ceiling also occurs in the first-floor gallery sequence of the Castelvecchio, where the subdivision of its cobalt lacquered surface is played against a central gridded ventilation grill, framed out in wood, and set flush with the ceiling. The subdividing wooden strips between the panels assume a slightly different pattern in each gallery.

41

Pierluigi Nicolin, "La Banca di Carlo Scarpa a Verona," *Lotus* 28 (1981), p. 51.

10 Postscriptum: The Tectonic Trajectory, 1903–1994

Epigraph: Aris Konstantinidis, "Architecture," translated by Marina Adams, in *Architectural Design,* May 1964, p. 212.

1

See the statement by Pier Luigi Nervi published in *Nervi: Space and Structural Integrity,* exhibition catalog (San Francisco: Museum of Art May/June 1961).

2

See Pieter Singelenberg, *H. P. Berlage: Idea and Style* (Utrecht: Haentjens Dekker & Gumbert, 1972), p. 11. Singelenberg writes of Berlage: "In 1905, roughly half a century after Semper's London publication, he wrote similarly in *Gedanken über Stil* that one could not talk about the evolution of the arts without involving political and economic relations. He too thought in terms of a hopeless state of affairs, saw the cause of the situation in the rule of capital and found the reaction to this, social democracy, the greatest movement ever known to history. Like Semper he worried about human freedom, but in a socialist society the danger would no longer lie in capitalism, but in the misuse of possibilities."

Berlage upheld Semper's theory that the "technical arts" preceded architecture, and his *Over Stijl in Bouw en Meubelkunst* (On Style in Architectural and Furniture Design), published in 1904, is a Semperian argument for the unity of style emerging out of a long period of evolution.

3

Chris Burrows, "H. P. Berlage: Structure, Skin, Space" (unpublished architecture thesis, Polytechnic of the South Bank, London, 1989), p. 80.

4

However, the case may be made that Johannes Duiker also developed this tradition of the expressive skeleton frame in Dutch architecture beginning with his Zonnestraal Sanatorium, Hilversum, of 1926.

5

Le Corbusier and P. Jeanneret, *Oeuvre Complète 1934–1938,* 6th ed. (Zurich: Girsberger, 1958), p. 125.

6

I am thinking in particular of the *pilotis* of the Unité d'Habitation, Marseilles, of 1952, which may be seen as Egyptoid on account of the battered profile, tapering upward.

7

The term *saku* is taken from Islamic architecture and refers to the recessed bench that establishes, as it were, the threshold of the typical Arabic urban dwelling.

8

Herman Hertzberger, in Arnulf Luchinger, ed., *Herman Hertzberger, Buildings and Projects 1959–1986* (The Hague: Arch-Edition, 1987), p. 62.

9

Ibid., p. 119.

10

Max Bill, *Form* (Basel: Karl Verner, 1952), p. 11.

11

See "Swiss National Exhibition, Lausanne," *Architectural Design,* November 1963, pp. 526–529.

12

See Andrew Peckham, "This Is the Modern World," *Architectural Design,* February 1979, pp. 2–26.

13

Konrad Wachsmann, *The Turning Point of Building: Structure and Design* (New York: Reinhold, 1961), p. 187.

14

Per Olaf Fjeld, *Sverre Fehn: The Thought of Construction* (New York: Rizzoli, 1983), pp. 46–47.

15

Ibid., p. 112.

16

While architects such as Ernesto Rogers sought a subtle reinterpretation of historical type form—even if only at the level of structure and silhouette, as in his twenty-nine-story Torre Velasca, built in Milan in 1957, a work that consciously attempted to echo the medieval fortress towers of Lombardy—others such as the Argentine Amancio Williams attempted to create an architecture in which structural invention was inseparable from spatial form and vice versa. In general, Italian work during this period tended toward a kind of "tectonic historicism," as in Franco Albini and Franca Helg's Treasury Museum of San Lorenzo, Genoa (1952–1956), or Ignazio Gardella's Zattere building completed in Venice between 1954 and 1958. Of the Torre Velasca, Manfredo Tafuri has written: "Rolled up in its materiality, the tower expanded toward the sky like an energized volcano, assuming the appearance of a medieval tower paradoxically magnified. It stands as a 'homage to Milan,' achieved through means that could not yet be accused of historicism. The Velasca took its place in the city, commenting lyrically on an urban corpus about to disappear. Once again, the expectation was that a catharsis would emerge from intentions hidden in the recesses of a single object." Elsewhere in the same passage he writes of Albini's "buried architecture" as possessing its own language. "Isolated from the external world, it elicits a dialogue between technical elegance—a further tool for achieving supreme detachment-forms." In a similar vein Tafuri would see Gardella's Zattere as a kind of coda to the Torre Velasca, one that was greeted at the time as indicative of a dangerously evasive historicist climate. See Tafuri, *History of Italian Architecture 1944–1985* (Cambridge: MIT Press, 1989), pp. 50–52.

While militant left-wing critics such as G. C. Argan would dub Gardella's Zattere the Ca'd'Oro of modern architecture, and others of more liberal Brutalist persuasion such as Reyner Banham would generally deplore the Italian "retreat" from the modern movement, the gap separating Italian contextualism of the 1950s from the ethical British Brutalist line hardly seems as great as it once was. Both positions were in any event equally committed to the tectonic.

17

Son of the Argentine composer Alberto Williams, Amancio Williams has been one of the most brilliant "theoretical" architects of this century, in the sense that very few of his works have been realized. In almost all of his work, including the house over a stream built for his parents in Mar del Plata in 1945, the fundamental structural idea of the work is inseparable from the tectonic and spatial concept. This is very evident in such works as the suspended office building (1946) or the canopied exhibition building erected in Palermo (1963). See Pablo and Claudio Williams et al., *Amancio Williams* (Buenos Aires, 1990), the complete works of Amancio Williams as published by Archivo Amancio Williams.

18

The fact that Lewerentz visited the site every day for two years during construction, from 1958 to 1960, surely testifies to his commitment to the actual act of construction. See Janne Ahlin's monograph *Sigurd Lewerentz Architect 1885–1975* (Stockholm: Bygförlaget, 1987), pp. 154–156.

19

See Colin St. John Wilson, "Sigurd Lewerentz and the Dilemma of the Classical," *Perspecta 24* (1988), pp. 72–73. Jan Hendrikson of Stockholm has suggested that a Greek architect, Michael Papadopoulos, who had previously worked with Dimitris Pikionis on the Philopapou Hill site adjacent to the Acropolis in Athens, also assisted Lewerentz at Klippan.

20

See Leonardo Fiori and Massimo Prizzon, eds., *La Rinascente: il progetto di architettura* (Milan: Abitare Segesta, 1982), pp. 39, 47.

21

Joseph Rykwert, "The Work of Gino Valle," *Architectural Design,* March 1964, p. 128.

22

See Eduard Sekler, "Architecture and the Flow of Time," *Tulane School of Architecture Review,* no. 9 (1990).

23

Peter Smithson, "A Parallel of the Orders," *Architectural Design,* November 1966, pp. 561–563.

24

Where they happen to be graduates of the school of Madrid, many of these architects have been equally influenced by both de la Sota and Javier Sáenz de Oiza, above all Moneo, who, after he returned from the Utzon atelier in Copenhagen, worked on Sáenz de Oiza's Torres Blancas apartments completed just outside Madrid in 1966. See Pauline Saliga and Martha Thorne, eds., *Building in a New Spain* (Barcelona: Gustavo Gili; Chicago: Art Institute of Chicago, 1992).

25

Esteve Bonell and Francesc Rius, "Velodrome of Barcelona," *Casabella* 49 (December 1985), p. 62.

26

Ibid.

27

This scientistic term was coined by the Soviet avant-garde in the early 1920s in order to refer to the newly invented socialist workers' club as an institution that was hypothetically capable of unifying and transforming the society. Using a more industrial electrical metaphor, El Lissitzky characterized the workers' club as a *soziales Kraftwerk.* See Anatole Kopp, *Town and Revolution* (New York: Braziller, 1970), pp. 115–126.

28

The reappearance of Brunel's technology here would appear to relate to a passing remark made by the engineer Peter Rice in his 1991 RIBA Gold Medal address: "The Victorians succeeded where we do not. Industry and its power and capacity were new to them. Designers enjoyed the freedom to experiment, to enjoy themselves, to innovate, to explore the possibilities of this new power to manufacture and create."

29

See Aris Konstantinidis, *Elements for Self-Knowledge: Towards a True Architecture* (Athens, 1975), p. 290.

30

Ibid., p. 313.

31

Paul Ricoeur, "Universal Civilization and National Cultures," in *History and Truth* (Evanston: Northwestern University Press, 1965).

The Owl of Minerva: An Epilogue, 1993

Epigraph: see Guy Debord, *Comments on the Society of the Spectacle* (London: Verso, 1988), pp. 38, 39, 50, 51.

1

See *Mies van der Rohe Pavilion. Award for European Architecture, 1988–1992.* The Commission of the European Community, the European Parliament, and the Mies van der Rohe Pavilion, Barcelona, gave this award for the first time in 1988 to Alvaro Siza for the Borges & Irmão Bank built in Vilo do Conde, Portugal, in 1982.

2

For the British attempt in this regard see Bryan Appelyard, "Demolishing the Architect," *The Independent,* September 22, 1993.

3

The department of architecture in the Technical University of Delft has introduced the so-called "Case Study" pedagogical method borrowed from the medical school in Maastricht. As a result, lecturing, as a method of instruction, has been reduced to a minimum.

4

Rafael de la Hoz, "Delenda est Architectura," address given at the AIA/UIA Convention, Chicago, July 1993, and at the Biennale de Arquitectura held in Buenos Aires in September of the same year.

5

I am alluding to the emergence of the construction manager as a separate profession standing between the architect and the client.

6

In the design of his Sainsbury Centre for the Visual Arts in the University of Norwich, Norman Foster was to utilize components manufactured by the aerospace industry. On another occasion Richard Rogers & Partners would employ insulated paneling produced by refrigerated truck manufacturers.

7

Fordism is the term adopted by radical economists to characterize the period of 1950 to 1970, when Taylorized productive processes, facilitated by massive investment in machine tool production and by guaranteed markets, dominated industrial production in the West. Daniel Legorgne and Alain Lipietz have characterized the emerging period of so called "post-Fordism" in the following terms: "History is alive again. On the ruins of Fordism and Stalinism, humankind is at a crossroads. No technological determinism will light the way. The present industrial divide is first and foremost a political divide. The search for social compromise, around ecological constraints, macroeconomic consistency, gender and ethic quality, all mediated by the nature and degree of political mobilization will decide the outcome." See Michael Storper and Allen J. Scott, eds., *Pathways to Industrialization and Regional Development* (London: Routledge, 1992).

8

In an essay entitled "Architecture and the Flow of Time" (*Tulane School of Architecture Review,* no. 9 [1990]), Eduard Sekler writes of the relation between time and tradition:

Architecture and time are interwoven in many ways and subject to mutual influence. Time (chronos), according to the Orphic philosophers, has as its mate necessity (ananke). But forgetting is also time's mate, and in the fight against its all-devouring power, architecture is one of man's most faithful allies.

In the past, a work derived its authenticity not only from the personality of the creator but also from the fact that the work was in keeping with the highest social and spiritual aims of the culture in which it originated.

Today such unifying goals are less easily definable. Often they have been replaced by the much vaunted ideal of individual self-realization, an ideal that forces the artist to rely exclusively on his/her own spiritual resources of strength; authenticity then becomes something very personal, something at times even questionable.

9

R. Gregory Turner, *Construction Economics and Building Design: A Historical Approach* (New York: Van Nostrand Reinhold, 1986).

10

See Edward Ford, *The Details of Modern Architecture* (Cambridge: MIT Press, 1990), p. 352. Rather polemically he writes of layered construction: "The idea that walls in ancient or medieval architecture were mo-

nolithic was largely an illusion. Marbles have always been veneered, interiors have always been plastered, and even in a simple stone wall quality stone was always placed on the surface. . . . In the traditional monolithic wall, all functions—structure, insulation, waterproofing and finish—are performed by one or two materials. In the modern layered wall, there is a separate component for each function."

11

D. Andrew Vernooy, "Crisis of Figuration in Contemporary Architecture," in *The Final Decade: Architectural Issues for the 1990s and Beyond,* vol. 7 (New York: Rizzoli, 1992), pp. 94–96.

12

Gottfried Semper, *Wissenschaft, Industrie und Kunst* (Brauschweig, 1852). For the pertinent extract in English see Hans M. Wingler, *The Bauhaus* (Cambridge: MIT Press, 1969), p. 18.

13

Unlike the nineteenth-century rail or harbor facilities, twentieth-century airports are never finished; they are always in a state of construction and reconstruction. Leonardo da Vinci Airport in Rome, built in 1961 to handle six million passengers a year, is a case in point. By the beginning of this decade the annual throughput was over 17 million. It is estimated that by the year 2005 this figure will have climbed to 40 million and by 2030 to 60 million. The consequences of escalating tourism on this scale hardly bear contemplation, let alone the impact it will have on the environment in general.

Other institutional types have become just as fungible in less dramatic ways, even as a matter of state policy. I have in mind in particular the policy established in 1992 by the Dutch State Architect Professor Ir Kees Rijnboutt, who declared that henceforth law courts should be designed and built as though they were ordinary office buildings.

14

See Vittorio Gregotti, "Cultural Theatrics," *Casabella,* no. 606 (November 1993), pp. 2, 3, 71: "The most distressing consequence of these attitudes is the distance, the enormous gap, which has been created between saying and doing. The valid efforts of its theorists apart, it is certain that the translation of languages from one discipline to another presents significant obstacles; even if we acknowledge its legitimacy, the more indirect it is the more effective it becomes, insinuating itself into the material of design. . . . In substance the attempt to directly transfer the inventions of visual artists or theoretical conclusions of philosophers into architecture nearly always results in caricatures or disasters."

15

See France Vanlaethem, "Pour une architecture épurée et rigoureuse" (interview with Alvaro Siza), *ARQ* (Montreal), no. 14 (August 1983), p. 16.

16

See "Renzo Piano Building Workshop 1964/1991: In Search of a Balance," *Process Architecture* (Tokyo), no. 700 (1992), pp. 12, 14.

17

See the RIBA catalogue *The Work of Peter Rice* (London: RIBA Publications, 1992).

18

Le Corbusier, *My Work,* trans. James Palmes (London: Architectural Press, 1960), p. 197.

Bibliography

Abalos, Inaki, and Juan Herreros. *Técnica y arquitectura en la ciudad contemporanea, 1950–1990*. Madrid: Nevea, 1992.

Abraham, Pol. *Viollet-le-Duc et le rationalisme médiévale*. Paris: Vincent Fréal, 1934.

Agacinski, Sylvianne. "Shares of Invention." *D: Columbia Documents of Architecture and Theory* 1 (1992), 53–68.

Ahlin, Janne. *Sigurd Lewerentz, Architect*. Cambridge: MIT Press, 1987.

Albertini, Bianca, and Sandro Bagnoli. *Carlo Scarpa: Architecture in Details*. Cambridge: MIT Press, 1988.

Albini, Franco, and Franca Helg. "Department Store, Rome." *Architectural Design* 32 (June 1962), 286–289.

Allen, Edward. *Stone Shelters*. Cambridge: MIT Press, 1969.

Ambasz, Emilio. *The Architecture of Luis Barragán*. New York: New York Graphic Society, 1976.

Anderson, Stanford. "Modern Architecture and Industry: Peter Behrens, the AEG and Industrial Design." *Oppositions* 21 (Summer 1980).

Ando, Tadao. "Shintai and Space." In *Architecture and Body*. New York: Rizzoli, 1988.

Angeli, Marc. "The Construction of a Meta-Physical Structure: Truth and Utility in Nineteenth Century Architecture." *Modulus* 22 (Charlottesville, 1993), 26–39.

Angerer, Fred. *Surface Structures in Building: Structure and Form*. New York: Reinhold, 1961.

Angrisani, Marcello. "Louis Kahn e la storia." *Edilizia Moderna* 86 (1965), 83–93.

Antoniades, E. "Poems with Stones: The Enduring Spirit of Dimitrios Pikionis." *A + U* 72 (December 1976), 17–22.

Appia, Adolphe. *L'Oeuvre d'art vivant*. Geneva: Atar, 1921.

Appleyard, Donald, Kevin Lynch, and John R. Myer. *The View from the Road*. Cambridge: MIT Press, 1964.

Arendt, Hannah. *The Human Condition*. Chicago: University of Chicago Press, 1958.

Arkitektur 7 (1963). (Entire issue devoted to P. V. Jensen-Klint and Kaare Klint.)

Arup, Ove. "Sydney Opera House." *Architectural Design* 35 (March 1965).

Arup, Ove. *Sydney Opera House*. Sydney: Sydney Opera House Trust, 1988. (Reprint of the 1969 retrospective paper by the engineers.)

Asplund, E. G., Gregor Paulson, et al. *Acceptera*. Tidem, Stockholm, 1931 (reprinted 1980).

Bachelard, Gaston. *The Poetics of Space*. Boston: Beacon, 1969. Translation of *La Poétique de l'espace*, 1958.

Badovici, Jean. *L'Architecture Vivante* (journal), 1923–1933. Reprint, New York, 1975.

Badovici, Jean. *Grandes constructions: béton armé—acier—verre*. Paris: Albat Morance, 1925.

Banham, Reyner. *The Architecture of the Well-Tempered Environment*. London: Architectural Press, 1969.

Banham, Reyner. *The New Brutalism*. New York: Reinhold, 1966.

Banham, Reyner. "On Trial: Louis Kahn and the Buttery-Hatch Aesthetic." *Architectural Review* 131 (March 1962).

Banham, Reyner. *Theory and Design in the First Machine Age*. New York: Praeger, 1960.

Bartholomew, Robert. "Jørn Utzon: His Work and Ideas." Thesis, University of New South Wales, Australia, 1981.

Beaux, D. "Maisons d'Islande et Génie du Lieu." *Le Carré Bleu* (March 1984).

Beaver, Patrick. *The Crystal Palace 1851–1936: A Portrait of Victorian Enterprise*. London: Hugh Evelyn, 1970.

Benedikt, Michael. *For an Architecture of Reality*. New York: Lumen Books, 1987.

Benevolo, Leonardo. *History of Modern Architecture*. 2 vols. Cambridge: MIT Press, 1971. Translation of *Storia dell'architettura moderna*, 1960.

Bergdoll, Barry. "Gilly, Friedrich." In *Macmillan Encyclopedia of Architects*. New York: Free Press, 1982.

Bergdoll, Barry. *Karl Friedrich Schinkel: An Architecture for Prussia*. New York: Rizzoli, 1994.

Bergdoll, Barry. "Primordial Fires: Frank Lloyd Wright, Gottfried Semper, and the Chicago School." Paper delivered at the Buell Center, Columbia University, 1988.

Bergdoll, Barry. "Schinkel, Karl Friedrich." In *Macmillan Encyclopedia of Architects*. New York: Free Press, 1982.

Berlage, H. P. *Gedanken über Stil in der Baukunst*. Leipzig: Julius Zeitler, 1905.

Berry, James Duncan. "The Legacy of Gottfried Semper: Studies in *Späthistoricismus*." Ph.D. dissertation, Brown University, 1989.

Bettini, S. "L'architettura di Carlo Scarpa." *Zodiac* 6 (1960), 140–187.

Bill, Max. *Form*. Basel: Karl Verner, 1952.

Bill, Max. *Robert Maillart: Bridges and Constructions*. Zurich, 1949; rpt. New York: Praeger, 1969.

Bill, Max. "Swiss National Exhibition, Lausanne." *Architectural Design* 33 (November 1963), 526–529.

Billington, David P. *Robert Maillart and the Art of Reinforced Concrete*. Cambridge: MIT Press, 1989.

Billington, David P. *Robert Maillart's Bridges: The Art of Engineering*. Princeton: Princeton University Press, 1979.

Bindman, David, and Gottfried Riemann. *Karl Friedrich Schinkel, "The English Journey": Journal of a Visit to France and Britain in 1826*. New Haven: Yale University Press, 1993.

Bisol, Giampiero Destro. "L'antimetodo di Carlo Scarpa." *Ricerca Progetto* (Bulletin of the Department of Architecture and Urbanism in the University of Rome), 15 (July 1991), 6–12.

Bjerknes, Kristian, and Hans-Emil Liden. "The Stave Churches of Kaupanger." Oslo, 1975.

Blake, Peter. *The Master Builders*. New York: Knopf, 1960.

Blaser, Werner. *Mies van der Rohe: The Art of Structure*. New York: Praeger, 1965.

Bletter, Rosemarie Haag. "On Martin Frohlich's Gottfried Semper." *Oppositions* 4 (October 1974).

Bletter, Rosemarie Haag. "Semper, Gottfried." In *Macmillan Encyclopedia of Architects*. New York: Free Press, 1982.

Bonell, Esteve. "Civic Monuments." *Architectural Review* 188 (July 1990), 69–74.

Bonell, Esteve. "Velodromo a Barcelonna." *Casabella* 519 (December 1985), 54–64.

Bonell, Esteve, and Francesc Rius. "Velodrome, Barcelona." *Architectural Review* 179 (May 1986), 88–91.

Borbein, Adolf Heinrich. "Tektonik: zur Geschichte eines Begriffs der Archäologie." *Archiv für Begriffsgeschichte* 26, no. 1 (1982).

Borradori, Giovanna. "Weak Thought and Postmodernism: The Italian Departure from Deconstruction." *Social Text* 18 (Winter 1987/88), 39–49.

Borsi, Franco, and Ezio Godoli. *Paris 1900*. New York: Rizzoli, 1978.

Bottero, Maria. "Carlo Scarpa il veneziano." *World Architecture/Two* (London, 1965).

Bottero, Maria. "Organic and Rational Morphology in the Architecture of Louis Kahn." *Zodiac* 17 (1967).

Bötticher, Karl. *Die Tektonik der Hellenen*. 2 vols. Potsdam, 1852.

Bourdieu, Pierre. "The Berber House or the World Reversed." *Social Science Information* 9 (April 1970), 151–170.

Bressler, Henri. "Windows on the Court." *Rassegna* 28 (1979).

Brownlee, David B., and David G. DeLong. *Louis I. Kahn: In the Realm of Architecture*. New York: Rizzoli, 1992.

Brusatin, Manlio. "Carlo Scarpa's Minimal Systems." *Carlo Scarpa; il progetto per Santa Caterina a Treviso*. Treviso: Ponzano, 1984.

Buddensieg, Tilman. *Industriekultur: Peter Behrens and the AEG*. 1979; rpt. Cambridge: MIT Press, 1984.

Buel, Albert W. *Reinforced Concrete*. New York: Engineering News Publishing Co., 1904.

Burrows, Chris. "H. P. Berlage: Structure, Skin, Space." Unpublished thesis, Polytechnic of the South Bank, London, 1989.

Burton, Joseph Arnold, and David van Zanten. "The Architectural Hieroglyphics of Louis I. Kahn: Architecture as Logos." Unpublished abstract.

Butler, E. M. *The Tyranny of Greece over Germany*. 1935; rpt. Boston: Beacon Press, 1958.

Cacciari, Massimo. *Architecture and Nihilism: On the Philosophy of Modern Architecture*. New Haven: Yale University Press, 1993.

Cacciari, Massimo. "Mies's Classics." *Res* 16 (Autumn 1988), 9–16.

Carter, Peter. "Mies van der Rohe: An Appreciation on the Occasion, This Month, of His 75th Birthday." *Architectural Design* 31 (March 1961).

Carter, Peter. *Mies van der Rohe at Work*. New York: Praeger, 1974.

Champigneulle, Bernard. *August Perret*. Paris: Arts et Métiers Graphiques, 1959.

Chermayeff, Serge, and Christopher Alexander. *Community and Privacy: Toward a New Architecture of Humanism*. Garden City: Doubleday, 1963.

Chewing, J. A. "Root, John Wellborn." In *Macmillan Encyclopedia of Architects*. New York: Free Press, 1982.

Choay, Françoise. *Das Unesco-Gebäude in Paris*. Teufen, Switzerland, 1958.

Choisy, Auguste. *Histoire de l'architecture*. 2 vols. Paris: E. Rouveyre, n.s., 1899.

Christie, Sigrid and Hakon. *Nord Kirker Akershus*. Oslo, 1969.

Cirlot, J. E. *A Dictionary of Symbols*. London: Routledge & Paul, 1962.

Clarke, Somers, and R. Engelbach. *Ancient Egyptian Construction and Architecture*. London: Oxford University Press, 1930; rpt. New York: Dover, 1990.

Clotet, Luis, and Ignacio Paricio, eds. *Construcciones*. Monografías de Arquitectura y Vivienda, no. 43. Madrid, 1993.

Coaldrake, William H. *The Way of the Carpenter: Tools and Japanese Architecture*. New York and Tokyo: Weatherhill, 1990.

Collins, George. "Antonio Gaudi: Structure and Form." *Perspecta* 8 (1963).

Collins, Peter. *Concrete: The Vision of a New Architecture*. London: Faber & Faber, 1959.

Collins, Peter. "Perret, Auguste." In *Macmillan Encyclopedia of Architects*. New York: Free Press, 1982.

Columbia University. *Architecture and Body*. New York: Rizzoli, 1988.

Conrads, Ulrich, and Bernhard Leitner. "Audible Space: Experiences and Conjectures." *Daidalos* 17 (1985), 28–45.

Cook, John W., and Heinrich Klotz. "Louis Kahn." In *Conversations with Architects*. New York: Praeger, 1973.

Cook, Peter. "Trees and Horizons: The Architecture of Sverre Fehn." *Architectural Review* 170 (August 1981), 102–106.

Coomaraswamy, A. K. *Selected Papers*. Ed. R. Lipsey. Princeton: Princeton University Press, 1977.

Correa, Charles. *The New Landscape—Bombay*. Bombay: Book Society of India, 1985.

Correa, Charles. "Regionalism and Architecture." Lecture at the Bienal, Buenos Aires, 1991.

Coulton, J. J. *Ancient Greek Architects at Work: Problems of Structure and Design*. Ithaca: Cornell University Press, 1977.

Crippa, Maria Antonietta. *Carlo Scarpa: Theory, Design, Projects*. Cambridge: MIT Press, 1986.

Dal Co, Francesco. *Figures of Architecture and Thought: German Architecture Culture, 1880–1920*. New York: Rizzoli, 1990.

Dal Co, Francesco, and Giuseppe Mazzariol. *Carlo Scarpa: The Complete Works*. Milan: Electa; New York: Rizzoli, 1985.

Damisch, Hubert. "The Space Between: A Structuralist Approach to the *Dictionnaire*." *Architectural Design* 50, nos. 3/4 (1980).

Debord, Guy. *Commentary on the Society of the Spectacle*. London: Verso, 1990. Translation of *Commentaires sur le société du spectacle*, 1988.

Denyer, Susan. *African Traditional Architecture*. London: Heinemann, 1978.

De Vere Allen, James, and Thomas H. Wilson. "Swahili Houses and Tombs of the Coast of Kenya." *Art and Archaeology Research Papers*, no. 16 (London, December 1979).

De Zurko, Edward R. *Origins of Functionalist Theory*. New York: Columbia University Press, 1957.

Dimitracopoulou, A. "Dimitris Pikionis." *AAQ* 2/3 (1982), 62.

Dini, Massimo. *Renzo Piano: Projects and Buildings, 1964–1983*. New York: Rizzoli, 1984.

Disosway, Mason Hollier, ed. "Craft and Architecture." *Modulus* 22 (Charlottesville, 1993).

Dormoy, Marie. "Interview d'Auguste Perret sur l'Exposition internationale des arts décoratifs." *L'Amour de l'Art* (May 1925).

Dotremont, Christian, ed. *Cobra 1948–51*. Paris: Jean-Michel Place, 1980.

Drew, Philip. *Leaves of Iron: Glenn Murcutt, Pioneer of an Australian Architectural Form*. Sydney: Law, 1985.

Drew, Philip. "The Petrification of the Tent: The Phenomenon of Tent Mimicry." *Architecture Australia* (June 1987), 18–22.

Drew, Philip. *Tensile Architecture*. Boulder: Westview Press, 1979.

Drew, Phillip. *The Third Generation: The Changing Meaning of Architecture*. New York: Praeger, 1972.

Drexler, Arthur. *The Architecture of Japan*. New York: Museum of Modern Art, 1955.

Drexler, Arthur, ed. *The Architecture of the Ecole des Beaux-Arts*. New York: Museum of Modern Art, 1977.

Duboy, Philippe, and Yukio Futagawa. "Banca Popolare di Verona Head Offices." *Global Architecture* 63 (Tokyo, 1983).

Durand, Jean-Nicolas-Louis. *Nouveau Précis des Leçons d'Architecture, donné à l'Ecole Impériale Polytechnique*. Paris, 1813.

Eastlake, Charles. *A History of the Gothic Revival*. 1872; rpt. New York: Humanities Press, 1970; 2d ed. 1978.

Eco, Umberto. "A Componential Analysis of the Architectural Sign/ Column/ ." *Semiotica* 5, no. 2 (1972). Translation by David Osmond-Smith.

Eliade, Mircea. *The Sacred and the Profane*. New York: Harcourt, Brace & World, 1959.

Elliot, Cecil D. *Technics and Architecture: The Development of Materials and Systems for Buildings*. Cambridge: MIT Press, 1992.

Engel, Heino. *The Japanese House*. Rutland, Vermont: Charles E. Tuttle, 1964.

Engel, Heino. *Measure and Construction of the Japanese House*. Rutland, Vermont: Charles E. Tuttle, 1985.

Evans, Robin. "Mies van der Rohe's Paradoxical Symmetries." *AA Files* 19 (Spring 1990).

Faber, Tobias. *Jørn Utzon, Houses in Fredensborg*. Berlin: Ernst & Sohn, 1991.

Fanelli, Giovanni. *Architettura moderna in Olanda 1900–1940*. Florence: Marchi & Bertolli, 1968. (English translation.)

Fanelli, Giovanni, and Roberto Gagliani. *Il principio del rivestimento: prolegomena a una storia dell'architettura contemporanea*. Rome: Laterza, 1994.

Fathy, Hassan. *Architecture for the Poor: An Experiment in Rural Egypt*. Chicago: University of Chicago Press, 1973.

Fehn, Sverre. "Archaic Modernism." *Architectural Review* 179 (February 1986), 57–60.

Fehn, Sverre. "Biennale di Venezia: 10 architetti per il nuovo palazzo del cinema al Lido." *Domus* 730 (September 1991), 54–56.

Fehn, Sverre. "Has a Doll Life." *Perspecta* 24 (1988).

Fehn, Sverre. *The Poetry of the Straight Line*. Helsinki: Museum of Finnish Architecture, 1992.

Fehn, Sverre. "Three Museums." *AA Files* 9 (Summer 1985), 10–15.

Fehn, Sverre. "The Tree and the Horizon." *Spazio e Società* 3 (1980).

Fichten, John. *Building Construction before Mechanization*. Cambridge: MIT Press, 1986.

Fichten, John. *The Construction of Gothic Cathedrals: A Study of Medieval Vault Erection*. Chicago: University of Chicago Press, 1961; 2d ed. 1981.

Fjeld, Per Olaf. *Sverre Fehn: The Thought of Construction*. New York: Rizzoli, 1983.

Fonatti, Franco. *Elemente des Bauens bei Carlo Scarpa*. Vienna: Wiener Akademiereihe, 1984.

Ford, Edward R. *The Details of Modern Architecture*. Cambridge: MIT Press, 1990.

Forster, Kurt W. "Schinkel's Panoramic Planning of Central Berlin." *Modulus* 16 (Charlottesville, 1983).

Forte, Giorgio. *Antiche ricette di pittura murale*. Venice: Noale, 1984.

Frampton, Kenneth. "Louis Kahn and the French Connection." *Oppositions* 22 (Fall 1980).

Frampton, Kenneth. *Modern Architecture: A Critical History*. London: Thames & Hudson, 1980.

Frampton, Kenneth, Anthony Webster, and Anthony Tischhauser. *Calatrava Bridges*. Zurich: Artemis, 1993.

Frascari, Marco. "The Body and Architecture in the Drawings of Carlo Scarpa." *Res* 14 (Autumn 1987), 123–142.

Frascari, Marco. "A Deciphering of a Wonderful Cipher: Eleven in the Architecture of Carlo Scarpa." *Oz* 13 (1991).

Frascari, Marco. "A Heroic and Admirable Machine: The Theatre of the Architecture of Carlo Scarpa, Architetto Veneto." *Poetics Today* 10 (Spring 1989), 103–124.

Frascari, Marco. "A 'Measure' in Architecture: A Medical-Architectural Theory by Simone Stratico, Architetto Veneto." *Res* 9 (Spring 1985).

Frascari, Marco. "A New Corporeality of Architecture." *Journal of Architectural Education* 40, no. 2 (1987).

Frascari, Marco. "The Tell-the-Tale Detail." In Paula Behrens and Anthony Fisher, eds., *The Building of Architecture*. Via no. 7. Philadelphia: University of Pennsylvania; Cambridge: MIT Press, 1984.

Frascari, Marco. "The True and the Appearance: Italian Facadism and Carlo Scarpa." *Daidalos* 6 (December 1982).

Frei, Hans. "Über Max Bill als Architect." In *Konkrete Architektur*. Baden: Verlag Lars Müller, 1991.

Fuerst, Walter René, and Samuel J. Hume. *Twentieth Century Stage Decoration*. 2 vols. New York: Alfred A. Knopf, 1929; rpt. New York: Dover, 1967.

Futagawa, Yukio, ed. *Frank Lloyd Wright Monograph*. Text by Bruce Breohs Pfeiffer. 12 vols. Tokyo, 1984–1988.

Gage, John, ed. *Goethe on Art*. Berkeley and Los Angeles: University of California Press, 1980.

Gans, Deborah, ed. *Bridging the Gap*. New York: Van Nostrand Reinhold, 1959.

Gehlen, Arnold. *Man in the Age of Technology*. New York: Columbia University Press, 1980.

Gehlen, Arnold. "Die Säkularisierung des Fortschritts." In Gehlen, *Einblicke*, ed. K. S. Rehberg, vol. 7. Frankfurt: Klochtermann, 1978.

Gelpke, Rudolf. "Art and Sacred Drugs in the Orient." *World Cultures and Modern Art*. Munich: Bruckman, 1972.

Geraniotis, Roula. "Gottfried Semper and the Chicago School." Paper delivered at Buell Center symposium on the German influence on American architects, Columbia University, 1988.

Ghermandi, Martino. "I moderni e gli antichi romani." *Costruire* 58 (June 1988), 90–93.

Giedion, Sigfried. *Architecture and the Phenomenon of Transition: Three Space Conceptions of Architecture*. Cambridge: Harvard University Press, 1971.

Giedion, Sigfried. *Architecture, You and Me*. Cambridge: Harvard University Press, 1958.

Giedion, Sigfried. *The Beginnings of Architecture*. Princeton: Princeton University Press, 1964.

Giedion, Sigfried. "Jørn Utzon and the Third Generation." *Zodiac* 14 (1965).

Giedion, Sigfried. *Mechanization Takes Command*. New York: Oxford University Press, 1948; 2d ed. 1955.

Giedion, Sigfried. *Space, Time and Architecture*. Cambridge: Harvard University Press, 1941; 3d ed. 1954.

Girsberger, H. *Alvar Aalto*. London, 1963.

Giurgola, Romaldo, and Jaimini Mehta. *Louis I. Kahn*. Boulder: Westview Press, 1975.

Glaeser, Ludwig. *Mies van der Rohe: Drawings in the Collection of the Museum of Modern Art*. New York, 1969.

Glaeser, Ludwig, and Yukio Futagawa. "Mies van der Rohe: Farnsworth House, Plano, Illinois 1945–1950." *Global Architecture* 27 (Tokyo, 1974).

Glahn, Else. "Chinese Building Standards in the 12th Century." *Scientific American* (May 1981), 162–173.

Glahn, Else. "*Yingzao Fashi*: Chinese Building Standards in the Sung Dynasty." In Paula Behrens and Anthony Fisher, eds., *The Building of Architecture*. Via no. 7. Philadelphia: University of Pennsylvania; Cambridge: MIT Press, 1984.

Glob, P. V. *Denmark: An Archaeological History from the Stone Age to the Vikings*. Ithaca: Cornell University Press, 1971.

Grassi, Giorgio. *L'architettura come mestiere*. Milan: Cluva, 1980.

Grassi, Giorgio. "Avant-Garde and Continuity." *Oppositions* 21 (Summer 1980).

Grassi, Giorgio. *La costruzione logica dell'architettura.* Padua: Marsillo, 1967.

Grassi, Giorgio. "Immagine di Berlage." *Casabella* 249 (March 1961), 38–46.

Grassi, Giorgio. "The Limits of Architecture." *Architectural Design* 52, nos. 5/6 (1982).

Grassi, Giorgio, and Manuel Portaceli. *Projecte di Restauricio i Rehabilitacio del Teatre Roma de Sagnut.* Valenciana, 1986.

Gratama, Jan. *Dr. H. P. Berlage, Bouwmeester.* Rotterdam: W. L. & J. Brusse's, 1925.

Gravagnuolo, Benedetto. "Gottfried Semper, architetto e teorico." *Gottfried Semper: architettura, arte e scienza.* Naples, 1987.

Gray, Christopher. "Cubist Aesthetic Theories." Ph.D. dissertation, Harvard University, 1951.

Gregotti, Vittorio. "Auguste Perret, 1874–1974: Classicism and Rationalism in Perret." *Domus* 534 (May 1974).

Gregotti, Vittorio. "Clues." *Casabella* 484 (October 1982).

Gregotti, Vittorio. *Dentro l'architettura.* Turin: Bollati Boringhieri, 1991.

Gregotti, Vittorio. "The Exercise of Detailing." *Casabella* (June 1983).

Gregotti, Vittorio. "The Obsession with History." *Casabella* 478 (March 1982).

Gregotti, Vittorio. "On Architectural Composition." *A + U* 2 (1970), 20.

Gregotti, Vittorio. "The Shape of Landscape." *Architecture aujourd'hui* (December 1981), 218.

Gregotti, Vittorio. *Il territorio dell'architettura.* Milan: Feltrinelli, 1966.

Gronwold, Ulf. "Archaic Modernism." *Architectural Review* 179 (February 1986), 57–60.

Gronwold, Ulf. "Fehn on Ice." *Architectural Review* 187 (June 1990), 57–59.

Gruber, Karl. *Die Gestalt der deutschen Stadt.* Rpt. Munich: Verlag Callwey, 1952.

Guadet, Julien. *Eléments et théorie de l'architecture.* 4 vols. Paris: Librairie de la Construction Moderne, 1902.

Habermas, Jürgen. *Towards a Rational Society.* New York: Beacon Press, 1970.

Hartoonian, Gevork. *Ontology of Construction.* Cambridge: Cambridge University Press, 1994.

Hauglid, Roar. *Norske Stavkirker; Bygningshistorisk Bakgrunn og Utviking.* Oslo, 1976.

Hearn, M. F. "A Japanese Inspiration for Frank Lloyd Wright's High-Rise Structures." *Journal of the Society of Architectural Historians* 50 (March 1991), 70.

Heidegger, Martin. "Building, Dwelling, Thinking." In *Poetry, Language, Thought.* New York: Harper & Row, 1971.

Heidegger, Martin. *The Question Concerning Technology and Other Essays.* New York: Garland, 1977.

Helm-Petersen, Kjeld. "A New Personality: Jørn Utzon." *Zodiac* 5 (1959), 70–105.

Henderson, Linda Dalrymple. *The Fourth Dimension and Non-Euclidean Geometry in Modern Art.* Princeton: Princeton University Press, 1983.

Hernandez, A. "J. N. L. Durand's Architectural Theory." *Perspecta* 12 (1969).

Herrmann, Wolfgang. *Gottfried Semper: In Search of Architecture.* Cambridge: MIT Press, 1984.

Herrmann, Wolfgang, trans. and intro. *In What Style Should We Build? The German Debate on Architectural Style.* Santa Monica: Getty Center for the History of Art and the Humanities, 1991.

Herrmann, Wolfgang. *Laugier and Eighteenth-Century French Theory.* London, 1962.

Herrmann, Wolfgang. *The Theory of Claude Perrault.* London, 1962.

Hersey, George. *The Lost Meaning of Classical Architecture.* Cambridge: MIT Press, 1988.

Hertzberger, A. "Architecture for People." *A + U* 77 (March 1977), 124–146.

Hertzberger, Herman. "Henri Labrouste, la réalisation de l'art." *Technique et Architecture* 375 (1987–1988).

Hertzberger, Herman. "Place, Choice and Identity." *World Architecture/Four* (London, 1967), 73–74.

Hilberseimer, Ludwig. *Mies van der Rohe.* Chicago: Theobald, 1956.

Hildebrand, Adolf von. *Das Problem der Form in der bildenden Kunst.* Leipzig, 1893. English translation by Max Meyer and Robert Morris Ogden as *The Problem of Form in Painting and Sculpture;* New York: G. E. Stechert and Co., 1907.

Hirt, Aloys Ludwig. *Architecture According to the Basic Principles.* 1809.

Hochstim, Jan. *The Paintings and Sketches of Louis I. Kahn.* New York: Rizzoli, 1991.

Hoffman, Donald. *The Architecture of John Wellborn Root.* Baltimore: Johns Hopkins University Press, 1973.

Honegger, Denis. "Auguste Perret: doctrine de l'architecture." *Techniques et Architecture* 9, nos. 1–2 (1949).

Honey, Sandra, ed. "Mies van der Rohe: European Works." Special issue of *Architectural Design.* London, 1986.

Honor, Hugh. *Neo-Classicism.* London: Penguin, 1968.

Hübsch, Heinrich. *In welchem Style sollen wir bauen?* 1828. English translation by Wolfgang Herrmann as *In What Style Should We Build?* Santa Monica: Getty Center for the History of Art and the Humanities, 1992.

Huff, William. "Louis Kahn: Sorted Reflections and Lapses in Familiarities." *Little Journal* (Society of Architectural Historians, New York Chapter) 5 (September 1981).

Humbert, Claude. *Islamic Ornamental Design.* New York: Hastings House, 1980.

Jamot, B. *A.-G. Perret et l'architecture du béton armé.* Brussels: G. Vanoest, 1927.

Joedicke, Jürgen. *Pier Luigi Nervi.* Milan: Edizioni di Comunità, 1957.

Johnson, Mark. *The Body in the Mind.* Chicago: University of Chicago Press, 1987.

Johnson, Nell E., ed. *Light Is the Theme: Louis I. Kahn and the Kimbell Art Museum.* Fort Worth, Texas, 1975.

Johnson, Philip C. *Mies van der Rohe.* New York: Museum of Modern Art, 1947. 3d ed. 1978.

Jones, Dalu, and George Michell, eds. "Mobile Architecture in Asia: Ceremonial Chariots, Floats and Carriages." *Art and Archaeology Research Papers,* no. 16 (London, December 1979).

Jones, Owen. *The Grammar of Ornament.* 1856; rpt. New York: Portland House, 1987.

Jørgensen, Lisbeth Balslev. "Jensen-Klint, P. V." In *Macmillan Encyclopedia of Architects.* New York: Free Press, 1982.

Kahn, Louis I. *Architecture d'Aujourd'hui* 33, no. 105 (December 1962–January 1963).

Kahn, Louis I. "Building Engineering." *Architectural Forum* (November 1952).

Kahn, Louis I. "Design with the Automobile: The Animal World." *Canadian Art* 19 (January–February 1962).

Kahn, Louis I. Foreword to *Carlo Scarpa architetto poeta.* London: Royal Institute of British Architects, Heinz Gallery, 1974.

Kahn, Louis I. "Form and Design." *Architectural Design* 31 (April 1961).

Kahn, Louis I. "Louis Kahn." *Architecture and Urbanism* (November 1983), whole issue.

Kahn, Louis I. "Louis Kahn." *Perspecta* 7 (1961).

Kahn, Louis I. "Monumentality." In Paul Zucker, ed., *New Architecture and City Planning: A Symposium.* New York: Philosophical Library, 1944.

Kahn, Louis I. "Order in Architecture." *Perspecta* 4 (1957).

Kahn, Louis I. "Order Is." *Perspecta* 3 (1955).

Kahn, Louis I. "Silence and Light." *Architecture and Urbanism* 3 (January 1973), whole issue.

Kahn, Louis I. "Toward a Plan for Midtown Philadelphia." *Perspecta* 2 (1953).

Kao, Kenneth Martin. "Frank Lloyd Wright: Experiments in Building." *Modulus* 22 (Charlottesville, 1993), 66–93.

Klotz, Heinrich. *Conversations with Architects.*

Kommendant, August E. *18 Years with Architect Louis I. Kahn.* Englewood, N.J.: Aloray, 1975.

Konstantinidis, Aris. *Elements for Self-Knowledge: Towards a True Architecture.* Athens, 1975.

Koulermos, P. "The Work of Konstantinidis." *Architectural Design* 34 (May 1964).

Kropotkin, Peter. *Factories, Fields, and Workshops.* London: Hutchinson; Boston: Houghton Mifflin, 1899. Rev. ed. 1913.

Ksiazek, Sarah. "Architectural Discourse in the Fifties: Louis Kahn and the National Assembly Complex in Dacca." *Journal of the Society of Architectural Historians* 52 (December 1993), 416–435.

Lambot, Ian. *The New Headquarters for the Hongkong and Shanghai Banking Corporation.* Hong Kong: Ian Lambot, 1986.

Lasdun, Denys. *Architecture in an Age of Skepticism.* New York: Oxford University Press, 1984.

Laugier, Marc-Antoine. *Essai sur l'architecture.* Paris, 1753. English translation as *An Essay on Architecture;* Los Angeles: Hennessey & Ingalls, 1977.

Laugier, Marc-Antoine. *Observations sur l'architecture.* The Hague, 1765.

Lawlor, Robert. *Sacred Geometry.* London: Thames and Hudson, 1982.

Le Corbusier. *Des Canons, Des Munitions . . . Merci! Des Logis, S.V.P.—Monographie du "Pavillon des Temps Nouveaux" à l'exposition internationale "art et technique de Paris."* 1937.

Le Corbusier. *The Modulor.* Cambridge: Harvard University Press, 1954.

Le Corbusier. *Précisions sur un état présent de l'architecture et de l'urbanisme.* Paris: Crès, 1930; rpt. Paris: Vincent Fréal, 1960.

Le Corbusier. *Vers une architecture.* Paris, 1923. English translation by Frederick Etchells as *Towards a New Architecture;* London: John Rodker, 1931.

Le Corbusier and François de Pierrefeu. *The Home of Man.* London, 1948.

Lefaivre, Liane, and Alexander Tzonis. "The Grid and the Pathway." *Architecture in Greece* 15 (1981), 164–178.

Lemoine, Bertrand. *Gustave Eiffel.* Paris: Hazan, 1984.

Lesourd, Paul. *The Pantheon,* trans. Anne Dorny. Paris: Caisse Nationale des Monuments Historiques et des Sites, 1965.

Levine, Neil. "The Romantic Idea of Architectural Legibility: Henri Labrouste and the Neo-Grec." In *The Architecture of the Ecole des Beaux-Arts,* ed. Arthur Drexler. New York: Museum of Modern Art, 1977.

Lindsay, Jack. *The Origins of Alchemy in Greco-Roman Egypt.* London: Muller, 1970.

Lipman, Jonathan. *Frank Lloyd Wright and the Johnson Wax Buildings.* New York: Rizzoli, 1986.

Lippard, Lucy R. *Ad Reinhardt.* New York: Abrams, 1981.

Lipps, Theodor. "Ranästhetic und geometrisch-optische Täuschungen." In *Gesellschaft für psychologische Forschungsschriften,* second collection, vol. IX–X. Leipzig, 1893.

Lobell, John. *Between Silence and Light: Spirit in the Architecture of Louis I. Kahn.* Boulder: Westview Press, 1979.

Lobell, Mimi. "Postscript: Kahn, Penn and the Philadelphia School." *Oppositions* 4 (October 1974).

Loos, Adolf. *The Architecture of Adolf Loos.* London: Arts Council of Great Britain, 1985.

Loos, Adolf. *Spoken into the Void: Collected Essays 1897–1900.* Cambridge: MIT Press, 1982.

Los, Sergio. *Carlo Scarpa: architetto poeta.* Venice: Edizioni Cluva, 1967.

Loud, Patricia Cummings. *The Art Museums of Louis I. Kahn.* Durham: Duke University Press, 1989.

Lüchinger, Arnulf. "Dutch Structuralism." *A + U* 77 (March 1977), 47–65.

Lüchinger, Arnulf. *Herman Hertzberger: Buildings and Projects 1959–1986.* The Hague: Arch-Edition, 1987.

Lüchinger, Arnulf. *Structuralism in Architecture and City Planning.* Stuttgart: Karl Kramer, 1981.

Magagnato, Licisco. *Carlo Scarpa a Castelvecchio.* Milan: Edizioni di Comunità, 1982.

Magagnato, Licisco. "Scarpa's Museum." *Lotus* 35 (1982), 75–85.

Malevich, Kazimir. *The Non-Objective World.* Trans. Howard Dearstyne, introduction by Ludwig Hilberseimer. Chicago: Paul Theobald & Co., 1959.

Mallgrave, Harry Francis. "Gustav Klemm and Gottfried Semper: The Meeting of Ethnological and Architectural Theory." *Res* 9 (Spring 1985).

Mallgrave, Harry Francis, and Eleftherios Ikonomou, intro. and trans. *Empathy, Form, and Space: Problems in German Aesthetics, 1873–1893.* Santa Monica: Getty Center for the History of Art and the Humanities, 1994.

Manson, Grant Carpenter. *Frank Lloyd Wright to 1910: The First Golden Age.* New York: Reinhold, 1958.

Manson, Grant Carpenter. "Wright in the Nursery: The Influence of Froebel Education on the Work of Frank Lloyd Wright." *Architectural Review* 113 (June 1953).

Mark, Robert. *Experiments in Gothic Structure.* Cambridge: MIT Press, 1982.

Mark, Robert. *Light, Wind and Structure.* Cambridge: MIT Press, 1990.

Marta, Roberto. *Architettura romana: tecniche costruttive e forme architettoniche del mondo romano.* Rome: Edizioni Kappa, 1985.

Mazzariol, Giuseppe. "Un opera di Carlo Scarpa: il riordino di un antico palazzo veneziano." *Zodiac* 13 (1964).

McAuliffe, Mary. "Small Craft Warnings, Thickening Horizons, Hollowing Walls." *Modulus* 22 (Charlottesville, 1993), 95–110.

McCleary, Peter. "Structure and Intuition." *AIA Journal* (October 1980), 57–119.

McEwen, Indra Kagis. *Socrates' Ancestor: An Essay on Architectural Beginnings.* Cambridge: MIT Press, 1993.

McQuade, Walter. "Architect Louis Kahn and His Strong-Boned Structures." *Architectural Forum* 107 (October 1957), 134–143.

Meagher, Robert. "Technê." *Perspecta* 24 (1988), 158–167.

Menocal, Narciso. *Architecture as Nature: The Transcendentalist Idea of Louis Sullivan.* Madison: University of Wisconsin Press, 1981.

Middleton, Robin. "The Abbé de Cordemoy and the Graeco-Gothic Ideal: A Prelude to Romantic Classicism." *Journal of the Warburg and Courtauld Institutes* 25 (July–December 1962), 278–320.

Middleton, Robin. "Architects as Engineers: The Iron Reinforcement of Entablatures in Eighteenth-Century France." *AA Files* 9 (Summer 1985).

Middleton, Robin, ed. *The Beaux-Arts and Nineteenth-Century French Architecture.* Cambridge: MIT Press, 1982.

Middleton, Robin. "The Rationalist Interpretations of Leonce Reynaud and Viollet-le-Duc." *AA Files* 11 (Spring 1986).

Middleton, Robin. "Viollet-le-Duc, Eugène-Emmanuel." In *Macmillan Encyclopedia of Architects.* New York: Free Press, 1982.

Mies van der Rohe, Ludwig. "Mies Speaks, I Do Not Design Buildings, I Develop Buildings." *Architectural Review* 144 (December 1968).

Mies van der Rohe, Ludwig. "L'Oeuvre de Mies van der Rohe." Interview with Christian Norberg-Schultz. *Architecture d'Aujourd'hui* 29, no. 79 (September 1958).

Miller, Richard, ed. *Four Great Makers of Modern Architecture.* New York: Columbia University, School of Architecture, 1963.

Møller, Henrik Sten. "'Can Lis': Jørn Utzon's Own House." *Living Architecture* 8 (1989), 146–167.

Møller, Henrik Sten. "Jørn Utzon on Architecture: A Conversation with Henrik Sten Møller." *Living Architecture* 8 (Copenhagen, 1989), 168–173.

Moneo, Rafael. "The Idea of Lasting." *Perspecta* 24 (1988).

Moneo, Rafael. "The Solitude of Buildings." Kenzo Tange Lecture, March 9, 1985, Graduate School of Design, Harvard University.

Mooney, Michael. *Vico in the Tradition of Rhetoric.* Princeton: Princeton University Press, 1985.

Morgan, Lewis H. *Houses and House-Life of the American Aborigines.* Chicago: University of Chicago, 1881; rpt. 1965.

Moser, Oskar. *Das Bauernhaus und seine landschaftliche und historische Entwicklung in Kärnten.* Klagenfurt: Verlag des Geschichtsvereines für Kärnten, 1992.

Müller, Karl Otfried. *Ancient Art and Its Remains, or a Manual of the Archaeology of Art.* Trans. J. Leitch. London, 1847.

Murphy, Richard. *Carlo Scarpa and the Castelvecchio.* London: Butterworth, 1992.

Muthesius, Hermann. *Style-Architecture and Building Art: Transformations of Architecture in the Nineteenth Century and Its Present Condition.* Intro. and trans. Stanford Anderson. Santa Monica: Getty Center for the History of Art and the Humanities, 1994.

Nakamura, Toshio. *Carlo Scarpa.* Tokyo: A + U, 1985.

Nakamura, Toshio. *Renzo Piano Building Workshop 1964–1988.* Tokyo: A + U, 1989.

Nervi, Pier Luigi. *Nervi: Space and Structural Integrity.* Exhibition catalog. San Francisco: San Francisco Museum of Art, 1961.

Neuenschwander, Eduard and Claudia. *Alvar Aalto and Finnish Architecture.* New York: Praeger, 1954.

Neumeyer, Fritz. *The Artless Word: Mies van der Rohe on the Building Art.* Trans. Mark Jarzombek. Cambridge: MIT Press, 1991.

Neumeyer, Fritz. "Iron and Stone: The Architecture of the Grossstadt." In Harry Mallgrave, ed., *Otto Wagner: Reflections on the Raiment of Modernity.* Santa Monica: Getty Center for the History of Art and the Humanities, 1993.

Newman, Oscar. *New Frontiers in Architecture: CIAM in Otterloo, 1959.* New York: Universe Books, 1961.

Nicolin, Pier Luigi. "The Unfinished: Bank by Carlo Scarpa in Verona." *Lotus* 28 (1981).

Nitschke, Gunter. "*en*—Transactional Space." *Daidalos* 33 (September 1989), 64–78.

Nitschke, Gunter. "Ma: Place, Space and Void." *Kyoto Journal* 8 (Fall 1988), 33–39.

Nitschke, Gunter. "Shime: Binding/Unbinding." *Architectural Design* 44 (1974), 747–791.

Nitschke, Gunter. "Shime: Building, Binding, and Occupying." *Daidalos* 29 (September 1988), 104–116.

Norberg-Schulz, Christian. "Church at Bagsvaerd." *Global Architecture* 61 (Tokyo, 1981).

Norberg-Schulz, Christian. "Kahn, Heidegger, and the Language of Architecture." *Oppositions* 18 (Fall 1979).

Norberg-Schulz, Christian. "The Sydney Opera House." *Global Architecture* 54 (Tokyo, 1980).

Norri, Marja-Ritta, and Maija Karkkainen, eds. *Sverre Fehn: The Poetry of the Straight Line.* Helsinki: Museum of Finnish Architecture, 1992.

Oechslin, Werner. "Soufflot, Jacques-Germain." In *Macmillan Encyclopedia of Architects.* New York: Free Press, 1982.

O'Gorman, James F. *The Architecture of Frank Furness.* Philadelphia: Philadelphia Museum of Art, 1973.

Okamura, T. "Interview with Tadao Ando." *Ritual: The Princeton Journal, Thematic Studies in Architecture* 1 (1983), 126–134.

Onians, John. *Bearers of Meaning: The Classical Orders in Antiquity, the Middle Ages and the Renaissance.* Princeton: Princeton University Press, 1988.

Paricio, Ignacio. "Tres observaciones inconvenientes sobre la construcción en la obra americana." *Mies van der Rohe, 1886–1986.* Monografías de Arquitectura y Vivienda, no. 6. Madrid, 1986.

(Paxton, Joseph). *The Building Erected in Hyde Park for the Great Exhibition, 1851.* London, 1971.

Peckham, Andrew. "This Is the Modern World." *Architectural Design* 49 (February 1979), 2–26.

Pehnt, Wolfgang. *German Architecture, 1960–1970.* New York: Praeger, 1970.

Pérez-Gómez, Alberto. *Architecture and the Crisis of Modern Science.* Cambridge: MIT Press, 1983.

Perrault, Claude. *Ordonnance for the Five Kinds of Columns after the Method of the Ancients.* Trans. Indra Kagis McEwen, introduction by Alberto Pérez-Gómez. Santa Monica: Getty Center for the History of Art and the Humanities, 1993.

Perret, Auguste. *Contribution à une théorie de l'architecture.* Paris: Cercle d'études architecturales André Wahl, 1952. First published in *Das Werk* 34–35 (February 1947).

Perret, Auguste. "Exposition des arts décoratifs et industriels modernes—Théâtre." *L'Architect* 2 (June 1925), 58–62.

Perret, Auguste. "Musée des Travaux Publics à Paris." *Techniques et Architecture* 3 (March-April 1943), 62–73.

Perret, Auguste. "Le Palais de Bois à l'Exposition de Paris 1925." *Architecture d'Aujourd'hui* 11, no. 44 (November 1938).

Perret, Auguste. "Perret: 25 bis rue Franklin." *Rassegna* 28 (1979), whole issue.

Perret, Auguste. *Techniques et Architecture* 9, no. 1–2 (1949).

Pertuiset, Nicole. "Reflective Practice." *Journal of Architectural Education* 40, no. 2 (1987), 59–61.

Peschken, Goerd. *Karl Friedrich Schinkel: Lebenswerke; Das architektonische Lehrbuch.* Berlin, 1979.

Peters, Tom F. "An American Culture of Construction." *Perspecta* 25 (1989), 142–161.

Pevsner, Nikolaus. *A History of Building Types.* Princeton: Princeton University Press, 1976.

Pevsner, Nikolaus. *Some Architectural Writers of the Nineteenth Century.* Oxford: Clarendon Press, 1972.

Pevsner, Nikolaus. *Studies in Art, Architecture and Design.* 2 vols. New York: Walker & Co., 1968.

Piano, Renzo. "Renzo Piano Building Workshop 1964–1991: In Search of a Balance." *Process: Architecture* 100 (Tokyo, January 1992).

Pica, Agnoldomenico. *Pier Luigi Nervi.* Rome: Editalia, 1969.

Pietropoli, Guido. "L'invitation au voyage." *Spazio e Società* 50 (June 1990), 90–98.

Pikionis, Dimitris. "Memoirs." *Zygos* (January-February 1958), 4–7.

Pikionis, Dimitris. "A Sentimental Topography." *The Third Eye* (Athens, November-December 1933), 13–17.

Polano, Sergio, ed. *Hendrik Petrus Berlage.* New York: Rizzoli, 1988.

Poley, Arthur F. E. *St. Paul's Cathedral, London: Measured, Drawn, and Described.* London: the author, 1927; rev. ed. 1932.

Portoghesi, Paolo. "The Brion Cemetery by Carlo Scarpa." *Global Architecture* 50 (Tokyo, 1979).

Posener, Julius. "Apparat und Gegenstand." In *Aufsätze und Votäge, 1931–1980.* Braunschweig: Vieweg, 1981.

Pugin, A. W. *Contrasts; or, A Parallel between the Noble Edifices of the Middle Ages and Corresponding Buildings of the Present Day; Showing the Present Decay of Taste.* London: C. Dolman, 1836; rpt. New York: Humanities Press, 1969.

Pugin, A. W. *The True Principles of Pointed or Christian Architecture.* London: John Weale, 1841; rpt. London: Academy Editions, 1973.

Pundt, Hermann G. *Schinkel's Berlin.* Cambridge: Harvard University Press, 1972.

Quetglas, José. "Fear of Glass: The Barcelona Pavilion." In Joan Ockman and Beatriz Colomina, eds., *Architectureproduction.* New York: Princeton Architectural Press, 1988.

Quinan, Jack. *Frank Lloyd Wright's Larkin Building: Myth and Fact.* Cambridge: MIT Press; New York: Architectural History Foundation, 1987.

Rasmussen, Steen Eiler. *Experiencing Architecture.* Cambridge: MIT Press, 1964.

Raymond, Antonin. *An Autobiography.* Rutland, Vermont: Charles E. Tuttle, 1973.

Redtenbacher, Rudolph. *Die Architektonik der modernen Baukunst.* Berlin, 1883.

Reichlin, Bruno. "The Pros and Cons of the Horizontal Window: The Perret-Le Corbusier Controversy." *Daidalos* 13 (September 1984), 65–77.

Reinhardt, Ad. *Art as Art: The Selected Writings of Ad Reinhardt.* Ed. Barbara Rose. New York: Viking Press, 1975.

Rice, Peter. *An Engineer Imagines.* London: Artemis, 1993.

Rice, Peter, and Hugh Dutton. *Le Verre structurel.* Paris: Moniteur, 1990.

Rietdorf, Alfred, ed. *Gilly: Wiedergeburt der Architektur.* Berlin: H. von Hugo, 1943.

Robb, David M., Jr. *Louis I. Kahn Sketches for the Kimbell Art Museum.* Fort Worth: Kimbell Art Foundation, 1978.

Robertson, J. Drummond. *The Evolution of Clockwork.* London: Cassell, 1931.

Rondelet, Jean. *Traité théorique et pratique de l'art de bâtir.* 3 vols. Paris: chez l'auteur, 1830.

Ronner, Heinz, Sharad Jhaveri, and Alessandro Vasella. *Louis I. Kahn: Complete Works, 1935–74.* Boulder: Westview Press, 1977.

Roth, Alfred. *La Nouvelle architecture. Presentée en 20 examples.* Zurich: Girsberger, 1940.

Roux-Spitz, Michael. "La Bibliothèque Nationale de Paris." *Architecture d'Aujourd'hui*, no. 3 (March 1938), 30–45.

Rowe, Colin. "Neoclassicism and Modern Architecture." *Oppositions* 1 (1973), 1–26.

Rudi, Arrigo, and Valter Rosetto. *La sede centrale della Banca Popolare di Verona.* Verona, 1983.

Rudofsky, Bernard. *Architecture without Architects.* New York: Museum of Modern Art, 1965.

Rykwert, Joseph. *The First Moderns: The Architects of the Eighteenth Century.* Cambridge: MIT Press, 1980.

Rykwert, Joseph. *The Idea of a Town.* Cambridge: MIT Press, 1988.

Rykwert, Joseph. *The Necessity of Artifice: Ideas in Architecture.* New York: Rizzoli, 1982.

Rykwert, Joseph. "Semper and the Conception of Style." In *Gottfried Semper und die Mitte des 19. Jahrhunderts.* Basel and Stuttgart: Birkhäuser, 1976.

Rykwert, Joseph. "The Work of Gino Valle." *Architectural Design* 34 (March 1964), 112–113.

Sachs, Hans. *The Creative Unconscious.* Cambridge, Mass.: Sci-Art Publishers, 1942.

Saddy, P. "Henri Labrouste: architecte-constructeur." *Les Monuments Historiques de la France* 6 (1975), 10–17.

St. John Wilson, Colin. "Sigurd Lewerentz and the Dilemma of the Classical." *Perspecta* 24 (1988), 50–77.

Santini, Pier Carlo, and Yukio Futagawa. "Banca Popolare di Verona by Carlo Scarpa." In *GA Document 4.* Tokyo: ADA Edita, 1981.

Santini, Pier Carlo, and Yukio Futagawa. "Olivetti Showroom, Querini Stampalia, and Castelvecchio Museum." *Global Architecture* 51 (Tokyo, 1979), entire issue.

Scarpa, Carlo. "Carlo Scarpa." *A + U* (October 1985), extra edition.

Scarpa, Carlo. "Carlo Scarpa, frammenti: 1926/1978." *Rassegna* 27 (1979), whole issue.

Schild, Erich. *Zwischen Glaspalast und Palais des Illusions: Form und Konstruktion in 19 Jahrhundert.* Berlin: Bauwelt Fundamente, Ullstein, 1967.

Schinkel, Karl Friedrich. *Sammlung architektonische Entwurfe.* 1841–1843; rpt. Chicago: Exedra Books, 1981.

Schmarsow, August. *Das Wesen der architektonischen Schöpfung.* Leipzig: K. W. Hiersemann, 1894.

Schmutzler, Robert. *Art Nouveau.* New York: Abrams, 1962.

Schnaidt, Claude. *Hannes Meyer: Buildings, Writings and Projects.* London: Tiranti, 1965.

Schofield, P. H. *The Theory of Proportion in Architecture.* Cambridge: Cambridge University Press, 1958.

Schopenhauer, Arthur. *The World as Will and Idea* (1818). 6th ed. London: K. Paul, Trench, Trubner & Co., 1907–1909.

Schulze, Franz. *Mies van der Rohe: A Critical Biography.* Chicago: University of Chicago Press, 1985.

Schwarzer, Mitchell. "Ontology and Representation in Karl Bötticher's Theory of Tectonics." *Journal of the Society of Architectural Historians* 52 (September 1993), 267–280.

Scully, Vincent J. *Louis Kahn.* New York: Braziller, 1962.

Searing, Helen. "Berlage, Hendrik Petrus." In *Macmillan Encyclopedia of Architects.* New York: Free Press, 1982.

Segger, Heinz Geret, and Max Peintner. *Otto Wagner 1841–1916.* New York: Praeger, 1970.

"Seiersted Bodtker House, Oslo, Norway." *GA Houses* 2 (1977), 158–165.

Sekler, Eduard F. "Architecture and the Flow of Time." *Crit* 18 (Spring 1987), 43–48.

Sekler, Eduard F. "The Stoclet House by Josef Hoffmann." In Howard Hibbard, Henry Millon, and Milton Levine, eds., *Essays in the History of Architecture Presented to Rudolf Wittkower.* London: Phaidon, 1967.

Sekler, Eduard F. "Structure, Construction, Tectonics." In Gyorgy Kepes, ed., *Structure in Art and Science.* New York: Braziller, 1965.

Semper, Gottfried. "The Development of the Wall and Wall Construction in Antiquity" and "On the Relation of Architectural Systems with the General Cultural Conditions." Edited with a preface by Harry Francis Mallgrave. *Res* 11 (Spring 1986), 33–53.

Semper, Gottfried. *The Four Elements of Architecture and Other Writings.* Trans. Harry Francis Mallgrave and Wolfgang Herrmann. Cambridge: Cambridge University Press, 1989.

Semper, Gottfried. "On Architectural Symbols." London lecture of autumn 1854. *Res* 9 (Spring 1985), 61–68.

Semper, Gottfried. "On the Origin of Some Architectural Styles." London lecture of December 1853. *Res* 9 (Spring 1985), 53–61.

Semper, Gottfried. *Der Stil in den technischen und tektonischen Kunsten oder praktische Aesthetik.* 2 vols. 1860–1863; 2d ed. Munich: F. Bruchmann, 1878–1879.

Sergeant, John. *Frank Lloyd Wright's Usonian Houses: The Case for Organic Architecture.* New York: Whitney Library of Design, 1976.

Sergeant, John. "Woof and Warp: A Spatial Analysis of Frank Lloyd Wright's Usonian Houses." *Environment and Planning B* 3 (1976), 211–224.

Service, Alastair, and Jean Bradbery. *Megaliths and Their Mysteries: The Standing Stones of Old Europe.* London: Weidenfeld & Nicholson, 1979.

Seymour, A.T., III. "The Immeasurable Made Measurable: Building the Kimbell Art Museum." In Paula Behrens and Anthony Fisher, eds., *The Building of Architecture.* Via no. 7. Philadelphia: University of Pennsylvania; Cambridge: MIT Press, 1984.

Shankland, Graeme. "Architect of the 'Clear and Reasonable': Mies van der Rohe." *The Listener,* 15 October 1959, 620–622.

Sharp, Dennis. *Modern Architecture and Expressionism.* London: Longmans, 1966.

Simonsen, Svend. *Bagsvaerd Church.* Bagsvaerd Parochial Church Council, Denmark, 1978.

Singelenberg, Pieter. *H. P. Berlage: Idea and Style, the Quest for Modern Architecture.* Utrecht: Haentjens Dekker & Gumbert, 1972.

Singer, Charles, et al. *A History of Technology.* London: Oxford University Press, 1958.

Skolimowski, Henryk. *Eco-Philosophy: Designing New Tactics for Living.* Boston: Boyars, 1981.

Skriver, Paul Erik. "Kuwait National Assembly Complex." *Living Architecture* 5 (1986), 114–127.

Skriver, Paul Erik. "The Platform and the Element in Utzon's Work." *Arkitektur* 3 (June 1964).

Smith, Kathryn. *Frank Lloyd Wright: Hollyhock House and Olive Hill.* New York: Rizzoli, 1992.

Smith, Vincent. *The Sydney Opera House.* 1974; rpt. Sydney: Paul Hamlyn, 1979.

Smiths, Norris Kelley. *Frank Lloyd Wright: A Study in Architectural Context.* Englewood Cliffs, N.J.: Prentice-Hall, 1966.

Smithson, Alison and Peter. *Without Rhetoric: An Architectural Aesthetic.* London: Latimer New Dimensions, 1973.

Snodin, Michael, ed. *Karl Friedrich Schinkel: A Universal Man.* New Haven: Yale University Press, 1991.

Sola-Morales, Ignasí de. "Critical Discipline: Review of Giorgio Grassi, 'L'architettura come mestiere.'" *Oppositions* 23 (1981), 140–150.

Sola-Morales, Ignasí de. "Weak Architecture." *Ottagono* 92 (1991), 88–117.

Somers, Clarke, and R. Engelbach. *Ancient Egyptian Construction and Architecture.* London: Oxford University Press, 1930; rpt. New York: Dover, 1990.

Spaeth, David. *Mies van der Rohe.* New York: Rizzoli, 1985.

Spence, Rory. "Constructive Education." *Architectural Review* 186 (July 1989), 27–33.

Staber, Margit. "Hans Scharoun: ein Beitrag zum organischen Bauen." *Zodiac* 10 (1963), 52–93.

Stace, W. T. *The Philosophy of Hegel.* 1924; rpt. New York: Dover, 1955.

Stanton, Phoebe. *Pugin.* New York: Viking, 1972.

Stanton, Phoebe. "Pugin, Augustus Welby Northmore." In *Macmillan Encylopedia of Architects.* New York: Free Press, 1982.

Steiner, George. *Martin Heidegger.* New York: Viking Press, 1979.

Steinhardt, Nancy Shatzman. *Chinese Traditional Architecture.* New York: China Institute in America, 1984.

Stokes, Adrian. *The Critical Writings of Adrian Stokes.* 3 vols. London: Thames and Hudson, 1978.

Stokes, Adrian. *Greek Culture and the Ego: A Psycho-Analytic Survey of an Aspect of Greek Civilization and of Art.* London: Tavistock, 1958.

Stokvis, Willemijn. *Cobra: An International Movement in Art after the Second World War.* New York: Rizzoli, 1988.

Suisman, Doug. "The Design of the Kimbell: Variations on a Sublime Archetype." *Design Book Review* (Winter 1987), 36–47.

Sullivan, Louis. "Suggestions in Artistic Brickwork." 1910; rpt. *Prairie School Review* 4 (2d Quarter 1967).

Sullivan, Louis. *A System of Architectural Ornament According with a Philosophy of Man's Power.* 1924; rpt. New York: Eakins Press, 1966.

"Sverre Fehn." *Byggekunst: The Norwegian Review of Architecture* 74 (1992), 76–127.

Sweeney, Robert L. *Wright in Hollywood: Visions of a New Architecture.* New York: Architectural History Foundation; Cambridge: MIT Press, 1994.

Tafuri, Manfredo. "Am Steinhof: Centrality and Surface in Otto Wagner's Architecture." *Lotus* 29 (1981), 73–91.

Tafuri, Manfredo. *History of Italian Architecture, 1944–1985.* Cambridge: MIT Press, 1989.

Tafuri, Manfredo, and Francesco Dal Co. *Modern Architecture.* New York: Abrams, 1979. Translation of *L'architettura contemporanea;* Milan: Electa Editrice, 1976.

Tange, Kenzo, and Noboru Kawazoe. *Ise: Prototype of Japanese Architecture.* Cambridge: MIT Press, 1965.

Taut, Bruno. *Die Stadtkrone.* Jena: Eugen Diederichs, 1919.

Taylor, Brian Brace, and Raul Shelder. "Technology and Image: Architects' Roles." *Mimar* 1 (1981), 24–45.

Taylor, Charles. *Hegel and Modern Society.* Cambridge: Cambridge University Press, 1979.

Tegethoff, Wolf. *Mies van der Rohe: The Villas and Country Houses.* New York: Museum of Modern Art, 1985.

Thompson, D'Arcy Wentworth. *On Growth and Form.* Ed. J. T. Bonner. Cambridge: Cambridge University Press, 1971. First published 1917; expanded and revised 1942.

Thompson, Fred S. "Manifestation of the Japanese Sense of Space in Matsuri." In *Fudo: An Introduction,* ed. A.V. Liman and F. Thompson. University of Waterloo, c. 1986.

Tyng, Alexandra. *Beginnings: Louis I. Kahn's Philosophy of Architecture.* New York: Wiley & Sons, l984.

Utzon, Jørn. "Atriumhaussiedlung in Kingo." *Bauen und Wohnen* 16 (February 1962), 74–75.

Utzon, Jørn. "Court Houses of Elsinore, Denmark." *Architectural Design* 30 (September 1960), 347–348.

Utzon, Jørn. "Elements in the Way of Life." Interview by Karkur Komonen. *Arkkitehti* 80, no. 2 (1983).

Utzon, Jørn. "Elineberg." *Zodiac* 5 (1959).

Utzon, Jørn. "Elviria." *Arkitektur* 3 (June 1964), 99.

Utzon, Jørn. "House in Majorca." *Quaderns* 153 (September 1982), 22–29.

Utzon, Jørn. "Jørn Utzon: Additiv arkitektur." *Arkitektur* 14, no. 1 (Copenhagen, 1970).

Utzon, Jørn. "Nordic Architects; Asplund, Aalto, Jacobsen and Utzon." Interview. *Quaderns* 137 (April/June 1983), 8–115.

Utzon, Jørn. "Nordisk ide-konkurrence om et Center for hojere Uddannelse og forskning i Odense." *Arkitekten* 69, no. 4 (1967), 69–104.

Utzon, Jørn. "Own Home at Hellebaek, Denmark." *Byggekunst* 5 (1951), 83.

Utzon, Jørn. "Platforms and Plateaus: The Ideas of a Danish Architect." *Zodiac* 10 (1962), 112–140.

Utzon, Jørn. RIBA Address, "Jørn Utzon, Royal Gold Medalist." *RIBA Journal* 85 (1978), 425–427.

Utzon, Jørn. "Schauspielhaus, Zürich." *Deutsche Bauzeitung* 10 (October 1965), 829.

Utzon, Jørn. "Silkeborg Art Gallery." *Arkitektur* 8 (February 1964), 1–5.

Utzon, Jørn. "Three Buildings by Jørn Utzon: Sydney Opera House, the Silkeborg Museum, the Zurich Theatre." *Zodiac* 14 (1965), 48–93.

Utzon, Jørn. "Three Houses in Denmark." *Architect's Yearbook* 6 (London, 1955), 173–181.

Utzon, Jørn, and Tobias Faber. "Tendenze: Notidens Arkitektur." *Arkitekten* (Copenhagen), 1947, 63–69.

Utzon, Jørn, with Tobias Faber and Mogens Irming. "Forslag til Crystal Palace i London." *Arkitekten* 49 (1947).

Valéry, Paul. "The History of Amphion." In *The Collected Works of Paul Valéry,* ed. Jackson Mathews. Vol. 3. Princeton: Princeton University Press, 1960.

Vallhonrat, Carlos. "Tectonics Considered between the Presence and Absence of Artifice." *Perspecta* 24 (1988), 122–135.

Van der Laan, Dom H. *Architectonic Space.* Leiden: Brill, 1983.

Van de Ven, Cornelis. *Space in Architecture.* Assen, The Netherlands: Van Gorcum, 1978.

Van Eck, Caroline. *Organicism in Nineteenth Century Architecture: An Inquiry into Its Theoretical and Philosophical Background.* Amsterdam: Architectura and Natura Press, 1994.

Van Eyck, Aldo. "Kinderhaus in Amsterdam." *Werk* (January 1962), 16–21.

Van Eyck, Aldo. "Labyrinthine Clarity." *World Architecture/Three* (London, 1966), 120–122.

Van Heuvel, Wim J. *Structuralism in Dutch Architecture.* Rotterdam: Uitgeverij, 1992.

Van Zanten, David T. "Jones, Owen." In *Macmillan Encyclopedia of Architects.* New York: Free Press, 1982.

Van Zanten, David T. "Labrouste, Henri." In *Macmillan Encyclopedia of Architects.* New York: Free Press, 1982.

Vattimo, Gianni. "Dialoghi fra Carlo Olmo e Gianni Vattimo." *Eupalino* 6 (1986), 2–6.

Vattimo, Gianni. *The End of Modernity.* Cambridge, England: Polity Press, 1988.

Vattimo, Gianni. "Myth and the Fate of Secularization." *Res* 9 (Spring 1985), 29–36.

Vattimo, Gianni. "Project and Legitimation 1." Conference held at Centro Culturale Polifunzionale, Bra, June 6, 1985.

Vattimo, Gianni. *The Transparent Society.* Baltimore: Johns Hopkins University Press, 1992.

Venene, Donald Phillip. "Vico's Philosophy of Imagination." In *Vico and Contemporary Thought,* ed. Giorgio Tagliacozzo et al. Atlantic Highlands, N.J.: Humanities Press, 1976.

Vesely, Dalibor. *Architecture and Continuity, Themes 1.* London: AA School of Architecture, 1985.

Vico, Giambattista. *Principia di scienza nuova.* Naples: Stamperia Muziana, 1744.

Viollet-le-Duc, Eugène-Emmanuel. *Discourses on Architecture.* Trans. Benjamin Bucknall. New York: Grove Press, 1959. Translation of *Entretiens sur l'architecture;* Paris, 1859–1872.

Vogt, Max Adolf. *Gottfried Semper und die Mitte des 19. Jahrhunderts.* Basel and Stuttgart: Birkhäuser, 1976.

Wachsmann, Konrad. *The Turning Point of Building: Structure and Design.* New York: Reinhold, 1961.

Wagner, Otto. *Modern Architecture: A Guidebook for His Students to This Field of Art.* Intro. and trans. Harry Francis Mallgrave. Santa Monica: Getty Center for the History of Art and the Humanities, 1988.

Wagner, Walter F. "Ludwig Mies van der Rohe: 1886–1969." *Architectural Record* 146 (September 1969), 9.

Wangerin, Gerda, and Gerhard Weiss. *Heinrich Tessenow: Ein Baumeister 1876–1950; Leben, Lehre, Werk.* Essen: Bacht, 1976.

Warnke, Georgia. *Gadamer: Hermeneutics, Tradition and Reason.* Stanford: Stanford University Press, 1987.

Weiner, Frank. "Fragrant Beams and Dazzling Furniture: The Architectural Thoughts of Paul Valéry." Unpublished paper, Virginia Polytechnic Institute, 1990.

Westcott, Pat. *The Sydney Opera House.* Sydney: Ure Smith, 1968.

Weston, Richard. "Confrontation with Nature: The Clarity and Precision of Sverre Fehn's Architecture." *Building Design* 856 (October 9, 1987), 16–19.

Weston, Richard. "A Sense of the Horizon." *Architect's Journal* 187 (November 9, 1988), 38–45.

White, Theo. B., ed. *Paul Philippe Cret: Architect and Teacher.* Philadelphia: Art Alliance Press, 1973.

Winckelmann, Johann Joachim. *History of Ancient Art* (1764). Trans. Henry Lodge. Boston: J. R. Osgood and Company, 1872–1873.

Worringer, Wilhelm. *Abstraction and Empathy* (1905). New York: International Universities Press, 1953.

Wright, Frank Lloyd. *An American Architecture.* New York: Horizon Press, 1955.

Wright, Frank Lloyd. *An Autobiography.* London: Faber & Faber, 1945.

Wright, Frank Lloyd. *Frank Lloyd Wright: Writings and Buildings.* Ed. Edgar Kaufman and Ben Raeburn. New York: Horizon Press, 1960.

Wright, Frank Lloyd. *In the Cause of Architecture: Essays by Frank Lloyd Wright for Architectural Record, 1908–1952.* Ed. Frederick Gutheim. New York: McGraw-Hill, 1975.

Wright, Frank Lloyd. *The Living City.* New York: Horizon, 1958.

Wu, Nelson I. *Chinese and Indian Architecture.* New York: Braziller, 1963.

Wurman, Richard Saul, and Eugene Feldman. *The Notebooks and Drawings of Louis I. Kahn.* Cambridge: MIT Press, 1973.

Wurman, Richard Saul, and Eugene Feldman. *What Will Be Has Always Been: The Words of Louis I. Kahn.* New York: Access Press; Rizzoli, 1986.

Yeomans, John. *The Other Taj Mahal: What Happened to the Sydney Opera House.* London: Longmans, 1968.

Yoshida, Tetsuro. *The Japanese House and Garden.* New York: Praeger, 1955; rpt. 1969.

Yuzawa, Masanobu. "Sant'Andrea al Quirinale of Borromini." Unpublished thesis, University of Toyko, 1975.

Zambonini, Giuseppe. "Process and Theme in the Work of Carlo Scarpa." *Perspecta* 20 (1983), 21–42.

Ziegler, Oswald L., ed. *Sydney Builds an Opera House.* Sydney: Oswald Ziegler, 1973.

Zimmerman, Michael E. *Heidegger's Confrontation with Modernity.* Bloomington: Indiana University Press, 1990.

Zunz, Jack. "Sydney Opera House Revisited." *The Arup Journal* (Spring 1988), 2–11.

Illustration Credits

Index